WordPerfect 5.1 for Windows By Example

Everything You Need to Know

Webster & Associates

Prima Publishing
P.O. Box 1260TW
Rocklin, CA 95677
(916) 786-0426

Typography by Webster & Associates
Production by Webster & Associates
Copyediting by Webster & Associates
Interior Design by Renee Deprey
Cover Design by Kirschner-Caroff Design

Prima Publishing
Rocklin,CA

How to Order:

Quantity discounts are available from the publisher, Prima Publishing, P.O. Box 1260TW Rocklin, CA 95677; telephone (916) 786-0426. On your letterhead, include information concerning the intended use of the books and the number of books you wish to purchase.

U.S. Bookstores and Libraries: Please submit all orders to St. Martin's Press, 175 Fifth Avenue, New York, NY 10010; telephone (212) 674-5151.

Library of Congress Cataloging-in-Publication Data

Webster, Tony 1940-
WordPerfect for Windows By Example: everything you need to know / by Webster & Associates

p. cm.
Includes bibliographical reference and index.
ISBN 1-55958-162-X
1. WordPerfect for Windows (Computer program) 2. Microsoft Windows (Computer program). 3. Word processing—Computer programs. I. Title.
Z52.5.W65W43 1991
652.5 536——dc20 91-34561
CIP

92 93 94 95 RRD 10 9 8 7 6 5 4 3 2 1
Printed in the United States of America

Acknowledgments

This book was produced by the the publication department of Webster and Associates. We wish to acknowledge the effort and dedication of Carrie Webster, David Webster, Jenny Hamilton, Paul Webster, Lesleigh Simms, and Jason Berman in the researching, writing, and editing of this book.

Webster and Associates also wishes to thank Dolf Leendert Boek and Doug Ruttan of WordPerfect Pacific, Roger Stewart of Prima Publishing, and Matt Wagner and Bill Gladstone from Waterside Productions, for their valuable assistance and cooperation.

Contents at a glance

Contents

16 Quick Lists 455

17 Advanced Text Editing 469

18 Merging 511

Introduction

WordPerfect

WordPerfect has, for many years, been the leading word processing program for personal computers. Recent estimates suggest that over seven million people world-wide use WordPerfect.

With the rising popularity of Microsoft Windows and the graphical operating environment that it creates, a Windows version of WordPerfect is now available.

This new version of WordPerfect retains all of the functions and features of the current DOS-based version of WordPerfect. Like the current DOS version, WordPerfect for Windows is also labeled as Version 5.1.

Command functions, embedded codes, and, optionally, even keyboard shortcuts remain the same for WordPerfect for Windows as they were under DOS. Perhaps most important of all, the WordPerfect file format, the way in which WordPerfect documents are stored on disk, remains identical to that of the DOS version. Files can be passed between the Windows and DOS versions of WordPerfect, and *vice versa*, without having to perform any special conversions.

If you are new to WordPerfect, you will find WordPerfect for Windows easy to learn and use. If you are an experienced user of WordPerfect under DOS, you will find that the transition to the Windows environment is not a difficult one.

Word processing

It was not until the early 1980s that personal computers became powerful enough, and economical enough, to attain widespread use both in the home and in the workplace.

With the spread of computing power came the spread of word processing programs; programs specially designed to simplify and facilitate the task of writing and editing letters and documents.

Over the past ten years, the effects of the word processor have made themselves felt over a wide range of fields: the use of personalized form letters as marketing and advertising tools has increased dramatically; newspapers and magazines have reported a significant increase in the number of unsolicited contributions they receive; the number of privately circulated newsletters has risen dramatically; and universities have noted a marked increase in the length of papers and reports submitted. All of these effects can be linked to the increasing availability of word processing programs.

Using a word processor, you need only write a document, in its entirety, once. From that point on, any changes, no matter how complex, can be incorporated into the existing document without the need to retype the surrounding text. In the time it would have taken to retype a single draft using a typewriter, you can enter second and third draft revisions using a word processing program.

In addition, the more sophisticated word processing programs, of which WordPerfect is a leading example, have automated such traditionally time consuming tasks as footnoting, indexing, and spell-checking. Word processors generally include a merging feature, which allows the multiple copies of a form letter to be personalized to individual recipients.

Finally, as computers become more sophisticated, their word processing programs follow suit. WordPerfect for Windows includes many advanced features, such as graphic editing, layout and typesetting, and the use of colors which, not long ago, were well out of the range of any word processor.

As personal computers become more commonplace, the impact of application programs, such as word processors, will become much more pronounced.

Windows

Text-based systems

Traditionally, IBM and compatible personal computers have operated on what is called a 'text-based' level. DOS itself is a typical text-based program.

In a text-based operating environment, such as that which is created by DOS, commands to the computer are typed in through the keyboard and appear on the screen as alphabetic and numeric characters. The computer communicates with its users by displaying messages and data on the screen; also in alphabetic and numeric form.

Under DOS, if a program is to have any graphical characteristics, these features would have to be created by the program itself.

One result of this limitation is that DOS-based programs require more disk and memory space. Each program has to contain its own commands for using and controlling graphics.

Another result, is that each DOS-based program, because it designs its own graphics, has a unique appearance. This uniqueness makes each program more difficult to learn. It also makes the mastery of one program of little, or no, help in the learning of another.

The Windows Graphic User Interface

The Windows program creates a graphics-based working environment on your computer called a Graphic User Interface (GUI). In Windows, commands are selected by positioning the mouse pointer over graphical pictures or symbols rather than by typing them in through the keyboard.

There are many advantages to using Windows. All programs written for use with Windows conform to a standard 'look and feel'. The way commands are entered, the way the screen is organized, and the way programs are manipulated, remain standard throughout a wide range of Windows applications.

Under Windows, each application program can concentrate on serving its specialized purpose, while such details as command menus, screen colors, the handling of peripheral devices (printers, monitors, etc.), and the allocation of memory, are left to Windows itself.

Because many aspects of Windows applications are handled by Windows itself, the appearance, and function, of most Windows programs have much in common. Windows applications can be learned and mastered more quickly. The usual confusion that one often faces when switching between programs is minimized in Windows, because there are fewer differences to overcome.

For a more detailed account of the advantages of using Windows, consult your Windows user's manual.

Command menus and dialog boxes

Windows uses a standardized set of on-screen methods to obtain information from its users. It is one of the advantages of Windows, that all Windows applications, including WordPerfect, use the same type of input media.

Command menus

Windows uses a device known as a 'menu' to accept commands from its users. Figure 1 shows the top of the WordPerfect editing screen.

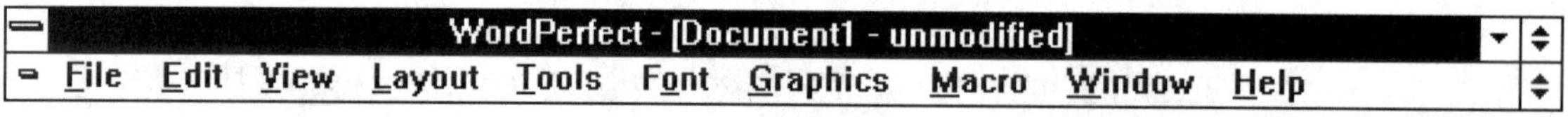

WordPerfect - [Document1 - unmodified]

File Edit View Layout Tools Font Graphics Macro Window Help

Figure 1. The Menu bar consists of a list of menu titles below the Title bar at the top of the WordPerfect for Windows editing screen.

The list of words below the Title bar is called the Menu bar. The Menu bar consists of the titles of each of the menus available. To view the commands available in a given menu, click the left mouse button once on the menu's title in the Menu bar.

As illustrated in Figure 2, a menu consists of a menu title above a list of menu commands. To select a command from a menu, position the mouse pointer over the desired command and click the button once.

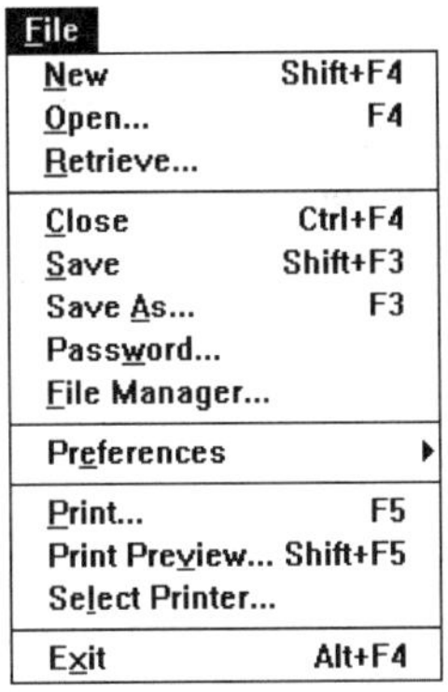

File	
New	Shift+F4
Open...	F4
Retrieve...	
Close	Ctrl+F4
Save	Shift+F3
Save As...	F3
Password...	
File Manager...	
Preferences	▸
Print...	F5
Print Preview...	Shift+F5
Select Printer...	
Exit	Alt+F4

Figure 2. In Windows programs, a menu consists of a menu title, in this case the word "File", above a list of menu commands.
The menu shown here is the ***File*** *menu from the WordPerfect for Windows editing screen.*

A quicker way of selecting a command from a menu is to click, and hold, the mouse button over the desired menu title and—while keeping the mouse button depressed—drag the mouse pointer to the desired command. The command will become selected when the mouse button is released.

In this book, menu titles are always stated in bold-faced type and menu commands are always shown in italics. Thus the command highlighted in Figure 3 would be referred to as the *Open* command in the **File** menu.

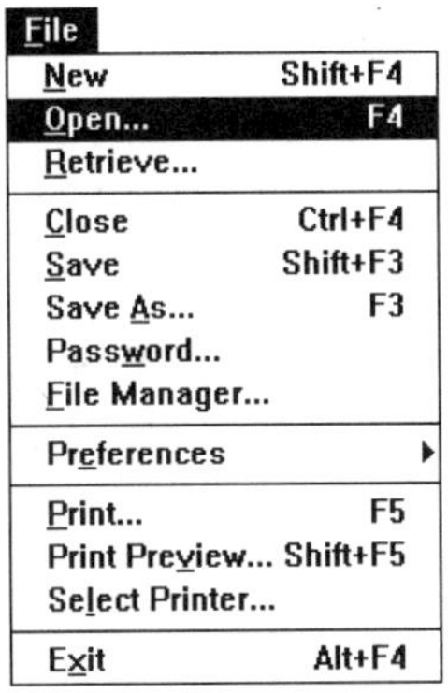

File	
New	Shift+F4
Open...	F4
Retrieve...	
Close	Ctrl+F4
Save	Shift+F3
Save As...	F3
Password...	
File Manager...	
Preferences	▸
Print...	F5
Print Preview...	Shift+F5
Select Printer...	
Exit	Alt+F4

Figure 3. In this figure, The Open command is highlighted in the ***File*** *menu.*

Figure 4 shows an example of a fly-out menu; a secondary menu invoked by a menu command. The command highlighted in Figure 4 would be described as the *Environment* command in the *Preferences* fly-out menu in the **File** menu. Because this description can be a bit cumbersome, it is often abbreviated as: the *Preferences/Environment* command from the **File** menu.

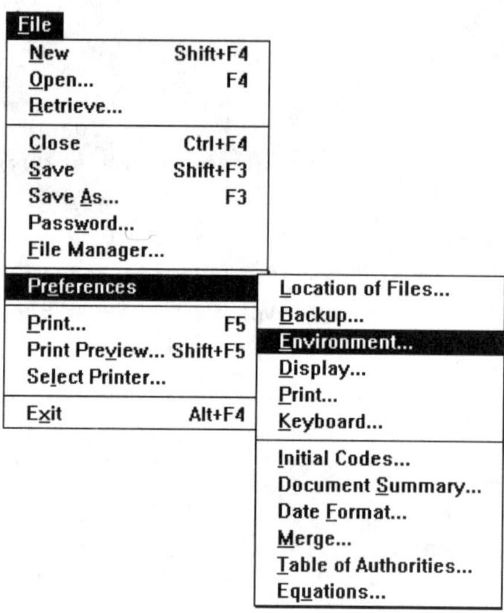

Figure 4. *In this figure, the Environment command in the Preferences fly-out menu from the* ***File*** *menu has been highlighted. This type of command is often abbreviated in this book as the Preferences/Environment command from the* ***File*** *menu.*

Dialog boxes

Sometimes you are required to provide additional information before a selected command can be carried out. To allow this information to be entered, Windows has features known as dialog boxes. Special devices, called input media, appear within dialog boxes to allow you to enter information as easily as possible.

Figure 5 shows two dialog boxes that contain examples of the major input media found within dialog boxes.

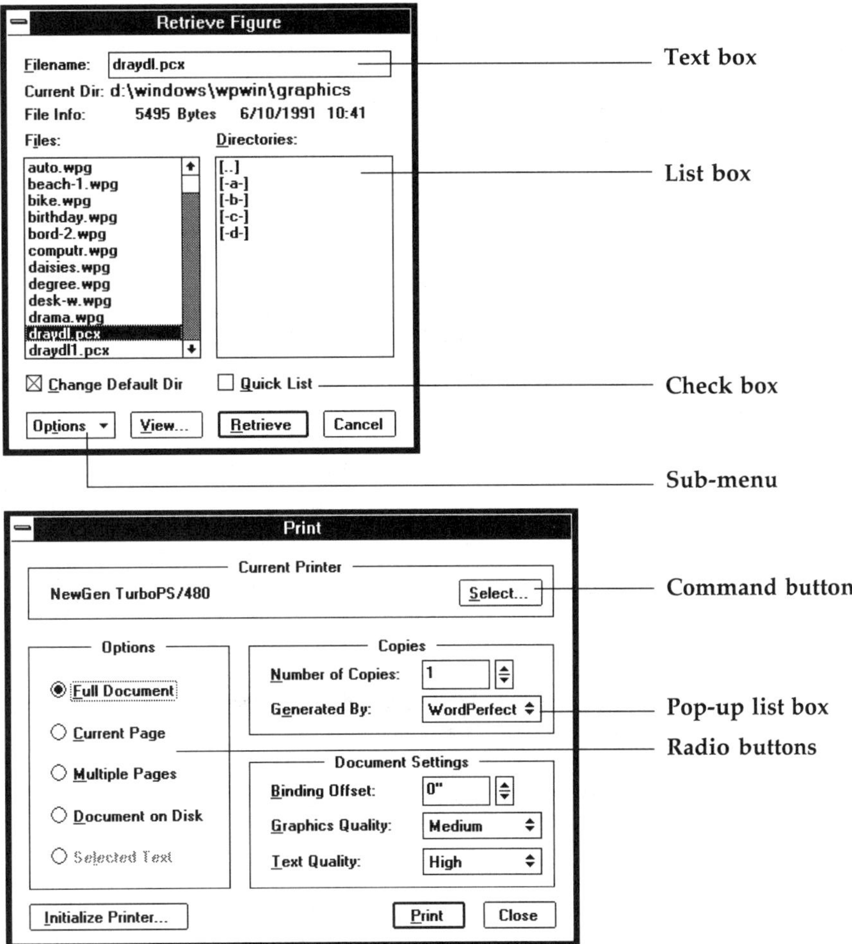

Figure 5. *These dialog boxes contain examples of most of the major input media found in dialog boxes in WordPerfect for Windows.*

In this book, the names of dialog boxes and of elements within them are always shown in italics. Thus, the dialog box at the top of Figure 5 would be called the *Retrieve Figure* dialog box.

Names of files and directories are indicated in bold italic type in this book. Thus, the file listed in the *Filename* text box, in Figure 5 (top figure), would be referred to as ***draydl.pcx***.

The By Example approach

WordPerfect for Windows By Example follows the unique *By Example* learning approach.

Graphic screen images

Because Windows programs rely heavily on graphics-based interaction with the user, *WordPerfect for Windows By Example* includes over one thousand screen images taken directly from WordPerfect for Windows itself.

At each step in the learning process, figures will show you the appearance of the WordPerfect screen or dialog box being discussed.

Figure 6 shows the WordPerfect for Windows editing screen as it appears when the program is first started.

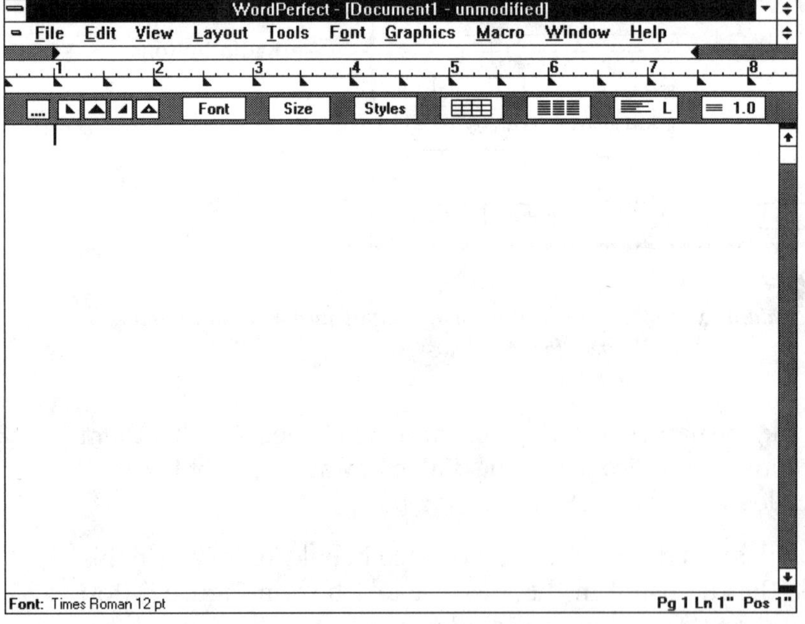

Figure 6. *This figure represents the appearance of the WordPerfect for Windows editing when the program is first started. Over one thousand screen images, such as this one, make the examples and exercises in this book easier to follow.*

Interactive examples

The best way to master any computer program, particularly a program such as WordPerfect for Windows which is very interactive, is to use it. The chapters in this book are designed in the form of interactive examples.

While each chapter can be read individually for reference, it will greatly enhance your learning process to follow through each chapter on your own computer. Each chapter will take you, step by step, through various WordPerfect features and commands. By actually following the steps yourself, you will learn much more quickly. As you follow the examples in each chapter, you can compare the screen images in the book with the appearance of your own screen.

Exercises

To reinforce the information being taught, and to provide additional hands-on training, most chapters include an exercise. While it is not essential to the learning process to complete every exercise, they can be helpful in strengthening your grasp on the material. The exercises can also give you an idea of how well you have mastered the subject matter.

Each exercise begins with a concise list of steps that incorporate the concepts and commands covered in the preceding chapter. If you feel comfortable enough with the material, you may wish to complete the steps as outlined at the start of the exercise.

Following the initial list of steps, each of the steps is restated, one at a time, along with a detailed account of the commands and selections required to carry out each step. As with the examples in the chapters, each step is accompanied by a complete series of screen images showing the progression from the beginning to the end of the exercise.

To ensure that all readers can derive maximum benefit from the exercises, many are based on the ***learn*** sample files included with WordPerfect for Windows. These files can be copied to your hard disk when WordPerfect for Windows is installed. Before using these files to complete the exercises, make a second copy of them on a different sub-directory to protect them from accidental modification.

Defaults settings and assumptions

The screen images and descriptions in this book try to follow, as closely as possible, the way the program will appear on your computer. However, as no two computer systems are organized in exactly the same way, differences between users are inevitable.

Thus, your screen may not always look the same as every screen image in this book and files may not always be located in the same subdirectories.

Because the figures in this book appear in black and white, and because no single color scheme will match the displays of every reader, the screen images displayed in this book are all displayed as they would appear on a monochrome monitor.

The ruler

Most of the images of the WordPerfect editing screen in this book, include the ruler along the top of the document window. In WordPerfect for Windows, the ruler display is optional. It has been included in this book because it is a useful addition to the screen which enhances the power of the program. We recommend that you use the ruler when using WordPerfect.

If the ruler does not appear on your editing screen, it can be activated by selecting the *Ruler* command from the **View** menu, as seen in Figure 7.

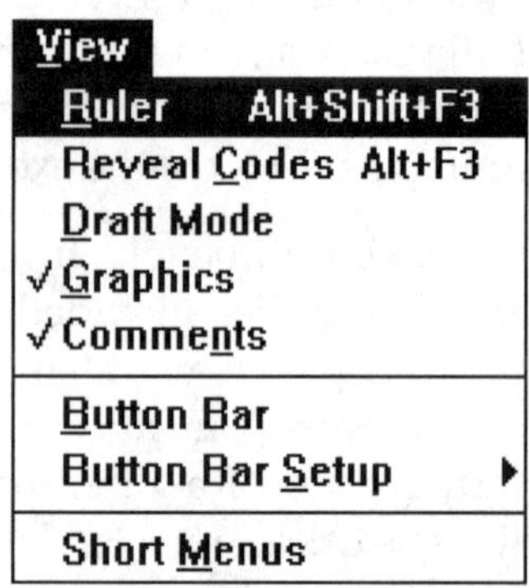

Figure 7. *Use the Ruler command from the* ***View*** *menu to activate (or deactivate) the ruler display at the top of the editing window.*

To make the ruler display by default, every time a new document is opened, select the *Environment* command from the *Preferences* fly-out menu in the **File** menu as shown in Figure 8, to activate the *Environment Settings* dialog box, seen in Figure 9.

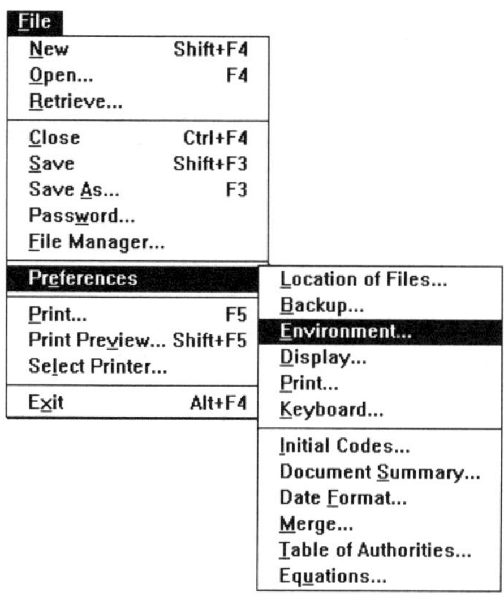

Figure 8. *Select the Preferences/ Environment command to invoke the Environment Settings dialog box seen in Figure 9.*

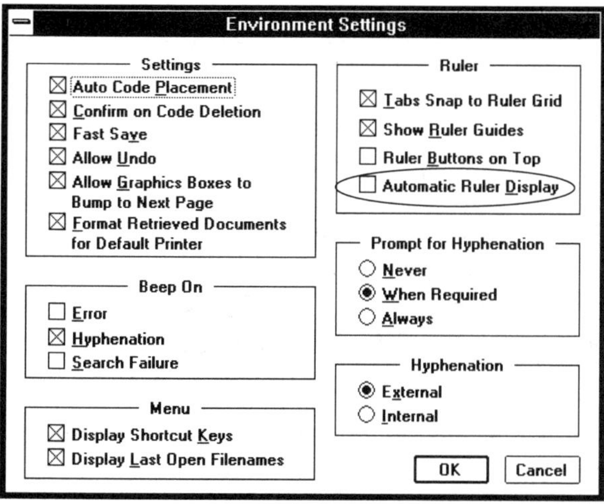

Figure 9. *To make the ruler appear, by default, every time a new document is opened, select the Automatic Ruler Display option from the Environment Settings dialog box shown here. Be sure that this option is marked with an 'X'.*

In the *Environment Settings* dialog box, select the *Automatic Ruler Display* check box. If this option is marked with an 'X', the ruler will display automatically when a new document is opened.

Sub-directories

When you install WordPerfect for Windows, you can decide which files are placed in which sub-directories. This decision will depend, in part, on your personal preference. It will also depend on the disk resources available on your computer and on the sub-directories that already exist on your disk before WordPerfect is installed.

In this book, a number of the most likely sub-directory structures have been represented throughout different chapters. Though your own system will not match all of our examples, it is likely that it will match with some of them.

Keyboard shortcuts

With WordPerfect for Windows, as with previous versions of WordPerfect, most of the commands and functions can be accessed through a combination of keyboard shortcuts. In WordPerfect for Windows you can modify these shortcuts to suit your needs.

Included with WordPerfect for Windows, are two sets of predetermined shortcut key systems. One set, stored on the file named ***wpdos51.wwk***, reproduces the keyboard shortcuts found in the DOS version of WordPerfect 5.1. Thus, using this system, the keyboard shortcut for the *Save As* command is F10.

The second set of keyboard shortcuts is the Common User Access (CUA) set. The CUA system conforms, as much as possible, to recognized keyboard standards under Windows. Thus, in the CUA system, the keyboard shortcut for the *Save As* command is F3.

When you install WordPerfect for Windows, you can select which of these two shortcut systems you wish to use by default. In this book, the CUA system has been selected.

For more information on keyboard shortcuts, see Chapter 9 **Preferences - 1**.

The Editing Screen

Most of the work you will do in WordPerfect for Windows will take place in the editing screen. To make the most of this program, you must be able to identify, and use, the various tools and components of this screen.

The editing screen is made up of many elements, which combine to give you access to WordPerfect's many functions and commands. In the following chapter, you will take a look at the different parts of the WordPerfect for Windows editing screen shown below in Figure 1-1. More detailed explanations of each of these elements will be found in later chapters of this book.

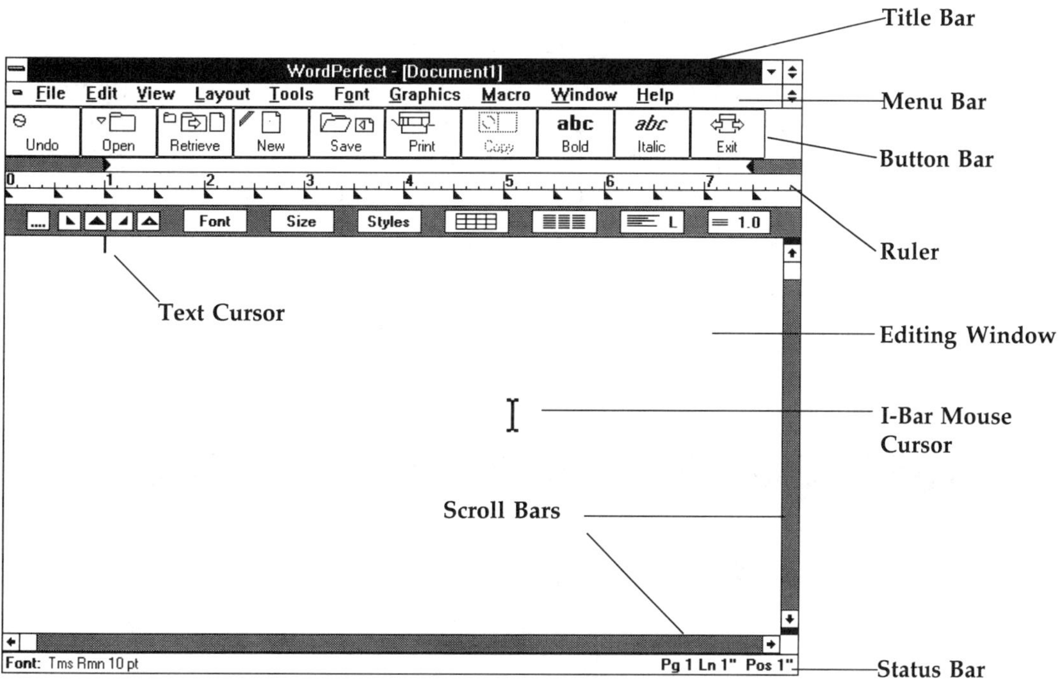

Figure 1-1. The WordPerfect for Windows editing screen.

Title bar

The Title bar, located at the top of the screen, tells you a number of things about the documents being edited. On starting WordPerfect, the Title bar on the screen will look like the one in Figure 1-2. The word *Document1* is displayed and remains until the document is saved. This title is a generic label used to identify and number documents that have not yet been given a unique name.

WordPerfect - [Document1 - Unmodified]

Figure 1-2. *The Title bar that appears on opening WordPerfect for Windows.*

When you save a document for the first time, you give it a name and assign it to a specific disk drive and sub-directory. Once a document has been saved, this information is displayed in the Title bar (Figure 1-3), in place of the generic *Document* title. Notice that the word *Unmodified* appears beside the Title bar text. This designation will disappear if you make any changes to the document.

When you open or retrieve a document into a window, the Title bar will change to reflect the correct drive, directory, and filename of the selected document.

Figure 1-3. *The Title bar of a saved document.*

Menu bar

At the top of your screen, below the Title bar, are the words **File**, **Edit**, **View**, **Layout**, **Tools**, **Font**, **Graphics**, **Macro**, **Window**, and **Help** displayed horizontally. These words are the titles of the command menus that make up the WordPerfect for Windows Menu bar.

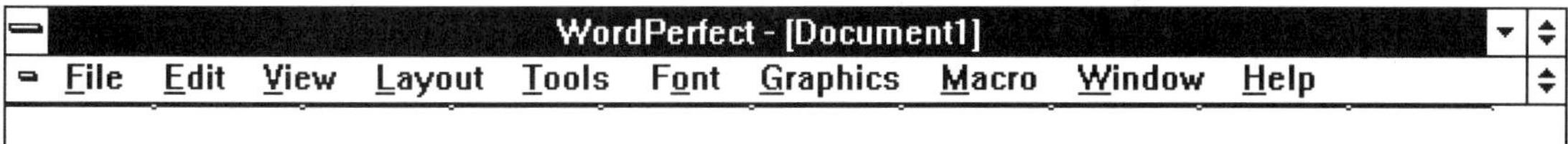

Figure 1-4. *WordPerfect for Windows Menu bar.*

Button bar

The Button bar, in WordPerfect for Windows, is used for quick access to commands in the menus. Clicking the mouse button on one of the buttons in the Button bar will activate the corresponding command in the menu.

Button bars are intended to save time and effort by providing quick and easy access to the most frequently used commands. The Button bar can be customized for use in different types of documents, because the most frequently used commands for one type of file may differ from those for another type. The Button bar can be positioned at either the top, bottom, left, or right of the editing screen. The Button bar is discussed in Chapter 14 of this book. The Button bar shown in Figure 1-1, and again here in Figure 1-5, has been positioned at the top of the editing screen.

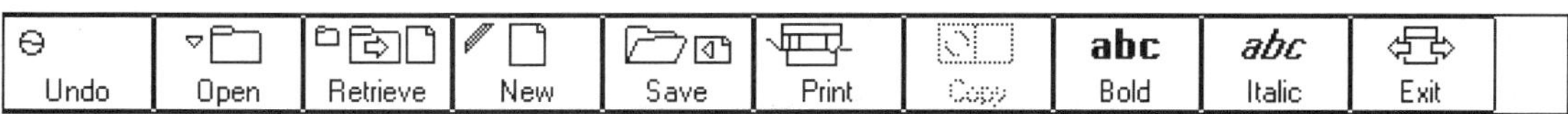

Figure 1-5. *Customized Button bar positioned at the top of the screen.*

Ruler

The ruler, if selected, appears at the top of the document window. Unlike the Button bar, which is independent of the document you are editing, the ruler's appearance will vary depending on the units of measure, margins, and tab settings of each document.

The ruler's measurements can be displayed in inches, centimeters, or points. Changing these units is discussed in Chapter 4 of this book. For consistency, most examples in this book will use inches as the units of measure.

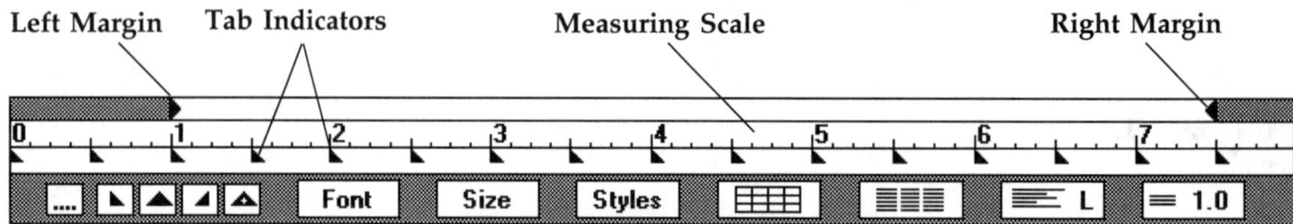

Figure 1-6. The WordPerfect ruler.

At the top of the ruler are the margin indicators, showing the exact positions of the left and right margins of the document. In Figure 1-6 we have set the left margin at 1 inch and the right margin at 7.50 inches.

In taking a closer look at the ruler, you will notice that below the measuring scale are triangular tab indicators. These indicators are used to show how the tabs have been set for each document. Tabs and their settings are discussed in Chapter 4 of this book.

Directly below the Tab settings are a number of command buttons (Figure 1-7). These command buttons are used as shortcuts when creating or formatting documents.

Figure 1-7. The selection of command buttons found on the ruler.

Each command button on the ruler has a corresponding command in one of the menus. The use of these command buttons is discussed in Chapter 4 of this book.

Scroll bars

The scroll bars are situated along the bottom and right-hand sides of the screen (Figure 1-1) and allow you to shift your view to any part of the document. Scroll bars are a standard Windows feature.

Because you can use the cursor keys to move around in your document, WordPerfect for Windows allows you to turn off one or both of the scroll bars.

Status bar

The Status bar appears at the bottom of the screen below the horizontal scroll bar. The Status bar's measurements are displayed in the same units you have selected for the ruler.

The current font and size selected for your document will be displayed on the left-hand side of the Status bar. On the right-hand side, the number of the page on which you are currently working and the exact position of the text cursor are indicated (Figure 1-8).

Font: Tms Rmn 10 pt	**Pg 1 Ln 1" Pos 1"**

Figure 1-8. *The Status bar showing the Font, Pitch and exact location of the text cursor.*

The Status bar shown in Figure 1-8 has the top and left margins set at 1 inch with the cursor positioned on the first line of page 1 of the document. The current font is Times Roman 10 point size.

Different messages appear from time to time replacing the font and its size on the left-hand side of the screen. These messages will be explained as they are encountered throughout this book.

Text cursor

The text cursor appears on the screen as a blinking vertical line, showing you exactly where text will next be entered in a document.

You may move the cursor around in the document by using either the mouse or the cursor movement keys. Each of these methods is discussed in Chapter 2 of this book.

Mouse cursor

The position of the mouse on the editing screen is marked by an 'I-bar' shaped icon: I, when the mouse is positioned over a part of the screen where text can be placed.

When the mouse pointer is in a part of the screen where it is used for selecting commands, such as the menus or the ruler, it takes the form of a hollow arrow: .

Short menus

Selecting the *Short Menus* command from the **View** menu removes commands that are not commonly used (in WordPerfect for Windows), leaving only the more frequently used commands. Figure 1-9 shows the **Edit** menu in both Normal and Short menu modes.

Edit	
Undo	Alt+Bksp
Undelete...	Alt+Shift+Bksp
Cut	Shift+Del
Copy	Ctrl+Ins
Paste	Shift+Ins
Append	
Link	▸
Select	▸
Convert Case	▸
Search...	F2
Search Next	Shift+F2
Search Previous	Alt+F2
Replace...	Ctrl+F2
Go To...	Ctrl+G

Edit	
Undo	Alt+Bksp
Undelete...	Alt+Shift+Bksp
Cut	Shift+Del
Copy	Ctrl+Ins
Paste	Shift+Ins
Append	
Search...	F2
Search Next	Shift+F2
Search Previous	Alt+F2
Replace...	Ctrl+F2
Go To...	Ctrl+G

*Figure 1-9. The **Edit** menu displayed in both Normal and Short menu modes.*

Typing a Document

In this chapter you will see how to create a simple document using WordPerfect for Windows.

When you start WordPerfect, the program places a blank page on your screen. A flashing cursor is automatically placed at the top left-hand side of the page. Entering a new document in WordPerfect is like typing on a clean piece of paper.

Typing text

To begin typing a document, start the WordPerfect for Windows program. Your screen will look like that shown in Figure 2-1.

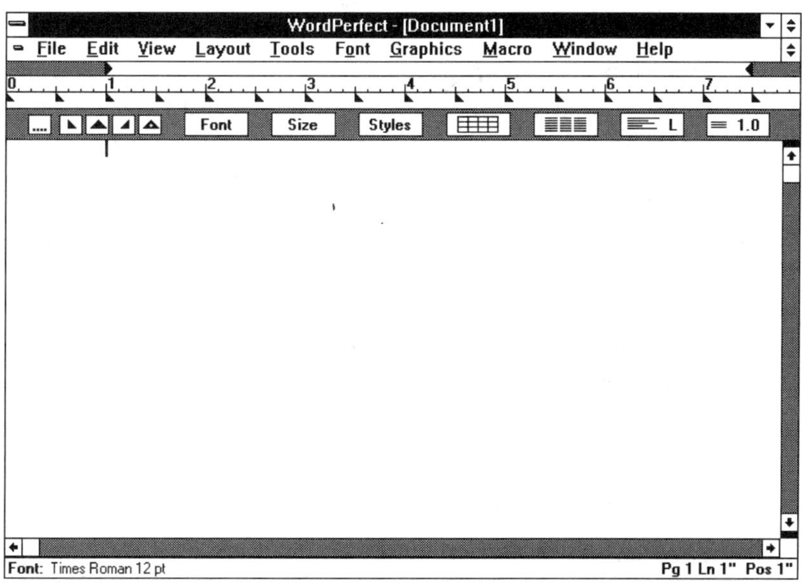

Figure 2-1. *The opening screen in WordPerfect for Windows.*

A sample business letter appears below. Begin typing this letter into your empty document page.

Some of the words in the sample document are written in **bold** or *italics*. To apply these text attributes, select the appropriate command from the **Font** menu, shown in Figure 2-2, before typing the bold or italic text. The text typed after selecting an attribute from the menu will automatically be given the attribute you have selected. To resume typing normal text, select the *Normal* command from the **Font** menu.

A faster way of activating these attributes is to use the Control key in conjunction with the B key, for **bold**, the I key for *italic*, and the N key for normal text.

Mrs. P. C. Computer
14 King Street
Sydney N.S.W. 2000

Dear Pam,

As a member of your local government I am writing to you to ask for your assistance in buying some *computer terminals* for our local school.

I would like to arrange a meeting with you to discuss this matter and the possibility of your heading a committee that will advise us on future purchases of computer equipment.

My secretary will call and make arrangements for us to meet at your convenience.

If you have any further queries please do not hesitate to contact me. I look forward to meeting with you soon.

Yours sincerely,

Peter Principal

Don't worry if you have made any mistakes while typing this letter. You will see how mistakes are corrected later in this chapter. For now, simply leave any errors in the document.

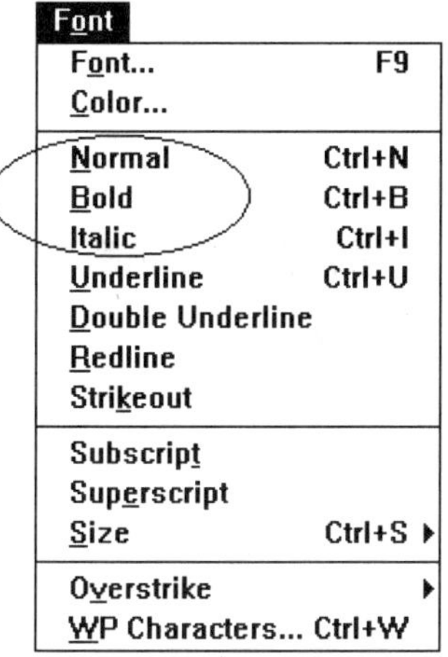

***Figure 2-2.** The Bold, Italic, and Normal commands in the **Font** menu.*

Moving the cursor

When you type a document, it is important to be able to move the cursor around the screen in order to insert text and correct errors. The cursor can be moved in two ways.

The first method of positioning the text cursor involves using the mouse. When you are typing or editing a document, the mouse cursor's position on the screen is represented by an I-bar: (I). This 'I-bar' only represents the mouse position and should not be confused with the flashing text cursor, which is the point in your document where text is inserted.

To select a position for the text cursor, using the mouse, place the I-bar at the point in the document where you would like the cursor to be and click the left mouse button. The flashing text cursor will then be inserted beneath the I-bar.

In the letter you have just typed, place the text cursor after the word "to" in the paragraph beginning with the phrase: "I would like to...". Place the I-beam after the word "to" and click the mouse button.

Now type ", sometime in the near future," after the word "to". Notice that the text you are typing is always entered immediately to the left of the text cursor. Your letter will now look like the document in Figure 2-3.

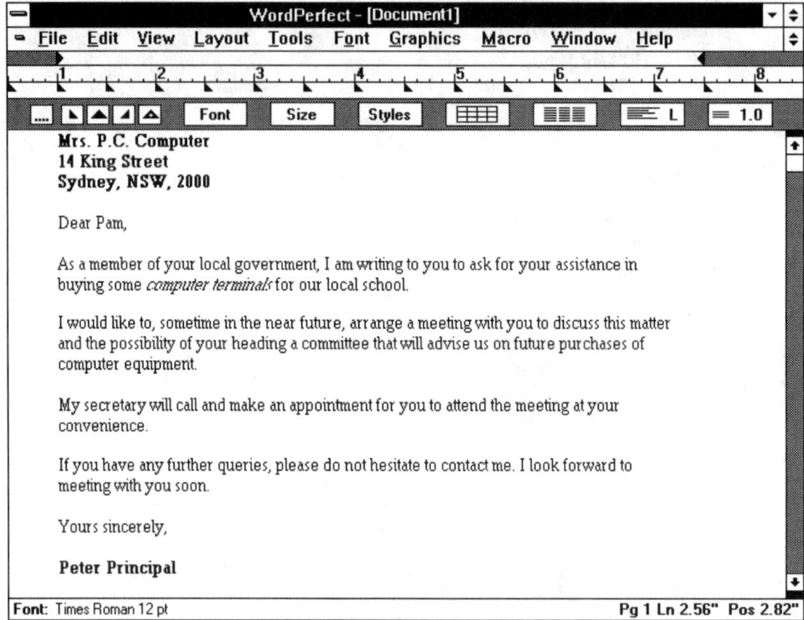

Figure 2-3. *The letter should now have the phrase "sometime in the near future" added to it.*

The second method of cursor movement involves the cursor keys on the keyboard. The flashing text cursor will move through a document in response to the cursor keys pressed. The left and right-facing cursor keys move the cursor one character in the appropriate directions, while the up and down cursor keys move the cursor up, or down, by a single line.

Sometimes another key, such as the Control key, is used in conjunction with the cursor keys to move the cursor greater distances. The direction and distance that the cursor will move depends on which keys you press.

To move the cursor one word at a time, hold down the Control key when pressing the appropriate cursor key. The Home key will place the text cursor at the beginning of the line and the End key will place it at the end of the line.

Try using the keyboard to position the cursor within this sample document. At the moment, the text cursor should still be positioned just to the right of the word "future,". Press the Left cursor key once and watch the cursor move one character to the left. Now try moving it two characters to the right by pressing the Right cursor key twice. To move to the end of the line press the End key. Try moving to the beginning of the line by pressing the Home key.

The **Hints and Tips** section, at the end of this chapter, includes a complete list of the different cursor keystrokes and their functions.

Positioning the cursor is a very important skill to master in order to use WordPerfect for Windows. If you still feel unsure about these two techniques, try moving the cursor around in the document until you feel more comfortable.

The editing keys

Some of the keys on the keyboard have specialized editing functions. In particular, the Backspace, Delete, and Insert keys each have special properties that are invaluable in typing and editing documents.

The Backspace and Delete keys

The Backspace and Delete keys on your keyboard are editing keys, used to delete text from your screen.

Using the Backspace key will delete the character to the *left* of the text cursor and move the cursor to this position. The Delete key deletes the character to the *right* of the cursor but the text cursor remains in its original position.

Try using these editing keys to remove some text from your screen. Place your cursor to the right of the word "future". Press the Backspace key to delete the letter "e". Keep pressing the Backspace key until the whole word has been removed from the document.

Now use the Delete key to remove the word "near". Place the cursor to the left of the word "near" using either the mouse or the cursor keys. Press the Delete key to remove the letter "n" from the screen. Press the Delete key four more times to delete the rest of the word and the space which follows it.

Using the Control key in conjunction with the Backspace key allows you to remove entire words from the screen.

Position the cursor to the left of the word "sometime". Now, hold down the Control key while pressing the Backspace key. The word "sometime" is deleted with one keystroke. Your cursor will now be automatically positioned in front of the word "in".

Use any of the deletion techniques to remove the words "in the" that remain from the original phrase. Be sure to remove any commas that are now no longer required. If there are any typing errors remaining in the document, use your newly acquired editing skill to correct them.

The Insert key

By default, WordPerfect operates in *Insert* mode. In *Insert* mode, when text is typed into a document, any characters already present to the right of the text cursor are pushed over to make room for the new text. Earlier, when you added the phrase "in the near future" to the sample letter, the words were inserted into the sentence without replacing any existing words.

An alternative to *Insert* mode is *Typeover* mode. When *Typeover* mode is in use, characters typed into a document will replace, or type over, text already present to the right of the cursor. Existing text is not pushed over to make room for the added text.

Typeover mode is activated by pressing the Insert key. The left-hand side of the Status bar, which normally shows the current text font and size, will display the word *Typeover* as seen in Figure 2-4. Pressing the Insert key again will return WordPerfect to *Insert* mode.

Typeover	Pg 1 Ln 1.58" Pos 1"

Figure 2-4. *The word Typeover appears on the left-hand side of the Status bar to show that Typeover mode has been activated.*

Use *Typeover* mode to replace a word in your letter with a new word. Place your cursor in front of the word "queries", in the last paragraph, and press the Insert key on your keyboard. Check the Status bar to be sure that *Typeover* mode has been activated. Now type in the word "questions", allowing it to overwrite the word "queries".

When "queries" has been completely overwritten, switch back to *Insert* mode to finish typing the word "questions".

The Undo command

The *Undo* command, which is located in the **Edit** menu, is a safety feature that can be used to correct accidental changes to a document. Selecting the *Undo* command will reverse the effects of the most recently completed function or command. Though a powerful tool, this command will only reverse the very last step you have taken.

For example, delete the word "sincerely" (second last line) in your letter. Now select the *Undo* command from the **Edit** menu (Figure 2-5). The word "sincerely" will be inserted back into the document. You might find it quicker and easier to use the Alt and Backspace keys together as a shortcut to activating the *Undo* command.

Try using the *Undo* command in a few other places. Always remember: only the most recently completed action will be 'undone'.

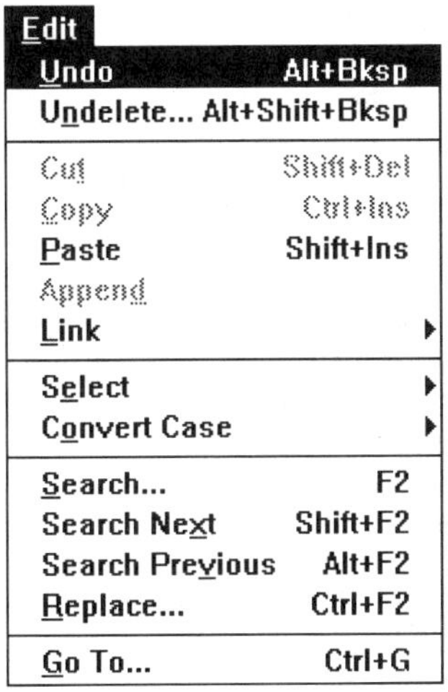

Edit	
Undo	Alt+Bksp
Undelete...	Alt+Shift+Bksp
Cut	Shift+Del
Copy	Ctrl+Ins
Paste	Shift+Ins
Append	
Link	▸
Select	▸
Convert Case	▸
Search...	F2
Search Next	Shift+F2
Search Previous	Alt+F2
Replace...	Ctrl+F2
Go To...	Ctrl+G

*Figure 2-5. The Undo command in the **Edit** menu.*

The Undelete command

The *Undelete* command, in the **Edit** menu, lets you restore up to the last three deletions that have been made to a document. By selecting this command, you can display these deleted passages on your screen and insert the desired text at the position of the text cursor.

To demonstrate this command, delete the words "local", "arrange", and "secretary" from the sample letter. Now use the *Undelete* command, as follows, to reinstate these deletions.

Place the text cursor immediately to the right of the word "your", in the first paragraph of the letter. Now, select the *Undelete* command from the **Edit** menu. The *Undelete* dialog box, shown in Figure 2-6, will appear on the screen. The last deletion you made, in this case the word "secretary", is displayed at the current cursor position.

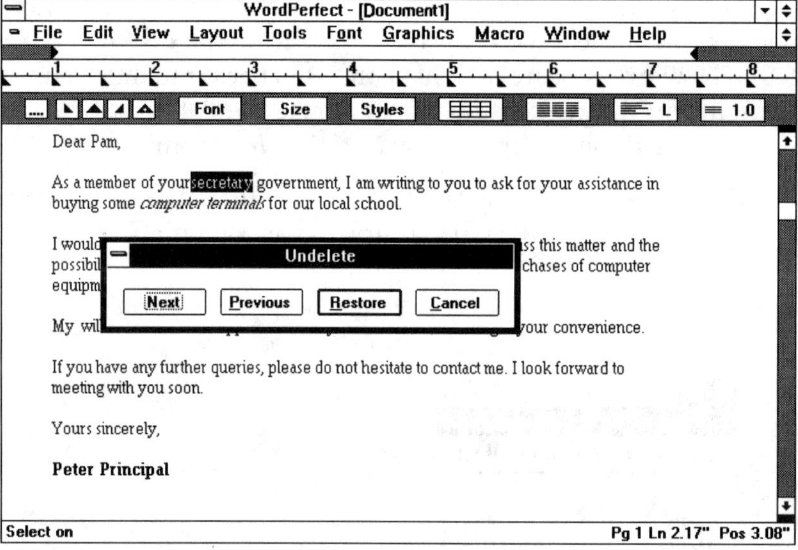

Figure 2-6. *The Undelete dialog box appears on the screen with the last deleted word, "secretary", placed at the current cursor position.*

The *Undelete* dialog box contains buttons labeled *Next, Previous* and *Restore.*

Press the *Previous* button once to replace the currently displayed word, in this case "secretary", with the word deleted prior to it, in this case the word "arrange". Press *Previous* again to display the word "local", which was deleted prior to "arrange".

As "local" is the correct word for this part of the document, press the *Restore* button. This command reinserts the word "local" into the document, and exits from the *Undelete* dialog box.

Now place the cursor to the right of the word "to", in the second paragraph, and use the *Undelete* command to restore the word "arrange" to the letter. Use the *Undelete* command once more to restore the word "secretary" to its original spot in the document.

The letter will now look like the example in Figure 2-7.

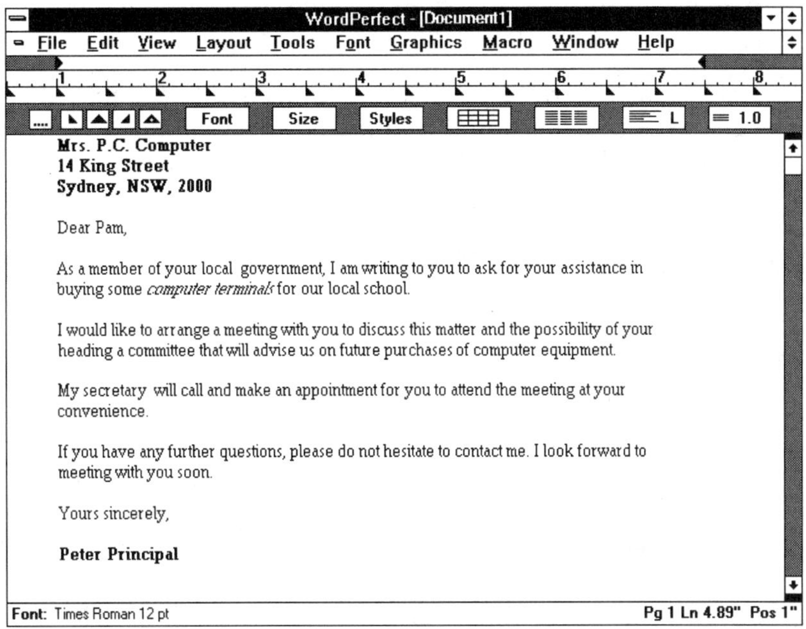

Figure 2-7. *This is how your completed document will now look, ready for you to save.*

Saving files

When you create or edit a document, it is important that you save your work to disk at regular intervals. When you work on a WordPerfect document, the changes that you make are stored temporarily in your computer's memory.

To have access to a document at a later date, and also to protect against accidental loss of data, a disk file of the document must be created. Such files are created using the *Save* or *Save As* commands in the **File** menu.

The Save As command

The first time a document is saved, it will not have a name. The Title bar of the WordPerfect window refers to it simply as a numbered document, in this case: *Document1*. The *Save As* command lets you create, and name, a file for the document currently being edited.

To demonstrate the *Save As* command, create a file for this sample document. Select the *Save As* command from the **File** menu and the *Save As* dialog box, shown in Figure 2-8, will appear.

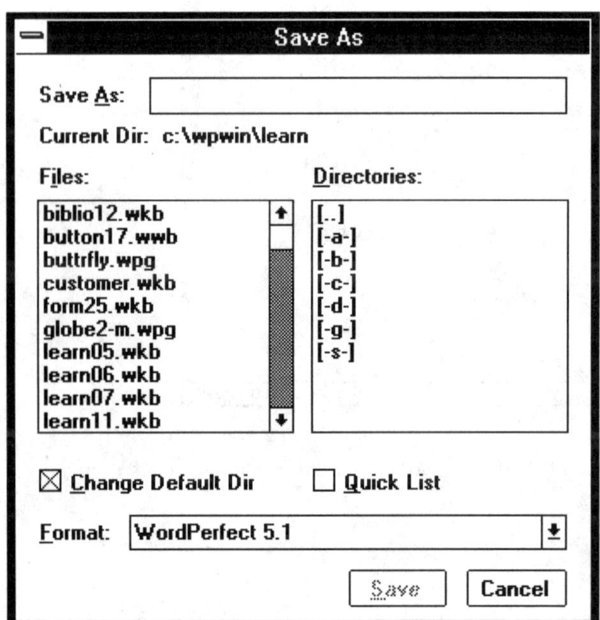

Figure 2-8. *The Save As dialog box with the flashing cursor automatically placed in the Save As: box, ready for you to type in the name of your letter.*

When the *Save As* dialog box appears, a flashing text cursor is automatically placed in the *Save As* text box, located at the top of this dialog box.

For this example, don't change the drive or directory where the document is saved. Simply type the name ***school.let*** in the *Save As* text box and click on the **OK** button. Notice that the new name of the document has been placed in the Title bar at the top of the screen (see Figure 2-9).

You may, when naming WordPerfect documents, select extensions that give some idea of the document's contents. For example, you may like to give your letters ***'let'*** extensions and your memos ***'meo'*** extensions. WordPerfect for Windows does not automatically place any extensions on documents.

Figure 2-9. *The sample document's new name: '**school.let**' has now been placed in the Title bar at the top of the WordPerfect screen.*

The Save command

The *Save* command is used when saving a file that has already been named using the *Save As* command described above. The *Save* command replaces the existing file on disk, with a new file of the same name, that is an up-to-date record of the document's contents. (Choosing *Save* before you name a document will automatically invoke the Figure 2-8 *Save As* dialog box.)

The *Save* command is convenient because it does not require you to supply the name of the file as you would using the *Save As* command.

A short-cut to using the *Save* command, is to hold the Control key while pressing the S key.

You can activate the *Save* and *Save As* commands, anytime you are working in WordPerfect for Windows, without losing your place in the document you are editing.

The Close command

Now that you have used the *Save As* command to give your document a name, it is time to close the window in which you have been working.

Select the *Close* command from the **File** menu. If the current version of the document which you have been editing has been saved, the current document window will close immediately.

If you have not saved the most recent version of the document, a warning dialog box, shown in Figure 2-10, will appear. In this dialog box you are given a final chance to save changes made to the document.

If the document does not yet have a name, selecting the *Yes* button will activate the *Save As* dialog box. If the document already has a name, but has been changed since it was last saved, selecting *Yes* will update the existing file.

Selecting the *No* button clears the screen without saving the latest changes to the file. If the document is not yet named, it will be completely deleted.

Selecting the *Cancel* button, cancels the *Close* command and returns you to the document without saving or closing it.

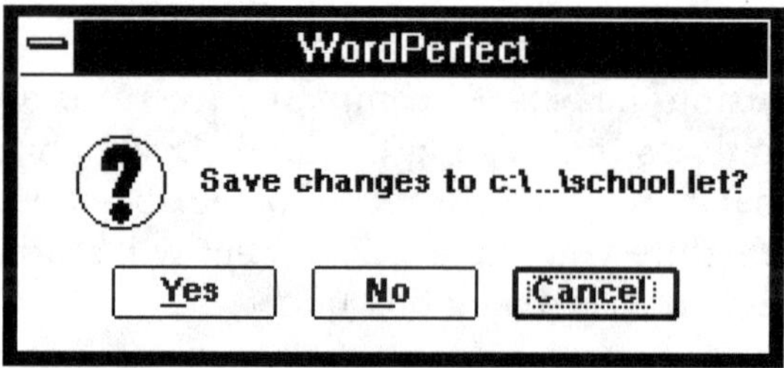

Figure 2-10. *A warning dialog box appears if you attempt to close a document that has yet to be saved or has been modified since it was last saved.*

Hints and Tips

Typing text

The following table summarizes key combinations often used when typing text.

Keyboard shortcuts	Function
Ctrl + B	Bold
Ctrl + I	Italics
Ctrl + N	Normal text
Ctrl + U	Underline
Enter	Start new paragraph

Moving the cursor

The following tables list key combinations used to move the cursor around in a document.

Keyboard shortcuts	Function
Left-arrow key	Positions the cursor to the previous character on the left
Ctrl+Left-arrow key	Positions the cursor to the beginning of the previous word.
Right-arrow key	Positions the cursor to the next character on the right
Ctrl+Right-arrow key	Positions the cursor to the beginning of the next word on the right
Up-arrow key	Positions the cursor up one line
Ctrl+Up-arrow key	Positions the cursor up one paragraph
Down-arrow key	Positions the cursor down one line
Ctrl+Down-arrow key	Positions the cursor down one paragraph
Home	Positions the cursor at the beginning of a line
Alt-Home	Positions the cursor at the top of the page
Ctrl-Home	Positions the cursor at the top of the document

Keyboard shortcuts	Function
End	Positions cursor at the end of a line
Alt+End	Positions cursor at the bottom of the current page
Ctrl+End	Positions cursor at the bottom of the current document
Page Up	Positions cursor up one screen
Alt+Page Up	Positions cursor up one page
Page Down	Positions cursor down one screen
Alt+Page Down	Positions cursor down one page

Editing keys

The table below lists key combinations used in deleting text from documents.

Keyboard shortcuts	Function
Backspace	Deletes the character to the left of the cursor
Ctrl + Backspace	Deletes the word adjacent to the cursor
Delete	Deletes the character to the right of the cursor
Ctrl + Delete	Deletes all text from the text cursor to the end of the line
Alt + Backspace	Undoes the last function your performed - a shortcut for the Undo command
Alt + Shift + Backspace	Invokes the Undelete dialog box and inserts the last deletion at the current cursor position

Typing a Document — Exercise 2ex

This training exercise is designed so that people of all levels of expertise with WordPerfect can use it to gain maximum benefit. In order to do this, the bare exercise is listed below this paragraph on just one page, with no hints. The following pages contain the steps needed to complete this exercise for those who need additional prompting.

Steps in brief

1. *Open up WordPerfect from the Windows icon.*
2. *Type in the following text:*

Headlines
Every one of your publications has a message to give to your target audience, and you should give it to them right away. Put it in the Headline.
Why? Because research has shown that five times as many people will read the headlines as the rest of the publication.
Research has also shown that clever headlines, puns, literary allusions and snappy words don't work.

---

3. *Move the cursor up to the word "target" and delete it.*
4. *Using Typeover mode, change the heading so it reads: "Making it Clear".*
5. *Save the file as header.doc.*

The details for completing these steps are on the following pages.

Steps in detail

1. Open up WordPerfect from the Windows icon.

Your program may already be open; in this case just select *New* from the **File** menu to start a new document. Your screen will then be the same as Figure 2x-2.

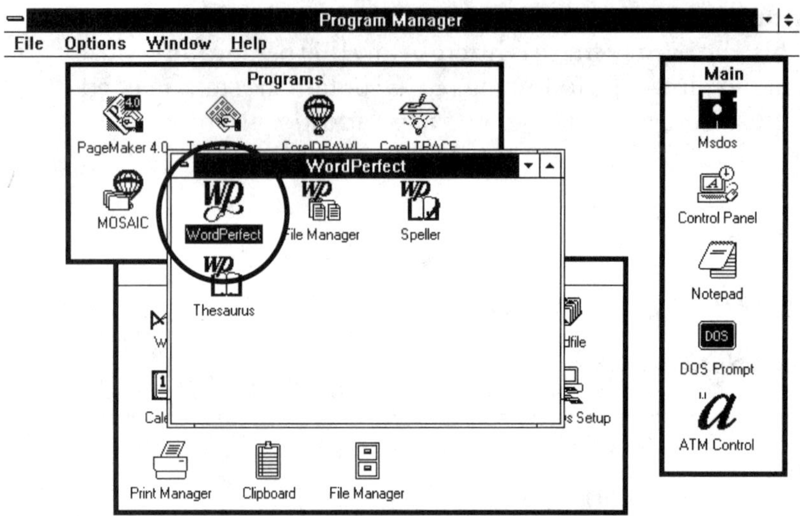

Figure 2x-1. *Double-click on the WordPerfect Windows icon to open WordPerfect.*

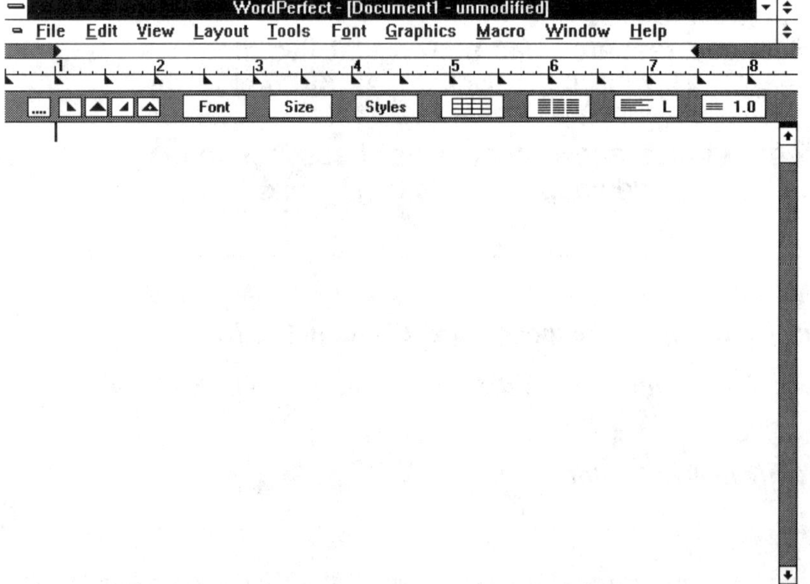

Figure 2x-2. *This is the WordPerfect editing screen ready for keying in the text.*

2. Type in the following text:

Headlines
Every one of your publications has a message to give to your target audience, and you should give it to them right away. Put it in the Headline.
Why? Because research has shown that five times as many people will read the headlines as the rest of the publication.
Research has also shown that clever headlines, puns, literary allusions and snappy words don't work.

The text cursor is positioned at the top left of the WordPerfect screen. All you need to do is start typing. Text characters will always appear to the right of the flashing cursor.

Note: *Only use the Enter key to start a new paragraph, as WordPerfect word-wraps the lines automatically.*

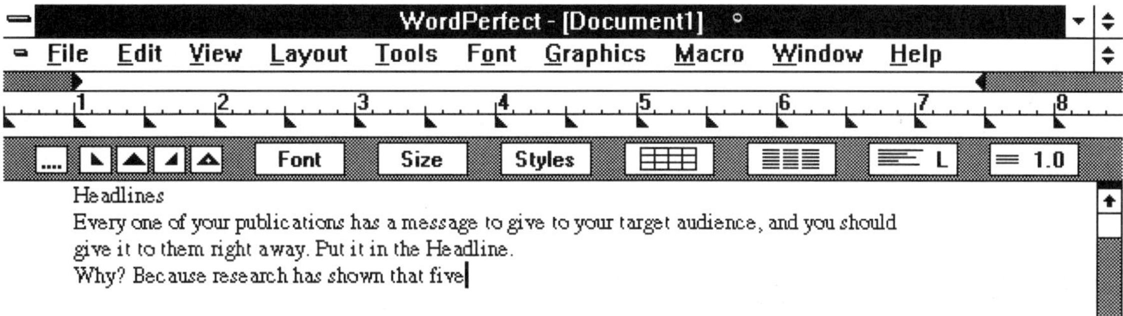

Figure 2x-3. *Start typing the text straight into WordPerfect. Don't worry about accuracy at this stage, but if you do type in the wrong character, use the Backspace key to delete it.*

3. Move the cursor up to the word "target" and delete it.

When you have finished typing the document, the flashing cursor will be at the end. An easy way to move the cursor to the word "target", other than using the mouse, is to use the Arrow keys on your keyboard. See Figures 2x-4 through 2x-6 captions to complete this step.

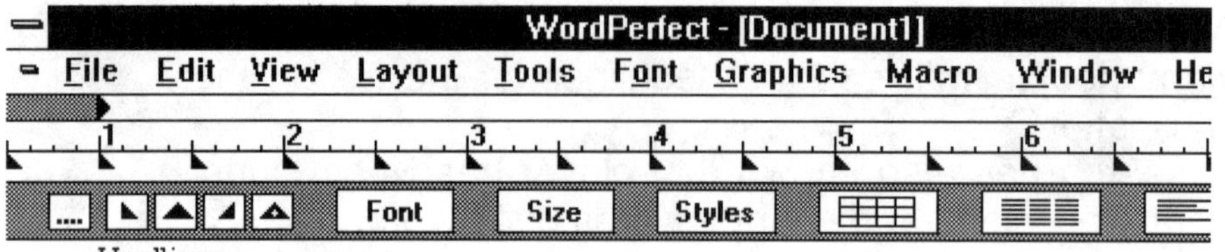

Figure 2x-4. *First locate the line containing the word "target" and move the cursor to this line using the Up Arrow key.*

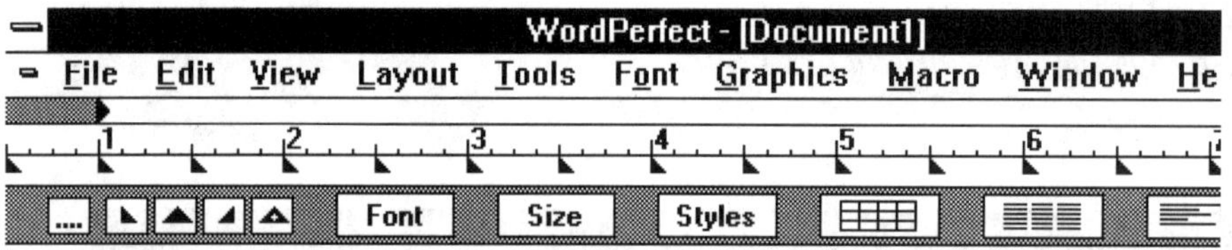

Figure 2x-5. *Using the shortcut keys, Ctrl+Right Arrow, (which moves the cursor right a word at a time) or Ctrl+ Left Arrow (depending where the word is on your screen), position the text cursor after the word "target".*

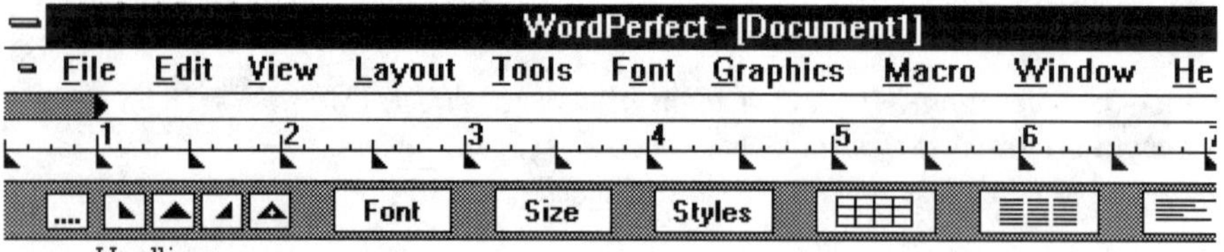

Figure 2x-6. *Use the Backspace key to delete "target" and the blank space that precedes it.*

4. ***Using Typeover mode, change the heading so it reads: "Making it Clear".***

Press the *Insert* key to activate *Typeover* mode (see Figure 2x-7). Perform the additional steps as indicated in the Figures 2x-8 and 2x-9 captions.

Typeover

Figure 2x-7. *Check the Status bar in the bottom left corner to see that Typeover mode has been activated by the Insert key.*

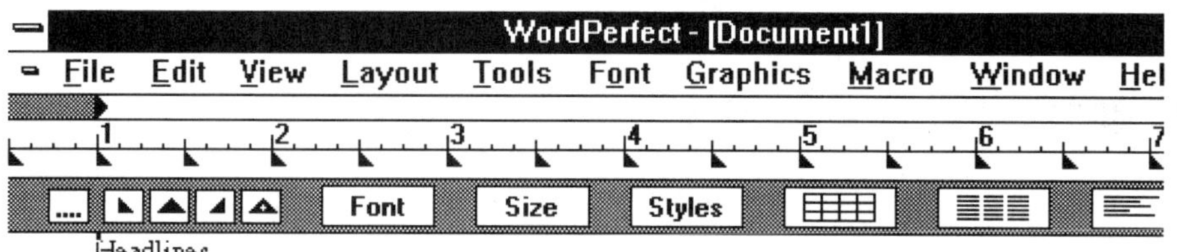

Figure 2x-8. *Click the mouse at the beginning of the document to insert the text cursor or, alternatively, press the Ctrl+Home keys.*

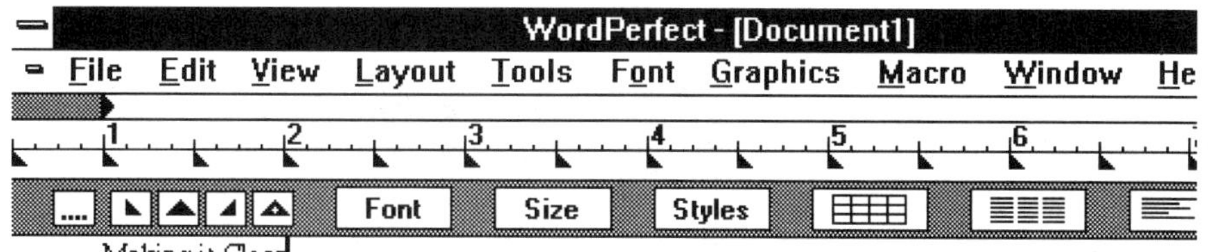

Figure 2x-9. *Type the new heading over the current one. Text in Typeover mode replaces existing text, as opposed to Insert mode, which pushes text to the right of the cursor.*

Note: *Typeover mode is de-activated by pressing the Insert key again.*

5. ***Save the file as header.doc.***

Select the *Save* command from the **File** menu to activate the *Save As* dialog box (Figure 2x-10). After keying in the name of the file, click on the *Save* button.

For this exercise, the file was saved in a sub-directory called ***learn*** which comes with WordPerfect. You may save it where you like.

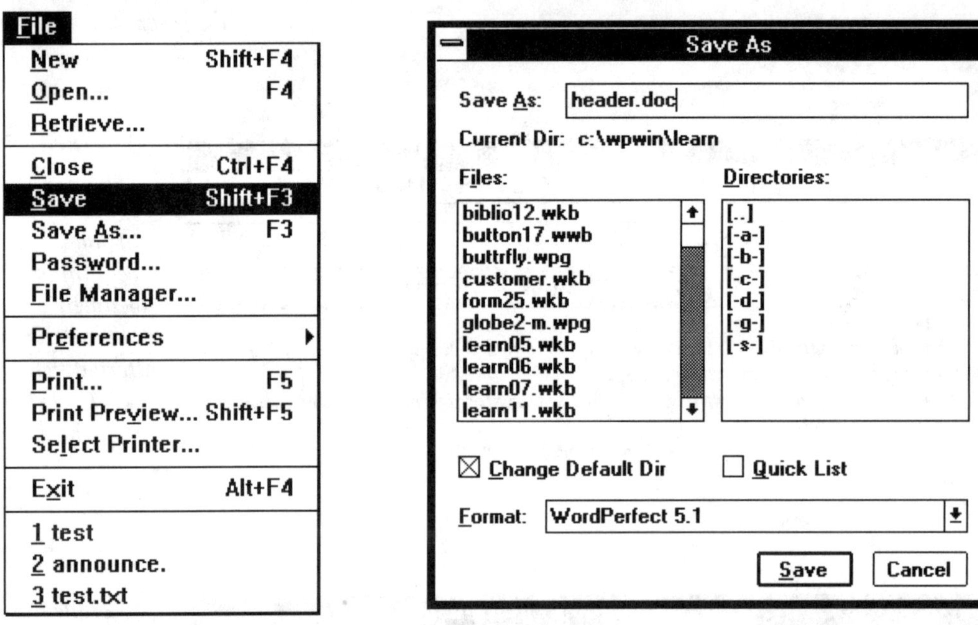

Figure 2x-10. *To save this document, select Save from the* ***File*** *menu to activate the Save As dialog box. In this dialog box, type the name of the file, in this case header.doc, and select Save.*

After exiting the *Save As* dialog box, the new name of the document will be reflected in the Title bar (Figure 2x-11).

Figure 2x-11. *When you return to the editing screen, the new name appears in the Title bar.*

Editing Text

At any time, while writing or editing a document, the document's text can be deleted, copied, moved, or have its attributes changed.

In this chapter you will be asked to edit the ***school.let*** file, that you created in the example in Chapter 2.

The Open command

The *Open* command, in the **File** menu, is used to load an existing WordPerfect document from a file into its own editing window. In this chapter you will use the *Open* command to edit the file ***school.let*** that you created in Chapter 2.

To open the file ***school.let***, select the *Open* command from the **File** menu. The *Open File* dialog box, seen in Figure 3-1, will appear. Notice that, while the *Open* command is selected, the words "Open an existing file and retrieve it into a window" replace the font and typesize information in the Status bar.

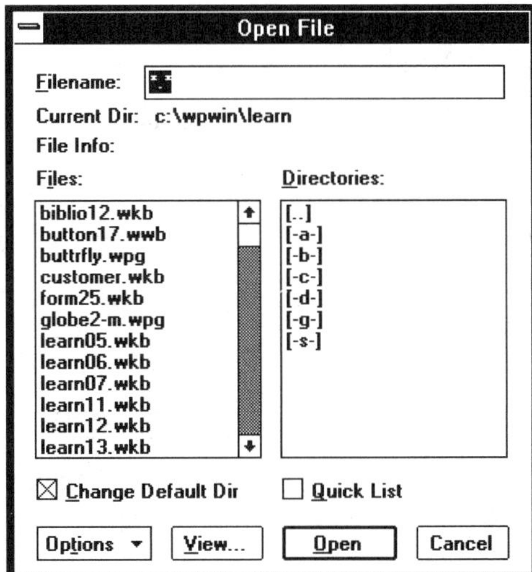

Figure 3-1. *The Open File dialog box appears when the Open command is selected from the **File** menu.*

Though it contains some special features that will be discussed in later chapters of this book, the *Open File* dialog box is very similar to any other Windows file selection box.

The *Directories* list box on the right lets you select the sub-directory in which the file to be loaded is located. Double-click on the appropriate drive letters and sub-directory names until the desired path is listed on the *Current Dir* line. Use this list box to select the directory in which you saved the file ***school.let*** in the last chapter.

The *Files* list box on the left of the *Open File* dialog box lists files from the selected directory. By default, the *Filename* text box contains the wild-card *.*, which allows all files in the current directory to be listed.

Locate the ***school.let*** file in the *Files* list box and highlight it by clicking on it once. Select the **Open** button to load the file. As with other Windows file selection dialog boxes, you may simply double-click on ***school.let*** to load it into the editing screen.

Once you select the file, it will load from disk and display on screen as shown in Figure 3-2.

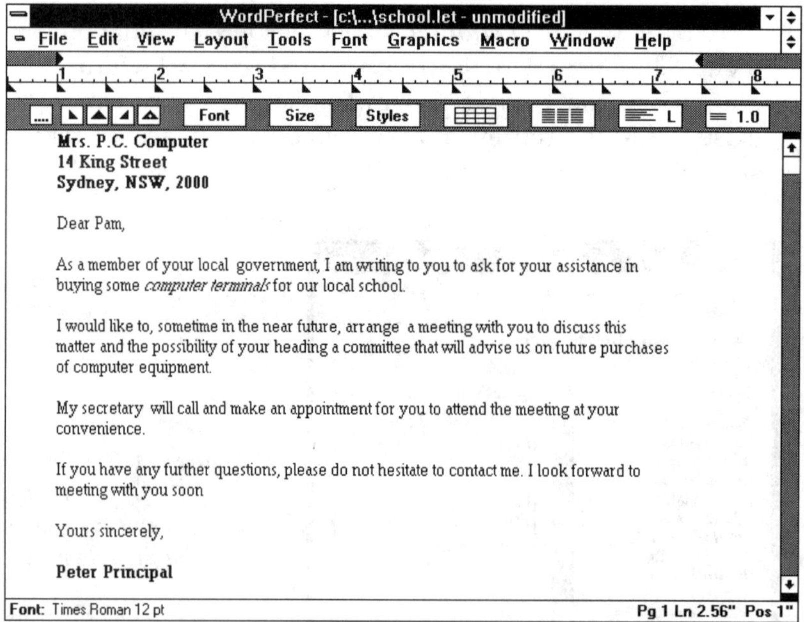

Figure 3-2. *The file* ***school.let*** *that was saved at the end of Chapter 2 has been loaded into the editing screen using the Open command.*

Selecting text

In Chapter 2, you saw how text could be modified letter-by-letter using the cursor control keys. Often, entire blocks of text must be edited in the same way and at the same time. In such cases, it is more efficient to be able to identify all of the text to be edited, and to apply a command or a process to all of the text simultaneously.

In WordPerfect for Windows, this process for identifying text is called 'selecting' and it involves highlighting the desired text so that it appears reversed—white on black instead of black on white—on the screen.

Swiping text

One of the easiest, and most efficient, ways of selecting text is the 'swiping' method. There are several ways in which you can swipe text in WordPerfect. By completing the following examples, you will see the two most useful swiping techniques; other methods are listed in the **Hints and Tips** section of this chapter.

To use the 'dragging' method of swiping text, place the cursor in front of the word "Dear" at the beginning of the letter. Click and hold the mouse button and, without releasing, move the cursor to the end of the last letter ("r") of this word. Release the mouse button. The word "Dear" now appears reversed, as seen in Figure 3-3, indicating that it is selected.

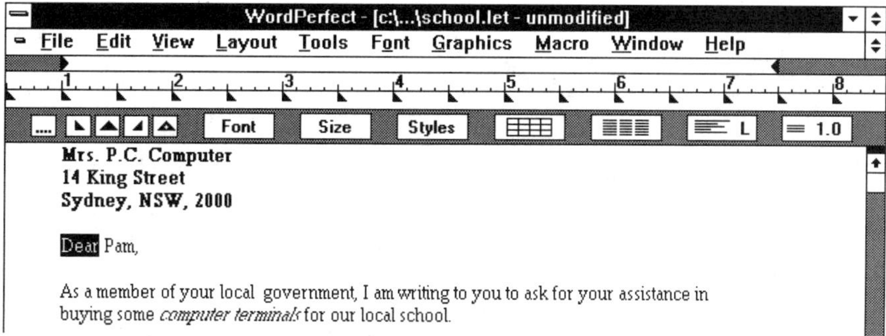

Figure 3-3. The word "Dear" has been highlighted by holding the mouse button down and dragging it across the word.

The 'shift-click' method of swiping is useful for selecting larger blocks of text. Insert the text cursor at the beginning of the word "As", in the first paragraph. Without clicking or holding the mouse button, position the I-bar mouse cursor at the end of the last word in the second paragraph: "equipment". Hold the Shift key and, while the mouse cursor remains positioned after "equipment", click the mouse button once. The first two paragraphs will now be entirely highlighted, as seen in Figure 3-4.

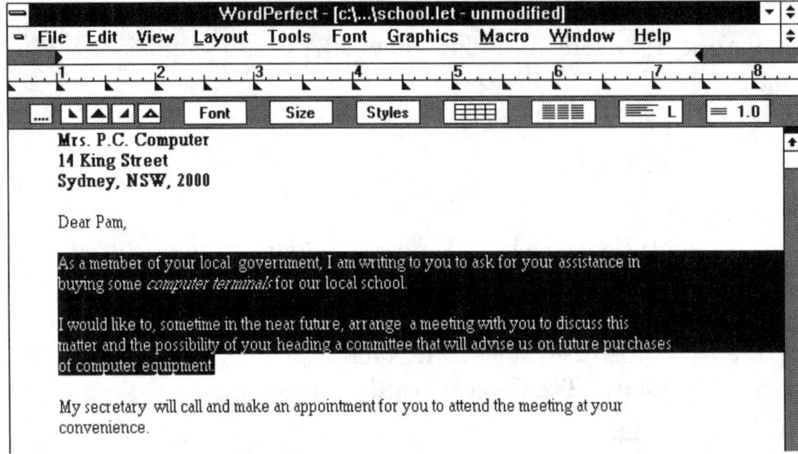

Figure 3-4. *The first two paragraphs of the sample letter are selected using the shift-click swiping technique.*

Clicking on text

Clicking with the mouse can be a quick and easy alternative to selecting text by swiping. By clicking the left mouse button a certain number of times, you can select specific quantities of text.

A single click simply places the text cursor into the document at the position of the I-bar mouse pointer. Place the flashing text cursor in the middle of the word "questions" in the last paragraph, by clicking the mouse button once.

Double-clicking the mouse button will highlight the word under the I-bar. Double-click the mouse over the word "questions" and the whole word will become highlighted.

A triple-click is used to select an entire sentence. Move the mouse cursor to the beginning of the last paragraph, and click the mouse button three times to select the entire first sentence.

Finally, a quadruple-click—four clicks of the left mouse button in succession—can be used to select an entire paragraph. For example, move your cursor to the last paragraph in the letter and click the mouse button four times. The entire last paragraph will now be highlighted.

Figure 3-5 shows the effect of each of these clicking actions on the last paragraph in the letter.

When text is selected in a document, as shown in Figure 3-5, the words *Select on* appear in the Status bar in place of the font and size information.

***Figure* 3-5.** *Clicking the left mouse button can be used to select text in a WordPerfect document.*

A single click places the text cursor into the document below the mouse cursor.

If you have any further questions, please do not hesitate to contact me. I look forward to meeting with you soon

A double-click selects the word below the mouse cursor.

If you have any further questions, please do not hesitate to contact me. I look forward to meeting with you soon

A triple-click selects the sentence below the mouse cursor.

If you have any further questions, please do not hesitate to contact me. I look forward to meeting with you soon

A quadruple-click selects the entire paragraph below the mouse cursor.

If you have any further questions, please do not hesitate to contact me. I look forward to meeting with you soon.

When text is selected, the words "Select on" appear in the Status bar.

Select on Pg 1 Ln 4.11" Pos 3.28"

The Date command

The *Date* command in the **Tools** menu is used to insert the current date into a document. This date comes from your computer system's date which is set by the computer's internal clock.

To insert today's date into the sample letter, place the text cursor to the left of the word "Mrs." at the beginning of the document. Now, select the *Date* command from the **Tools** menu, activating the *Date* fly-out menu shown in Figure 3-6.

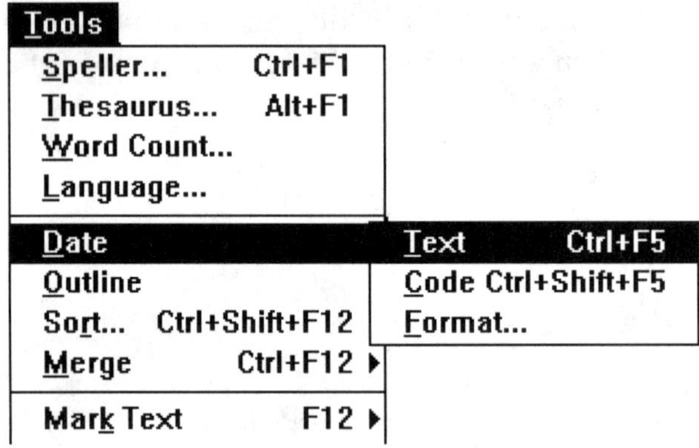

Figure 3-6. *Selecting the Date command from the* ***Tools*** *menu activates a fly-out menu.*

Select the *Text* command from this list. The *Text* command from the *Date* fly-out menu will automatically type the date into the document at the position of the text cursor.

As a shortcut to selecting the *Text* command from the *Date* fly-out menu in the **Tools** menu, you may find it easier to hold the Control key while pressing the F5 key.

Once you have entered the date into the document, press the Enter key twice to move the phrase: "Mrs. P.C. Computer", down to a separate line. The letter should now look like the example shown in Figure 3-7.

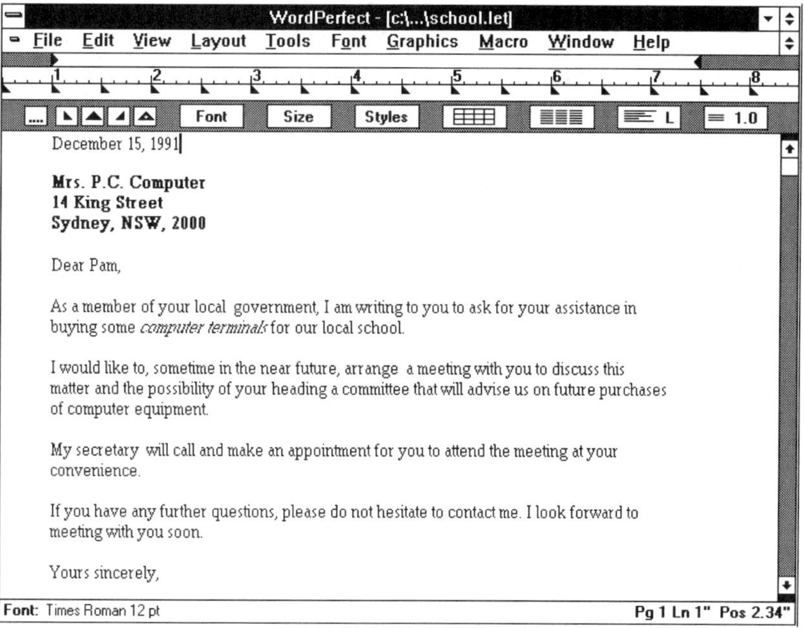

Figure 3-7. *Using the Date command, the date has been inserted into the sample letter.*

The Flush Right command

The *Flush Right* command is used to position text, such as dates, titles, or headings so that the last letter is aligned with the right margin.

For example, align the date inserted above, with the right margin. Select the text associated with the date, making sure that the entire date is properly highlighted. Now, select the *Line* command in the **Layout** menu to activate the fly-out menu seen in Figure 3-8. Select the *Flush Right* command from this list. The date text will now be automatically placed against the right margin.

Holding the Alt key while pressing F7 is a quick and easy short-cut to selecting the *Flush Right* command from the *Line* fly-out menu in the **Layout** menu.

Figure 3-8 shows how the letter will look after the date has been aligned to the right margin.

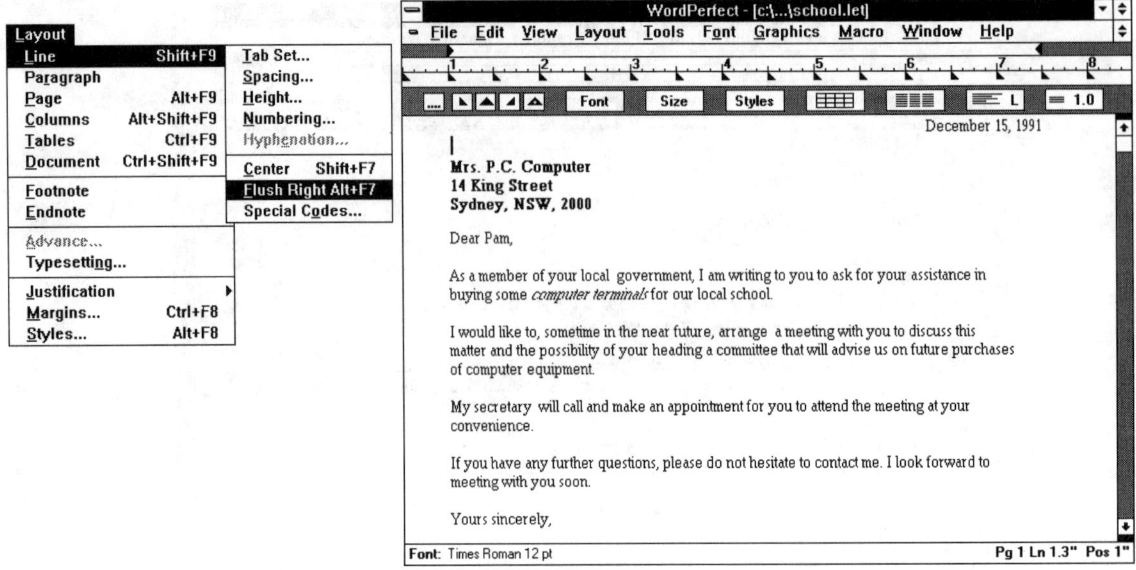

***Figure 3-8.** The Line/Flush Right command in the **Layout** menu positions lines of text so that they are aligned with the right margin.*

The Center command

The Center command is used to align a single line, horizontally, in the middle of the page. Add a line of text to the sample letter, and center it as follows.

Place the text cursor at the beginning of the first paragraph of the letter and type the words "Re: Purchase of Computer Terminals". Press the Enter key twice to move the first paragraph down to a separate line. The letter will now look like the excerpt shown in Figure 3-9.

Now, highlight the line of text you have just typed. Select the *Line* command from the **Layout** menu. From the fly-out menu that appears (already shown in Figure 3-8), select the *Center* command. You might find it quicker and easier to use the Shift and F7 keys as a shortcut.

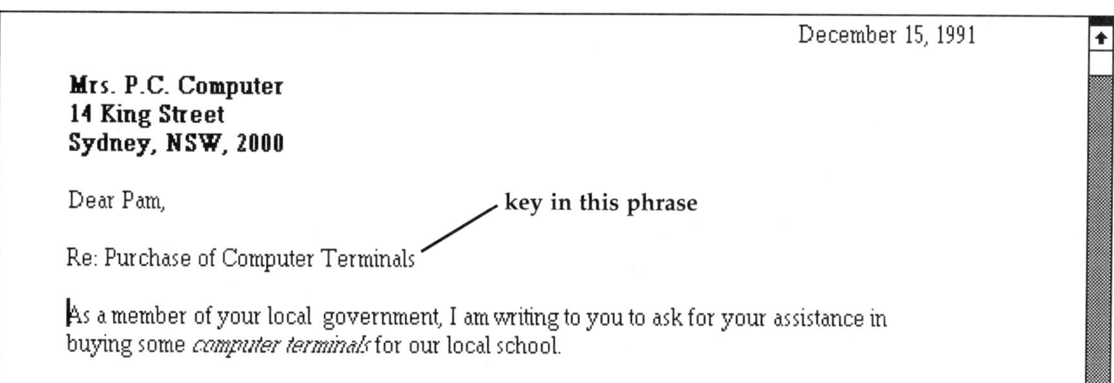

Figure 3-9. Insert the phrase "Re: Purchase of Computer Terminals" at the beginning of the letter.

The line of text you have selected will be centered between the right and left margins. The letter will now look like the example in Figure 3-10.

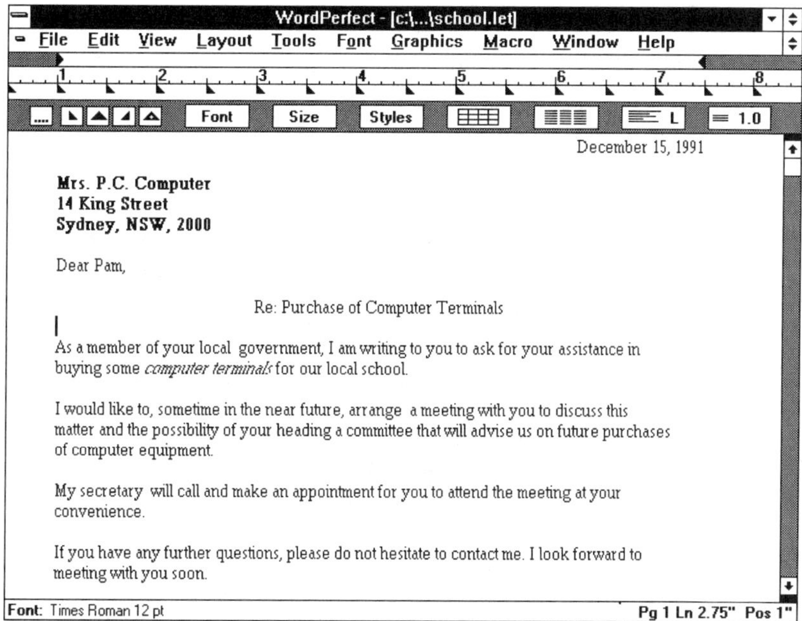

Figure 3-10. *The Line/Center command in the* ***Layout*** *menu centers lines of text between the left and right margins.*

The Font command

The font styles and sizes available in WordPerfect for Windows depend on the capabilities of your printer. In the following example, a PostScript printer is used. If you have a different type of printer, some of the dialog box options which follow may differ from those you see on your own screen.

The *Font* command in the **Font** menu, Figure 3-11, allows you to change the size and appearance of printed text.

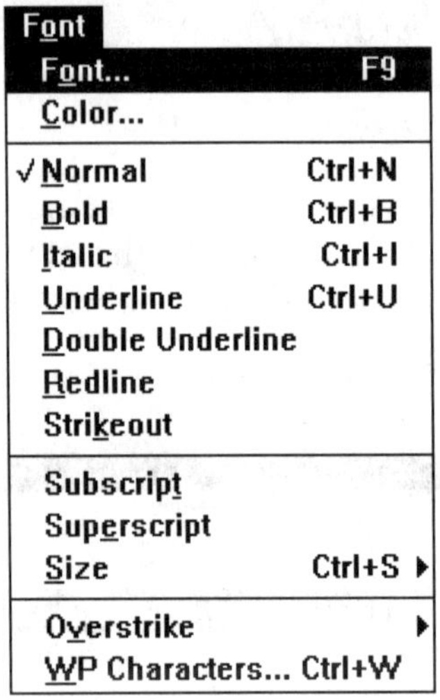

Font
Font... F9
Color...
√ Normal Ctrl+N
Bold Ctrl+B
Italic Ctrl+I
Underline Ctrl+U
Double Underline
Redline
Strikeout
Subscript
Superscript
Size Ctrl+S ▸
Overstrike ▸
WP Characters... Ctrl+W

Figure 3-11. *The Font command in the **Font** menu.*

Highlight the text in the third paragraph (commencing with "My secretary...") and select the *Font* command from the **Font** menu. The *Font* dialog box, shown in Figure 3-12, will appear. Because the fonts available depend on the selected printer, the currently selected printer is listed at the top of the dialog box.

The *Font* list box contains the names of all the available fonts. Most printers will have several fonts available. The font currently in use is highlighted in this list. Beside the *Font* list box, the *Point Size* list box is used to select the size of the font.

The *Appearance* and *Size* areas of the *Font* dialog box allow you to select a variety of text attributes you may want to apply to the fonts. In Chapter 2, you have already seen other ways of applying some of these attributes. In fact, nearly all of the *Appearance* and *Size* attributes in this dialog box can also be applied directly through the **Font** menu.

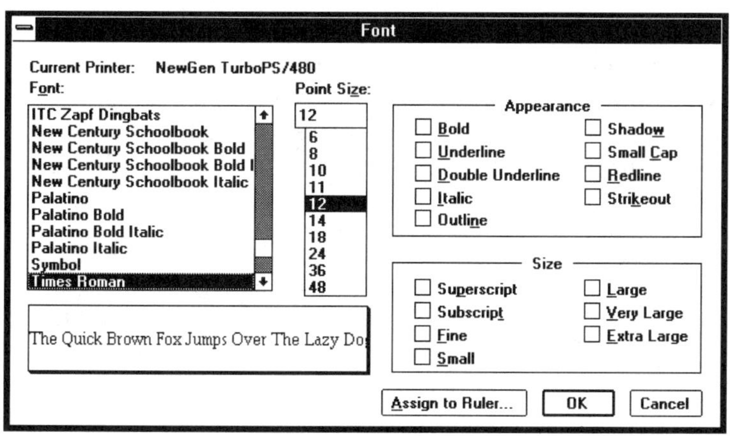

*Figure 3-12. The Font dialog box appears when the Font command is selected from the **Font** menu. Twelve point Times Roman font is selected and the sample text is displayed in this font and type-size.*

A sample box below the *Font* list box contains the traditional typing sentence: "The Quick Brown Fox Jumps Over The Lazy Dog". As different fonts and type attributes are selected, the text in this box alters to represent the selected attributes. In the dialog box in Figure 3-12, the selected font is Times Roman, and the size is 12 point. In Figure 3-13, 24 point Helvetica has been selected. Note how the sample text has altered to represent the new settings.

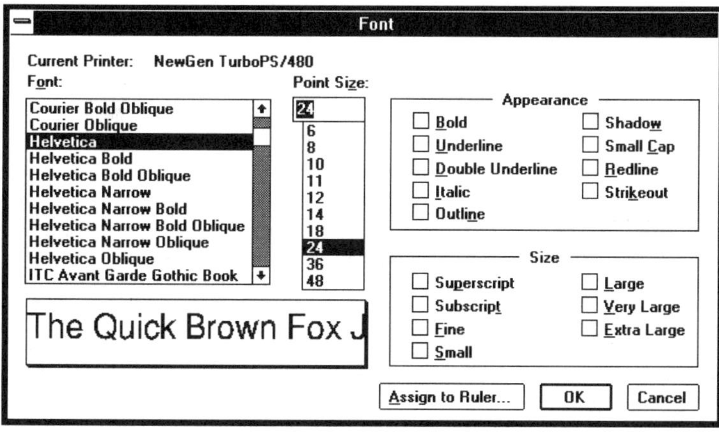

Figure 3-13. The Font dialog box with 24 point Helvetica as the selected font and type-size. Note the difference between the sample text here and in Figure 3-12.

Without selecting **OK**, try highlighting a few different fonts and font attributes, to see their effects on the sample text. Finally, select a new font and size for the highlighted third paragraph of the document. For this example, 14 point Courier has been selected. When you have selected the desired font, click on **OK** to return to the editing screen. Figure 3-14 shows the document as it will now appear.

Use the mouse to place the text cursor in the third paragraph of the letter and note the font information in the Status bar. Now move the text cursor into the second paragraph and again note the font listed in the Status bar. Figure 3-14 shows the two versions of the Status bar.

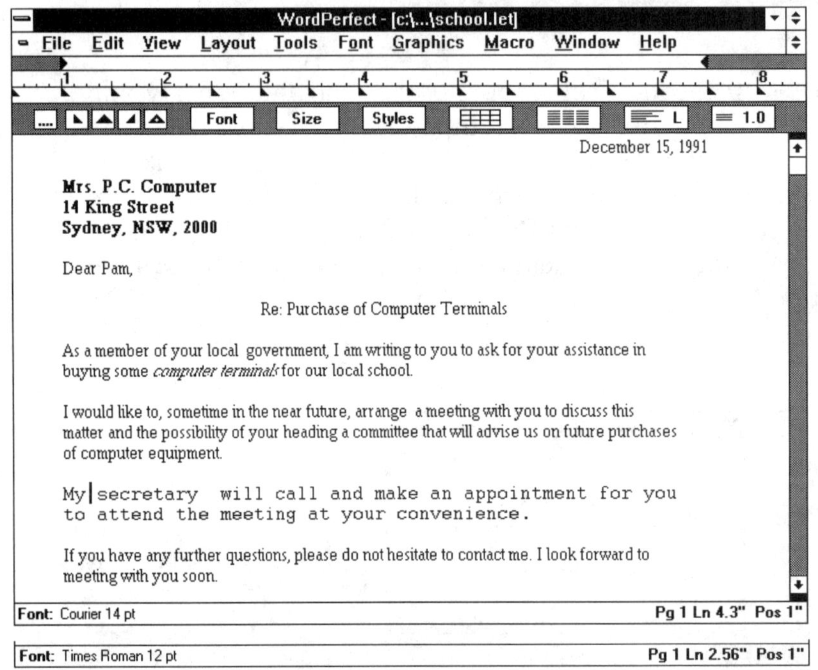

Figure 3-14. *The third paragraph of the sample letter has been converted to 14 point Courier font.*

The Status bar displays the font and size of the text adjacent to the text cursor.

The Size command

The *Size* command, in the **Font** menu, allows you to set certain font size attributes. The attributes in the *Size* fly-out menu, seen in Figure 3-15, are the same size attributes that can be selected in the *Font* dialog box (in Figures 3-12 and 3-13).

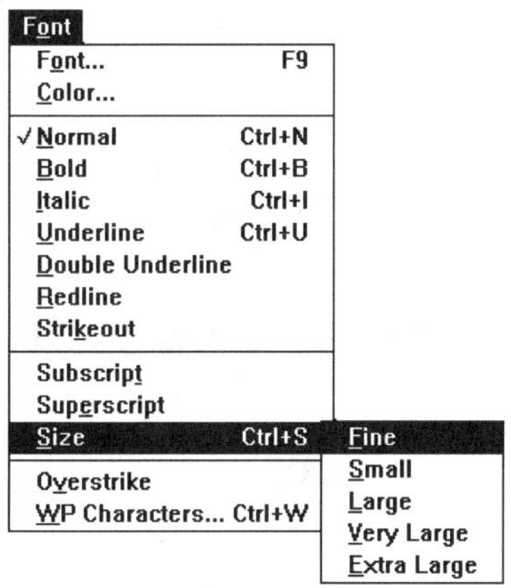

Figure 3-15. *The Size command in the* ***Font*** *menu invokes a fly-out menu from which you can select a number of text size attributes. These same attributes could also be selected from the Font dialog box (Figures 3-12 and 3-13).*

Rather than imposing a new font, these size attributes are relative to the current font in use. By default, with a PostScript printer, the *Large*, *Very Large*, and *Extra Large* attributes increase the text size by 120%, 150%, and 200% respectively. The *Fine* and *Small* attributes reduce text to 60% and 80% of its original size, respectively. You will see how to adjust these settings in Chapter 9 of this book.

Assign the *Large* attribute to the words "computer terminals" in the second line of the first paragraph of the letter. Highlight these words in the letter and select the *Size* command from the **Font** menu. From the fly-out menu, select the *Large* command. The words "computer terminals" now appear in a larger size. The document should now resemble the example shown in Figure 3-16.

Dear Pam,

Re: Purchase of Computer Terminals

As a member of your local government, I am writing to you to ask for your assistance in buying some *computer terminals* for our local school.

I would like to, sometime in the near future, arrange a meeting with you to discuss this matter and the possibility of your heading a committee that will advise us on future purchases of computer equipment.

Figure 3-16. *An excerpt from the sample letter as it should look (when formatted for a PostScript printer) after the words "computer terminals" have been given the Large font size attribute.*

The Convert Case command

The *Convert Case* command in the **Edit** menu, shown in Figure 3-17, is used to convert selected text to either all upper or all lower-case letters.

Assign the *Uppercase* attribute to the text you last typed into your letter: "Re: Purchase of Computer Terminals". Select this text in the letter and, once it is highlighted, select the *Convert Case* command in the **Edit** menu. In the fly-out menu that appears, select the *Uppercase* command.

The selected sentence now appears in all capital letters. When the highlighting is removed, by placing the text cursor in the document, the document will look like the example in Figure 3-17.

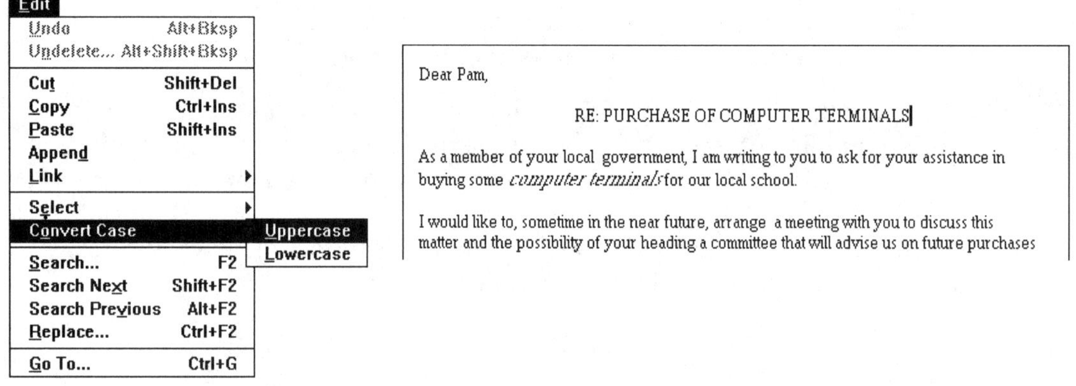

Figure 3-17. *Using the Convert Case command to capitalize a sentence of text.*

Justification

The justification feature in WordPerfect for Windows is used to align multiple lines of text in a document. The *Justification* command, in the **Layout** menu, activates a fly-out menu, seen in Figure 3-18, containing four justification commands: *Left*, *Right*, *Center*, and *Full*.

If you chose the *Left* justification command, text will be aligned to the left margin while leaving an unaligned, or ragged, right margin.

Choosing the *Right* justification command aligns the selected text to the right margin leaving a "ragged" left margin.

Text formatted with the *Center* justification command will be centered between the right and left margins, like most of the figure captions in this book.

The *Full* justification command aligns your text with both the left and right margins, like most of the paragraphs in this book.

Assign full justification to the second paragraph in your letter, that begins "I would like to...". Highlight this paragraph, and, when it is highlighted, select the *Justification/Full* command from the **Layout** menu.

All other types of justification—*Left, Right,* and *Center*—can be assigned to text using this same method.

The letter will now look like the example in Figure 3-18.

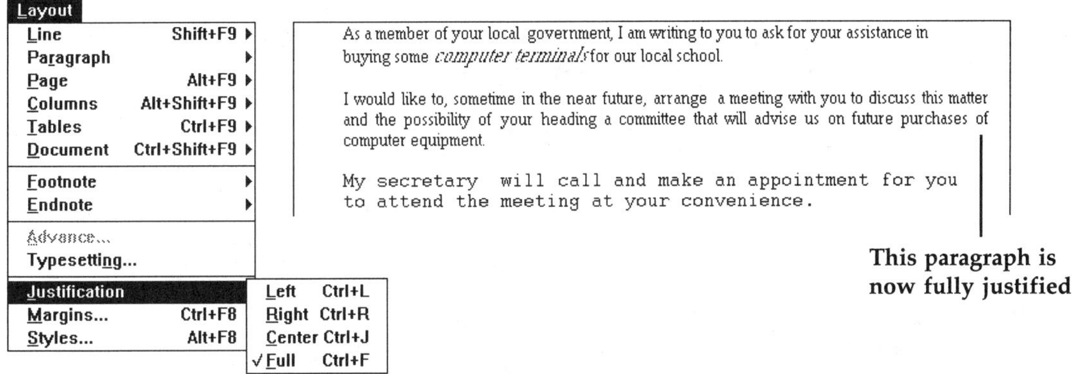

***Figure 3-18.** In this figure, the Justification/Full command has been used to align the second paragraph in the sample letter. Compare this paragraph with how it looks in Figure 3-2.*

The Page Break command

The point in a document where a new page begins, is called a 'page break'. WordPerfect for Windows keeps track of the number of lines which will fit on a page. A new page is automatically started when text is entered below the bottom margin.

This kind of automatically generated page-break is called a 'soft' page break, because it is generated by the program, or *soft*ware. These breaks will be displayed on the editing screen, shown in Figure 3-19, as a single line.

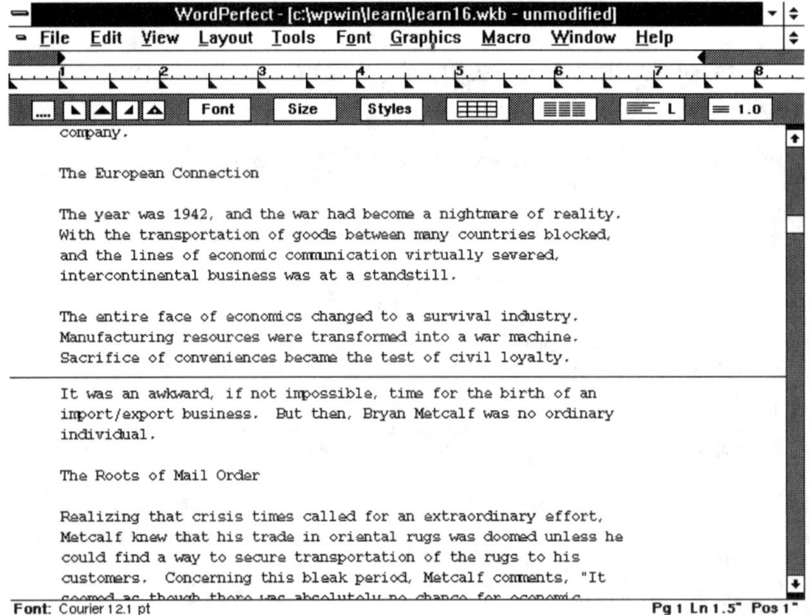

Figure 3-19. *A sample WordPerfect document showing an automatically inserted, or soft, page break.*

At times, while typing or editing a document, you will want to impose a page break when there is still room on the page for more text. Such breaks are called 'hard' page breaks and will display across your page as double lines, seen in Figure 3-20.

In Figure 3-19 and Figure 3-20, both pages of the document are visible at once. When the document is printed, each page will, of course, appear on a separate sheet of paper.

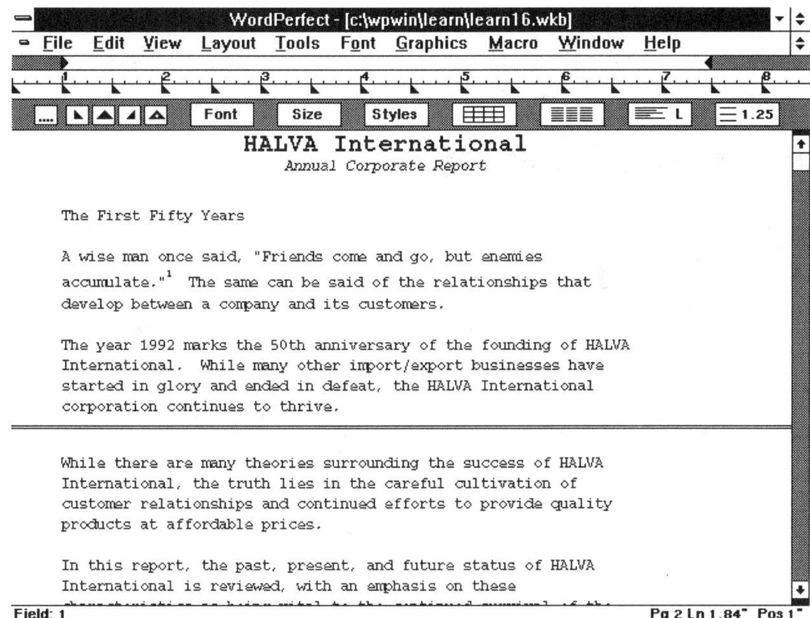

Figure 3-20. *A sample WordPerfect document showing a manually entered, or hard, page break.*

Insert a hard page break into the sample letter document. Place the text cursor at the end of the last line of text, "Peter Principal", and press the Enter key once to move down to a new line. Now select the *Page* command from the **Layout** menu.

From the fly-out menu that appears, shown in Figure 3-21, select the *Page Break* command. A double line is now placed into the letter, indicating the presence of a hard page break.

You can also use the Control and Enter keys together as a shortcut to selecting the *Page Break* command from the *Page* fly-out menu in the **Layout** menu.

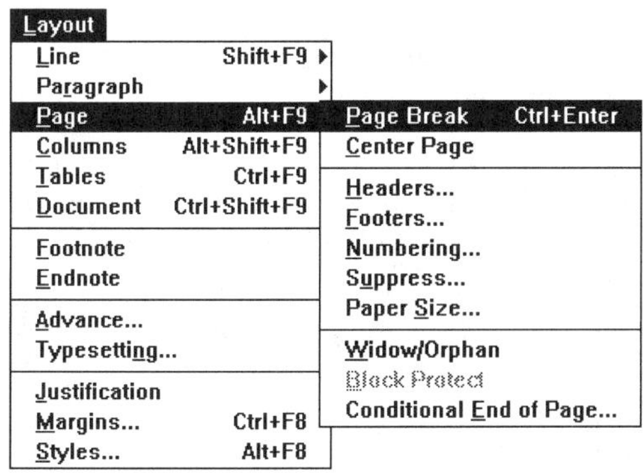

Figure 3-21. *The Page command's fly-out menu in the **Layout** menu.*

The document will now look like the example in Figure 3-22. Note that the information on the right-hand side of the Status bar now indicates that the text cursor is at the beginning of a new page.

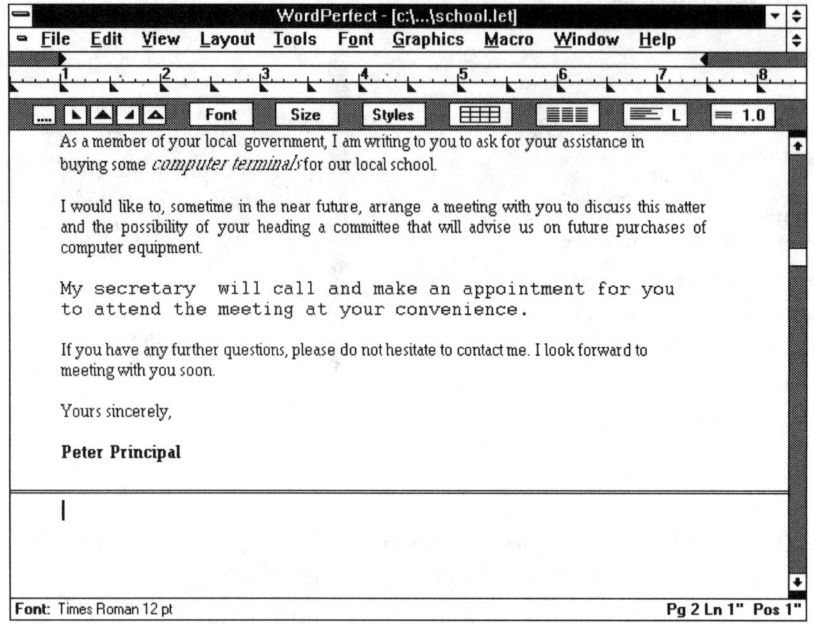

Figure 3-22. *A hard page break has been inserted into the sample letter document. Note the information on the right-hand side of the Status bar, indicating that the text cursor is positioned at the beginning of the new second page.*

The Clipboard commands

Four commands in the **Edit** menu, shown in Figure 3-23, allow you to use the Windows Clipboard as an editing tool in WordPerfect. These commands are: *Cut*, *Copy*, *Paste*, and *Append*.

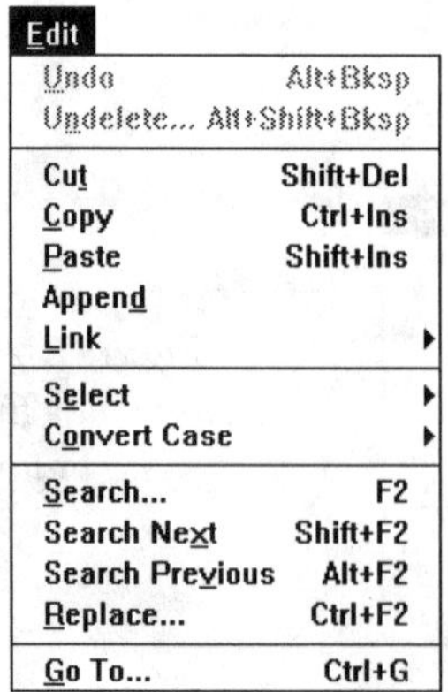

Figure 3-23. *The Cut, Copy, Paste, and Append commands, in the **Edit** menu, deal with the Windows Clipboard.*

The *Copy* command is used to place a copy of selected text, or graphics, into the Clipboard. The selected text is not removed from your document.

Highlight the words *"computer terminals"* from the first paragraph of the letter. Select the *Copy* command from the **Edit** menu. The selected text is now placed in the Clipboard, complete with its text attributes—*Italic* and *Large*— and will replace any previous Clipboard contents.

Move the text cursor to the top of the second page of the letter. Select the *Paste* command from the **Edit** menu to insert the Clipboard's contents at the cursor position. The document will now look like the example in Figure 3-24.

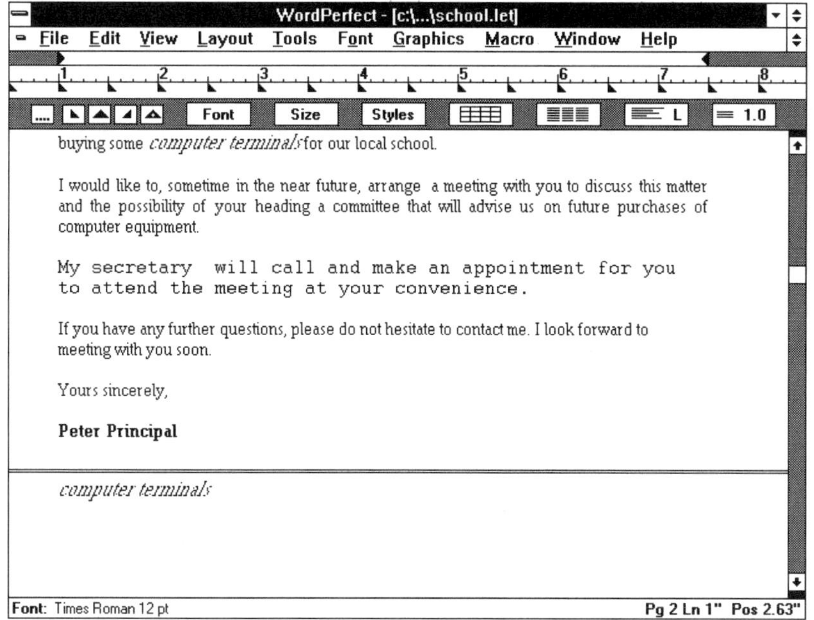

***Figure 3-24.** The Paste command from the **Edit** menu is used to insert the contents of the Windows Clipboard into the document at the position of the text cursor.*

The *Cut* command works in a similar fashion to the *Copy* command, except that it removes the selected text from the document while placing it into the Clipboard. Highlight the date at the top of the letter and select the *Cut* command from the **Edit** menu. Notice that the date is now removed from your letter. Without moving the cursor, select the *Paste* command from the **Edit** menu again. The date will now be re-inserted at the text cursor's position.

The *Append* command in the **Edit** menu is used when you want to add selected text or graphics to the Clipboard without replacing its earlier contents. Any selections you append to the Clipboard are placed after the contents already there and will remain until replaced with either the *Cut* or *Copy* commands.

All items on the Clipboard will remain if you exit from WordPerfect for Windows and run another Windows application. This feature of the Clipboard allows data to be passed between Windows applications and is one of the principal advantages of using Windows.

Saving the document

The sample letter, ***school.let***, that you have modified in this chapter will be used in the next chapter.

Please update the existing ***school.let*** file on your disk by using the *Save* command in the **File** menu.

Hints and Tips

Selecting text

The text selecting techniques described in this chapter all involve the mouse. There are however, keyboard shortcuts for selecting text as well. As you grow more familiar with WordPerfect for Windows, you may find some of these shortcuts convenient.

The following tables list the keyboard shortcuts for selecting text.

Selection Method	Result
Double-click the mouse button	Selects a word
Triple-click the mouse button	Selects a sentence
Quadruple-click the mouse button	Selects a paragraph
Insert the flashing text cursor at the beginning of a block of text. Move the mouse cursor to the end of the block and, holding down the Shift key, click the mouse button once.	Selects the text between the text cursor and the mouse cursor
Shift+Right arrow key	Selects the character to the right of the flashing text cursor
Shift+Left arrow key	Selects the character to the left of the flashing text cursor
Shift+End key	Selects to the end of a line

Selection Method	Result
Shift+Home key	Selects to the beginning of a line
Shift+PgUp key	Selects to the top of the screen, then up one screen at a time when you press the PgUp key again
Shift+PgDn key	Selects to the bottom of the screen, then down one screen at a time when you press PgDn again
Shift+Alt+PgUp	Selects to the first line of the previous page
Shift+Alt+PgDn	Selects to the first line on the next page
Shift+Ctrl+Right arrow key	Selects the word to the right of the cursor
Shift+Ctrl+Left arrow key	Selects the word to the left of the cursor
Shift+Ctrl+Up arrow key	Selects up one paragraph
Shift+Ctrl+Down arrow key	Selects down one paragraph

Editing Text — Exercise

3ex

This training exercise is designed so that people of all levels of expertise with WordPerfect can use it to gain maximum benefit. In order to do this, the bare exercise is listed below this paragraph on just one page, with no hints. The following pages contain the steps needed to complete this exercise for those who need additional prompting.

Steps in brief

1. *Open up the WordPerfect file, learn12.wkb, located in the learn sub-directory of the wpwin sub-directory (within the windows directory).*
2. *Select the words "The First" and delete them.*
3. *Insert the date in the line under "Annual Corporate Report".*
4. *Move the date so that it is flush right.*
5. *Center the words "Fifty Years".*
6. *Change the font of "Fifty Years" to Helvetica Bold 12 point.*
7. *Fully justify the text from the line beginning with: "A wise man once said..." until the end of the document.*
8. *Insert a page break after the heading "The European Connection".*
9. *Cut "The European Connection" from page one and paste it at the beginning of page two.*

The details for completing these steps are on the following pages.

Steps in detail

1. ***Open up the WordPerfect file, learn12.wkb, located in the learn sub-directory of the wpwin sub-directory (within the windows directory).***

Follow Figures 3x-1 and 3x-2 to open the file ***learn12.wkb.*** (Depending upon how your machine is setup, your ***learn*** sub-directory may not be in exactly the same place as Figure 3x-2.)

Figure 3x-1. *Select the Open command from the **File** menu to activate the Open File dialog box .*

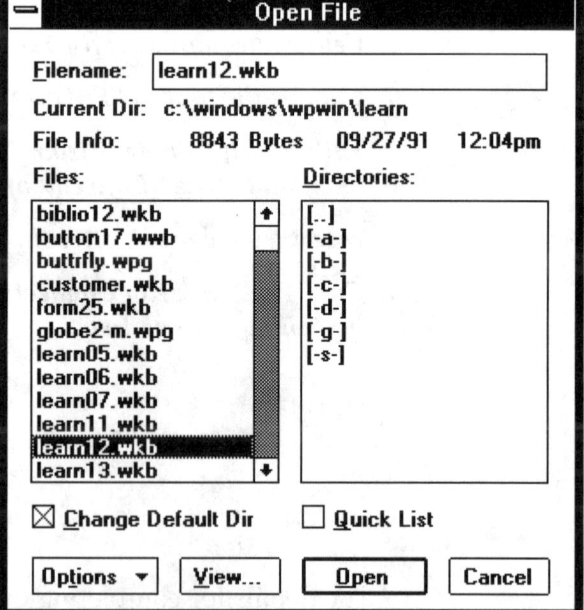

Figure 3x-2. *In this dialog box, locate the **learn12.wkb** file in the **learn** sub-directory of the **wpwin** sub-directory. Highlight the file name with the mouse and click on the Open button.*

2. *Select the words "The First" and delete them.*

Use the swiping method to select this text. Click the mouse cursor so that it is inserted just before the word "The". Hold the mouse button down, move the mouse to the right until both words are highlighted, and then release the mouse.

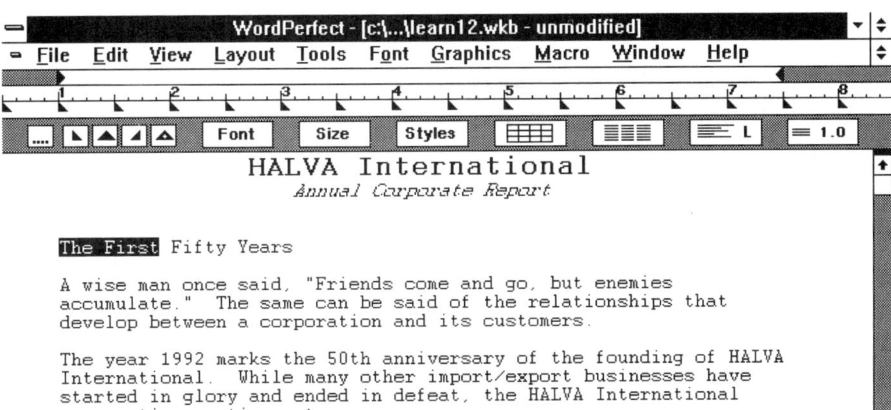

Figure 3x-3. Highlight the two words "The First" by swiping them with the mouse.

Now that the text has been highlighted, all you need do is press the Delete key to erase the highlighted words. Figure 3x-4 shows the result.

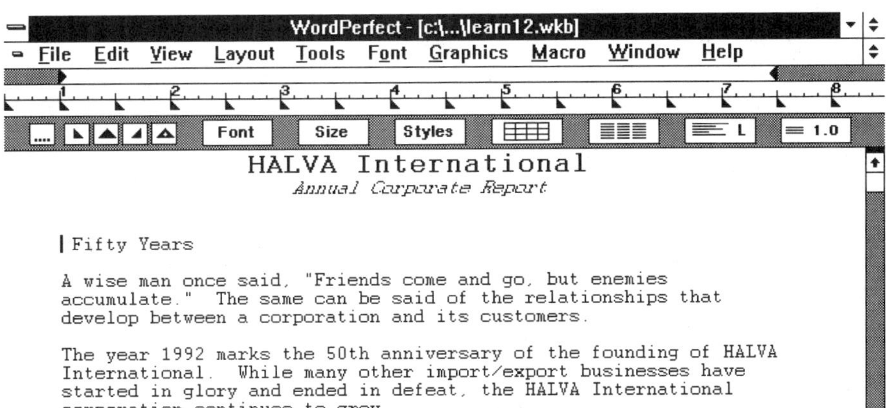

***Figure 3x-4.** This is how the screen looks after the words have been deleted.*

3. Insert the date in the line under "Annual Corporate Report".

Move the cursor up one line with the Up Arrow key so that it is above "Fifty Years". Follow Figures 3x-5 and 3x-6 for instructions on how to insert the date.

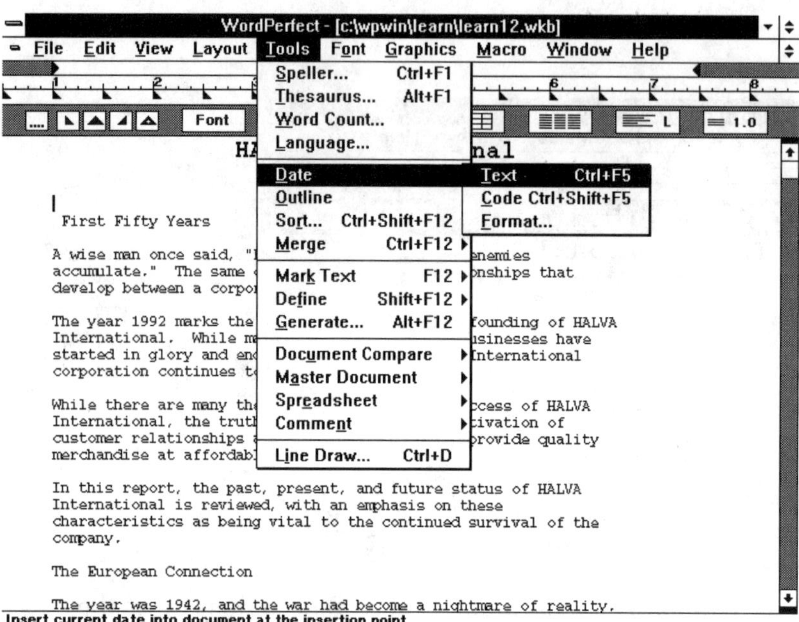

Figure 3x-5. *Once your cursor is in the correct position, select the Date command from the **Tools** menu, and click on the Text option.*

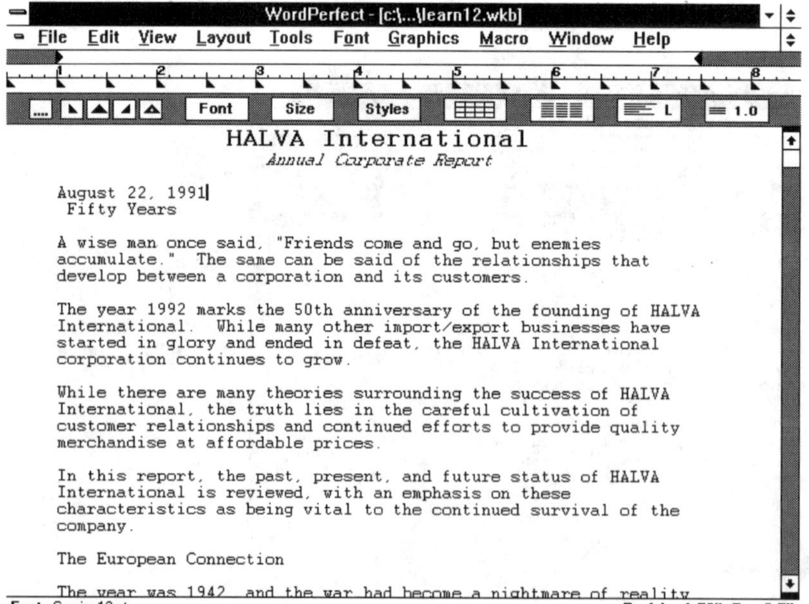

Figure 3x-6. *After returning to the screen, today's date will appear to the left of the cursor.*

4. *Move the date so that it is flush right.*

To move the date so that it is flush with the right margin, relocate the text cursor to the beginning of the date. Next, select the *Flush Right* command from the *Line* fly-out menu in the **Layout** menu (Figure 3x-7). The date will now be aligned with the right margin as shown in Figure 3x-8.

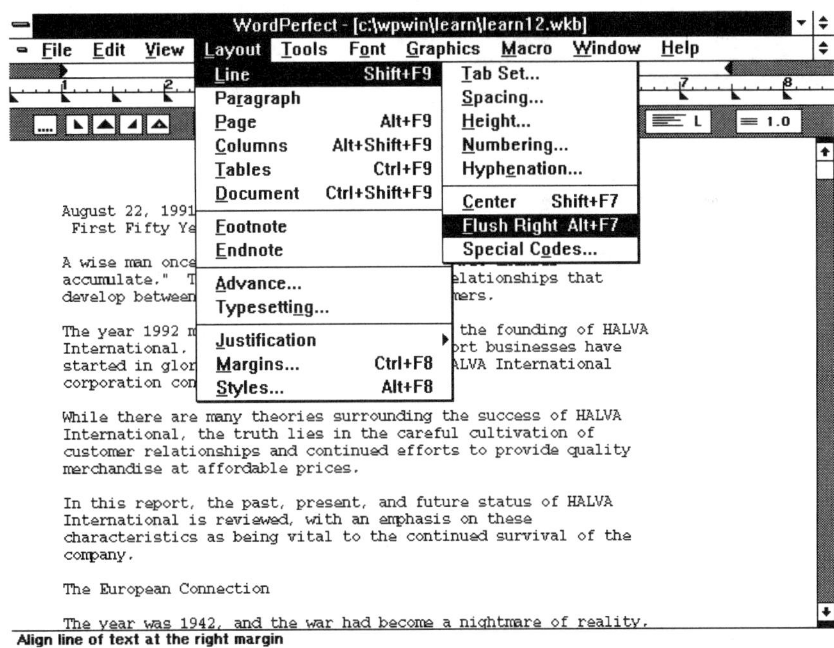

Figure 3x-7. Select the Line/Flush Right command from the **Layout** menu, to align the date with the right margin.

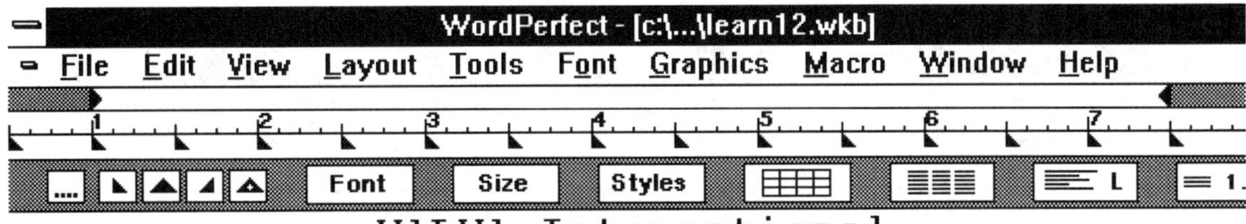

Figure 3x-8. This is how the date will appear with its new alignment.

5. *Center the words "Fifty Years".*

Make sure the cursor is positioned at the beginning of the words "Fifty Years". You can click your mouse at the beginning of the line to reposition it or, alternatively, use the directional Arrow keys. The next step is to select the *Center* command from the *Line* fly-out menu, as shown in Figure 3x-9. The result is shown in Figure 3x-10.

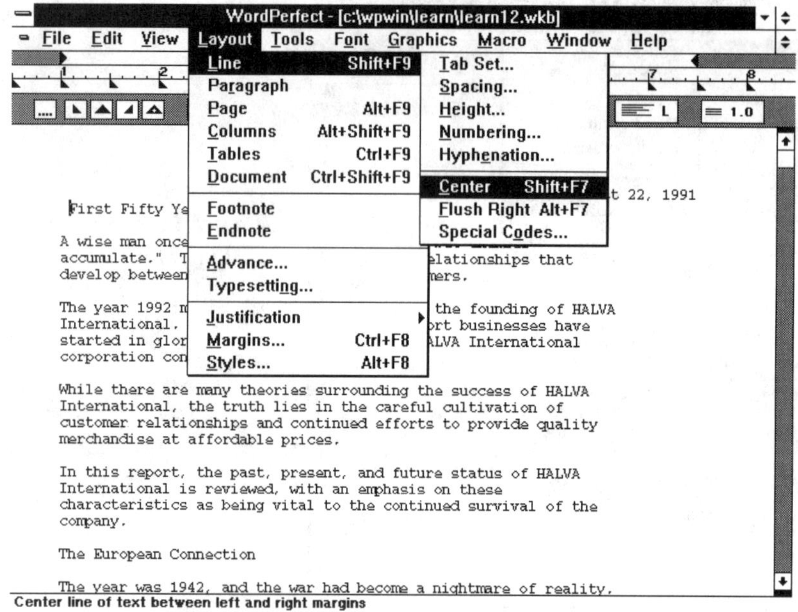

Figure 3x-9. *Select the Center command after the cursor is correctly positioned.*

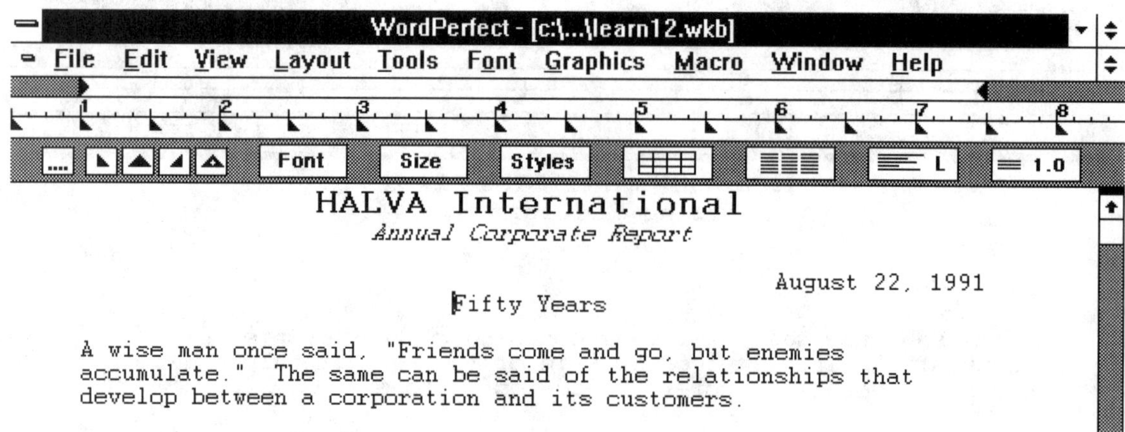

Figure 3x-10. *The required line of text is now center aligned.*

6. Change the font of "Fifty Years" to Helvetica Bold 12 point.

Because you only need to change the font of two single words, it is necessary to select these two words with the mouse. Follow Figures 3x-10 through 3x-13 for instructions on changing the font.

Figure 3x-10. *Swipe the two words "Fifty Years" with the mouse so they are highlighted.*

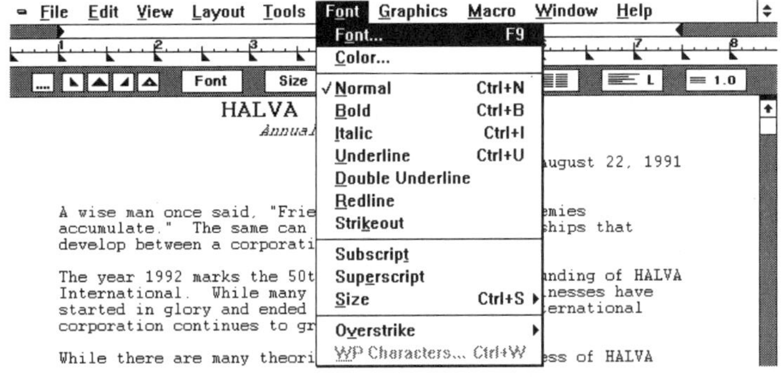

Figure 3x-11. *Select the Font command from the* ***Font*** *menu.*

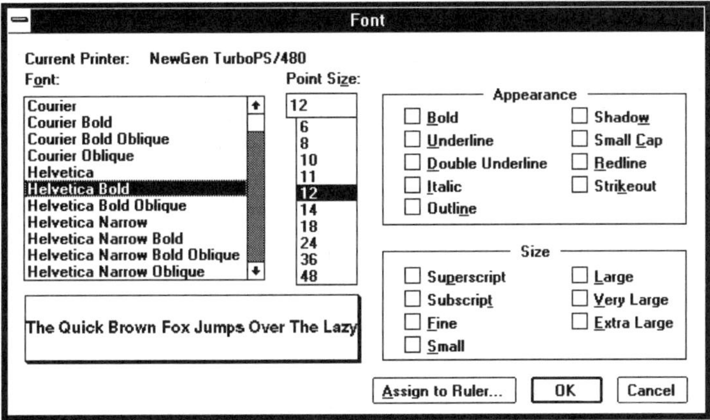

Figure 3x-12. *In the Font dialog box, select Helvetica Bold for the Font and 12 for the Point Size as shown here.*

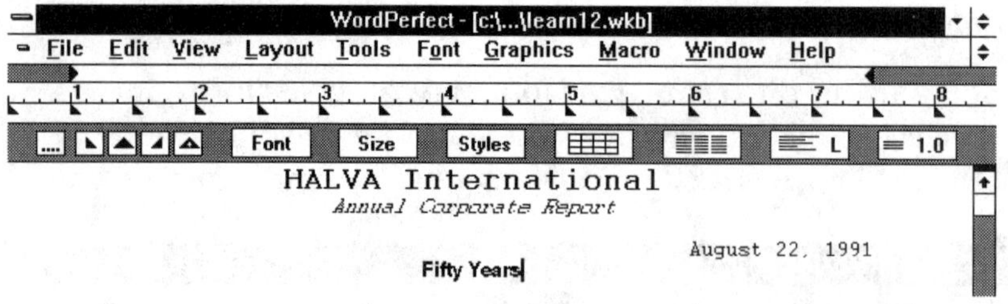

Figure 3x-13. When you return to the screen, the text will look like this.

7. *Fully justify the text from the line beginning with: "A wise man once said..." until the end of the document.*

To fully justify the text from the first body text paragraph onwards, the flashing cursor must be inserted at the beginning of the paragraph commencing "A wise man...". Move the cursor to this position with the directional Arrow keys. Refer to Figures 3x-14 and 3x-15 for further instructions.

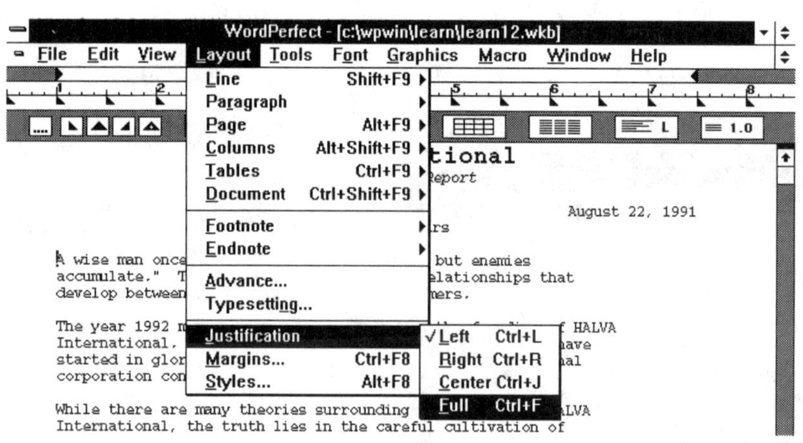

*Figure 3x-14. After you have positioned the cursor, select the Justification/Full command from the **Layout** menu.*

HALVA International
Annual Corporate Report

August 22, 1991

Fifty Years

A wise man once said, "Friends come and go, but enemies accumulate." The same can be said of the relationships that develop between a corporation and its customers.

The year 1992 marks the 50th anniversary of the founding of HALVA International. While many other import/export businesses have started in glory and ended in defeat, the HALVA International corporation continues to grow.

While there are many theories surrounding the success of HALVA International, the truth lies in the careful cultivation of customer relationships and continued efforts to provide quality merchandise at affordable prices.

In this report, the past, present, and future status of HALVA

Figure 3x-15. This is how the text will look with Full justification selected for alignment.

8. Insert a page break after the heading "The European Connection".

To insert a page break into this document, the cursor must again be positioned correctly. For this exercise, use the mouse to insert the cursor after the heading "The European Connection". Refer to Figures 3x-16 and 3x-17 for further instructions.

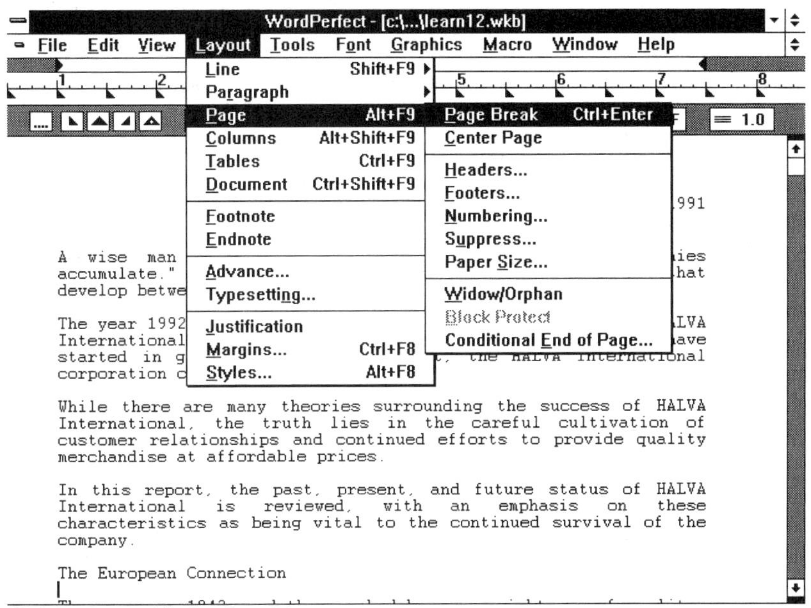

Figure 3x-16. *Insert the cursor after the heading, then select the Page/Page Break command as shown here.*

```
In this report, the past, present, and future status of HALV
International is reviewed, with an emphasis on thes
characteristics as being vital to the continued survival of th
company.

The European Connection
═══════════════════════════════════════════════════════════════
|
The year was 1942, and the war had become a nightmare of reality
With the transportation of goods between many countries blocked
```

Figure 3x-17. *On returning to the page, the page break is indicated by a double line across the screen.*

9. *Cut "The European Connection" from page one and paste it at the beginning of page two.*

Performing this last step involves the *Cut* and *Paste* commands from the **Edit** menu. Follow Figures 3x-18 through 3x-21 for further instructions.

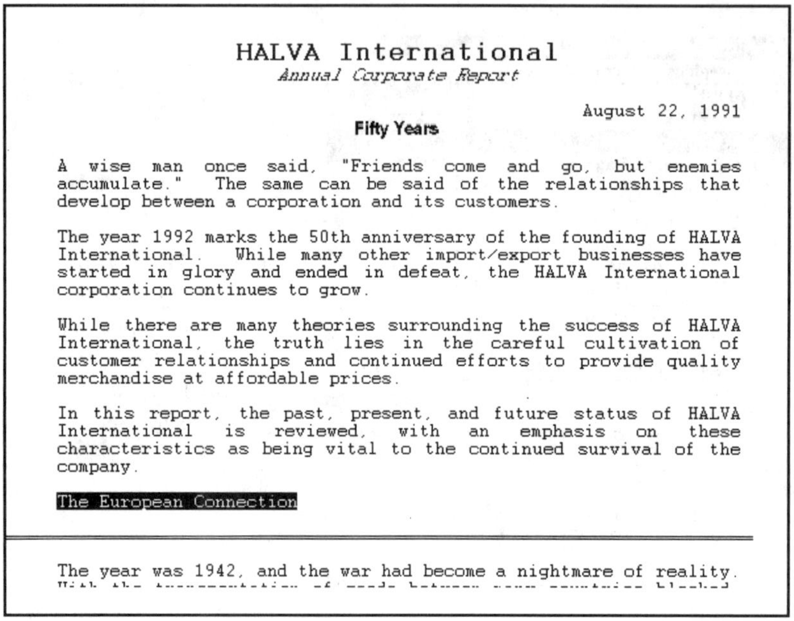

HALVA International

Annual Corporate Report

August 22, 1991

Fifty Years

A wise man once said, "Friends come and go, but enemies accumulate." The same can be said of the relationships that develop between a corporation and its customers.

The year 1992 marks the 50th anniversary of the founding of HALVA International. While many other import/export businesses have started in glory and ended in defeat, the HALVA International corporation continues to grow.

While there are many theories surrounding the success of HALVA International, the truth lies in the careful cultivation of customer relationships and continued efforts to provide quality merchandise at affordable prices.

In this report, the past, present, and future status of HALVA International is reviewed, with an emphasis on these characteristics as being vital to the continued survival of the company.

The European Connection

The year was 1942, and the war had become a nightmare of reality.

Figure 3x-18. *Swipe the required text with the mouse.*

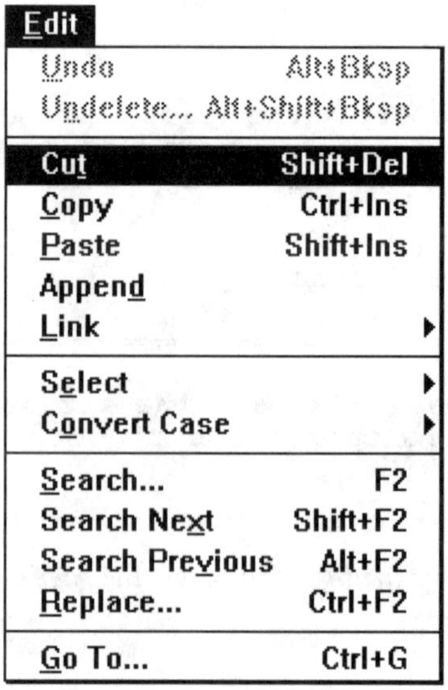

Edit	
Undo	Alt+Bksp
Undelete...	Alt+Shift+Bksp
Cut	Shift+Del
Copy	Ctrl+Ins
Paste	Shift+Ins
Append	
Link	▸
Select	▸
Convert Case	▸
Search...	F2
Search Next	Shift+F2
Search Previous	Alt+F2
Replace...	Ctrl+F2
Go To...	Ctrl+G

Figure 3x-19. *Select the Cut command from the* **Edit** *menu.*

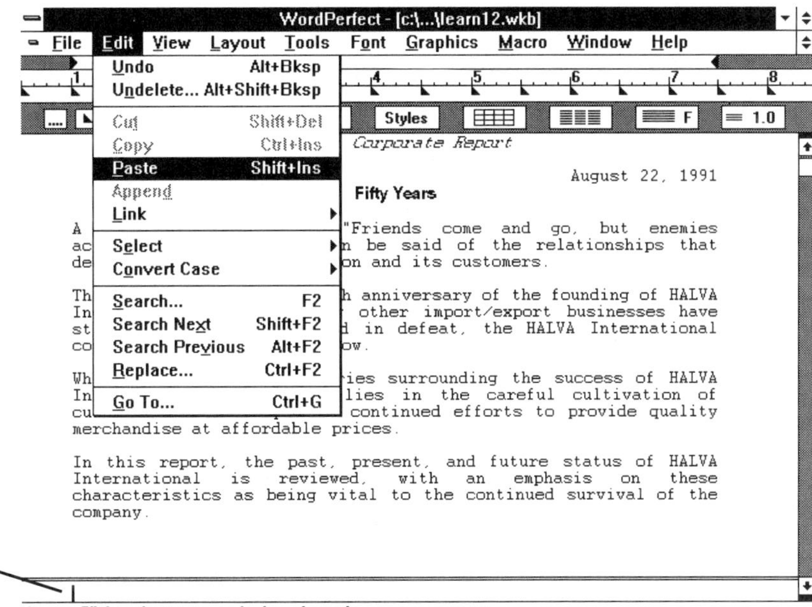

Position of text cursor

Figure 3x-20. *Reposition the text cursor just below the page break, using the directional Arrow keys, and select Paste from the **Edit** menu.*

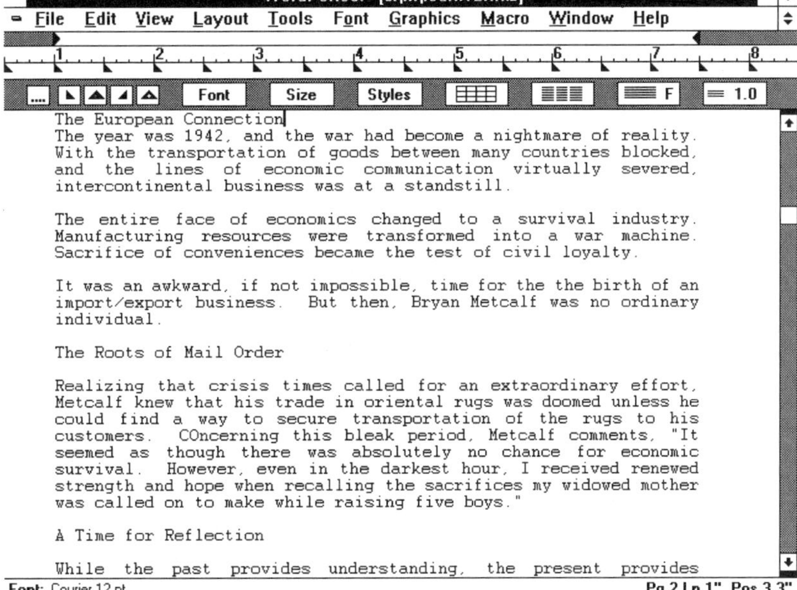

Figure 3x-21. *The text has been pasted at the top of page 2. You can insert an extra carriage return by pressing the Enter key if you wish. Note that the start of page 2 is showing at the top of the screen.*

The Ruler

The ruler, in WordPerfect for Windows, provides easy access to a variety of frequently-used commands.

This chapter is written with the assumption that the *Auto Code Placement* option in the *Environment Settings* dialog box is selected. This is the default setting in WordPerfect for Windows and will only be set differently if you have made the change yourself. This, and other default settings, will be discussed in detail in Chapters 10 and 13 of this book.

In this chapter you will use the various ruler functions to modify the document, ***school.let,*** that you created in Chapter 2 of this book. If ***school.let*** is not already loaded into the editing screen, use the *Open* command, as described in Chapter 3, to retrieve the document from disk. The document, including the changes made in Chapter 3, should now look like the example in Figure 4-1.

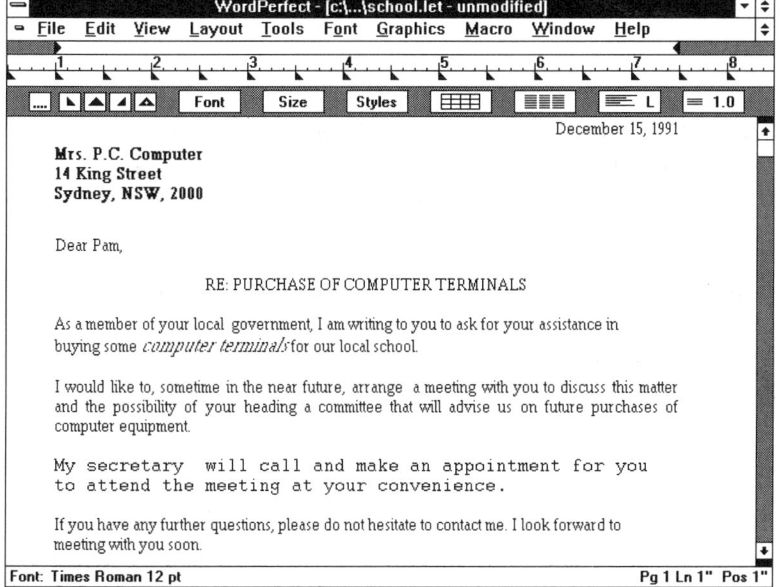

Figure 4-1. *The file,* ***school.let,*** *that was created in Chapter 2 and modified in Chapter 3.*

Displaying the ruler

If the ruler is not already visible at the top of the editing screen, it can be activated by selecting the *Ruler* command from the **View** menu, as shown in Figure 4-2. A short-cut to selecting the *Ruler* command, is to press the Alt, Shift and F3 keys together.

Figure 4-2. *Use the Ruler command in the* ***View*** *menu to activate the ruler display, if it is not already visible on the screen.*

The ruler can be displayed in either inches, centimeters, points, or 1200th of an inch. Chapter 10 of this book discusses how these settings can be selected. Throughout most of this book, the default setting for measurements is inches.

Setting margins

Margins are the areas, forming the perimeter of the page, where there is no text. The top of the ruler displays the positions of the left and right margins in the form of the elongated rectangle shown in Figure 4-3.

The areas on the screen, below the shaded portions of this rectangle, represent the left and right margins. The area of the editing screen below the clear portion of this rectangle, represents the area of the page where text will appear.

Both the left and right shaded areas terminate in arrow heads called margin indicators. The margin indicators (Figure 4-3) mark the boundaries between the margins and the text area of the page.

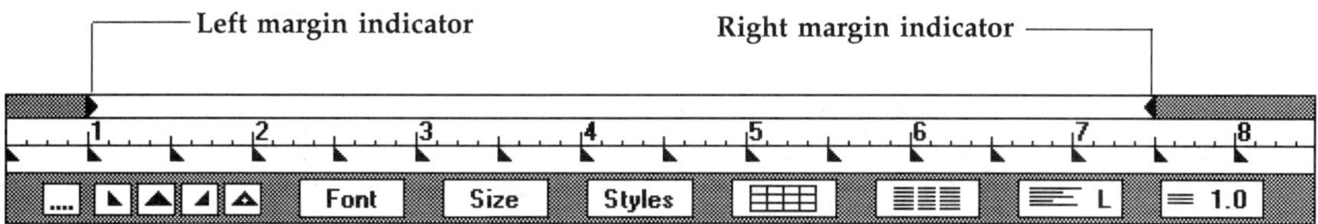

***Figure 4-3.** The margin guides on the ruler mark the left and right margins of the document.*

In WordPerfect for Windows, the default for each of the margin settings (top, bottom, left, and right) is 1 inch. There are several methods of setting the margins in WordPerfect for Windows.

The Margins dialog box

Position the text cursor at the top of page two of the letter. Move the mouse cursor to the shaded area adjacent to either the left or right margin indicator, and double-click. This action activates the *Margins* dialog box shown in Figure 4-4. (Selecting the *Margins* command from the **Layout** menu will achieve the same result.) Use this dialog box to set both the left and top margins to 1.5 inches. When the desired values have been entered, click on the **OK** button.

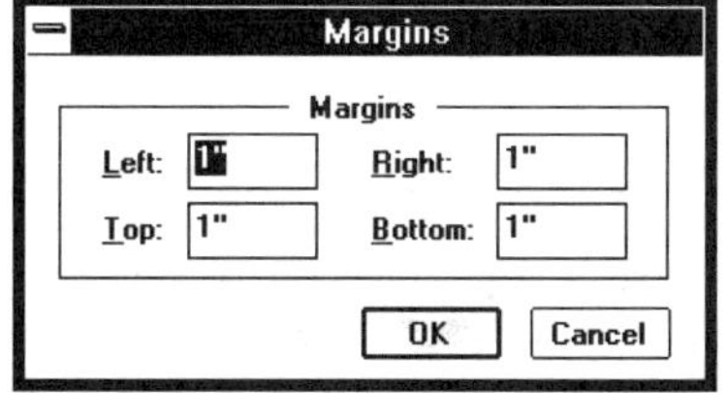

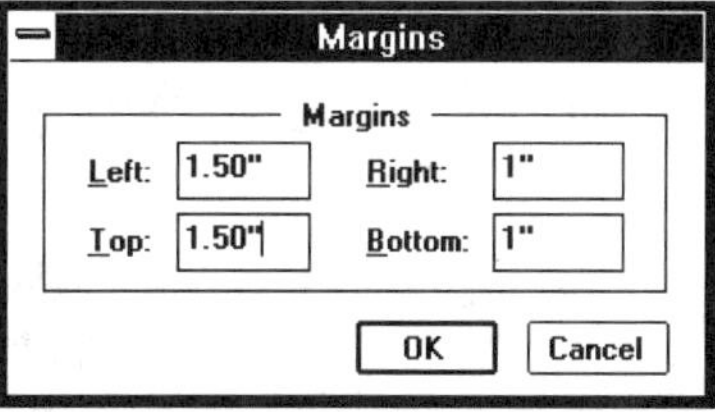

***Figure 4-4.** The Margins dialog box is used to set the margins for a document. The dialog box will first appear as it does on the left in this figure. In the dialog box on the right, the required changes to the margins have been entered.*

Notice, as seen in Figure 4-5, that the left margin indicator now shows the left margin at 1.5 inches. When margin settings are changed using the ruler, the change in margins takes effect at the beginning of the paragraph in which the text cursor is located.

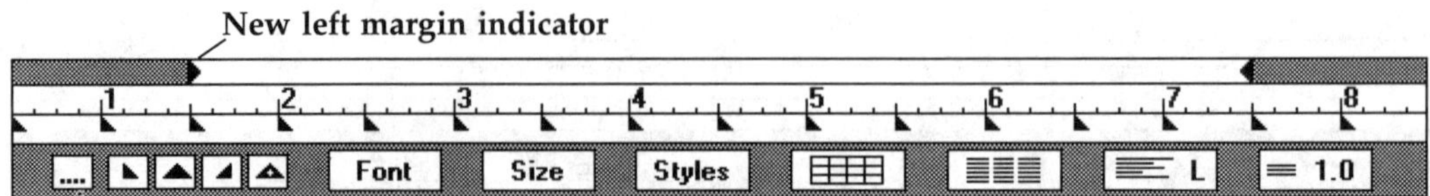

Figure 4-5. *The margin guides on the ruler show the new left margin setting (1.5 inches).*

Move the text cursor up into the first page of the letter and note that the left margin indicator reverts to its initial 1 inch setting. Move the cursor back to the second page and the left margin indicator will again show 1.5 inches. The margin indicators always show the current margins for the position in the document where the text cursor is located.

Dragging the margin indicator

Now, move the text cursor back to page one and change the left margin to 2 inches using a different, more visual, method. Position the cursor at the top of the page. Hold the mouse down on the left margin indicator and, as shown in Figure 4-6, drag the indicator to the 2 inch graduation on the ruler before releasing the mouse button.

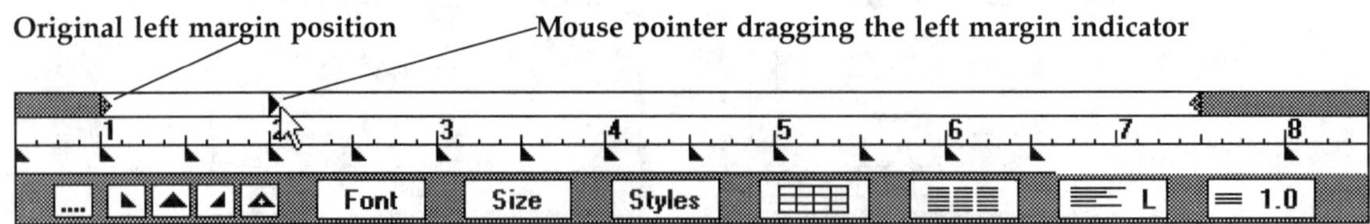

Figure 4-6. *To change the left margin visually, hold the mouse button down on the left margin indicator and drag it to the 2.0 inch graduation on the ruler. While the margin indicator is being dragged, the triangle remaining in the old margin position turns gray while the black triangle follows the mouse. When the mouse button is released, the left margin is reset to the position of the mouse pointer.*

Notice, as shown in Figure 4-7, that as you drag the margin indicator, the right-hand side of the Status bar displays the changing position of the margin. To help you align the margin relative to the text in the document, a vertical line, also shown in Figure 4-7, follows the margin indicator while its position is being set.

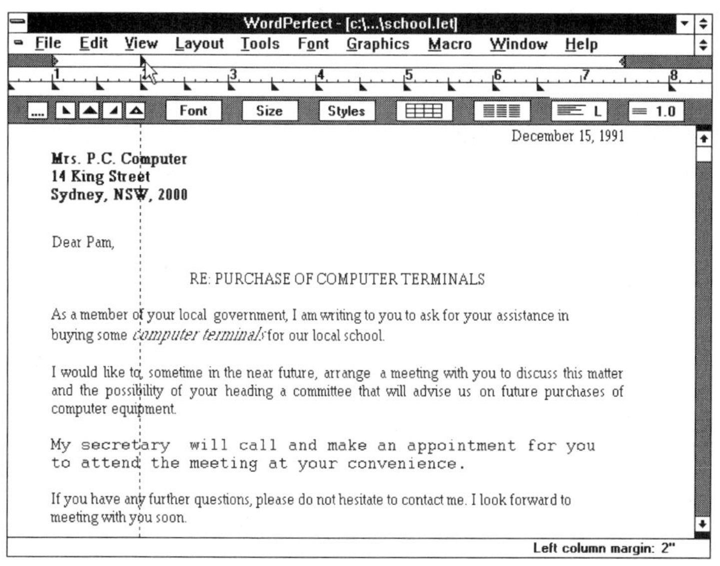

Figure 4-7. Note that as the left margin is adjusted, a vertical line marks its position relative to the text in the document. Note also that the position of the margin, as it is adjusted, is indicated in the right-hand side of the Status bar.

Once you release the margin indicator at the desired position—in this case, 2 inches—the text on the page automatically aligns with the left margin indicator. The letter will now look like the example in Figure 4-8.

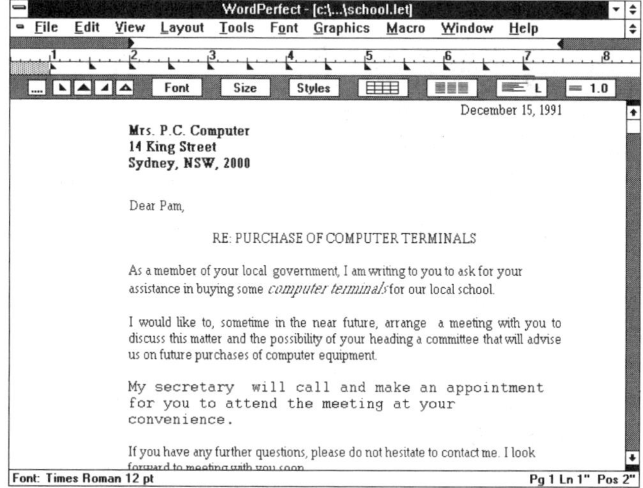

Figure 4-8. When the left margin is set to 2.0 inches, the text in the affected area of the document is automatically moved over to fit the new margin.

Tabs

Tabs are positions on a page, usually measured from the left margin, where the text cursor can automatically be positioned using the Tab key. Pressing the Tab key will immediately move the text cursor to the right until it reaches the next tab position. Tabs are normally used to indent text in a paragraph or to align columns or lists of data in a document.

Below the ruler's graduations are the tab markers. These triangular symbols, shown in Figure 4-9, mark the tab settings for the document. These markers can be used to move, or remove, any of the tabs that have been set. By default, tabs are set every 0.5 inches.

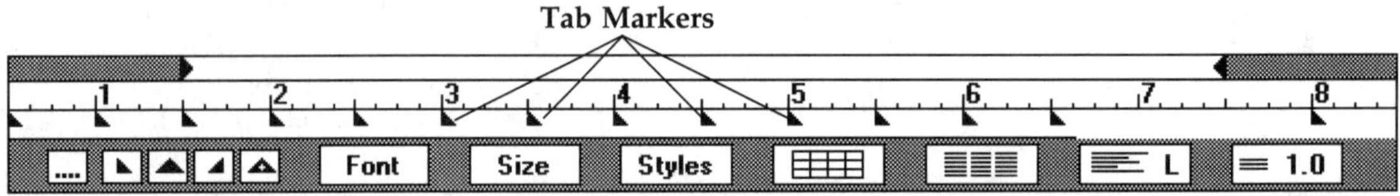

Figure 4-9. The triangular tab markers are positioned directly below the ruler's graduations.

Types of tabs

Below the actual tab markers, on the left side of the ruler, are a cluster of tab buttons, shown in Figure 4-10. These buttons are used to add tab settings to those already on the ruler.

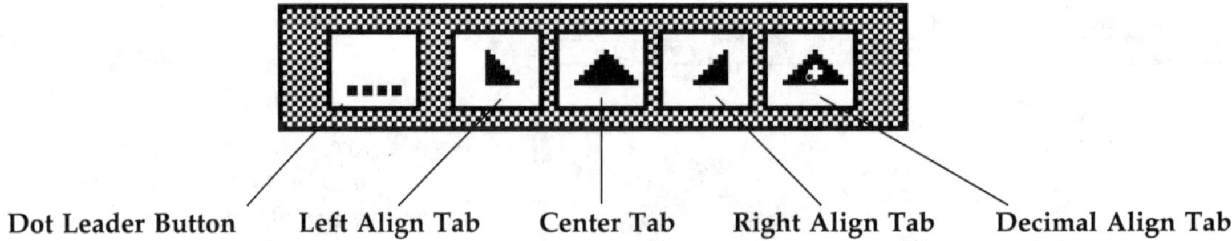

Figure 4-10. Each type of tab is represented by its own tab button on the ruler.

There are four different types of tab, each represented by a different triangular symbol. The types are: *Left Align, Right Align, Center* and *Decimal Align*.

Left Align tabs align the left side, or beginning, of a block of text with the tab position. *Right Align* tabs align the right side, or end, of a block of text with the tab position. *Center* tabs align the text so it is centered around the tab position.

Decimal Align tabs are used to align columns of figures by their decimal points. The decimal will automatically be placed on the tab position.

A *Dot Leader* is a row of periods, or dots, that fills the space between the text cursor's position before the Tab button was pressed and the text at that tab position. This attribute can be applied to any of the four types of tabs.

Setting tabs

Move the text cursor to the top of the second page in the sample document. Place the text cursor below the first line of text on this page, "computer terminals", as shown in Figure 4-11.

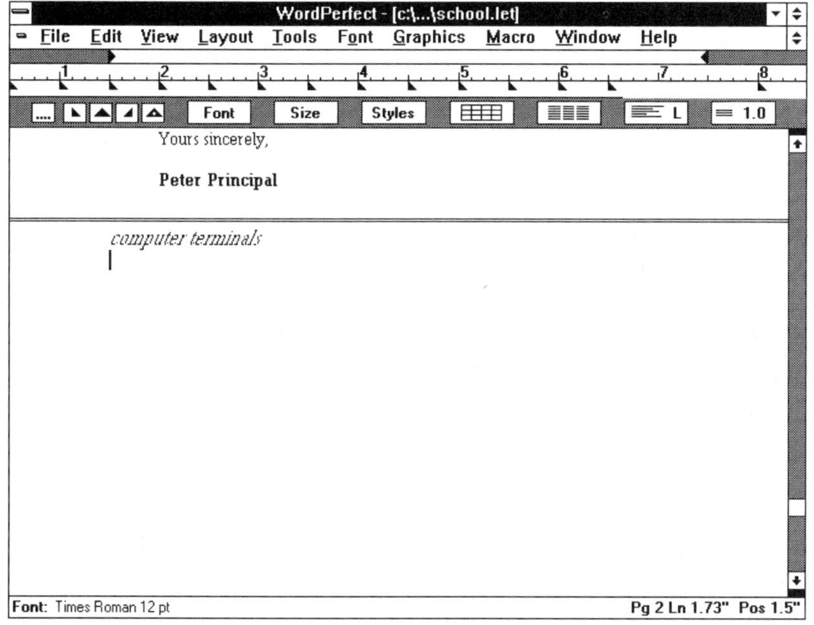

Figure 4-11. *Place the text cursor below the line containing the words "computer terminals" on the second page of the sample letter.*

If the cursor will not move beyond this line, position it after the word "terminals" and press the Return (or Enter) key to advance to a new line.

Clear the tabs that are already marked on the ruler using the *Tab Set* dialog box. To activate the *Tab Set* dialog box, double-click on any of the tab buttons on the ruler, as seen in Figure 4-10. When the *Tab Set* dialog box appears, as seen in Figure 4-12, click on the *Clear Tabs* button.

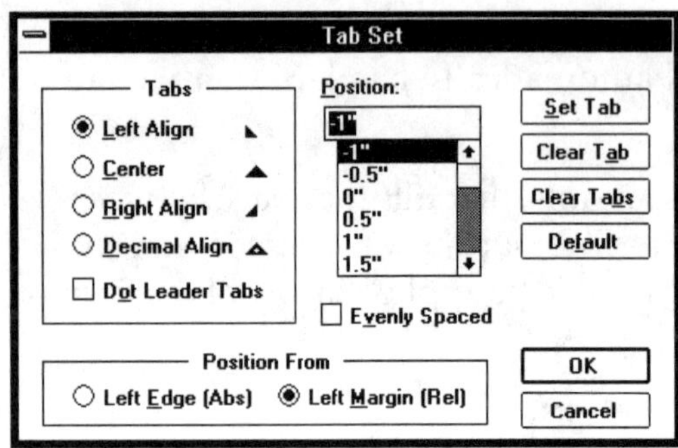

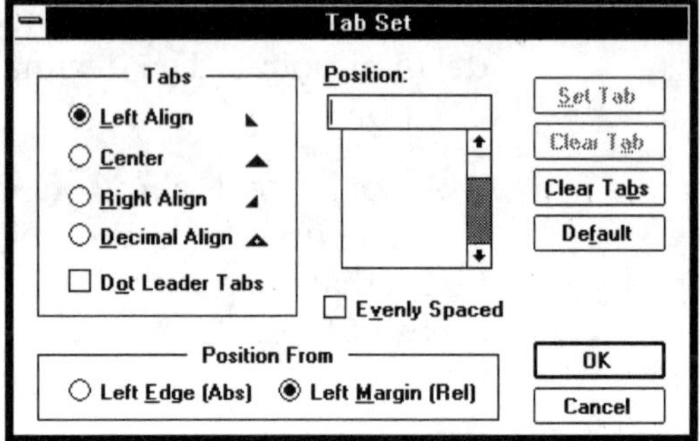

Figure 4-12. *The Tab Set dialog box. The example on the left shows this dialog box as it appears when it is first selected. The example on the right shows the effect of the Clear Tabs button.*

In the *Position From* section make sure the *Left Margin* radio button is selected. Select **OK** now, to clear the tab markers from the ruler and ensure that any new tab will be measured from the left margin of your document, rather than the left edge of the page.

To begin, set a left aligned tab at 3.5 inches on the ruler. Hold the mouse button down on the *Left Align* tab button, as shown in Figure 4-13 and, without releasing the mouse, drag the marker to the 3.5 graduation on the ruler.

As you drag the mouse, a triangular tab symbol will follow the mouse pointer. Notice, as seen in Figure 4-13, that as you drag the tab marker, the right-hand side of the Status bar displays the position of the new tab. As with the setting of margins, a vertical line follows the mouse pointer to help you align the setting with the text.

When the tab marker is correctly positioned, release the mouse button and the tab marker will remain on the ruler.

Next, set a center aligned tab at 5.5 inches on the ruler. Hold the mouse button down on the *Center Align* tab button, as seen in Figure 4-14, and, without releasing the mouse button, drag the tab marker to the 5.5 graduation on your ruler.

Finally, set a decimal aligned tab at 7.0 inches on the ruler. Select and move a decimal tab marker in the same way you set the previous tabs. The tab markers on the ruler will now be arranged as seen in Figure 4-15.

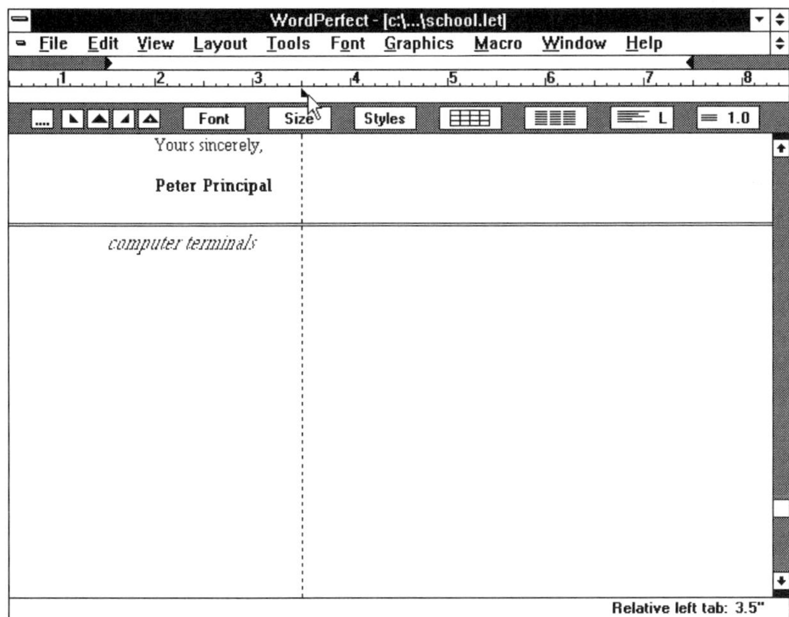

Figure 4-13. Use the Left Align tab button to position a tab marker at the 3.5 inch graduation on the ruler. A vertical line in the document will follow the mouse pointer as you move it across the ruler. The right-hand side of the Status bar will indicate the exact ruler position of the mouse pointer.

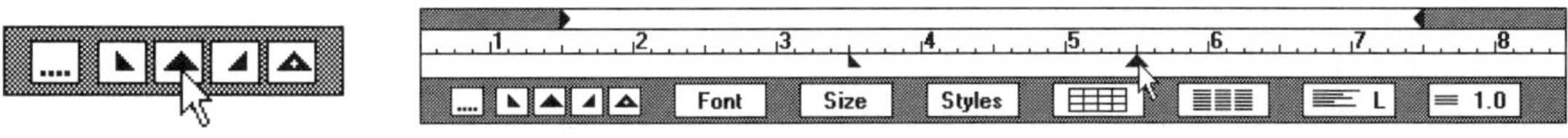

Figure 4-14. Use the Center tab button to drag a tab marker to the 5.5 inch graduation on the ruler.

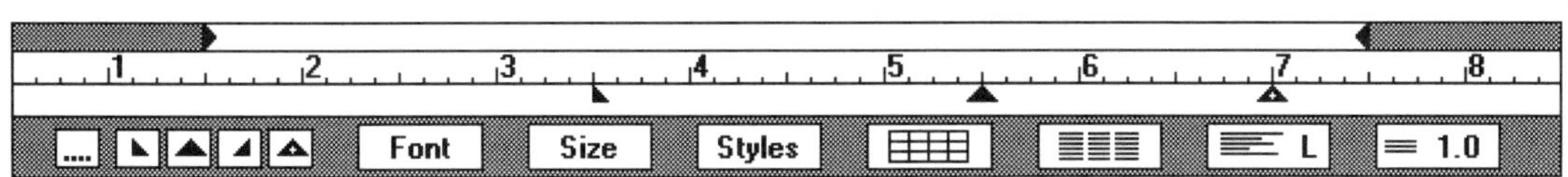

Figure 4-15. After you have set the three tabs required for this part of the document, the ruler will look like the one shown above. Note that each of the four tab types has a different tab marker symbol. You can tell, at a glance, where the tabs are positioned and what type of tab each one is.

Making sure that the text cursor is still positioned below the words "computer terminals", type the first four lines of text that appear in Figure 4-16. Use the Tab key to move the text cursor between columns of text or numbers.

computer terminals

Type	Location	Qty	Price
IBM 386	English Dept.	2	6,950.00
COMPAQ	Science Dept.	4	28,350.00
EPSON	Sports Dept.	2	5,250.00

Authorized by.................................. Date ....

Figure 4-16. *Type the above text into the second page of the sample letter.*

For the last line of text seen in Figure 4-16, you must change the tab settings. Position the text cursor below the rest of the document by pressing the Return key four times. Now, remove the three tab markers you have just set.

To remove tab settings, hold the mouse down on the marker to be removed and drag it off the ruler, as shown in Figure 4-17. The removed tab setting will now be deleted from the ruler. Remove all three tab settings in this way.

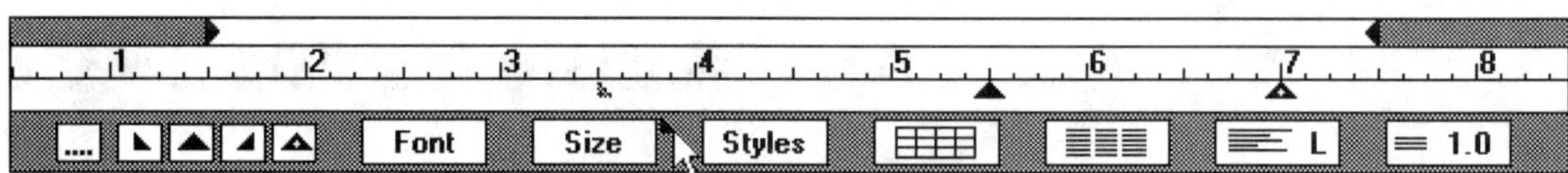

Figure 4-17. *To remove a tab marker, drag it into the gray region on the ruler.*

Place a left aligned tab with a dot leader at 5.0 inches on the ruler. Select the *Dot Leader* tab button. As seen in Figure 4-18, the four tab buttons now contain a set of dots, to show that the *Dot Leader* option has been activated.

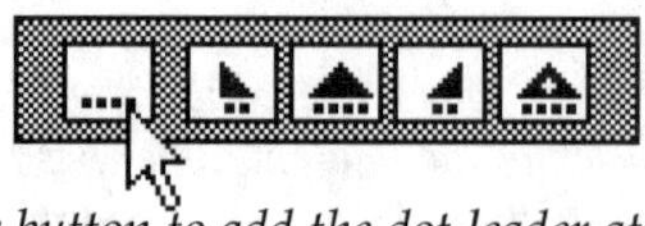

Figure 4-18. *Use the Dot Leader button to add the dot leader attribute to the four tab buttons.*

Hold the mouse button down on the *Left Align* tab marker and drag it to the 5.0 inch graduation on the ruler. Click on the *Dot Leader* button once more to turn it off and drag the *Left Align* marker to the 5.5 inch ruler graduation.

You can also use the ruler to copy tabs from one position to another without removing the original tab. Copy the first tab you just set (a left aligned tab with a dot leader at the 5.0 inch mark on the ruler) and place it at 7.0 inches on the ruler. To copy a tab, hold the Control key, then drag the tab marker with the mouse button held down, to the desired position on the ruler; in this case the 7.0 inch mark. Once this is done, release the mouse and the Control key.

Type the last line of text using the Tab key to move from one column of text to another. You will need to press the Tab key twice after the word "by" before typing the word "Date". Press the Tab key once after the word "Date".

The second page of this document will now look like the example in Figure 4-19.

Use the *Save* command from the **File** menu to save the changes you have made so far in this chapter.

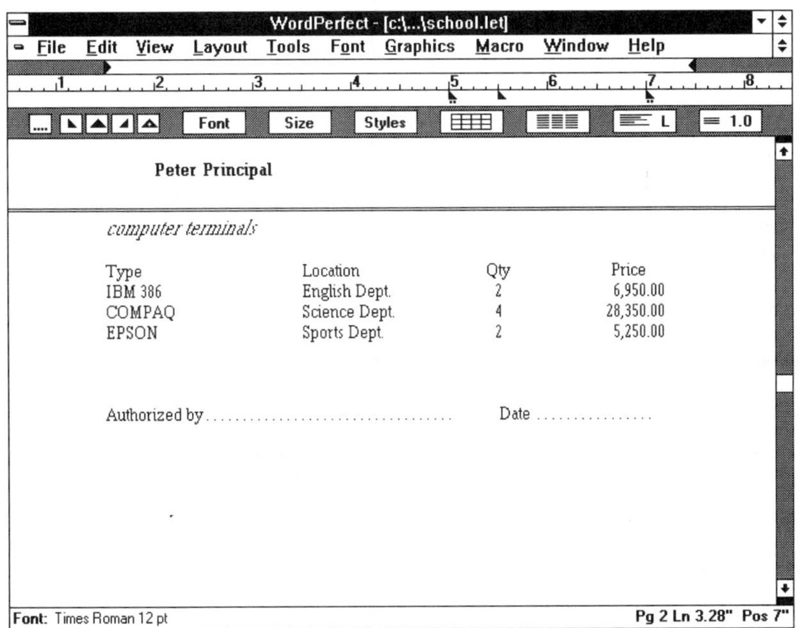

***Figure 4-19.** This is how the second page of the sample letter will look after the text in Figure 4-16 has been entered using the correct tabs.*

The Font button

The *Font* button on the ruler, seen in Figure 4-20, is used to assign fonts quickly and easily to selected text. You can use an option in the *Font* dialog box—activated by the *Font* command in the **Font** menu—to add frequently used fonts to the *Font* button.

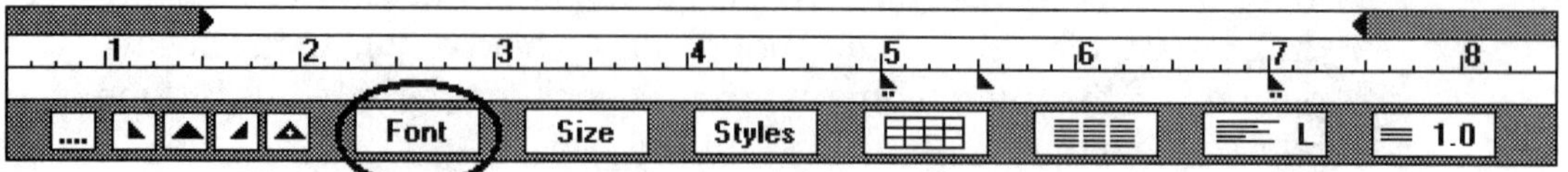

Figure 4-20. *The Font button on the ruler can be used as a convenient shortcut to invoking the Font command in the **Font** menu.*

To add a font to the ruler, double-click on the *Font* button. This is an alternative method of activating the *Font* dialog box, seen in Figure 4-21, which is more fully described in Chapter 3. When the *Font* dialog box has appeared, click on the *Assign to Ruler* button to obtain the *Ruler Fonts Menu* dialog box, shown in Figure 4-22.

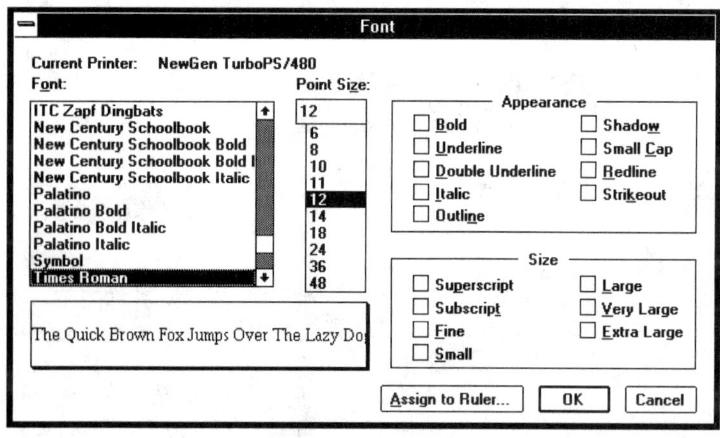

Figure 4-21. *The Font dialog box can be activated by double-clicking on the Font button in the ruler.*

The *Ruler Fonts Menu* dialog box contains two list boxes. The *Font List* list box, on the left, lists all the fonts available on the currently selected printer. The *Fonts on Ruler* list box, on the right, lists the fonts that can currently be selected from the ruler.

If this is the first time that you are using this dialog box on your copy of WordPerfect for Windows, the *Fonts on Ruler* list box will only contain one font.

To add a font from the *Font List* list box to the *Fonts on Ruler* list box—in this example, the font Helvetica is being added—highlight the font's name in the left-hand list box and click on the *Add* button. As seen in Figure 4-22, the font will be added to the list box on the right.

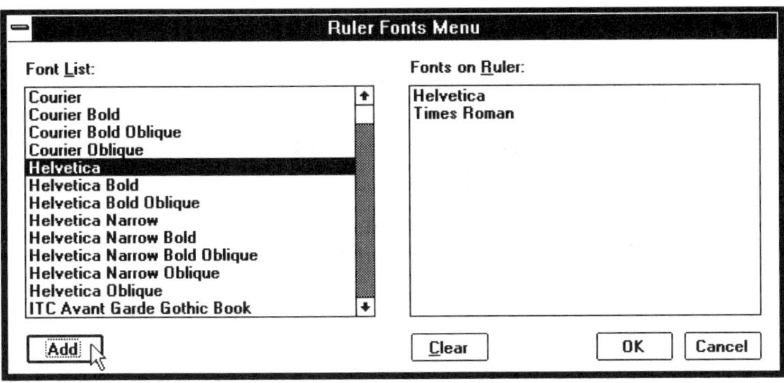

Figure 4-22. *The Ruler Fonts Menu dialog box is activated to add frequently-used fonts to the Font button sub-menu on the ruler. In this example, the Helvetica font has just been added.*

When you have finished adding fonts to the ruler, click on **OK** to return to the *Font* dialog box. Click on **OK** again to return to the editing screen. In the example of Figure 4-23, the fonts: Courier, Helvetica, Palatino, and Times Roman have been included in the ruler.

Now, use the *Font* button on the ruler to change the line of text, on page two of the sample, beginning with "Type...." to the Helvetica font. Select this first line of text, then hold down the mouse button on the *Font* button in the ruler. As seen in Figure 4-23, a pull-down menu, listing all the fonts which have been assigned to the ruler, appears while the mouse button remains depressed.

Without releasing the mouse button, move the mouse pointer down until the desired font, in this case Helvetica, is highlighted. Release the mouse button to implement the selection. As seen in Figure 4-23, the first line of text in the table is now in Helvetica font.

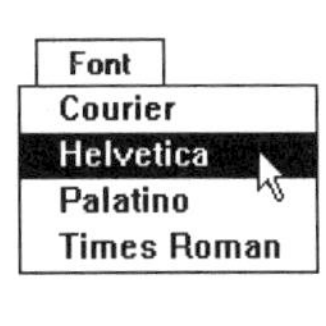

computer terminals

Type	Location	Qty	Price
IBM 386	English Dept.	2	6,950.00
COMPAQ	Science Dept.	4	28,350.00
EPSON	Sports Dept.	2	5,250.00

Authorized by.................................. Date ....

Figure 4-23. *Use the Font button in the ruler to convert the line of text beginning with "Type..." in the sample letter to Helvetica font.*

This procedure has the same effect as selecting a font from the *Font* dialog box as discussed in Chapter 3. Because the ruler's *Font* button is conveniently located at the top of the editing screen, this method of applying a font is often more efficient than using the menus.

The Size button

Most fonts—depending, as always, on the available printer—can be displayed in a variety of sizes. In Chapter 3, you have seen how font size can be selected using the *Font* dialog box. The *Size* button on the ruler provides a convenient shortcut for selecting font size.

Change the size of the text you just finished making Helvetica, to 18 point size. Select this line of text, then hold the mouse button down on the *Size* button. As seen in Figure 4-24, a list of font sizes appears in a pull-down menu. Without releasing the mouse button, move the mouse cursor down until *18* is highlighted.

When you release the mouse button, the size of the selected text will be changed to 18 point. The letter will now look like the example in Figure 4-24.

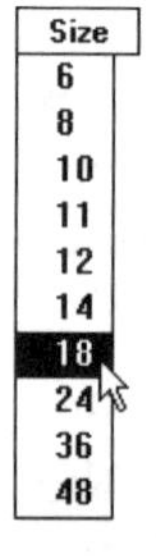

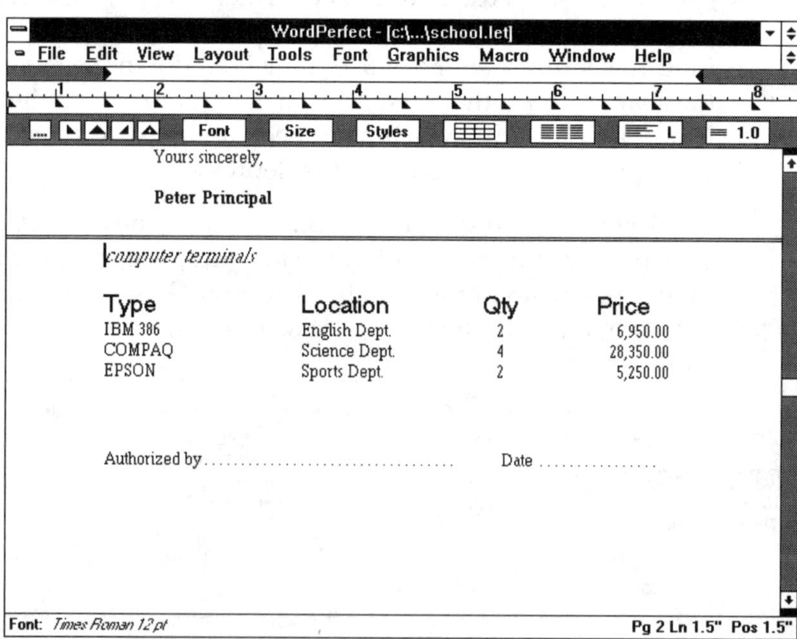

Figure 4-24. *Use the Size button to change the size of the second line of this page to 18 point.*

Select the last line of text, beginning with "Authorized by...", and assign the size of 14 point to it. The document will now look like the example in Figure 4-25.

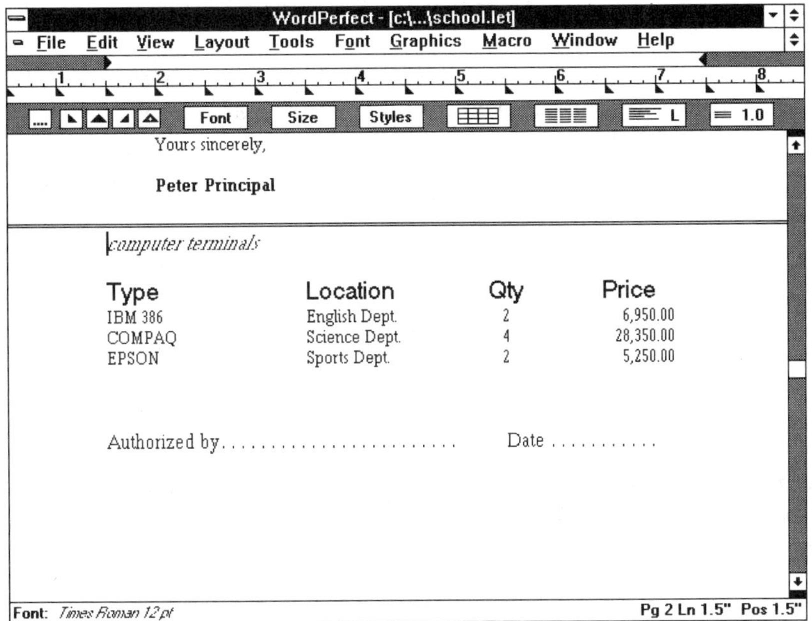

Figure 4-25. *This is how the second page of the sample letter will now look on the editing screen.*

All these adjustments were made without using the menus.

The Styles button

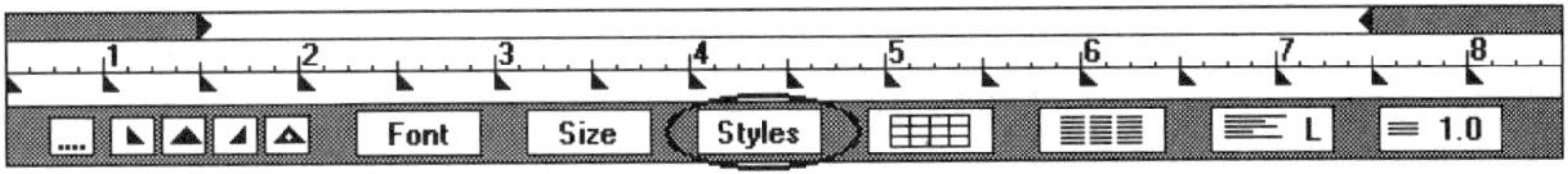

The *Styles* button on the ruler is used as a shortcut for inserting styles. Styles are a special text formatting feature of WordPerfect that are discussed in Chapter 15 of this book.

The Tables button

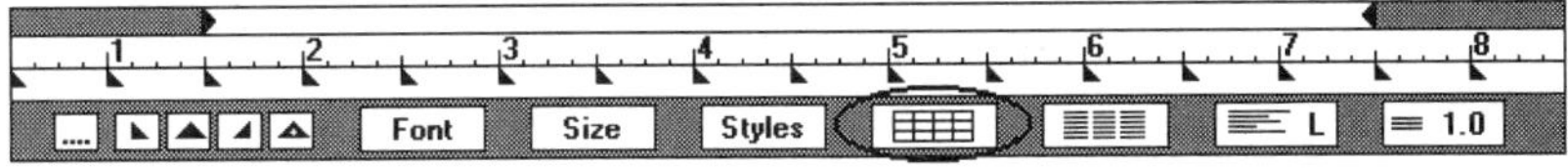

The *Tables* button on the ruler is used to create and insert a table into a document. Tables are explained in Chapter 21 of this book.

The Columns button

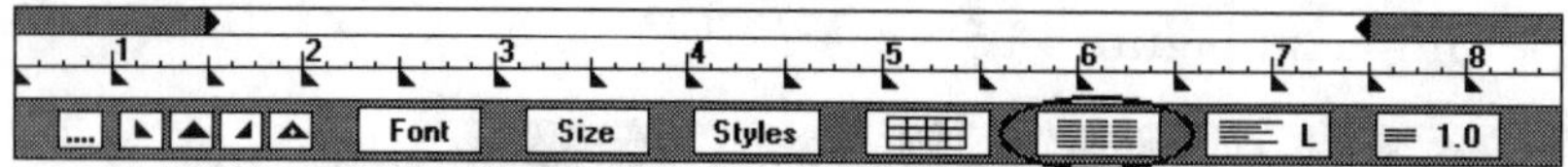

The *Columns* button on the ruler is used to create between two and five evenly-spaced newspaper-type columns. Columns are discussed in Chapter 7 of this book.

The Justification button

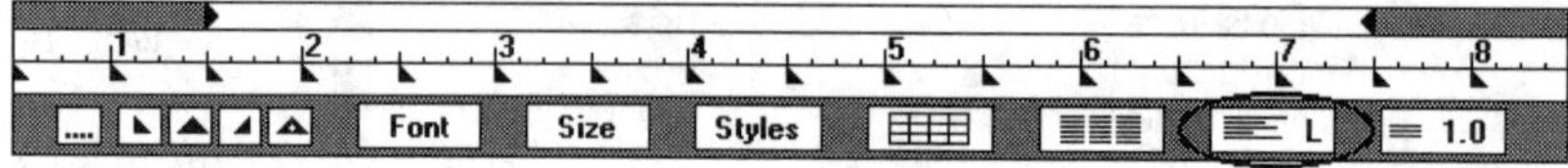

The *Justification* button on the ruler provides a shortcut to assigning the *Left, Right, Center,* and *Full* justification attributes to selected text. The current setting is shown on the button by the setting's first initial and a graphic symbol showing the setting's effect. Above, the letter "L" indicates that *Left* justification is currently set.

Place the text cursor at the end of the last line of text on page two of the letter. Press the Enter key three times to move the text cursor down three lines. Type the words: "The above prices do not include Federal Goods and Services tax." Page two of the letter will now look like the example in Figure 4-26.

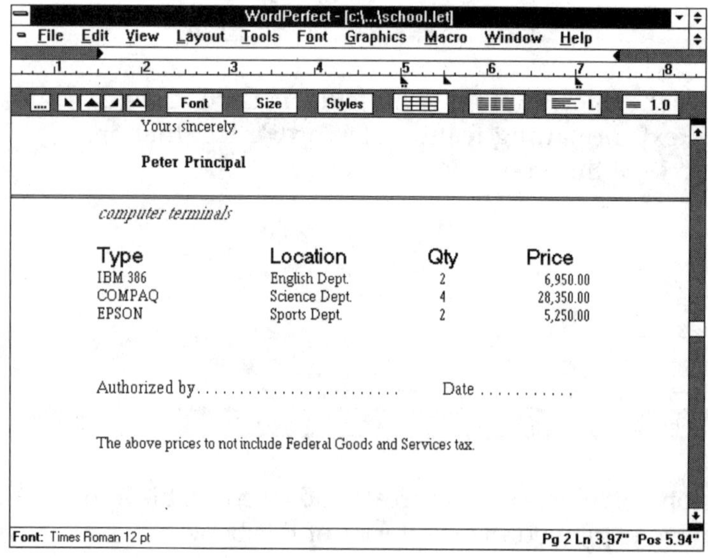

Figure 4-26 *Add the sentence: "The above prices do not include Federal Goods and Services tax." to the bottom of page two of the sample letter.*

Select this newly typed line of text, then press and hold the mouse button on the *Justification* button in the ruler. A pop-up list box will appear, as seen in Figure 4-27, showing the different justification types.

As with the other pop-up list boxes in WordPerfect for Windows, the current selection is automatically highlighted when the list box appears. Without releasing the mouse button, move the mouse pointer until the *Center* command is highlighted. Release the mouse button to assign this justification command to the selected text (Figure 4-28).

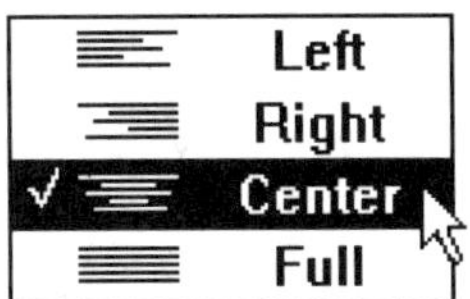

Figure 4-27. *Clicking on the Justification button causes this pop-up list box to appear. For this example, select the Center option from the list.*

Now, assign *Center* justification to the words "computer terminals" on the first line of text. Page two of the letter will now look like the example in Figure 4-28.

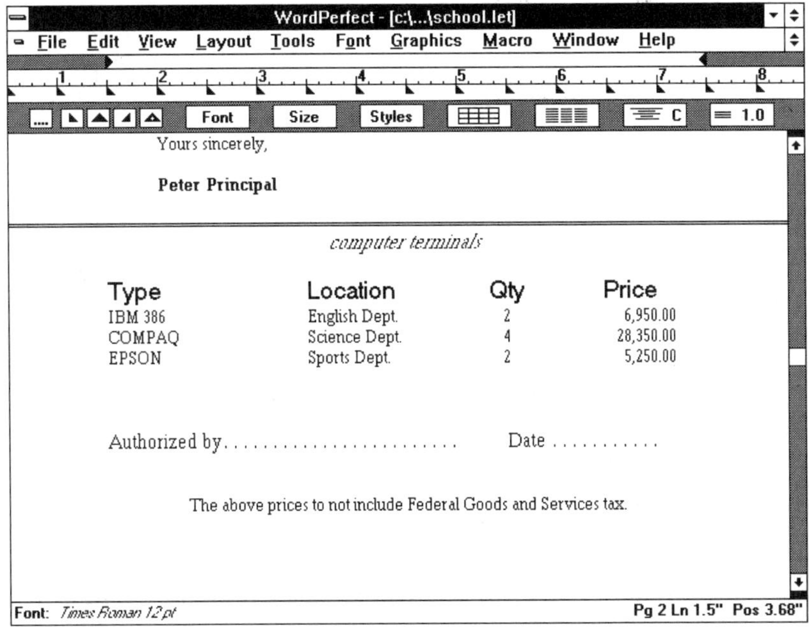

Figure 4-28. *The first and last lines on page two of the sample letter have been centered using the Justification button on the ruler.*

The Line Spacing button

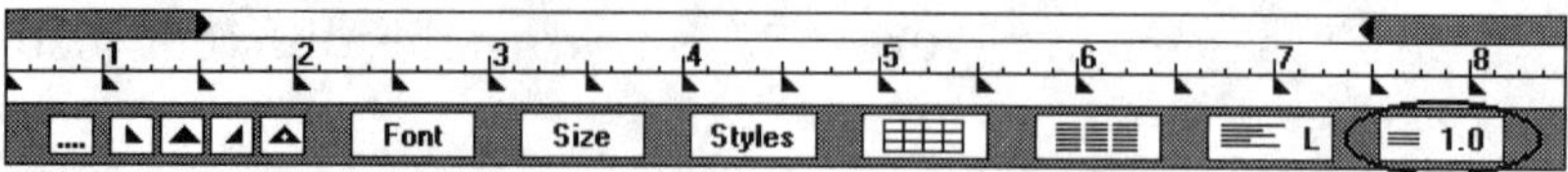

The *Line Spacing* button is the last button found on the ruler. This button is used as a shortcut to change the line spacing within documents. In WordPerfect, the default for this setting is single-spacing. The current setting can be read from the button, which displays a number and a graphic image representing the line spacing.

Change the line spacing for some of the text on page two of your letter. Select the third, fourth, and fifth lines, on the second page of the sample letter. Select the *Line Spacing* button, as you did for the previous buttons on the ruler. In the pop-up list box that appears, select the 2.0 spacing. Releasing the mouse button assigns double-spacing to the selected text. The second page of the letter will now look like the example in Figure 4-29.

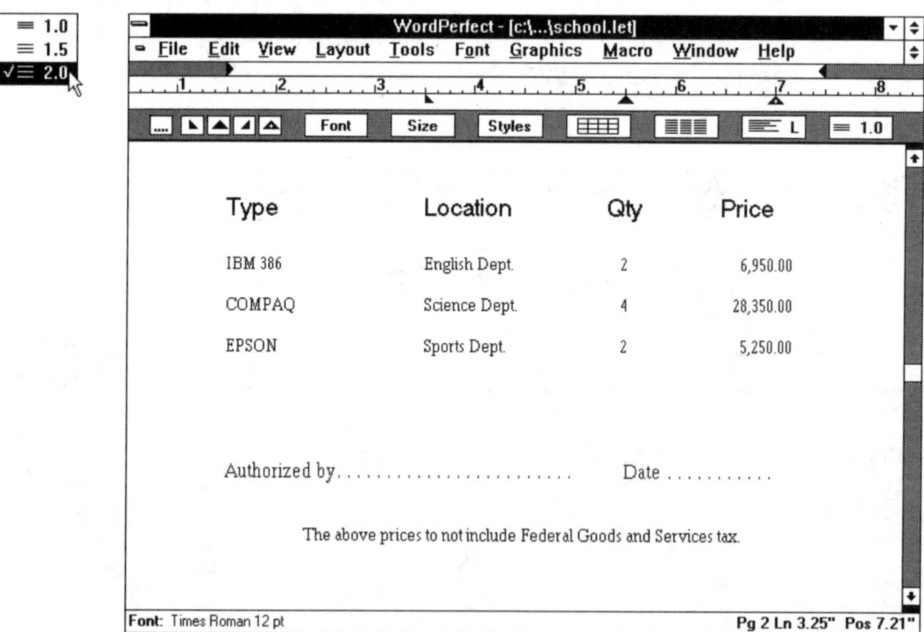

Figure 4-29. *Use the Line Spacing button to double-space the text on the second page of the sample letter.*

Select the *Save* command from the **File** menu to save the changes you have made to your letter.

Hints and Tips

Tab settings

Tabs can also be set using the menus. To set tabs without using the ruler, select the *Line* command in the **Layout** menu. In the fly-out menu that appears, select the *Tab Set* command. The *Tab Set* dialog box, Figure 4-30, will be activated.

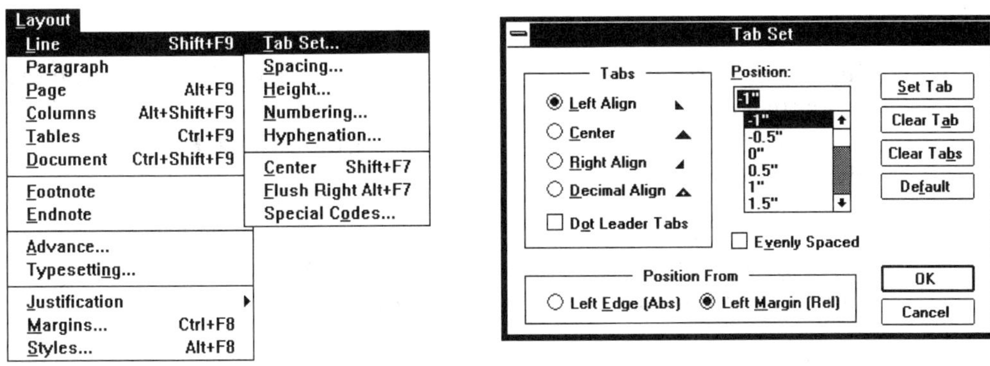

*Figure 4-30. The Tab Set dialog box can be activated by selecting the Line/Tab Set command in the **Layout** menu.*

The position of the current tab settings is displayed under *Position* in this dialog box. You can change the type and position of tab settings by following the steps below.

1. Type a new tab setting in the *Position* text box.
2. Select the type of tab from the *Tabs* group box.
3. Select the *Set Tab* command button.
4. Select the **OK** command button to accept the changes made and return you to the editing screen.

When you change or insert a tab, the new settings will continue from the current cursor position to the end of your document, or until a new tab setting is inserted.

The Font button

Another way to activate the *Font* dialog box, instead of double-clicking on the *Font* button on the Ruler, is to press the F9 key.

When you change a font using the *Font* button on the Ruler, the font you have selected will be assigned to all text from the current cursor position to the end of the document, or until you make another change.

The Line Spacing button

An alternate method of changing the line spacing, rather than using the *Line Spacing* button on the ruler, is to select the *Spacing* command from the *Line* fly-out menu in the **Layout** menu, shown in Figure 4-30. You may find it quicker and easier to press the Shift+F9 keys to activate the *Line* command.

When you make a change to the line spacing of a document, all line spacing is changed from the current position of the cursor to the end of the document, or until you make another line spacing alteration.

The Ruler — Exercise

4ex

This training exercise is designed so that people of all levels of expertise with WordPerfect can use it to gain maximum benefit. In order to do this, the bare exercise is listed below this paragraph on just one page, with no hints. The following pages contain the steps needed to complete this exercise for those who need additional prompting.

Steps in brief

1. *Open up the WordPerfect file, learn06.wkb, from the learn sub-directory within the wpwin sub-directory.*
2. *Activate the ruler.*
3. *Set the left margin to 1.5" and the right margin to 6.5", as measured by the ruler.*
4. *Select the four paragraphs shown in Figure 4x-6 and delete the tabs at 2" and 2.5". Add a left aligned tab at 2.75".*
5. *Use the Font button to activate the Font dialog box and change the font of the heading,"Corporate Memo", to Courier.*
6. *Use the Justification button to center the last paragraph.*
7. *Double-space the whole document using the Line Spacing button.*

The details for completing these steps are on the following pages.

Steps in detail

1. ***Open up the WordPerfect file, learn06.wkb, from the learn sub-directory within the wpwin sub-directory.***

After selecting the *Open* command from the **File** menu, locate the ***learn06.wkb*** file in the ***learn*** sub-directory (Figure 4x-1). Double-click on this file, or select it and click on *Open*, to bring this document onto your screen.

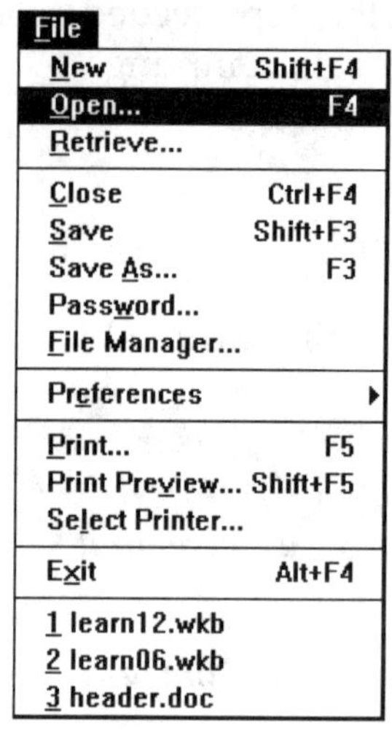

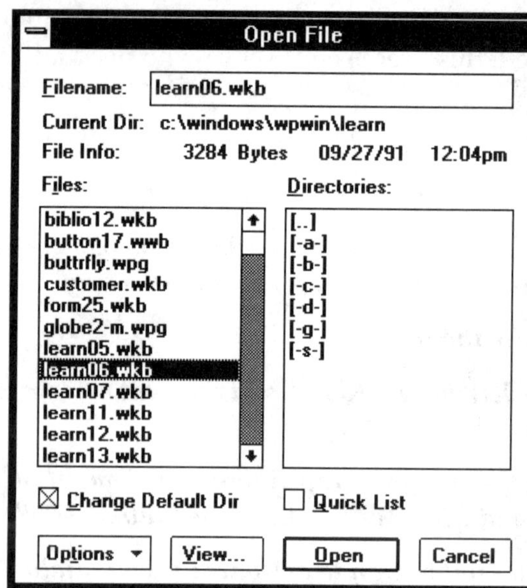

*Figure 4x-1. Select the Open File command from the **File** menu. In the Open File dialog box, select **learn06.wkb,** and click on the Open button.*

WordPerfect - [c:\...\learn06.wkb - unmodified]

File Edit View Layout Tools Font Graphics Macro Window Help

Corporate Memo

To: All Marketing Managers
From: Jan Sills
Date:
Subject: Corporate Marketing Conference

We have ***tentatively*** arranged a Marketing Conference for September 4, 5, and 6 to be held at the Parkway Hotel in Buffalo, New York. All marketing managers and sales representatives are required to attend. If you wish to bring your spouse, please let Beverly know by the end of the month so that arrangements can be made.

I will let you know when final approval has been given for the time and place.

Figure 4x-2. This is how the file will look on screen.

Please note that your screen may differ slightly from this one. WordPerfect occasionally modifies these files with later versions of WordPerfect.

2. *Activate the ruler.*

To activate the ruler on your screen, select the *Ruler* command from the **View** menu (Figure 4x-3). You only need to do this if your ruler is not currently showing.

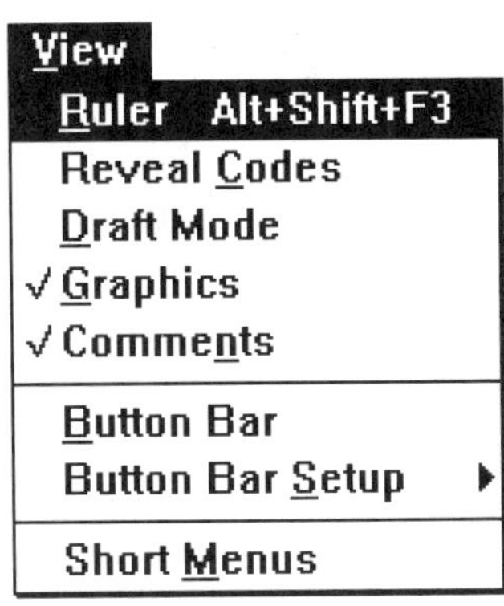

Figure 4x-3. Select the Ruler command in the **View** menu to activate the ruler.

3. *Set the left margin to 1.5" and the right margin to 6.5", as measured by the ruler.*

One way of changing the margins in WordPerfect is to use the mouse in conjunction with the ruler. Follow Figures 4x-4 and 4x-5 for further instructions.

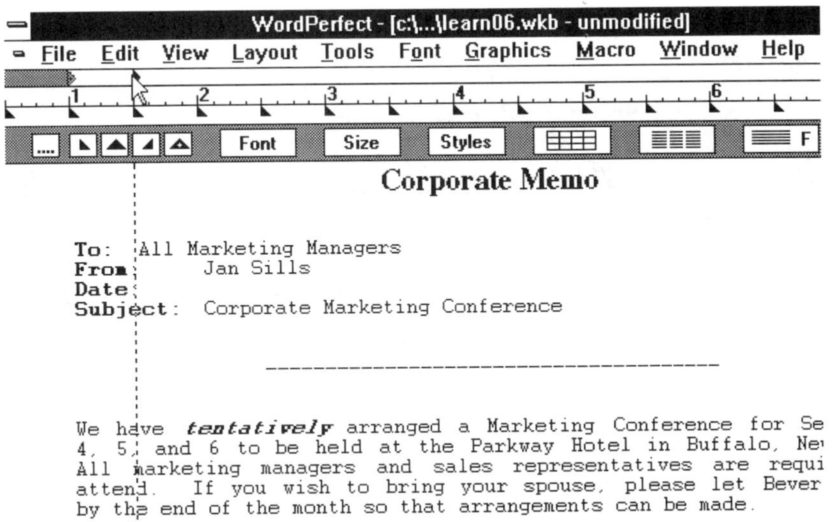

Figure 4x-4. Hold the mouse button down on the left margin indicator and reposition it at 1.5". When you release the mouse, all text will reformat automatically. This figure assumes that the left margin was originally at 1.0", the default setting.

Repeat the same procedure, as described in Figure 4x-4, to reposition the right margin indicator at 6.5". Figure 4x-5 shows the result.

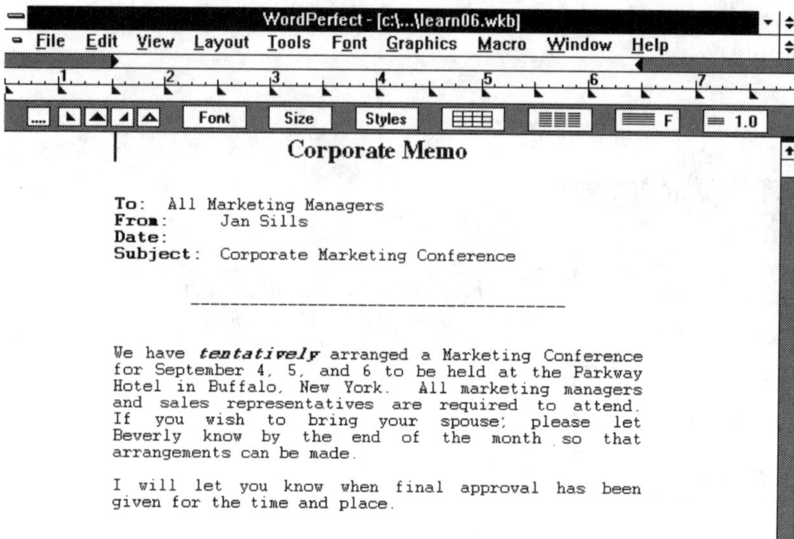

Figure 4x-5. *Both margins have been repositioned with the mouse, and the text has moved accordingly.*

4. ***Select the four paragraphs shown in Figure 4x-6 and delete the tabs at 2" and 2.5". Add a left aligned tab at 2.75".***

Highlight these paragraphs using the mouse to swipe the text. Now refer to Figures 4x-6 through 4x-8 for further instructions.

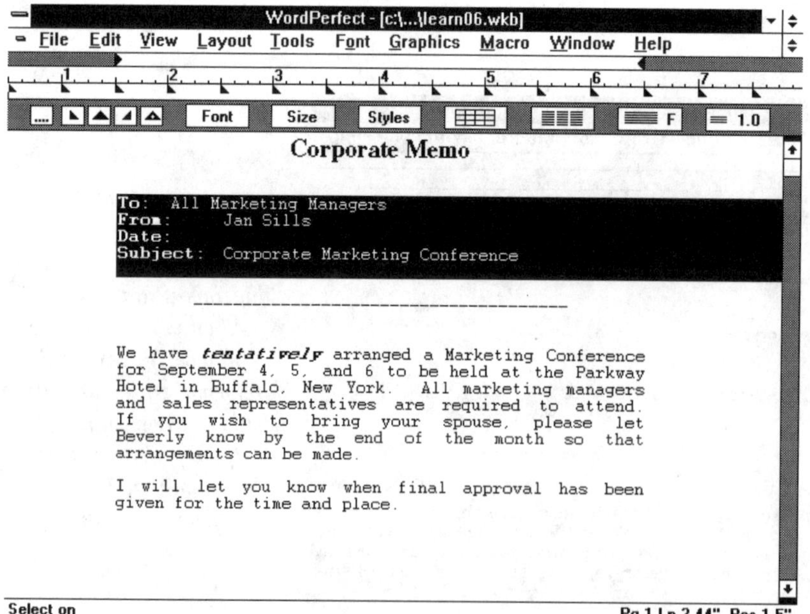

Figure 4x-6. *After you have selected the text, two tabs need to be deleted from the ruler. These two deleted tabs will affect the selected text only.*

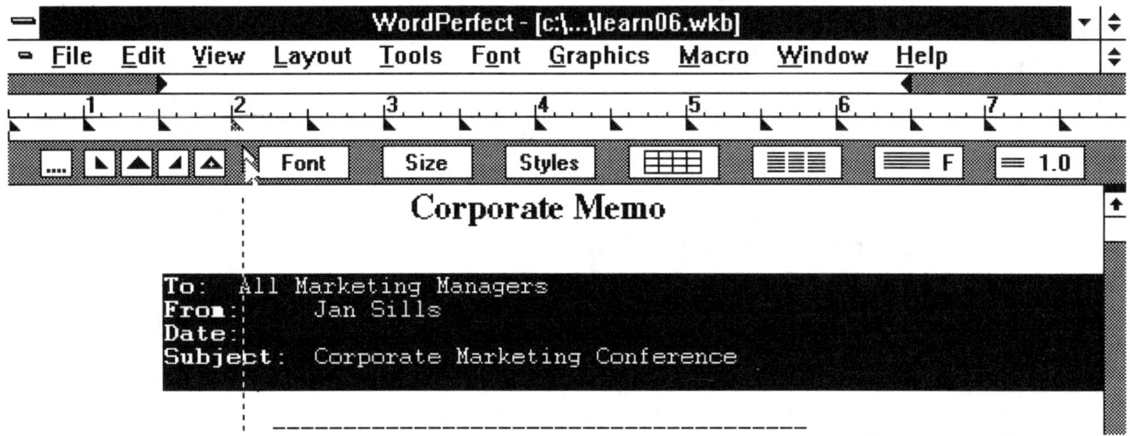

Figure 4x-7. With the mouse held down, select the tab at 2" and drag it down into the gray area of the ruler. When you release the mouse, the tab will be deleted. Repeat this procedure for the tab at 2.5".

To add a left aligned tab at 2.75", see Figure 4x-8.

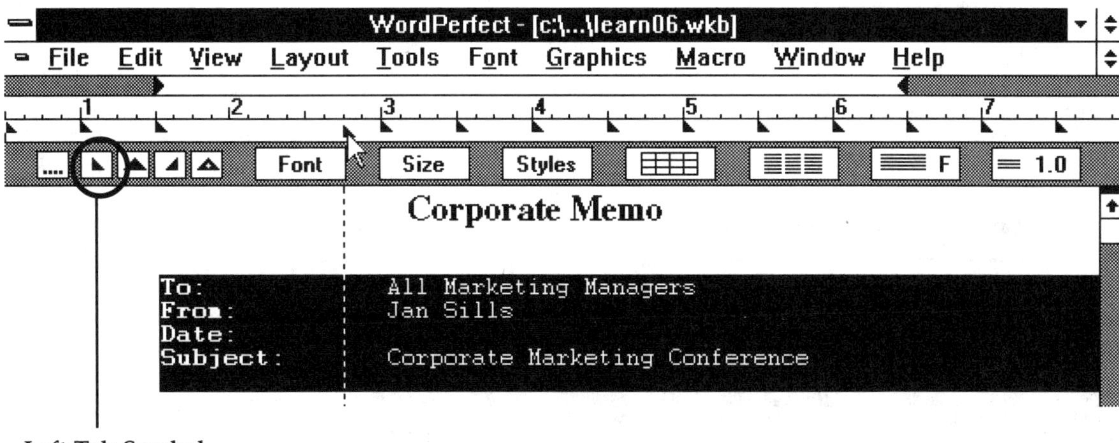

Figure 4x-8. Hold the mouse down on the left tab symbol and drag it to 2.75" on the ruler; then release the mouse. The text will realign accordingly when you release the mouse button. To be more precise with the tab placement, refer to the bottom right-hand corner of the screen, which displays the tab's exact location as it is moved by the mouse.

5. ***Use the Font button to activate the Font dialog box and change the font of the heading, "Corporate Memo", to Courier.***

To change the font of the heading, "Corporate Memo", select this text now with the mouse. To change the font of the selected text, double-click on the **Font** button in the Ruler to activate the *Font* dialog box of Figure 4x-10. Select Courier from the list of available fonts, and click on OK. Figure 4x-11 shows the result.

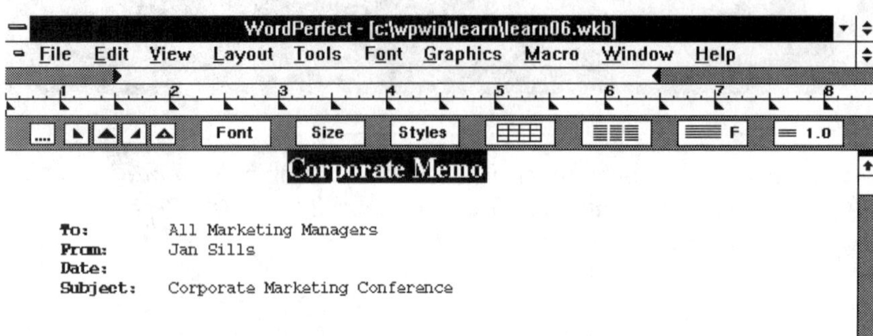

Figure 4x-9. After the words "Corporate Memo" have been selected, double-click on the Font button in the Ruler to activate the Font dialog box..

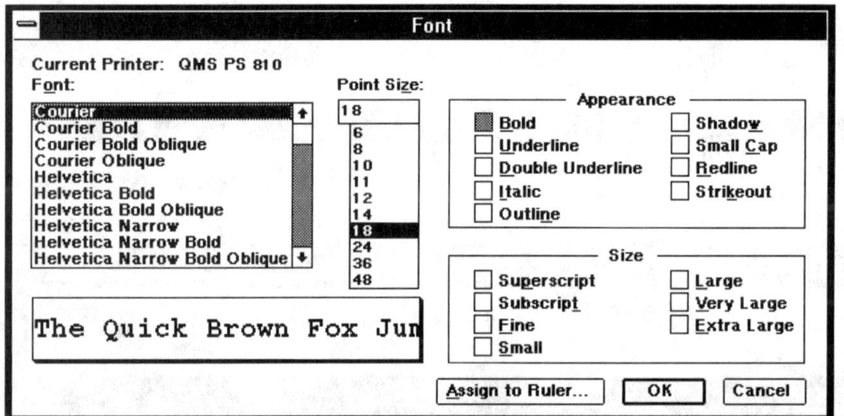

Figure 4x-10. Select Courier from the list of fonts in the Font dialog box and click on OK.

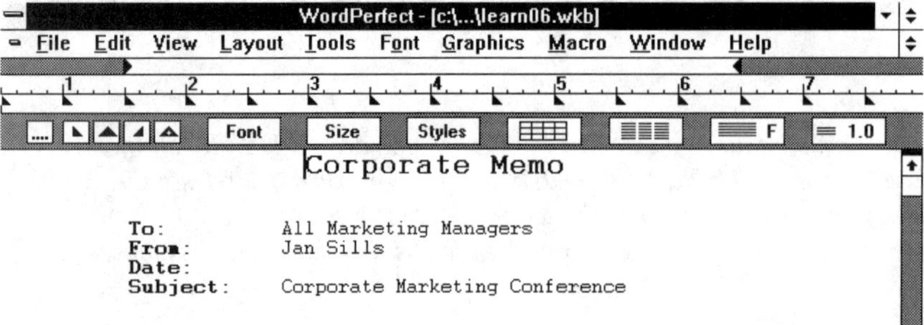

Figure 4x-11. The result of the font change to Courier.

6. Use the Justification button to center the last paragraph.

To center the last paragraph of text, it is not necessary to select the whole paragraph or to position the cursor at the beginning of the paragraph. All you need do is insert the cursor anywhere within the paragraph, as shown in Figure 4x-12, and select the *Center* command from the ruler *Justification* button.

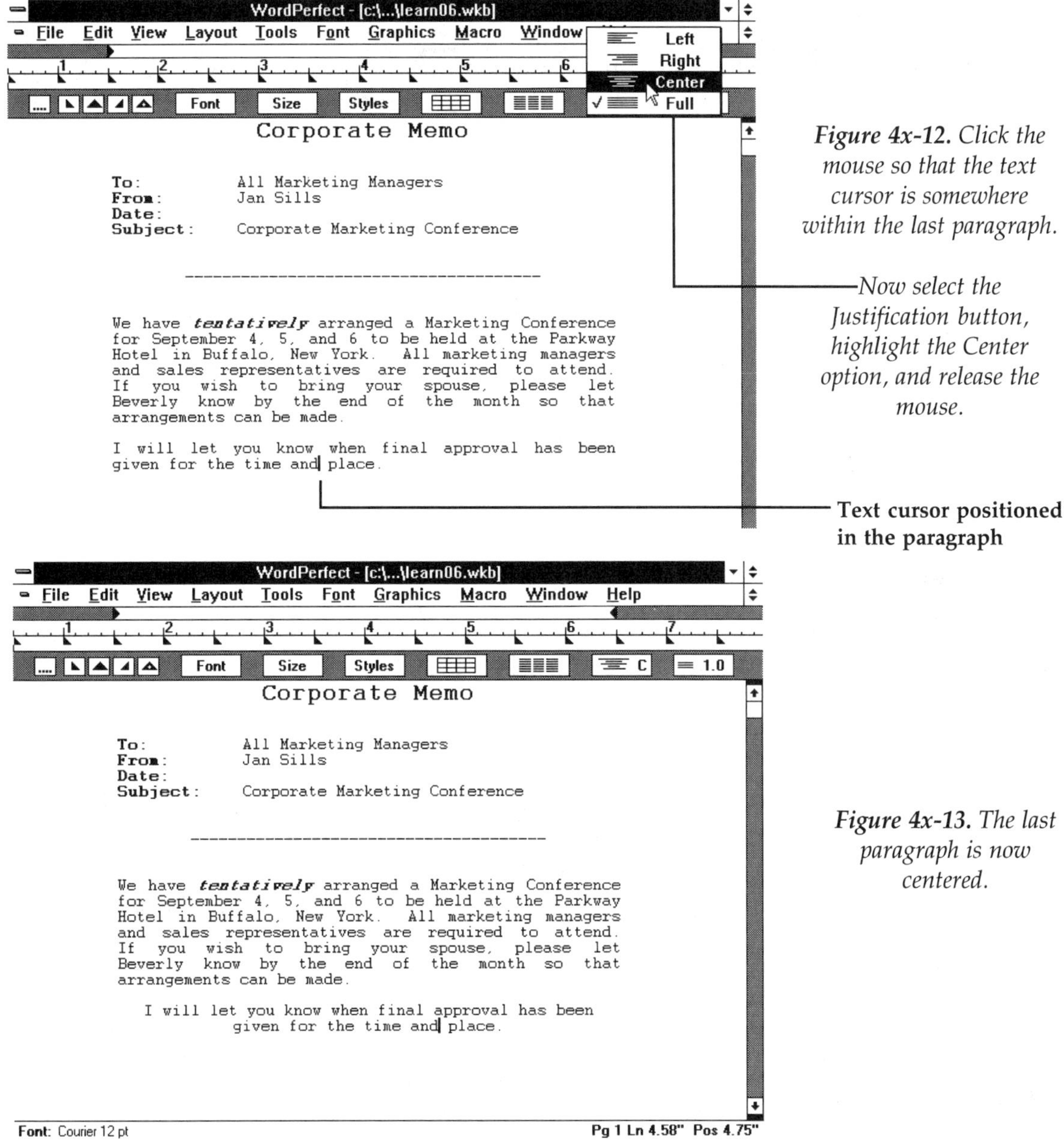

Figure 4x-12. *Click the mouse so that the text cursor is somewhere within the last paragraph.*

Now select the Justification button, highlight the Center option, and release the mouse.

Text cursor positioned in the paragraph

Figure 4x-13. *The last paragraph is now centered.*

7. Double-space the whole document using the Line Spacing button.

To perform this step, the cursor must be positioned at the beginning of the document. Use the Ctrl+Home keys to move the cursor. Figure 4x-14 shows the next step.

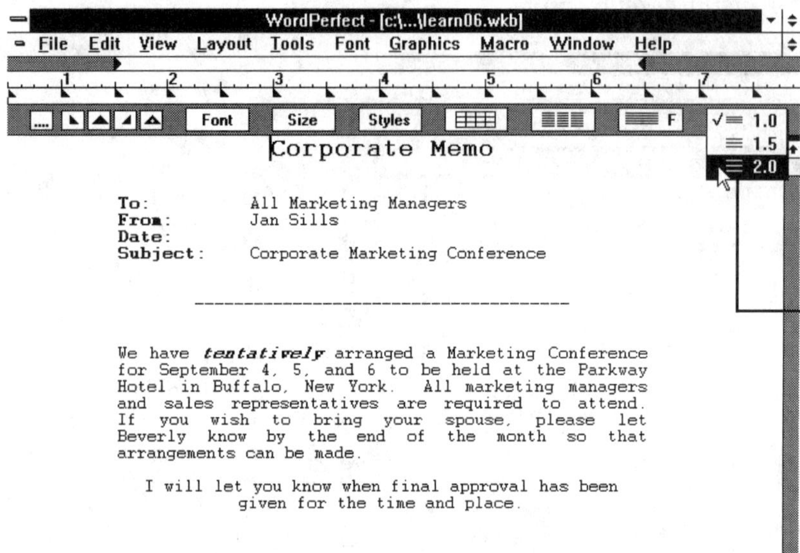

__Figure 4x-14.__ After the cursor has been inserted at the beginning of the document, select the Spacing button, highlight 2.0, and release the mouse.

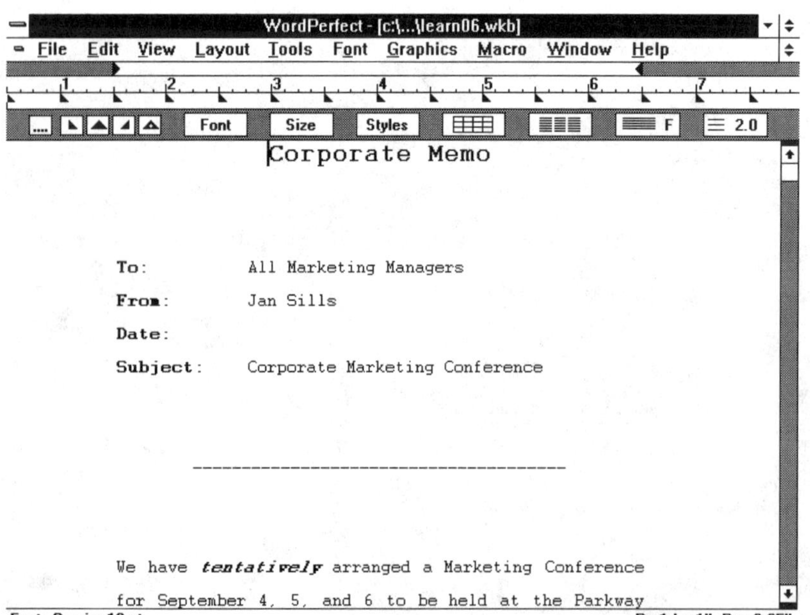

__Figure 4x-15.__ This is how double-spacing will look after the operation of Figure 4x-13.

Codes

Theory

WordPerfect for Windows is a WYSIWYG (What you see is what you get) program. This means text and graphics will display on screen as closely as possible to how they will appear when printed. However, formatting codes, which are not visible on the editing screen, are also inserted into documents. These codes are very important, as they determine the properties of such things as text, pages, paragraphs, tables, columns and graphics—in fact everything that can possibly appear within a WordPerfect document.

As you will have experienced from the use of WordPerfect to this stage, the normal editing screen does not display hidden codes that control the formatting of text. Rather, the text (and graphics) appear as they will print.

For a simple demonstration of codes, enter the string "This is a test of WordPerfect codes" into a fresh WordPerfect document window (Figure 5-1). This can be achieved by selecting the *New* command from the **File** menu.

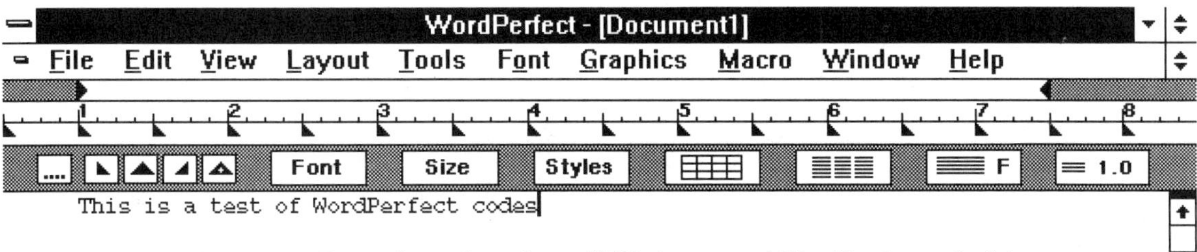

Figure 5-1. *Enter the string of text "This is a test of WordPerfect codes" into a new document window.*

To view the codes within a document, you select the *Reveal Codes* command from the **View** menu (Figure 5-2).

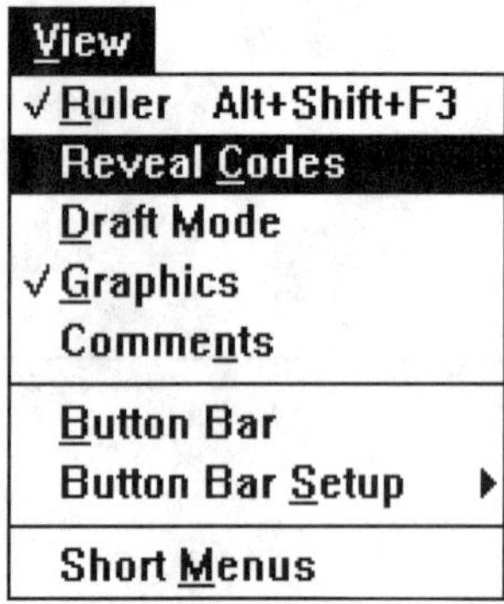

Figure 5-2. The Reveal Codes command from the ***View*** *menu splits the screen into two halves—the editing screen on the top half, and the codes and text on the bottom half (Figure 5-3).*

On selecting this command, your screen splits horizontally—editing screen on the top half and *Reveal Codes* section on the bottom half, as shown in Figure 5-3.

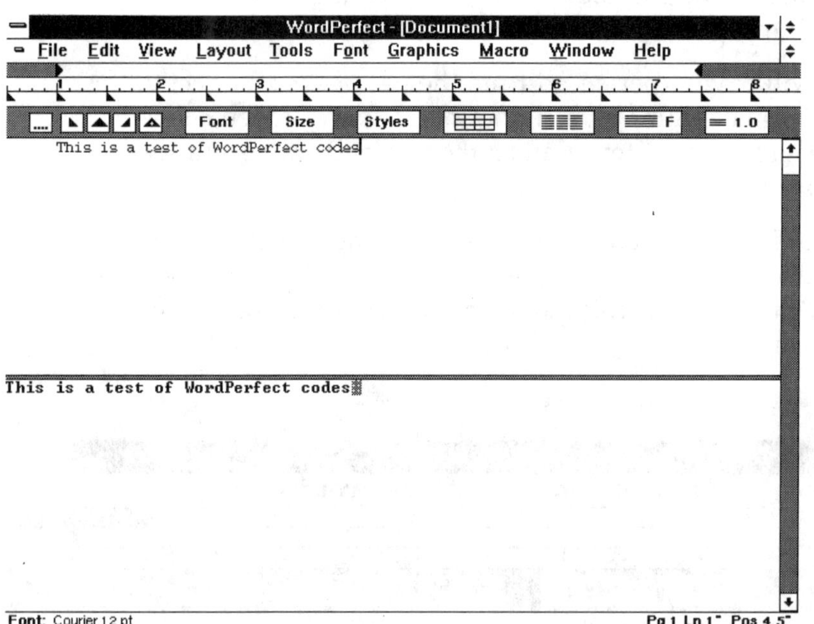

Figure 5-3. The Reveal Codes screen appears along the bottom half of the screen.

The appearance of text and codes in the *Reveal Codes* section of the screen (colors and shades), is determined by the *Display* command from the *Preferences* fly-out menu in the **File** menu. This is discussed in Chapter 10, **Preferences - (1)** under the *Reveal Codes Colors* section.

In Figure 5-3, the *Reveal Codes* section appears very similar to the editing screen section—this is because no codes have currently been inserted—the text is totally unformatted. All editing is still performed in the top half of the screen.

Every time you insert a text formatting or other instruction into text in the normal editing screen, a code is also placed in the text. To illustrate this, select the word "WordPerfect" (by double-clicking on it) from the text on your screen (Figure 5-4).

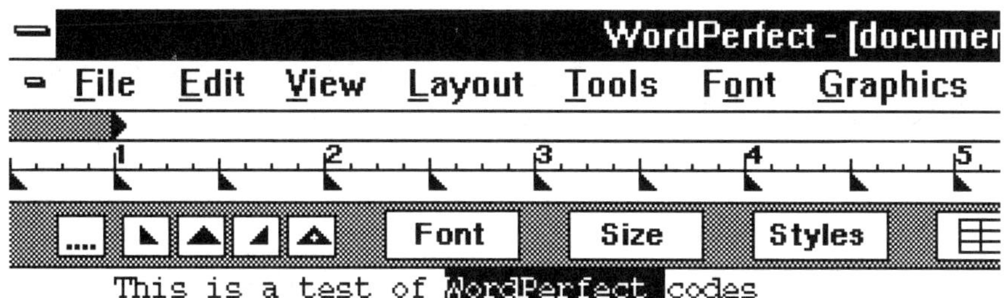

This is a test of [Select]WordPerfect codes

Figure 5-4. *Select the word "WordPerfect" from the top half of the screen. This selection is reflected in the bottom half of the screen by the text "[Select]" before the word "WordPerfect".*

Now select the *Bold* command from the **Font** menu to bold this word (Figure 5-5).

Font
Font... F9
Color...
✓Normal Ctrl+N
Bold Ctrl+B
Italic Ctrl+I
Underline Ctrl+U
Double Underline
Redline
Strikeout
Subscript
Superscript
Size Ctrl+S ▸
Overstrike ▸
WP Characters... Ctrl+W

Figure 5-5. *Select the Bold command from the **Font** menu to bold the selected word in Figure 5-4.*

The selected text becomes bold in the editing screen and, in the *Reveal Codes* screen, is surrounded by two codes—[*Bold On*] and [*Bold Off*]. The [*Bold On*] code tells you and WordPerfect that every character encountered after this code is bolded—until such time as a [*Bold Off*] code is encountered.

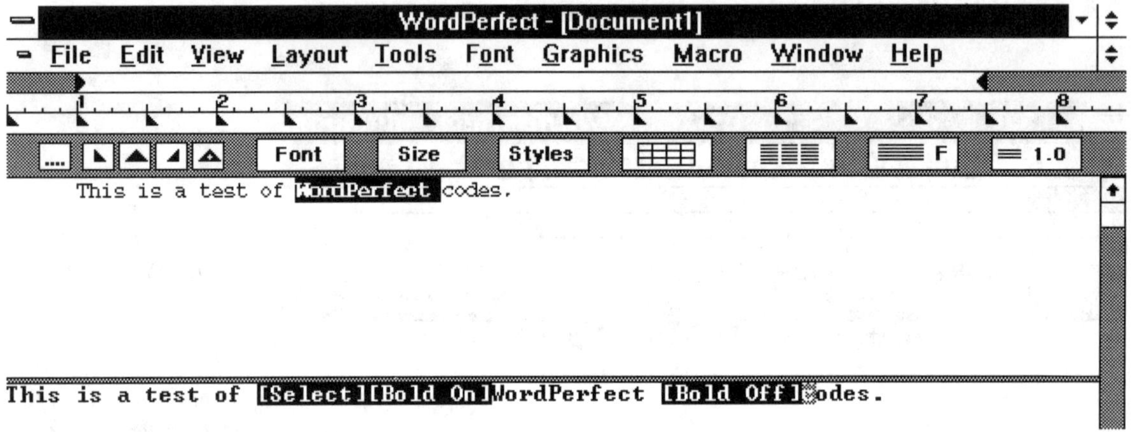

Figure 5-6. *After bolding a selected word, that word becomes surrounded by a [Bold On] and a [Bold Off] code.*

No matter what you do to text in WordPerfect, a code is always inserted into the text—whether you change margins, change fonts, add columns, import a graphic, whatever.

On the next page, in Figure 5-7, is an example WordPerfect file—it has had many codes inserted. You may recognize the meaning of many codes (some tend to be a little obscure).

In the figure, there are codes for *Left* and *Right Margin* settings [*L/R Mar:*], font changing commands (*Font:*), justification commands [*Just: Left*], and others, appearing in the bottom half of the screen—the *Reveal Codes* section.

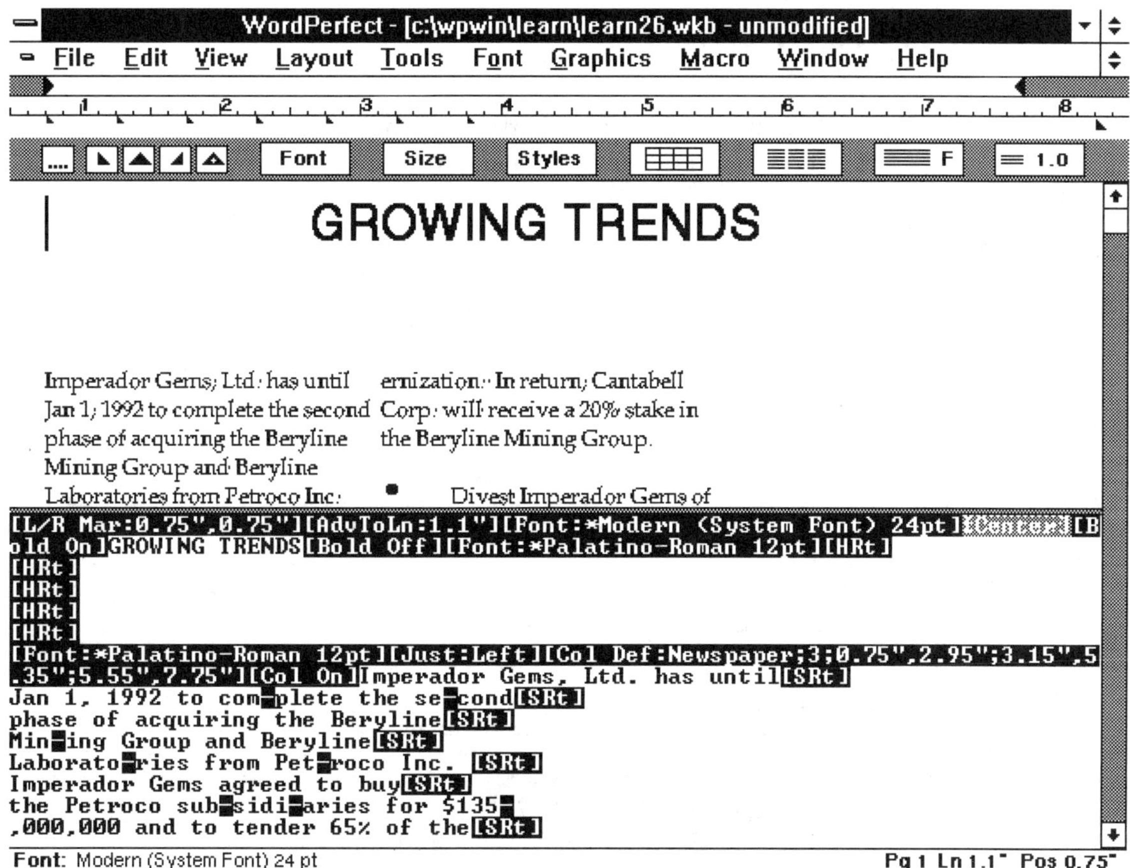

Figure 5-7. Many text and document formatting codes can be seen within the Reveal Codes section of this document.

Why do you need to know about codes?

As WordPerfect is a WYSIWYG package, using *Reveal Codes* when working with a document is not necessary all that often. Knowing how to deal with codes, and how codes work, could save you quite a bit of heartache, however, as you become more proficient in the program.

Different types of codes

Depending on the type of formatting you apply to a document, one of several types of codes may be inserted in the document.

Simple codes

Codes are inserted into text to denote such things as tabs, carriage returns, line wraps, and new pages. See Figure 5-8 as an illustration of this.

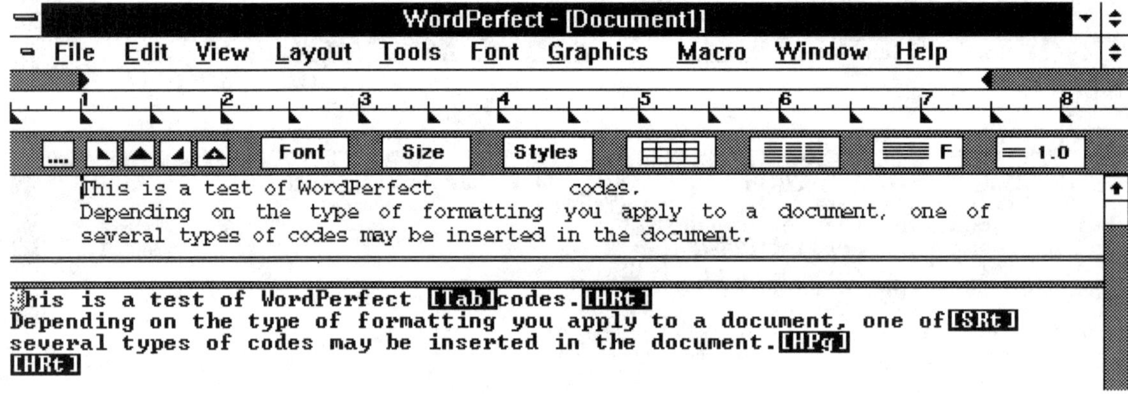

Figure 5-8. Illustrated in this text are four different simple codes. Towards the end of the first line, a tab is indicated [Tab]. At the end of the first line, a carriage return (or hard return) is indicated [HRt]. At the end of the second line, a line wrap (soft return) is indicated [SRt]. At the end of the third line, a new page is indicated [HPg].

Paired codes

The easiest type of codes to use are the *paired codes*—codes that work on the function on/function off principle. The [*Bold On*] and [*Bold Off*] codes of Figure 5-6 are an example of a *paired code*.

If text is selected, and a *paired code* then applied, a [*Function On*] code is placed at the start of the selection, and a [*Function Off*] is placed at the end of the selection. The function is applied to all text between the [*Function On*] and [*Function Off*] codes.

In most cases, if you apply a function that uses a *paired code*, and no text is selected, a [*Function On*] code is placed in the text, followed immediately by a [*Function Off*] code. All text that you insert between these two codes uses that function.

Figures 5-9 and 5-10 are examples of *paired codes*.

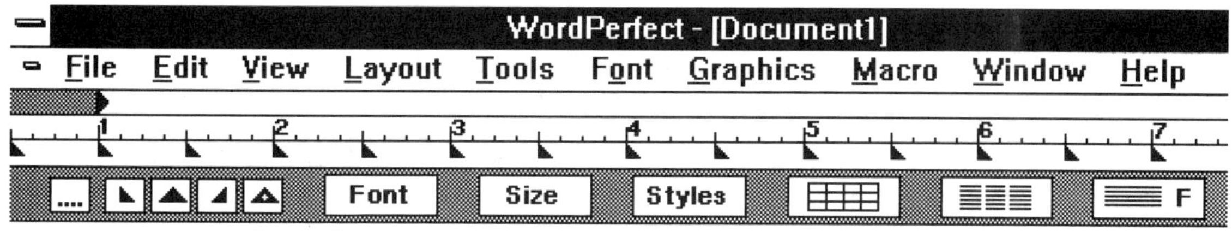

Figure 5-9. *Here is an example of the Paired Codes [Vry Large On] and [Vry Large Off] surrounding the word "test". On the editing part of the screen, you can see that the word "test" does indeed use a larger font.*

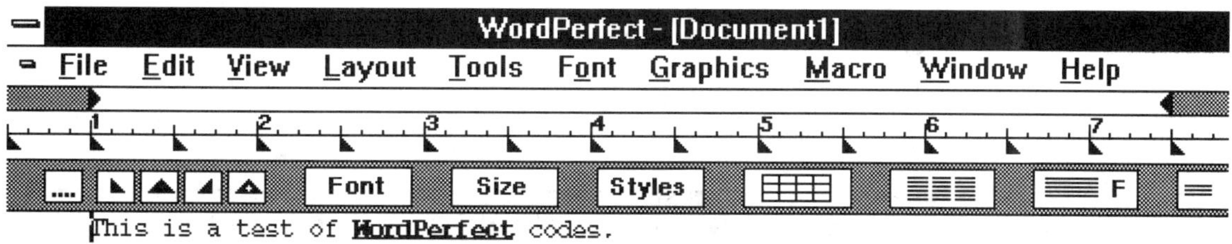

Figure 5-10. *Here is an example of the Paired Codes [Und On] and [Bold On] and [Und Off] and [Bold Off] surrounding the word "WordPerfect". On the editing section of the screen, you can see that the word "WordPerfect" is underlined and bolded.*

Open codes

Open codes are used by WordPerfect to change the format of text from a certain point in documents onwards. These codes are not turned off, and will remain in a document until they are replaced by another *open code* of the same type.

For example, if you change the font used by text in a document to Times Roman 10pt in a certain point in a document, Wordperfect inserts a code that reads [*Font: Tms Rmn 10pt*] in the document. Everything following that code will use the font specified in that code until another [*Font:*] code is found.

Figure 5-11 has inserted the mouse cursor before the "W" in "WordPerfect", and used the *Font* command in the **Font** menu to set the font to Times Roman 10pt. As you can see, a code representing this change appears in the text.

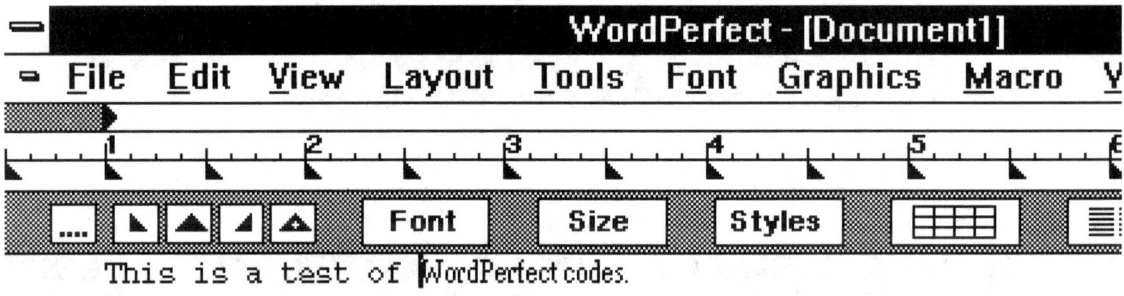

Figure 5-11. *Changing text font is an example of an open code—there are no On and Off codes—simply a code.*

In Figure 5-11, all text following the inserted code changes to the font specified in the code. This will continue until such time as a contradictory font code is found (Figure 5-12).

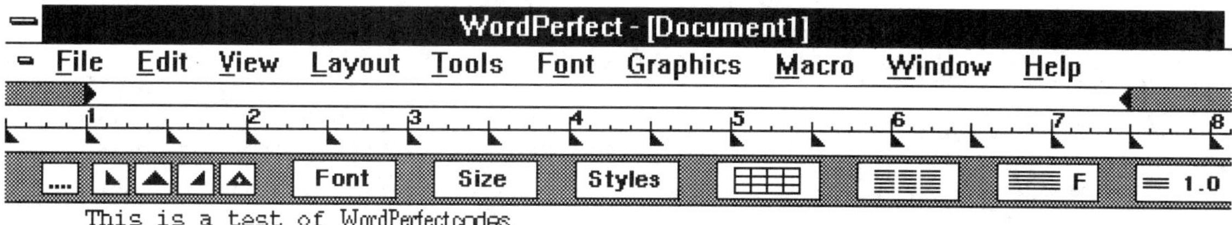

This is a test of [Font:Tms Rmn 10pt]WordPerfect [Font:Helvetica 10pt]codes.

Figure 5-12. *This example is the result of inserting the text cursor before the word "codes" and changing the font again. As you can see, another font code is inserted in the text. The text following this code uses the font specified in this code.*

Figure 5-12 illustrates what *open codes* are all about—when an *open code* is set, the text in the document following that code obeys that code, until another code of the same type or the end of the document is reached.

Editing codes

From time to time, you may find that using the *Reveal Codes* screen, and actually editing the codes in this screen, makes it very much easier to create, format, and edit documents.

Being able to view the codes in a document makes it absolutely clear why text and pages are formatted the way they are.

When *Reveal Codes* is on, you can still edit text in the editing section of the screen, as normal. However, as the text cursor is moved around the editing screen, a similar cursor moves around the *Reveal Codes* screen. As text is deleted from the editing screen, it is deleted from the *Reveal Codes* screen, as well.

In the editing screen, it is impossible to see, and therefore very difficult to delete, codes. However, in the *Reveal Codes* screen, a code can be selected by clicking the mouse on it, or moving the text cursor onto it (Figure 5-13).

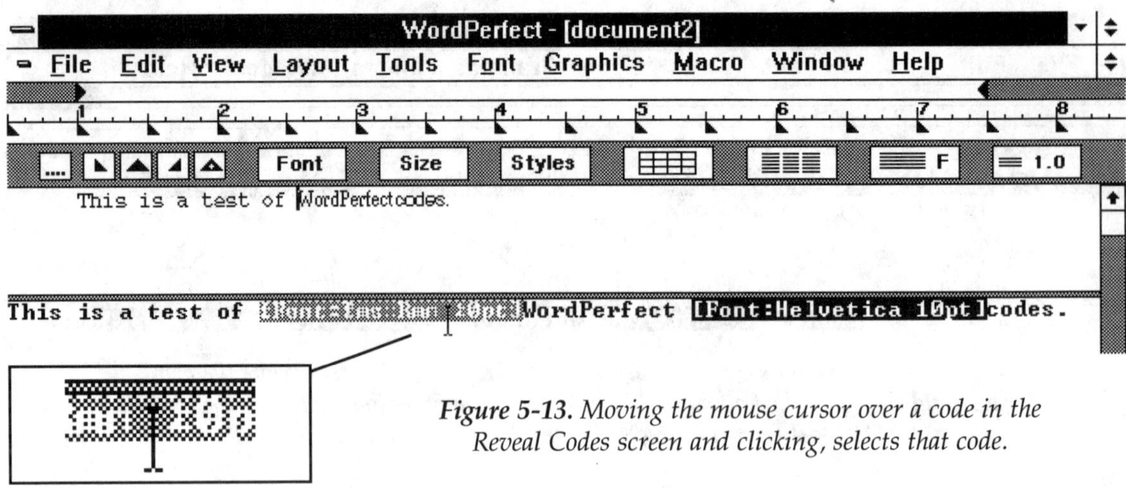

Figure 5-13. Moving the mouse cursor over a code in the Reveal Codes screen and clicking, selects that code.

The appearance of text and codes in the *Reveal Codes* section of the screen (colors and shades), is determined by the *Display* command from the *Preferences* fly-out menu in the **File** menu. This is discussed in Chapter 10, **Preferences - (1)** under the *Reveal Codes Colors* section.

The appearance of codes as they are selected can be quite different, depending on how the *Display* command from the *Preferences* fly-out menu in the **File** menu is used. In Figure 5-13, a selected code appears as white text over a gray, stippled background.

Once a code is selected, it can be deleted, by pressing the Del key on the keyboard. If a code is deleted, the effect of that code is removed from following text (Figure 5-14).

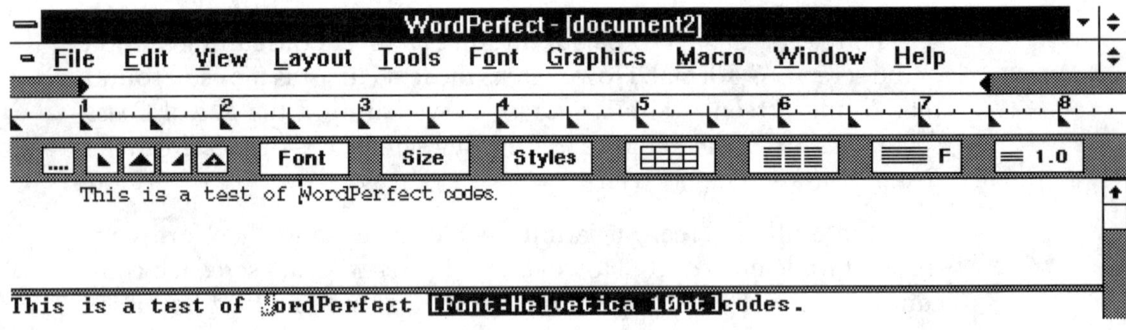

***Figure 5-14.** Once a code is selected (Figure 5-13), pressing the Del key on the keyboard removes that code from the text. The effect of that code is also removed from the text on the editing screen.*

In Figure 5-14, the code [*Font: Tms Rmn 10pt*] from Figure 5-13 has been removed. Also removed is the effect of this code. Before it was deleted, it caused the text following it to use the Times Roman 10pt font—now the text reverts to the font used prior to the code.

Deleting a paired code

When you select an [*On*] or an [*Off*] code from a *paired code*, and delete that code, the corresponding [*Off*] or [*On*] code is also deleted.

Deleting an open code

Deleting an *open code* requires more forethought than deleting a *paired code*, as *open codes* generally affect much larger portions of a document, often entire documents. Thus, when deleting an *open code*, it is quite possible that most, if not all, of the document may be affected.

Using codes for problem solving

Using *Reveal Codes* is often a way to discover why something is going wrong—why WordPerfect is not doing what you think it should be doing.

It is quite possible to leave 'stray' codes in a document—codes that you did not even realize still existed in the file. Sometimes the only time you realize that a code is still in your document is when it causes a problem.

Let's say, for example, that you insert the text cursor at the start of a document, and set the font to Helvetica 10 pt. For some reason, only half the document changes to Helvetica 10 pt—the last half of the text remains the same.

If this sort of thing occurs, use *Reveal Codes* to examine your document. Chances are, as in the above example, there is a stray code in the file, which is causing the text from a certain point in the document to use another font. As any code will only remain in effect until another code of the same type is found (or the document end reached), the effect of the code inserted at the start of the document will run out when it reaches another font code—the font code that you may not even have realized was there.

Searching for/replacing codes

It is possible, using the standard WordPerfect search and replace facilities, to search for codes of a certain type, and even perform a replace function on these codes if you wish.

To do this, first select any of the *Search* or *Replace* commands in the **Edit** menu. In this case, use as an example the simple *Search* command from the **Edit** menu (Figure 5-15).

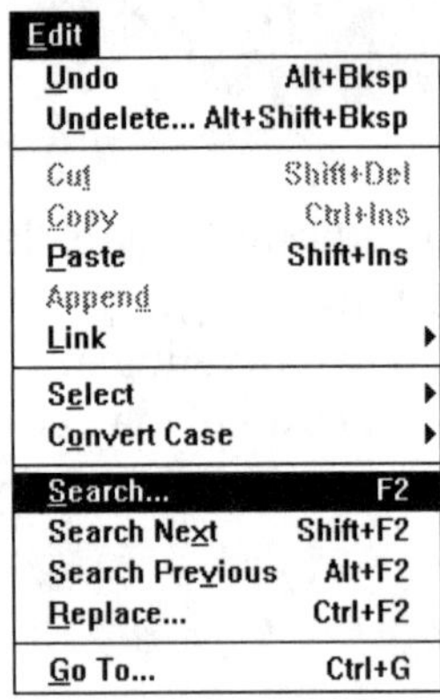

***Figure 5-15.** The Search command from the **Edit** menu can be used to search for certain codes in a document.*

The *Search* command activates the dialog box of Figure 5-16.

Search
Search For:
Search Document Body Only
Direction: Forward
Codes...
Search
Cancel

***Figure 5-16.** The Search command dialog box—all Search and Replace dialog boxes are very similar. They all contain the Codes button in the bottom left-hand corner.*

The use of the *Search* command normally involves your entering text into the *Search For* text box, and clicking on the *Search* button. However, you may wish to click on the *Codes* button in the bottom left-hand corner of the screen, if you would like to search for codes. You will then be presented with the *Codes* dialog box of Figure 5-17.

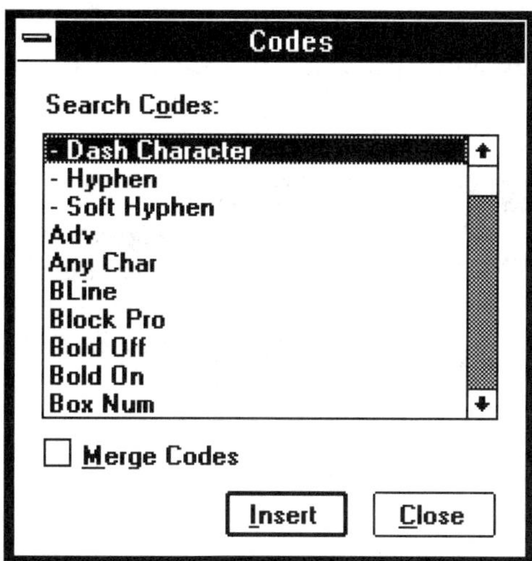

Figure 5-17. *After selecting the Codes button of Figure 5-16, this dialog box appears. Quite simply, it is a list of all the possible codes that can be found in a WordPerfect document.*

The Figure 5-17 dialog box lists all possible code types that you can find in a WordPerfect document. From here, you locate the code for which you wish to search and select that code by clicking on it (Figure 5-18).

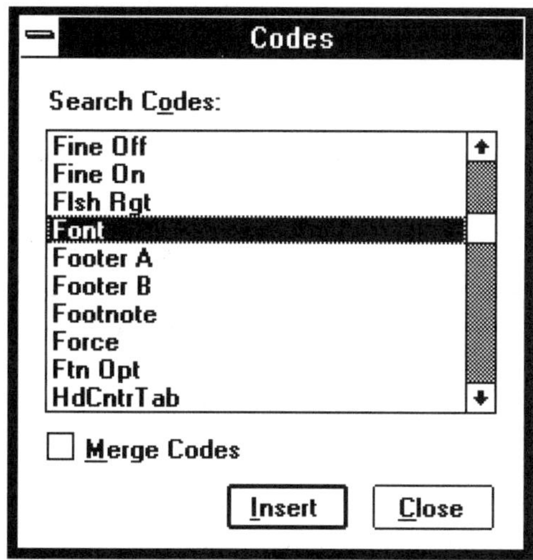

Figure 5-18. *Here the 'Font' code has been selected from the list of codes in Figure 5-17.*

Once you have located and selected the code for which you are searching, click on the *Insert* and then the *Close* buttons.

After selecting the *Insert* and *Close* buttons, the selected code will appear in the *Search For* text box (Figure 5-19) of the *Search* dialog box.

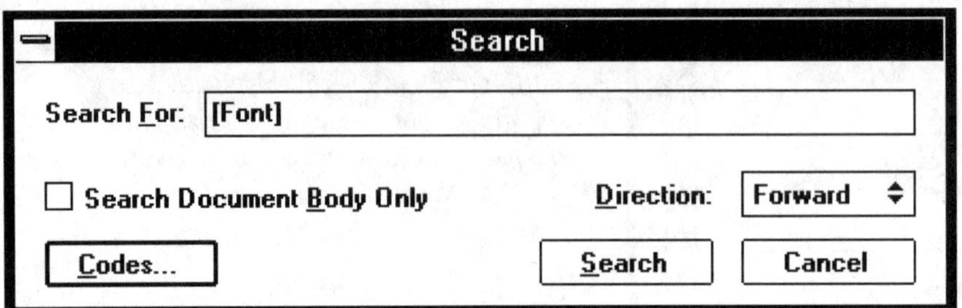

Figure 5-19. *The code selected in the list, after selecting the Insert and Close buttons (Figure 5-18), now appears in the Search For text box.*

Once the code is inserted in the *Search For* text box, the *Search* command operates in the same manner as always—the search is initiated using the *Search* button.

For more information regarding the use of the *Search/Replace* features, see Chapter 17, **Advanced Text Editing**.

Hints and Tips

Options affecting the use of codes

There are two options within the *Preferences/Environment* command (Figure 5-20) in the **File** menu, that affect the use of codes in WordPerfect documents. While these are covered in Chapter 10, they are worth covering again here, while discussing codes.

The first option, *Auto Code Placement*, is an extremely handy option—make sure it is enabled at all times.

WordPerfect expects certain types of codes to be placed at certain points in a document—the page size for example. It likes this to be at the start of the page. If margins change, they should not change in the middle of a paragraph, etc.

Auto Code Placement ensures that all codes are placed in the correct positions in a document. If, for example, you changed the page size half way through a page, WordPerfect moves this code to the beginning of the page, regardless of where the text cursor was when the page size was changed. It acts as a kind of automatic code manager—always moving codes to the correct position in text.

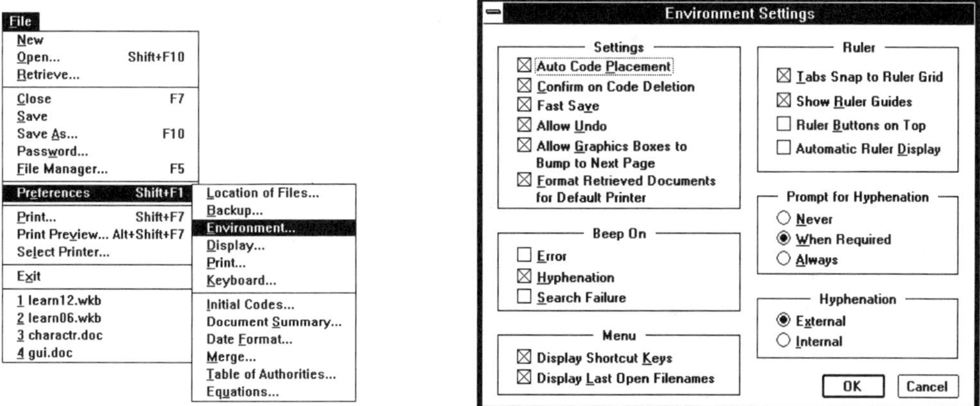

Figure 5-20. *The Preferences/Environment command and dialog box.*

The second option, *Confirm on Code Deletion*, is used to prevent accidental deletion of codes.

When you are using *Reveal Codes*, it is very easy to see codes and much harder to accidentally delete them. For this purpose, you are never given a warning if you attempt to delete a code while using *Reveal Codes*.

If, however, you are not using *Reveal Codes* and you are using the Backspace or Delete key to remove text, you may be in danger of accidentally deleting a code (as these are invisible on the editing screen). WordPerfect can warn you about this with the dialog box of Figure 5-21.

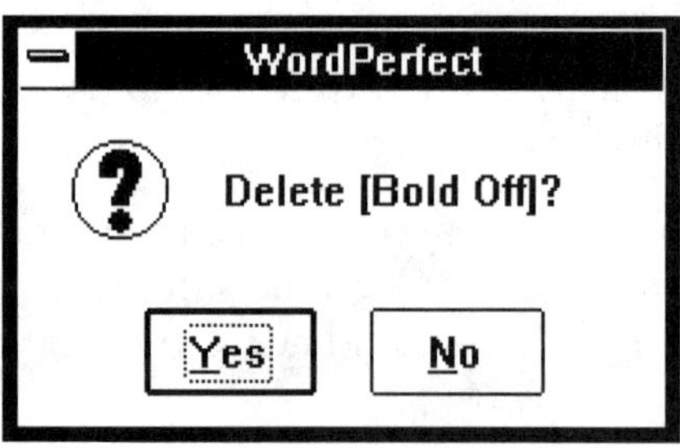

Figure 5-21. *Here WordPerfect warns that a code (in this case, the [Bold Off] code) is about to be deleted. You now have the option on how to handle this.*

Codes — Exercise

5ex

This training exercise is designed so that people of all levels of expertise with WordPerfect can use it to gain maximum benefit. In order to do this, the bare exercise is listed below this paragraph on just one page, with no hints. The following pages contain the steps needed to complete this exercise for those who need additional prompting.

Steps in brief

1. *Open the WordPerfect file, biblio12.wkb, in the learn sub-directory of the wpwin sub-directory.*
2. *Activate the Reveal Codes screen.*
3. *Using the Replace command, search for all Underline codes and delete them.*
4. *Bold all the book names by selecting them and applying the Bold command.*
5. *Delete the Bold codes for the first two bolded book titles.*

The details for completing these steps are on the following pages.

Steps in detail

1. ***Open the WordPerfect file, biblio12.wkb, in the learn sub-directory of the wpwin sub-directory.***

Using the *Open* command from the **File** menu, locate and double-click on the file ***biblio12.wkb*** in the *Open File* dialog box (Figure 5x-1). Figure 5x-2 shows the open file on the screen.

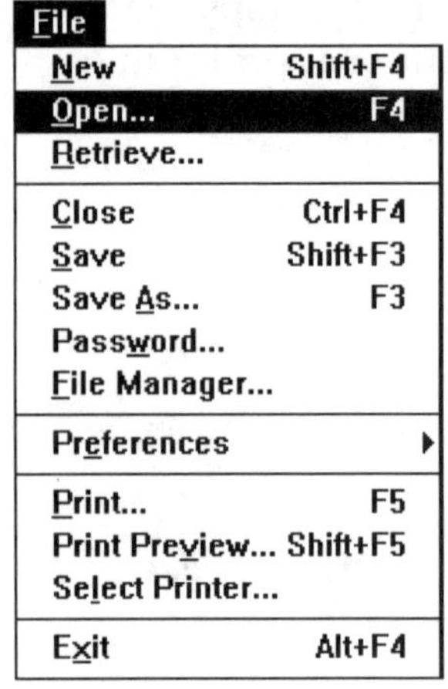

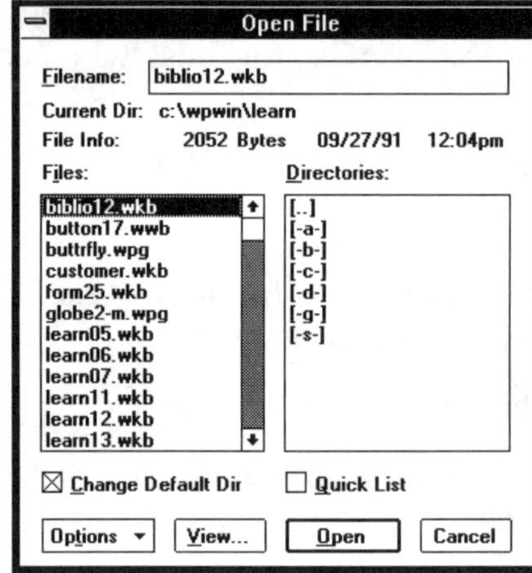

Figure 5x-1. *After selecting Open from the* ***File*** *menu, double-click on the file* ***biblio12.wkb*** *to open it on your screen.*

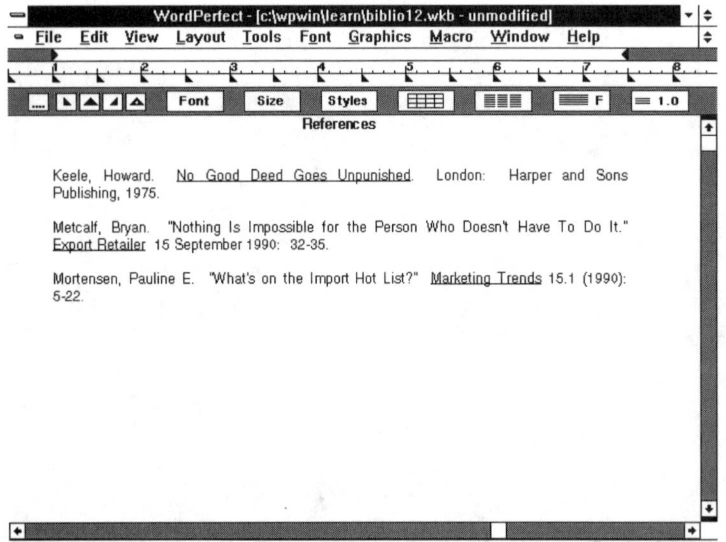

Figure 5x-2. *This is how the opened file looks on screen.*

2. *Activate the Reveal Codes screen.*

You need to activate the *Reveal Codes* screen to see the code placement for any document. To do this, select the *Reveal Codes* command from the **View** menu (Figure 5x-3).

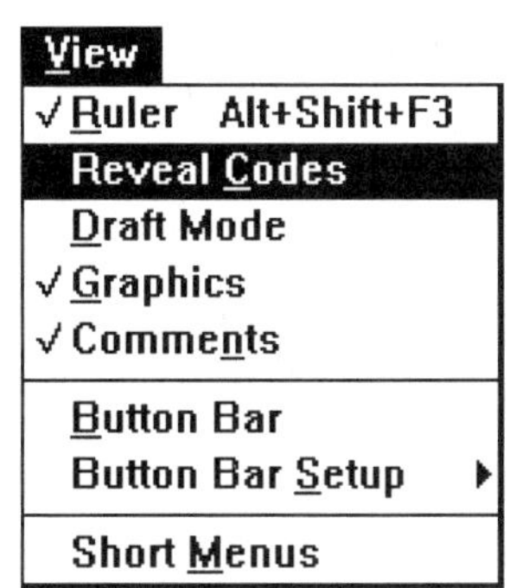

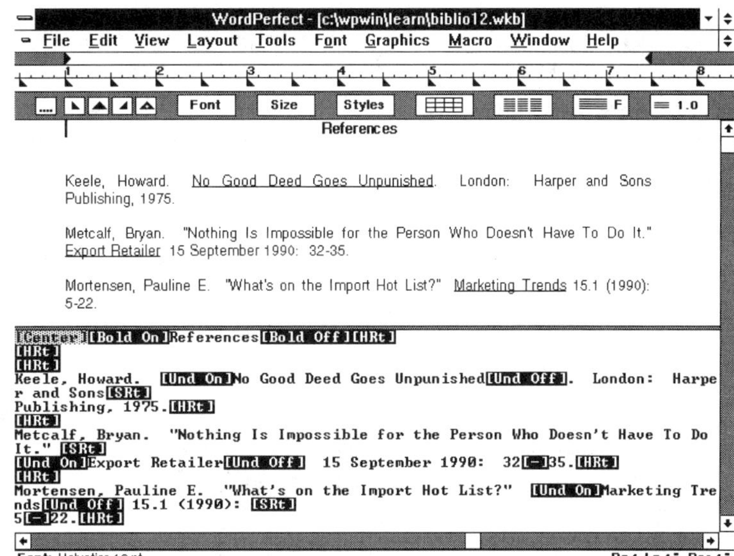

*Figure 5x-3. By selecting the Reveal Codes command from the **View** menu, the Reveal Codes screen appears in the bottom half of the document screen. Note the Und On and Und Off codes at the start and end of each underlined text string.*

3. *Using the Replace command, search for all Underline codes and delete them.*

You now need to remove all underlining in this document. To do this, first select the *Replace* command in the **Edit** menu to activate the *Search and Replace* dialog box (Figure 5x-4).

Edit
Undo Alt+Bksp
Undelete... Alt+Shift+Bksp
Cut Shift+Del
Copy Ctrl+Ins
Paste Shift+Ins
Append
Link
Select
Convert Case
Search... F2
Search Next Shift+F2
Search Previous Alt+F2
Replace... Ctrl+F2
Go To... Ctrl+G

Search and Replace
Search For:
Replace With:
Search Document Body Only
Direction: Forward
Codes... Replace All Find Next Replace Close

Figure 5x-4. Select the Replace command from the **Edit** menu to activate the Search and Replace dialog box.

Because you will be searching for a specific code, select the *Codes* button (bottom left corner) to activate the *Codes* dialog box. Highlight the code *Und On*, using the scroll bars to move through the list (Figure 5x-5).

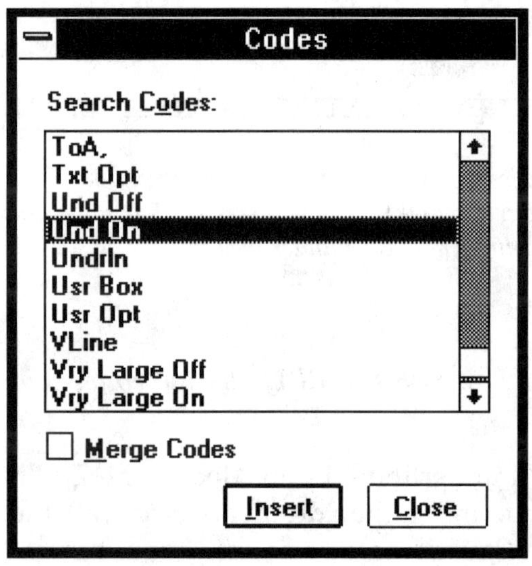

Figure 5x-5. After clicking on the Codes button in Figure 5x-4, the list of codes appears. Move down the list using the scroll bars and highlight the code Und On.

After locating the correct code, click on the *Insert* button to place it in the *Search For* line in the dialog box of Figure 5x-4 and click on the *Close* button. This will bring you to the dialog box of Figure 5x-6.

Search and Replace

Search For: [Und On]

Replace With:

Search Document Body Only

Direction: Forward

Codes... | Replace All | Find Next | Replace | Close

Figure 5x-6. *You now have a code to search for in the Search For line; the Replace With line remains empty.*

Because you want WordPerfect to delete the underline code without replacing it, leave the *Replace With* line empty, so that the code will be deleted and replaced with nothing. To activate this next process, click on the *Replace All* command. When WordPerfect has finished deleting all the underline codes, which should only take a couple of seconds, click on the *Close* button. Your screen will now look like the one in Figure 5x-7.

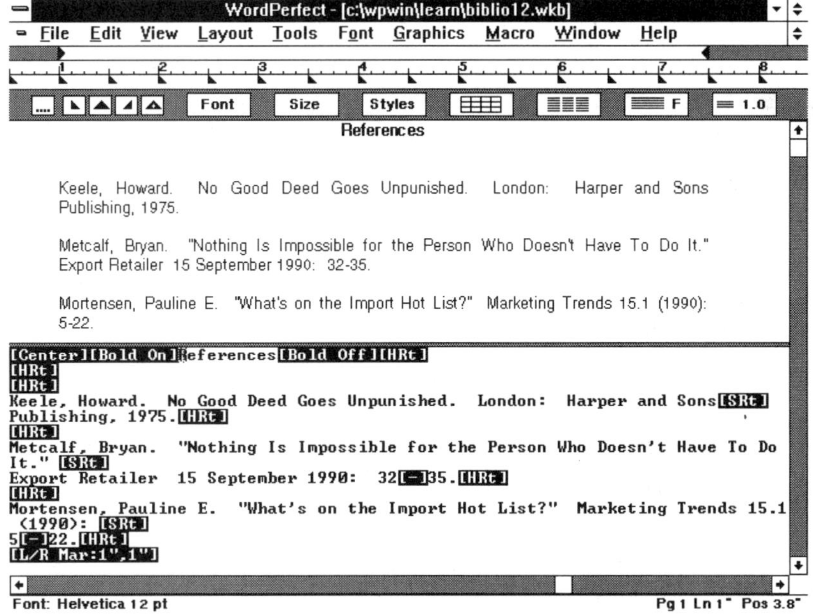

Figure 5x-7. *This is how the text on screen looks after the underline codes have been deleted.*

4. ***Bold all the book names by selecting them and applying the Bold command.***

Use the scroll bar to move back to the top of the screen. Now select the book title *"No Good Deed Goes Unpunished"* as shown in Figure 5x-8.

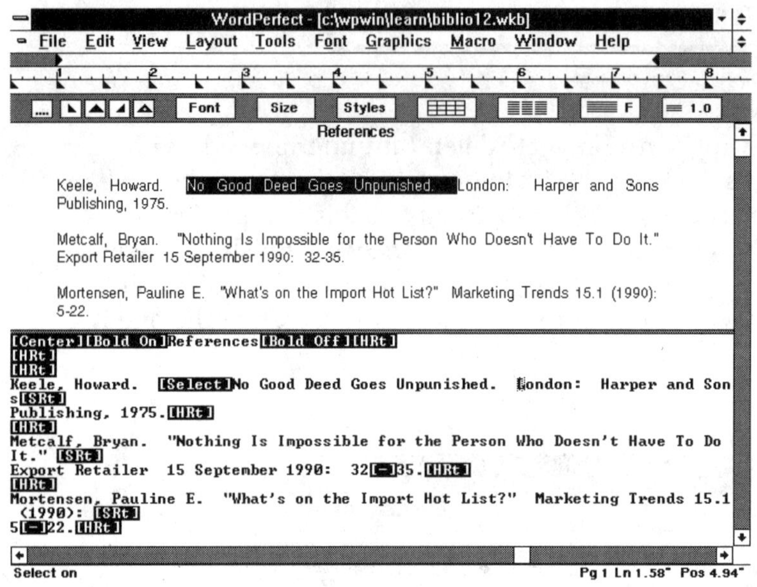

Figure 5x-8. *Select the first book title with the mouse, as shown in this figure.*

With the text still highlighted, go to the **Font** menu and select the *Bold* command (Figure 5x-9). The result is seen in Figure 5x-10.

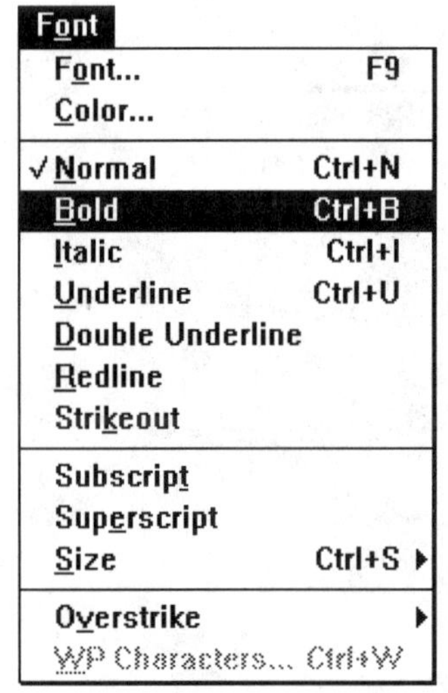

Figure 5x-9. *Select the Bold command from the* ***Font*** *menu.*

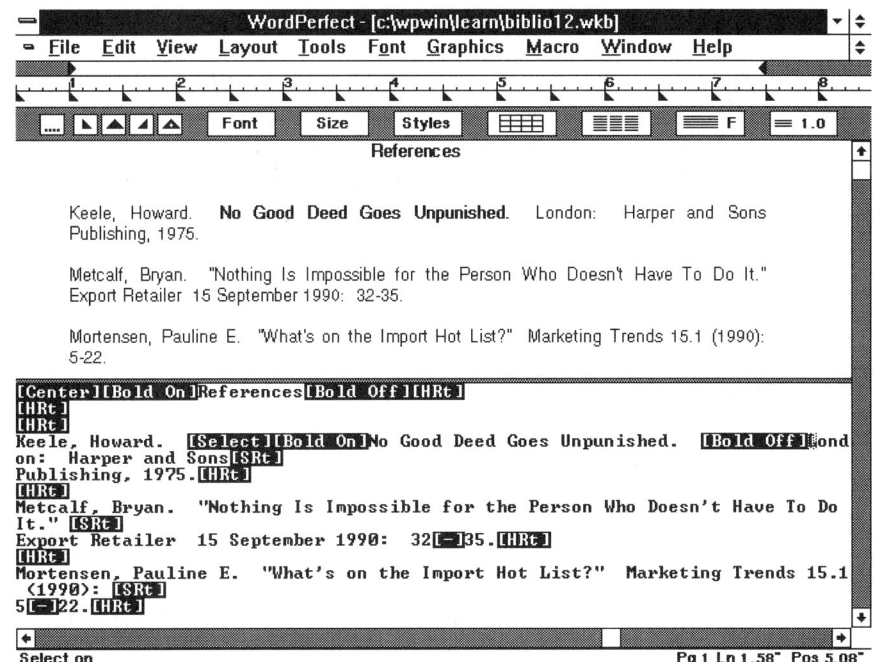

Figure 5x-10. *Here you see the result of the bolded text. Note where the paired codes appear in the Reveal Codes screen.*

Repeat this process with the other two book titles. The result is shown in Figure 5x-11.

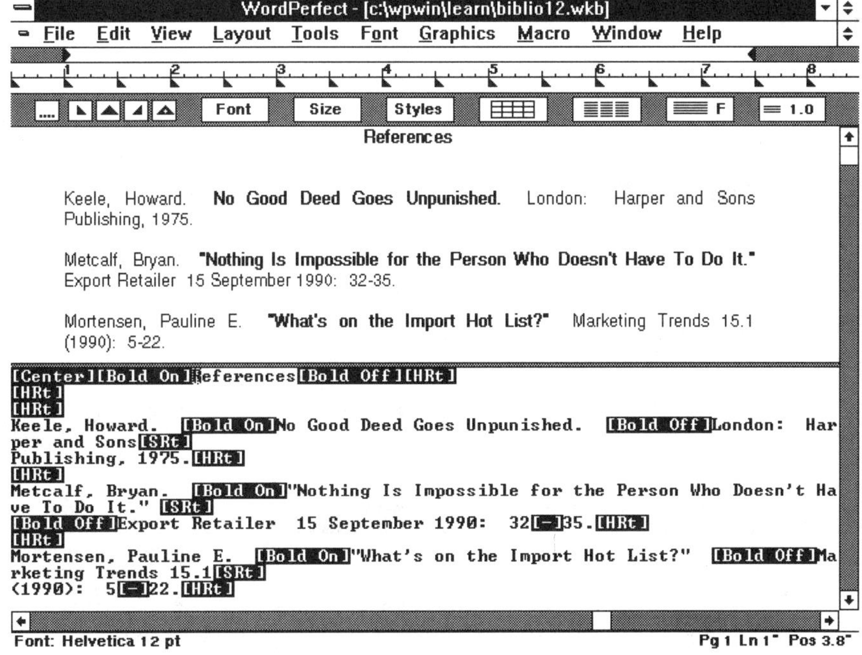

Figure 5x-11. *This figure shows all three book titles bolded, which is the required result. Note the three sets of Bold On/Bold Off paired codes.*

5. Delete the Bold codes for the first two bolded book titles.

Click once on the *Bold On* code in front of the first book title (Figure 5x-12) and press the Del key on your keyboard. Both the *Bold On* and *Bold Off* codes are automatically removed from the document (Figure 5x-13). For the second book title, click once on the *Bold Off* code and press the Del key. Note how this also removes both the *Bold On* and *Bold Off* codes.

```
[Center][Bold On]References[Bold Off][HRt]
[HRt]
[HRt]
Keele, Howard.  [Bold On]No Good Deed Goes Unpunished.  [Bold Off]London:  Har
per and Sons[SRt]
Publishing, 1975.[HRt]
[HRt]
Metcalf, Bryan.  [Bold On]"Nothing Is Impossible for the Person Who Doesn't Ha
ve To Do It." [SRt]
[Bold Off]Export Retailer  15 September 1990:  32[-]35.[HRt]
[HRt]
Mortensen, Pauline E.  [Bold On]"What's on the Import Hot List?"  [Bold Off]Ma
rketing Trends 15.1[SRt]
(1990):  5[-]22.[HRt]
Font: Helvetica 12 pt                                    Pg 1 Ln 1" Pos 3.8"
```

Figure 5x-12. *Click on the Bold On code (in the Reveal Codes screen) in front of the first book title. Note, that in the Reveal Codes screen, the code become highlighted. (In this case, the code appears on a gray background rather than a black. On your system, it may appear on a black background, rather than a gray.)*

```
[Center][Bold On]References[Bold Off][HRt]
[HRt]
[HRt]
Keele, Howard.  No Good Deed Goes Unpunished.  London:  Harper and Sons[SRt]
Publishing, 1975.[HRt]
[HRt]
Metcalf, Bryan.  [Bold On]"Nothing Is Impossible for the Person Who Doesn't Ha
ve To Do It." [SRt]
[Bold Off]Export Retailer  15 September 1990:  32[-]35.[HRt]
[HRt]
Mortensen, Pauline E.  [Bold On]"What's on the Import Hot List?"  [Bold Off]Ma
rketing Trends 15.1[SRt]
(1990):  5[-]22.[HRt]
[L/R Mar:1",1"]
Font: Helvetica 12 pt                                    Pg 1 Ln 1.58" Pos 2.26"
```

Figure 5x-13. *After pressing the Del key on the keyboard, both the Bold On and Bold Off codes are deleted from around the first book title. The book title itself is no longer bolded.*

Handling Files

WordPerfect for Windows provides many features that make the opening, saving, protection, using, closing, and viewing of files far easier than many other packages.

WordPerfect allows multiple files (up to nine) to be opened and edited at once. This feature makes it very easy to compare files and to swap data between files.

In this chapter, we review many of the commands from the **File** menu that facilitate file handling, and also look at many of the features from WordPerfect which facilitate the use of multiple files.

To work through this chapter, it is best to close down WordPerfect completely and then start it again.

Document windows

Every text file used within WordPerfect appears within a document window—a window very much like a traditional Windows window in that it can be resized, moved, maximized, and minimized. (Moving, resizing, maximizing, and minimizing document windows are covered later in this chapter.) The document window always appears within the WordPerfect window itself, below the Menu bar.

The use of the document window will become more apparent in this chapter, particularly as you start to resize and move these windows. For now, simply understand that a document window is the area in which a text file is displayed and edited.

New files

When WordPerfect is started, it opens a new file for you—in effect an empty window in which you can begin to enter or import text, graphics, and other objects. The new file that WordPerfect creates initially has the name ***Document 1 - unmodified*** which is shown in the Title bar (Figure 6-1).

WordPerfect - [Document1 - unmodified]

Figure 6-1. *The name of the new file in the Title bar as WordPerfect opens.*

Whenever a file name appears in the WordPerfect Title bar with the word ***"unmodified"*** beside it, this denotes that the file has been unchanged in any way since it was created or opened. As soon as a change is made to this file, the word ***"unmodified"*** will disappear.

To create a new file of your own, select the *New* command from the **File** menu as shown in Figure 6-2.

File

New	Shift+F4
Open...	F4
Retrieve...	
Close	Ctrl+F4
Save	Shift+F3
Save As...	F3
Password...	
File Manager...	
Preferences	▸
Print...	F5
Print Preview...	Shift+F5
Select Printer...	
Exit	Alt+F4
1 learn13.wkb	
2 learn26.wkb	
3 learn12.wkb	
4 document	

Figure 6-2. *The New command from the* ***File*** *menu creates a new file, which will open into a new document window.*

When a new document is created by selecting the *New* command of Figure 6-2, a new document window is created to hold that document. WordPerfect also gives this file a temporary name—in this case, ***"Document2 - unmodified"*** (Figure 6-3). You should see this name in your Title bar now. The document is named ***"Document2"*** because, in this case, you already have a ***"Document1"*** (Figure 6-1) which was created when WordPerfect was opened. If the *New* command of Figure 6-2 was now used again, a new window would be created with a ***"Document3 - unmodified"*** title.

WordPerfect - [Document2 - unmodified]

Figure 6-3. *As new files are opened, WordPerfect gives them a temporary name, beginning with the word "Document", followed by a number (which depends on the number of currently open files).*

You are now free to enter text into this new window. The text cursor appears in the top left-hand corner when a new document window is opened.

In other parts of this chapter, you will look at how to open files, switch between currently open files, retrieve and concatenate files, close files, and save files.

Open File dialog box

Opening a new file recalls an existing file from disk and displays it, ready for editing, in a new document window. Files are opened using the *Open* command from the **File** menu (Figure 6-4).

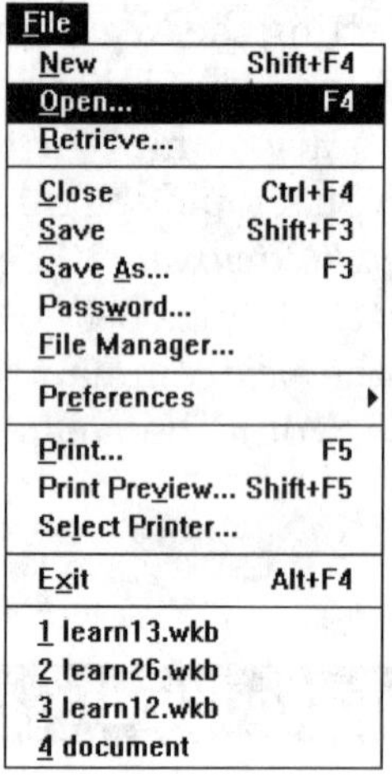

Figure 6-4. The Open command recalls existing documents from disk and displays them, ready for editing, in a new document window.

The *Open* command invokes the *Open File* dialog box, as seen in Figure 6-5, which allows you to choose the file you wish to open.

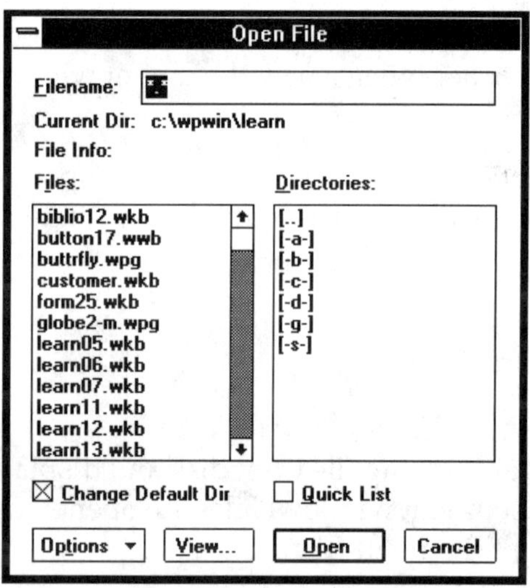

Figure 6-5. After selecting the Open command (Figure 6-4), you are asked to specify the file you wish to open.

The Figure 6-5 *Open File* dialog box is similar to other file open/save/retrieve dialog boxes found in almost all Windows programs. You may already be familiar with the structure of this type of dialog box; however, the remainder of this section briefly explains its operation.

If you understand how this dialog box operates, skip to the next section in this chapter (**Opening files**).

At the top of the *Open File* dialog box is the *Filename* text box (Figure 6-6). Here, the file you wish to open can be specified by clicking on its name or, if you wish, by entering the name through the keyboard.

Most of the time, however, the *Filename* text box contains the filter that controls the files displayed in the *Files* list box (Figure 6-7) further down the dialog box. In Figure 6-6, the *Filename* text box reads *"*.*"*, which means all file types are listed in the *Files* list box. If you were to change the string in the *Filename* text box to read ***"*.txt"***, only files with a file extension of ***"txt"***, will be listed in the *Files* list box.

Figure 6-6. *You may enter the name of the file you wish to open/save/retrieve in the Filename text box or, alternatively, specify the file filter used to determine the files listed in the Files list box.*

The *Filename* text box will also reflect the name of a file as it is selected from the *Files* list box. The *Files* list box provides the list from which the file to be opened is selected.

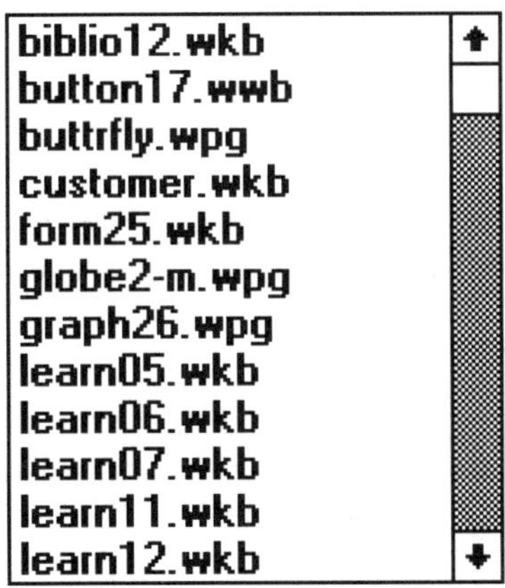

Figure 6-7. *The Files list box lists the files in the current directory, based on the file filter in the Filename text box (Figure 6-6). The file filter in Figure 6-6 is "*.*", which means display all files.*

Between the *Filename* text box and the *Files* list box are two lines—the first being the *Current Dir* line (Figure 6-8). This line reflects the subdirectory in which the files in the *Files* list box are located.

Current Dir: c:\wpwin\learn

Figure 6-8. The Current Dir line reflects the sub-directory from which the files in the Files list box are displayed.

Do not expect the *Current Dir* line in your *Open* dialog box to be exactly the same as the one in Figure 6-8—the directory that is viewed initially is determined by how WordPerfect was installed on your system, and what preferences have previously been set.

Below the *Current Dir* line is the *File Info* line of Figure 6-9. This line will remain blank until a file is selected from the *Files* list (a file is selected from the *Files* list by clicking on it once). Once a file has been selected in this manner, the size of the file, and the date and time that it was last modified, are displayed.

File Info: 17578 Bytes 07/24/91 12:00PM

Figure 6-9. The File Info line reflects current file information about the file currently highlighted in the Files list box.

To the right of the *Files* list box is the *Directories* list box (Figure 6-10). This list box is used to move into different sub-directories, or to different disk drives, from which to select a file. Two kinds of items can be denoted in this list box: sub-directories and disk drives.

Disk drives are denoted in this fashion:

`[-a-]` represents the ***a:*** drive, `[-b-]` represents the ***b:*** drive, and so on. Double-clicking on any drive name in this list changes the drive listed in the *Current Dir* line to the disk drive selected.

Sub-directories are denoted in this fashion:

`[windows]` represents the ***windows*** sub-directory, `[wpwin]` represents the ***wpwin*** sub-directory, etc. Double-clicking on a sub-directory name changes the sub-directory listed in the *Current Dir* line to the sub-directory selected.

The only exception to the sub-directories rule is the directory denoted by `[..]`. This symbol represents the directory one level higher than the current sub-directory. Each time you double-click on this symbol, you move a level closer to the root directory.

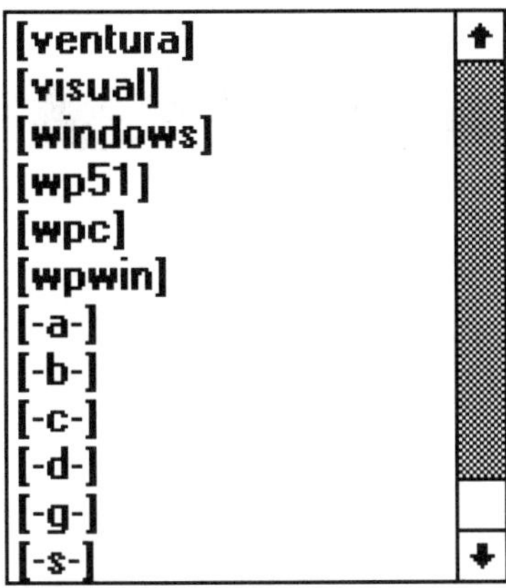

Figure 6-10. *The Directories list box is used to change the disk drive and subdirectory from which files to be opened can be selected.*

Opening files

Towards the bottom of the *Open File* dialog box (Figure 6-5) is the *Change Default Dir* check box (Figure 6-11). If selected, this causes WordPerfect to remember the directory and drive from which you last loaded a file and to move directly to that directory when you next use this command.

Figure 6-11. *The Change Default Dir check box causes WordPerfect to remember, and to set as a default, the last directory from which you loaded a file.*

The *Quick List* option towards the bottom of the dialog box is covered in Chapter 16 within this book.

The other interesting option of the Figure 6-5 *Open File* dialog box is the *View* button (Figure 6-12). This button allows you to quickly see the contents of any file selected from the *Files* list before it is opened. Using this button will save you time when loading a file—it makes it hard to load the wrong file.

View...

Figure 6-12. *The View button makes it nice and easy to view the contents of a file before that file is actually loaded.*

Select the *View* button on your machine now (Figure 6-13).

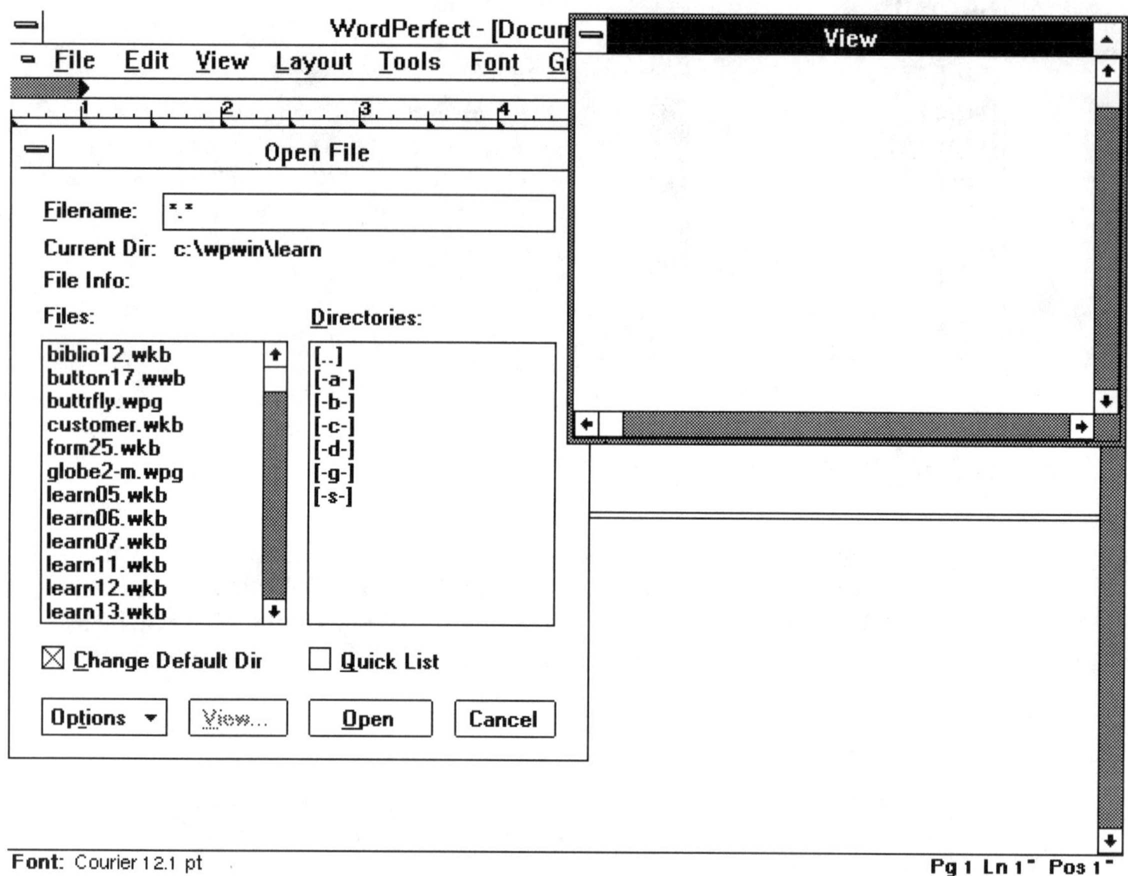

Figure 6-13. *As the View button is selected, a new window opens, which WordPerfect uses to display the contents of any file selected within the Files list.*

After selecting the *View* button, select any file in your *Files* list and it will be displayed in the *View* window (Figures 6-14 and 6-15). Some files (those which are not text files) may display as a series of zeros and ones, or as other strange characters.

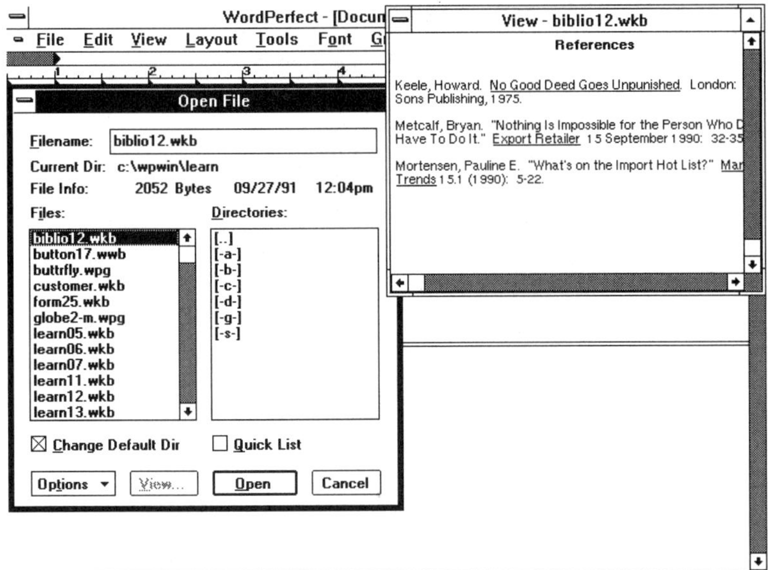

Figure 6-14. A text file appears as text in the View window.

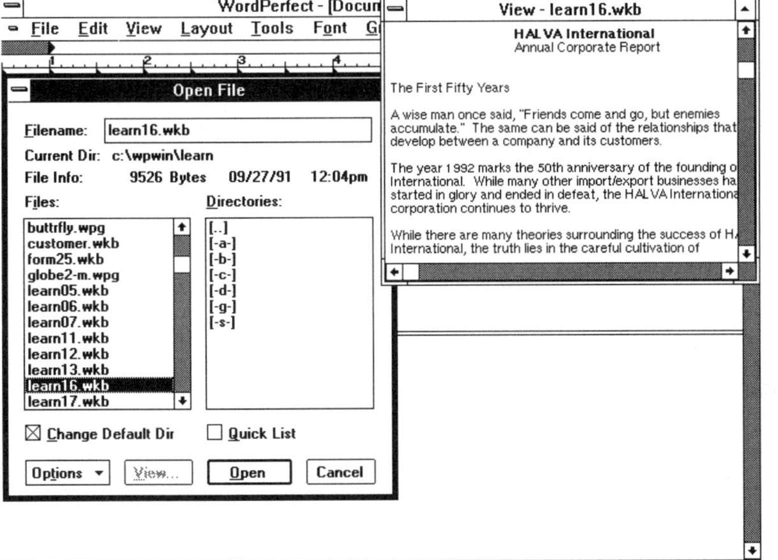

Figure 6-15. A separate text file is now selected from the Files list box and is, in turn, displayed in the View window.

Once you locate the file you are after, it can be opened using the *Open* button after it is selected in the *Files* list box. The file that will be opened in this example is ***biblio12.wkb*** (actually selected in Figure 6-14) from the ***wpwin\learn*** sub-directory. Figure 6-16 shows this file now open on the WordPerfect page. If you cannot locate this file, open another text file.

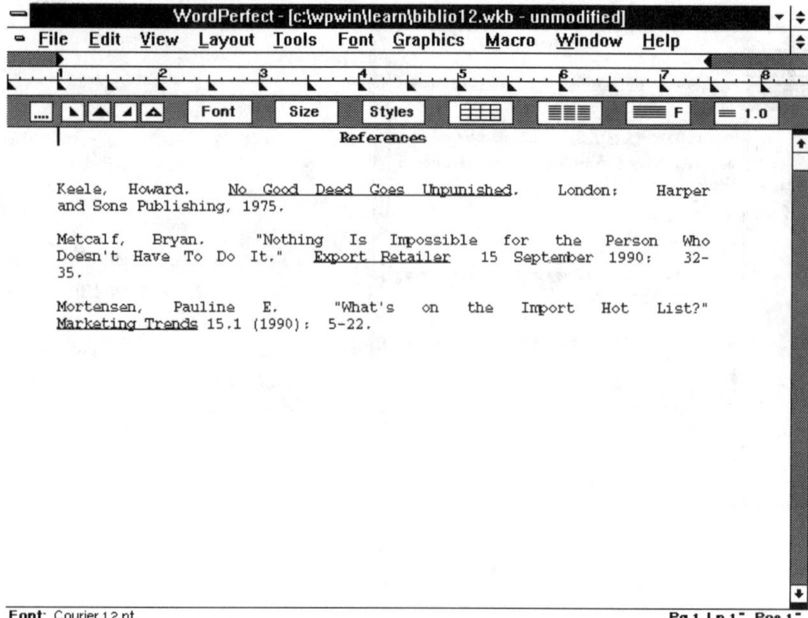

Figure 6-16. *The file **biblio12.wkb** is opened into a new window by selecting it (Figure 6-14) and clicking on Open.*

Because the *Open* command was used to load it, the file ***biblio12.wkb*** is opened into a new document window. The title of the file is now reflected in the Title bar (the word ***"unmodified"*** will also appear in the Title bar, until such time as the file is modified).

Multiple files

At this stage there are actually several files open within WordPerfect. One you can see, ***biblio12.wkb***; the files ***Document1*** and ***Document2***, that were created earlier in this chapter, are still open as well.

There are several ways to determine how many files are open. One way is to click on the **Window** menu in Figure 6-17 and check its contents.

Window

Cascade
Tile

1 Document1 - unmodified
2 Document2 - unmodified
√ 3 c:\wpwin\learn\biblio12.wkb - unmodified

Figure 6-17. *The bottom part of the **Window** menu lists the names of all currently open document windows.*

The bottom part of the **Window** menu (Figure 6-17) indicates that three documents are currently open—***Document1, Document2***, and ***c:\wpwin\learn\biblio12.wkb*** (all unmodified).The file ***c:\wpwin\learn\biblio12.wkb*** has a check mark next to it—indicating that this is the file that occupies the currently active document window.

To make any other files the active ones, select them from this menu. In this example, select the file ***Document1 - unmodified*** (Figure 6-18). This file will now become the active file as shown in Figure 6-19.

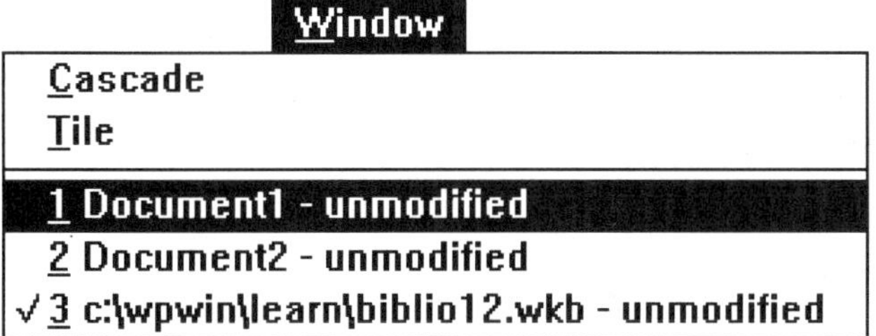

Figure 6-18. *Selecting the name of any open file, as if it were a command, will make the document window of that file the active one.*

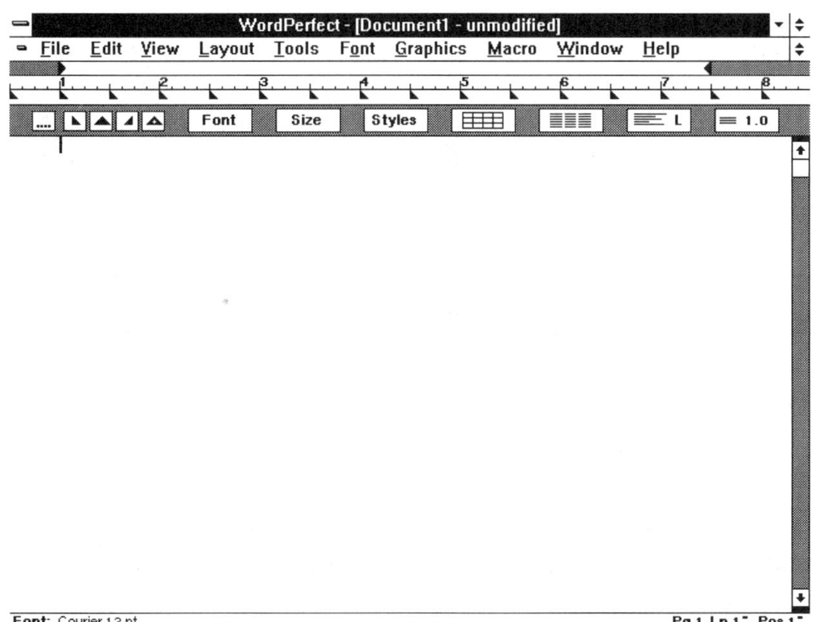

Figure 6-19. *Note the name of the document in the Title bar after selecting* ***Document1 - unmodified*** *from the* **Window** *command in Figure 6-18.*

Cascade and Tile commands

Another method of viewing the currently open files, is to select the *Cascade*, or *Tile*, command from the **Window** menu. Select the *Cascade* command (Figure 6-20) now. All currently open document windows are now arranged in the WordPerfect window (Figure 6-21).

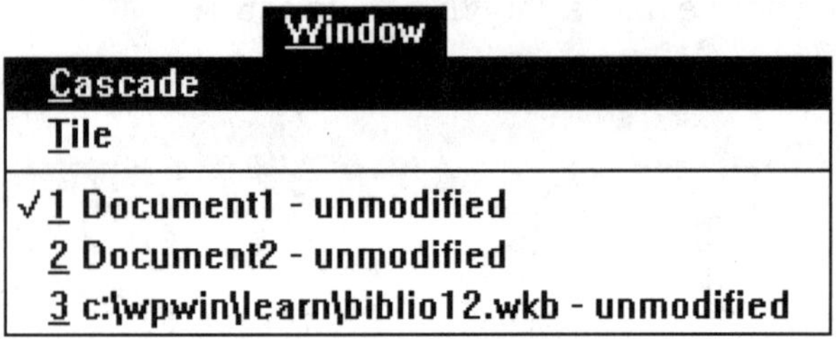

***Figure 6-20.** Selecting the Cascade command from the **Window** menu arranges all currently open document windows in the WordPerfect window.*

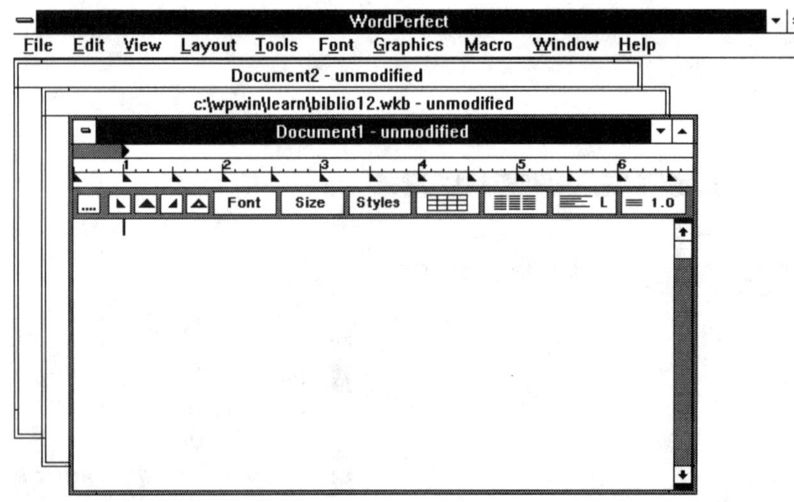

***Figure 6-21.** See how the various document windows are arranged so that they overlap and the Title bar of each window can be viewed.*

The *Tile* command from the **Window** menu has a similar effect, but document windows are arranged in a non-overlapping pattern (Figure 6-22).

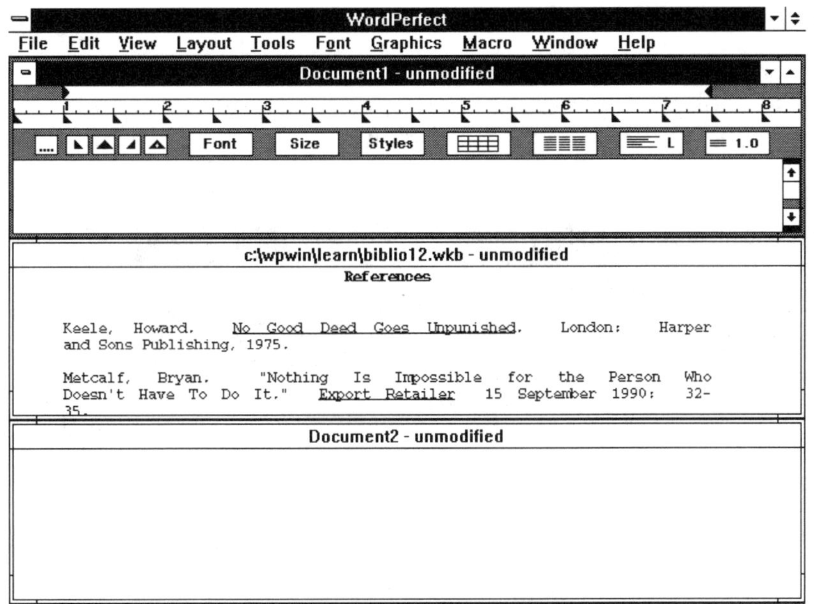

__Figure 6-22.__ The result of using the Tile command from the __Window__ menu—all currently open files are arranged in document windows that do not overlap.

Once you can view all open document windows (either Figure 6-21 or Figure 6-22), you can make any of these document windows the active one by clicking the mouse anywhere on that window.

For example, in Figure 6-21, the document window on the top (***Document1 - unmodified***) is the active window. Selecting any window behind it (by clicking on it), makes the selected window the active window as shown in Figure 6-23.

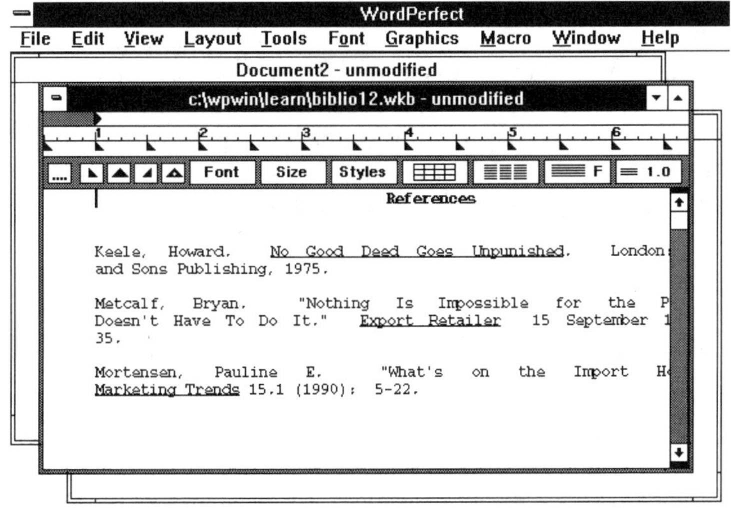

__Figure 6-23.__ In this example, click on the Title bar that reads __c:\wpwin\learn\biblio12.wkb - unmodified__ (Figure 6-21), and that window becomes the active window.

Minimize and Maximize buttons

Take a closer look at a document—more specifically, the document window that you just made the active document window (Figure 6-24).

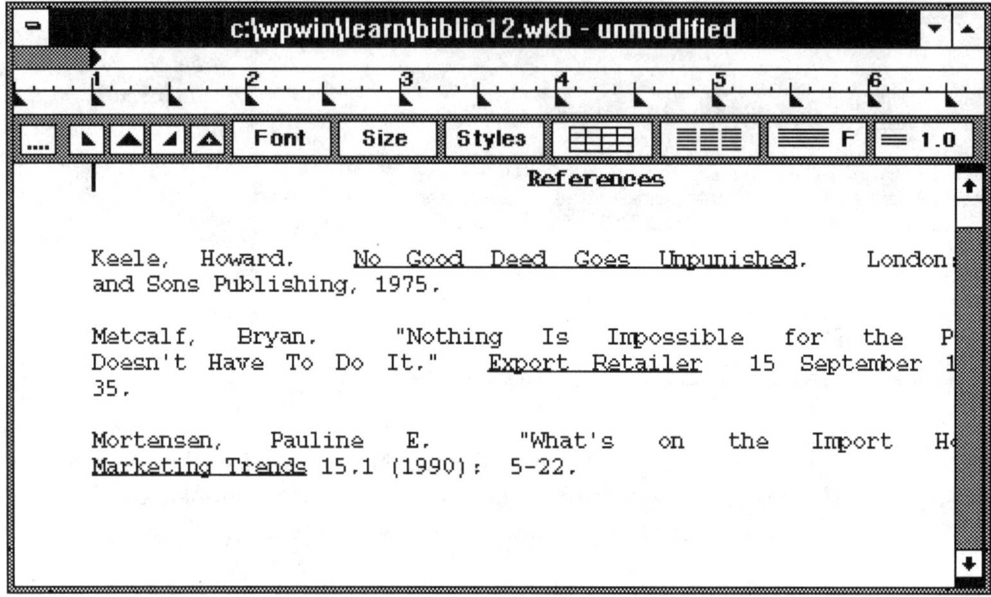

Figure 6-24. *A close up of a document window (once the Tile, or Cascade commands from the* ***Window*** *menu have been used).*

This document window is much like a normal Windows window—it contains Maximize and Minimize buttons, a Title bar, and a control menu box. These items can be used to move, resize, minimize, and maximize the document window. For example, click on the Minimize button (Figure 6-25) in the right-hand corner of this document window. The result of this action is shown in Figure 6-26.

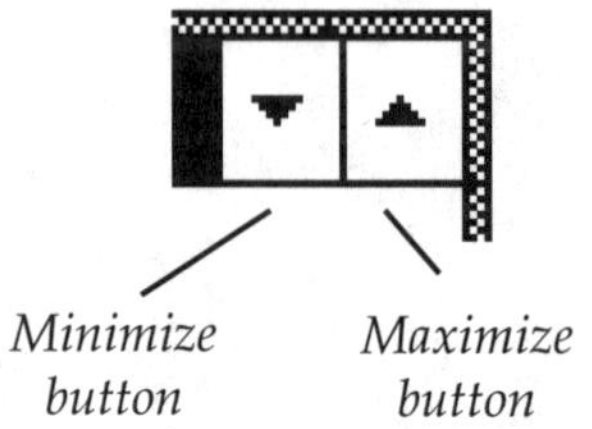

Figure 6-25. *The Minimize and Maximize buttons of the current document window of Figure 6-24.*

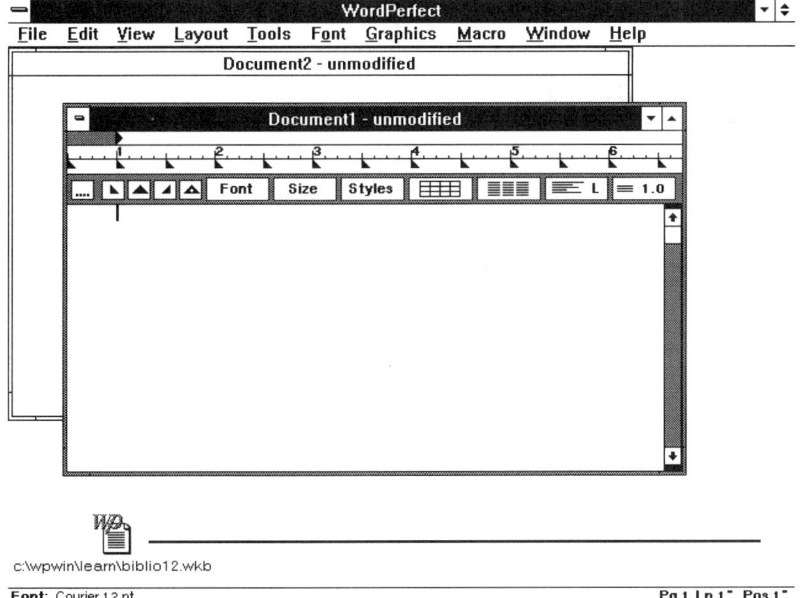

Figure 6-26. *The result of selecting the Minimize button. See the bottom left-hand corner of the screen? The document window, in which the Minimize button was clicked, is now minimized to an icon.*

The document minimized in Figures 6-24 and 6-25 is reduced to an icon.

The minimizing of documents can help reduce screen clutter—in Figure 6-26, there are only two overlapping windows on the screen at once. If you wish, you could minimize all of your document windows in this manner.

To retrieve the document window that you have minimized, double-click on the icon of that document window (Figure 6-27). The document window then re-appears as shown in Figure 6-28.

Figure 6-27. *Minimized windows appear as icons along the bottom of the WordPerfect window (with a filename underneath them). Double-click on these icons to re-open the document window.*

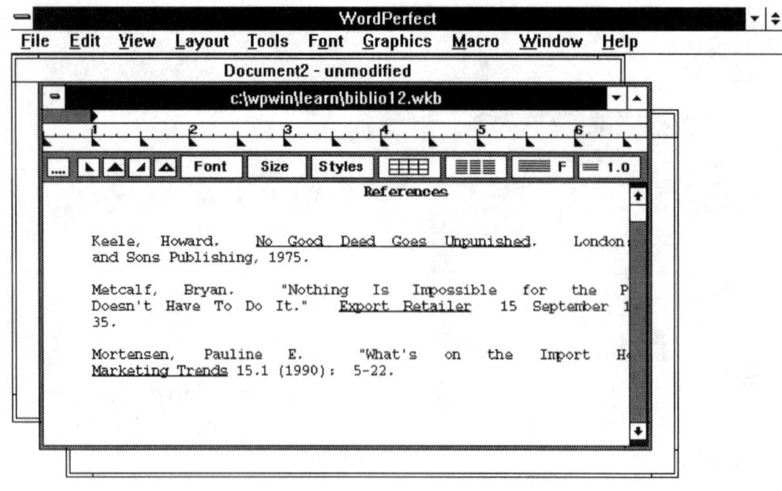

Figure 6-28. The minimized window is restored by double-clicking on the icon of that window.

To make any window appear at its maximum size, click on that window's Maximize button (Figure 6-25). The maximized window will cover all other document windows (Figure 6-29).

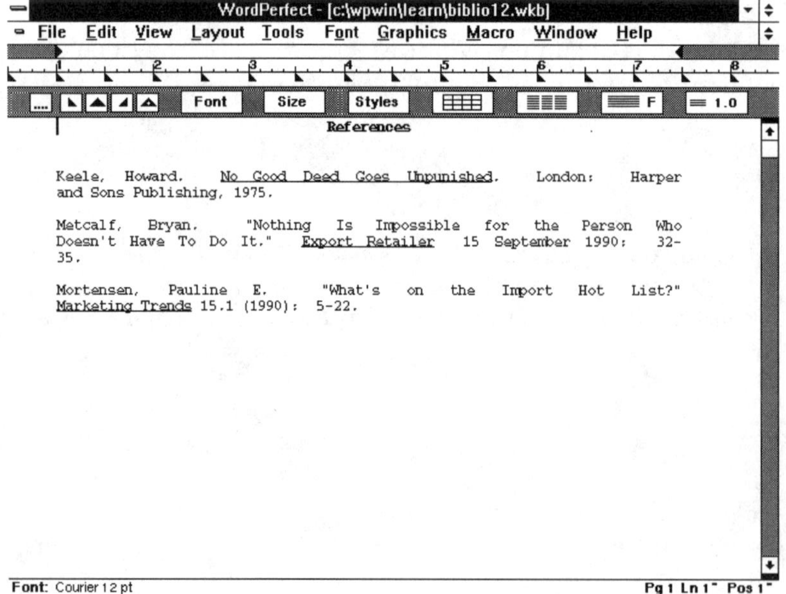

***Figure 6-29.** Clicking on the Maximize button of a window causes that window to fill the entire area below the WordPerfect Menu bar. This figure is the result of clicking on the Maximize button of the front window of Figure 6-28.*

Once a document window is maximized, as in Figure 6-29, clicking on the Maximize button again will cause the window to return to its original appearance of Figure 6-28.

Cutting/copying/pasting between document windows

As you learn to move between document windows at will, it becomes very easy to transfer data between them—you can copy data from one window, activate another window, and paste the data directly into that other window.

Retrieving files/concatenating files

The *Retrieve* command in the **File** menu (Figure 6-30) is much like the *Open* command but with one difference; rather than opening the selected document file into its own document window, the file is loaded into the active document window, at the text cursor. This feature allows you to join, or concatenate, two or more files into a single document.

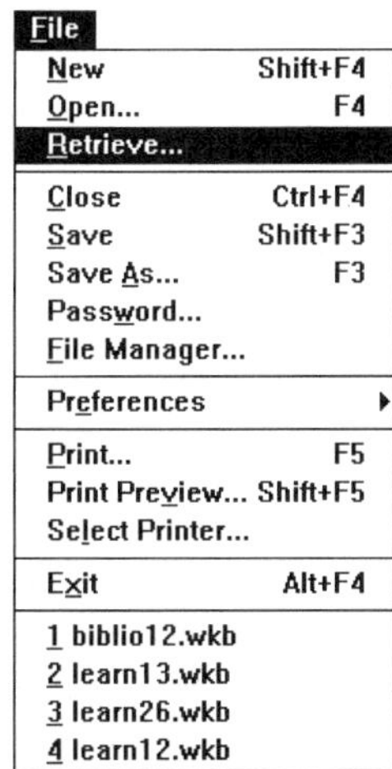

Figure 6-30. *The Retrieve command is much like the Open command, but files are retrieved into the currently open document window, rather than into a new window.*

There are two slightly different ways in which retrieving a file can work—you may retrieve a file into an existing document or into a new file.

First, look at what is now on screen—the document window containing the file *c:\wpwin\learn\biblio12.wkb* should be active (Figures 6-28 or 6-29). The text cursor should be flashing in the top left-hand corner of the document window.

Move the text cursor so that it appears at the beginning of the third paragraph—starting "Metcalf, Bryan" as shown in Figure 6-31.

Keele, Howard. No Good Deed
and Sons Publishing, 1975.

Metcalf, Bryan. "Nothing]
Doesn't Have To Do It." Expo
35.

Figure 6-31. *Position the text cursor so that it appears just before the M in "Metcalf" at the start of the third paragraph.*

Now select the *Retrieve* command from the **File** menu (Figure 6-30). You will be presented with the same dialog box as for the *Open* command earlier in this chapter (Figure 6-32).

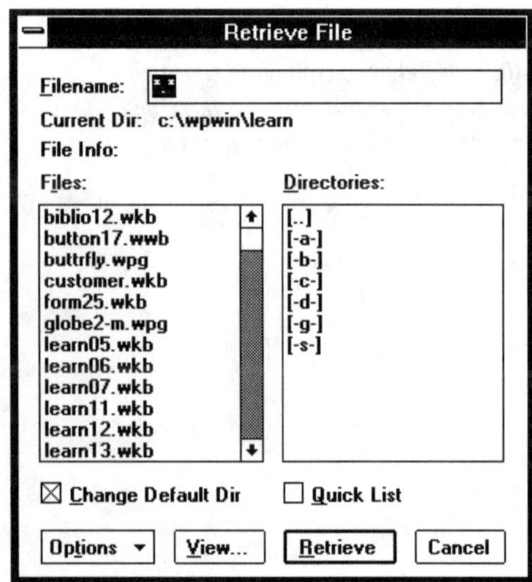

Figure 6-32. *To retrieve a file, use exactly the same steps as you would to open a file. The dialog boxes for the Retrieve and Open commands are almost identical.*

If you can find it, select the file ***learn05.wkb*** (Figure 6-33) from the list, and click on the *Retrieve* button. This file is contained in the ***learn*** sub-directory, within the ***wpwin*** sub-directory. If you cannot find this file (it may have been deleted from your system), select another text file.

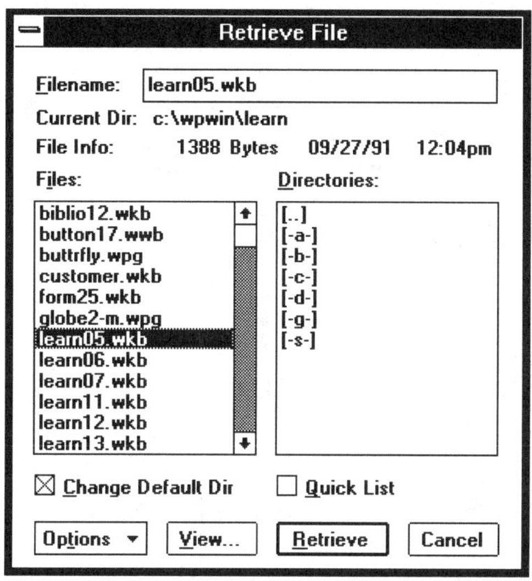

Figure 6-33. *Click on the **learn05.wkb** file to retrieve it into your document.*

After selecting the *Retrieve* button, you will be asked to confirm this operation (Figure 6-34).

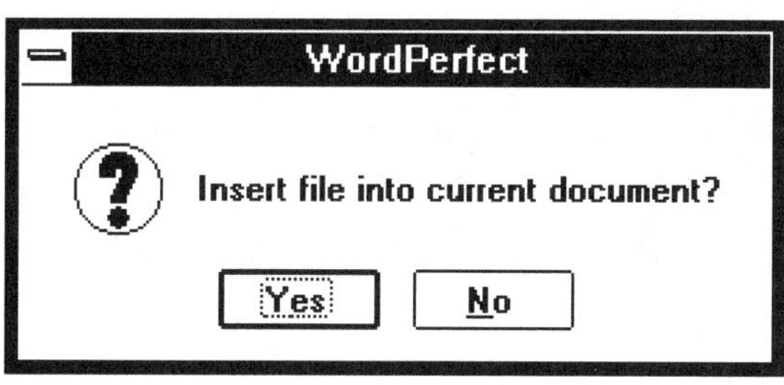

Figure 6-34. *The Retrieve operation will require confirmation. In this case, click on **Yes**.*

After selecting *Yes* from the warning in Figure 6-34, your document will appear as shown in Figure 6-35.

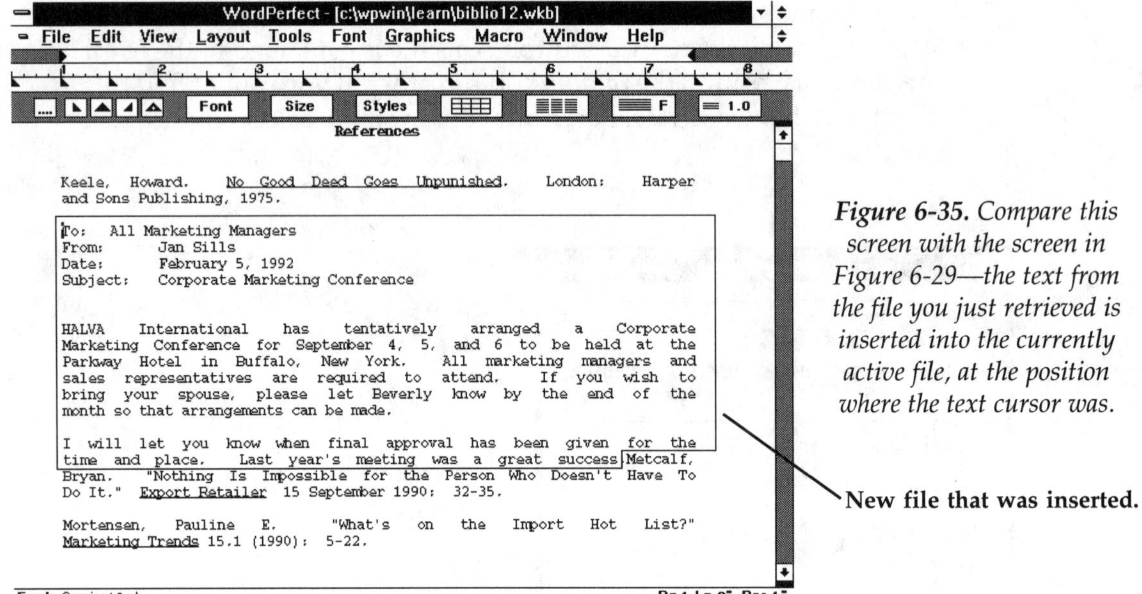

Figure 6-35. *Compare this screen with the screen in Figure 6-29—the text from the file you just retrieved is inserted into the currently active file, at the position where the text cursor was.*

The text from the document you retrieved (***learn05.wkb***) is inserted into the current file, at the text cursor. In effect, the two files (***biblio12.wkb***, and ***learn05.wkb***) have been joined. Note that the Title bar in Figure 6-35 no longer says *unmodified*, as the file has now been changed.

If a file is retrieved into a completely empty window (i.e., the result of the *New* command), then you are given no warning as in Figure 6-34, and the Title bar will change to reflect the name of the file that was retrieved. If text already exists in the active window when you use the *Retrieve* command (as was the case for the Figures 6-31 through 6-35 example), the name in the Title bar will remain unchanged, and you will be asked to confirm the *Retrieve* operation.

Closing files

Files can be closed by first making them the active document window, if multiple files are opened, and then selecting the *Close* command from the **File** menu (Figure 6-36).

If you are following this example on screen, select the *Close* command now. You will be presented with the dialog box of Figure 6-37.

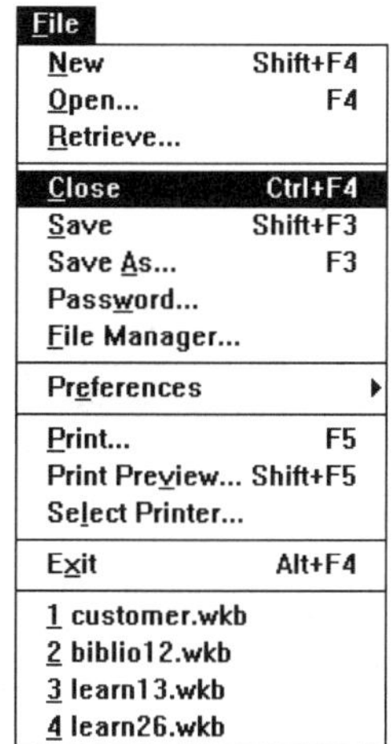

Figure 6-36. *The Close command from the* ***File*** *menu closes the currently active document window.*

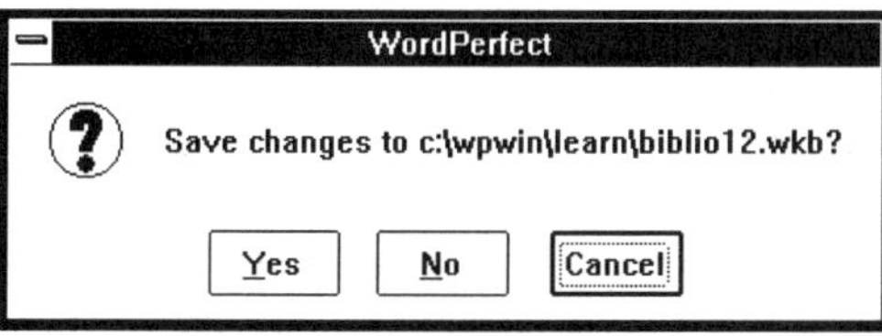

Figure 6-37. *This dialog box warns you that changes have been made to the file since it was opened, and asks you if you would like to save them.*

If no changes have been made to a file since it was opened, or if the changes have already been saved to disk, the file will be closed and the dialog box of Figure 6-37 will not appear.

However, in this case, the currently active file had been modified, and WordPerfect asks you if you would like to save changes to that file before closing. **Yes** will save the file, and **No** will close the file and abandon changes. In this case, chose **No** to abandon the changes made to the file. The file and document window are then closed.

Saving files

Saving files is the process of writing the contents of the currently active document window to a file on disk. Files can be saved using the *Save* or *Save As* command from the **File** menu (Figure 6-38).

Figure 6-38. *Either the Save, or Save As, command can be used to save the contents of the currently active document window to a file on disk.*

The very first time a document is saved, it needs to be given a name, a location on disk, and a file format.

In the example of this chapter, the currently active window should now be ***Document1 - unmodified***. This file has never been saved and does not yet have a name (only the temporary name assigned to it by WordPerfect). To save this file with a name, select the *Save* command from the **File** menu (Figure 6-38). The *Save As* dialog box of Figure 6-39 will appear.

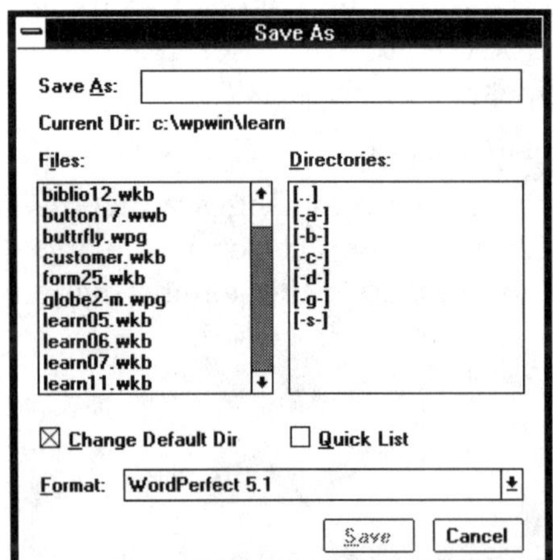

Figure 6-39. *The Save As dialog box appears when a file is saved for the very first time (i.e. before it has been named).*

To save a file, all you need do is enter a name for that file in the *Save As* text box at the top of the *Save As* dialog box. The text cursor will already be positioned at the correct place for you. In this case, enter the name ***"myfile.wkb"***.

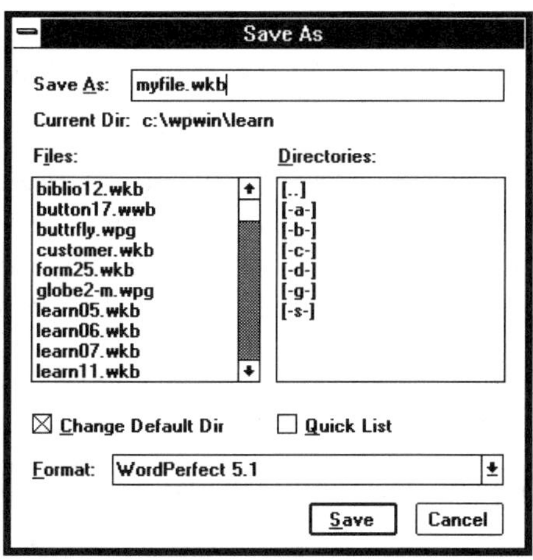

Figure 6-40. *The name that you wish to call this file is entered on the Save As line.*

You can determine the location of this file, by selecting a different drive or directory from the *Directories* list box in Figure 6-40. In this example, the file will be saved in the ***c:\wpwin\learn*** sub-directory denoted on the *Current Dir* line.

Once you have entered the name of the file, you may, if you wish, select a file format for this file. Files, by default, will be saved in WordPerfect format. However, other text formats are available. To access other formats, click the mouse on the down facing arrow to the right of the *Format* sub-menu (Figure 6-41).

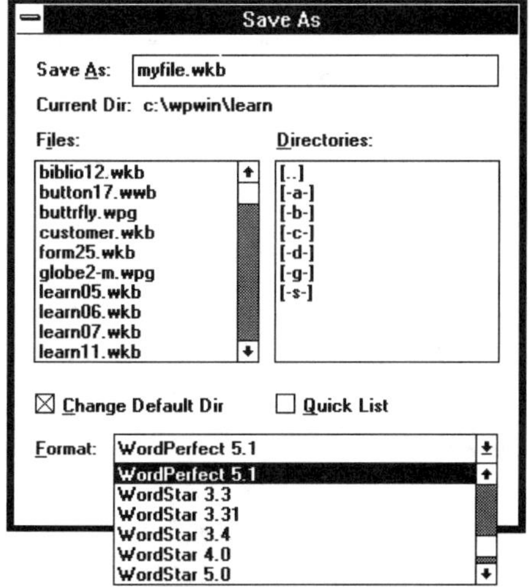

Figure 6-41. *To save this file in a format other than WordPerfect format, click on the Format sub-menu to display and locate other file formats.*

Saving a file in any other format than WordPerfect's, is only necessary if you wish to use this file in another software package that does not accept WordPerfect format files.

Once you have selected the correct directory, entered a file name, and selected a file format, click on the *Save* button to save the document to disk and remove this dialog box. The Title bar of the file will show that the file has now been saved under this new name (Figure 6-42).

Figure 6-42. *Once a file is saved, the name of that file appears in the Title bar.*

Once a file has been saved with a name (as was just done), each subsequent time you use the *Save* command, you do not have to name the file. Changes are saved to the filename shown in the Title bar automatically.

Using the *Save As* command, however, will always ask you to name the file, using the *Save As* dialog box in Figure 6-40. *Save As* is a command that allows you, in effect, to make copies of files—it leaves the original file intact while creating a new file.

When using the *Save* or *Save As* command to save a file, it is possible that the name selected for the file is already being used. If this is the case, you will see the dialog box of Figure 6-43.

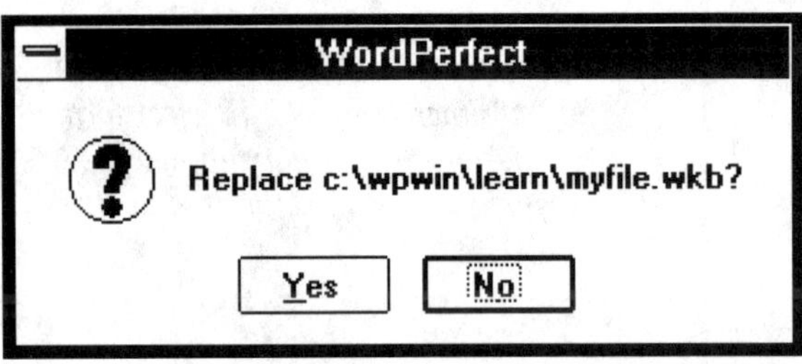

Figure 6-43. *If you attempt to save a file under a name that is already in use, you are presented with this dialog box.*

If this dialog box appears, you can either click on **Yes** to replace the existing file with the current document, or **No** to give the current document a new filename.

Hints and Tips

Opening files using the File menu

Another chapter in this book, Chapter 10—**Preferences - (1),** discusses the *Environment* command from the *Preferences* fly-out menu in the **File** menu. One of the options within this command is *Display Last Open Filenames* (Figure 6-44).

Menu

☒ Display Shortcut Keys

☒ Display Last Open Filenames

Figure 6-44. *The Display Last Open Filenames option in the Preferences/ Environment command from the* ***File*** *menu.*

With this option selected, WordPerfect adds the names of the four most recently opened files to the bottom of the **File** menu. This feature allows you to open these files quickly, simply by selecting the name of the file you wish to open (Figure 6-45).

File	
New	Shift+F4
Open...	F4
Retrieve...	
Close	Ctrl+F4
Save	Shift+F3
Save As...	F3
Password...	
File Manager...	
Preferences	▸
Print...	F5
Print Preview...	Shift+F5
Select Printer...	
Exit	Alt+F4
1 myfile.wkb	
2 customer.wkb	
3 biblio12.wkb	
4 learn13.wkb	

Figure 6-45. *Selecting a file name from the bottom of the* ***File*** *menu is exactly the same as using the Open command but, in this case, you do not have to locate the file.*

Loading files in different formats

WordPerfect has the capability to open files that were not originally created within WordPerfect itself. WordPerfect can read a wide range of file formats, from simple ASCII text files, to Microsoft Word, XYWrite, and many other text formats.

To open a file in a different format, you do not have to do anything special—the file can be loaded using either the *Open* or *Retrieve* commands, as explained earlier in this chapter.

However, as WordPerfect loads a file that it senses is in a format other than WordPerfect format, it provides a dialog box, asking you to confirm the exact type of file (Figure 6-46).

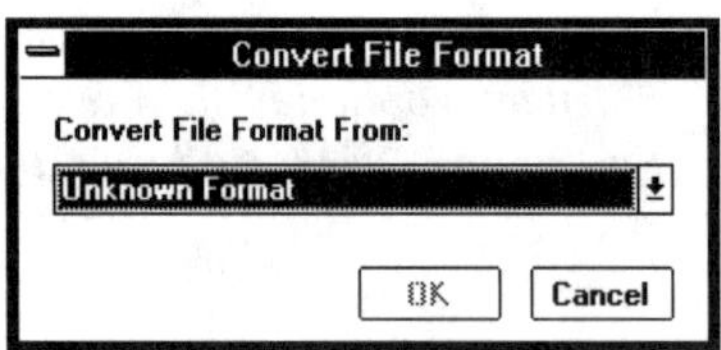

Figure 6-46. *This dialog box appears as WordPerfect loads a text file in a format other than WordPerfect format.*

In Figure 6-46, WordPerfect cannot determine exactly what sort of file it has been asked to load, and uses the expression *Unknown Format* in the *Convert File Format From* sub-menu. This situation is actually quite rare—generally WordPerfect can tell exactly what type of file it is loading, in which case, you can click on **OK**, and the file is converted as it is loaded.

If, for whatever reason, you feel that the file format listed in the *Convert File Format From* sub-menu is incorrect (or reads *Unknown Format*), you can click on the down facing arrow to the right of this sub-menu, and a list of formats will appear (Figure 6-47). It is from this list that you can tell WordPerfect the actual file format of the file you are loading.

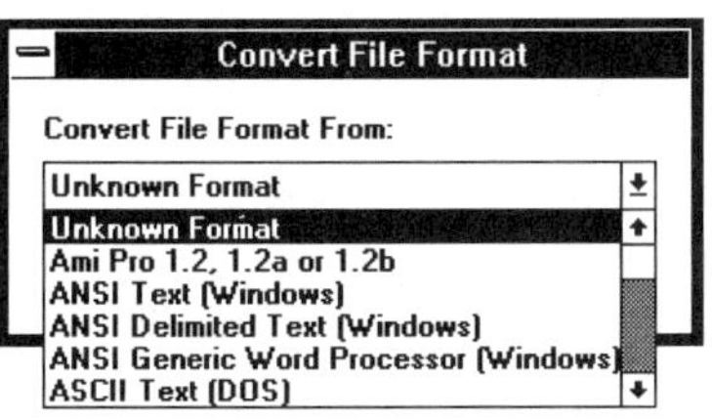

Figure 6-47. *Selecting the Convert File Format From sub-menu arrow will present you with a large list of file formats from which to choose the correct one.*

There are some file formats that WordPerfect cannot load using the *Open* or *Retrieve* commands. For example, if you attempt to load a WordPerfect graphic file using the *Open* command, you will see the warning message of Figure 6-48.

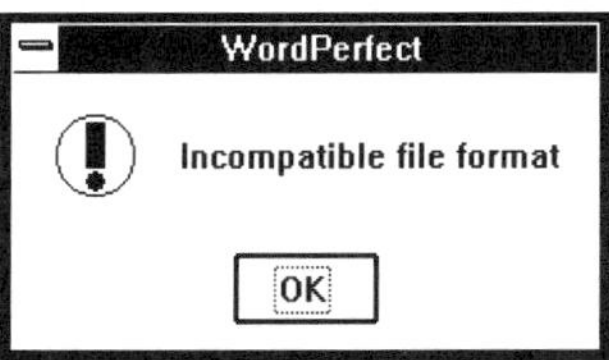

Figure 6-48. *This warning message appears to alert you that this file cannot be loaded. You will be given another chance to load a file after you click on* ***OK.***

File extensions

When a file is saved in WordPerfect, WordPerfect does not, unlike other programs, suggest a file extension for that file. You have complete freedom as to the file extension of all files you create.

While this feature gives you flexibility in naming files, it could possibly lead to confusion, as on personal computers people generally associate a particular file extension with a particular program. Therefore, it may be wise to restrict the use of file extensions to a common extension or as small a number of extensions as possible.

Handling Files — Exercise

6ex

This training exercise is designed so that people of all levels of expertise with WordPerfect can use it to gain maximum benefit. In order to do this, the bare exercise is listed below this paragraph on just one page, with no hints. The following pages contain the steps needed to complete this exercise for those who need additional prompting.

Steps in brief

1. *Restart WordPerfect.*
2. *Retrieve the file biblio12.wkb from the learn sub-directory in the wpwin sub-directory.*
3. *Without closing the current document, view and open the file learn07.wkb from the learn sub-directory.*
4. *Without closing the current documents, start a new WordPerfect document.*
5. *Tile the three documents.*
6. *Copy the first paragraph of text from the biblio12.wkb document.*
7. *Maximize Document3 and paste in the copied text.*
8. *Save Document3.*

The details for completing these steps are on the following pages.

Steps in detail

1. *Restart WordPerfect.*

For this exercise to work correctly, particularly with the later steps, you will need to totally restart WordPerfect. This is because, from step 5 onwards, you are working only with files opened during this exercise.

2. ***Retrieve the file biblio12.wkb from the learn sub-directory in the wpwin sub-directory.***

Selecting the *Retrieve* command from the **File** menu (Figure 6x-1) activates the *Retrieve File* dialog box of Figure 6x-2.

Figure 6x-1. *The Retrieve command in the **File** menu activates the Retrieve File dialog box.*

In the *Retrieve File* dialog box, locate the ***learn*** sub-directory inside the ***wpwin*** sub-directory. Once the files in the ***learn*** sub-directory are displayed in the list of files, click once on the ***biblio12.wkb*** file and then click on the **Retrieve** button. Alternatively, double-click on the file name ***biblio12.wkb.***

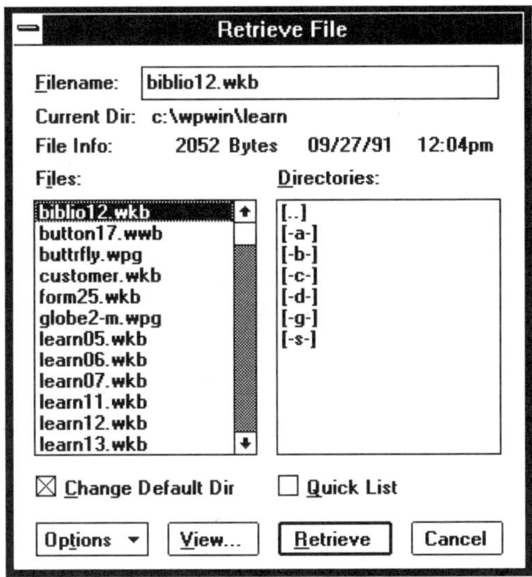

*Figure 6x-2. In the Retrieve File dialog box, select the file **biblio12.wkb** and click on the Retrieve button.*

Either of the two methods previously described will retrieve the file into the current document. Because no changes have been made to the current document, the Title bar will now contain the path and file name of the file just retrieved (Figure 6x-3).

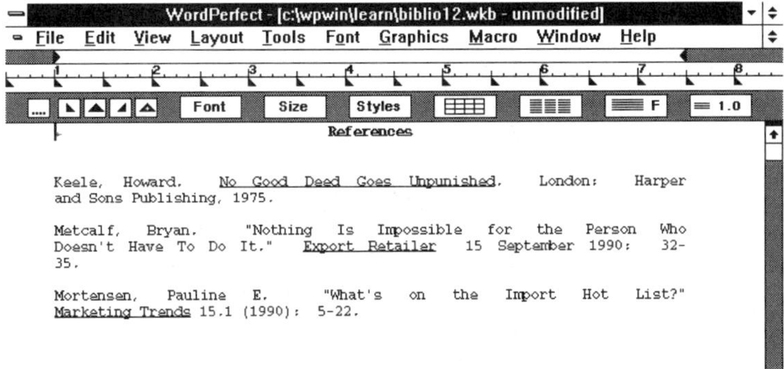

*Figure 6x-3. The file **biblio12.wkb** is now in the current document and the Title bar reflects this.*

3. ***Without closing the current document, view and open the file learn07.wkb from the learn sub-directory.***

Because WordPerfect allows you to have multiple files open at once, it is now possible to open another file. To do this without closing the current document, simply select the *Open* command from the **File** menu (Figure 6x-4).

*Figure 6x-4. Select the Open command from the **File** menu to activate the Open File dialog box. This will not close the currently active document you retrieved in steps 1 and 2.*

The file you want to open is also located in the ***learn*** sub-directory in the ***wpwin*** sub-directory. Your list of files should be the same or similar to Figure 6x-5.

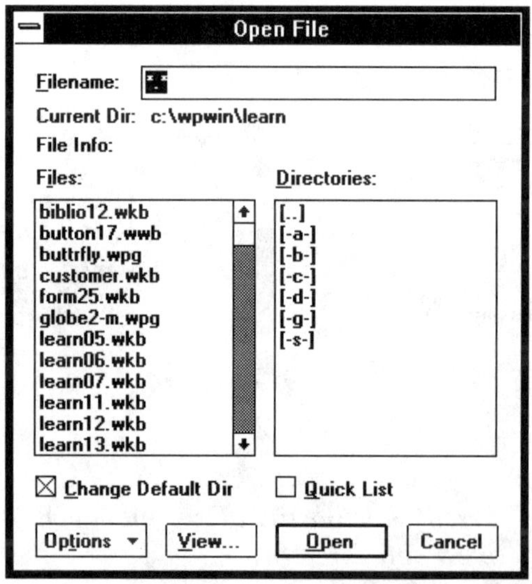

*Figure 6x-5. Here the Open File dialog box lists the files available in the **learn** sub-directory. The file you want is **learn07.wkb.***

Before you open the ***learn07.wkb*** document, you are going to view it. To do this, click once on the file name in the list of files and then click on the *View* button, as shown in Figure 6x-6.

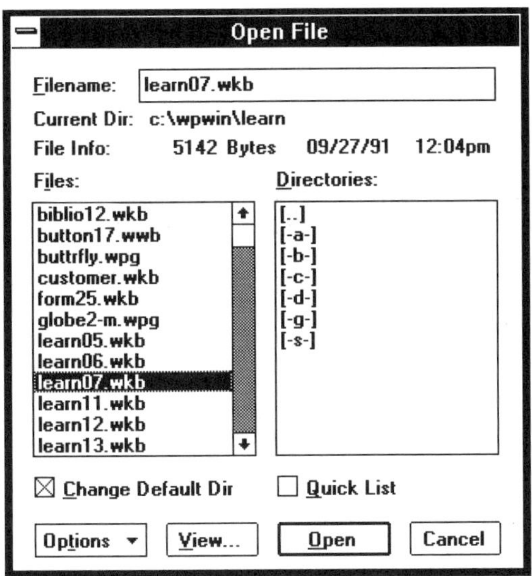

Figure 6x-6. To view a file, select it from the list of files and click on the View button.

After clicking on the *View* button, the *View* window appears in the top right-hand side of the screen (Figure 6x-7).

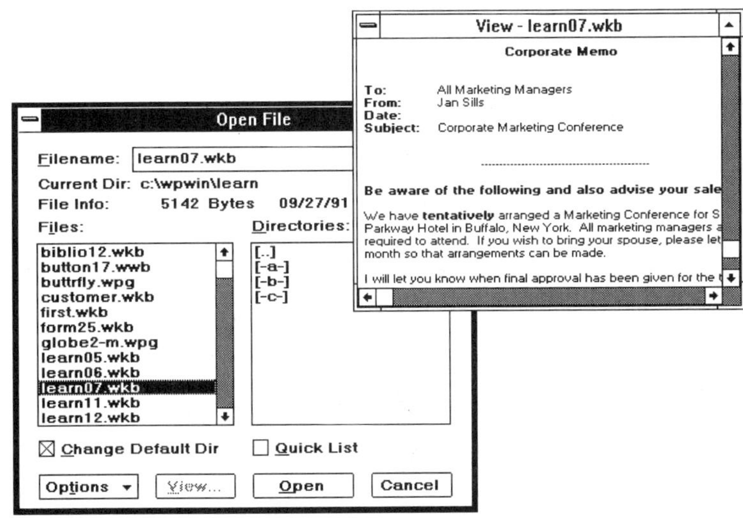

*Figure 6x-7. After clicking on the View button, the View - **learn07.wkb** window appears, indicating the contents of the file.*

Now that you have viewed the file, you can open it. This is done by clicking on the *Open* button (Figure 6x-8), making sure you still have the ***learn07.wkb*** file name selected in the list of files.

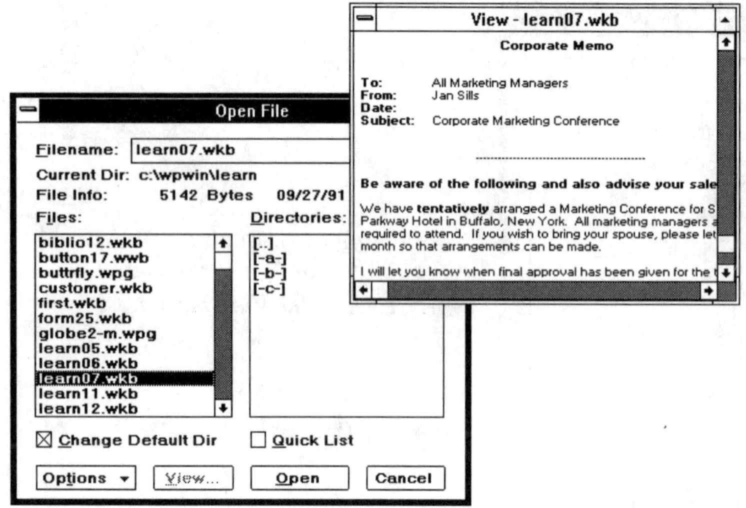

Figure 6x-8. To now open the file, click on the Open button.

After clicking on *Open*, the ***learn07.wkb*** file appears on the WordPerfect screen. The Title bar, as shown in Figure 6x-9, now reflects this document name.

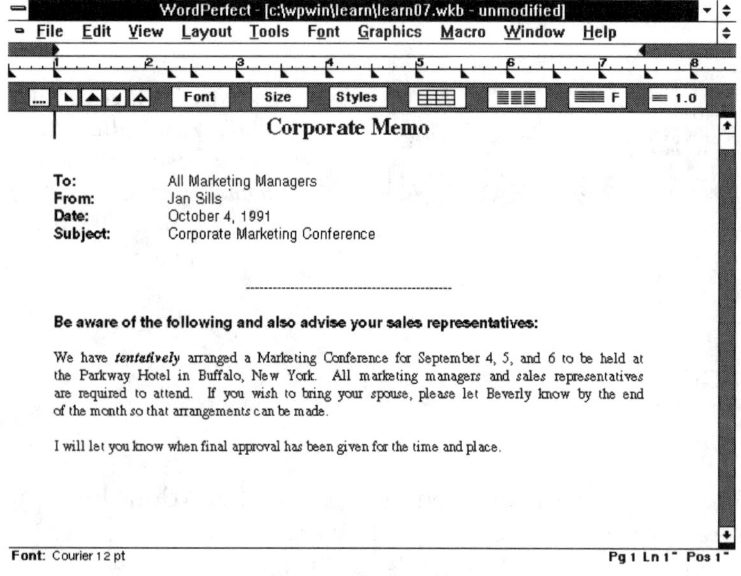

*Figure 6x-9. The **learn07.wkb** file has now been opened.*

4. ***Without closing the current documents, start a new WordPerfect document.***

To now start a third and new document, select the *New* command from the **File** menu (Figure 6x-10). An empty document window appears with ***Document3 - unmodified*** in the Title bar (Figure 6x-11).

File
New Shift+F4
Open... F4
Retrieve...
Close Ctrl+F4
Save Shift+F3
Save As... F3
Password...
File Manager...
Preferences
Print... F5
Print Preview... Shift+F5
Select Printer...
Exit Alt+F4
1 learn07.wkb
2 biblio12.wkb
3 school.let
4 learn12.wkb

*Figure 6x-10. Selecting the New command from the **File** menu will start a new WordPerfect document.*

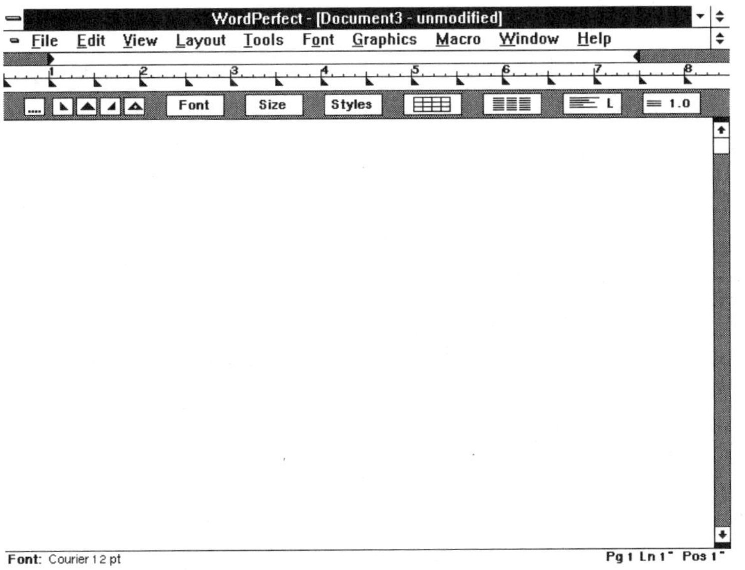

*Figure 6x-11. After selecting the New command, an empty document window appears. Because you have two other documents open, the Title bar of the new document reads **Document3 - unmodified.***

5. *Tile the three documents.*

The *Tile* command is located in the **Window** menu. On selecting this menu, you will see the names of the three files that are open. The check mark next to the third option indicates this is the currently active document. Tiling the documents is as simple as selecting the *Tile* command from this menu (Figure 6x-12).

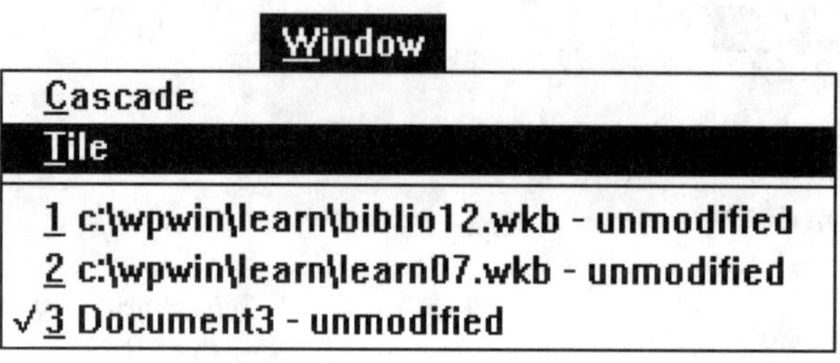

***Figure 6x-12**. Select the Tile command from the **Window** menu to execute step 5.*

The *Tile* command will display the three document windows one after the other as shown in Figure 6x-13.

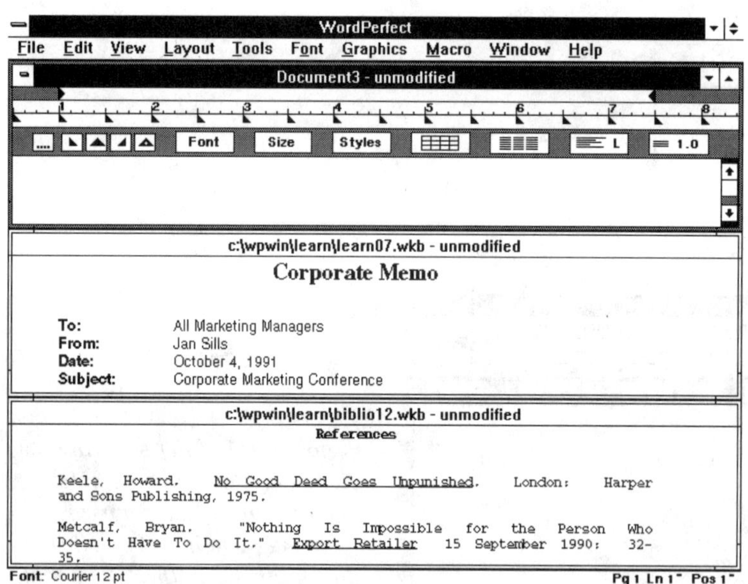

***Figure 6x-13**. This is the result of tiling the three current document windows.*

6. *Copy the first paragraph of text from the biblio12.wkb document.*

After tiling the documents, the third unmodified document will still be active. To make another document active, simply click inside the document window once with the mouse. In this case you want to copy text from the ***biblio12.wkb*** document into the Clipboard, so you must click inside that window.

Once you have clicked inside the ***biblio12.wkb*** document window, select the first paragraph of text by holding down the mouse at the beginning of the paragraph and dragging it to the end. As shown in Figure 6x-14, this paragraph is only two lines long. You may have to use the scroll bar at the right of the window to maneuver the first paragraph of text into view.

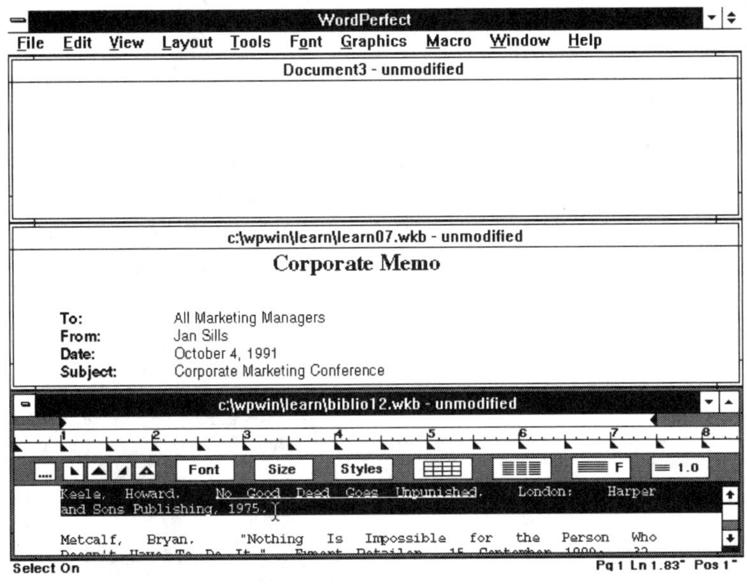

*Figure 6x-14. Select the first paragraph of text in the **biblio12.wkb** file, so that it can be copied to the Clipboard.*

Once you have selected the text, choose the *Copy* command from the **Edit** menu in the Menu bar at the top of the screen (Figure 6x-15).

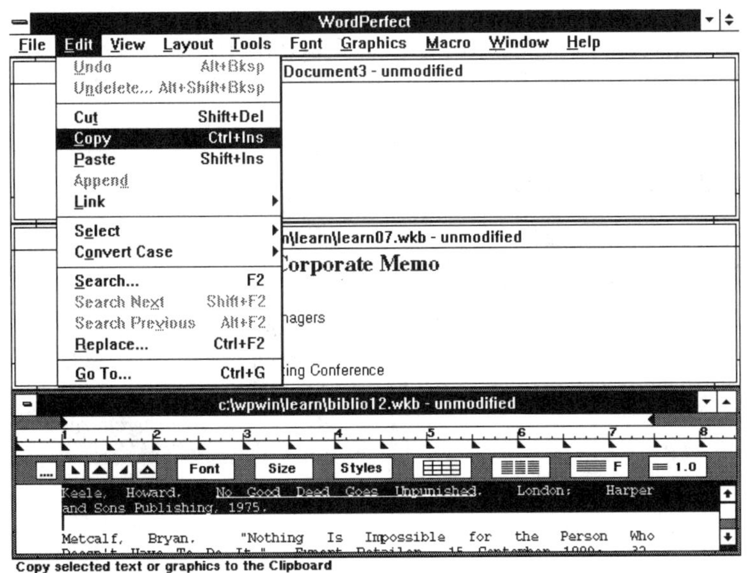

*Figure 6x-15. Select the Copy command from the **Edit** menu to make a copy of the selected text into the Windows Clipboard.*

7. Maximize Document3 and paste in the copied text.

Maximizing ***Document3*** will make it the active document again and increase the size of the window to full screen. To maximize the ***Document3*** window, click on its window to make it active, and then click on the Maximize button as in Figure 6x-16. Alternatively, you could just click on the Maximize button, without first making ***Document3*** the active window.

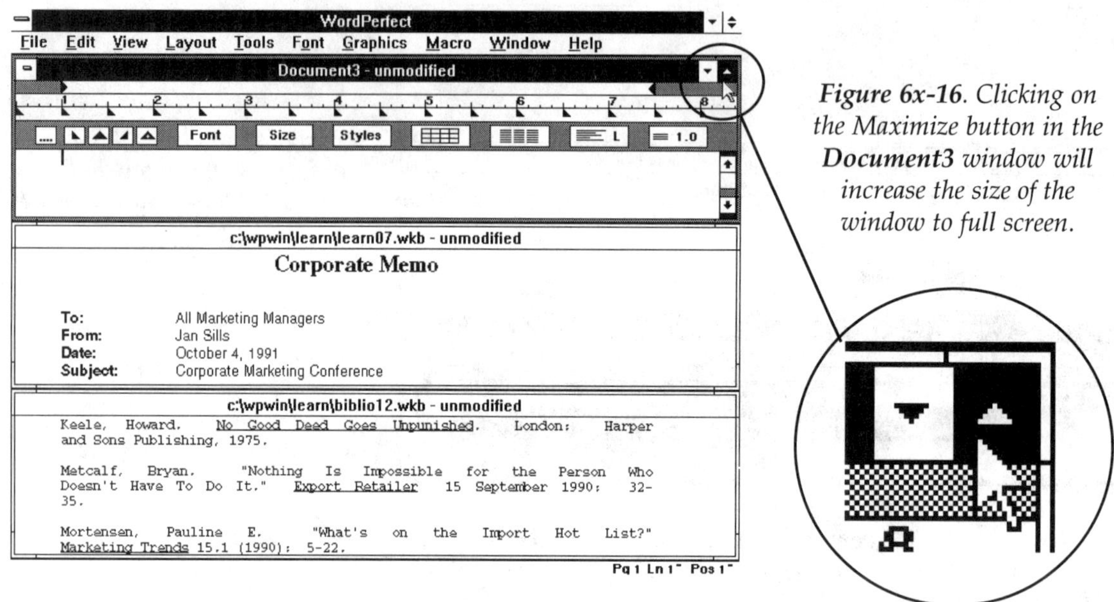

*Figure 6x-16. Clicking on the Maximize button in the **Document3** window will increase the size of the window to full screen.*

Once you have maximized the window of ***Document3***, you can paste in the copied text from step 6. To do this, select the *Paste* command from the **Edit** menu (Figure 6x-17).

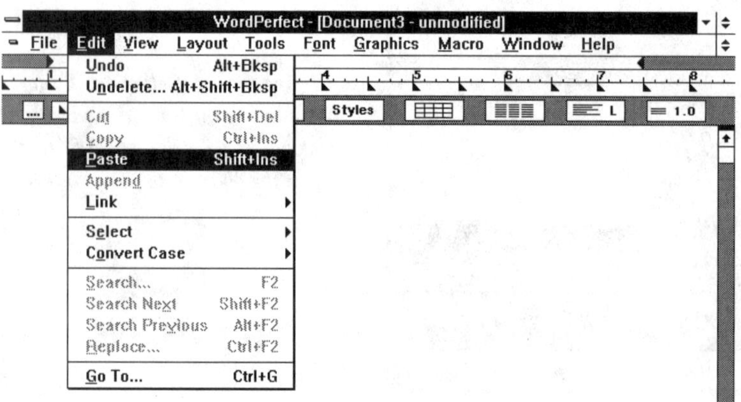

Figure 6x-17. The Paste command will bring the text, copied in step 6, from the Clipboard into the current document.

The text is pasted into the document where the cursor was positioned, which in this case was at the very beginning of the document. Figure 6x-18 shows the result of this step.

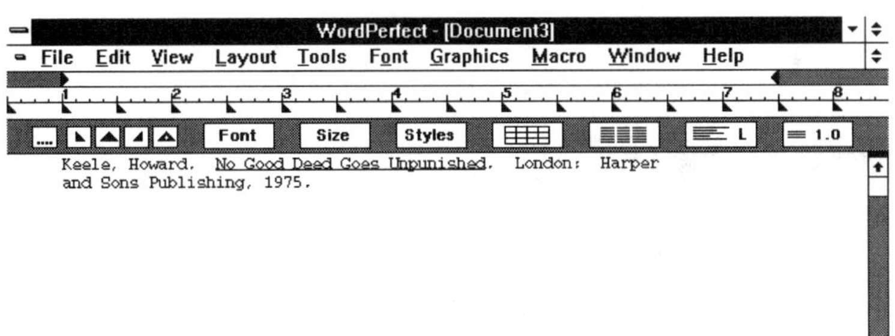

Figure 6x-18. The text copied from the ***biblio12.wkb*** *document in step 6 has now been pasted into* ***Document3****.*

8. Save Document3.

The last step of this exercise is to save the current document, which is ***Document3***. Select the *Save* command from the **File** menu (Figure 6x-19) to activate the *Save As* dialog box of Figure 6x-20.

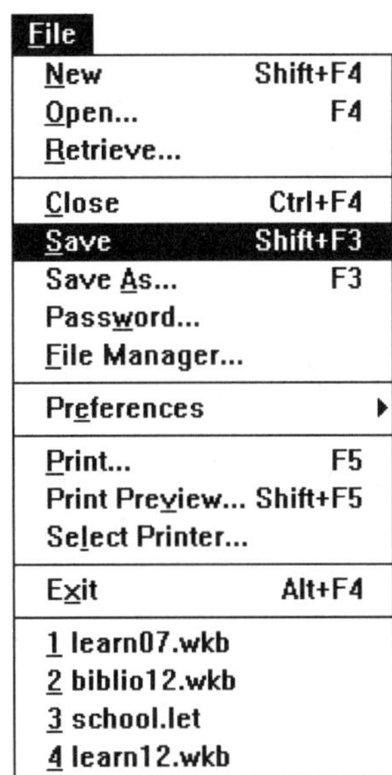

Figure 6x-19. Select the Save command from the ***File*** *menu, as the final step in this exercise, to save the untitled* ***Document3****.*

In the *Save As* dialog box, choose the drive and directory where you would like to save the file. For this exercise, we are saving the file in the ***learn*** sub-directory. You may have another directory where you would like to save the file; it's up to you.

Once you have chosen where to save the file, you need to give it a name. For this exercise the file is being saved as ***myfile.paw.*** You may prefer to call it something else and use your initials for the extension. After keying in the name, click on the *Save* button to finalize the procedure.

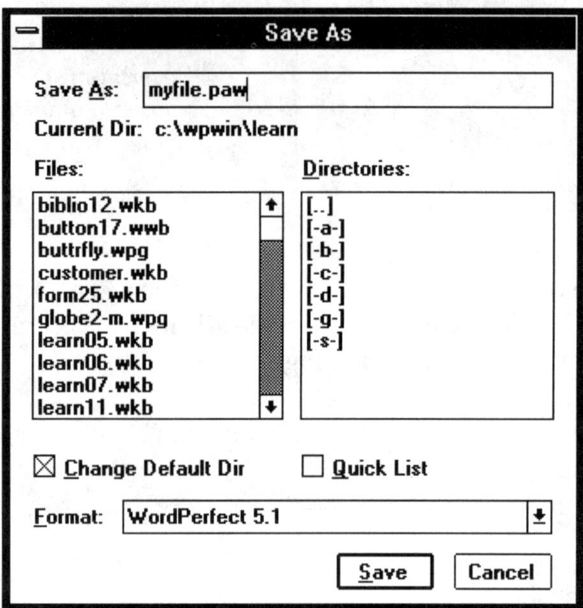

Figure 6x-20. *In the Save As dialog box, you choose where you are going to save the file and give it a name. Then click on the Save button.*

After clicking on the *Save* button, you will be returned to the document which will have the new name of the file in the Title bar. When you next *Exit* out of WordPerfect, you will be asked if you want to save the changes to the other two files. Click on the *No* option.

Margins and Columns

This chapter discusses the application of margins and columns to text and pages within a WordPerfect document.

Throughout this chapter, we will be using the sample file, ***learn13.wkb,*** to demonstrate the use of margins and columns.

Note: This chapter assumes that you have the *Auto Code Placement* option of the *Environment* command from the *Preferences* fly-out menu in the **File** menu enabled—this is the default setting.

Margins

Margins can be defined as the white area around the edge of the page within which text and graphics appear (Figure 7-1). In WordPerfect, the default margin around the inside of a page is 1 inch. However, you have the ability to alter the top, bottom, left, or right margins as you wish.

Figure 7-1. *The dotted line on this sample page represents the page margin—the area around the inside of the page within which text and graphics flow.*

As well as being able to define a global margin which affects an entire document, specific paragraphs, tables, or graphics can have individual margins defined for them alone. Chapter 4, **The Ruler**, looked at changing margin dimensions using the ruler. This chapter looks at more detailed use of the *Margins* dialog box for adjusting WordPerfect margins.

In Figure 7-2, the sample document, ***learn13.wkb,*** has been opened and the text cursor is positioned at the very start of the document—this is the best place for the cursor when creating or editing a margin setting for a document.

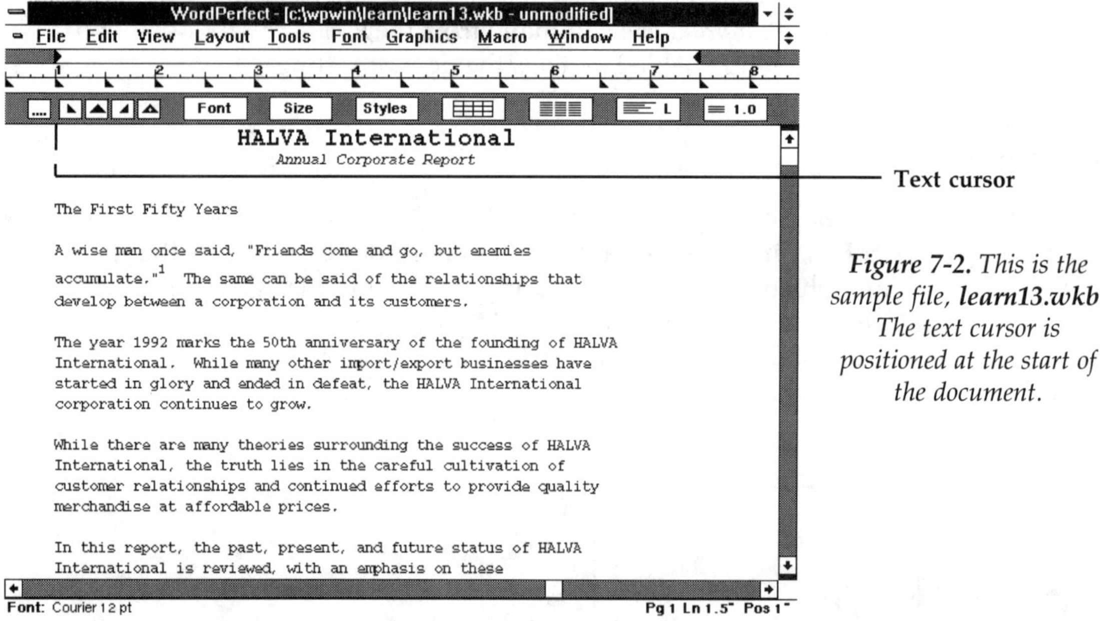

Figure 7-2. *This is the sample file,* ***learn13.wkb****. The text cursor is positioned at the start of the document.*

To view or edit the current margin settings, select the *Margins* command from the **Layout** menu to activate the *Margins* dialog box (Figure 7-3).

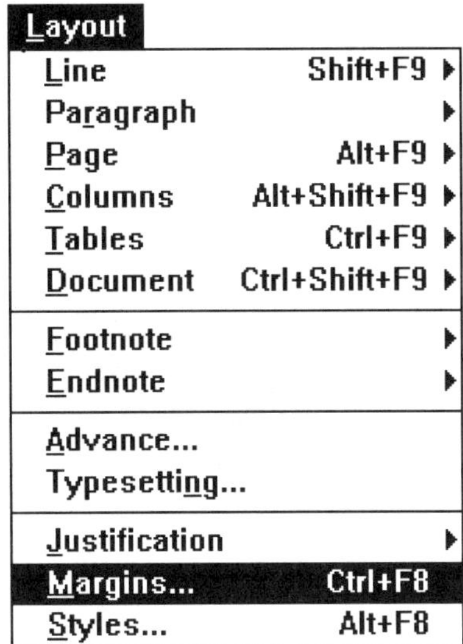

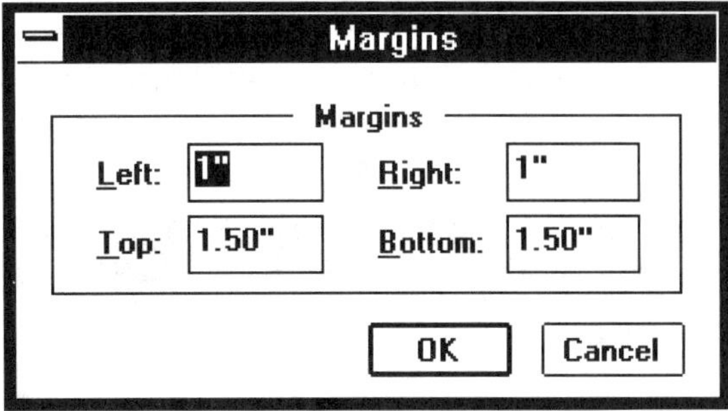

Figure 7-3. *The Margins command from the* ***Layout*** *menu is used to view and/or edit current margin settings.*

There are four options within this dialog box (Figure 7-3)—*Left*, *Right*, *Top*, and *Bottom*. The text box for each option displays the current margin for that side of the page. As you can see, the left and right margins for this page are set to one inch, while the top and bottom margins are set to 1.5 inches.

The left and right margins for the page are also shown in the ruler (Figure 7-4), if the ruler is currently displayed. See Chapter 4 in this book, for more details on altering margins with the ruler.

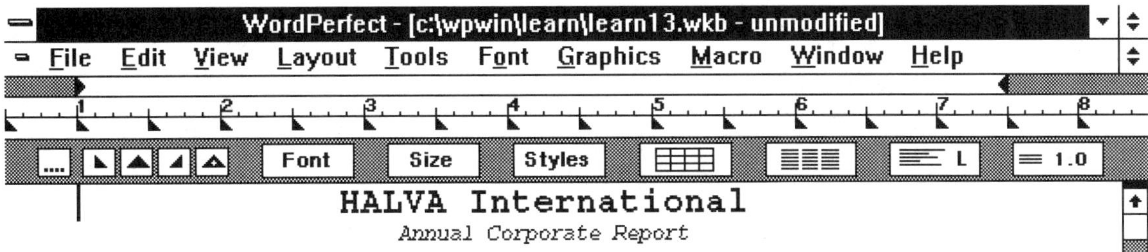

Figure 7-4. *A close up view of the ruler reveals that the Left margin is set to one inch. The right margin setting is a little more obscure, as it depends on the size of the page. On an 8.5" wide page, and a 1.0" right margin, the ruler margin indicator is set at 7.5", as this ruler shows.*

To edit the current margin setting, enter a new figure in any of the text boxes within the *Margins* dialog box. In Figure 7-5, the left and right margins for the page have been altered to 2.0 inches each.

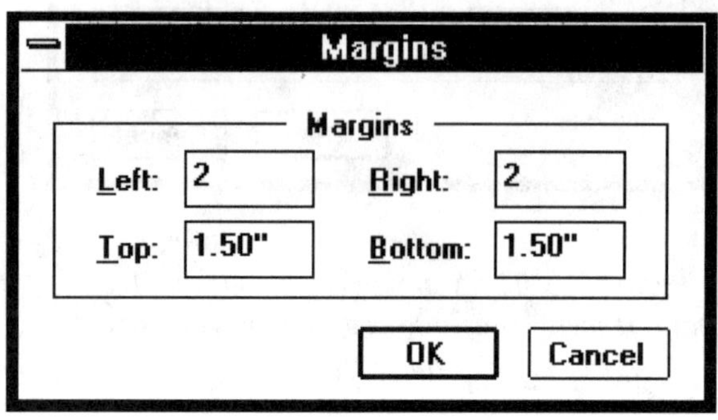

Figure 7-5. *Both the Left and Right margins in this dialog box have been changed from 1.0" to 2.0".*

Clicking on **OK** applies these margins to the currently open document. Compare the appearance of text in Figure 7-6 (with the new 2 .0 inch left and right margins) to the text in Figure 7-2 (with 1.0 inch margins).

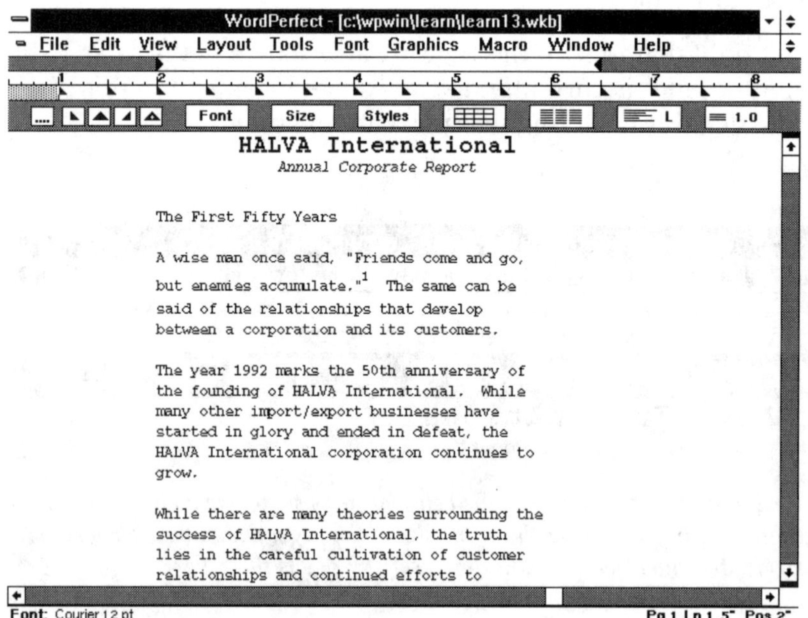

Figure 7-6. *The left and right margins have been increased to 2.0" each—hence the text area has been reduced.*

Applying margins to part of a page

Setting a margin in the method described will set the page margin for the entire document (unless, of course, a margin setting has been placed elsewhere in the document). What if you want to alter the margin for only a few paragraphs?

In Figure 7-7, left and right margins have been reset to 1.0 inch—please do this now if you wish to work through with this example. Then, select any part of the text in the fourth paragraph, as indicated in Figure 7-7. Because some text has been selected, you can apply a new margin now, and it will only affect this paragraph.

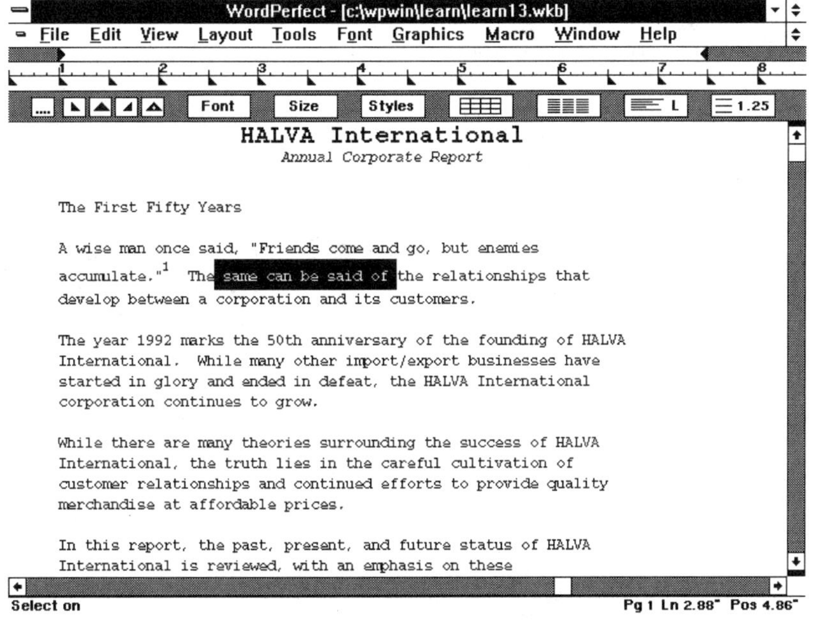

Figure 7-7. *To apply a margin to a single paragraph, or to several paragraphs, select text from that paragraph(s) before selecting the Margins command from the* ***Layout*** *menu.*

After selecting some text from a paragraph, select the *Margins* command from the **Layout** menu (Figure 7-3).

In the dialog box that appears, set the new *Left* and *Right* margins for this paragraph as shown in Figure 7-8.

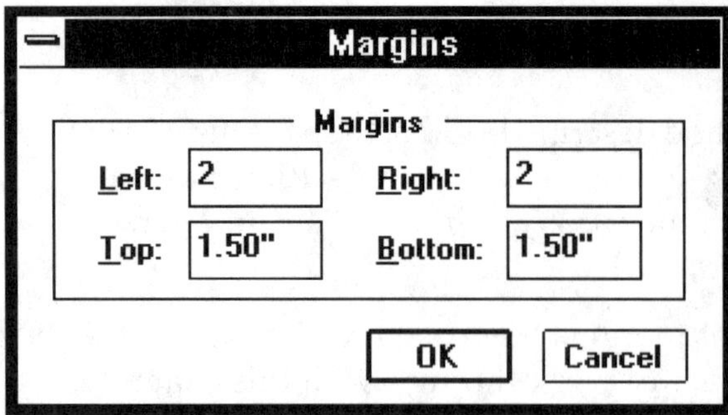

Figure 7-8. *Set the new Left and Right margins for the selected paragraph. Here, both these margins have been set to 2.0".*

Figure 7-9 shows the result in the sample document. Note that only the paragraph from which text was selected in Figure 7-7 has been indented.

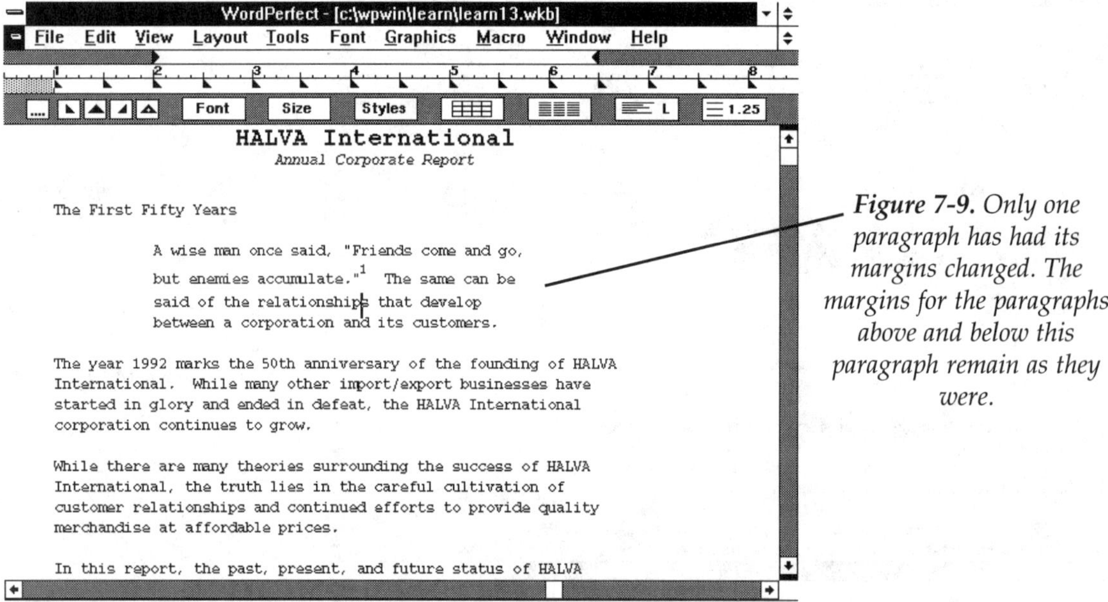

Figure 7-9. *Only one paragraph has had its margins changed. The margins for the paragraphs above and below this paragraph remain as they were.*

When margins are applied in this fashion, *Margin* codes are automatically placed at the beginning and end of the paragraph with the selected text (Figure 7-10). Codes are discussed in Chapter 5.

margin codes

```
[L/R Mar:2",2"]A wise man once said, "Friends come and go,[SRt]
but enemies accumulate."[Footnote:1;[Note Num]Howard Keele, [Und On]N
ed Goes Unpu[ ... ] The same can be[SRt]
said of the relationships that develop[SRt]
between a corporation and its customers.[HRt]
[L/R Mar:1",1"][HRt]
```

Figure 7-10. *This figure shows the codes from the text in Figure 7-9. Note that the new margin settings appear at the start of the paragraph, and the margin code required to set the margins back to the way they were appears at the end of the paragraph.*

If the *Margins* command is selected to alter margins, and no text is currently selected on the page, then the new margin settings will affect all text following the text cursor, until such time as another margin code is encountered.

Columns

The theory of applying columns is quite similar to that of applying margins. Once again, for this example, the document ***learn13.wkb*** is used to illustrate the use of columns. To follow this example, reload the ***learn13.wkb*** file using the *Open* command in the **File** menu.

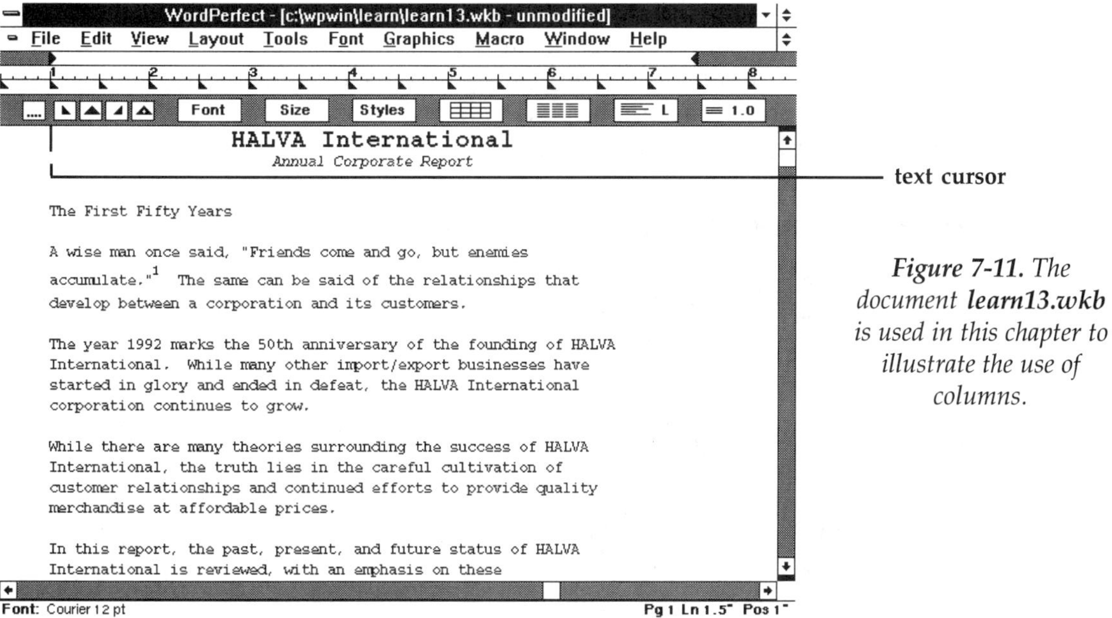

Figure 7-11. *The document **learn13.wkb** is used in this chapter to illustrate the use of columns.*

Note where the text cursor is in Figure 7-11—at the beginning of the text file. This is the place to position the cursor when setting columns for the entire document.

To apply columns to a document, select the *Define* command from the *Columns* fly-out menu in the **Layout** menu (Figure 7-12).

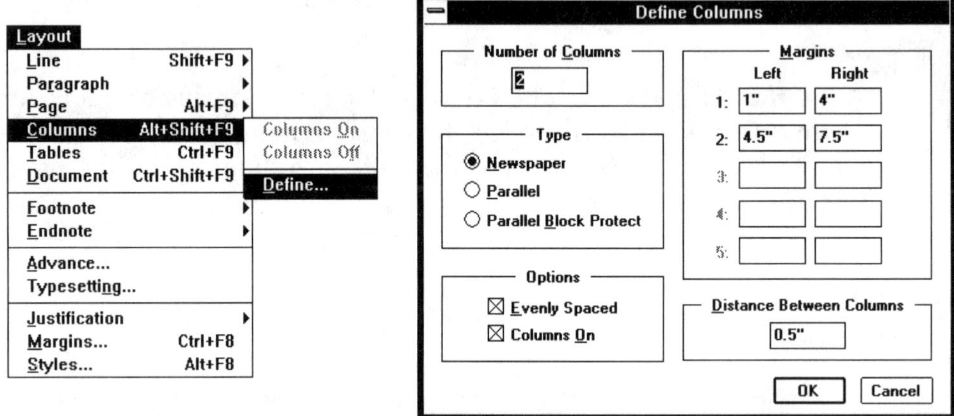

*Figure 7-12. The Columns/Define command in the **Layout** menu is used to apply columns to a document.*

There are several different options within the Figure 7-12 dialog box that control the appearance, properties, and number of columns. However, by default, WordPerfect will suggest two columns, of equal width. To see how these columns appear on the page, you can click on **OK** in the *Define Columns* dialog box (Figure 7-13).

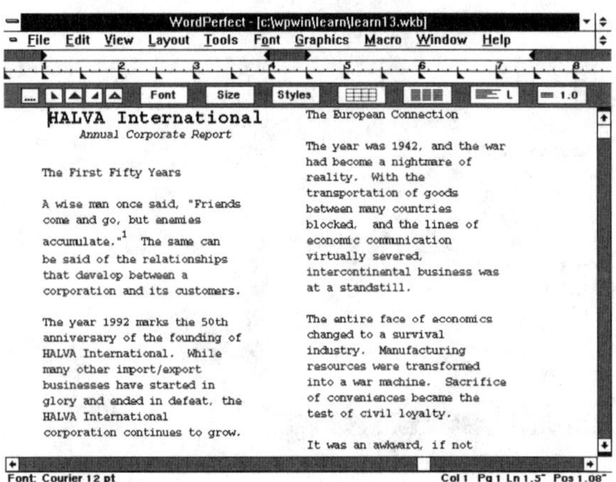

Figure 7-13. The text on the page now flows into two columns.

The text on screen flows neatly into two columns, assuming that you have the *Display Columns Side by Side* option enabled (Figure 7-14) in the *Display* command from the *Preferences* fly-out menu in the **File** menu. The text will print in multiple columns regardless of how this option is set.

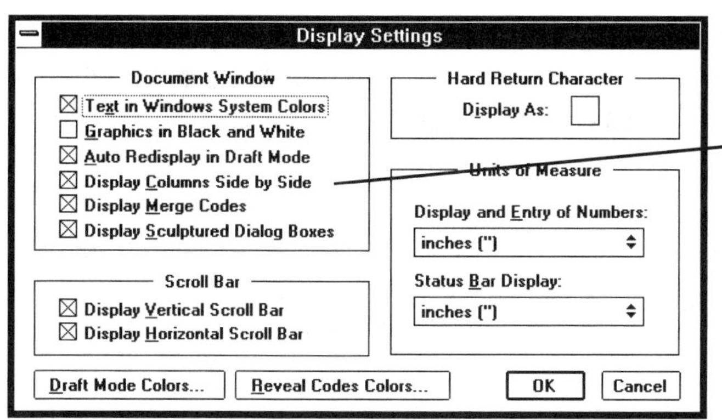

Figure 7-14. *In order for columns to appear side by side on the editing screen (Figure 7-13), the Display Columns Side by Side option must be enabled in the Preferences/ Display command from the* ***File*** *menu.*

The following figures (Figures 7-15 through 7-19) refer to the options within the *Define Columns* dialog box seen in Figure 7-12.

In the *Number of Columns* text box (Figure 7-15), you can insert the number of columns you want on the page—from 2 to 24.

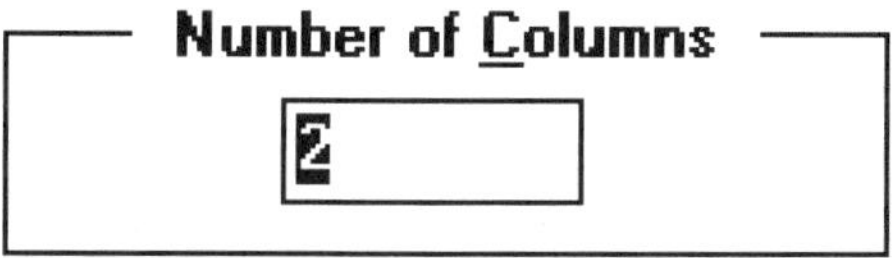

Figure 7-15. *In the Number of Columns text box, insert the number of columns you would like on the page, from 2 to 24.*

In the *Type* section of the *Define columns* dialog box (Figure 7-16), you can select the *Type* of columns that you want to use.

Type
Newspaper
Parallel
Parallel Block Protect

Figure 7-16. *The Type section of the Figure 7-12 dialog box lets you select one of three types of columns.*

Newspaper columns are traditional columns—text flows from the bottom of one column to the top of the next.

Parallel columns are slightly different—text stays in the column into which it is keyed; not unlike setting up multiple columns using the WordPerfect *Tables* feature (see Chapter 21).

The *Parallel Block Protect* option creates *Parallel* columns where each row stays together on a page. If a particular column in a row is too long for a page, block protect moves the entire row of columns to the new page.

In the *Options* section of the *Define Columns* dialog box are two options (Figure 7-17): *Evenly Spaced* and *Columns On*. *Evenly Spaced* ensures that all columns on the page are equal in width. *Columns On* ensures that the columns set in this dialog box appear on screen. The *Columns On* option will, by default, be checked in this dialog box—clicking on this option will disable the columns from appearing on the page.

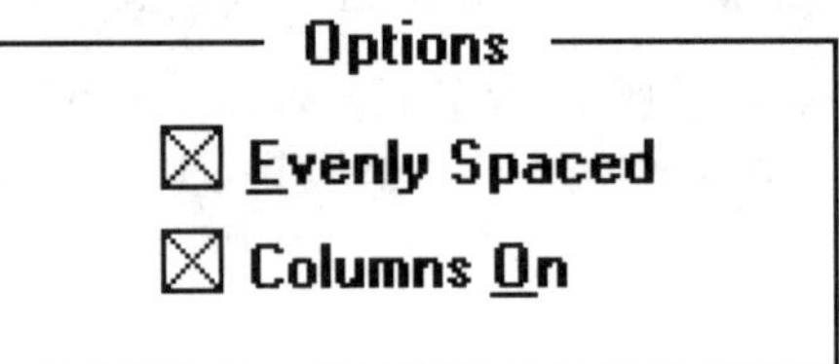

Figure 7-17. *The Options section in the Figure 7-12 dialog box.*

The *Margins* section of the *Define Columns* dialog box (Figure 7-12) lists the *Left* and *Right* margins of each column defined. Each measurement is taken from the left-hand side of the page. The *Left* margin of the first column and the *Right* margin of the last column should correspond to the actual page margins (Figure 7-18).

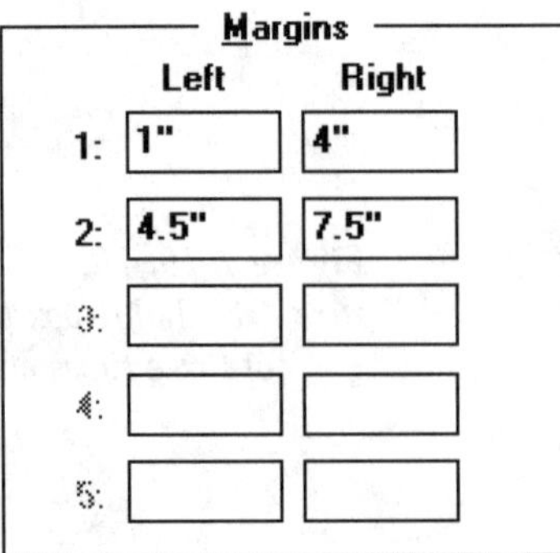

Figure 7-18. *The Margins section in the Figure 7-12 dialog box.*

The *Distance Between Columns* setting, often referred to as the gutter width, is set through the section of the *Define Columns* dialog box shown in Figure 7-19. Note the relationship between Figure 7-18 and Figure 7-19. The right margin of column one and the left margin of column two are 0.5 inches apart—the same measurement as Figure 7-19—the *Distance Between Columns.*

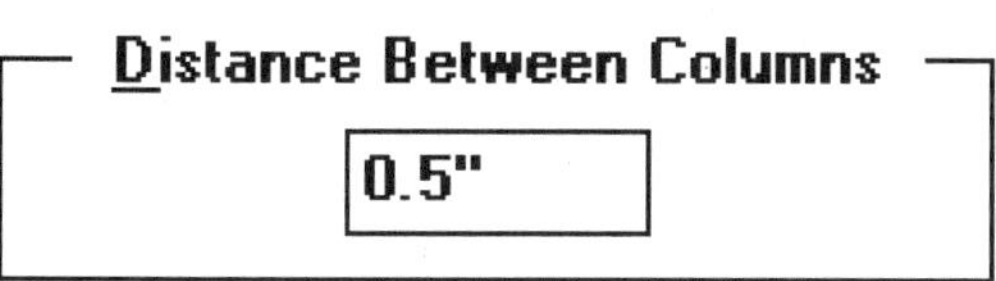

Figure 7-19. *The default setting for distance between columns is 0.5 inches.*

Columns, like margins, will commence from wherever the flashing text cursor appears in the text until another column code, or the end of the document, is reached.

In Figure 7-20, where the number of columns has been set back to one, note where the text cursor appears—just in front of the fifth paragraph in the text. If the number of columns is changed now, the effect will start at the fifth paragraph.

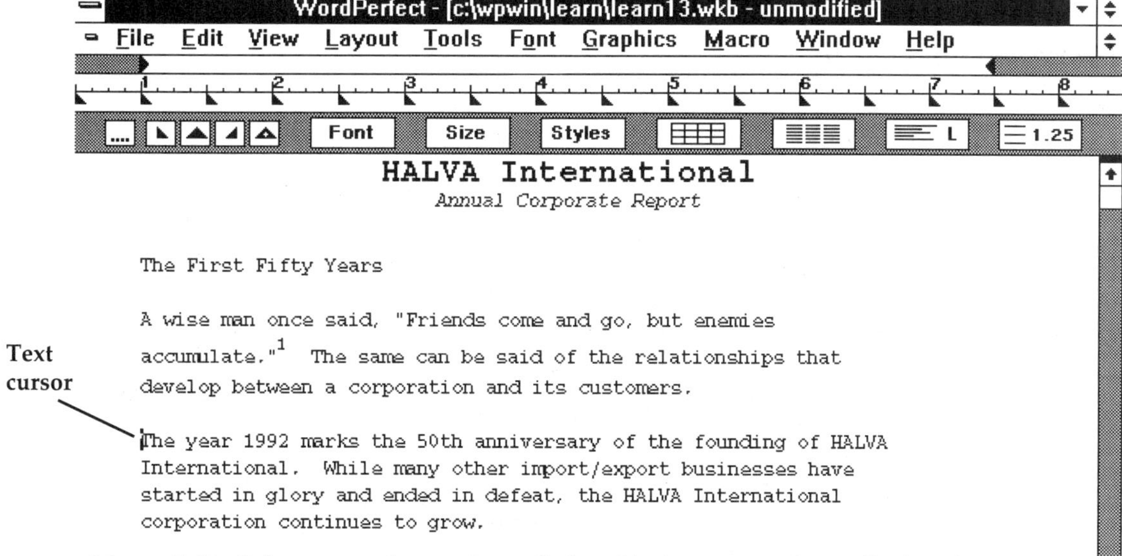

Figure 7-20. *Columns are about to be applied to this document—they will take effect from the position of the flashing text cursor to the end of the document (or until another code is found).*

Figure 7-21 shows the result of using the *Columns/Define* command of Figure 7-12 to select two columns and clicking on **OK**.

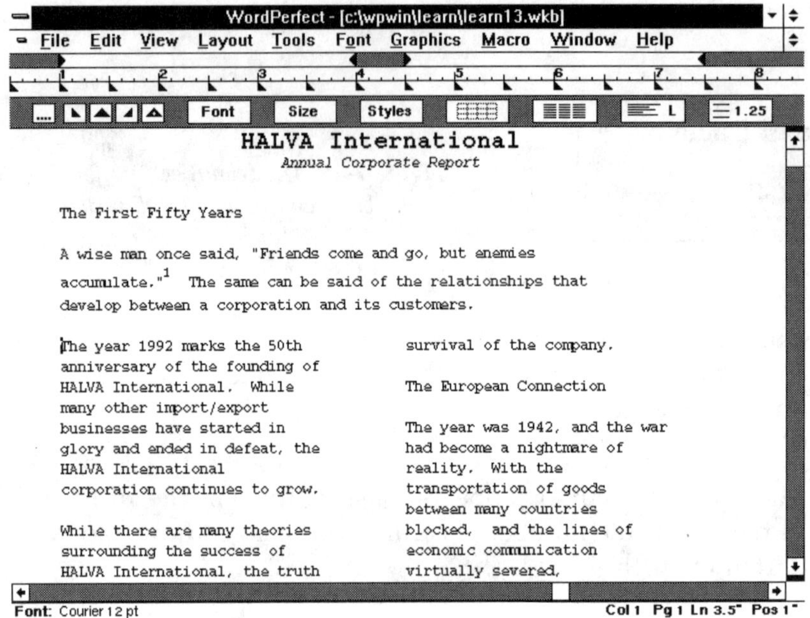

Figure 7-21. Because of the position of the flashing text cursor in Figure 7-20, columns are applied to only the text following the flashing text cursor.

Turning columns on/off

Two other commands appear in the *Columns* fly-out menu from the **Layout** menu (Figure 7-12). These are the *Columns On* and *Columns Off* commands.

Using the *Columns Off* and *Columns On* commands, you can temporarily disable columns for one or more pages, paragraphs, or any block of text. By disabling columns with the *Columns Off* command, there is no need to redefine the column. When you want to return to a columned document, simply use the *Columns On* command to restore the previous column definition.

The following figures (Figures 7-22 through 7-28) illustrate how the *Columns On* and *Columns Off* commands can be used.

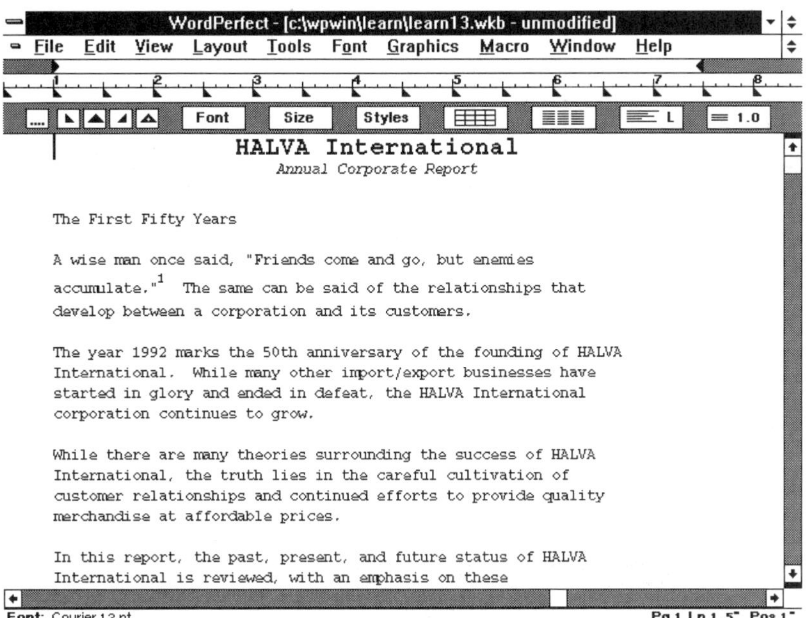

Figure 7-22. Once again, the columns previously set for this document have been removed. To make sure all column codes have been removed, you may choose to either reload the document, or use Reveal Codes to check that column codes have been removed.

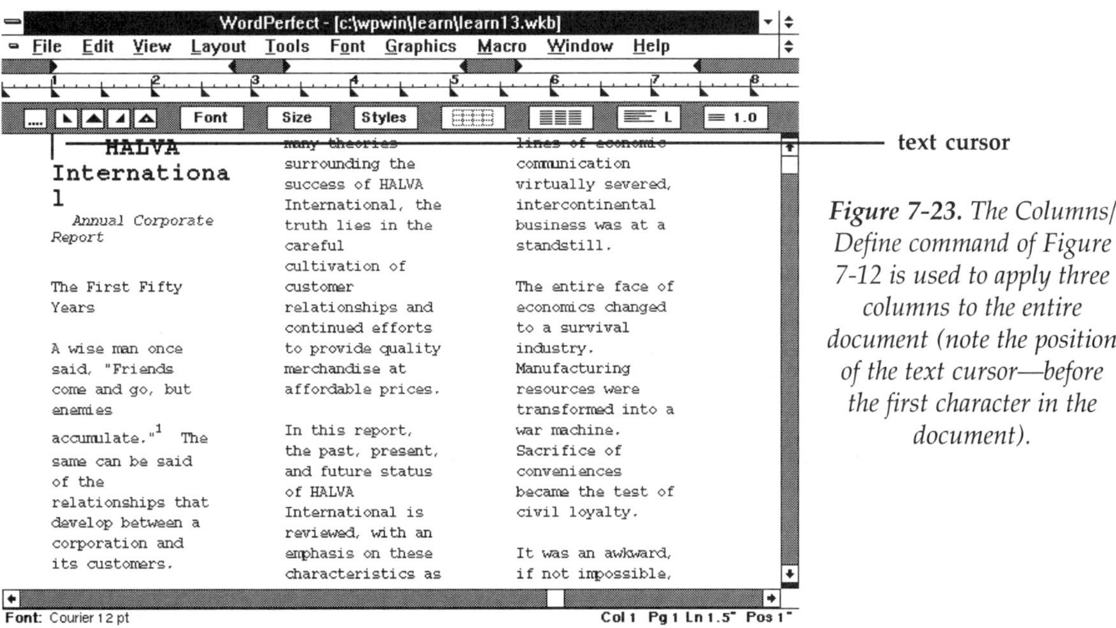

Figure 7-23. The Columns/ Define command of Figure 7-12 is used to apply three columns to the entire document (note the position of the text cursor—before the first character in the document).

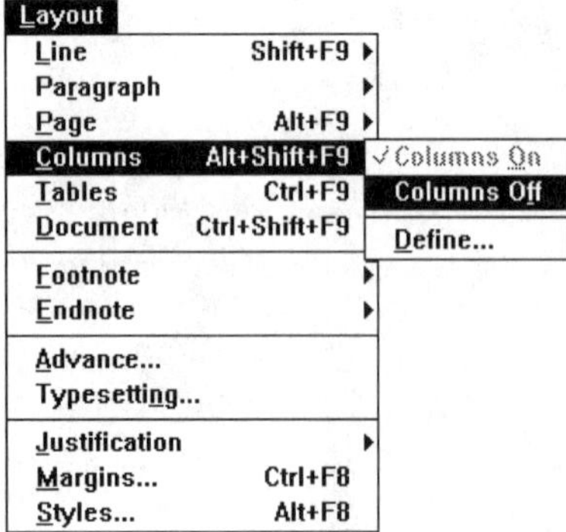

Figure 7-24. Because the first few paragraphs (the headings and subheads) should not really appear within the columns, the Columns Off command can be used to disable columns for these paragraphs. Note the position of the text cursor in Figure 7-23 before this command was selected—it appeared just before the paragraphs that should not appear in columns.

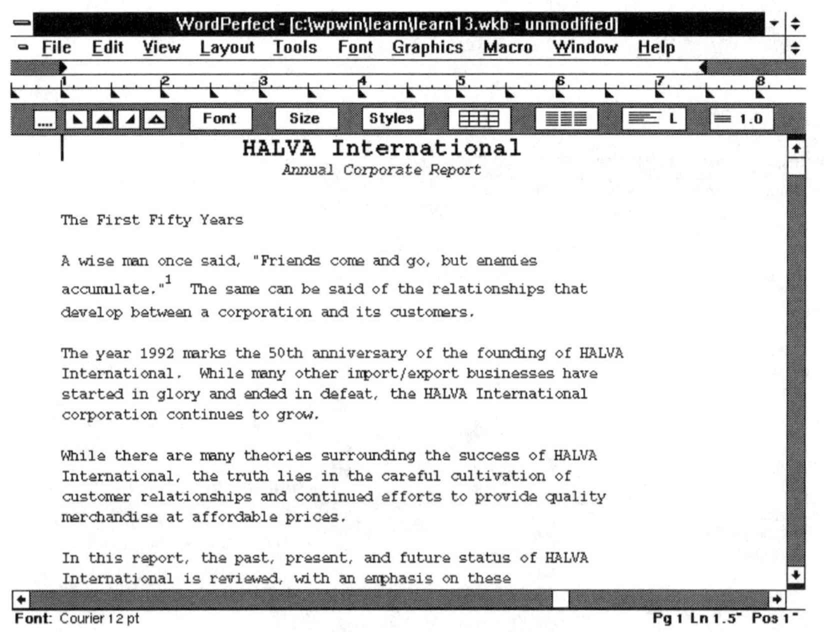

Figure 7-25. After selecting the command in Figure 7-24, it appears that the columns have been removed from the document. However, they have only been turned off for all text following the text cursor (in this case, this is the entire document).

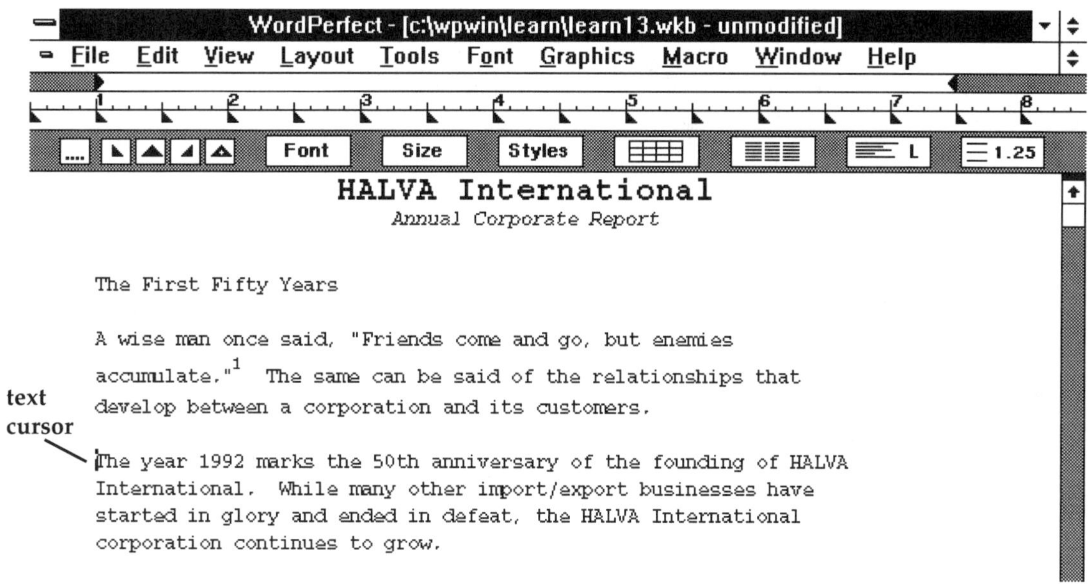

Figure 7-26. *The text cursor is now moved down to the start of the fifth paragraph. This is where the columns should start again.*

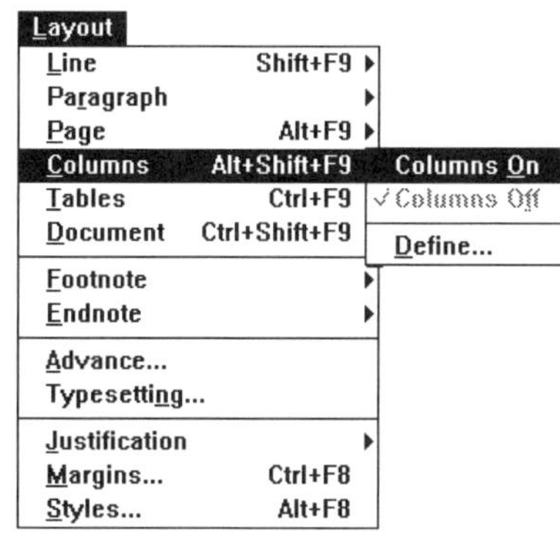

Figure 7-27. *The Columns/Columns On command from the* ***Layout*** *menu is used to turn columns back on from the position of the cursor in Figure 7-26.*

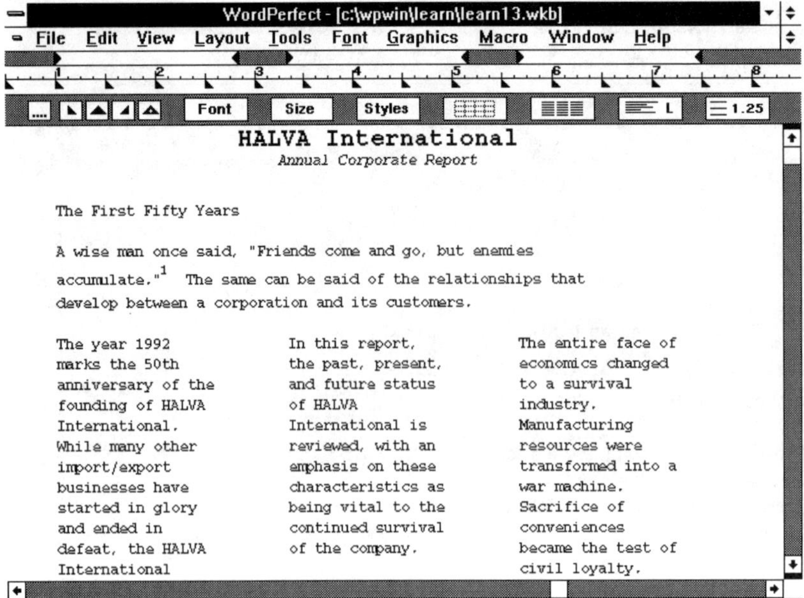

Figure 7-28. *The most recently defined columns (see Figure 7-23) are then turned back on again, for all text following the mouse cursor position of Figure 7-26.*

Margins and Columns — Exercise

This training exercise is designed so that people of all levels of expertise with WordPerfect can use it to gain maximum benefit. In order to do this, the bare exercise is listed below this paragraph on just one page, with no hints. The following pages contain the steps needed to complete this exercise for those who need additional prompting.

Steps in brief

1. *Start a new WordPerfect file.*
2. *Change the left and right margin settings to 2 inches.*
3. *Retrieve the learn13.wkb file from the learn sub-directory.*
4. *Change the left margin to 0.75 of an inch for the whole document.*
5. *Apply a 2 inch left margin to the second paragraph of body text.*
6. *Apply three newspaper columns, with 0.25 of an inch distance between each column, from the first paragraph of body text onwards.*

The details for completing these steps are on the following pages.

Steps in detail

1. Start a new WordPerfect file.

If you have just opened WordPerfect, you will be in a new WordPerfect file. If you are working on another WordPerfect document, select the *New* command from the **File** menu. If you are not in WordPerfect, start the program from Windows.

2. Change the left and right margin settings to 2 inches.

Before starting this step, ensure your paper size is set to Letter (8.5" x 11"). If you are using a Windows printer driver, this is done through the *Select Printer* command (**File** menu). If you are using a WordPerfect printer driver, this is done through the *Page/Paper Size* command in the **Layout** menu.

The default setting for the left and right margins is 1 inch. In this step of the exercise, you will change the settings for the left and right margins to 2 inches. Use the *Margins* dialog box, which is activated by selecting the *Margins* command from the **Layout** menu (Figure 7x-1).

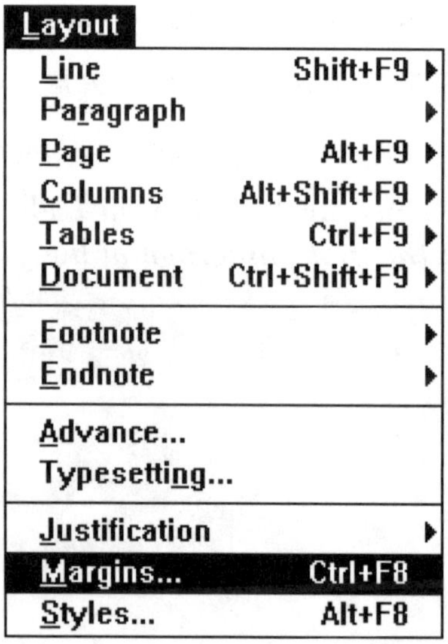

Layout
Line Shift+F9
Paragraph
Page Alt+F9
Columns Alt+Shift+F9
Tables Ctrl+F9
Document Ctrl+Shift+F9
Footnote
Endnote
Advance...
Typesetting...
Justification
Margins... Ctrl+F8
Styles... Alt+F8

*Figure 7x-1. The Margin dialog box is activated by selecting the Margins command from the **Layout** menu.*

Once the *Margins* dialog box appears, as seen in Figure 7x-2, the number in the *Left* option box will automatically be highlighted, allowing you to key in the value "2" (representing 2 inches). If, for some reason, this number is not highlighted, select the number in the *Left* text box with the mouse and key in "2". Do the same for the *Right* option.

After keying in the new value for the *Left* option, you can press the Tab key and the figure in the right text box will become highlighted automatically.

Once your *Margins* dialog box looks like the example in Figure 7x-2, click on the **OK** button.

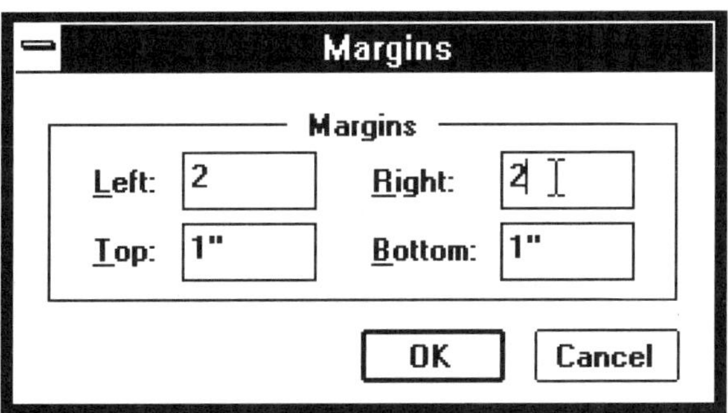

Figure 7x-2*. Change the settings for the Left and Right margins to 2 inches.*

When you return to the document window, you will see that the left and right margin markers in the ruler have moved. The left marker will be at the 2 inch position on the ruler and the right-hand marker will be positioned two inches short of the right-hand end of the page; in this case, at 6.5 inches in the ruler, as seen in Figure 7x-3. The flashing cursor will also move to reflect the new left margin; note its position in the next figure.

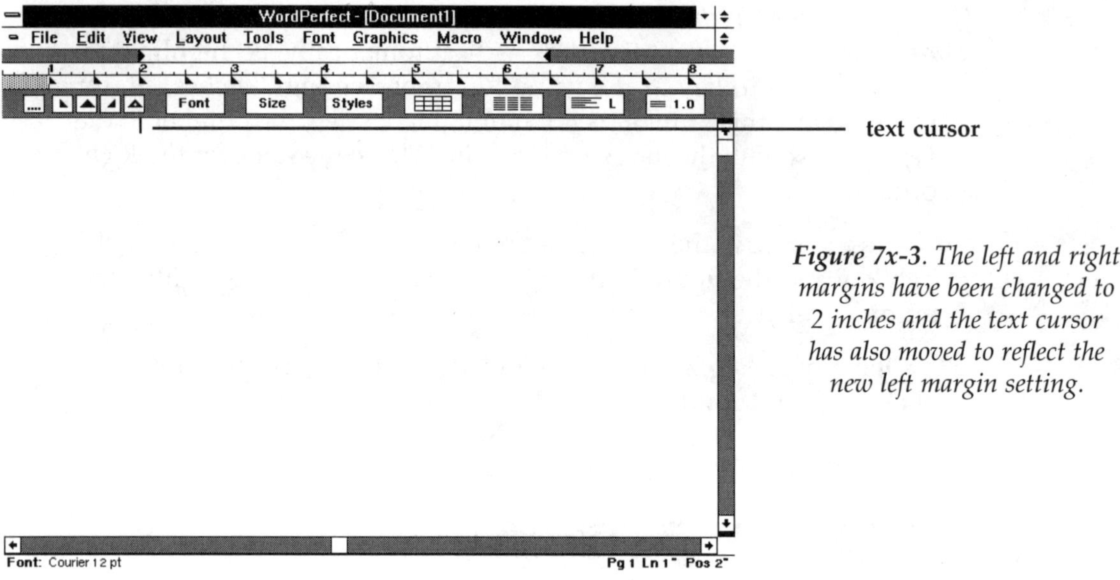

Figure 7x-3. The left and right margins have been changed to 2 inches and the text cursor has also moved to reflect the new left margin setting.

3. Retrieve the learn13.wkb file from the learn sub-directory.

To retrieve this file, first select the *Retrieve* command from the **File** menu (Figure 7x-4) to activate the *Retrieve File* dialog box of Figure 7x-5.

*Figure 7x-4. Selecting the Retrieve command from the **File** menu will activate the Retrieve File dialog box of Figure 7x-5.*

In the *Retrieve File* dialog box, locate the ***learn*** sub-directory in the ***wpwin*** sub-directory. Select the ***learn13.wkb*** file from the list of files that appears and then click on the *Retrieve* button (Figure 7x-5).

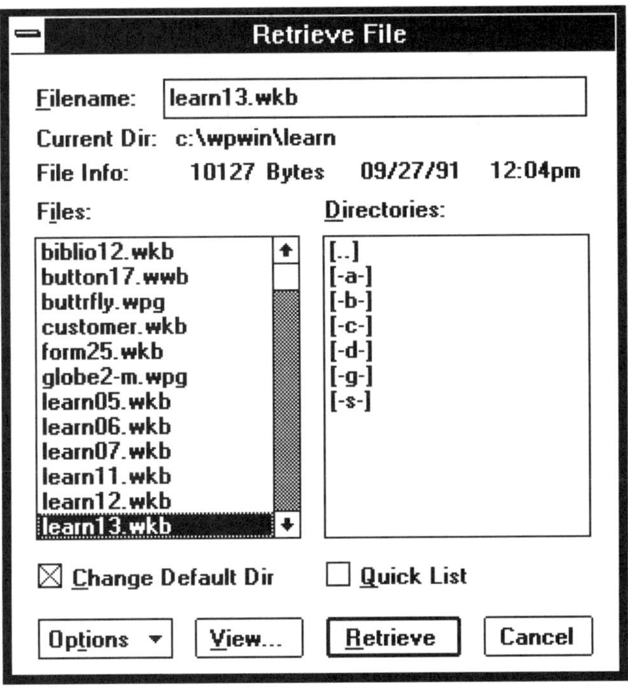

Figure 7x-5. *Locate the **learn13.wkb** file in the **learn** sub-directory and select it. To finalize the retrieve procedure, click on the Retrieve button.*

Because you have altered the current empty document (by changing the margins), WordPerfect will alert you with the screen prompt of Figure 7x-6. For this exercise click on the *Yes* option.

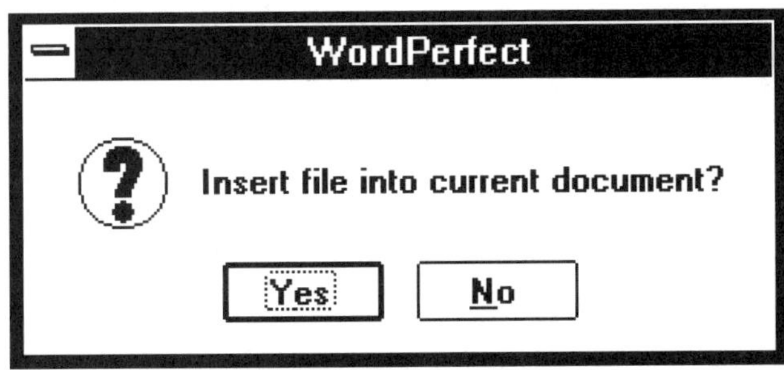

Figure 7x-6. *This screen prompt will appear after clicking on the Retrieve button in Figure 7x-5. Click on the Yes option.*

If you click on **Yes** in Figure 7x-6, the ***learn13.wkb*** file will be inserted into the document as displayed in Figure 7x-7. Because you are retrieving a document into an existing file, the text follows the settings you have chosen for the left and right margins.

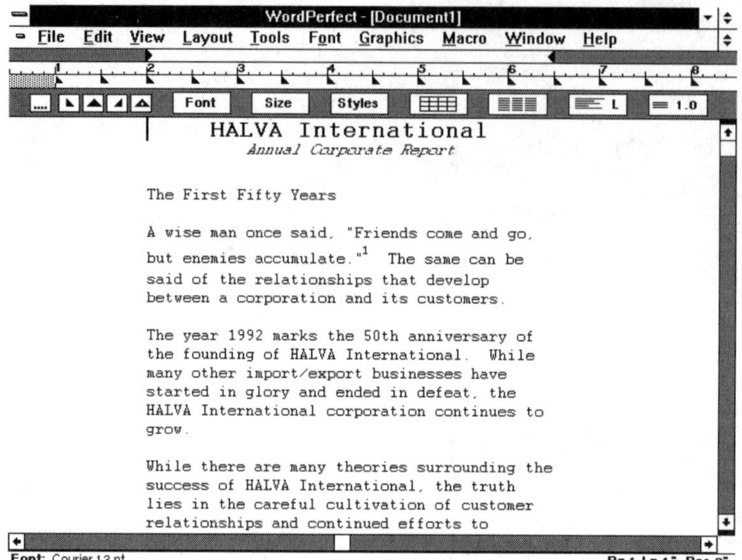

Figure 7x-7. *The file* ***learn13.wkb*** *has been successfully retrieved into the current document.*

4. Change the left margin to 0.75 of an inch for the whole document.

After you have retrieved the file in the previous step, the cursor will automatically be at the top left of the page. If you change the margin settings now, all text after the cursor will be affected (in this case, the whole document).

Select the *Margins* command from the **Layout** menu (Figure 7x-8). The *Margins* dialog box, in Figure 7x-9, will again be activated.

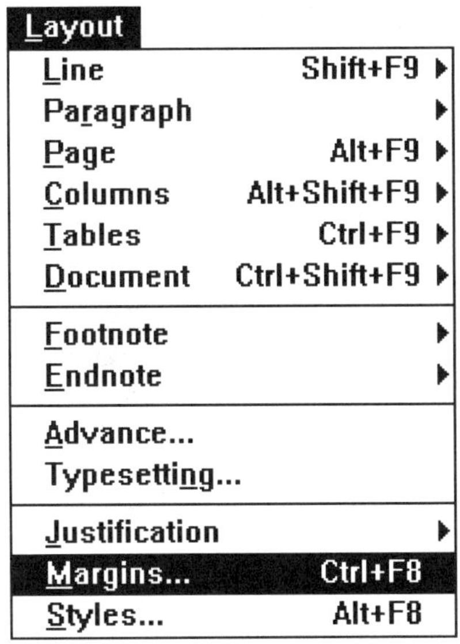

*Figure 7x-8. To alter the left margin again, first select the Margins command from the **Layout** menu to activate the Margins dialog box.*

The *Left* and *Right* settings in the *Margins* dialog box will both read 2 inches. To complete step four of this exercise, change the setting in the *Left* option to 0.75 as seen in Figure 7x-9.

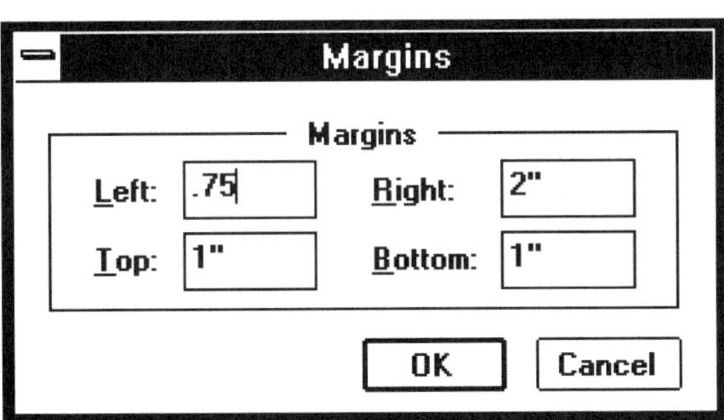

Figure 7x-9. Change the setting in the Left option of the Margins dialog box to 0.75.

After changing the *Left* setting, click on the **OK** button. The left margin marker in the ruler will move to the 0.75 position. The text in the document will reformat to match the new left margin setting as shown in Figure 7x-10.

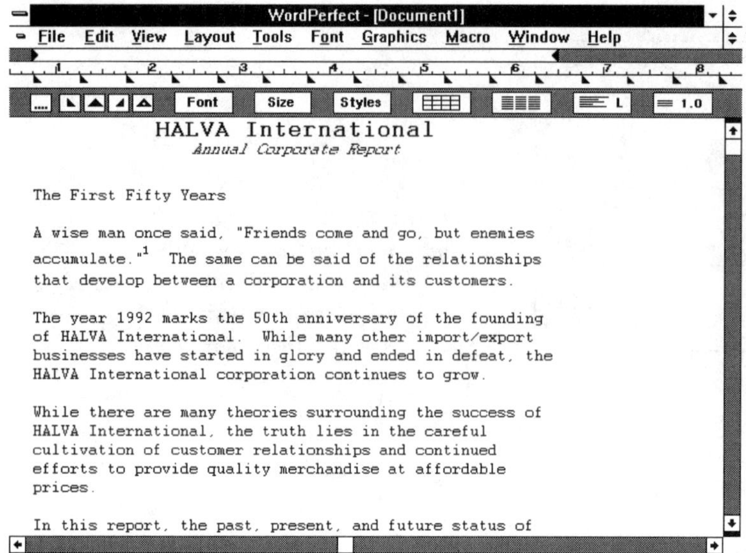

Figure 7x-10. After changing the Left setting in the Margins dialog box, the text will reformat so that it begins 0.75 of an inch from the left side of the page.

5. ***Apply a 2 inch left margin to the second paragraph of body text.***

To apply a different margin to only one paragraph, select some text from the paragraph you wish to adjust. In Figure 7x-11, the first few words of the second paragraph have been selected.

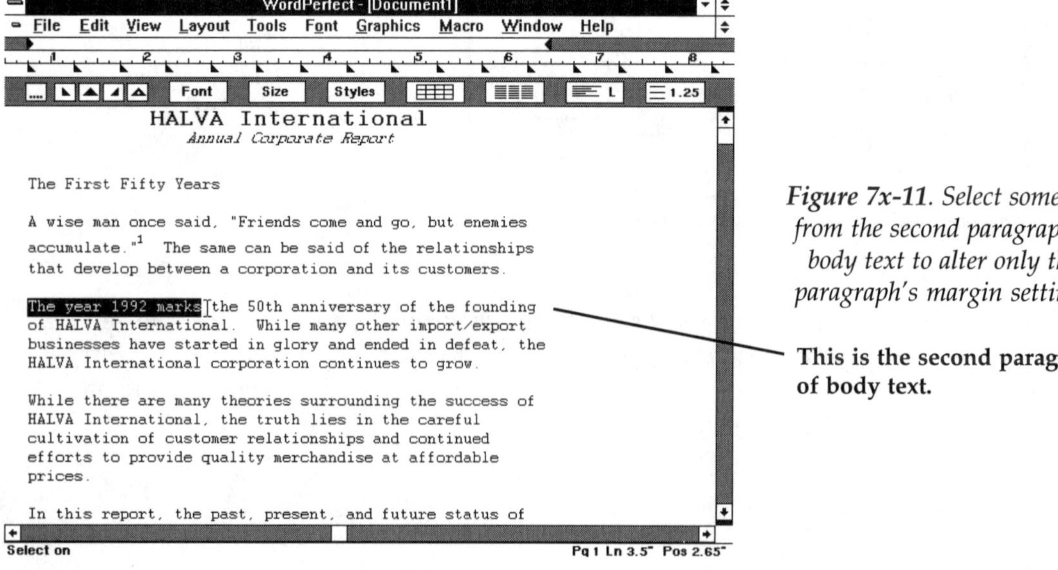

Figure 7x-11. Select some text from the second paragraph of body text to alter only this paragraph's margin settings.

Once you have selected some text in paragraph two, choose the *Margins* command from the **Layout** menu (Figure 7x-12).

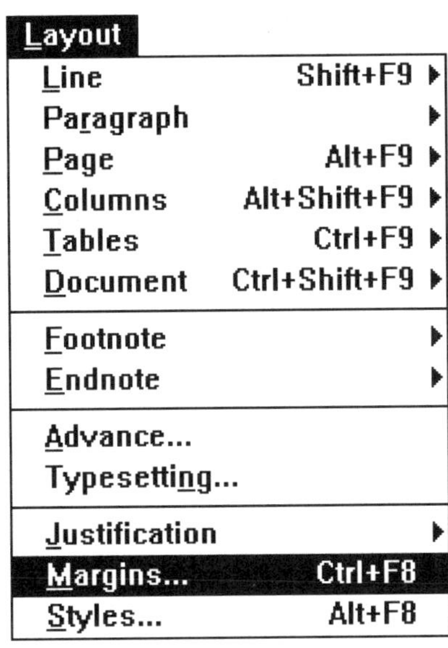

***Figure 7x-12**. After selecting the text in paragraph two, choose the Margins command from the **Layout** menu.*

This time in the *Margins* dialog box, change the *Left* setting to 2, as in Figure 7x-13, and then click on **OK**.

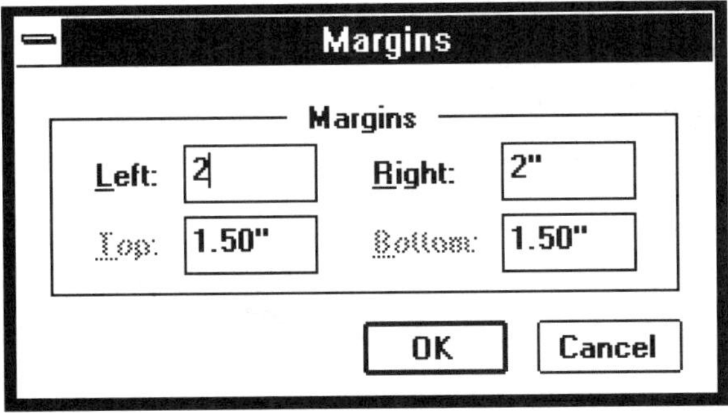

***Figure 7x-13**. Change the Left setting to 2. The changes made in the Margins dialog box this time will only affect the second paragraph.*

After clicking on **OK** in the *Margins* dialog box of Figure 7x-13, the text in the second paragraph will have a 2 inch left margin as indicated in Figure 7x-14.

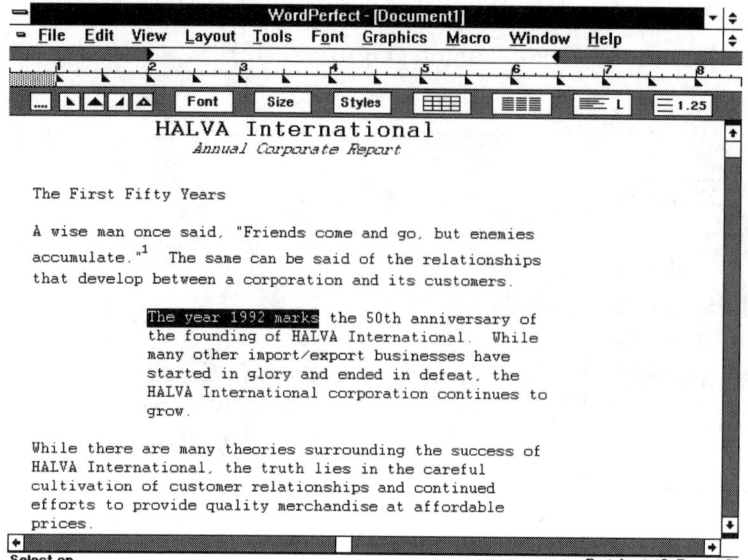

Figure 7x-14. The second paragraph now has a 2 inch left margin.

6. ***Apply three newspaper columns, with 0.25 of an inch distance between each column, from the first paragraph of body text onwards.***

You are now going to reformat the text, beginning with the first paragraph of body text, with three newspaper columns. Place your cursor at the beginning of the first paragraph, as shown in Figure 7x-15.

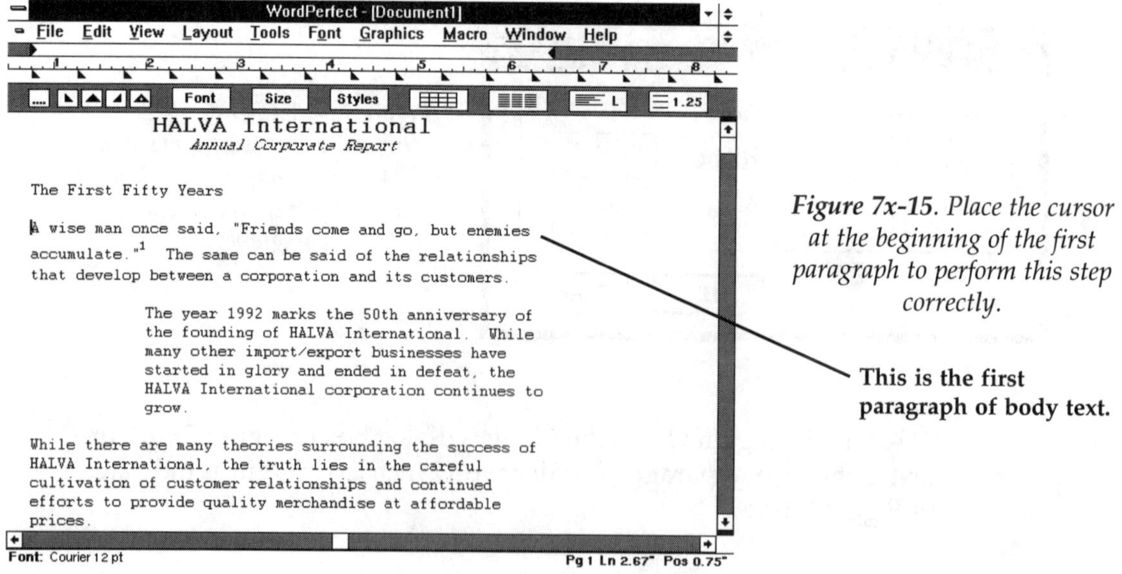

Figure 7x-15. Place the cursor at the beginning of the first paragraph to perform this step correctly.

Once the cursor has been placed at the beginning of the first paragraph, select the *Define* command from the *Columns* fly-out menu in the **Layout** menu (Figure 7x-16). This command will activate the *Define Columns* dialog box of Figure 7x-17.

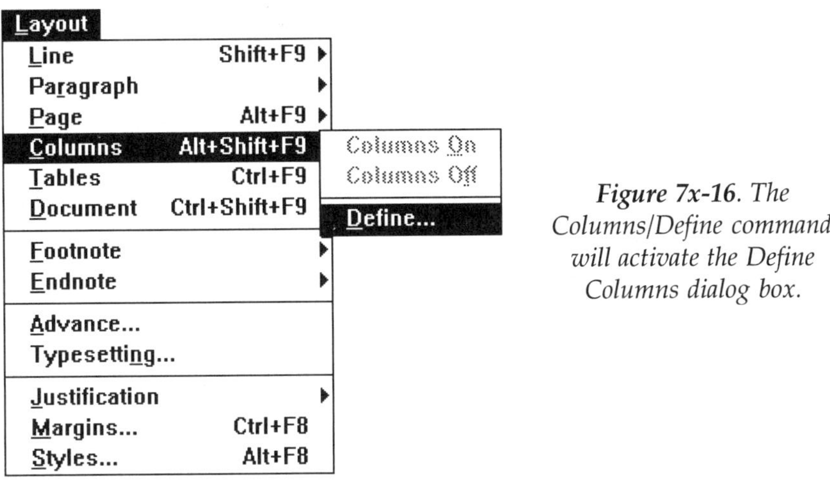

***Figure 7x-16**. The Columns/Define command will activate the Define Columns dialog box.*

In the *Define Columns* dialog box, change the *Number of Columns* to 3, leave the default *Type* setting of *Newspaper* as it is, and change the *Distance Between Columns* setting to 0.25 of an inch (Figure 7x-17).

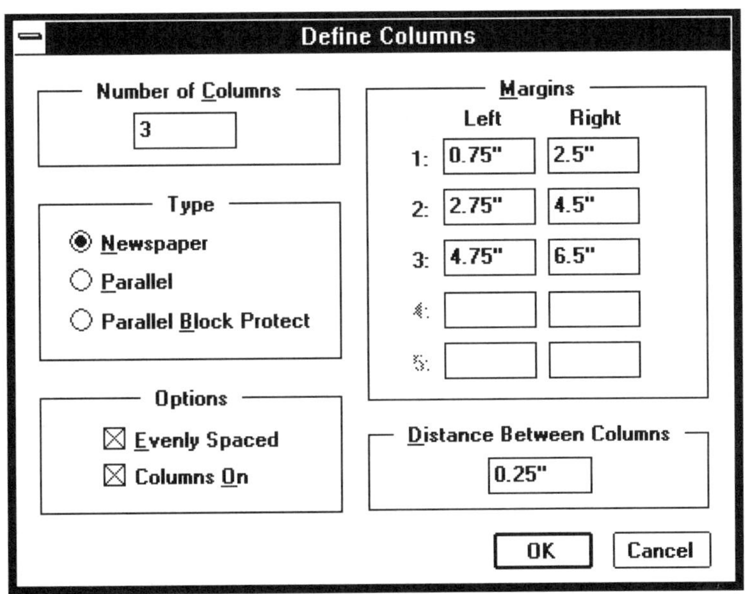

***Figure 7x-17**. Once you have set your Define Columns dialog box up as shown here, click on the **OK** button.*

After you click on **OK** in the *Define Columns* dialog box, your text will look like the document shown in Figure 7x-18.

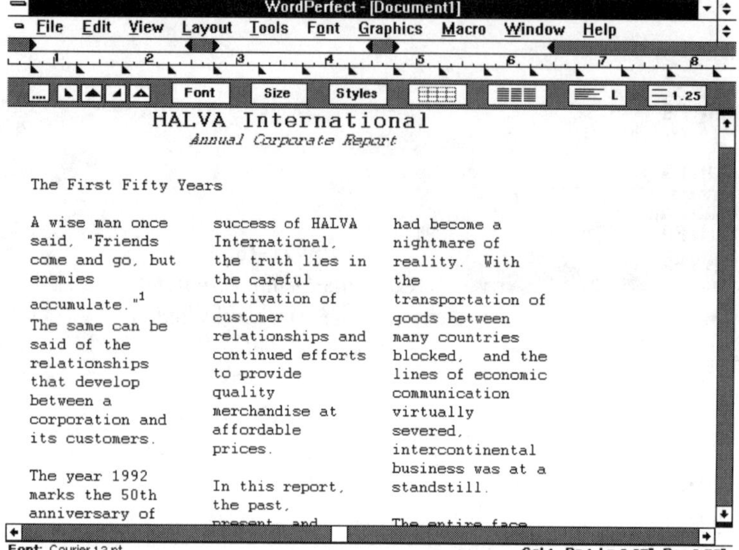

Figure 7x-18. The text from paragraph one onwards has been formatted into three columns.

Layout

This chapter looks at many of the commands in the **Layout** menu and how they are used to help format text and pages.

Some of the commands found in the various fly-out menus of the **Layout** menu have been discussed in earlier chapters in this book, or will be discussed in future chapters. Where this occurs, the relevant chapter will be pointed out.

If you wish to follow through in this chapter, load the sample file called ***learn18.wkb*** from the ***learn*** sub-directory (Figure 8-1).

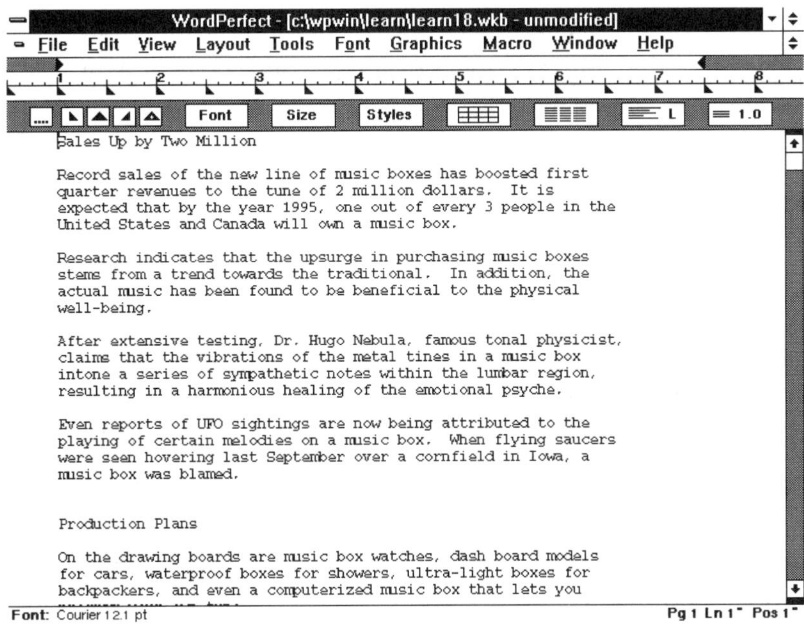

*Figure 8-1. This chapter uses the sample file **learn18.wkb** from the **learn** sub-directory, to illustrate the different layout functions.*

The various formatting and layout features discussed in this chapter are all found in the **Layout** menu shown in Figure 8-2.

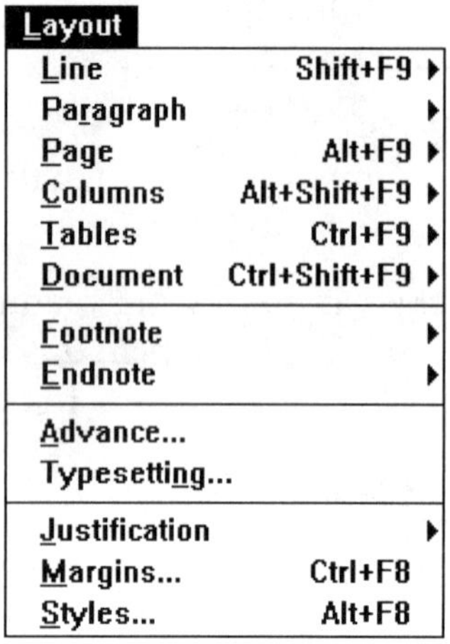

Layout	
Line	Shift+F9 ▸
Paragraph	▸
Page	Alt+F9 ▸
Columns	Alt+Shift+F9 ▸
Tables	Ctrl+F9 ▸
Document	Ctrl+Shift+F9 ▸
Footnote	▸
Endnote	▸
Advance...	
Typesetting...	
Justification	▸
Margins...	Ctrl+F8
Styles...	Alt+F8

*Figure 8-2. The **Layout** menu.*

In almost all cases in this chapter, changes affect the text following the flashing text cursor or, if text is selected, only the selected text. Any differences, where applicable, will be pointed out.

Adjusting line height

Adjusting line height is quite a simple task; it is similar to adjusting line spacing in WordPerfect. Line spacing, which can be adjusted using the *Line Spacing* button in the ruler or through the *Line/Spacing* command in the **Layout** menu, is relative to the size of the font in use, whereas line height allows you to set a fixed spacing for line height.

Make sure your flashing text cursor is positioned before the first character in the document you have opened.

To adjust line height, select the *Height* command from the *Line* fly-out menu in the **Layout** menu (Figure 8-3).

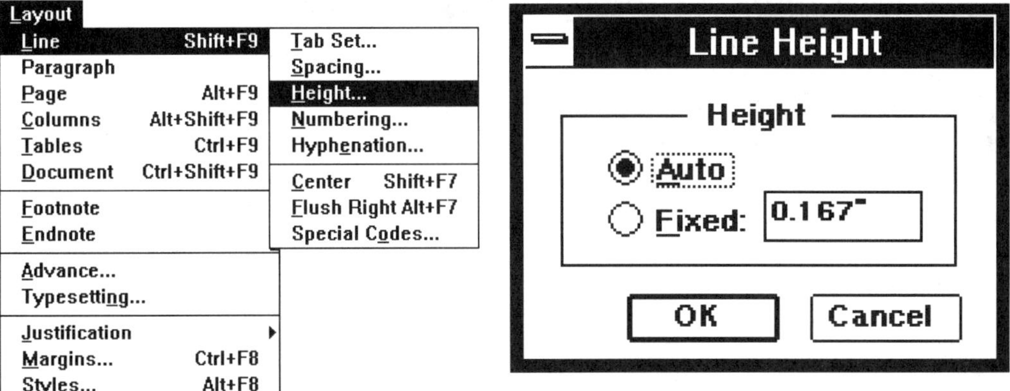

Figure 8-3. *The Line/Height command from the* ***Layout*** *menu and its dialog box.*

In Figure 8-3, the *Line Height* dialog box indicates two choices for line height: *Auto* (where WordPerfect decides the optimum line height based on the font size), or *Fixed* (where you decide line height).

Line height is measured from baseline to baseline. In this example, select the *Fixed* radio button from Figure 8-3. The current line height will be listed in the *Fixed* text box (Figure 8-4).

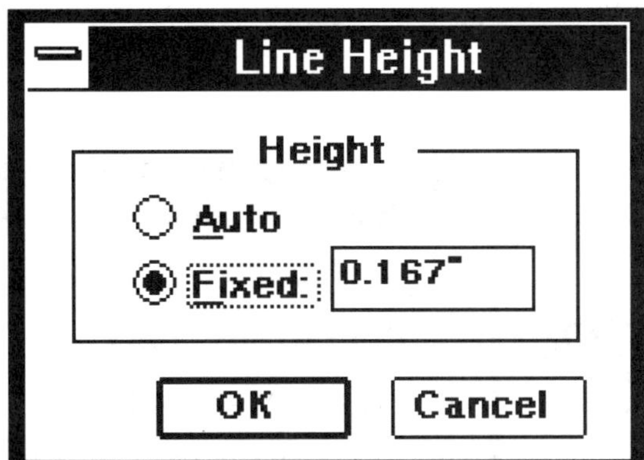

Figure 8-4. *The current line height is displayed when you select the Fixed radio button.*

Currently, the line height is set to 0.167 inches. To illustrate the difference a change in line height can make, edit this figure to read 0.3 inches, and click on **OK.** Your screen will appear as shown in Figure 8-5.

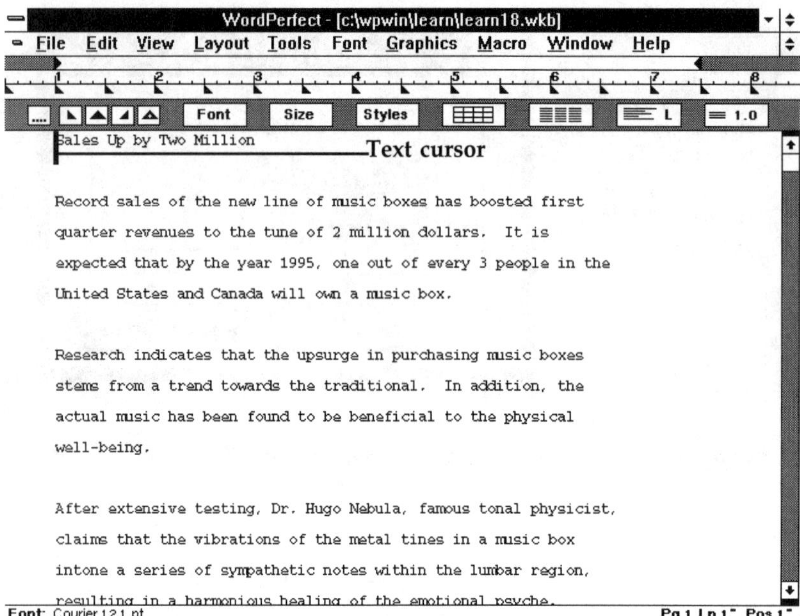

Figure 8-5. *Compare this screen display with Figure 8-1. The line height has almost doubled.*

Hyphenation

WordPerfect can automatically hyphenate documents, if this is required. The control that enables and disables this feature is found in the *Hyphenation* command from the *Line* fly-out menu in the **Layout** menu (Figure 8-6).

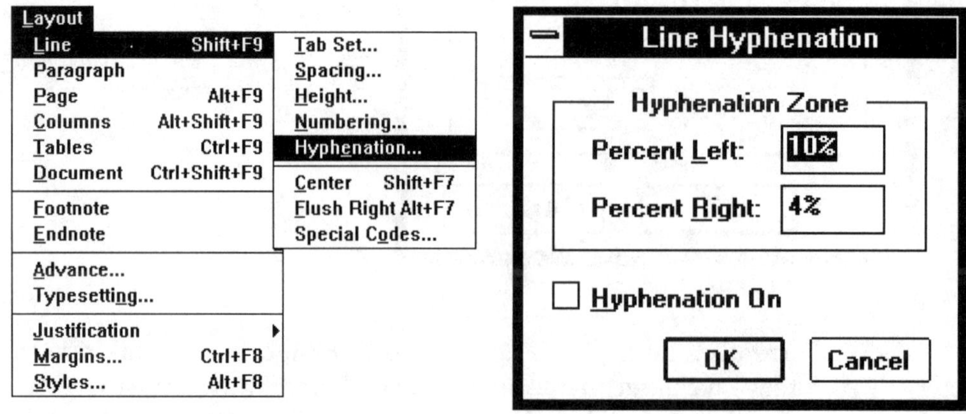

Figure 8-6. *The Line/Hyphenation command in the* ***Layout*** *menu and its dialog box.*

In Figure 8-6, the main option appears at the bottom of the *Hyphenation* dialog box—the *Hyphenation On* check box. If checked, automatic hyphenation will occur. Select this option now, by clicking in the box.

The *Hyphenation Zone* options determine exactly how hyphenation is to take place. Although it sounds a little complex, the settings for *Percent Left* and *Percent Right* are quite easy to follow.

WordPerfect will only hyphenate a word that starts before the *Percent Left* setting from the right-hand side of any line and continues past the *Percent Right* setting. For example, if a line is five inches wide (margin to margin), and *Percent Left* and *Percent Right* are set to 20% and 10%, respectively, this is equivalent to 20% and 10% of five inches, or one inch and half an inch, respectively. This means any word that begins more than one inch from the right-hand side of the line, and extends past the half inch setting will be hyphenated.

In Figure 8-7, hyphenation has been turned on, and the **OK** button clicked. Turning hyphenation on gives no guarantee that words will actually be hyphenated—this depends totally on how the text falls on each line. However, at least one line in the document has been hyphenated (Figure 8-7).

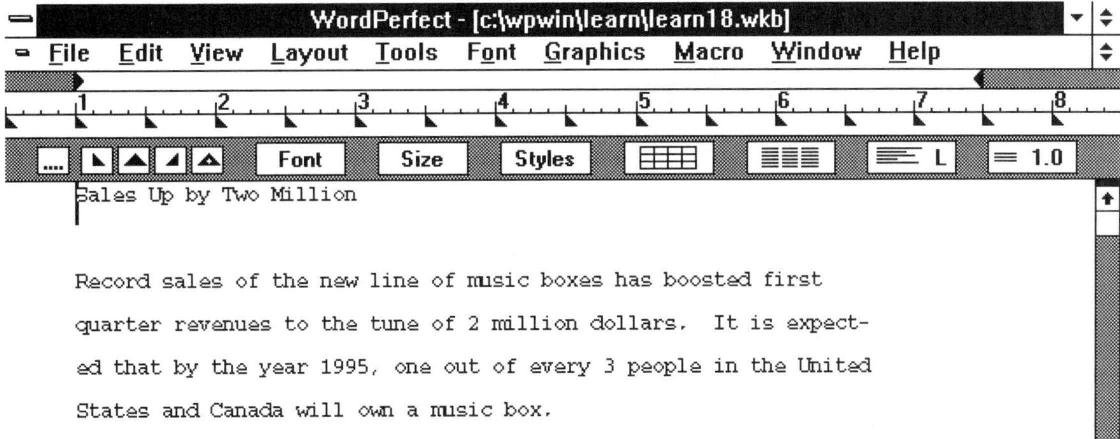

Figure 8-7. WordPerfect has hyphenated the second line in this document.

In the *Preferences/Environment* command in the **File** menu, there are several options that can affect how hyphenation occurs within WordPerfect. These are the *Hyphenation Options* and a *Beep On* option. This command is discussed in Chapter 10, **Preferences - (1)**.

Other codes that help when manually hyphenating can be found in the *Line/Special Codes* command in the **Layout** menu, in the *Hyphenation Codes* section. Chapter 22, **Advanced Features**, provides more information on this feature.

Paragraph indenting

Paragraph indenting affects the margins of a paragraph. WordPerfect provides several options relating to paragraph indenting.

For this command, you may wish to insert the text cursor before the first character of the second paragraph of this document (Figure 8-8). Paragraph indenting options are far more apparent when observed on a multi-line document.

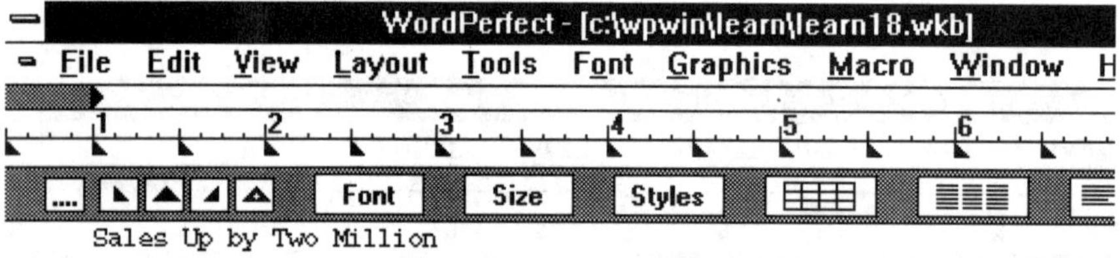

Figure 8-8. Note the position of the text cursor—just before the first character in the second paragraph.

Before indenting this paragraph, note that its left margin is the same as all other paragraphs.

To indent the paragraph, select the *Indent* command from the *Paragraph* fly-out menu in the **Layout** menu (Figure 8-9). Figure 8-10 illustrates the result of selecting this command.

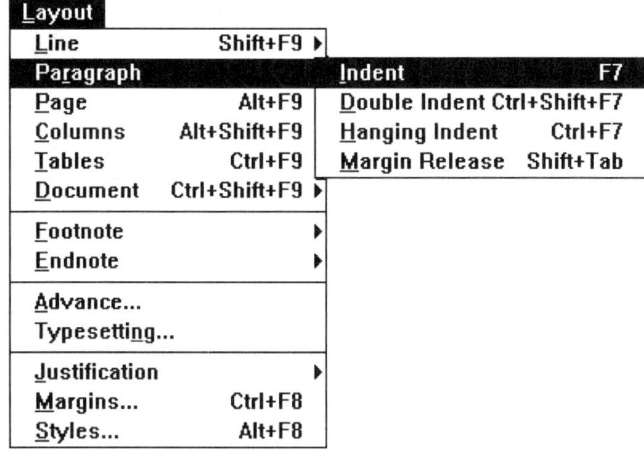

Figure 8-9. *The Paragraph/ Indent command will indent the current paragraph.*

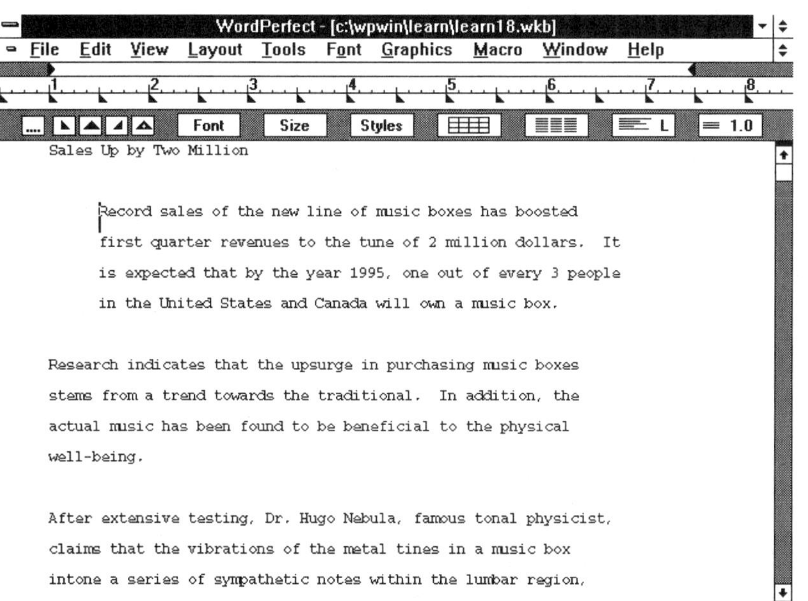

Figure 8-10. *The paragraph in which the text cursor was inserted has been indented.*

In Figure 8-10, and on your screen, the paragraph in which the text cursor was inserted has now been indented by one tab position. Note, in the ruler, how this paragraph now lines up with the 1.5 inch tab marker.

If no text is selected, the *Indent* commands in the *Paragraph* fly-out menu in the **Layout** menu will affect the text following the text cursor, until the end of the paragraph. If the text cursor has been inserted at a point other than before the very first character in the paragraph, only the part of the paragraph that follows the text cursor will be affected by the command.

A paragraph is indented to the next tab stop each time the *Paragraph/ Indent* command is selected. If you have not yet used tabs, the default tab setting is one at every half an inch.

The *Paragraph/Double Indent* command (Figure 8-11) indents both the left and right margins of the paragraph in one tab position. In other words, the *Double Indent* command indents a paragraph from both sides. Figure 8-12 shows the result of applying the *Paragraph/Double Indent* command to the paragraph of Figure 8-10.

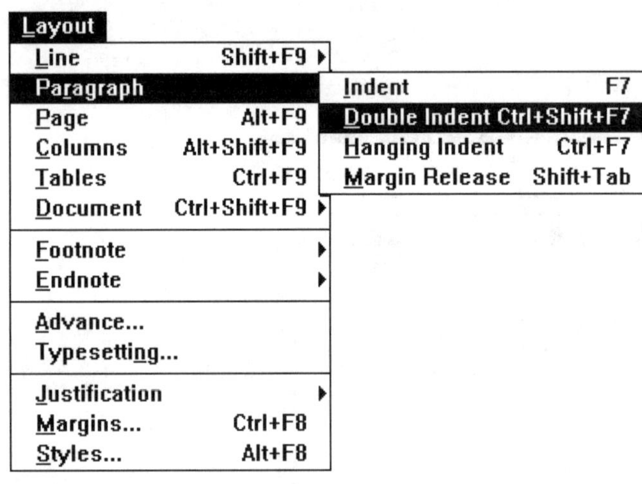

Figure 8-11. Paragraph/Double Indent indents a paragraph from both the left and right hand sides by one tab stop, each time the command is selected.

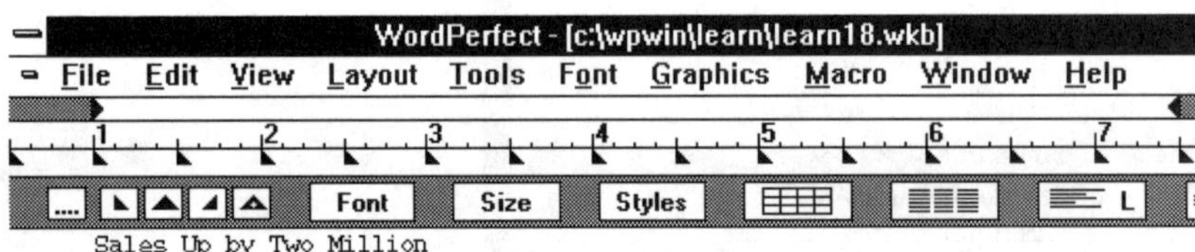

Figure 8-12. The Paragraph/Double Indent command indents a paragraph from both sides, as seen in this figure.

The *Paragraph/Hanging Indent* command (Figure 8-13) is much the same as the *Paragraph/Indent* command, although the first line of the paragraph remains as it was—all other lines are indented one tab stop as shown below.

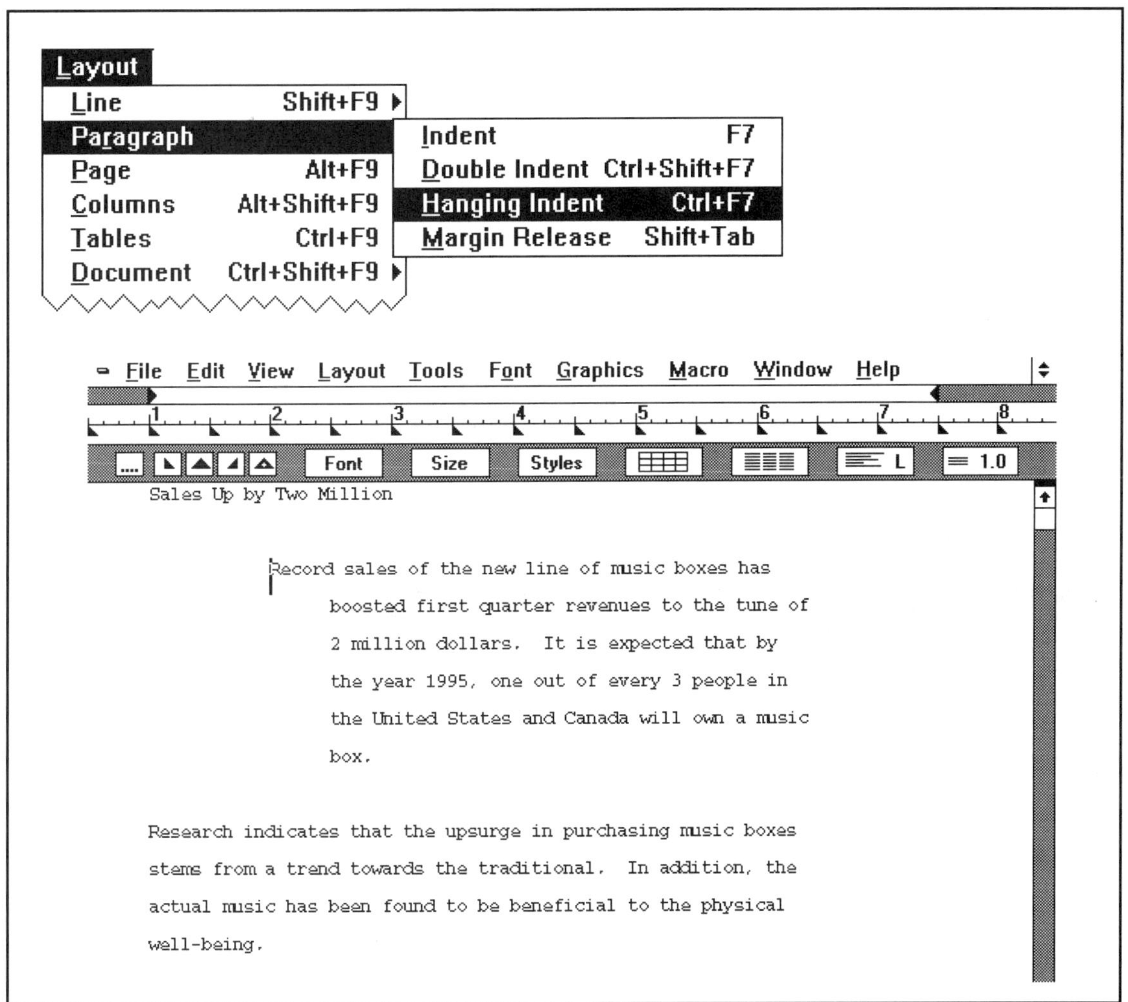

Figure 8-13. *The Paragraph/Hanging Indent command. The paragraph on your screen will be indented for every line except the first—this is known as a hanging indent.*

The final command in the *Paragraph* fly-out menu in the **Layout** menu is the *Margin Release* command (Figure 8-14). This command will move the text cursor and the text back one tab stop, even beyond the left margin if necessary.

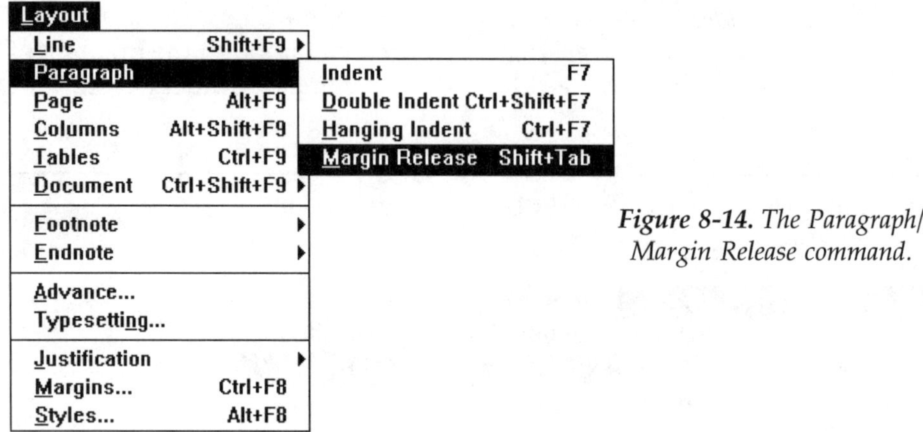

Figure 8-14. *The Paragraph/ Margin Release command.*

This commands only works on one line at a time. It is, in effect, the reverse of a tab. Figure 8-15 shows the result of using this command in your example.

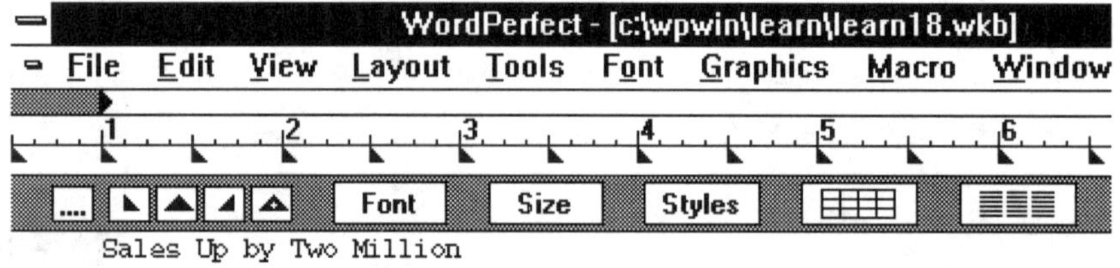

Figure 8-15. *Compare this figure with Figure 8-13—the first line of this paragraph has moved back one tab stop.*

Page breaks

WordPerfect will automatically create new pages as needed, to hold text and graphics. There are cases, however, when you may wish to force the creation of a new page, independent of whether or not the current page has been filled.

Before creating such a page break, move the text cursor to the start of the third paragraph in this document (Figure 8-16). This is where you will force a page break to occur—at the left of the text cursor's position.

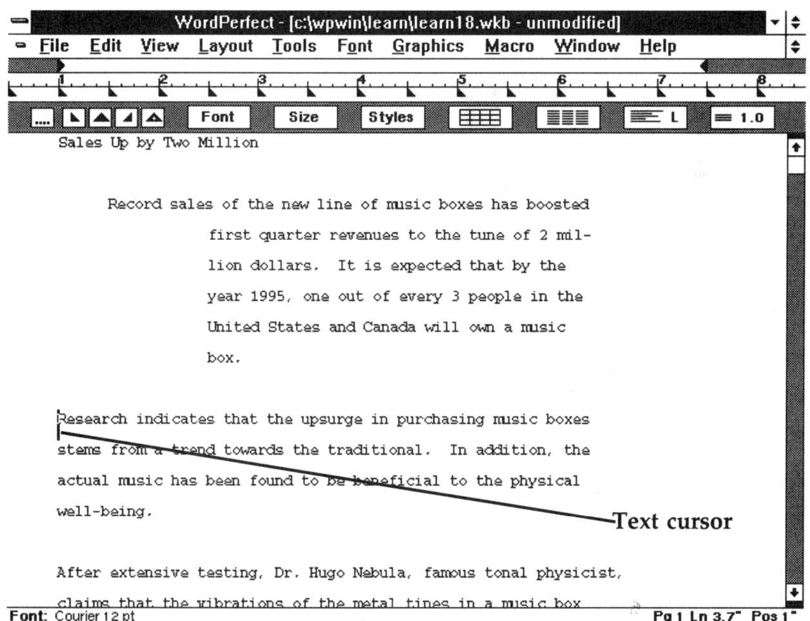

Figure 8-16. *Insert the text cursor at the start of the third paragraph.*

To insert a page break at the text cursor, select the *Page Break* command from the *Page* fly-out menu in the **Layout** menu (Figure 8-17).

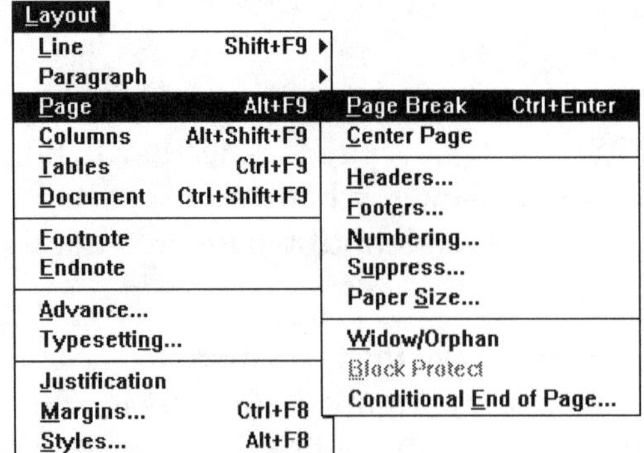

Figure 8-17. This command creates a page break in a WordPerfect document at the text cursor's position.

A page break is indicated in a document by two horizontal lines running across the page as shown in Figure 8-18.

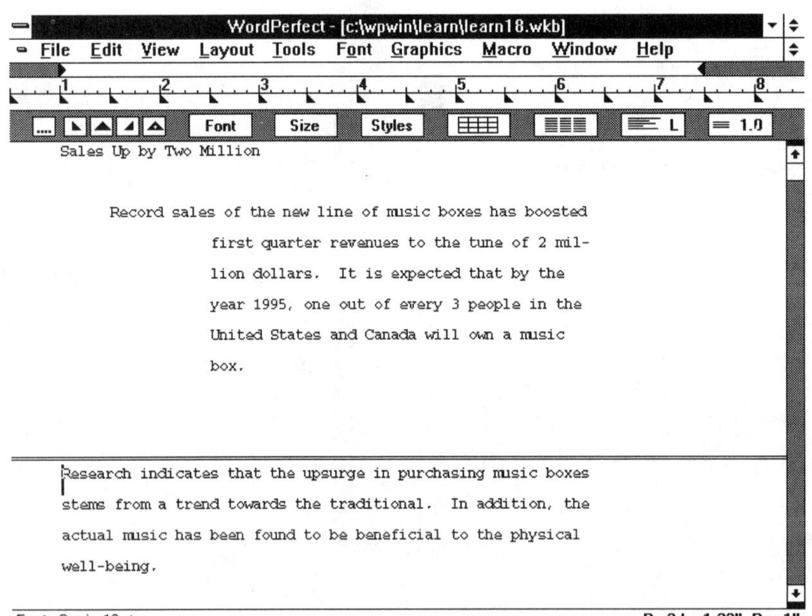

Figure 8-18. The two horizontal lines on this page indicate the point where one page ends, and another page starts.

The keyboard shortcut for creating a page break is to hold down the Ctrl key, and press the Enter key. This has exactly the same effect as selecting the command of Figure 8-17.

Headers and footers

Headers and footers are the text that is repeated across the top (header) or bottom (footer) of pages in a document. In this book, for example, there is a header on all left-hand pages that reads ***WordPerfect for Windows By Example***. On the right pages, the header changes with each chapter—in this chapter, it reads ***Chapter 8 — Layout***. The footer in this book, consists of the current page number.

Header

Sales Up by Two Million

Record sales of the new line of music boxes has booste first quarter revenues to the tune of 2 million dollars. is expected that by the year 1995, one out of every 3 people in the United States and Canada will own a mu box.

Research indicates that the upsurge in purchasing musi boxes stems from a trend towards the traditional. In addition, the actual music has been found to be beneficial to the physical well-being.

After extensive testing, Dr. Hugo Nebula, famous tonal physicist, claims that the vibrations of the metal tines a music boxintone a series of sympathetic notes within the lumbar region, resulting in a harmonious healing of the emotional psyche.

Even reports of UFO sightings are now being attributed the playing of certain melodies on a music box. When flying saucers were seen hovering last September over a cornfield in Iowa, a music box was blamed.

On the drawing boards are music box watches, dash board models for cars, waterproof boxes for showers, ultra-light boxes for backpackers, and even a computerized music box that lets you program your owr tune.

Music boxes with figurines depicting the following occupational motifs will be available in November:

Footer

Figure 8-19. *A header is information repeated at the top of all, or most pages, in a document, and a footer is information repeated at the bottom.*

As with most WordPerfect features, a header or footer becomes active from the point in the document where the text cursor is located when the command is entered. For a header or footer to appear on all pages in a document, the text cursor must be placed at the very beginning of the document when the command is given.

If the text cursor is positioned within the text of a page, the header or footer defined will only become active from the following page (except for the conditions of the next paragraph).

If the option *Auto Code Placement*, from the *Preferences/Environment* command from the **File** menu is enabled (see Chapter 10, **Preferences - (1)**), you can insert the text cursor anywhere in a page, and WordPerfect will automatically move the header or footer reference to the top of the page.

Creating a header

In this example, insert the text cursor before the very first character in the document (Figure 8-20).

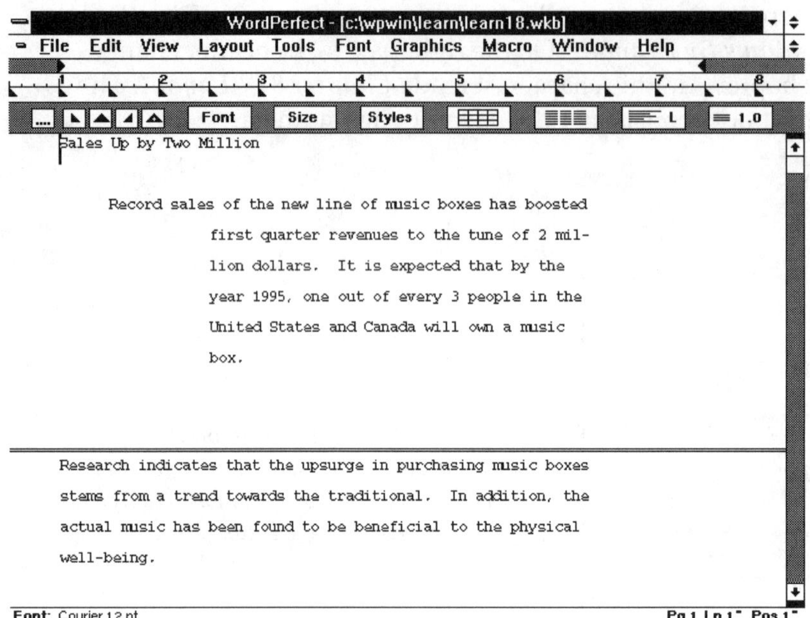

Figure 8-20. *Before you define a header or footer, you should move the text cursor to the beginning of the page from where you first want the header or footer to appear. In this case it is the start of the document.*

To define a header starting from this page, select the *Headers* command from the *Page* fly-out menu in the **Layout** menu as shown in Figure 8-21.

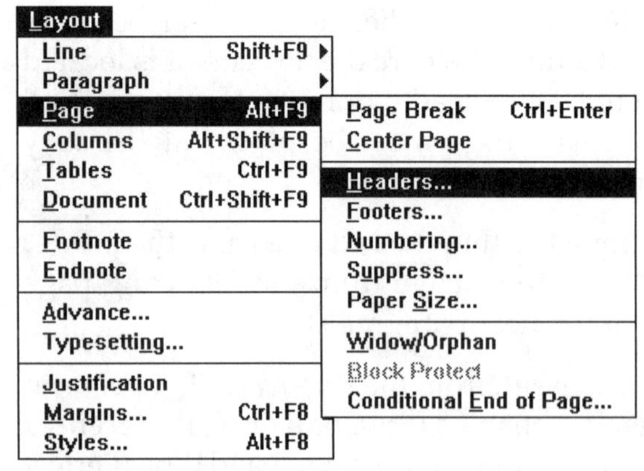

Figure 8-21. *The Page/Headers command from the **Layout** menu is used to define a repeating header for a document.*

The *Headers* dialog box of Figure 8-22 will then appear.

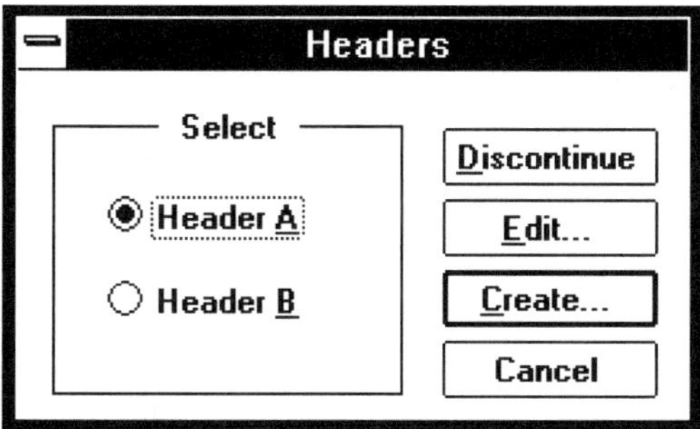

Figure 8-22. *The Headers dialog box.*

Your first option in this dialog box is under the *Select* heading. Here, there are two choices—*Header A*, and *Header B*.

If you are using the same header on both pages of a document, and in the same position, only the *Header A* option would be selected, as only one piece of header information is required. However, if a header is required with different text appearing on the right and left-hand sides of the page, or different headers on the even and odd pages of a document, then two separate headers would need to be created.

For example, if the name of a book is to be displayed on the left-hand side of even pages and the chapter title displayed on the right-hand side of odd pages (as for this book), two separate headers would be needed: *Header A* and *Header B*.

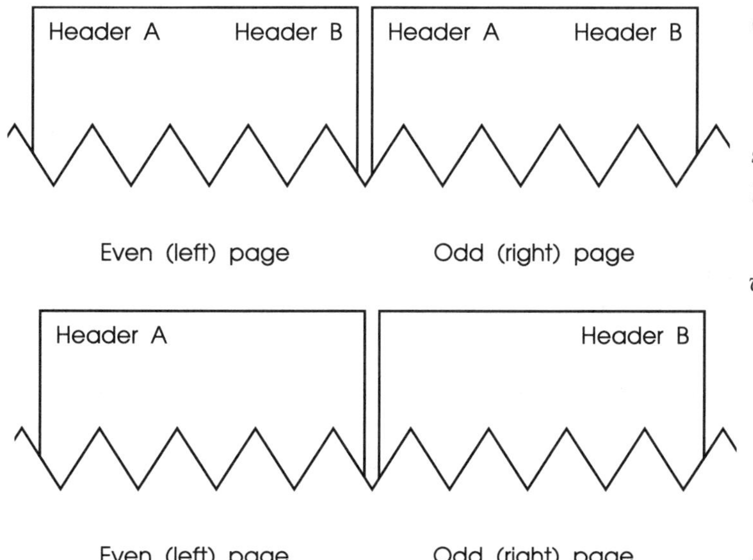

(a)

Figure 8-23. *This diagram shows even (left) and odd (right) pages. It provides two examples of header options. Option (a) shows two headers per page—with the same details for odd and even pages. Option (b) shows different headers for odd and even pages (which is the same example as this book). The same principle applies for footers.*

(b)

You can have a maximum of two headers and two footers on each page. You can, however, define new headers and footers on other pages. The new header (footer) definition continues until another new header (footer) is defined. For example, you can create a header on pages one to ten of a document, saying "Chapter 1" and then define a new header saying "Chapter 2", from pages eleven to twenty.

To create a header that will appear on all pages, click on the *Create* button in the *Headers* dialog box of Figure 8-22. The *Header A* editing screen of Figure 8-24 will appear.

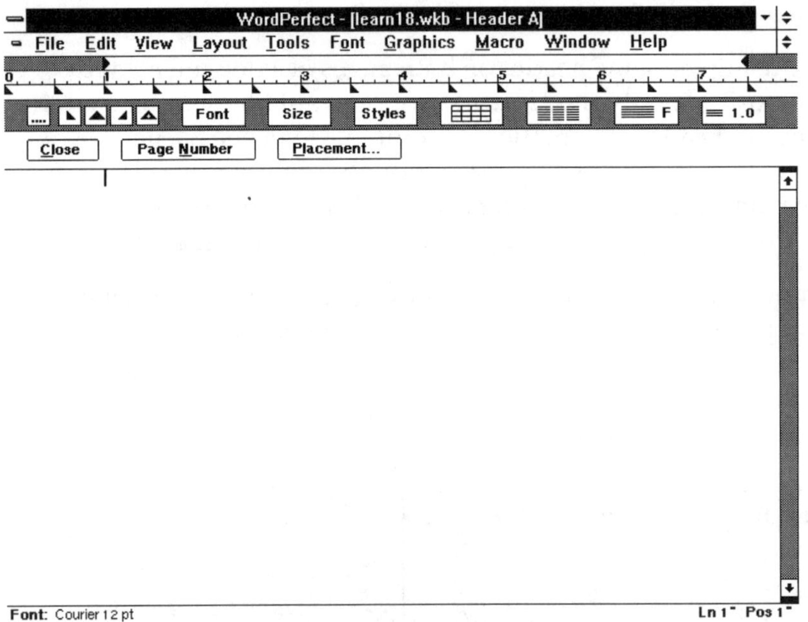

Figure 8-24. *When the Create button is selected from the Headers dialog box, the editing screen disappears and the Header A editing screen appears.*

In the *Header A* editing screen, enter the heading that is to appear at the top of each page in this document. In this case, enter "This is a sample header." (Figure 8-25). A maximum of one page of text can be defined for a single header or footer.

The default setting for headers (and footers) allows this text to appear on all pages. Shortly, you will see how to create headers for even or odd pages, and how to turn headers (footers) off on one or multiple pages.

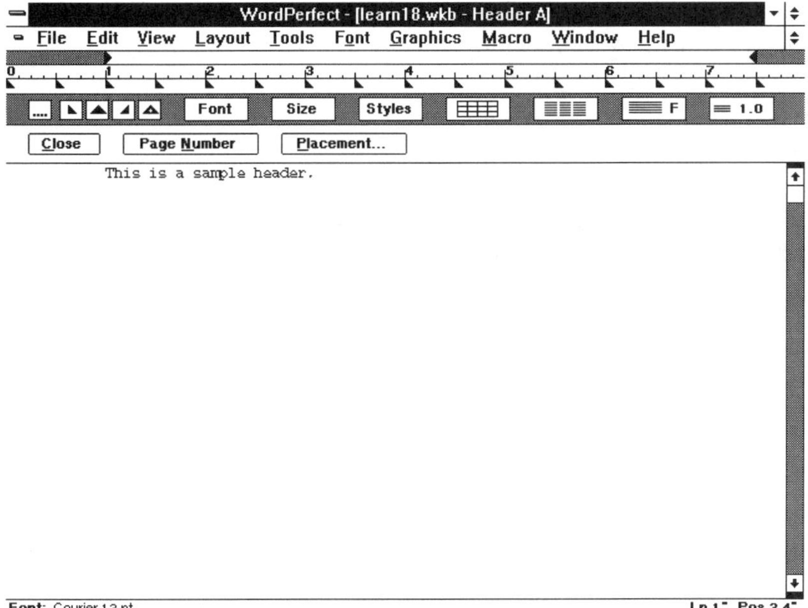

Figure 8-25. Enter "This is a sample header." in the Header editing screen.

The text for the header has now been defined.

Formatting a header

The header, as defined in Figure 8-25, will appear on all pages exactly as it is in this figure. Therefore, you are free to apply any formatting to this text that you wish to—as if this text was on the editing screen. In Figure 8-26, the text that was entered in Figure 8-25 was selected and the *Bold* command from the **Font** menu applied.

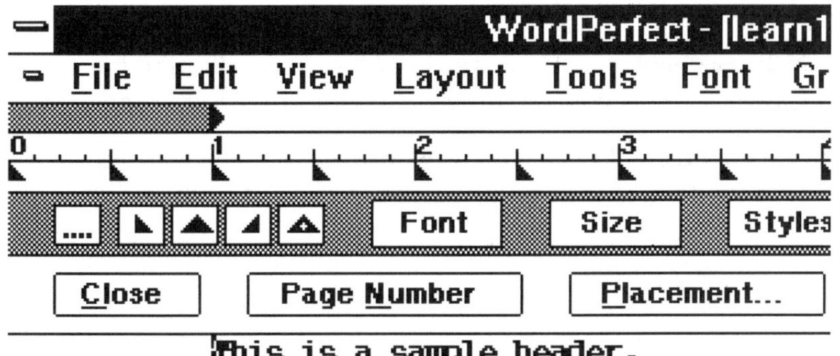

Figure 8-26. Any formatting applied while creating the header, will stay with the header when it appears on the page. Here, the text has been bolded.

To see how this header appears on the page, the first step is to select the *Close* button (Figures 8-25 or 8-26).

Viewing headers

On returning to the editing screen, you will initially see no difference, as headers and footers do not appear on this screen. The only way to see a header or footer is to select the *Print Preview* command from the **File** menu (Figure 8-27). (The *Reveal Codes* screen, however, will display the header and footer, as well as the codes.)

Figure 8-27. *The Print Preview command, from the* ***File*** *menu, is the only way that a header or footer can be seen in WYSIWYG format.*

Figure 8-28 illustrates the header on the *Print Preview* screen.

You may wish to check the **Printing** chapter, in particular the reference to *Print Preview,* if you are unfamiliar with this command.

All pages in this document now have the same header as shown in Figure 8-28. To return back to the editing screen from the *Print Preview* screen, select the *Close* command from the **File** menu.

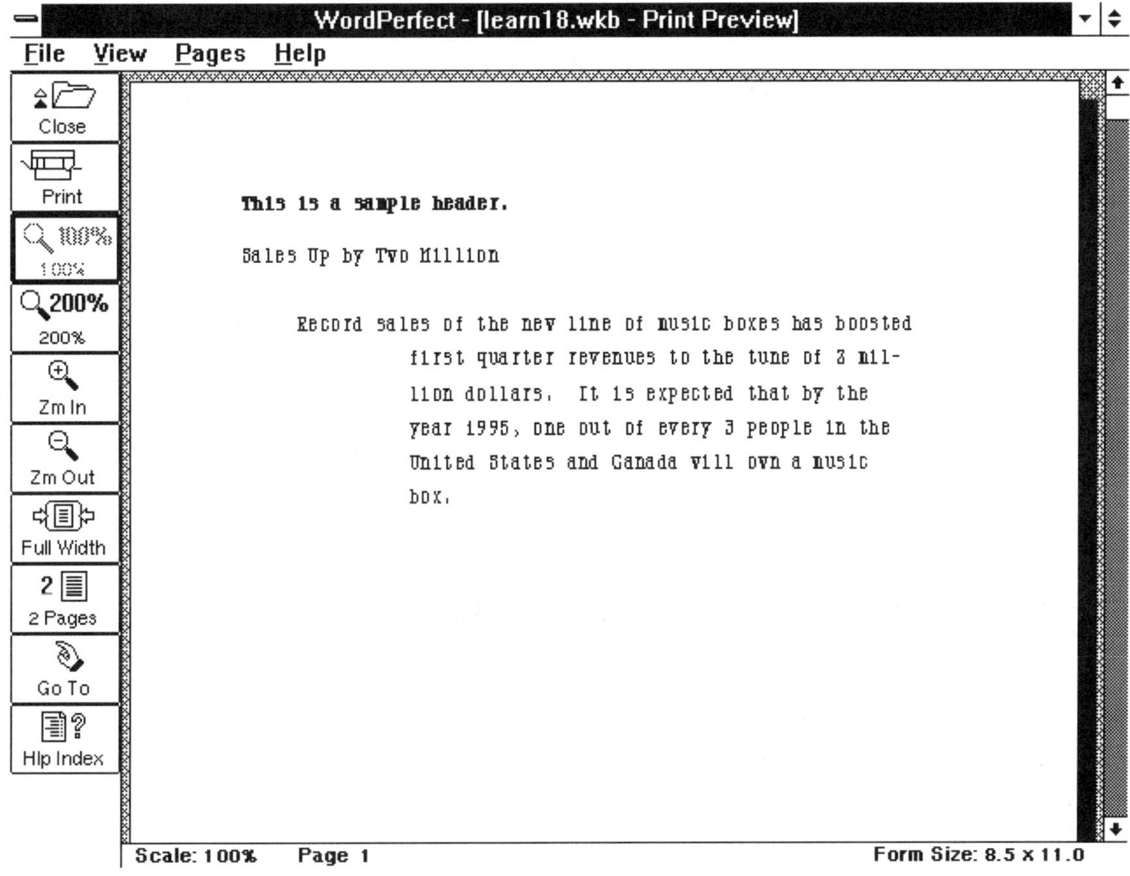

Figure 8-28. *The header, as defined in Figures 8-25 and 8-26, appears on the Print Preview screen.*

Creating, formatting, and viewing a footer

A footer is created in the same way as a header, replacing the dialog box of the *Page/Headers* command with the dialog box of the *Page/ Footers* command. Other than this difference (and the fact that headers appear at the top and footers at the bottom of a page), footers are created, edited and manipulated in exactly the same way as headers.

Throughout the rest of this chapter, any reference to options and commands relating to headers, will also apply to footers.

Editing a header

A header can be edited by selecting the *Page/Headers* command from the **Layout** menu once again. However, when the *Headers* dialog box of Figure 8-22 appears, select the *Edit* button, rather then the *Create* button. The *Header A* editing screen will appear as with the *Create* command. The current header will be displayed on this screen to be edited, if required.

The text cursor does not need to be at the start of a document to edit a header—it can be anywhere in the document.

Select the *Page/Headers* command from the **Layout** menu now, and select the *Edit* button from the dialog box that appears (Figure 8-22). The *Header A* editing screen will appear as shown in Figure 8-29.

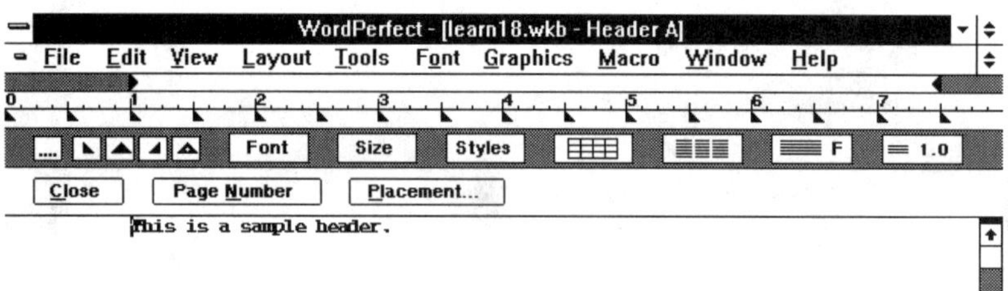

***Figure 8-29.** On selecting the Edit button from the Headers dialog box, the current header appears, ready to be edited.*

Edit the header to read "This is a header." rather than "This is a sample header."; then click on the *Close* button to return to the document. On selecting the *Print Preview* command again, the header will appear as shown in Figure 8-30.

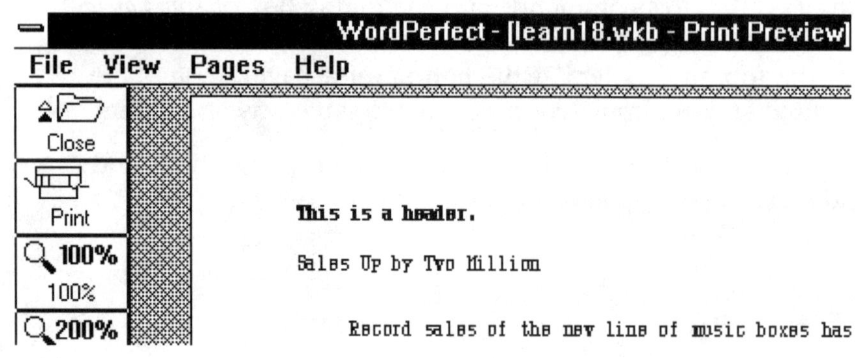

***Figure 8-30.** The Print Preview screen shows how the new edited header will appear for all following pages.*

Creating alternating headers

Creating a different header for odd and even (right and left) pages in a document can be achieved in two steps. Create the header (say, *Header A*) for the odd pages, then do the same (but as *Header B*) for the even ones.

Selecting the *Placement* button from the *Header A* editing screen (Figure 8-29) invokes the *Placement* dialog box (Figure 8-31). This dialog box, through the *Place On* options, allows you to choose on which pages the header is placed.

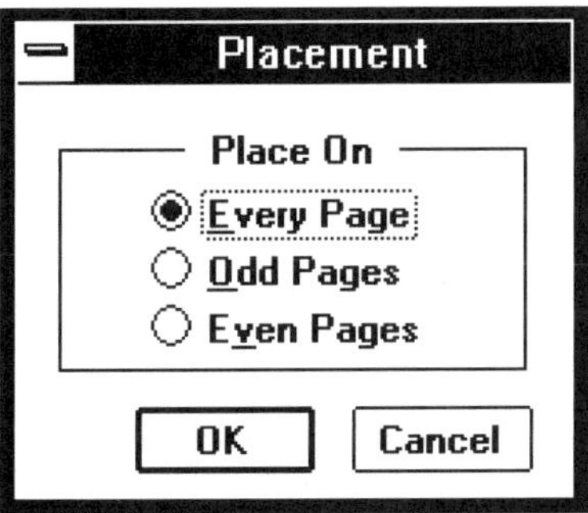

Figure 8-31. *When creating or editing a header, select the Placement button to access the Place On options for this header. Then choose the pages on which the header (or footer) is to appear.*

The *Every Page* option forces the header to appear on all pages in the document.

Odd Pages forces the header to appear on all pages with an odd page number (always right-hand pages as for this book).

Even Pages forces the header to appear on all pages with an even page number (left-hand pages as for this book).

For the example just completed, you used the *Header A* option from the Figure 8-22 dialog box. As the *Every Page* option in Figure 8-31 is selected, by default, this header will appear on all pages. If you selected *Odd Pages* from the *Place On* options (Figure 8-31), this header would only appear on odd numbered pages. You could then define a *Header B*, and make it appear only on *Even Pages*. This is how the alternating headers used in this book could have been achieved.

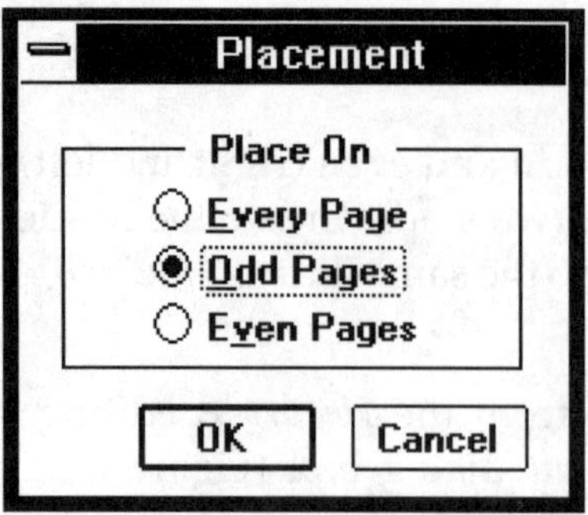

Figure 8-32. *To create a header designed purely for odd pages, select the Odd Pages option from the Placement dialog box.*

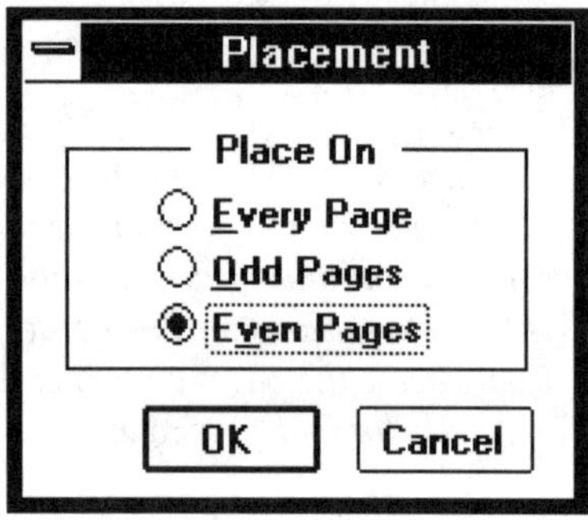

Figure 8-33. *Select the Even Pages option from the Placement dialog box to create a header for even pages.*

Positioning a header

A header appears on a page at a vertical position defined by the current margins. If, for example, the current margins are one inch top and bottom, the header will appear one inch below the top of the page. The footer will be one inch up from the bottom of the page.

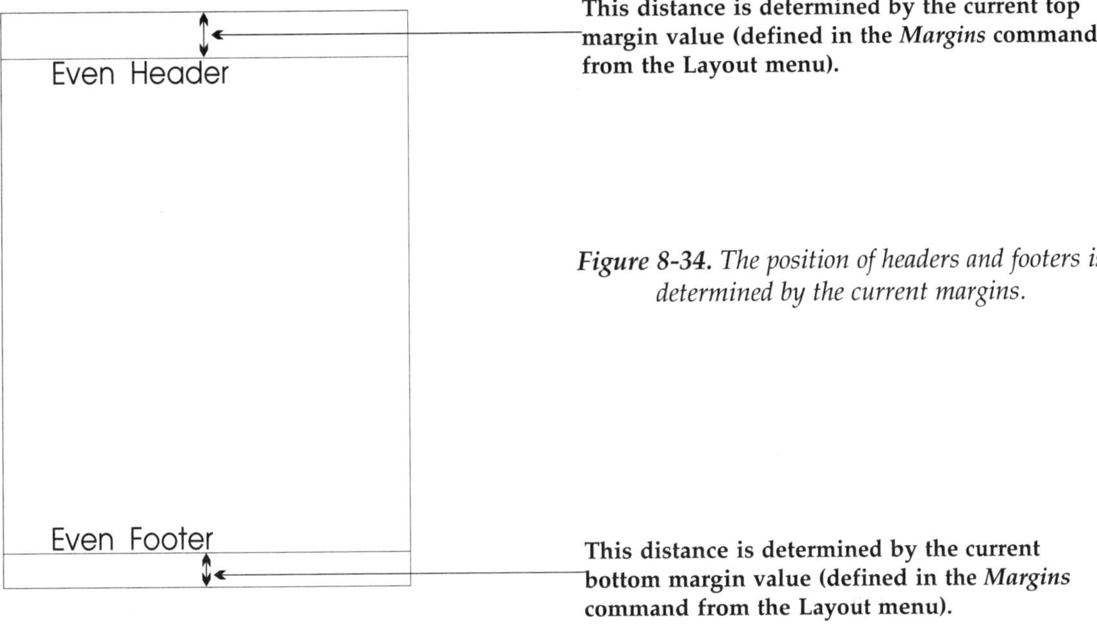

Figure 8-34. The position of headers and footers is determined by the current margins.

To move the header or footer up or down, you must alter the margin on the page, using the *Margins* command from the **Layout** menu (see Chapter 7, **Margins and Columns**).

Discontinuing a header

To discontinue a header for the rest of the document (Figure 8-35), you first position the text cursor at the start of the page where the header will stop, then select the *Headers* command from the *Page* fly-out menu in the **Layout** menu.

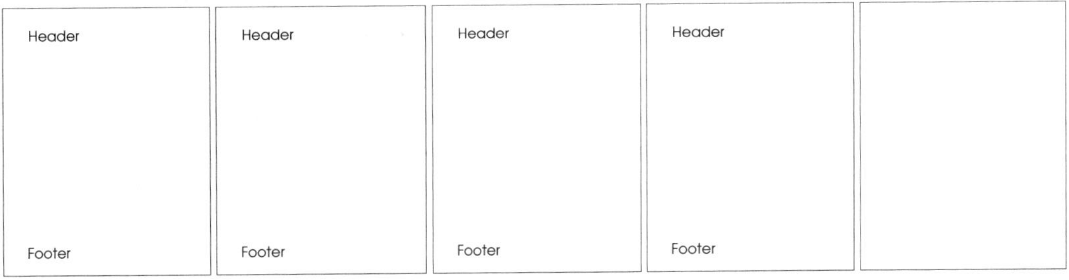

Figure 8-35. *An example of a discontinued header—after page 4, the header no longer appears.*

When the *Headers* dialog box (Figure 8-22) appears, select the header you would like to discontinue, using the *Select* option, then click on the *Discontinue* button. The header will no longer appear on any pages in the document, past the current page.

Removing a header from one page only

Header or footers can be removed from individual pages without discontinuing their use in the document. To achieve this effect, move to the page on which the header or footer should not appear and select the *Suppress* command from the *Page* fly-out menu in the **Layout** menu.

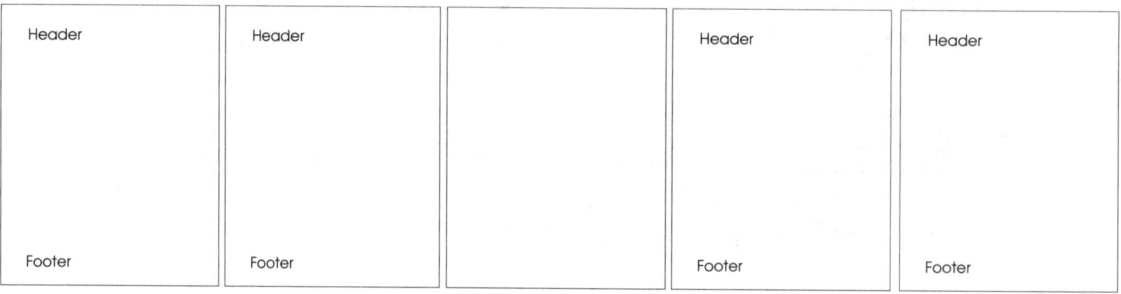

Figure 8-36. *In this example, page three does not use a header or footer, while all other pages in the document do. This effect can be achieved by selecting the Page/Suppress command in the* ***Layout*** *menu.*

In the currently opened document (***learn18.wkb***), position the mouse cursor at the beginning of the second page (this will be just after the double horizontal line in page two—Figure 8-37).

Now select the *Page/Suppress* command from the **Layout** menu (Figure 8-38).

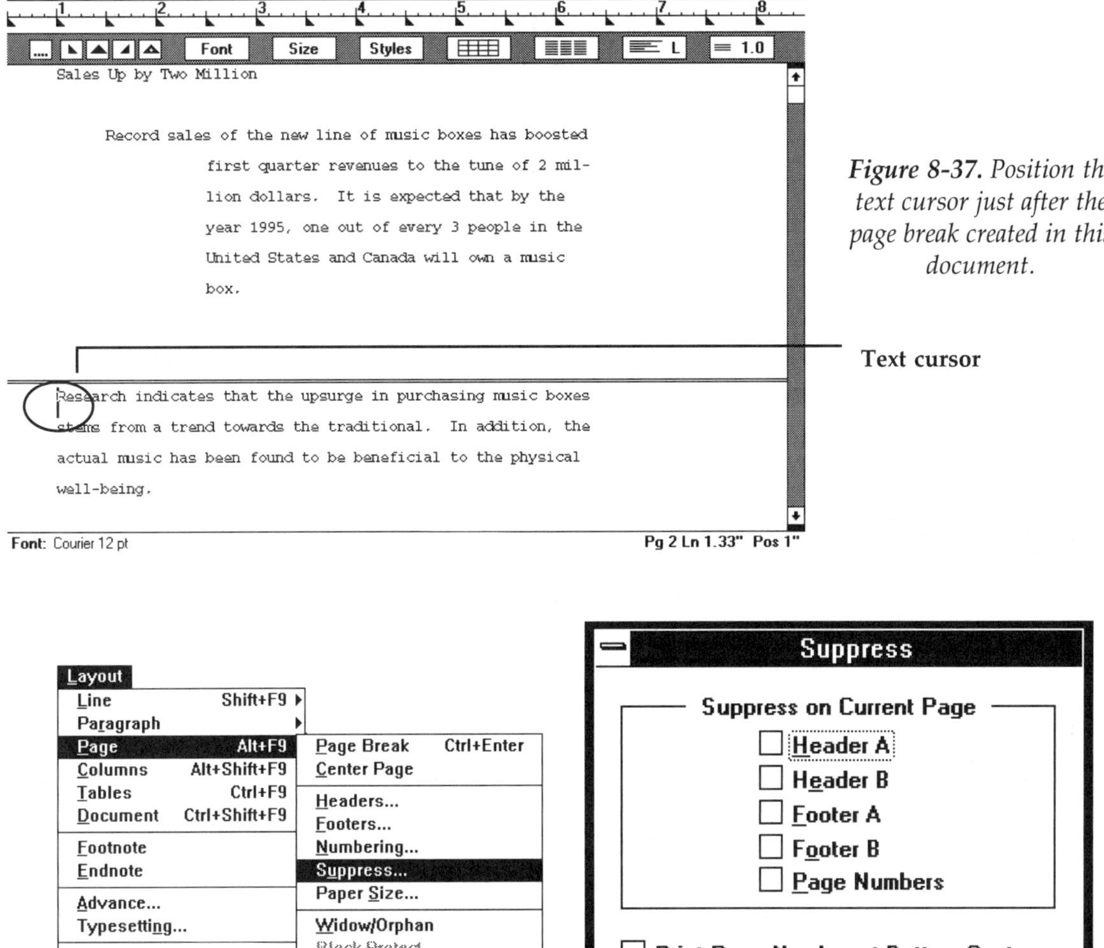

Figure 8-37. *Position the text cursor just after the page break created in this document.*

Figure 8-38. *The Page/Suppress command from the* ***Layout*** *menu can stop a header or footer from appearing on a particular page. On the right is the Suppress dialog box.*

When the *Suppress* dialog box appears, select the option you would like to suppress on this page. In this case, you only have *Header A*, but you can see how any header or footer you have defined can be suppressed. Select the *Header A* check box, and click on **OK**.

When the *Print Preview* command is used to view the document, you will notice that every page except page two displays the header. (You may wish to use the *Previous Page* and *Next Page* commands in the **Pages** menu to check this.)

Deleting a header

The best way to fully delete a header or footer reference in a document is to delete the code from the document. Turn on the *Reveal Codes* command, from the **View** menu. Select this command now and locate the *Header* code in the text; it will appear at the top of page 1 (Figure 8-39). Use the mouse to position the cursor on the code and press the Delete key.

```
[Ln Height:0.3"][Hyph On][Header A:Every page;[Bold On]This is a header.[Bold
Off]]Sales Up by Two Million[HRt]
[HRt]
[Indent][Dbl Indent][Indent][Mar Rel][Mar Rel]Record sales of the new line of
music boxes has boosted[SRt]
first quarter revenues to the tune of 2 mil-
lion dollars.  It is expect-ed that by the year[SRt]
1995, one out of every 3 people in the United[SRt]
States and Canada will own a music box.[HRt]
[HRt]
[HPg]
[Suppress:HA]Research indicates that the upsurge in purchasing music boxes[SRt
]
stems from a trend towards the traditional.  In addition, the[SRt]
actual music has been found to be beneficial to the physical[SRt]
Font: Courier 12 pt                                          Pg 1 Ln 1.33" Pos 1"
```

Figure 8-39. The header code appears in this illustration on the top line "[Header A:Every Page;[Bold On]This is a header[Bold Off]]".

Header page numbering

Automatic page numbering can be incorporated quite easily into a header or footer. Just above where the text is entered in the *Header* editing screen is a *Page Number* button (Figure 8-40).

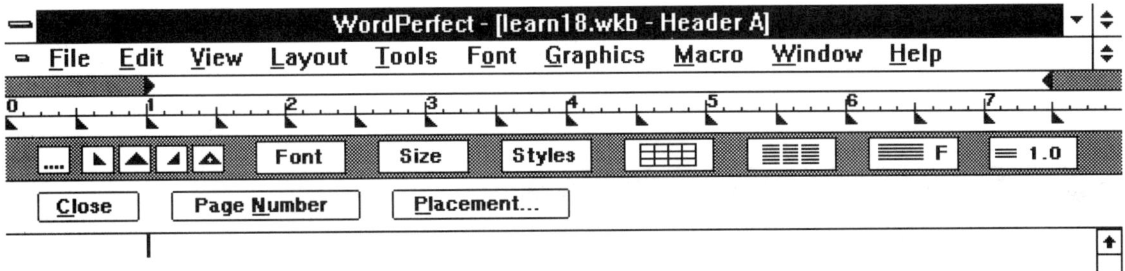

Figure 8-40. *The Page Number button appears to the right of the Close button in the Header editing screen.*

Click on this button to insert the characters "^B" into the header. This symbol indicates that the page number will be placed in the header, at the position where this symbol appears.

You are free to type in whatever text you wish around the page number symbol. For example, you may enter "Page " before you click on the *Page Number* button, so that the header will read Page 1, Page 2, Page 3, etc.

To include page numbering in the document currently open, return to the editing screen, and select the *Page/Headers* command from the **Layout** menu. Select the *Edit* button from the *Headers* dialog box. You will see a screen very similar to that of Figure 8-29. Just before the string "This is a header.", type the word "Page", press the Spacebar once, and click on the *Page Number* button. Then press the period, and the Spacebar again. Your screen will now look like Figure 8-41.

If you have deleted your header by following the actions of Figure 8-39, instead of selecting *Edit*, as suggested above, select *Create* to re-create the header as shown in Figure 8-41.

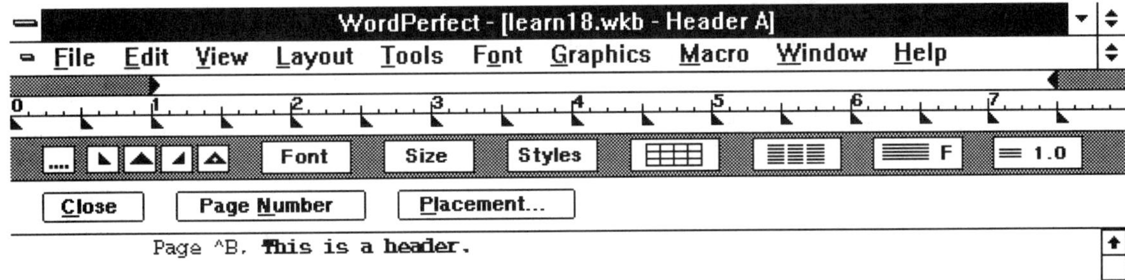

Figure 8-41. *This header will appear back on the page including the current page number.*

Figure 8-42 shows a sample page, viewed through the *Print Preview* command.

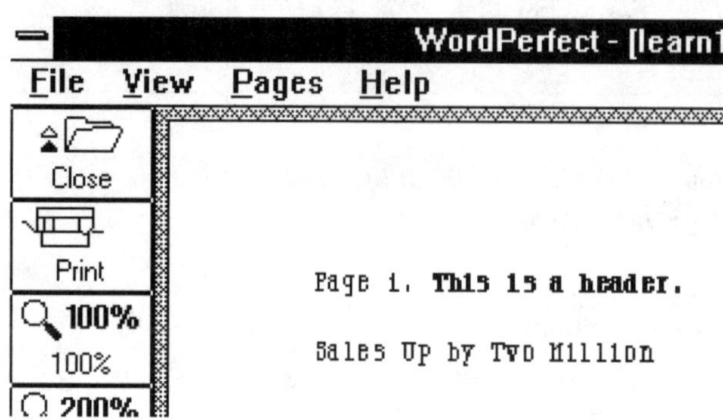

Figure 8-42. *The header now includes the current page number, as will all pages that use the header. This page number is constantly updated by WordPerfect as pages are added or deleted.*

Page numbering

Automatic page numbering can be achieved not only with the *Page/ Headers* or *Page/Footers* commands, but also through the *Numbering* command from the *Page* fly-out menu in the **Layout** menu (Figure 8-43). Select this command now.

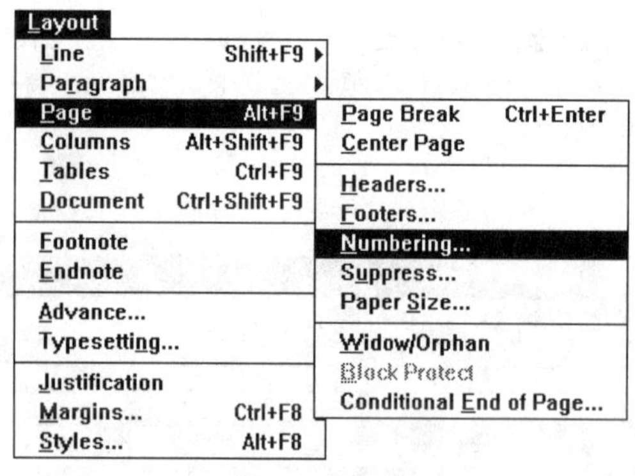

Figure 8-43. *The Page/Numbering command from the* ***Layout*** *menu automatically adds page numbers to a document, in almost any position you choose.*

Figure 8-44 illustrates the *Page Numbering* dialog box.

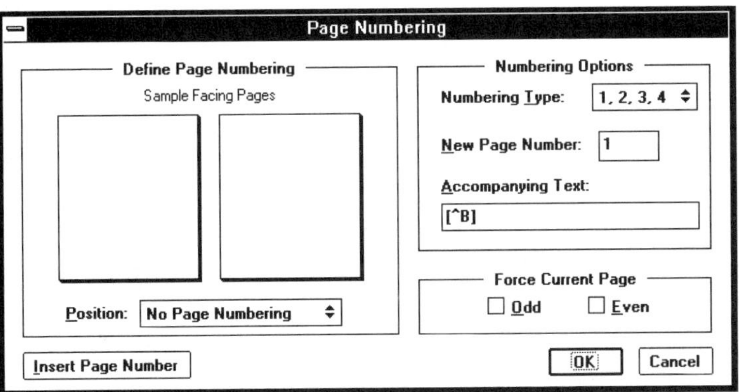

Figure 8-44. *The Page Numbering dialog box.*

The *Page Numbering* dialog box provides many options as to how and where a page number can be inserted on document pages.

Under the heading *Sample Facing Pages* are two pages—much like the two pages used as examples earlier in this document to define headers and footers (Figure 8-23)—representing an odd and an even page.

Below the *Sample Facing Pages* is a pop-up list box with the name *Position*. This option determines where page numbers are placed on a page. In Figure 8-44, this currently reads *No Page Numbering*. However, you may wish to hold the mouse button down on this pop-up list, and select one of the many options within this list.

After a selection is made, sample page numbers will appear on the *Sample Facing Pages* (Figure 8-45).

Figure 8-45. *In this example, Alternating Bottom has been selected for the page number Position. Sample Facing Pages show where Alternating Bottom page numbers will appear on the pages of the document.*

Under the *Numbering Options* heading are three choices.

The first, *Numbering Type,* determines how page numbers will appear. The options are: Arabic numerals (1,2,3,4, etc.), lower case Roman numerals (i,ii,iii,iv, etc.), and upper case Roman numerals (I,II,III,IV, etc.).

The second choice, *New Page Number,* reflects the current page number of the page in which the cursor is located. In addition, changing the value in this text box allows you to change the actual page numbering sequence, from this page onwards. In Figure 8-44, this value reads "1". If it was changed to 45, for example, the page number would appear as 45, the next page number as 46, and so on.

The third, *Accompanying Text,* allows you to add some text to either side of the page number. In Figure 8-46, the word "Page" has been added before the page number code in the *Accompanying Text* text box. In the *Sample Facing Pages* section, once *Position* is clicked on again, the effect this change has on the page number display can be seen.

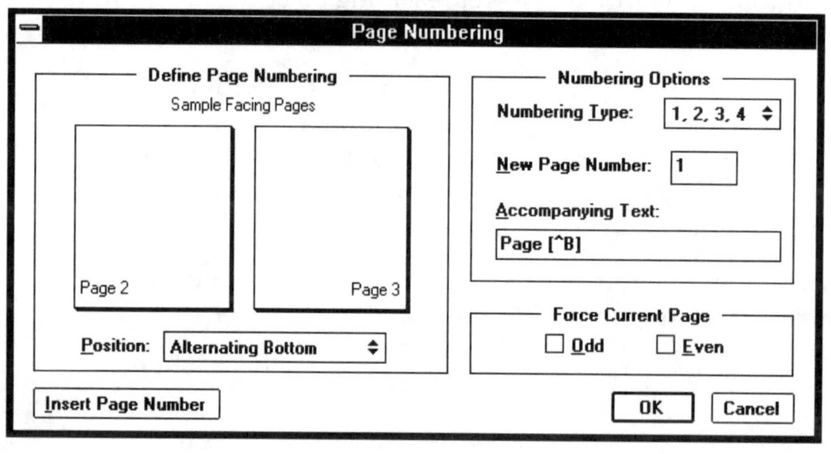

Figure 8-46. *Note the text inserted in the Accompanying Text text box. This is reflected in the Sample Facing Pages to the left.*

In the *Force Current Page* section, you can force the current page to be *Odd* or *Even*. In most cases, this is decided automatically by the way pages fall but you may have a particular reason for wanting a particular page to be numbered odd or even.

The *Insert Page Number* option will insert the current page number into the text, at the position of the text cursor. The page number is inserted as a code and will be updated if the current page number ever changes.

As with headers and footers, the only way to see how page numbers will appear in a document is to use the *Print Preview* command (Figure 8-47).

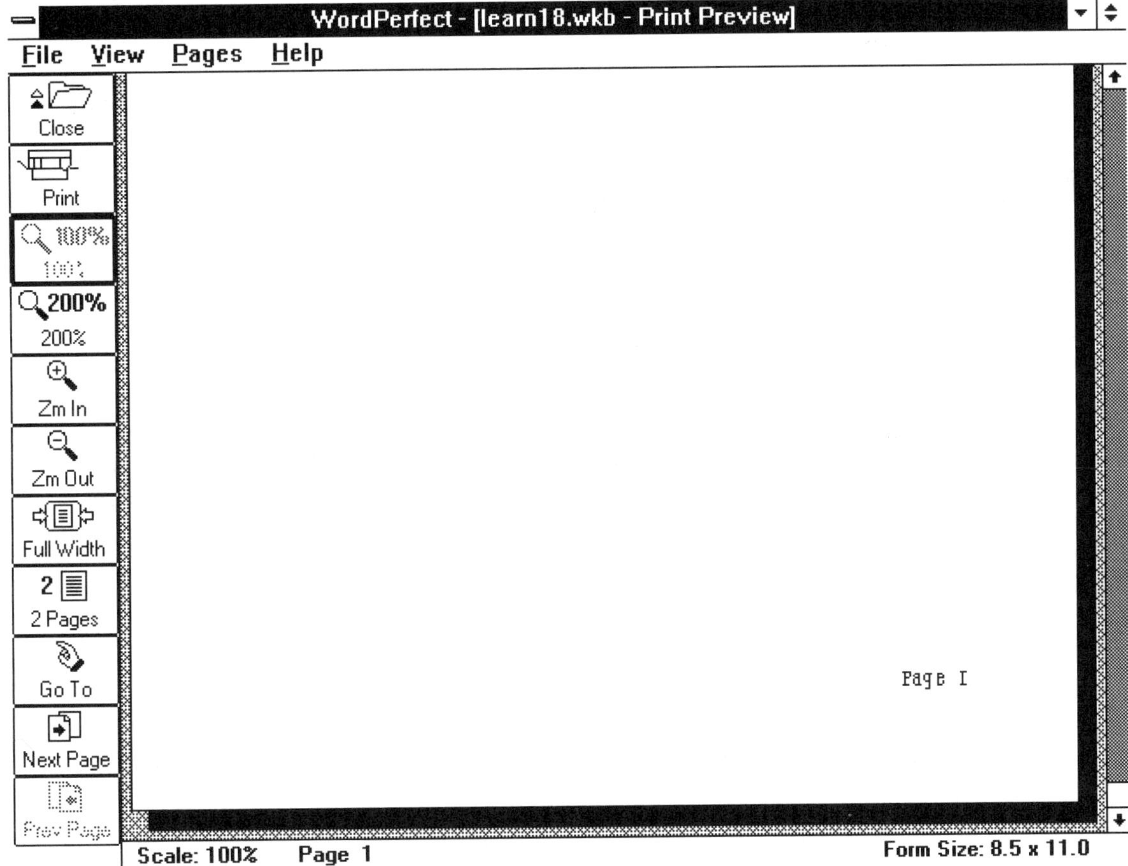

Figure 8-47. *The bottom of Page 1 indicates an automatically inserted page number, using the settings selected in the Figure 8-46 dialog box.*

Setting paper size

The paper size for a document can be set in two different ways depending on whether a Windows or WordPerfect printer driver has been selected. (Selecting a printer driver is covered in Chapter 9, **Printing**.)

Paper size and the Windows printer driver

When using a Windows printer driver, the paper size is set using the Windows *Control Panel.* More specifically, the *Setup* dialog box for a Windows printer driver (Figure 8-48) can be accessed when a Windows printer driver is selected within WordPerfect (see once again the **Printing** chapter).

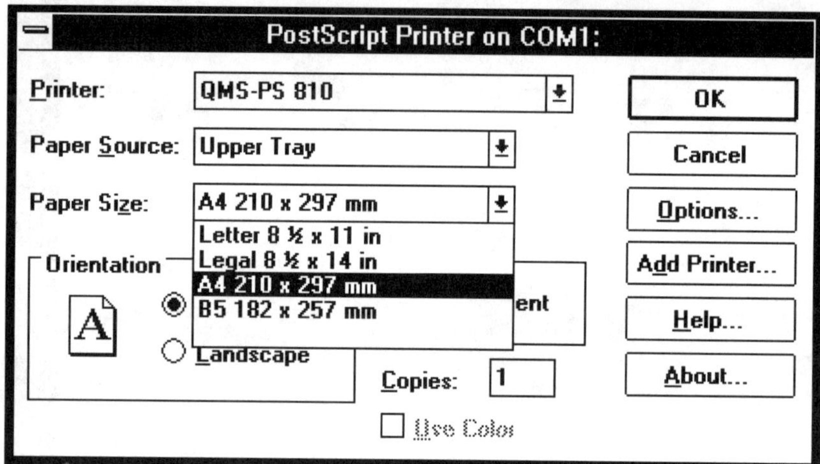

***Figure 8-48.** Although this dialog box will look a little different depending on the actual printer you have selected (PostScript, HP LaserJet, etc.), all printer setup dialog boxes will have a paper size option, where different paper sizes can be selected.*

The *Printer Setup* dialog box for any Windows printer driver also lets you set the page orientation.

Paper size and the WordPerfect printer driver

Before you select a page size when using a WordPerfect printer driver, you should make sure that you insert the text cursor at the very start of the document, so that the entire document uses this particular page size.

You have many more options about paper size and orientation when specifying a WordPerfect printer driver. To set the paper size, in this case, you must select the *Paper Size* command from the *Page* fly-out menu in the **Layout** menu (Figure 8-49).

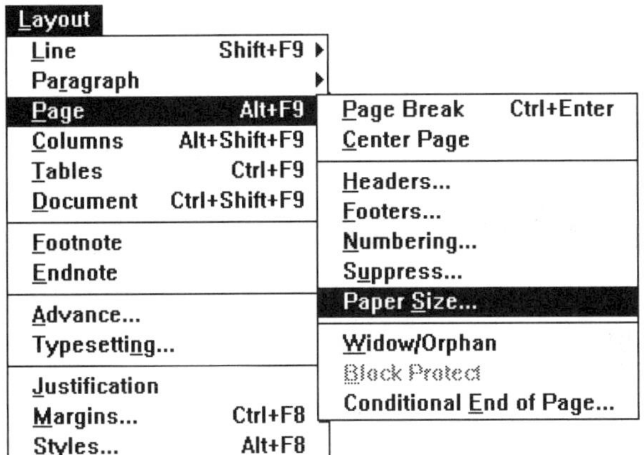

Figure 8-49. When using a WordPerfect printer driver, the Page/Paper Size command can be used to select the desired paper size.

Once again, depending on the actual WordPerfect printer driver selected, your choices may be a little varied. However, the *Paper Size* dialog box will look much like Figure 8-50.

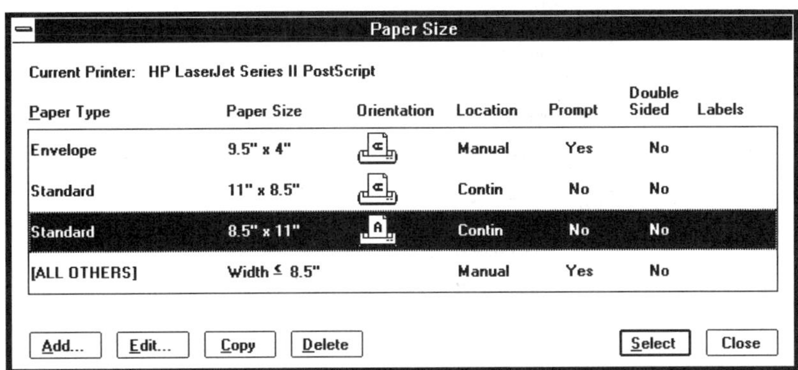

Figure 8-50. The Paper Size dialog box.

In this dialog box, you can make a selection from the options listed. The basic forms for your printer will be listed here, along with several options for those forms.

For example, in Figure 8-50, there are three main options—the first is an *Envelope* option, the second a *Portrait* Letter page, and the third a *Landscape* Letter page. This information can be gleaned by looking at the entries below the various headings—*Paper Type* (the name of the form), *Paper Size* (the actual size of the page), *Orientation* (either portrait (vertical), or landscape (horizontal)), *Location* (*Contin* for a paper tray or tractor feed, *Manual* for hand feed), *Prompt* (*Yes* for hand feed, *No* for paper tray or tractor feed), *Double Sided* (*Yes*, or *No*), and whether *Labels* are being used.

If none of the standard forms matches the desired size, click on the *Add* button to add a form to this list. Figure 8-51 illustrates the *Add Paper Size* dialog box.

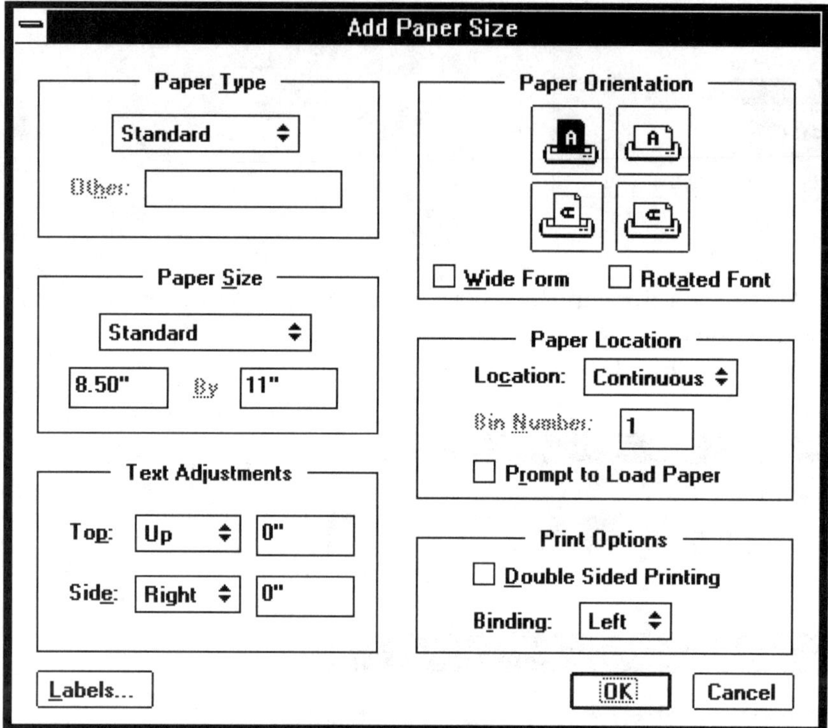

Figure 8-51. *The Add Paper Size dialog box.*

The *Paper Type* pop-up list box specifies what type of paper is being used: *Standard, Envelope, Transparency, Bond,* etc.

The *Paper Size* pop-up list box specifies the size of paper you wish to use, and reflects the paper size dimensions just below this list.

Text Adjustments allows you to move the page position around on the printed page. This feature should only be used if, after you print, you feel that the margins in WordPerfect are not correctly reflected on the printed page. You can move the page *Up, Down, Left* or *Right* any distance required to correct this discrepancy.

The *Paper Orientation* options decide whether the page is portrait (vertical) or landscape (horizontal). Most laser printers can print horizontal fonts but some dot matrix printers cannot. In this case, if you need to print a landscape page, you may be able to select *Wide Form*, which allows the equivalent of landscape printing to be achieved.

The *Paper Location* option determines how the paper is loaded into the printer. The setting here may be *Continuous* (for tractor feed, or a printer with one bin), *Manual* (for manual feed), or *Bin* (and bin number for multi-bin printers). Check the *Prompt* check box if you wish to be prompted to load paper when using a manually fed form.

Print Options let you specify double-sided printing, if your printer is capable of duplex printing—not many printers possess this feature. You can also specify a binding edge (either *Left*, or *Top*).

A *Labels* button at the bottom left of this dialog box lets you customize a label form.

Once you have set your options here, click on **OK** to add this form to the *Paper Size* dialog box (Figure 8-50). In Figure 8-52, some options have been set to create an A4 portrait paper page, on a normal laser printer.

Figure 8-53 shows the results of adding the form of Figure 8-52 to the Figure 8-50 dialog box.

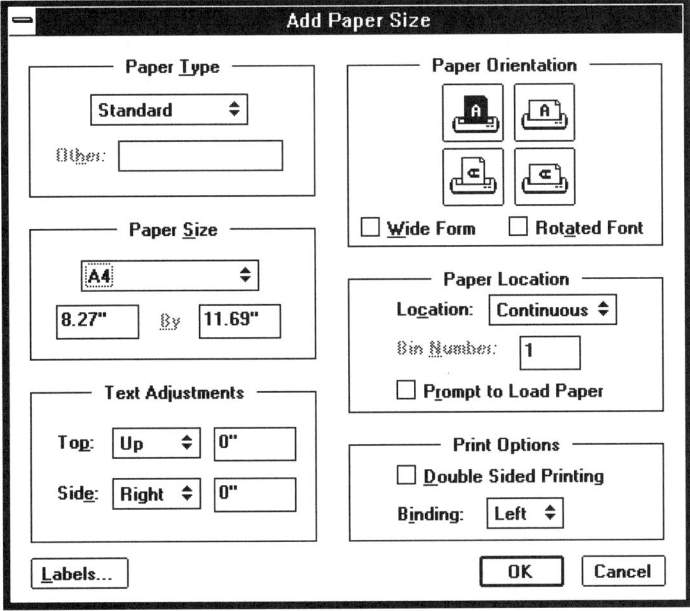

Figure 8-52. *This Add Paper Size dialog box is set up to add a standard A4 portrait paper size for a standard laser printer to the Paper Size dialog box of Figure 8-50.*

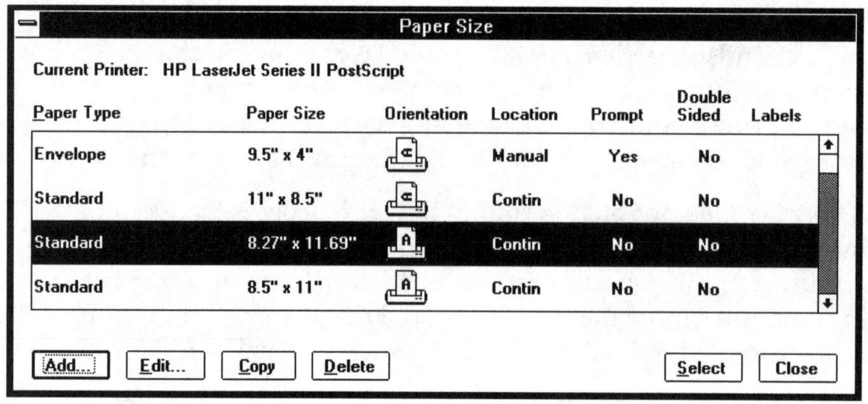

Figure 8-53. *The Paper Size created in Figure 8-52 now becomes one of the standard selections when the Page/ Paper size command from the* ***Layout*** *menu is selected.*

As this form has now been added to the list, it can be selected any time the *Page/Paper Size* command is activated from the **Layout** menu.

The other controls along the bottom of the dialog box of Figure 8-53 allow you to *Edit*, *Copy*, or *Delete* a selected form.

Once you select the form you wish to use, click on the *Select* button to assign this form size to the current document.

Document command

The fly-out menu from the *Document* command in the **Layout** menu lists commands that are relevant only to the currently active document window (Figure 8-54).

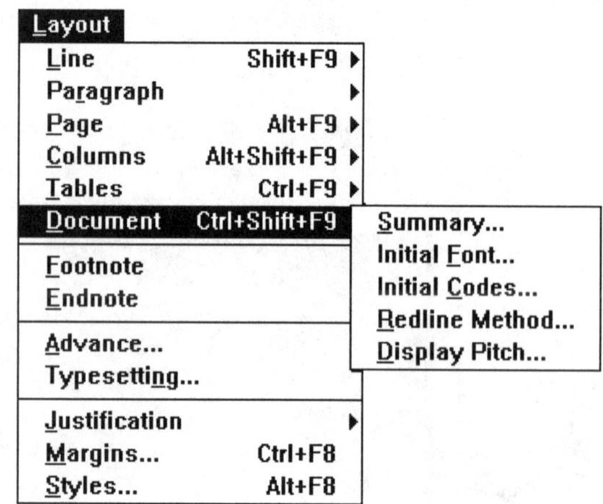

Figure 8-54. *The Document command fly-out menu from the* ***Layout*** *menu.*

Commands in the *Document* fly-out menu are similar to commands in the *Preferences* fly-out menu, in the **File** menu. These commands are discussed in Chapter 10, **Preferences - (1)** and Chapter 13, **Preferences - (2).** The commands in the *Preferences* fly-out menu, however, are concerned with setting defaults for all new documents; the *Document* fly-out menu sets defaults for only the currently active document window.

All settings made using the commands in the *Document* fly-out menu will override any settings made using the commands in the *Preferences* fly-out menu.

The *Document/Summary* command is discussed in the **Preferences - (2)** chapter, under the *Preferences/Document Summary* command.

The *Document/Initial Font* command allows you to set an initial font for your printer, affecting only the current document. This setting overrides any *Initial Font* settings made through the *Printer Setup* dialog box, as discussed in Chapter 9, **Printing**.

The *Document/Initial Codes* command is identical to the *Preferences/ Initial Codes* command, discussed in the **Preferences - (2)** chapter. The latter command sets codes for all new documents as well, while the former applies only to the active document.

The *Document/Redline Method* command will override the *Redline Method* preferences set using the *Preferences/Print* command, and discussed in the **Preferences - (1)** chapter.

The *Document/Display Pitch* command is the only unique command in this menu. It is used to alter the pitch (or width) of characters on screen. It will only affect text on screen when you are working in *Draft Mode*.

This mode is potentially useful in cases where there are a number of different fonts, columns and graphics in a document; in such a case *Draft Mode* may be a faster method of operation. This mode is selected through the *Draft Mode* command in the **View** menu.

Layout — Exercise

This training exercise is designed so that people of all levels of expertise with WordPerfect can use it to gain maximum benefit. In order to do this, the bare exercise is listed below this paragraph on just one page, with no hints. The following pages contain the steps needed to complete this exercise for those who need additional prompting.

Steps in brief

1. *Start a new WordPerfect file.*
2. *Open the learn18.wkb file from the learn sub-directory.*
3. *Change the line height for the entire document to 0.25 of an inch.*
4. *Indent the heading two tab stops.*
5. *Give paragraph two a Double Indent and a Hanging Indent.*
6. *Create a page break after paragraph four.*
7. *Create Header A for all pages in your document, from page two onwards, saying "Chapter 1". Make the header 14 point, Helvetica Bold.*
8. *Set up page numbering for the entire document. Make the numbers appear in the bottom center of each page.*

The details for completing these steps are on the following pages.

Steps in detail

1. Start a new WordPerfect file.

If you have just opened WordPerfect, you will be in a new WordPerfect file. If you are working on another WordPerfect document, select the *New* command from the **File** menu. If you are not in WordPerfect, start the program from Windows.

2. Open the learn18.wkb file from the learn sub-directory.

To open the ***learn18.wkb*** file, select the *Open* command from the **File** menu of Figure 8x-1. This will activate the *Open File* dialog box of Figure 8x-2.

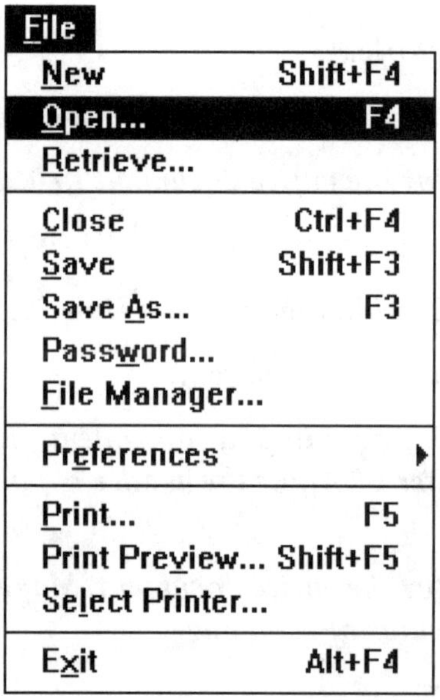

Figure 8x-1*. Select the Open command from the* ***File*** *menu to activate the Open File dialog box.*

In the *Open File* dialog box, first locate the ***learn18.wkb*** file in the ***learn*** sub-directory. Highlight this file in the list of files and click on the *Open* button. Alternatively, double-clicking on the file name will open this document.

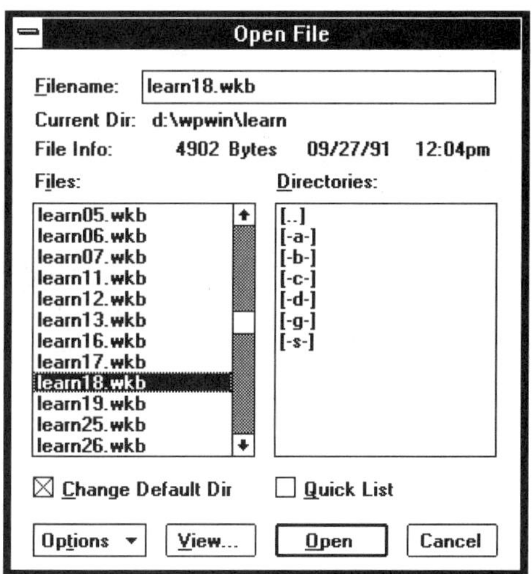

Figure 8x-2. In the Open File dialog box, locate the ***learn18.wkb*** *file in the* ***learn*** *sub-directory and open it.*

Once the file is opened it will look like Figure 8x-3.

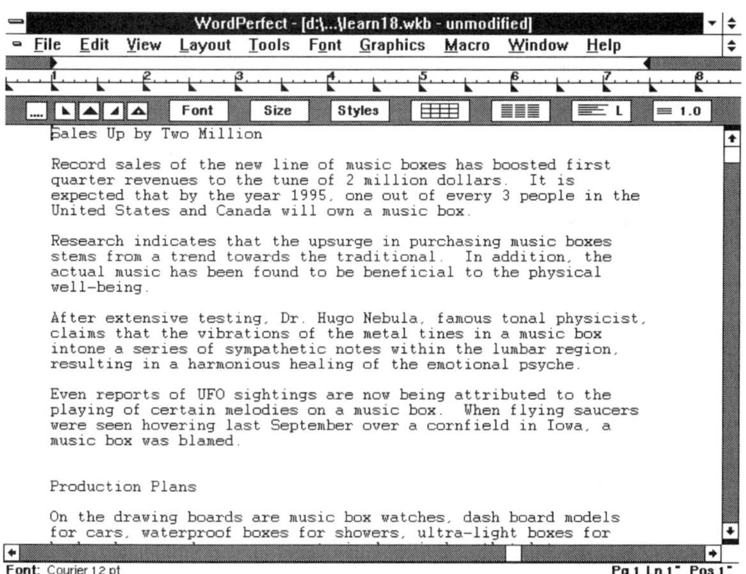

Figure 8x-3. This is how the ***learn18.wkb*** *file will look on your screen.*

3. Change the line height for the entire document to 0.25 of an inch.

To change the line height for the entire document, make sure the cursor is located at the start and select the *Line/Height* command from the **Layout** menu (Figure 8x-4). This will activate the *Line Height* dialog box of Figure 8x-5.

Figure 8x-4. *Select the Line/Height command from the* ***Layout*** *menu to activate the Line Height dialog box.*

In the *Line Height* dialog box, select the *Fixed* option, where a default value will appear. You are now free to key in 0.25 for the new *Fixed* figure (Figure 8x-5). Click on **OK** once you have done this.

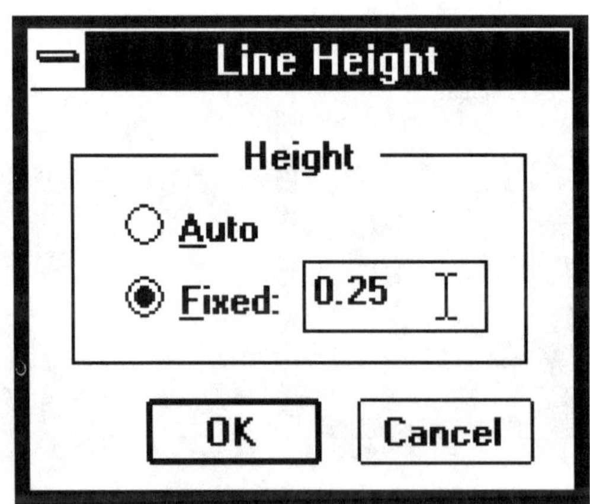

Figure 8x-5*. In the Line Height dialog box, select the Fixed option, change the setting to 0.25, and click on* ***OK****.*

The text on the screen will now show a 0.25 inch space between each line (Figure 8x-6).

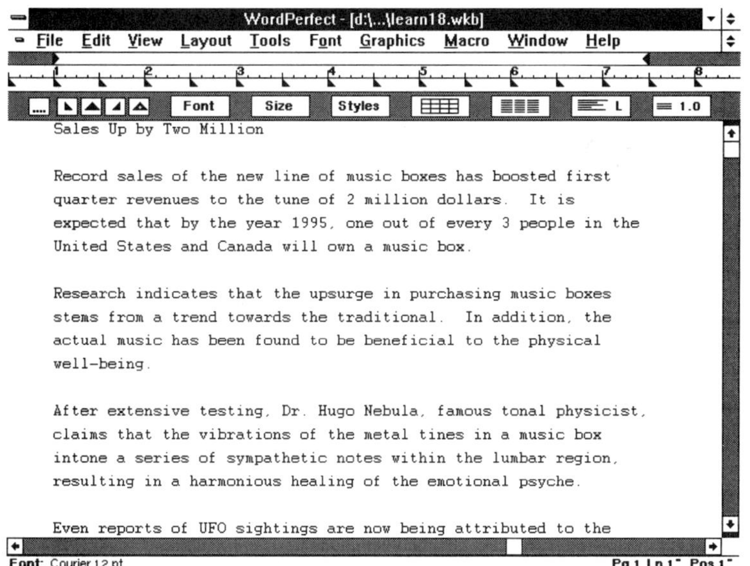

Figure 8x-6. *The document now has a 0.25 inch line height.*

4. *Indent the heading two tab stops.*

If the cursor is not currently at the beginning of the document, position it at this point. This is done simply by clicking the mouse before the first word in the heading. Once the cursor is in place, select the *Paragraph/Indent* command from the **Layout** menu (Figure 8x-7).

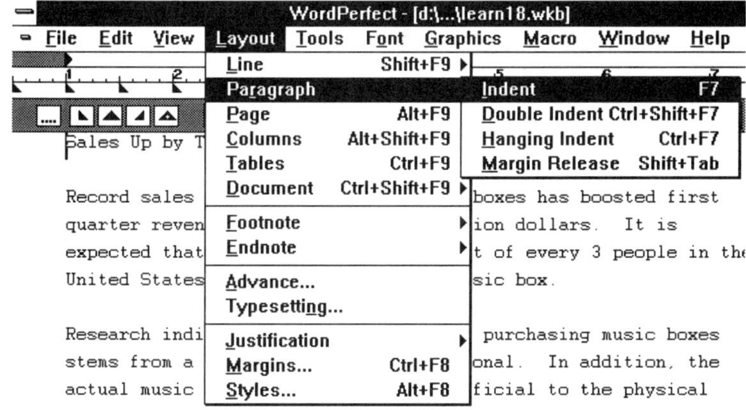

Figure 8x-7. *With the cursor at the beginning of the document, select the Paragraph/Indent command from the* ***Layout*** *menu.*

Each time you select the *Indent* command, it will push the heading over one tab stop. For this step you want it to move two stops, so for the second time just press the F7 key; this is the default keyboard shortcut for the *Indent* command.

After indenting the heading twice, it will appear as shown in Figure 8x-8.

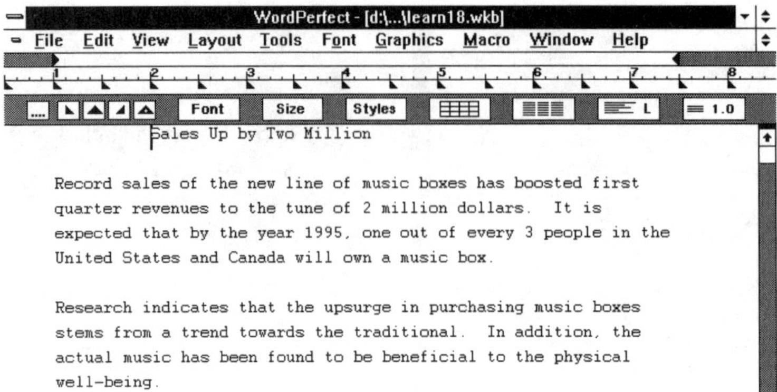

Figure 8x-8. The heading has now been indented twice.

5. *Give paragraph two a Double Indent and a Hanging Indent.*

Position the cursor at the beginning of paragraph two and select the *Paragraph/Double Indent* command from the **Layout** menu (Figure 8x-9).

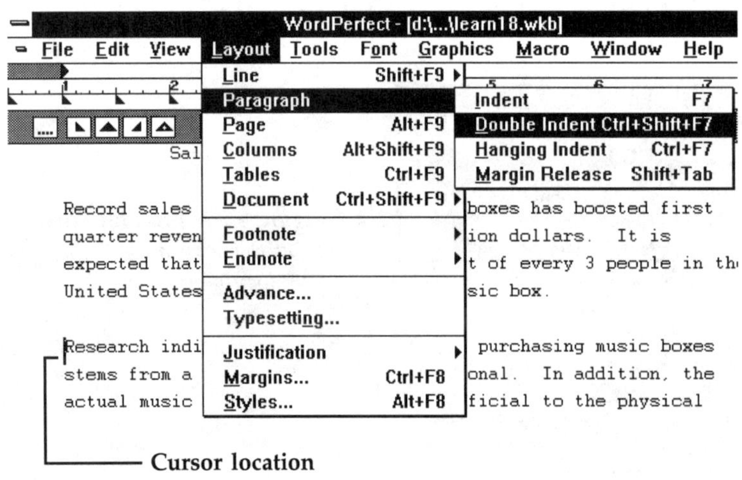

Figure 8x-9. Once the cursor is at the beginning of paragraph two, select the Paragraph/ Double Indent command from the ***Layout*** *menu.*

The second paragraph has now been indented from the left and from the right one tab stop, which can be seen in Figure 8x-10. Compare this paragraph with the ones above and below it.

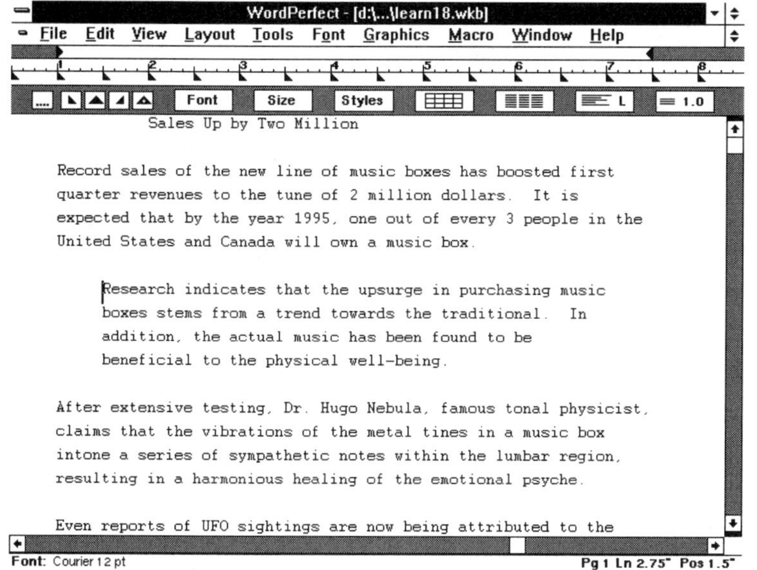

Figure 8x-10*. After applying the Double Indent command to the second paragraph, you can see that it has been indented from both the left and right.*

With the cursor still at the start of paragraph two, select the *Paragraph/Hanging Indent* command from the **Layout** menu (Figure 8x-11). This will force all lines, except the first, to move forward one tab stop (Figure 8x-12).

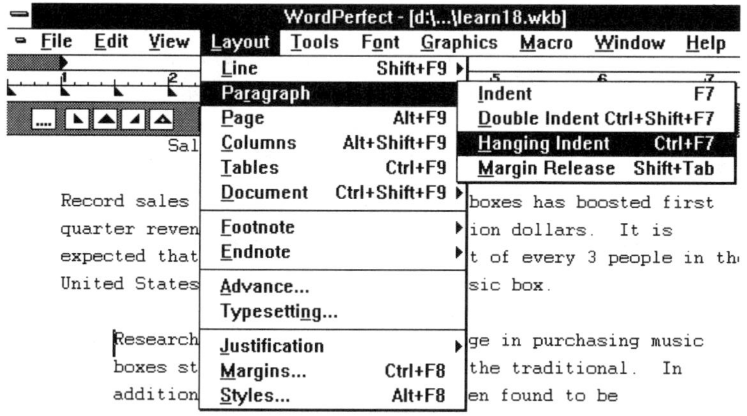

Figure 8x-11*. To produce a Hanging Indent, select the Paragraph/Hanging Indent command from the* ***Layout*** *menu.*

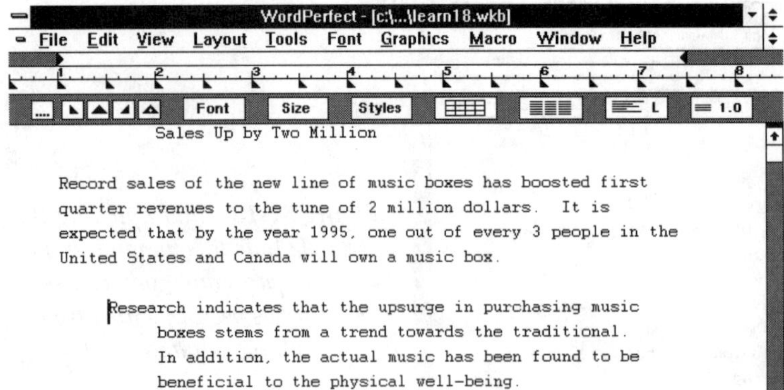

Figure 8x-12. From the actions of Figure 8x-11, the second paragraph now includes a hanging indent.

6. Create a page break after paragraph four.

Using the vertical scroll bar, move through the document until all of paragraph four is visible and insert the cursor at the end of this paragraph. Then select the *Page/Page Break* command from the **Layout** menu (Figure 8x-13).

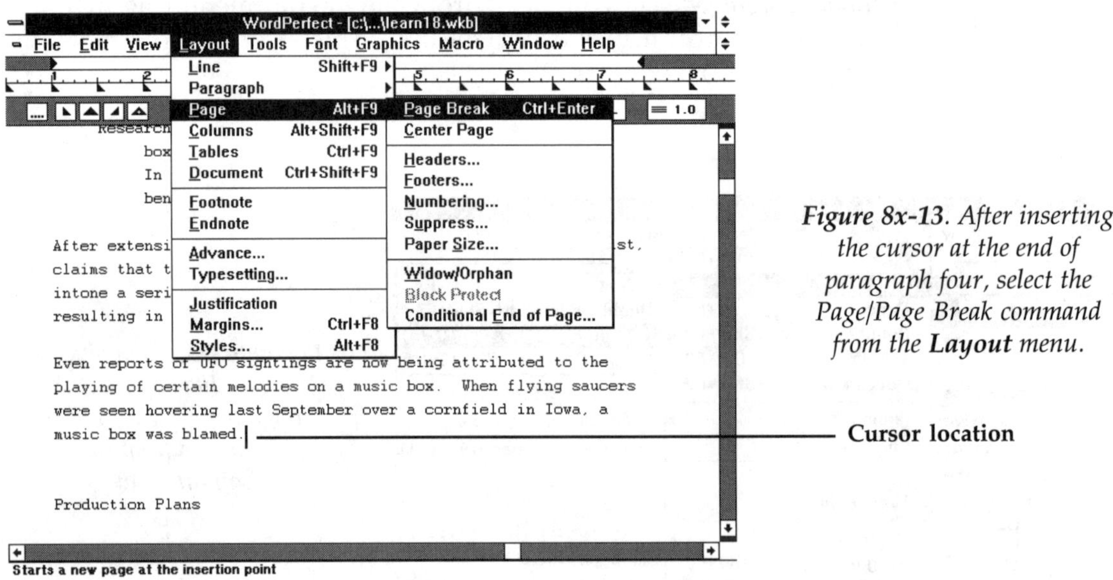

*Figure 8x-13. After inserting the cursor at the end of paragraph four, select the Page/Page Break command from the **Layout** menu.*

The text after paragraph four will now be on a new page as shown in Figure 8x-14.

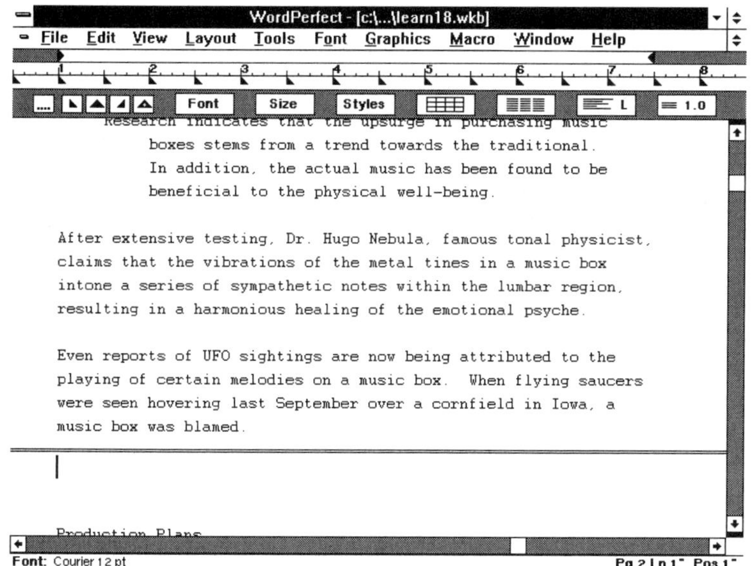

Figure 8x-14. A page break has been inserted after paragraph four.

7. ***Create Header A for all pages in your document, from page two onwards, saying "Chapter 1". Make the header 14 point, Helvetica Bold.***

Because the header you are about to create starts from page two, leave the flashing cursor where it is after the previous step. This means it will be at the top of page two; if for some reason it is not, insert it there.

Now, select the *Page/Headers* command from the **Layout** menu (Figure 8x-15).

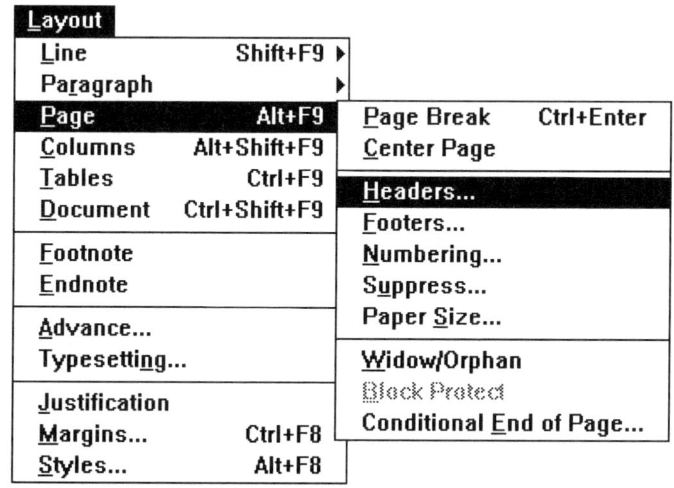

*Figure 8x-15. To create a header for your document, select the Page/Headers command from the **Layout** menu.*

In the *Headers* dialog box that appears after selecting the *Headers* command, click on the *Create* button (Figure 8x-16). The *Header A* option will already be selected by default.

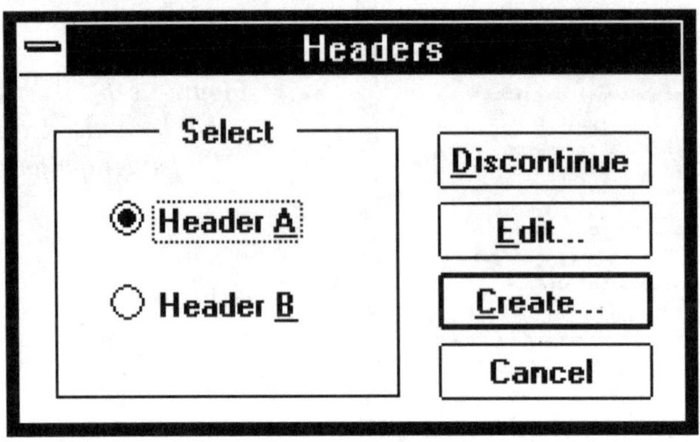

Figure 8x-16*. Select the Create button from the Headers dialog box.*

In the *Header* editing screen that appears after clicking on the *Create* button, select the *Font* command from the **Font** menu (Figure 8x-17).

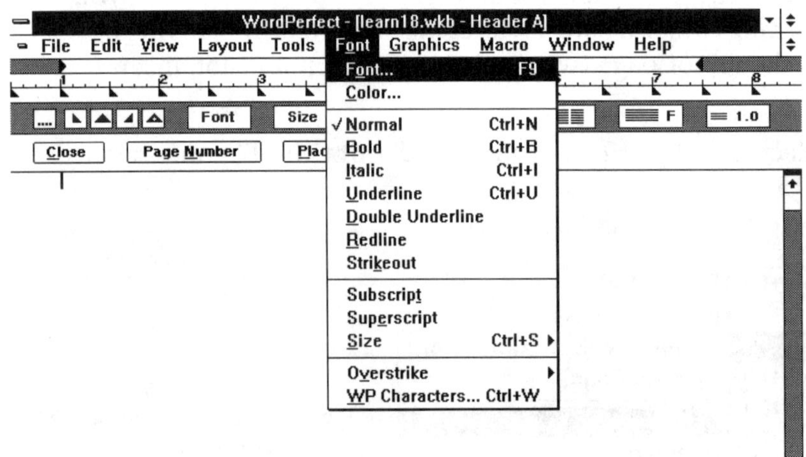

Figure 8x-17*. Once inside the Header editing screen, select the Font command from the* ***Font*** *menu.*

The *Font* command from the **Font** menu activates the *Font* dialog box of Figure 8x-18. The first option you select here is the type of *Font*. Locate and click on the *Helvetica Bold* font from the list available. Then click on 14 in the *Point Size* list. Once your dialog box is identical to the *Font* dialog box of Figure 8x-18, click on **OK**.

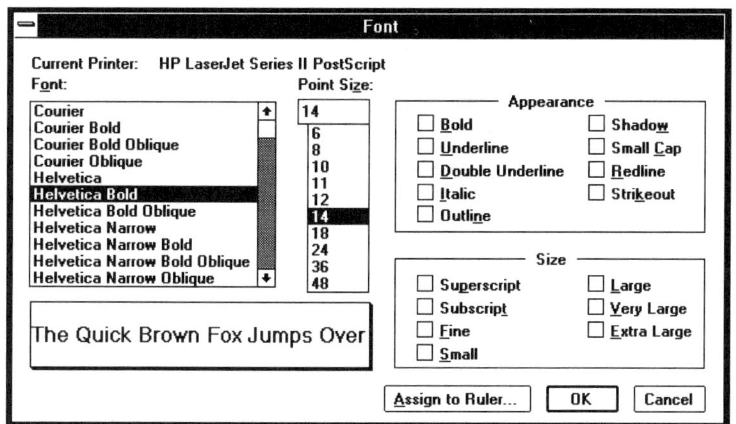

Figure 8x-18. In the font dialog box, select the Helvetica Bold and 14 point options before clicking on ***OK****.*

Once you have made the changes to the font and size and are back in the *Header* editor screen, key in "Chapter 1". The text appearing on screen will reflect the settings you chose in the *Font* dialog box of Figure 8x-18. After keying in the required text (Figure 8x-19), click on the *Close* button to return to the document.

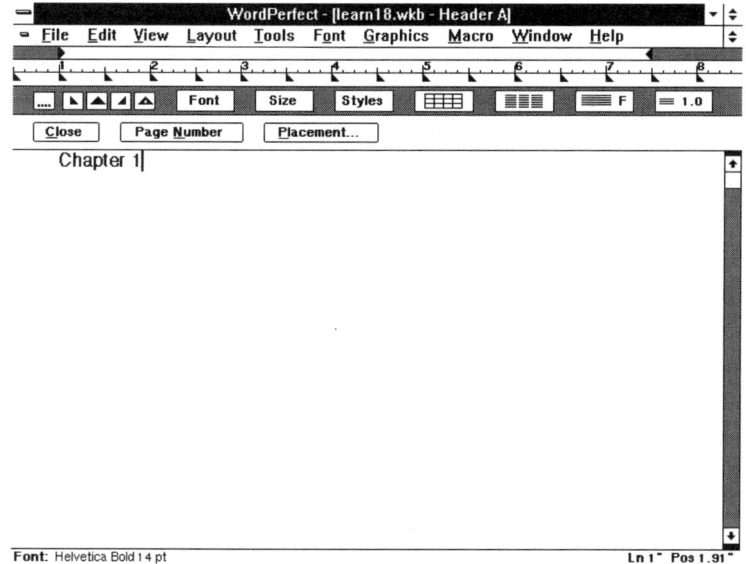

Figure 8x-19. The text you key in will display in the font and size you selected previously in the Font dialog box. After keying in this text, click on the Close button.

8. ***Set up page numbering for the entire document. Make the numbers appear in the bottom center of each page.***

To set up page numbering for the entire document, the cursor must be positioned at the beginning of page one .

Use the scroll bar to position the page to the top of the document; then insert the cursor before the first word. Once this is done, select the *Page/Numbering* command from the **Layout** menu (Figure 8x-20). This will activate the *Page Numbering* dialog box of Figure 8x-21.

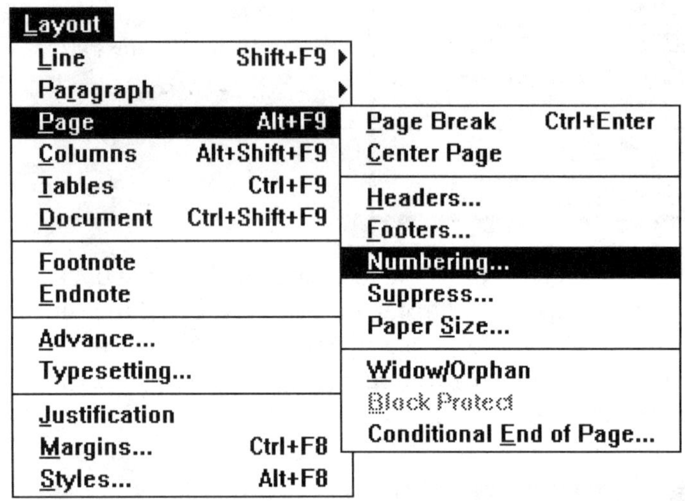

Figure 8x-20. *With the cursor at the beginning of the document, select the Page/ Numbering command from the* ***Layout*** *menu.*

In the *Page Numbering* dialog box, select the *Bottom Center* option from the *Position* pop-up list (Figure 8x-21).

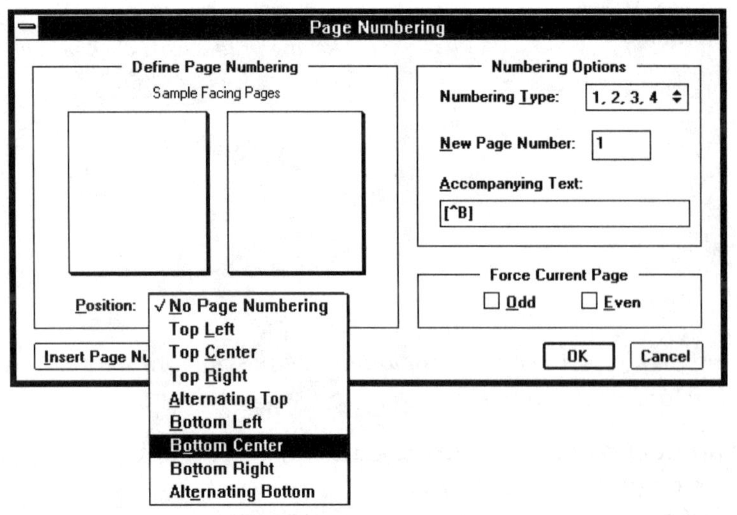

Figure 8x-21*. Select the Bottom Center option from the Position pop-up list.*

After selecting the *Bottom Center* option from the *Position* pop-up list in the *Page Numbering* dialog box, the numbers will appear in this position in the *Sample Facing Pages* representation (Figure 8x-22). You can now exit this dialog box by clicking on **OK**.

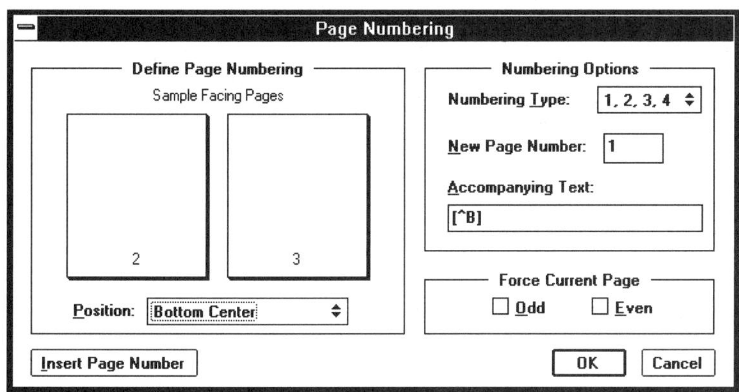

***Figure 8x-22**. After selecting the Bottom Center option, click on the **OK** button to exit the dialog box.*

All even pages in the document will now have a header and all pages will be numbered in the bottom center of each page. To see this, select the *Print Preview* command from the **File** menu, which activates the *Print Preview* screen of Figure 8x-23 and Figure 8x-24.

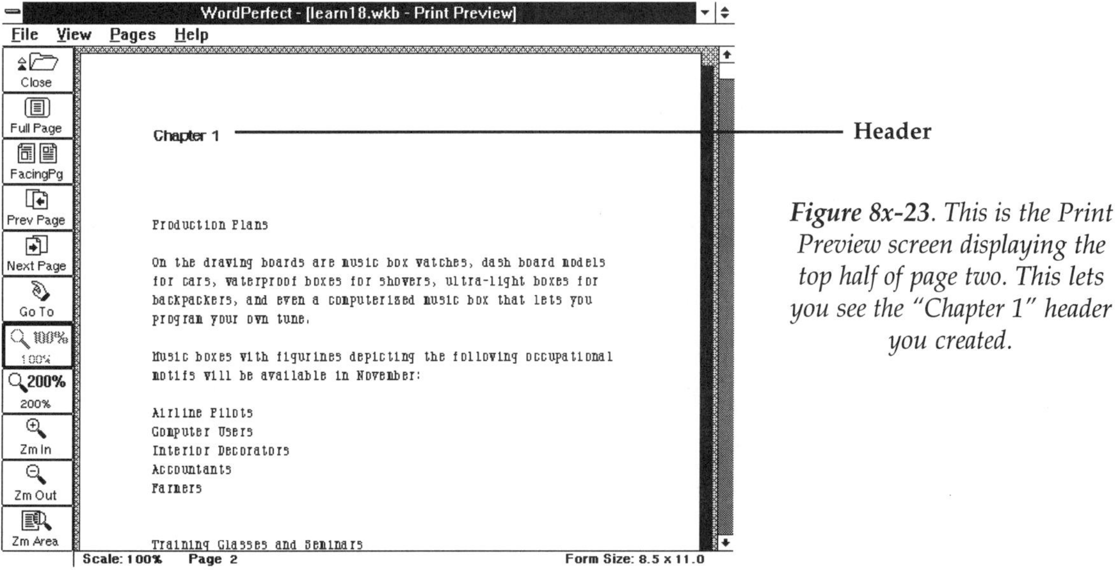

***Figure 8x-23**. This is the Print Preview screen displaying the top half of page two. This lets you see the "Chapter 1" header you created.*

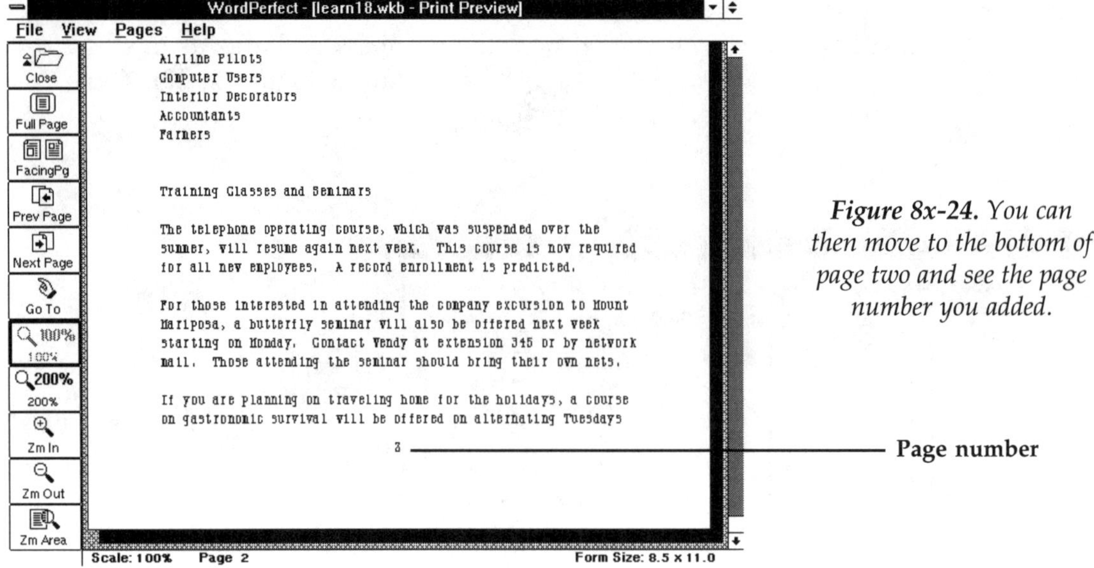

Figure 8x-24. *You can then move to the bottom of page two and see the page number you added.*

Printing

Although printing a WordPerfect document is quite simple, there are many options available that control such things as printer model selection, print quality, and print type.

Selecting a printer

Before you can print to your printer from WordPerfect, you must tell WordPerfect which printer you are using. Printers are selected using the *Select Printer* command in the **File** menu. Figure 9-1 shows this command and the associated dialog box.

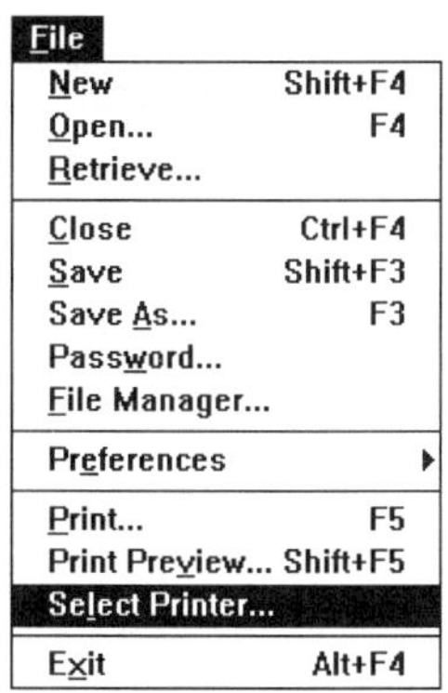

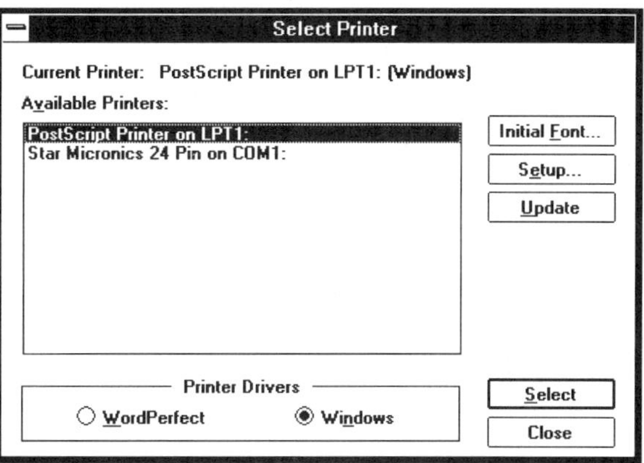

Figure 9-1. The Select Printer command from the ***File*** *menu is used to let WordPerfect know which printer you wish to use.*

As mentioned above, this command basically lets WordPerfect know which printer it will be using. WordPerfect needs this information so it can format the document correctly and give you access to the correct fonts.

Initially, the most important part of the *Select Printer* dialog box is the *Printer Drivers* options towards the bottom (Figure 9-2).

WordPerfect printer drivers versus Windows printer drivers

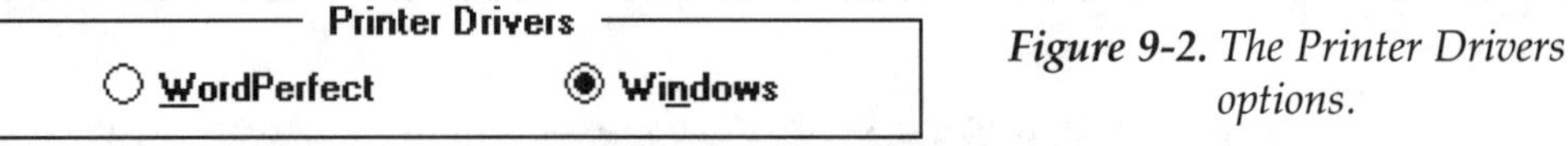

Figure 9-2. *The Printer Drivers options.*

Using the *Printer Drivers* options, you can decide whether to use the printer drivers provided with Microsoft Windows or those provided with WordPerfect for Windows.

A printer driver is a file used by a program to communicate with the printer. It acts as an intermediary—translating commands from the program into a language that the printer will understand.

Most programs that run under the Windows interface use Windows drivers—Windows provides printer drivers for a large range of output devices.

WordPerfect, although it can use Windows printer drivers, provides a large range of drivers specifically designed for WordPerfect. These include drivers for some printers that Windows itself does not directly support and drivers with different capabilities than those provided by Windows.

Using a Windows printer driver

In this section, assume that the *Windows* option is selected from the *Printer Drivers* section of the Figure 9-1 dialog box.

At the top of the *Select Printer* dialog box (Figure 9-1) is the *Current Printer* line (Figure 9-3). This line lists the name of the printer driver which is currently selected. If the word "Windows" appears in brackets after the printer name, this indicates that the printer driver is provided by Windows, rather than WordPerfect.

Current Printer: PostScript Printer on LPT1: [Windows]

Figure 9-3. *The Current Printer line, at the top of the Figure 9-1 dialog box, reflects the name of the printer driver currently in use.*

Clicking on the *Windows Printer Drivers* button, as shown in Figure 9-2, sets up the dialog box to choose a new printer driver. Nothing happens until you click on the *Select* button. The *Current Printer* line could therefore be listing either a WordPerfect or Windows printer driver at this stage.

Below the *Current Printer* line is the list of *Available Printers* (Figure 9-4). This list will differ quite markedly, depending on whether you are using WordPerfect, or Windows, printer drivers.

When Windows printer drivers are in use, the *Available Printers* list box will list only those printer drivers that have been installed using the Windows Control Panel or during Windows installation. Therefore, if you wish to print to a printer not currently in this list, using Windows printer drivers, you must use the Windows Control Panel to install a new printer.

Figure 9-4. *Two printers are currently available in the list of Available Printers.*

In Figure 9-4, there are two printers listed—the only two Windows printer drivers currently installed. If you only ever use one printer, you may find that only one printer is listed here. If there are multiple printers listed, a printer can be selected by clicking the mouse on its name.

An option to the right of the *Available Printers* list is the *Initial Font* button (Figure 9-5). This is only selectable if a Windows printer driver is already highlighted.

Initial Font...

Figure 9-5. *The Initial Font button lets you set a default font for all documents using this printer.*

When you select the *Initial Font* button of Figure 9-5, the *Printer Initial Font* dialog box of Figure 9-6 will appear.

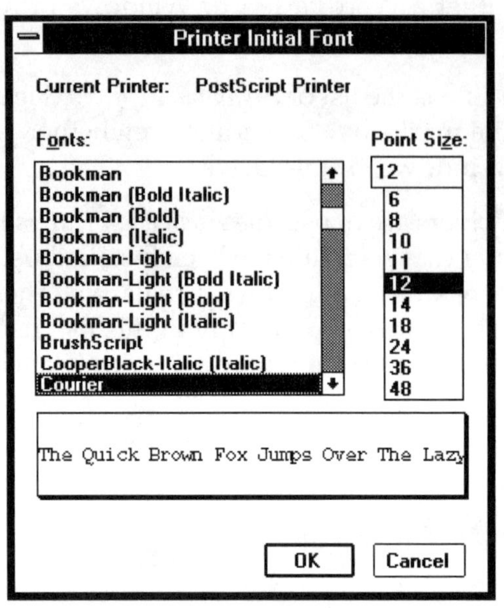

Figure 9-6. *The Initial Font for documents using this printer driver can be selected from the Fonts list box which appears when you select the button in Figure 9-5.*

Selecting the *Initial Font* for a printer sets the default font used for text in the document, including headers, footers, and equations, for all documents created while this printer is selected. Please note that the *Initial Font* set using the *Document/Initial Font* command from the **Layout** menu (see Chapter 8) overrides the *Initial Font* selected using the *Initial Font* button in the *Select Printer* command as discussed here.

Other options relating to the printer you have selected, can be set using the *Setup* button from the *Select Printer* dialog box (Figure 9-7).

Setup...

Figure 9-7. *The Setup button lets you set all options relating to the printer you have selected.*

The dialog box that appears upon selecting the *Setup* button in Figure 9-7 depends entirely on the name of the printer selected in the list of *Available Printers* (Figure 9-4). Each printer has different capabilities and options, and hence a different dialog box. Figure 9-8 shows the dialog box as it would appear for a PostScript printer.

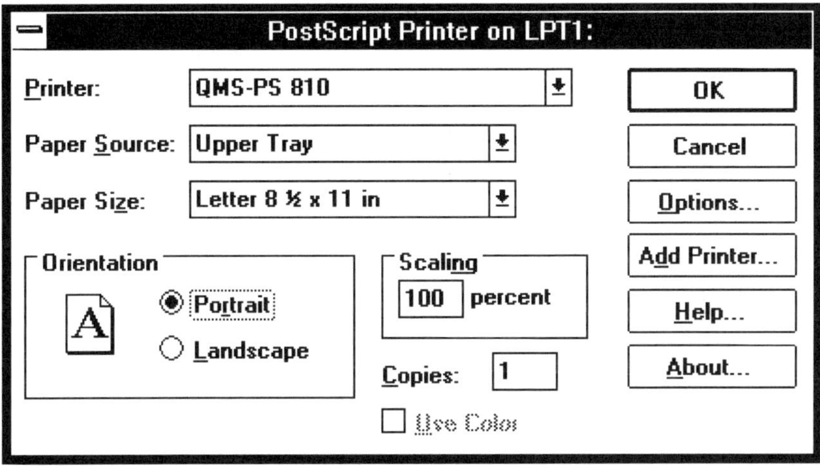

Figure 9-8. *The Printer Setup dialog box that appears when the Setup button of Figure 9-7 is selected, while a PostScript printer is highlighted in the Available Printers list box.*

When using a Windows printer driver, the dialog box that appears in Figure 9-8 is actually from Windows rather than from WordPerfect. In effect, WordPerfect has guided you into the Windows Control Panel.

As there are a huge variety of dialog boxes that can appear in place of Figure 9-8, it is very difficult to explain all types. Basically, however, you are being asked to supply information like the exact name of the printer you are using, the size of the paper used by that printer, the orientation of the printer, the number of copies to print, the amount of memory contained in the printer, and the font cartridge used by the printer.

If you are having trouble here, select the *Help* button from the Figure 9-8 dialog box, or consult the Windows manual.

Once you have selected the appropriate options from this dialog box, click on the **OK** button to confirm these options.

To update the selected printer, click on the *Update* button of Figure 9-1, shown again in Figure 9-9. This ensures that WordPerfect knows about all current options you just set for the current printer and formats the document accordingly. No dialog box will appear, but WordPerfect will take a few seconds to update the selected printer.

Update

Figure 9-9. *The Update button updates WordPerfect with all current settings for the selected printer.*

At this stage, to make sure that the currently selected printer becomes the WordPerfect default printer, you would need to click on the *Select* button of the *Select Printer* dialog box (Figure 9-1).

Using a WordPerfect printer driver

WordPerfect printer drivers may well provide more printing flexibility, quicker printing, and a wider range of printer models.

Even with a WordPerfect printer driver selected (Figure 9-10), all printing will still be handled by the Windows Print Spooler, if it is enabled through the Windows Control Panel.

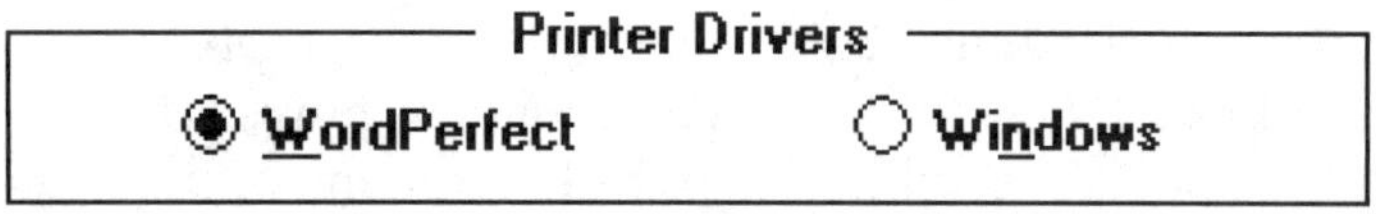

Printer Drivers

(•) WordPerfect ( ) Windows

Figure 9-10. *A WordPerfect printer driver can be selected by first selecting WordPerfect from the Printer Drivers section of the Figure 9-1 dialog box.*

At the top of the *Select Printer* dialog box (Figure 9-1) is the *Current Printer* line (Figure 9-3). This line shows the name of the printer driver currently selected. If the word "Windows" appears in brackets after the printer name, the printer driver is provided by Windows, rather than WordPerfect. In Figure 9-3, a Windows printer driver is currently selected.

Below the *Current Printer* line is the list of *Available Printers*, this time for those with WordPerfect drivers (Figure 9-11). Initially, this list box may be empty. However, you will be adding printers to this list in a moment.

If the list of *Available Printers* does contain entries, a printer can be selected by clicking on its name.

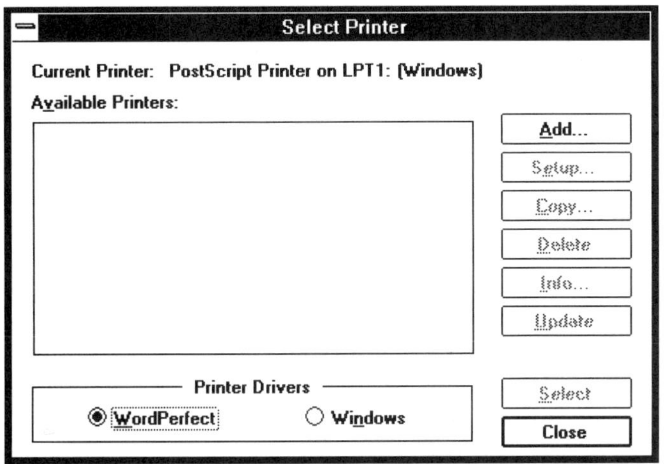

Figure 9-11. *The list of Available Printers may be empty at this stage. In a moment, you will be adding printers to this list.*

Adding a printer

To add a printer to the list of *Available Printers*, click on the *Add* button to the right of this list (Figure 9-12).

Figure 9-12. *The Add button is used to add other WordPerfect printer drivers to the list of Available Printers.*

The dialog box of Figure 9-13 will appear when the *Add* button (Figure 9-12) is selected.

Selecting *Add* forces WordPerfect to look into the directory specified by the *Printer Files* options of the *Location of Files* command from the *Preferences* fly-out menu in the **File** menu (see Chapter 10).

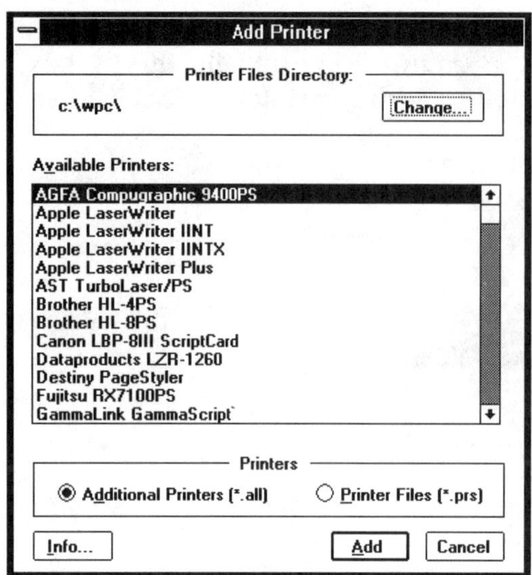

Figure 9-13. *After selecting the Add button of Figure 9-12, this list of WordPerfect printer drivers will appear.*

If your Figure 9-13 dialog box appears with no printers in the *Available Printers* list, you may need to use the *Change* button near the top of the dialog box, to move to another directory. The default directory for the installation of WordPerfect printer drivers is the ***wpc*** directory.

It is also possible that these WordPerfect printer drivers were not installed at all, as this is an option during installation. You may have to reinstall WordPerfect, at least partially, to gain access to these printer drivers.

The *Available Printers* list box displays all currently available WordPerfect printer drivers. From this list, you can make a selection by clicking on the name of a certain printer—your actual printer. In Figure 9-14, we have selected the printer *Apple LaserWriter Plus.*

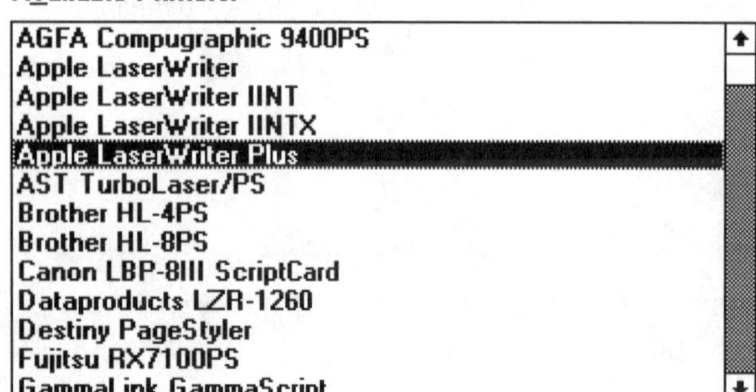

Figure 9-14. *The printer driver selected here is the Apple LaserWriter Plus printer.*

Once the printer you are using is selected from this list, click on **OK**. The dialog box of Figure 9-15 will then appear.

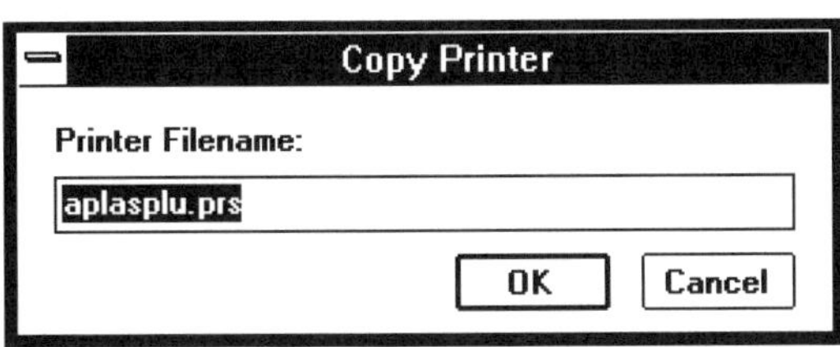

Figure 9-15. *This dialog box appears suggesting a printer settings file name.*

When you select a WordPerfect printer driver, you will be modifying the settings for that driver to suit your own needs. All the settings you make for a selected printer are stored in a file with a "***prs***" extension—-in this case, the name of the file in the *Copy Printer* dialog box of Figure 9-15. It only becomes important to memorize or note the names of the ***prs*** files being used when you start using multiple ***prs*** files.

After clicking on **OK** in the *Copy Printer* dialog box, the printer *Apple LaserWriter Plus* now appears in the list of *Available Printers,* as shown in Figure 9-16.

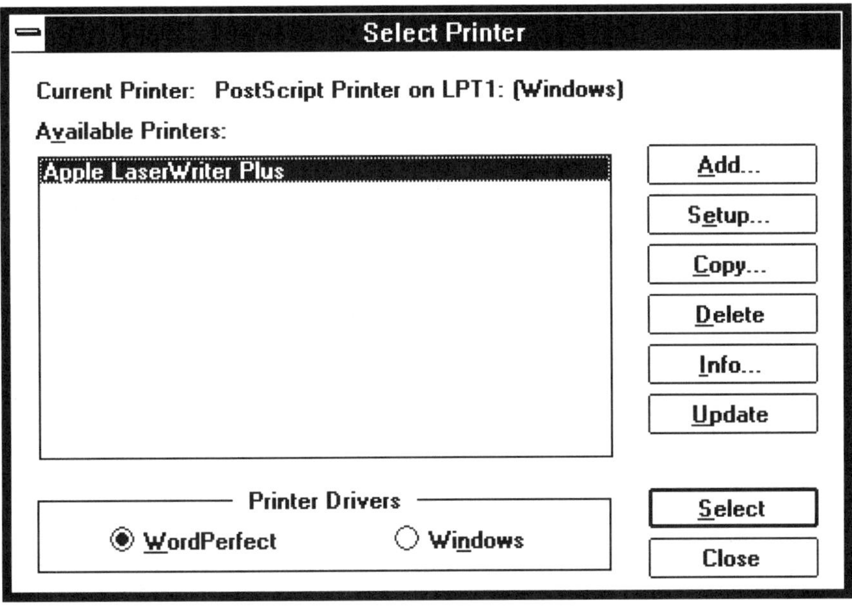

Figure 9-16. *Once a printer is selected from the dialog box of Figure 9-14 and you have clicked on* ***OK*** *in Figure 9-15, you will return to this dialog box, with the printer selected in the list of Available Printers.*

Selecting the *Add* button again enables you to select another printer to add to this list, if you wish.

Setting up a printer

The *Setup* button (Figure 9-17) enables you to specify some printer options.

Setup...

Figure 9-17. *The Setup button allows you to set Printer options.*

Selecting the *Setup* button of Figure 9-16 presents you with the dialog box of Figure 9-18 .

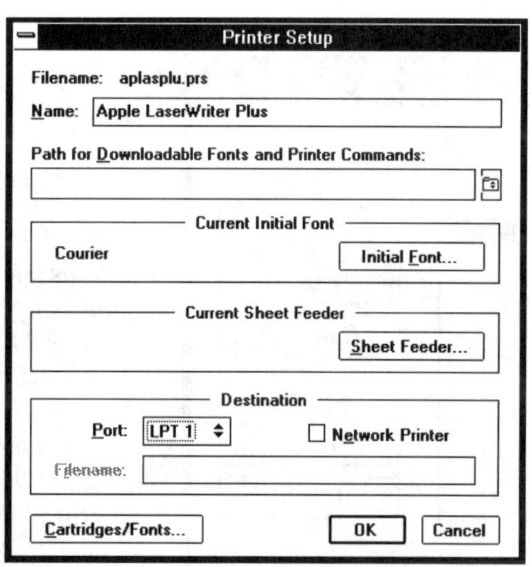

Figure 9-18. *The Printer Setup dialog box appears for the selected printer, once the Setup button of Figures 9-16 or 9-17 is selected.*

The top line of this dialog box, *Filename,* lists the name of the printer settings file on disk (Figure 9-19). This is the same file name as seen in Figure 9-15.

Filename: aplasplu.prs

Figure 9-19. *The name of the printer settings file in this case is* ***aplasplu.prs.*** *WordPerfect suggests this name as the printer driver is selected (Figure 9-15).*

Below the *Filename* line is the actual *Name* of the printer (Figure 9-20) selected in the Figure 9-16 dialog box—in this case, *Apple LaserWriter Plus.*

Name: Apple LaserWriter Plus

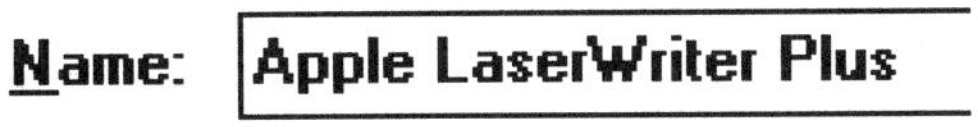

Figure 9-20. *The name of the printer selected appears in the Name text box of the Figure 9-18 dialog box.*

In the *Location of Files* command from the *Preferences* fly-out menu in the **File** menu (see Chapter 10), there is an option called *Printer Files,* which lets WordPerfect know where printer information, including downloadable fonts, are stored. If some information, downloadable fonts for example, are stored in a different directory, you must let WordPerfect know which directory, using the *Path for Downloadable Fonts and Printer Commands* option (Figure 9-21).

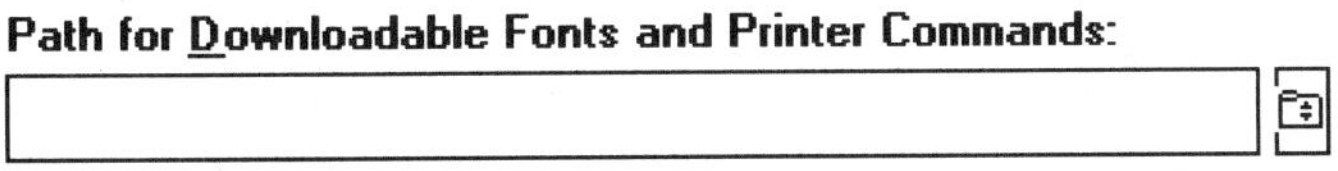

Path for Downloadable Fonts and Printer Commands:

Figure 9-21*. This option is used if downloadable fonts, or printer commands, are stored in a location other than that specified by the Printer Files option within the Preferences/Location of Files option.*

The *Current Initial Font* (Figure 9-22) sets the *Initial Font* for this printer. Selecting the *Initial Font* for a printer sets the initial font used for text in the document, including headers, footers, and equations, for all documents created while this printer is selected. Please note that the *Initial Font* set using the *Document/Initial Font* command from the **Layout** menu (see Chapter 8) overrides the *Initial Font* selected using the *Initial Font* button in the *Printer Setup* dialog box of Figure 9-18.

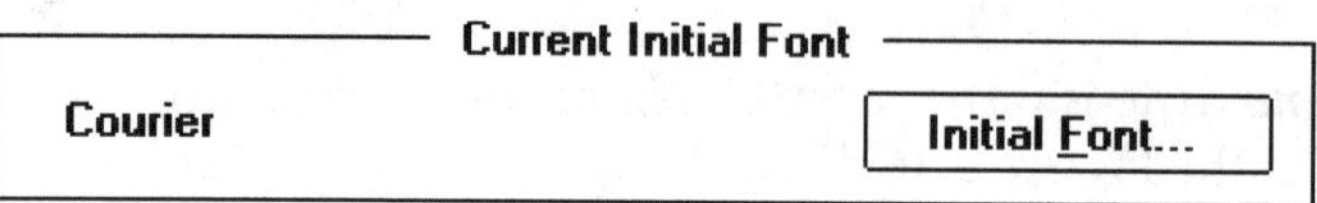

Figure 9-22. *This option sets the Current Initial Font for this printer. Click on the Initial Font button if you wish to change the font.*

The *Printer Initial Font* dialog box that appears when selecting the *Initial Font* button of Figure 9-22 is shown in Figure 9-23. You can simply select a font from the list of fonts available for the printer.

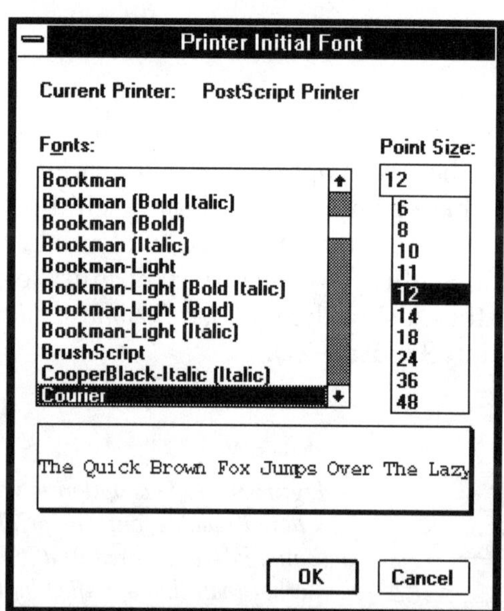

Figure 9-23. *Selecting a font from this list will set the Current Initial Font for the selected printer.*

Many printer models can use sheet feeders or several printer trays. Selecting the *Sheet Feeder* button from Figure 9-18, from the *Current Sheet Feeder* section (shown again in Figure 9-24) allows you to select a sheet feeder and peruse information about this option. The dialog box of Figure 9-25 will appear when the *Sheet Feeder* button is selected.

Figure 9-24*. The Current Sheet Feeder section lets you select a sheet feeder, and peruse information about that sheet feeder.*

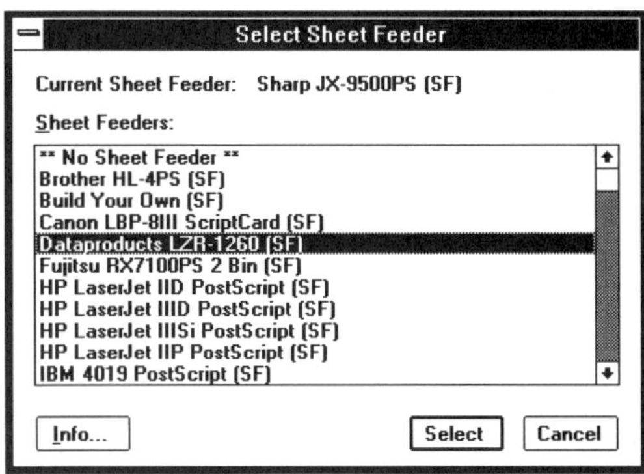

Figure 9-25. *After selecting the button in Figure 9-24, the Select Sheet Feeder dialog box appears, illustrating a list of possible sheet feeders, and dual bin printers. You may select a sheet feeder from this dialog box.*

Choose *Info* in the *Select Sheet Feeder* dialog box of Figure 9-25 to obtain the bin information for the selected sheet feeder (Figure 9-26). This information is then used to specify the *Paper Location* in the *Paper Size* dialog box (under the *Page* command in the **Layout** menu). *Paper Location* is found by clicking on the *Add* or *Edit* button in the *Paper Size* dialog box.

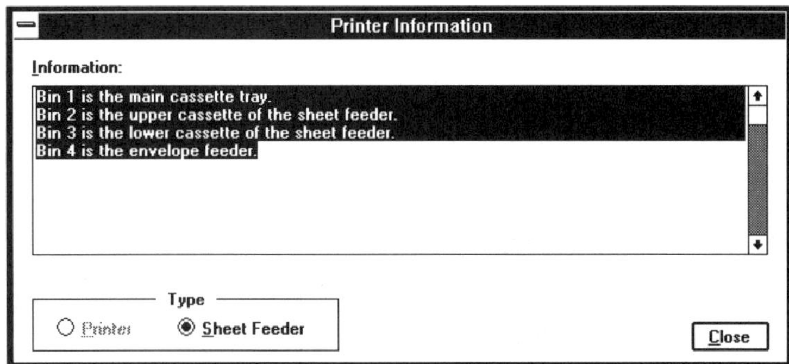

Figure 9-26*. Here, the Info button of Figure 9-25 was selected. This dialog box contains information about the bins available with the selected sheet feeder.*

Printing destination

Below the *Sheet Feeder* section of the Figure 9-18 *Printer Setup* dialog box is the *Destination* section (Figure 9-27). This determines such information as which output port the printer is using.

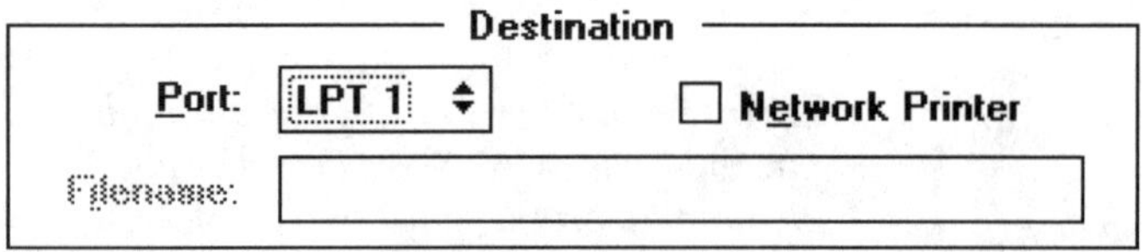

Figure 9-27. The Destination section determines whether or not you are using a network printer, and to which port the printer is connected.

Holding the mouse down on the *Port* button produces the *Port* pop-up list box of Figure 9-28. From this list, choose the port to which your printer is connected. As well as listing possible machine ports, this pop-up list box also contains the option, *File*.

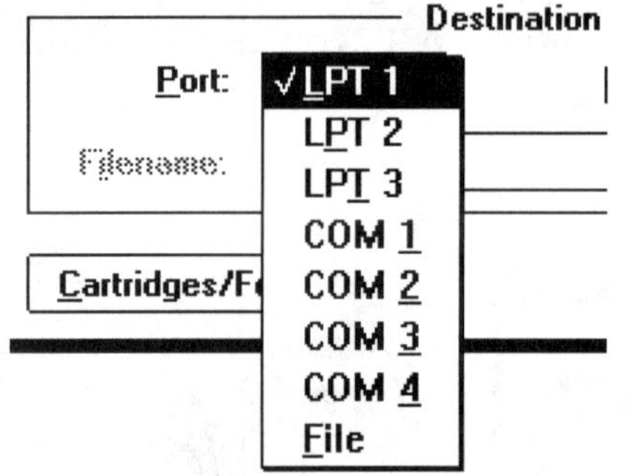

Figure 9-28. Selecting the Port pop-up list box presents you with these choices—simply select the port that the printer is connected to, or File, if you wish to print directly to disk.

In Figure 9-28, identify to which port your printer is connected. LPT identifies parallel ports; COM identifies serial ports.

If you select *File* from the Figure 9-28 pop-up list box, WordPerfect will create a print file on disk next time you print, instead of sending the information to the printer. You must also specify a print file name and directory path, on the *Filename* text box of the *Destination* section (Figure 9-29), so that WordPerfect knows to where it should save the print file.

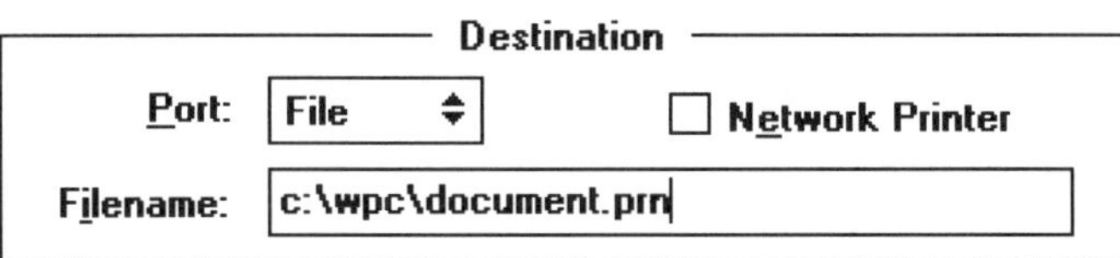

Figure 9-29*. Here, File has been selected from the Figure 9-28 pop-up list box and a filename and directory path has been entered into the Filename text box.*

If you are using a network printer, you can alert WordPerfect to this fact by selecting the *Network Printer* check box of Figures 9-27 or 9-29.

To let WordPerfect know what downloadable or cartridge fonts are available to the selected printer, select the *Cartridges/Fonts* button from Figure 9-18, shown below in Figure 9-30.

Cartridges/Fonts...

Figure 9-30*. The Cartridges/Fonts button allows you to alert WordPerfect to what cartridges and soft fonts are going to be available to your printer.*

If you select the *Cartridges/Fonts* button of Figure 9-30, you are presented with the *Cartridges and Fonts* dialog box (Figure 9-31). Under the *Font Source* heading, are listed several different options—*Built-In* (these are the fonts resident in the printer selected) and *Soft Fonts* (fonts purchased as software for downloading to your printer). Double-clicking on any of these options allows you to edit the list of fonts in each section. Choosing *Close* from Figure 9-31 returns you to the Figure 9-18 *Printer Setup* dialog box.

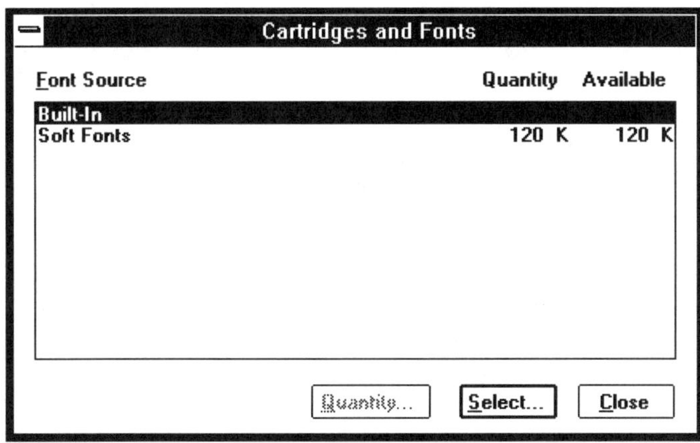

Figure 9-31. *WordPerfect contains information for all type of fonts available for a specific printer.*

Once you have reached this stage (i.e., back to Figure 9-18), select **OK** to save the settings you have selected for this printer. You will then be returned to the *Select Printer* dialog box of Figure 9-16.

Copying (duplicating) a printer driver

If you wish to have the same printer listed in the list of *Available Printers* twice, you can achieve this by selecting the *Copy* button from Figure 9-16. Having the same printer listed twice lets you create two different settings for the same printer, perhaps for different jobs.

Select the printer from the *Available Printers* you would like to *Copy* and click on the *Copy* button. The message box of Figure 9-32 will then appear.

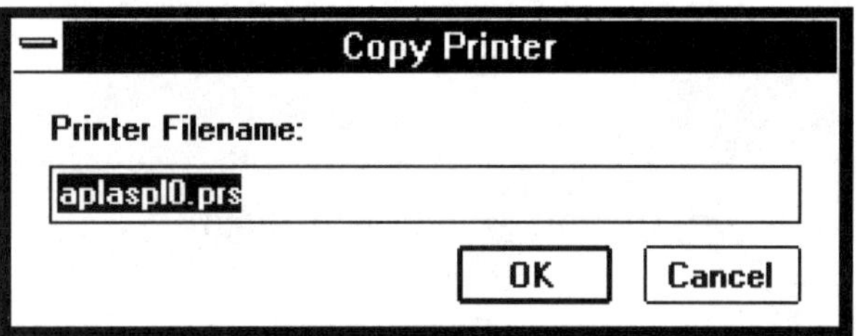

Figure 9-32. The Copy Printer dialog box.

Earlier in this chapter, ***prs*** files were mentioned in Figure 9-15 and the paragraph below it. A ***prs*** file is a set of printer settings that you create as you select a printer and modify as you adjust settings using the *Setup* button (described earlier). In Figure 9-32, the name of the file in the *Printer Filename* text box will differ slightly to the original ***prs*** filename (Figure 9-15), so that you can create two different files with different settings.

Because different ***prs*** files can be created for different jobs in WordPerfect, you may wish to alter the suggested name for ***prs*** files into something more meaningful to you or your colleagues.

For example, you may have a ***prs*** file called ***letters.prs*** which sets the printer up with no downloadable fonts and a certain initial font. You may also have a ***prs*** file called ***bureau.prs*** which sets the printer to print directly to disk and may use a set of downloadable fonts.

Clicking on **OK** in Figure 9-32 returns you to the Figure 9-33 *Select Printer* dialog box, with an additional copy of the *Apple LaserWriter Plus* printer name.

Later in this chapter, you will see how you can select a printer based on *prs* files, rather than just printer names—see the **Selecting from multiple prs files** section.

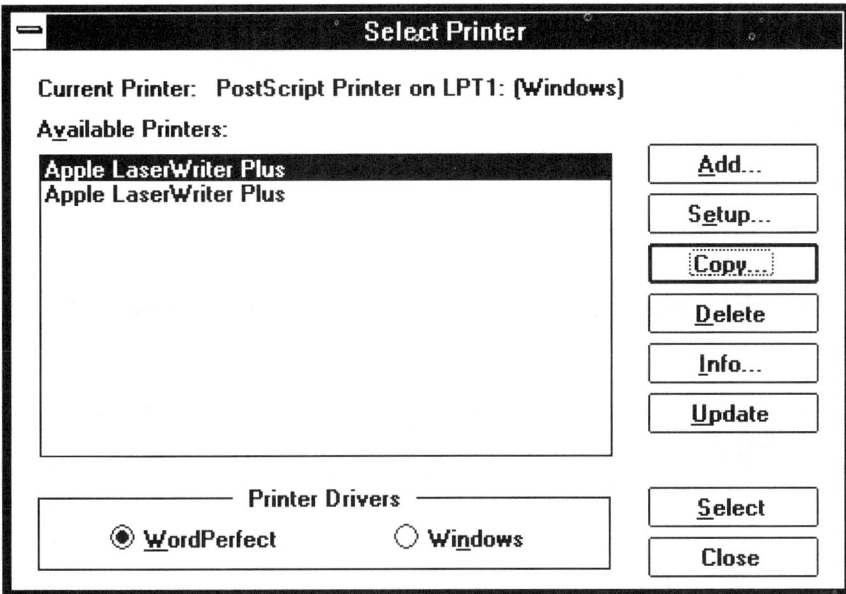

Figure 9-33. After using the Copy button to copy a selected printer, that printer name will appear twice in the list of Available Printers.

Deleting (removing) a printer

To delete a printer from the list of *Available Printers*, you first select that printer and then the *Delete* button. The dialog box of Figure 9-34 will then appear.

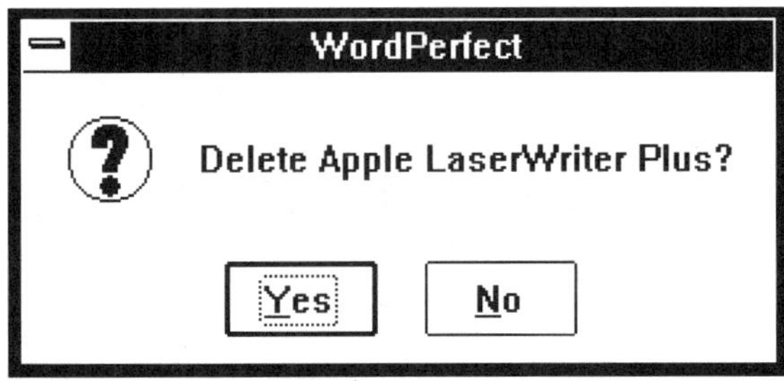

Figure 9-34. You will be asked to confirm the deletion of this printer from the list of Available Printers through this dialog box.

Selecting *Yes* will remove the named printer from the list of *Available Printers*, and *No* will keep it there. Nothing will be deleted from disk, in either case. Selecting *Yes* will remove one of the two *Apple LaserWriter Plus* printer drivers of Figure 9-33.

Selecting the *Info* button from Figure 9-33 will display a *Printer Information* dialog box about the printer currently selected in the list of *Available Printers*. This information box will inform you of any special characteristics of the selected printer.

Figure 9-35 displays the *Printer Information* dialog box for the printer *Destiny PageStyler*. This printer has been used as an illustration here because many printers (including the *Apple LaserWriter Plus*) have no special characteristics when working with WordPerfect.

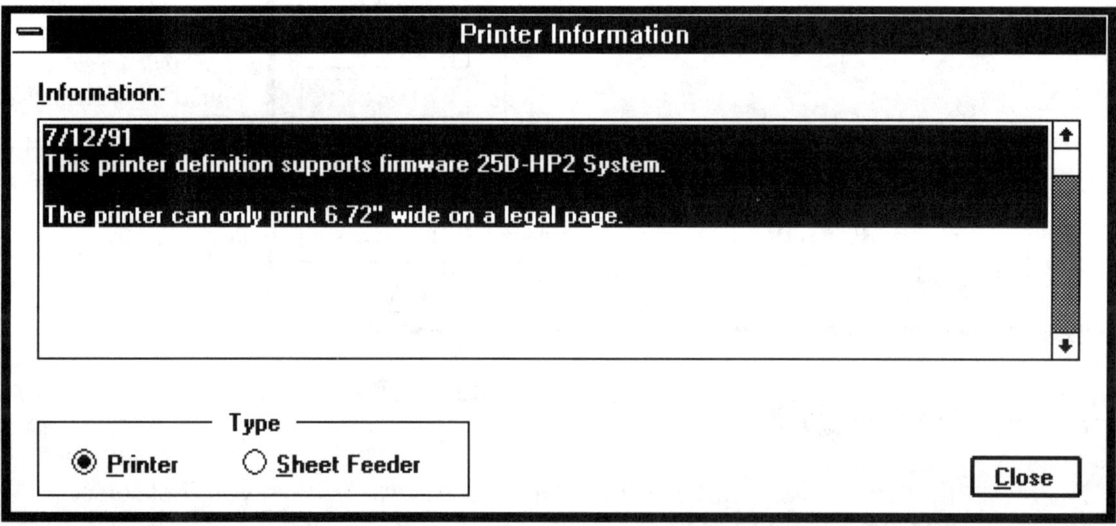

Figure 9-35. *The Printer Information dialog box for the printer type Destiny PageStyler.*

WordPerfect printer drivers are stored in a file with the extension ***"all"***. If you ever receive an updated version of ***all*** files (perhaps containing new, or updated printer drivers), you must update all the ***prs*** files you have created by selecting the *Update* button of Figure 9-33. No dialog box will appear, but WordPerfect will spend a few seconds updating all files.

Finally, to select the printer you wish to use, make sure the printer is highlighted in the list (if you only have one printer in the list, it should still be highlighted), and press the *Select* button. The *Close* button will remove this dialog box without selecting a new printer.

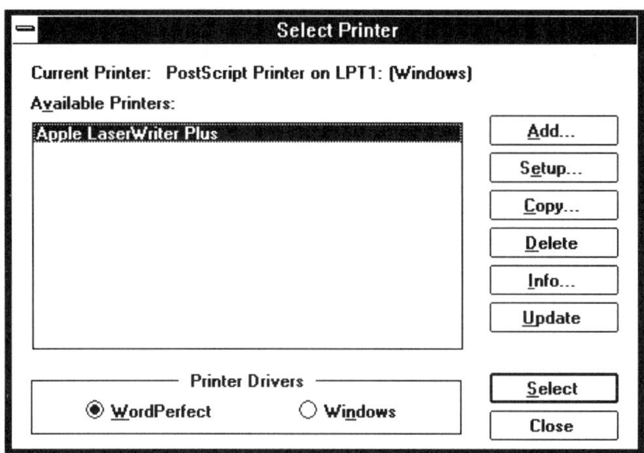

Figure 9-36. *As there is only one printer in this list, clicking on the Select button will select that printer for use with WordPerfect.*

Printing a document

Regardless of what type of printer you have selected, or whether you are using a Windows or a WordPerfect printer driver, the printing process is the same—select the *Print* command from the **File** menu (Figure 9-37).

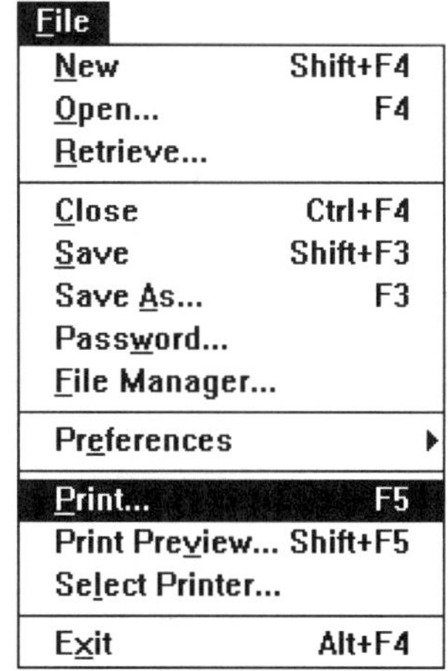

Figure 9-37. *The Print command from the* ***File*** *menu, through the Figure 9-38 Print dialog box, allows you to print a document.*

After selecting the *Print* command (Figure 9-37), you will be presented with the dialog box of Figure 9-38.

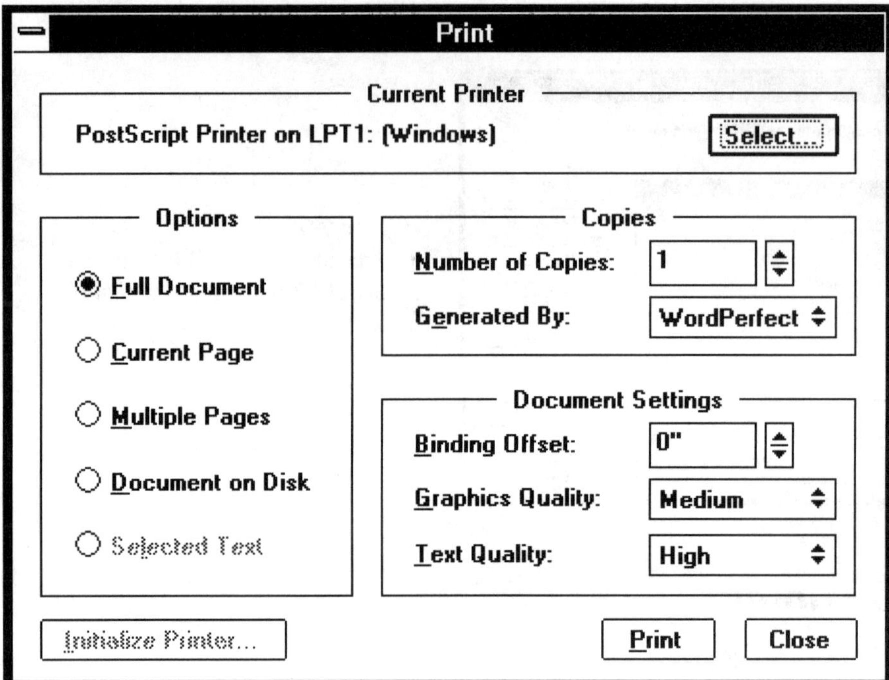

Figure 9-38. The Print dialog box.

The *Print* dialog box provides flexibility in printing your work. You are given several options from which to select, before printing takes place.

At the very top of the dialog box is the *Current Printer* section (Figure 9-39). This is the printer on which the printing will take place. If this printer is incorrect, you can use the *Select* button to present you with the *Select Printer* dialog box and options, as described from Figure 9-1 onwards in this chapter.

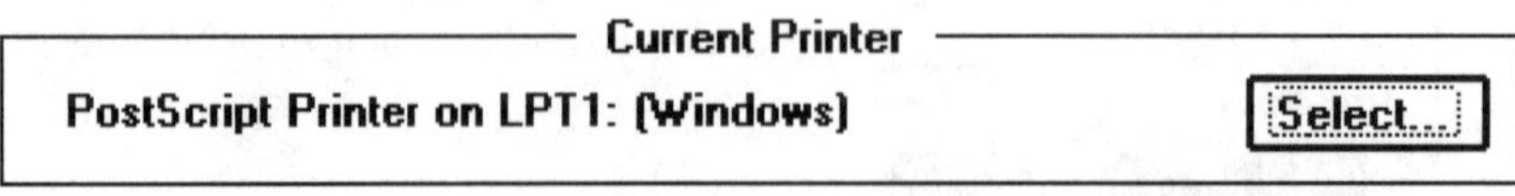

***Figure 9-39.** The Current Printer, in this case a PostScript Printer, uses the Windows, rather than the WordPerfect, printer driver.*

Below the *Current Printer* are the print *Options* radio buttons (Figure 9-40). These buttons let you select what part of the document to print. As with all radio buttons, only one option can be selected at any one time.

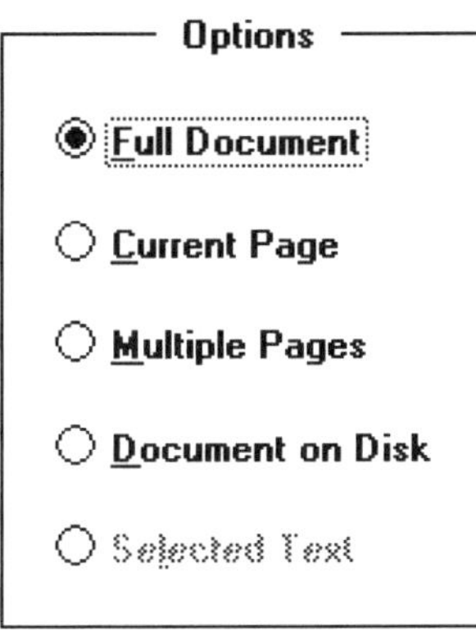

Figure 9-40. *The print Options let you select exactly what you wish to print.*

Selecting *Full Document* will ensure that every page in the current document will print.

Selecting *Current Page* means that only one page, the current page, from the current document will print.

Multiple Pages allows you to specify a page range from the current document to print—for example, print pages two through five from the current ten page document. You will not be asked what pages you would like to print until you actually select the *Print* button.

Document on Disk allows you to print a file that is not currently open. You will be asked to name the file you wish to print, after you select the *Print* button.

Selected Text will only be highlighted within the *Print* dialog box if there is text currently selected on the page before the *Print* command is activated. If so, selecting this option will print only the selected text.

The *Copies* section of this dialog box (Figure 9-41) lets you determine how many copies of this print job you would like to print, by editing the *Number of Copies* text box.

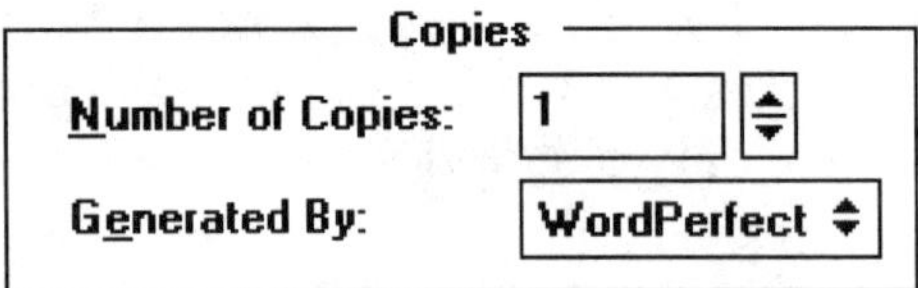

Figure 9-41. The Copies section lets you control how many copies of this document are to be printed.

The *Generated By* pop-up list box lets you make a choice between *WordPerfect* and *Printer*. If *WordPerfect* is selected, it is up to the WordPerfect program to generate the desired number of copies and send them to the printer. If *Printer* is selected, WordPerfect creates only one copy of the document, sends it to the printer, and tells the printer to make the desired number of copies of this document.

The *Document Settings* section of the *Print* dialog box (Figure 9-42) provides even more options as to how the document is to be printed.

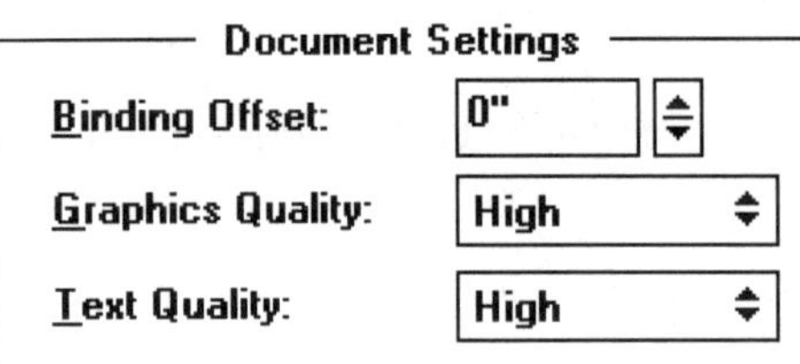

Figure 9-42. The Document Settings section of this dialog box determines several other options, mainly relating to print quality.

The *Binding Offset* is the distance that WordPerfect will shift, or offset, pages as they are printed. It will offset odd pages to the right, and even pages to the left, to allow additional room for binding.

If, for example, you are printing a booklet, that is going to be comb bound, then the inside margin of the book must be a little larger than the outside margin, to allow room for comb binding. To allow this room, set a small measure in the *Binding Offset* text box.

Graphics Quality and *Text Quality* determine, at what quality, objects on the page will print. Your choices are *High*, *Medium*, *Draft*, and *Do not Print*. Depending on your printer, and the type of fonts and graphics you use, you can speed printing time tremendously by selecting a lower quality output for either text or graphics. (If you are using a Windows, rather than a WordPerfect printer driver, you may not be able to select as wide a range of options from the *Graphics Quality*, or *Text Quality* pop-up list boxes.)

Whether or not the *Initialize Printer* button can be selected (Figure 9-43) depends on whether you are using a WordPerfect, rather than a Windows printer driver (see **Selecting a printer** earlier in this chapter), and whether, during the setup of the selected WordPerfect printer driver, you specified that soft fonts were to be used (Figure 9-3). Selecting this button will download the preselected fonts to your printer.

Initialize Printer...

Figure 9-43. *The Initialize Printer button from Figure 9-38.*

Selecting the *Print* button now will send the document to the printer. However, if you selected *Multiple Pages* for *Options* (Figure 9-40), you will be presented with the *Multiple Pages* dialog box of Figure 9-44.

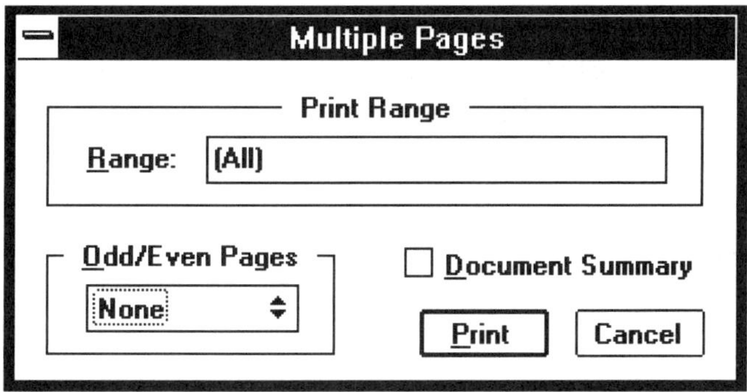

Figure 9-44. *If you selected Multiple Pages from Figure 9-40, you will be asked to specify what pages you would like to print after you select the Print button.*

In the Figure 9-44 dialog box, insert the numbers of the pages you wish to print. WordPerfect will print the pages between the highest and lowest numbers on this line. For example, in Figure 9-45, pages two through five will print.

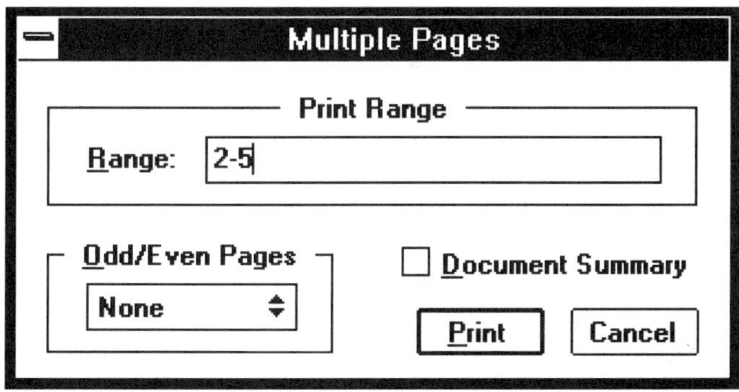

Figure 9-45. *WordPerfect will print the pages between the highest and the lowest numbers it finds on this line; in this case, pages 2 through 5.*

If you selected *Document on Disk* for *Options* (Figure 9-40), you will be presented with this dialog box (Figure 9-46).

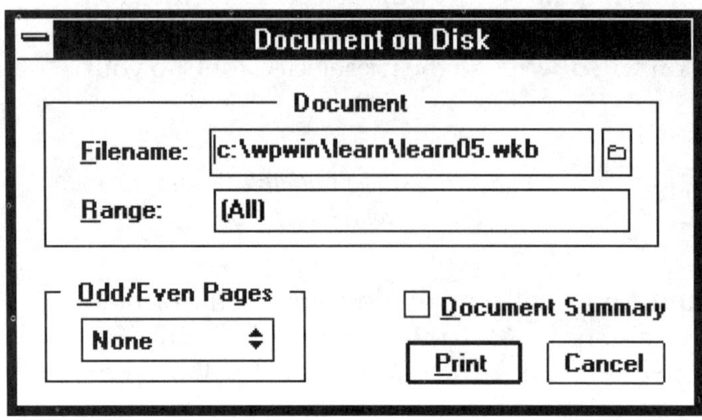

***Figure 9-46.** This dialog box will appear after selecting the Print button, if Document on Disk was the option selected from Figure 9-40.*

In Figure 9-46, a document name has already been inserted on the *Filename* line. However, you can click on the small folder icon to the right of the *Filename* box, and you will be presented with a dialog box similar to an open dialog box. You can then select a file to be inserted automatically on this *Filename* line.

In a similar method as described for Figure 9-44, you may insert the page range for the pages you would like printed from this document, in the *Range* text box.

When printing starts, WordPerfect displays a dialog box as shown in Figure 9-47, indicating the current page number, copy, message and action for the print job.

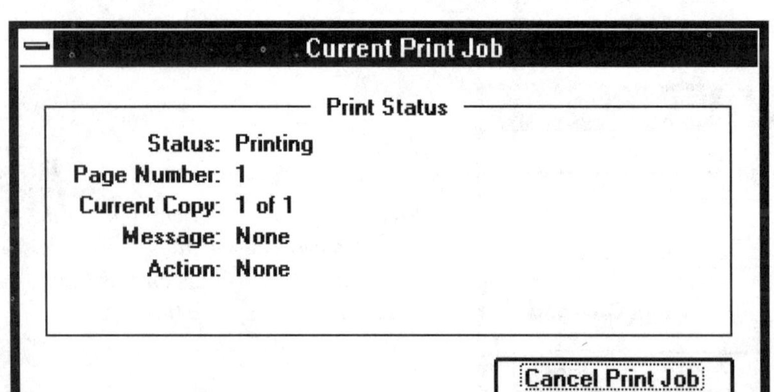

***Figure 9-47.** The dialog box that appears on selecting Print signifies that printing has begun.*

Using the Print Preview screen

Although WordPerfect is a WYSIWYG product, it can sometimes be difficult to tell how a particular document will appear once printed, without first printing it.

To overcome this problem, WordPerfect provides the *Print Preview* command in the **File** menu. This command allows you to look at single and multiple pages, using different view options, as they will appear when printed (Figure 9-48).

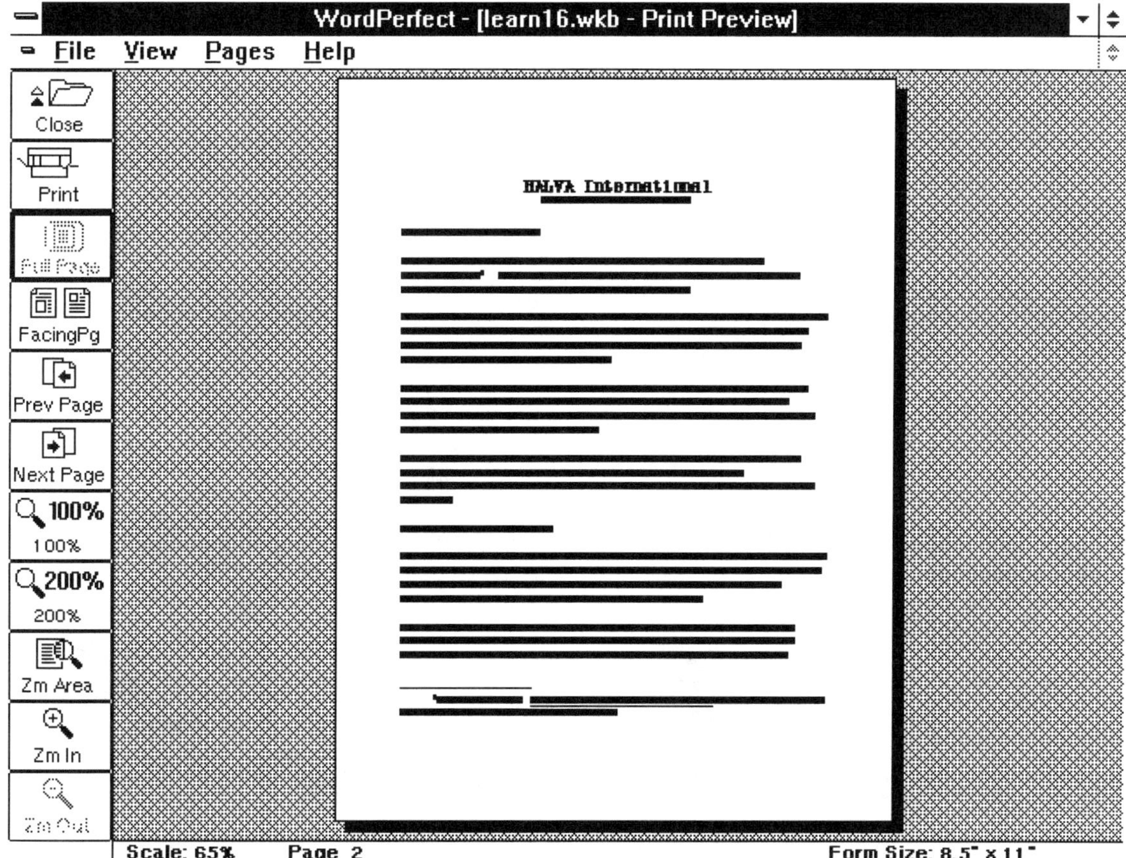

Figure 9-48. *A sample print preview, showing the actual page as it will print.*

In the *Print Preview* screen, you have many options in order to view your print job. The **View** menu (Figure 9-49) and the **Pages** menu (Figure 9-50), for example, let you view single pages or facing pages (pages 2 and 3, for example), at a range of sizes.

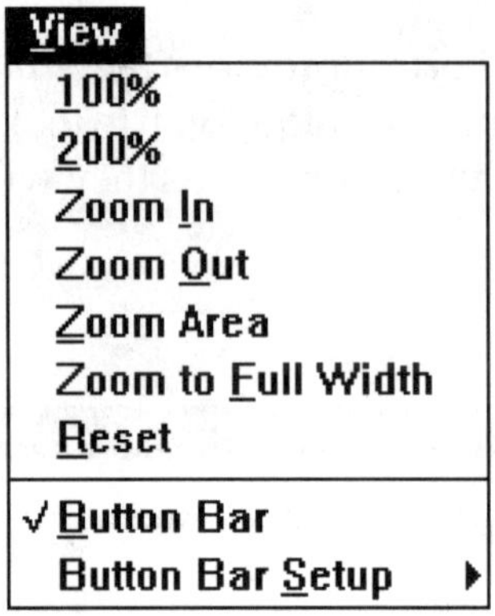

View
100%
200%
Zoom In
Zoom Out
Zoom Area
Zoom to Full Width
Reset
✓Button Bar
Button Bar Setup ▸

***Figure 9-49.** The **View** menu provides many options as to how a page, or pages, can be viewed in the Print Preview screen.*

Pages
Full Page
Facing Pages
Go To Page
Previous Page
Next Page

***Figure 9-50.** The **Page** menu provides options that allow multiple pages, or selected pages in a document, to be viewed in the Print Preview screen.*

Using the *Print* command from the **File** menu (or the *Print* button from the Button bar), you can even go directly to print from here. (The Button bar is the vertical icon bar at the left of the screen in Figure 9-48. The Button bar is described in detail in Chapter 14.)

You can return to the editing screen by selecting the *Close* command from the **File** menu, or the *Close* button. The following figures (Figures 9-51 and 9-52) illustrate some *Print Preview* options.

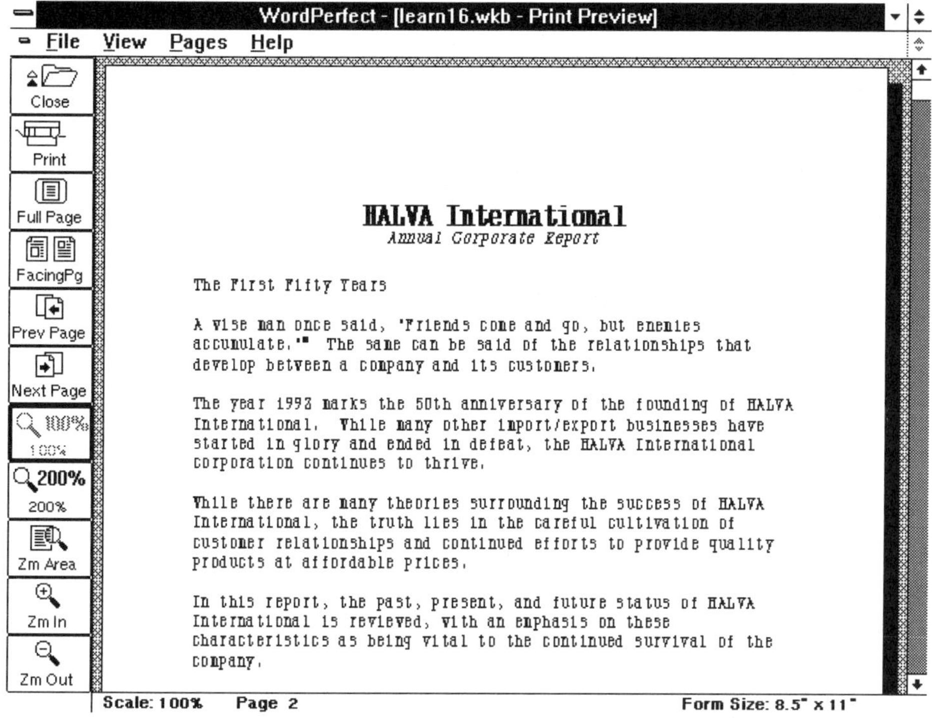

Figure 9-51. This page view results from selecting the 100% button in the Button bar.

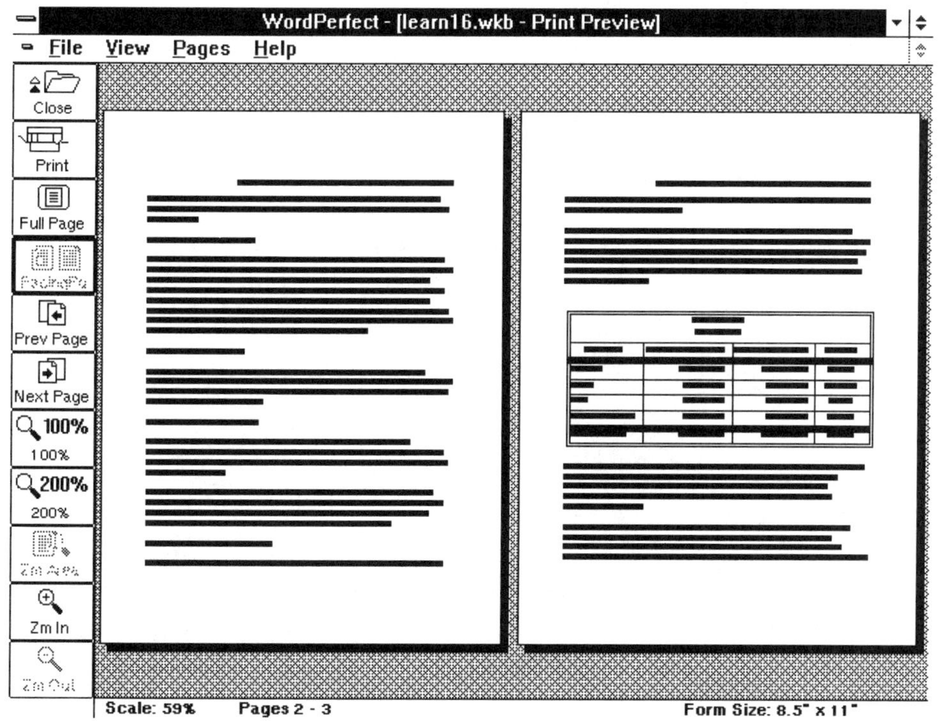

*Figure 9-52. Facing pages may be viewed simultaneously, by selecting the Facing Pages command from the **Pages** menu.*

Depending on the selected view, scroll bars may appear along the bottom, and the right, of the *Print Preview* screen. The scroll bars can be used to help you move around a page.

Along the bottom of the *Print Preview* screen is a Status bar which shows the viewing scale, the current page(s) viewed, and the current Form Size.

Selecting from multiple prs files

The comments here will only make sense if you have worked through the **Using a WordPerfect printer driver** section earlier in this chapter.

In Figure 9-13, you looked at how a WordPerfect printer could be selected from a list of drivers supplied with the program. This is shown again in figure 9-53. One part of this dialog box that was not explained was the *Printers* section at the bottom of the box (Figure 9-54).

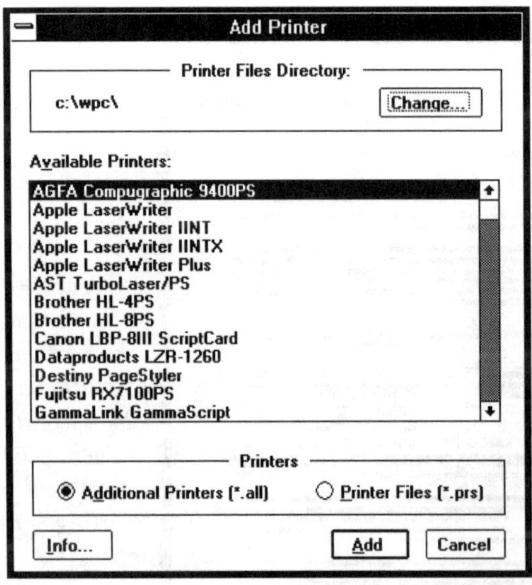

Figure 9-53. *The Add Printer dialog box, as described in Figure 9-13 and surrounding text.*

There are two choices in this section (Figure 9-54)—*Additional Printers* (**.all*), and *Printer Files* (**.prs*).

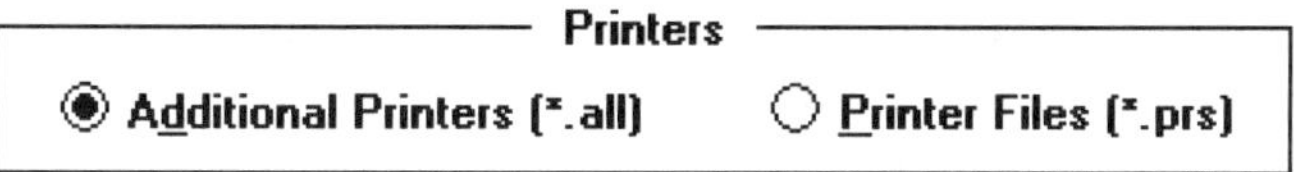

Figure 9-54. The Printers section of the Figure 9-53 dialog box.

With the *Additional Printers* option selected, the list of *Available Printers* will reflect simply the available WordPerfect drivers on disk—these drivers are contained in files with an *"all"* extension.

With the *Printer Files* option selected, the list of *Available Printers* lists the current ***prs*** files; files that are created by the user, every time a printer is selected in the method described earlier in this chapter. A default ***prs*** file is created for each printer selected as WordPerfect was installed. To refresh your memory, check the section on **Copying (duplicating) a printer driver** earlier in this chapter. Figure 9-55 illustrates the Figure 9-53 dialog box now listing only ***prs*** files.

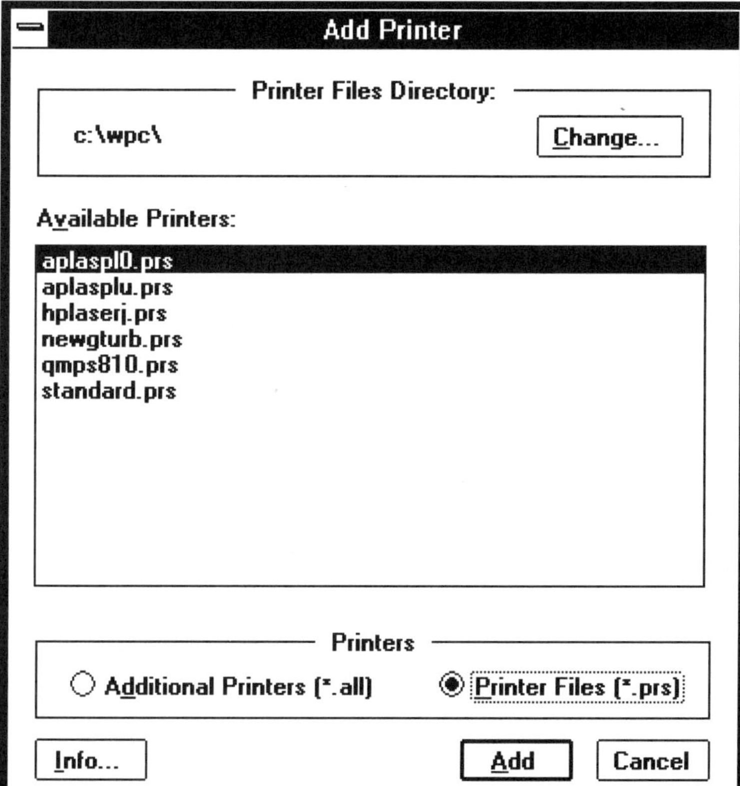

*Figure 9-55. The Add Printer dialog box, listing six **prs** files (note the option selected in the Printers section at the bottom of the dialog box).*

It is quite probable that you are not going to select printer drivers in this way—at least until you have used WordPerfect for a while and had a chance to create multiple ***prs*** files.

Setting printer defaults

In the **File** menu, there is a command called *Preferences/Print*. In this command, you can set up numerous print defaults. This command is discussed in detail in Chapter 10, **Preferences - (1)**.

Printing—Exercise

This training exercise is designed so that people of all levels of expertise with WordPerfect can use it to gain maximum benefit. In order to do this, the bare exercise is listed below this paragraph on just one page, with no hints. The following pages contain the steps needed to complete this exercise for those who need additional prompting.

Note: This exercise will only work if you have the WordPerfect PostScript printer drivers installed.

Steps in brief

1. ***Open the learn17.wkb file from the learn sub-directory.***
2. ***In the Select Printer dialog box, choose the WordPerfect Printer Drivers option.***
3. ***Add the HP LaserJet Series II PostScript printer to the Available Printers list.***
4. ***In the Printer Setup dialog box, alter the Destination options so the document is printed to disk.***
5. ***Preview, then print page two to disk.***

The details for completing these steps are on the following pages.

Steps in detail

1. *Open the learn17.wkb file from the learn sub-directory.*

If you are already in WordPerfect, you do not have to close the current document, as WordPerfect can open multiple files at once. If you are not in WordPerfect, start the program from Windows.

For this exercise you are opening a file from the ***learn*** sub-directory in the ***wpwin*** sub-directory. To access this file, select the *Open* command from the **File** menu (Figure 9x-1). This will activate the *Open File* dialog box of Figure 9x-2.

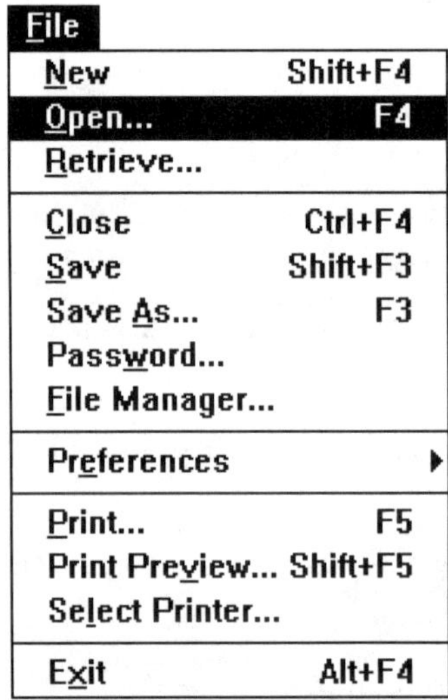

***Figure 9x-1**. Select the Open command from the **File** menu to activate the Open File dialog box of Figure 9x-2.*

In the *Open File* dialog box, locate the ***learn*** sub-directory in the ***wpwin*** sub-directory. Then, using the scroll bar to the right of the list of files, find the ***learn17.wkb*** file and click on it. To then open the file, click on the *Open* button (Figure 9x-2). Alternatively, double-click on the ***learn17.wkb*** file and it will automatically open.

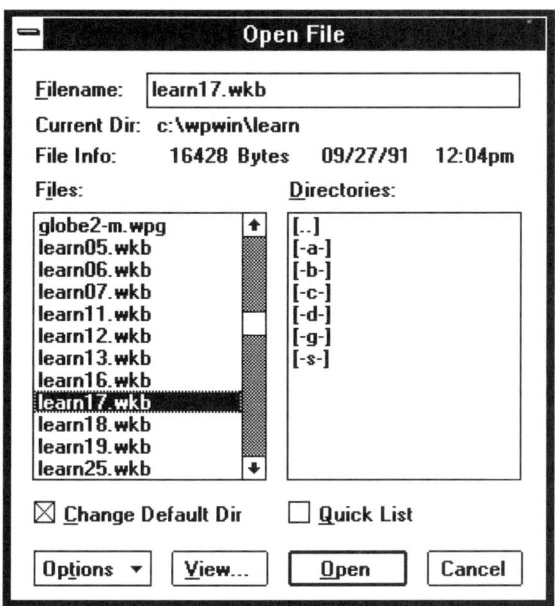

Figure 9x-2. *Select the **learn17.wkb** file from the list of files in the **learn** sub-directory, and click on the Open button.*

After clicking on the *Open* button in the Figure 9x-2 dialog box, the selected file (***learn17.wkb***) will be opened into the current document window, which is reflected in the Title bar (Figure 9x-3).

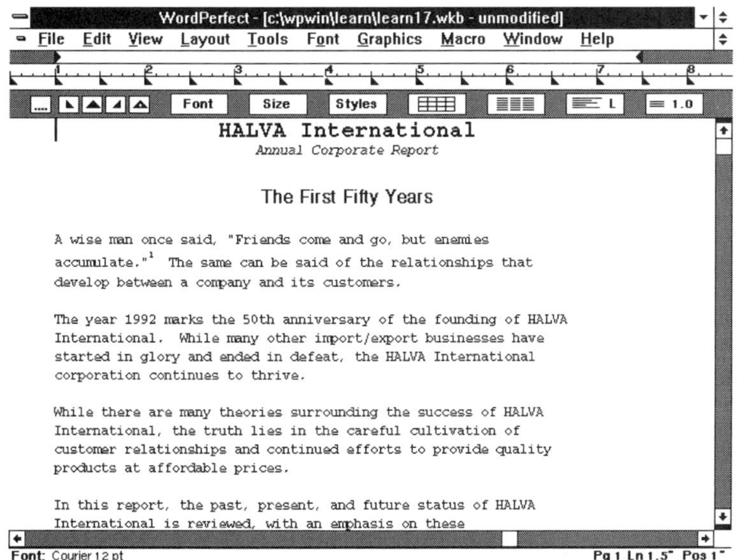

Figure 9x-3. *The **learn17.wkb** file is now open.*

2. ***In the Select Printer dialog box, choose the WordPerfect Printer Drivers option.***

To activate the *Select Printer* dialog box, choose the *Select Printer* command from the **File** menu (Figure 9x-4).

File
New Shift+F4
Open... F4
Retrieve...
Close Ctrl+F4
Save Shift+F3
Save As... F3
Password...
File Manager...
Preferences
Print... F5
Print Preview... Shift+F5
Select Printer...
Exit Alt+F4

***Figure 9x-4**. The Select Printer command in the **File** menu will activate the Select Printer dialog box of Figure 9x-5.*

In the *Printer Drivers* section of the *Select Printer* dialog box, click on the *WordPerfect* option (Figure 9x-5). It is quite possible that you may have some WordPerfect printer drivers already listed in the Figure 9x-5 dialog box under *Available Printers.*

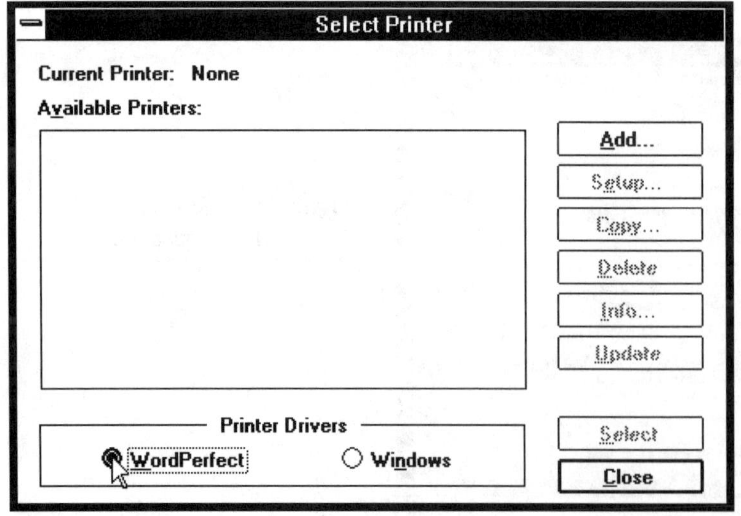

***Figure 9x-5**. Click on the WordPerfect option in the Printer Drivers section of the Select Printer dialog box.*

3. *Add the HP LaserJet Series II PostScript printer to the Available Printers list.*

To now add printers to the list of *Available Printers* in the *Select Printer* dialog box, click on the *Add* button (Figure 9x-6). This will activate the *Add Printer* dialog box of Figure 9x-7.

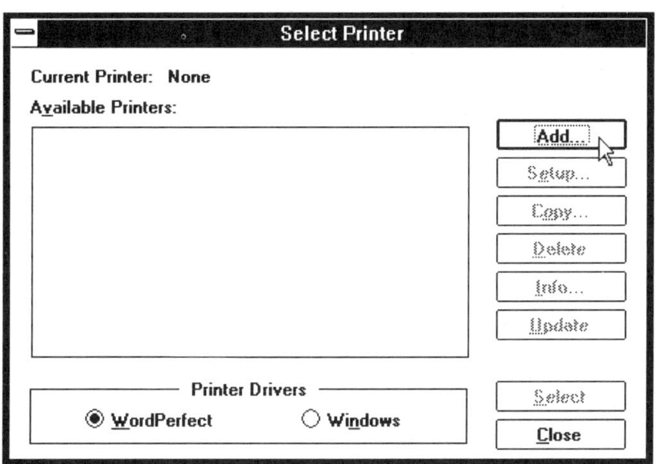

***Figure 9x-6**. Click on the Add button to get access to the Add Printer dialog box.*

Use the scroll bar to the right of the list of *Available Printers* to find the HP LaserJet Series printers (Figure 9x-7).

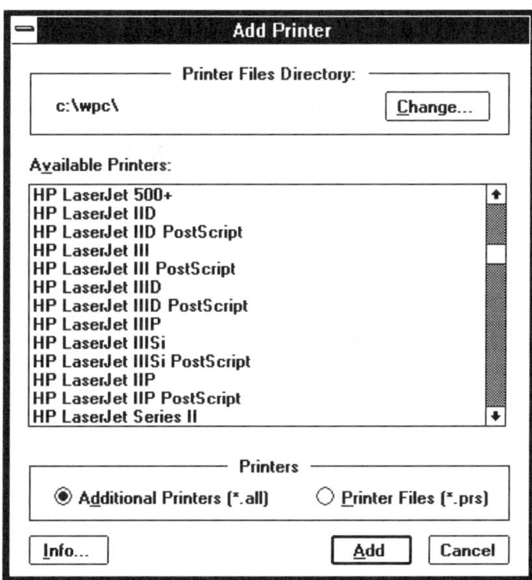

***Figure 9x-7**. To locate the HP LaserJet Series printers, use the scroll bar to the right of the Available Printers list.*

Click on the HP LaserJet Series II PostScript option and then click on the *Add* button as shown in Figure 9x-8. You may prefer to select another printer.

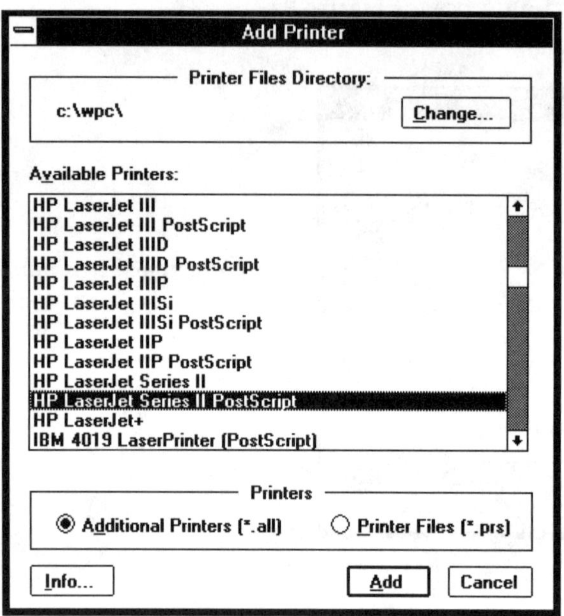

Figure 9x-8. *After selecting the correct printer from the list, click on the Add button.*

After clicking on *Add* in the dialog box of Figure 9x-8, the *Copy Printer* screen prompt of Figure 9x-9 appears. This indicates the filename of the printer you just selected. It is possible to change this name by keying in your own, but for this exercise leave it as is. If you do change it, make sure you keep the ***.prs*** extension, so that the file can be recognized as a printer file. Click on **OK** in the *Copy Printer* dialog box.

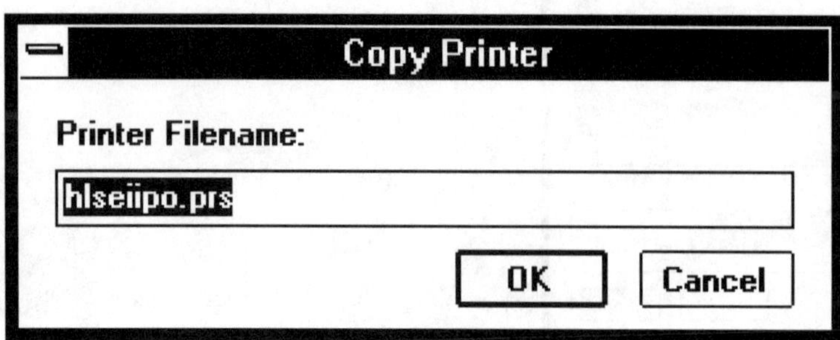

Figure 9x-9. *After you click on the Add button in the Add Printer dialog box, the Copy Printer screen prompt appears. Here the Printer Filename is established.*

After exiting the *Copy Printer* dialog box of Figure 9x-9, you will be returned to the *Select Printer* dialog box of Figure 9x-10. The printer you selected in the *Add Printer* dialog box of Figure 9x-8 is now in the list of *Available Printers*.

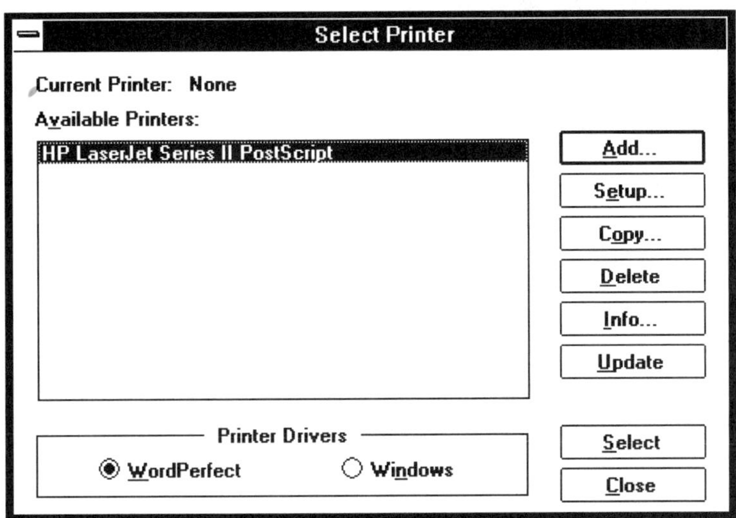

Figure 9x-10*. The printer selected in the Add Printer dialog box is now in the Select Printer dialog box.*

4. ***In the Printer Setup dialog box, alter the Destination options so the document is printed to disk.***

Once the printer has been added, click on the *Setup* button in the *Select Printer* dialog box. This will activate the *Printer Setup* dialog box of Figure 9x-11. In the *Destination* section of this dialog box, hold the mouse down on the *Port* pop-up list. Run your mouse down this list and select the *File* option. You are now able to insert a path and filename for the print file you are going to create.

For this exercise, create the print file on the C drive, and call it ***test***. Give the file a ***.prn*** extension so it can be recognized as a print file. Once you have set up your dialog box as for Figure 9x-11, click on **OK**.

After setting up the *Printer Setup* dialog box to create a print file, click on **OK** and you will be returned to the *Select Printer* dialog box of Figure 9x-12. To finalize the adding of the printer to the list, and the changes made in the *Printer Setup* dialog box, click on the *Select* button.

Printer Setup

Filename: hlseiipo.prs

Name: HP LaserJet Series II PostScript

Path for Downloadable Fonts and Printer Commands:

Current Initial Font

Courier

Initial Font...

Current Sheet Feeder

Sheet Feeder...

Destination

Port: File

Network Printer

Filename: c:\test.prn

Cartridges/Fonts...

OK

Cancel

This is the section you need to change in this dialog box

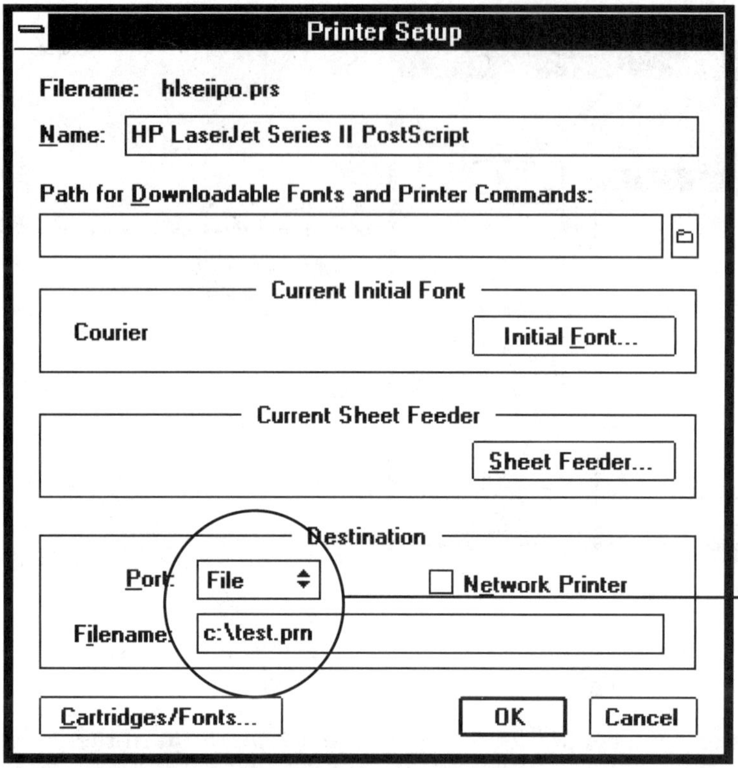

Figure 9x-11*. Set up your dialog box as shown here in preparation for creating a print file. Then click on* ***OK*** *to return to the Select Printer dialog box.*

Select Printer

Current Printer: HP LaserJet Series II PostScript

Available Printers:

HP LaserJet Series II PostScript

Add...

Setup...

Copy...

Delete

Info...

Update

Printer Drivers

WordPerfect

Windows

Select

Close

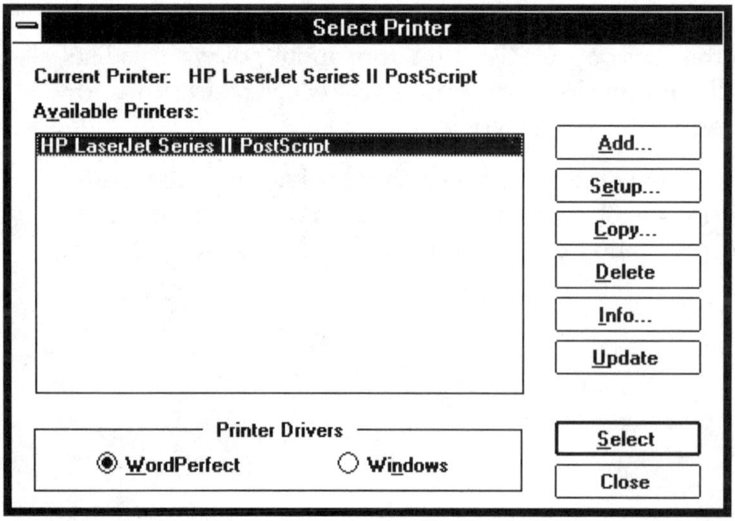

Figure 9x-12*. Click on the Select button in the Select Printer dialog box and you will be returned to the document window.*

5. *Preview, then print page two to disk.*

Before previewing page two, move to page two in the document window. To do this, first select the *Go To* command in the **Edit** menu (Figure 9x-13).

Edit
Undo Alt+Bksp
Undelete... Alt+Shift+Bksp
Cut Shift+Del
Copy Ctrl+Ins
Paste Shift+Ins
Append
Link
Select
Convert Case
Search... F2
Search Next Shift+F2
Search Previous Alt+F2
Replace... Ctrl+F2
Go To... Ctrl+G

***Figure 9x-13**. Before previewing page two, you are going to move to this page. As one way to do this, select the Go To command from the **Edit** menu.*

The *Go To* command from the **Edit** menu activates the *Go To* dialog box of Figure 9x-14. In this dialog box, key in 2 in the *Go To Page Number* text box, as shown in Figure 9x-14, and click on **OK**.

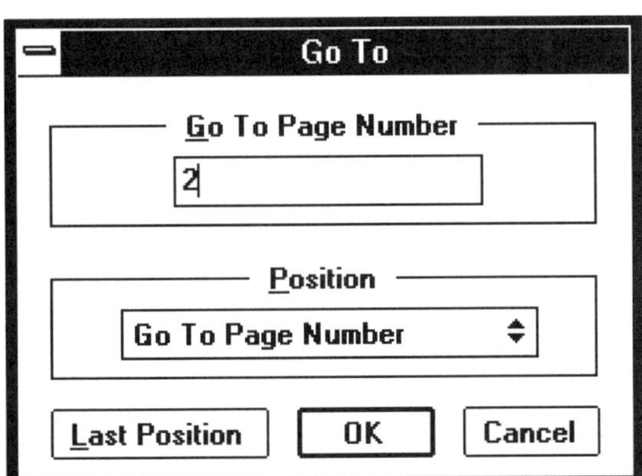

***Figure 9x-14**. Key in 2 in the Go To Page Number text box and click on the **OK** button.*

After clicking on **OK** in the *Go To* dialog box, the beginning of page two will appear at the top of the screen (Figure 9x-15).

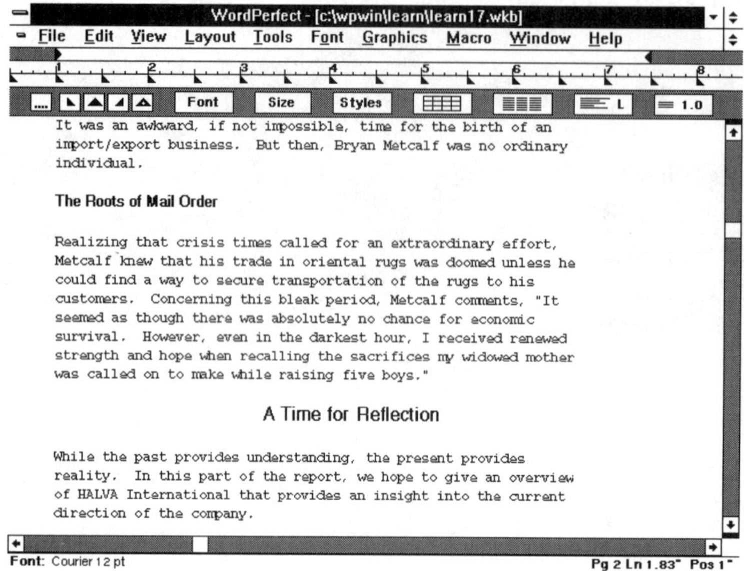

Figure 9x-15. *Page two is now at the top of the document window.*

Once page two is at the top of the document window, select the *Print Preview* option from the **File** menu (Figure 9x-16).

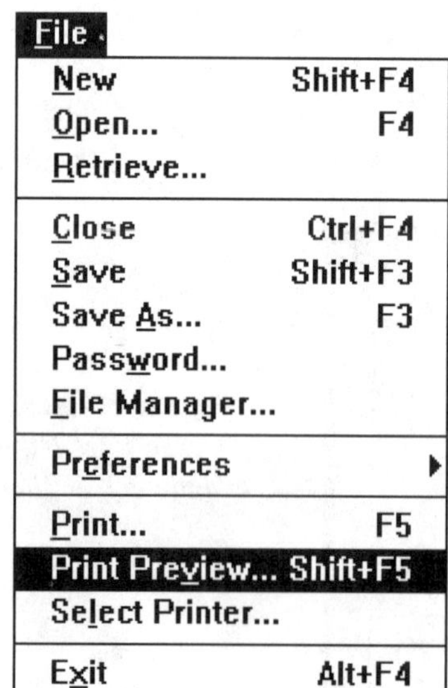

Figure 9x-16. *Select the Print Preview command from the* ***File*** *menu.*

The *Print Preview* command activates the *Print Preview* window. This shows you what the page will look like when printed. Page two should be the current page in the *Print Preview* window (Figure 9x-17).

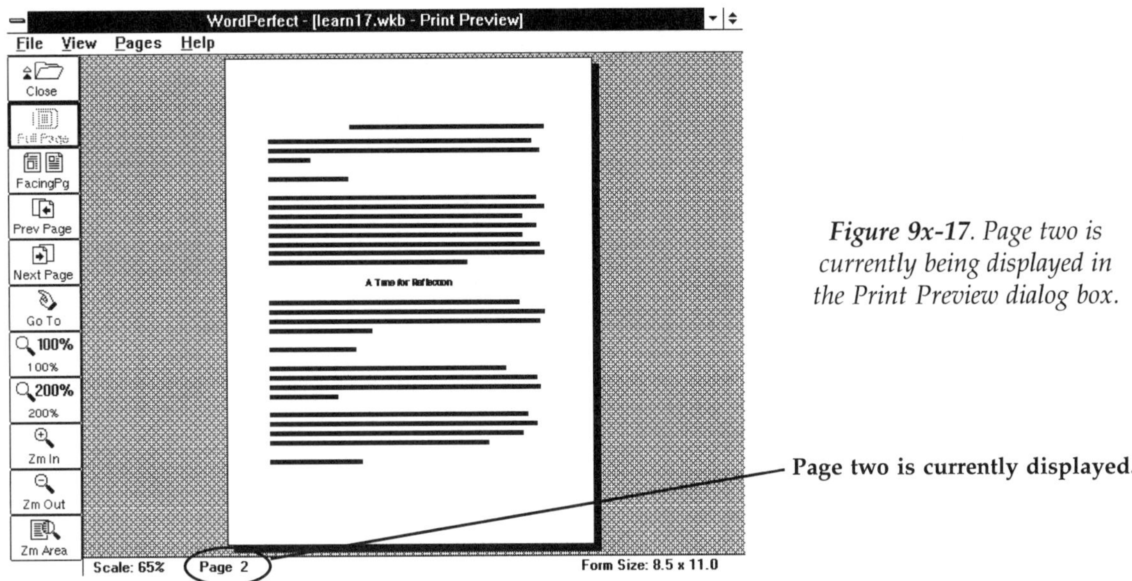

***Figure 9x-17**. Page two is currently being displayed in the Print Preview dialog box.*

It is now possible to print page two from inside the *Print Preview* window. To do this, select the *Print* command from the **File** menu in the *Print Preview* window (Figure 9x-18).

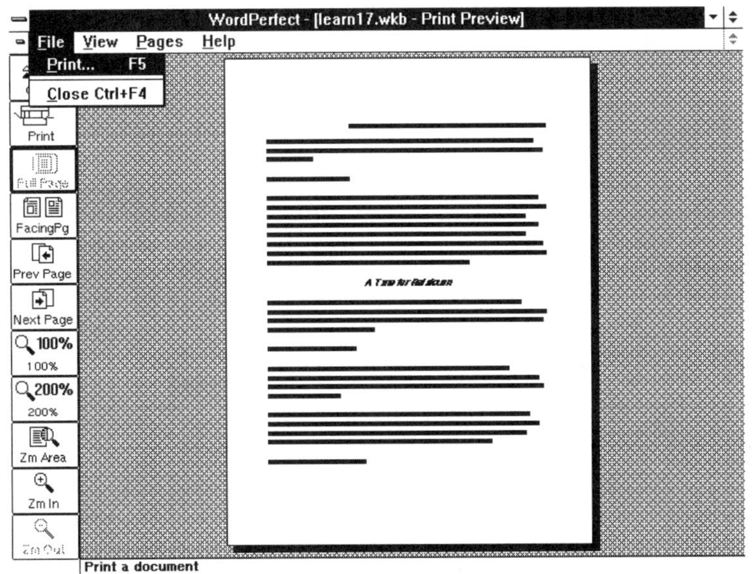

***Figure 9x-18**. To print from inside the Print Preview window, select the Print command from the **File** menu.*

Selecting the *Print* command, while in the *Print Preview* window, will activate the *Print* dialog box of Figure 9x-19. This is the same dialog box that you get when you select the *Print* command in the normal WordPerfect document window.

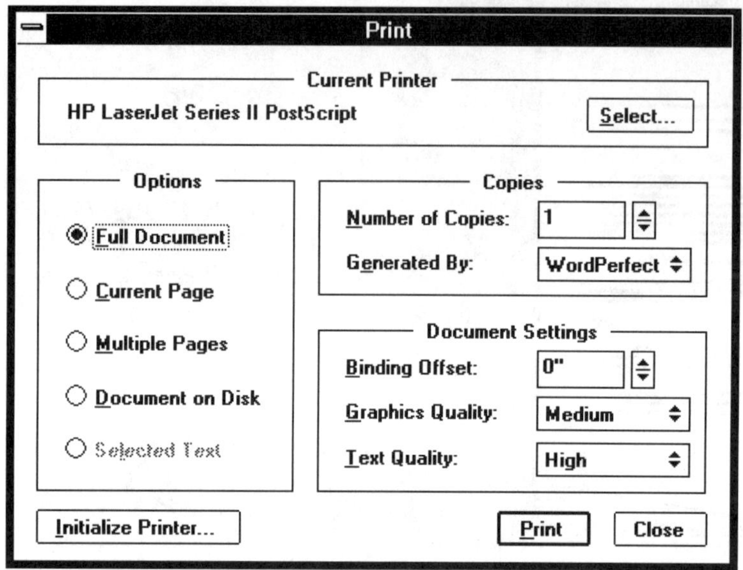

***Figure 9x-19**. The Print command activates this Print dialog box.*

To now print page two only, the change you make in the *Print* dialog box is in the *Options* section. Click on the *Current Page* option, as in Figure 9x-20, and then on the *Print* option.

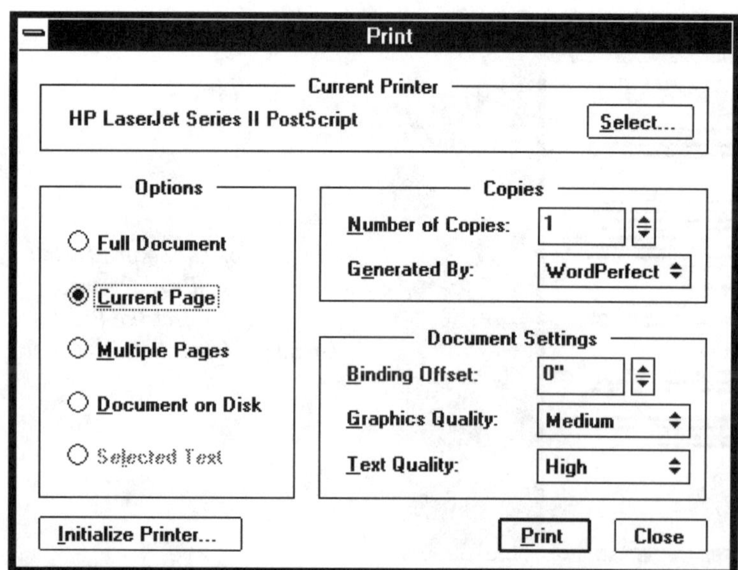

***Figure 9x-20**. In the Print dialog box, change the Options setting to Current Page and click on the Print button.*

After clicking on *Print*, the *Current Print Job* screen prompt of Figure 9x-21 appears. This gives you the current information on your print job. This will disappear once the print job is completed.

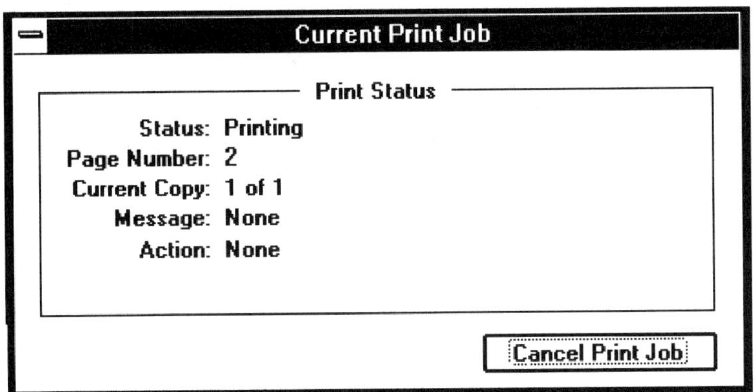

***Figure 9x-21**. The Current Print Job screen prompt appears while the document is printing.*

Preferences - (1)

Setting *Preferences*, in almost all software packages, is important in determining exactly how a program operates—i.e., what settings it uses by default. Successfully setting defaults, or preferences, means the program runs the way you want it to run; it looks for files where you keep files, etc. Because preferences are remembered even after you exit WordPerfect, these preferences only need be set once—unless of course you wish to modify them again.

All of the preferences discussed within this chapter are contained within the *Preferences* fly-out menu in the **File** menu as shown in Figure 10-1.

Preferences/Location of Files

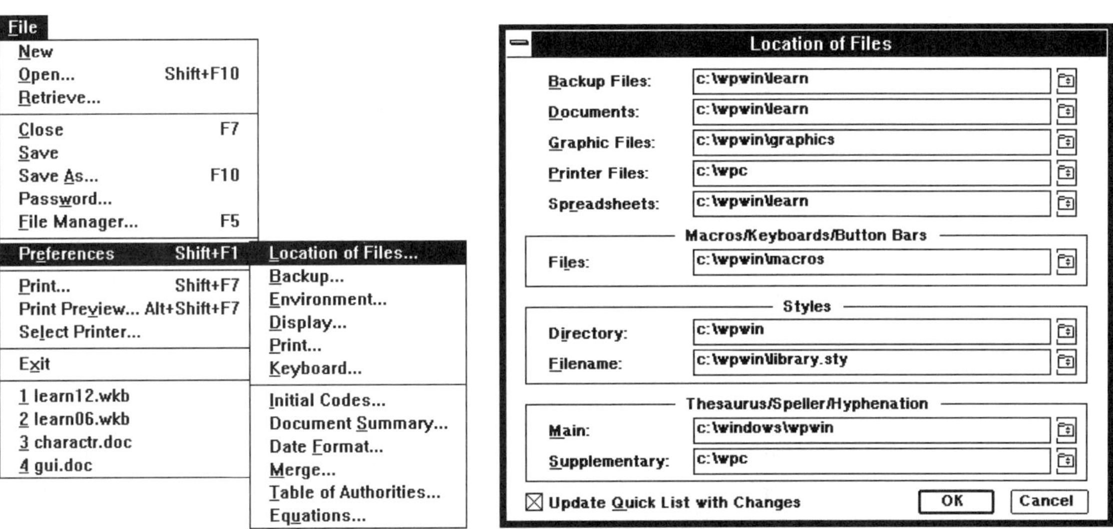

Figure 10-1. *The Preferences/Location of Files command and the Location of Files dialog box.*

The *Location of Files* command lets WordPerfect know where to look for certain types of files. This dialog box is organized as a series of file types, with an accompanying text box displaying the directory currently used to access these types of files.

Figure 10-2. A portion of the Location of Files dialog box, displaying the directories currently used to access/store Backup, Document, Graphic, Printer and Spreadsheet files.

Backup Files:	c:\wpwin\learn
Documents:	c:\wpwin\learn
Graphic Files:	c:\wpwin\graphics
Printer Files:	c:\wpc
Spreadsheets:	c:\wpwin\learn

Many of these entries will be filled out automatically by WordPerfect during either the installation process or the normal use of WordPerfect. However, this command provides the control needed for any modifications you wish to make.

For example, note in Figure 10-2, that the directory specified for Documents is ***c:\wpwin\learn***. This is now the directory that will be displayed every time you select the *Open* or *Retrieve* commands to load a file.

There are two ways to change the name of a directory used to access or store certain file types. The first way is simply to click the mouse cursor on any directory name in Figure 10-2 and edit the directory name.

Perhaps the more accurate way is to click on the *List* button provided on the right-hand side of every directory name. These buttons are indicated in Figure 10-3.

Backup Files:	c:\wpwin\learn
Documents:	c:\wpwin\learn
Graphic Files:	c:\wpwin\graphics
Printer Files:	c:\wpc
Spreadsheets:	c:\wpwin\learn

Figure 10-3. The List button at the right side of every directory name in the Location of Files dialog box can be used to select a new drive and directory.

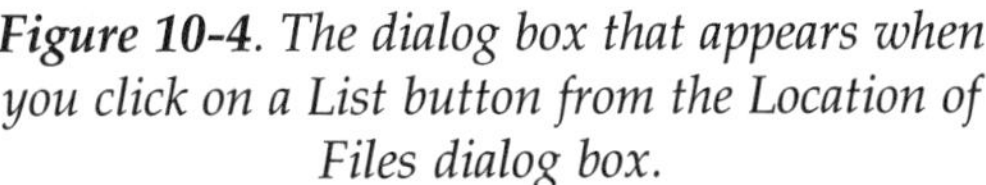

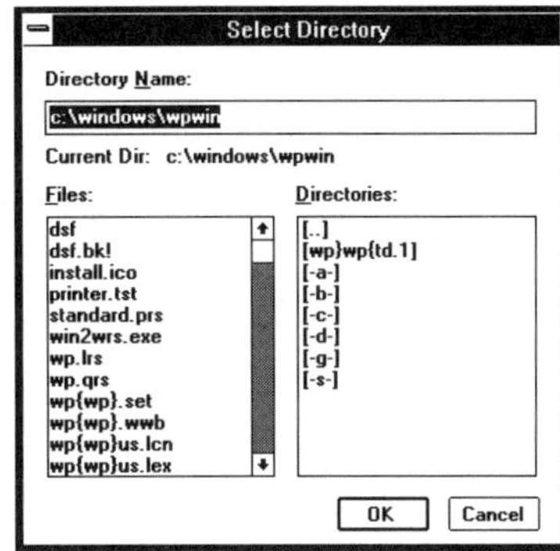

***Figure 10-4**. The dialog box that appears when you click on a List button from the Location of Files dialog box.*

In Figure 10-4, you can see the result of selecting one of these *List* buttons. The *Select Directory* dialog box appears, allowing you to move through and select any drive and directory you wish from the *Directories* box on the right. When you click on **OK** in Figure 10-4, the name of the current path is copied to the text rectangle of the *list box* that you selected from the *Location of Files* dialog box in Figure 10-3.

Once you have customized every Figure 10-1 file location that you wish, by repeating the above procedures, selecting **OK** will save all these settings as the default for all WordPerfect documents.

Preferences/Backup

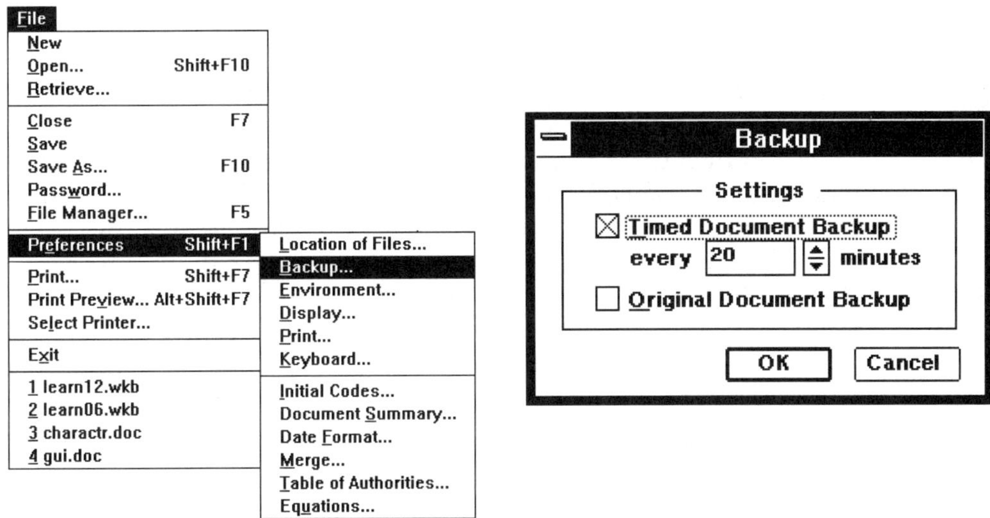

***Figure 10-5**. The Preferences/Backup command and its dialog box.*

WordPerfect includes an optional autobackup feature. This automatically saves the currently open file to disk, at predetermined intervals. This takes some responsibility from the user's shoulders, as in the event of some sort of power failure or user error, you only lose as much work as can be squeezed into each predetermined interval.

The *Timed Document Backup* option, within this dialog box, controls whether this feature is on or off. If a check appears in the box next to this option, the feature is on.

Under *Timed Document Backup* is the setting, in minutes, that determines how often WordPerfect saves to disk. By default, this setting is 20 minutes—you can edit this setting if a different time interval is more appropriate to your needs. If *Timed Document Backup* is enabled, and your session ends abnormally, then the Figure 10-6 dialog box will appear when you re-enter WordPerfect.

Figure 10-6*. This is the dialog box that appears if Timed Document Backup has been set on, and WordPerfect has ended abnormally in the last session. You are given the option of opening, renaming, or deleting any of the backup files that were created in the last session.*

Original Document Backup is a slightly different option. If this option is activated (i.e. has a check in the box next to it), WordPerfect will first create, and then update, a backup file of the currently opened document when the *Save* command from the **File** menu is selected. The first time you save the opened document, a backup file is created, and after that, the *Save* command will update both the open file and its backup. A backup file will have the same name as the file you are saving, but with the extension ***.bk!***.

Preferences/Environment

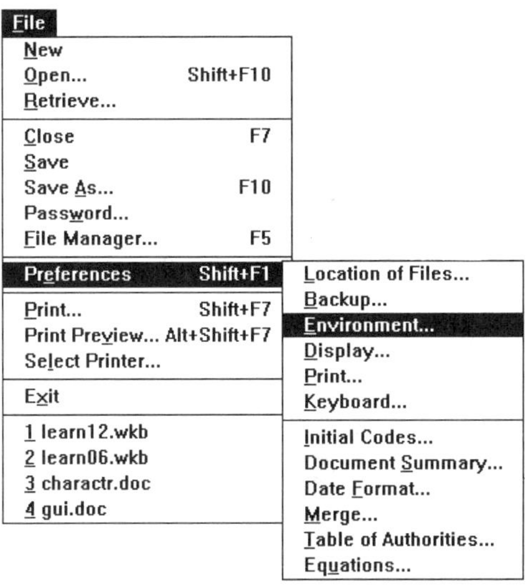

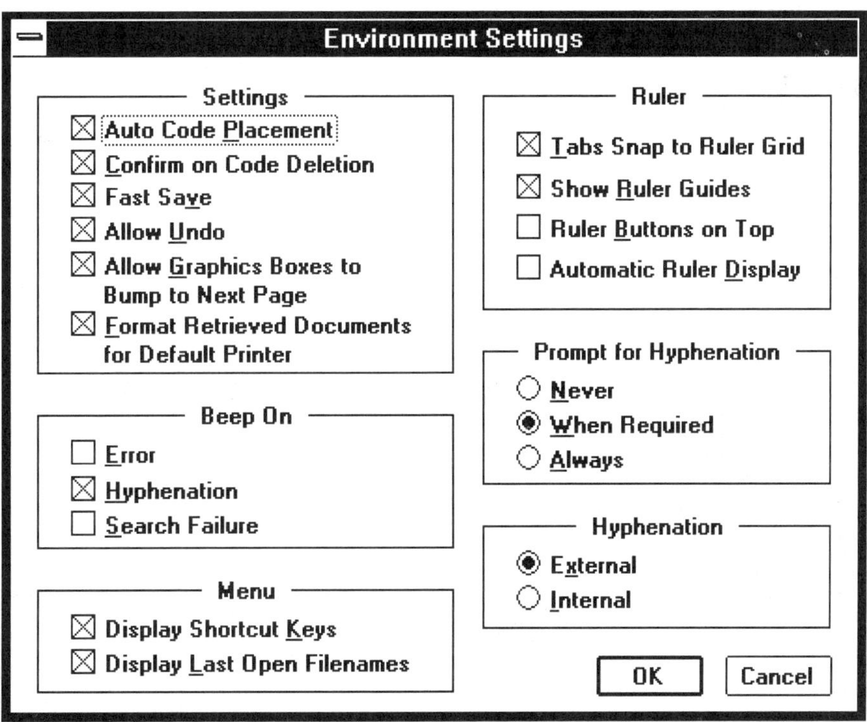

Figure 10-7. The Preferences/Environment command and dialog box.

The *Environment* command from the *Preferences* fly-out menu in the **File** menu is designed to set a variety of preferences in the WordPerfect environment.

Settings

Auto Code Placement, when selected, forces WordPerfect to automatically shift any codes inserted in text to the correct position within that text. For example, if you insert a page header or footer right in the middle of a paragraph, WordPerfect will force the code for this header or footer to the start of the page. This is a handy option to have on, particularly if you are a little fuzzy about codes in general (Figures 10-8 and 10-9). Codes are explained in detail in Chapter 5.

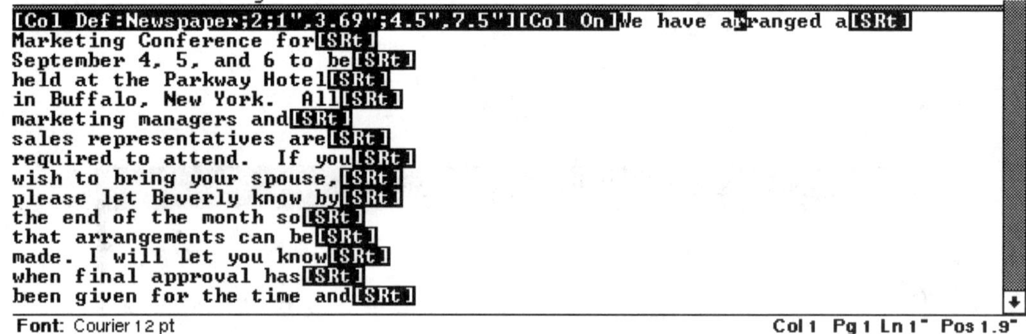

[Col Def:Newspaper;2;1",3.69";4.5",7.5"][Col On]We have arranged a[SRt]
Marketing Conference for[SRt]
September 4, 5, and 6 to be[SRt]
held at the Parkway Hotel[SRt]
in Buffalo, New York. All[SRt]
marketing managers and[SRt]
sales representatives are[SRt]
required to attend. If you[SRt]
wish to bring your spouse,[SRt]
please let Beverly know by[SRt]
the end of the month so[SRt]
that arrangements can be[SRt]
made. I will let you know[SRt]
when final approval has[SRt]
been given for the time and[SRt]

Font: Courier 12 pt   Col 1 Pg 1 Ln 1" Pos 1.9"

Figure 10-8. With Auto Code Placement on, most codes are automatically shifted to their correct position in the text (the correct position depends on the type of code). In this example, the code for columns has automatically been shifted to the beginning of a paragraph—making it easier to edit and find at a later date.

We have arranged a Marketing[Col Def:Newspaper;2;1",4";4.5",7.5"][HRt]
[Col On]Conference for September 4, 5,[SRt]
and 6 to be held at the Parkway[SRt]
Hotel in Buffalo, New York. [SRt]
All marketing managers and[SRt]
sales representatives are[SRt]
required to attend. If you[SRt]
wish to bring your spouse,[SRt]
please let Beverly know by the[SRt]
end of the month so that[SRt]
arrangements can be made. I[SRt]
will let you know when final[SRt]
approval has been given for the[SRt]
time and place.

Font: Courier 12 pt   Col 1 Pg 1 Ln 1.17" Pos 1"

***Figure 10-9.** If Auto Code Placement is disabled, codes appear in the text where they are created.*

Confirm on Code Deletion forces WordPerfect to issue a warning whenever an inserted code is about to be deleted (perhaps by accident). Once again, a handy option to turn on, as a code deleted by accident may cause unexpected results in a document. With this option on, you at least get the choice to confirm whether you think a particular code should be deleted (Figure 10-10).

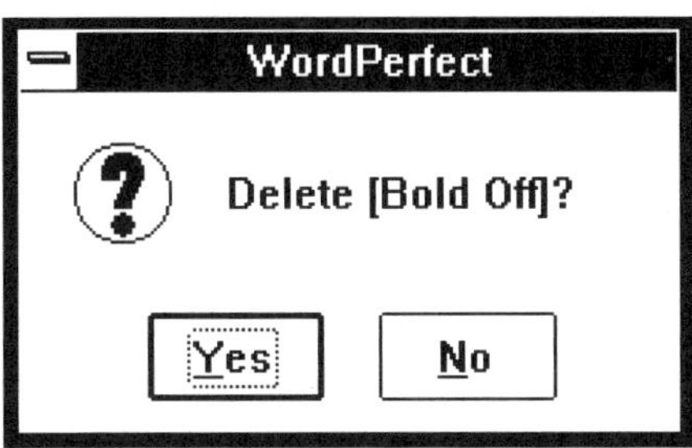

***Figure 10-10**. Using Confirm on Code Deletion, you are warned if a code is about to be deleted.*

Fast Save controls the two saving methods WordPerfect can use. With *Fast Save* on, documents are saved without printer formatting. This results in a faster save. Without this option on, documents are formatted for the printer each time the document is saved. With the *Fast Save* option on, saving is faster, but documents take longer to print, because the document must be formatted for printing at print time.

Allow Undo is an option that enables the *Undo* command in the **Edit** menu. This command allows you to undo the last formatting or editing change you made to your document.

Format Retrieved Documents for Default Printer, when selected, will format all documents, as they are opened, based on the currently selected printer, regardless of the printer selected when the document was originally created. Without this option enabled, WordPerfect will attempt to format the incoming document for the original printer. If the original printer is unavailable, the document is then formatted for the current printer.

Beep On

The options within this setting—*Error, Hyphenation, Search Failure*—determine whether WordPerfect 'beeps' if one of these errors occurs.

Menu

You may have noticed within most Windows applications, including WordPerfect, that the shortcut keys used to select commands are listed alongside the command in the menu. If you wish to disable this feature (not the shortcut key itself, just the display of the shortcut key in the menu), you must disable the *Display Shortcut Keys* option.

The *Display Last Open Filenames* option controls the display, in the form of a menu command at the bottom of the **File** menu, of the last four files opened (see Figure 10-11). Selecting one these file names from the **File** menu is exactly the same as opening that file.

File	
New	
Open...	Shift+F10
Retrieve...	
Close	F7
Save	
Save As...	F10
Password...	
File Manager...	F5
Preferences	Shift+F1 ▸
Print...	Shift+F7
Print Preview...	Alt+Shift+F7
Select Printer...	
Exit	
1 biblio12.wkb	
2 charactr.doc	
3 learn06.wkb	
4 learn12.wkb	

Figure 10-11. *The four most recently opened files can be listed at the bottom of the* ***File*** *menu, using the Display Last Open Filenames option.*

Ruler

The *Ruler* options control a range of visual options for the WordPerfect ruler.

The only option we mention here is *Automatic Ruler Display*. This option determines whether or not the WordPerfect ruler (Figure 10-12) is automatically displayed on screen as new documents are created and opened. For more information about the ruler and its options, see Chapter 4, **The Ruler**.

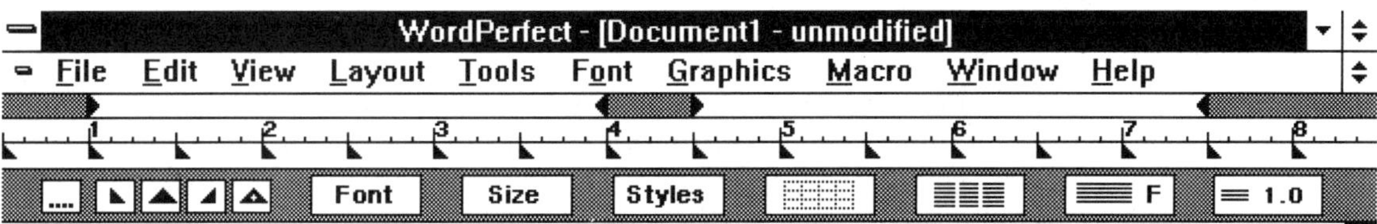

Figure 10-12. *The WordPerfect ruler.*

Prompt for Hyphenation

This section of the dialog box enables you to determine how often WordPerfect will request assistance in hyphenating words. The three options, *Always*, *When Required*, or *Never*, alter the frequency for which you will be asked for help.

Always forces WordPerfect to stop and request assistance whenever a word requires hyphenation.

When Required forces WordPerfect to ask for assistance when it needs to hyphenate a word that does not exist in its hyphenation dictionary.

Never forces WordPerfect not to hyphenate a word it cannot find in its dictionary—it simply wraps the entire word onto the next line.

Hyphenation

Automatic hyphenation can occur in WordPerfect in one of two ways—*Internal* or *External*.

With *Internal* hyphenation, WordPerfect searches an internal dictionary to determine how certain words need to be hyphenated. External hyphenation is much the same, except that an external dictionary is searched rather than in *Internal* one. *External* dictionaries are generally more complete and take up more space on disk.

Preferences/Display

The *Preferences* command for *Display Settings* controls many options, as with the *Environment* command, but these options are more concerned with the appearance of WordPerfect and its options. Figure 10-13 shows the command and its associated dialog box.

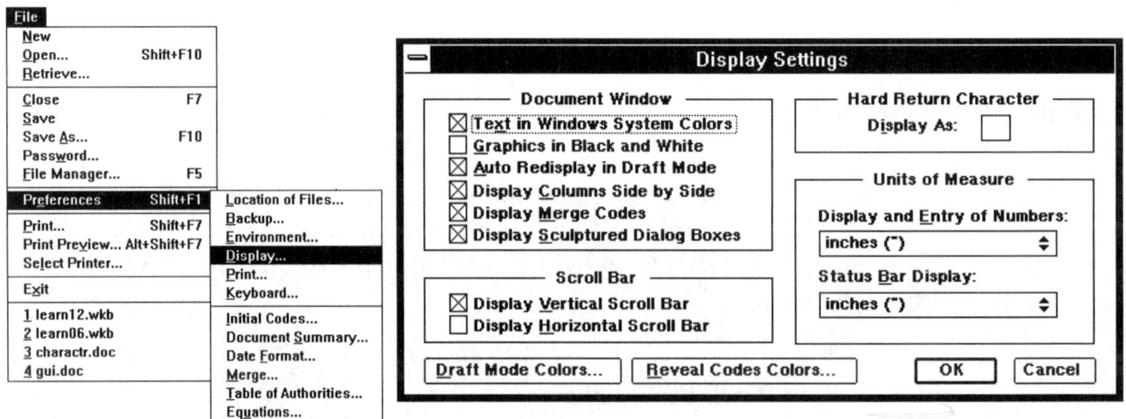

Figure 10-13*. The Preferences/Display command and dialog box.*

Document Window

Text in Windows System Colors is an option that determines whether the color of text in WordPerfect windows is controlled by the Microsoft Windows Control Panel, or by WordPerfect itself.

Graphics in Black and White is an option that can, in some cases, speed screen display quite markedly. Although it can be very handy at times to display graphics in full color, there is very little point if the final page will be printed in black and white. Choosing this option gives you an accurate idea of how a particular graphic will print.

Auto Redisplay in Draft Mode is an option only applicable if you are using the *Draft Mode* available in WordPerfect to view and edit documents. When on, it forces WordPerfect to update the screen after virtually all editing changes, rather than waiting for the user to choose *Redisplay*, or move the text cursor.

Using *Display Columns Side by Side*, all columns appear in the editing window next to each other, much as they will when they are printed. However, turning this option off will force WordPerfect to display only one long column, which can speed recalculation and screen redrawing after editing changes. Regardless of whether this option is enabled or disabled, multi-column documents will always print with multiple columns.

When using WordPerfect for merge operations, it can be handy to display, on screen, the codes associated with that merge operation. This option can be enabled or disabled using the *Display Merge Codes* option.

Display Sculptured Dialog Boxes is an option you can use to enhance the appearance of standard Windows dialog boxes, giving them a three dimensional, chiseled, appearance. This is a purely visual preference—it alters nothing other than the appearance of dialog boxes (Figure 10-14).

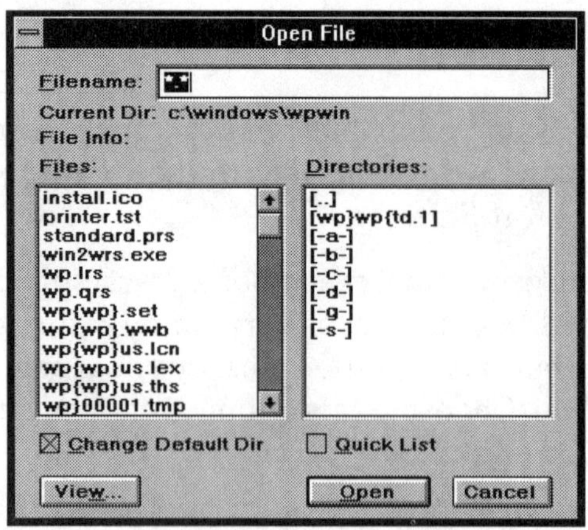

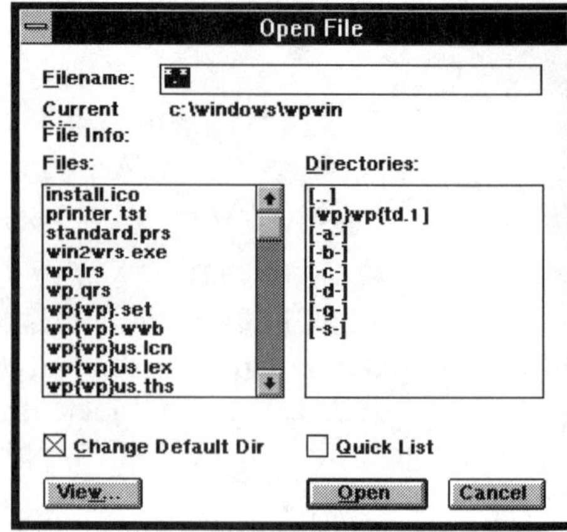

***Figure 10-14.** On the left, a sculptured dialog box, on the right, a normal dialog box. This choice is controlled by the Display Sculptured Dialog Boxes option in the Preferences/Display command.*

Scroll Bar

These settings, *Display Vertical Scroll Bar*, and *Display Horizontal Scroll Bar*, determine whether these scroll bars are displayed on the WordPerfect editing screen (Figure 10-15).

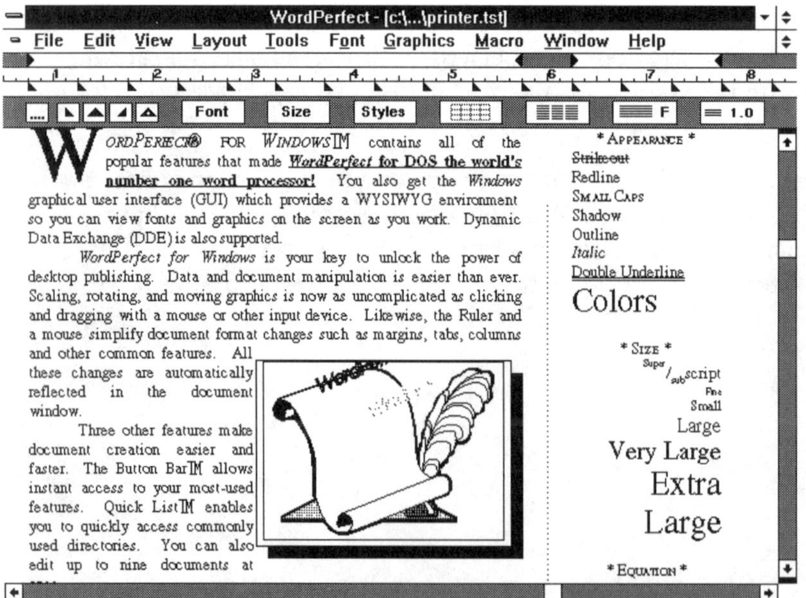

***Figure 10-15.** A WordPerfect document using both horizontal and vertical scroll bars.*

Hard Return Character

By default, the editing screen displays no character to represent a hard return, or enter character. If you wish, you can enter a character in the *Display As* text box that will represent the hard return characters on the editing screen.

If you press Ctrl+W while the text cursor is flashing in the *Display As* text box, it provides access to the WordPerfect special character sets, from which any character can be selected.

Units of Measure

In various dialog boxes throughout WordPerfect, you are asked to enter or edit a measurement—such as column widths or margins widths. As you can imagine, many units can be used in these measurements. The measurement unit used by default is the unit selected from the pop-up list box that appears when you hold the mouse button down on the *Display and Entry of Numbers* option (see Figure 10-16).

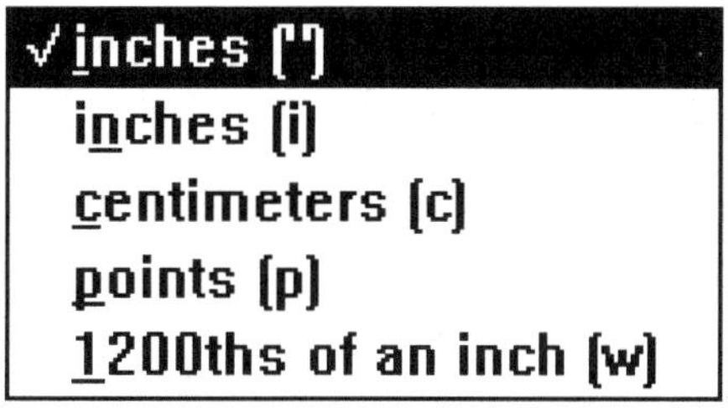

√ inches (")
inches (i)
centimeters (c)
points (p)
1200ths of an inch (w)

Figure 10-16. *The list box that appears when you hold the mouse button down on either the Status Bar Display, or Display and Entry of Numbers option from Figure 10-13. Note that with inches, you may select either of the top two options. The first option will display as 2.0", while the second will display as 2.0i.*

The *Status bar*, along the bottom of the screen, constantly indicates the horizontal position of the text cursor and uses the measurement unit selected from the *Status Bar Display* list box (see Figure 10-16). The *Status Bar Display* list box options also determine the unit of measurement used in the ruler.

Note the character in brackets after each measurement unit in Figure 10-16. This character can be used to override the current measurement unit. For example, if you would like a margin to be 2.0 centimeters, and the current measurement unit is inches, simply enter 2.00c. Similarly, with inches, you can enter 2.0" or 2.0i, to override what might be a centimeter or points current measurement unit.

Draft Mode Colors

Towards the bottom of the *Display Settings* dialog box of Figure 10-13 is the *Draft Mode Colors* button. Clicking on this button causes the Figure 10-17 dialog box to appear.

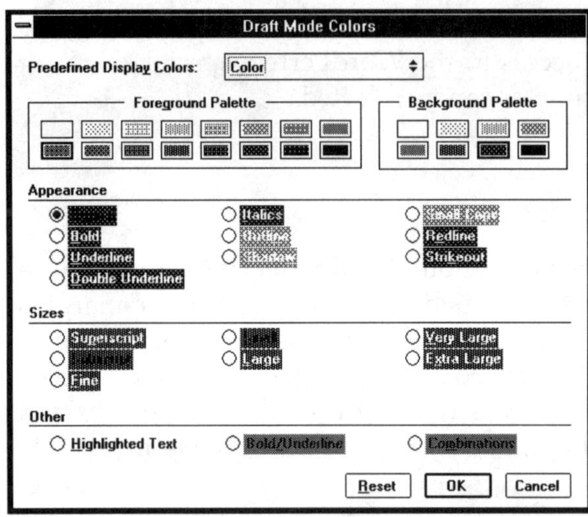

Figure 10-17. *The dialog box that appears when the Draft Mode Colors button is selected from the Preferences/Display command.*

The options within this dialog box control how various text attributes appear in color, when you are using the *Draft Mode* setting with WordPerfect. Simply select an option (e.g. *Bold*), and a foreground and background color, or shade, to represent that option in *Draft Mode*.

Of particular interest to laptop and notebook computer owners is the *Color Display Settings* list box near the top of the Figure 10-17 dialog box, which lets you select display modes specifically for a range of mono or LCD screens.

√ Color
Monochrome
Blue On White
LCD Display
LCD Display - No Intensity
Plasma Display
Custom

Reveal Codes Colors

In much the same way as with *Draft Mode Colors*, you can select the *Reveal Codes Colors* from the *Preferences/Display* dialog box of Figure 10-13.

As with *Draft Mode Colors*, you are free to select foreground and background colors or shades for text, codes, and the text cursor (see Figure 10-18 dialog box).

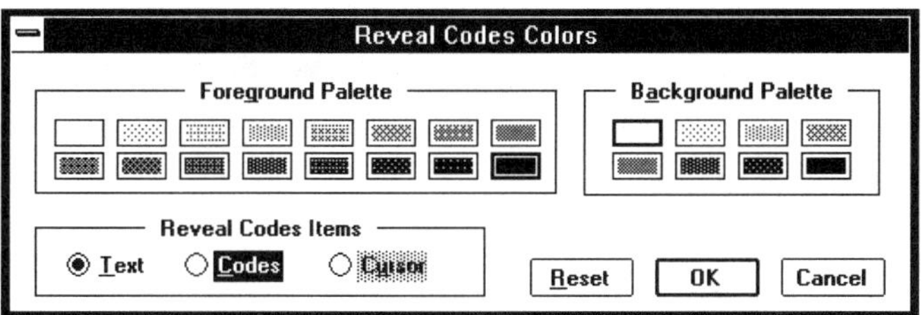

Figure 10-18. The Reveal Codes Colors dialog box.

Preferences/Print

The options set in the *Preferences/Print Settings* dialog box of Figure 10-19 act as default values for each time you attempt to print a document. Remember, however, that as these settings are only defaults, they can be overridden at print time by changing settings in the normal *Print* command dialog box.

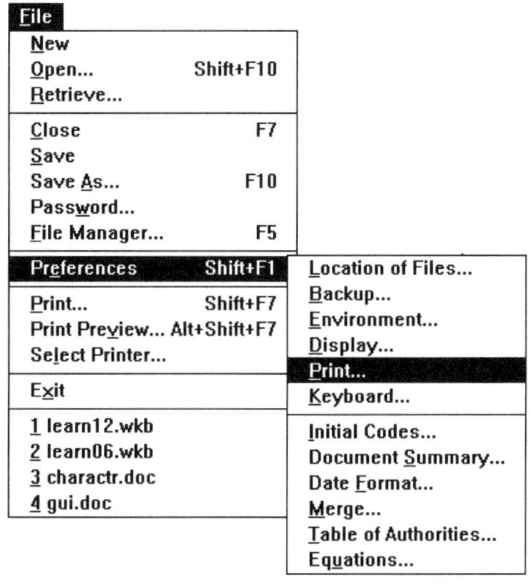

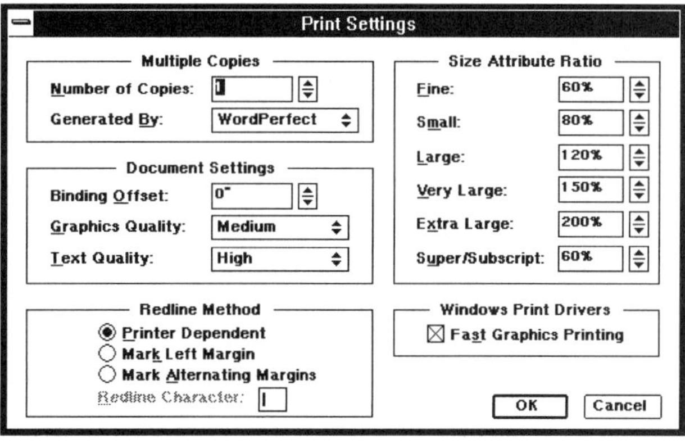

Figure 10-19. The Preferences/Print dialog box, used to set various printer defaults.

Multiple Copies

The *Number of Copies* option is quite simple—you enter a value that becomes the default for the number of copies of each page printed in the future.

Whether the number of copies is *Generated By* WordPerfect or by Windows itself is up to you. You may find it simpler to let WordPerfect handle multiple copies, as the process for setting a printer to print multiple copies using Windows controls can be rather complex.

Document Settings

The *Binding Offset* is a setting that causes WordPerfect to shift odd numbered pages to the right and even numbered pages to the left, to allow for some form of binding. The measure that you enter in this setting is determined by the binding method of the final job—different binding methods (e.g. comb bound, perfect bound, staple bound) may require different settings. A setting of 0 disables this option.

Graphics Quality determines the printed quality of graphics from WordPerfect, but perhaps more importantly, the speed at which these graphics print. The lower the quality of the graphic, the faster it prints —great for quick draft prints.

For printers that rely on bit-mapped fonts (this does not include PostScript printers), using the *Text Quality* option to reduce the quality of the text can also mean faster print times, but at a lower quality.

Redline Method

Redline is an attribute that can be assigned to text to indicate that the text has been added at a later date (helpful when editing documents). The *Redline Method* options determine how *Redline* text is represented on the printed page.

Printer Dependent is an option that marks *Redline* text according to the capabilities of the printer—on most printers, this translates to a shaded background.

Mark Left Margin or *Mark Alternating Margins* forces the specified *Redline Character* to appear in the page margin next to *Redline* text.

Size Attribute Ratio

The options within *Size Attribute Ratio* determine how a command within the **Font** menu, called *Size*, behaves when applied to selected text (see Figure 10-20).

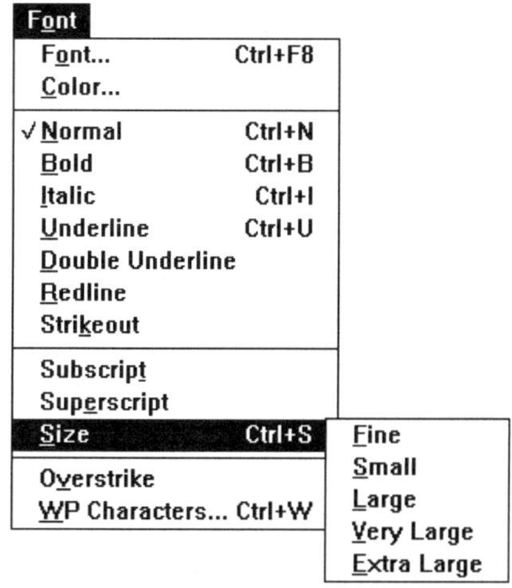

Figure 10-20. *The size that selected text becomes when any of these size commands from the* ***Font*** *menu are applied to it is determined by the Preferences/Print command.*

You can determine, by altering the percentages in the boxes next to the *Fine, Small, Large, Very Large, Extra Large, Superscript* and *Subscript* options of Figure 10-19, by exactly how much selected text is increased or decreased when the commands from Figure 10-20 are applied.

Windows Print Drivers

This option is available to WordPerfect users who select to use a Windows printer driver rather than a WordPerfect printer driver. When *Fast Graphics Printing* is selected, it causes graphics from WordPerfect to print substantially faster than would be the case just using the Windows driver, with no reduction in quality. This option should always be selected. If, for some reason, your printer is not printing graphics correctly, try turning *Fast Graphics Printing* off.

Preferences/Keyboard

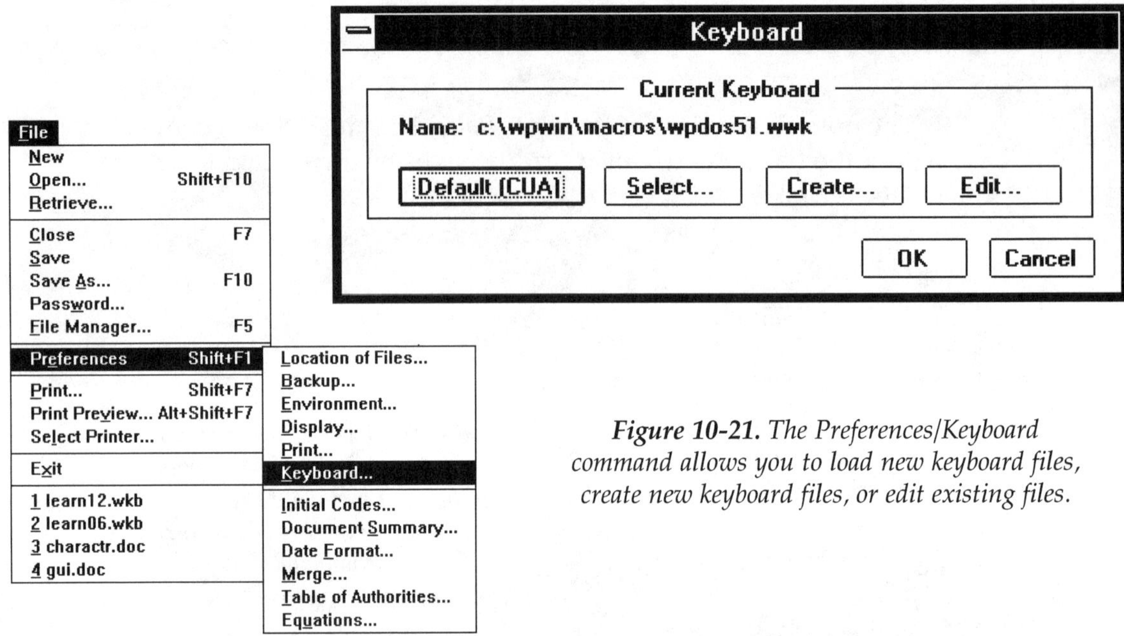

Figure 10-21. *The Preferences/Keyboard command allows you to load new keyboard files, create new keyboard files, or edit existing files.*

When WordPerfect is being installed, you are given a choice for the keyboard file to be loaded. The keyboard file is a file that determines what keyboard shortcuts are available for commands.

The default keyboard is called the **CUA**, or **Common User Access** keyboard. The keyboard shortcuts defined by the **CUA** conventions were determined by Microsoft, IBM *et al* to help form a common group of shortcut commands between Windows applications (e.g. F4 always activates the *Open* command). Note that the keyboard shortcut commands for the File menu, as seen in Figure 10-21, are not for the **CUA** keyboard.

However, WordPerfect has provided the ability for you to either edit an existing keyboard file, or create your own keyboard file, containing keyboard shortcuts designed by you. This may be a great help, particularly for those users moving from another word processing program, and who may have some keyboard shortcuts ingrained in their fingers.

The Default button

Using this button in Figure 10-21 will load the keyboard shortcuts as defined by **CUA** conventions. It removes any other keyboard files from memory.

The Select button

This button allows you to load a new set of keyboard shortcuts, by selecting a file from disk. WordPerfect includes one keyboard file, other than the standard **CUA** conventions, called ***wpdos51.wwk.*** This file provides keyboard shortcuts for those users who may be upgrading from WordPerfect 5.1 and are familiar with the keyboard shortcuts used with that product.

As you create other keyboard shortcut files, you can select the one you wish to use, perhaps for different tasks or even different people.

The Create button

The *Create* button allows you to create your very own set of keyboard shortcut commands and, if you wish, have these commands appear in the menus. Clicking on the *Create* button from Figure 10-21 provides you with the Figure 10-22 dialog box.

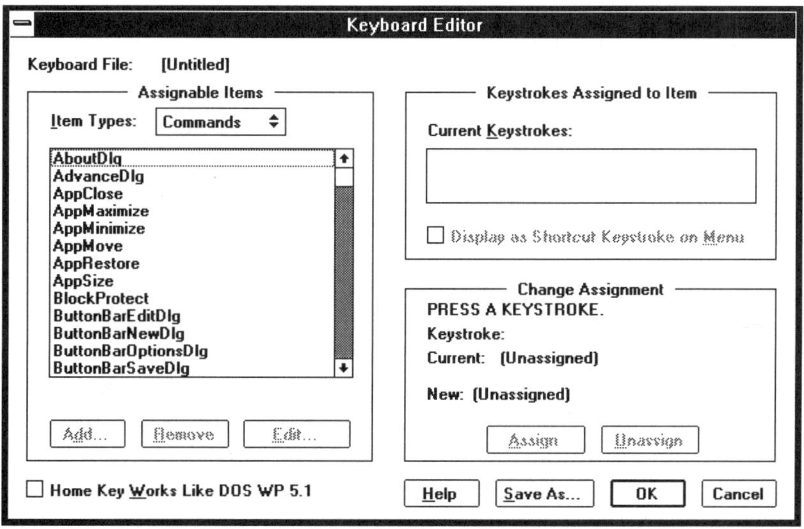

Figure 10-22. *The Keyboard Editor for WordPerfect dialog box.*

At the top of this dialog box is the current *Keyboard File*. When you create a new keyboard file, this line will initially read *[Untitled]*.

In the *Assignable Items* section, you can select one of several *Item Types* to which to apply a keyboard shortcut. In Figure 10-23, the selected *Item Type* is *Commands*—you can also select *Submenus, Text*, or *Macros*.

Underneath *Item Types* is a list of the available objects based on the current *Item Type*. In Figure 10-23, the current *Item Type* is commands. Therefore, the list under *Item Types* is the list of commands available within WordPerfect. It is from this list that you select a command to which to apply a shortcut key.

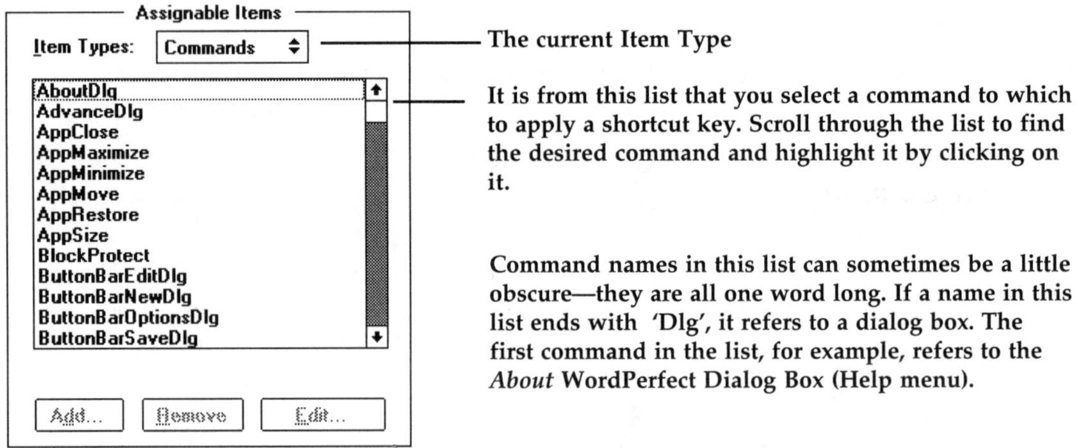

Figure 10-23. *The command list.*

Once a command is selected from the list, you can use the *Change Assignment* section of the Figure 10-22 dialog box in order to apply a shortcut key to the command, or to see if a shortcut key has already been applied to it.

Once the command to which you wish to apply a shortcut key is selected, your next step is to press the new shortcut key combination you wish to apply to this command. In the example of Figures 10-24 and 10-25, we have selected the *AboutDlg* command and are choosing the F4 key. In general, most shortcut keys are either function keys, or the Ctrl or Alt keys in combination with other keyboard keys (e.g. Ctrl+K).

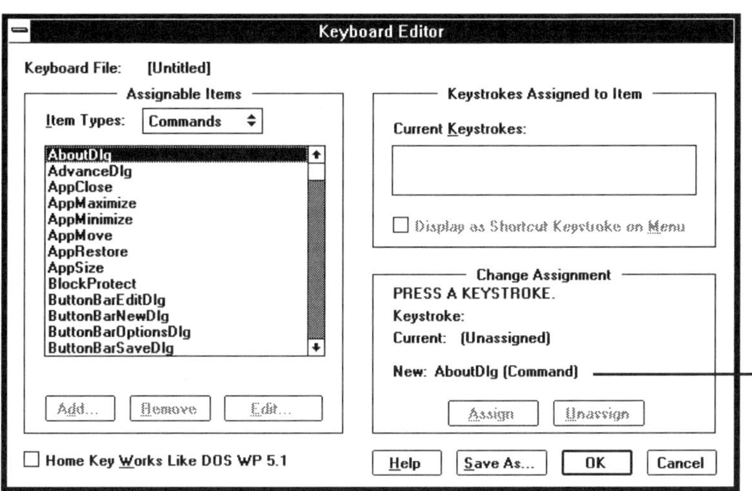

Figure 10-24*. Here we selected the command AboutDlg. Note the Change Assignment section of the dialog box (bottom right-hand corner) also reflects the fact, on the New line, that the AboutDlg command has been selected.*

Change Assignment
PRESS A KEYSTROKE.
Keystroke: F4
Current: FileOpenDlg (Command)
New: AboutDlg (Command)
Assign | Unassign

Figure 10-25. *In this exercise, on pressing the F4 key, another command name appears in the Current option in the Change Assignment section of this dialog box. This indicates that the keyboard shortcut selected (F4), has already been applied to another command—the File Open dialog box.*

As mentioned in the caption of Figure 10-25, the F4 key is used in this case for another command. If you wish, you could use the *Unassign* button to remove this keyboard shortcut from the *FileOpenDlg* command.

However, it may be wiser to select another keyboard shortcut, simply by entering it again—in Figure 10-26, for example, the shortcut Ctrl+E.

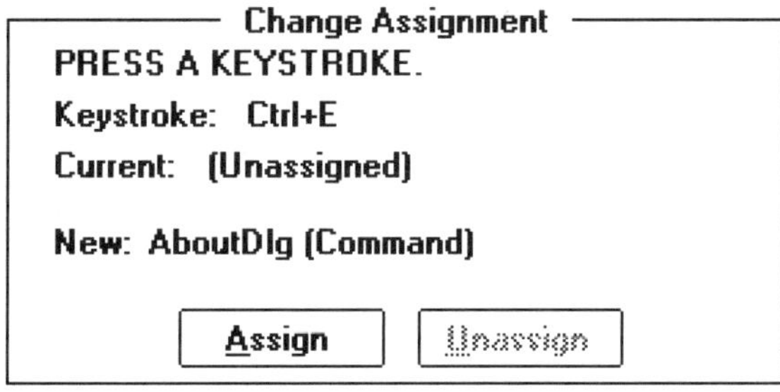

Figure 10-26. *Here, the keystroke we entered (Ctrl+E) is reflected on the Keystroke line. The Current line reflects that this keystroke is currently unassigned.*

If, after selecting a keyboard shortcut by pressing it on the keyboard, the *Current* line says *(Unassigned)*, it means that you are free to assign this keyboard shortcut to the currently selected command. This is achieved by selecting the *Assign* button of Figure 10-26.

After selecting the *Assign* button, the *Keystroke* is applied to the command displayed on the *New* line (Figure 10-27). If you wish, you can select another shortcut command through the keyboard. Each command can have several shortcut keys applied to it.

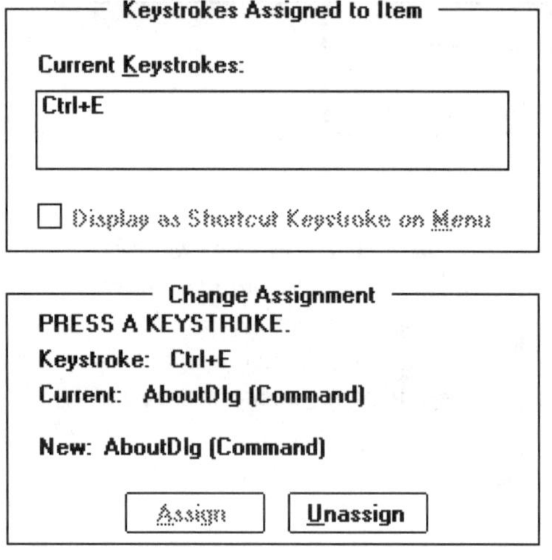

Figure 10-27. *After selecting the Assign button, the shortcut key is now the Current shortcut key for the command on the New line. Also, at the top of the dialog box in the Current Keystrokes section, the shortcut Ctrl+E is recorded.*

When you select a keystroke from the *Current Keystrokes* area, another option is activated (Figure 10-28).

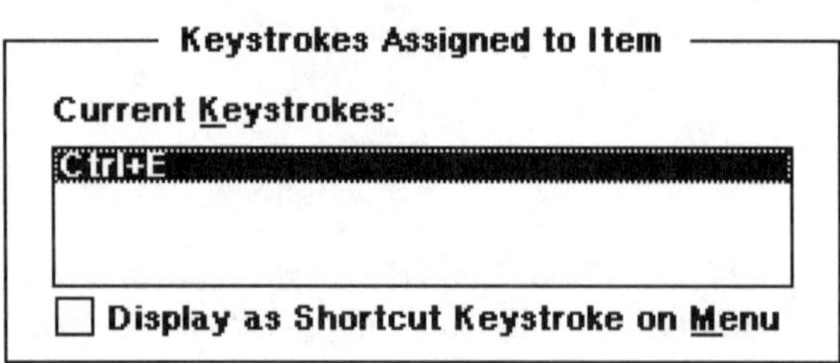

Figure 10-28. *Selecting a keyboard shortcut from the Current Keystrokes area enables the Display as Shortcut Keystroke on Menu option.*

Selecting the *Display as Shortcut Keystroke on Menu* option will cause, in this case, the keyboard shortcut Ctrl+E to appear next to the *About* command in the menu in which this command appears.

You are now free to select another command from the command list, and apply a keyboard shortcut to it.

When you have finished creating your own keyboard shortcuts, and press **OK**, you will be asked to save this series of keyboard shortcuts as a file (Figure 10-29).

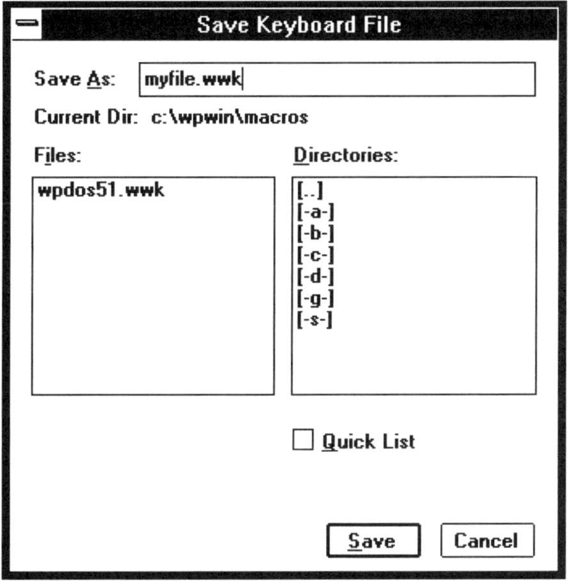

Figure 10-29*. After creating or editing your own keyboard shortcuts, you will be asked to save these keyboard shortcuts in a file as you exit the dialog box.*

Summary of keyboard shortcut creation

1. Select the *Keyboard* command from the *Preferences* fly-out menu in the **File** menu (Figure 10-21).

2. Select *Create* from the *Keyboard* dialog box of Figure 10-21 (select the *Create* key to create a new keyboard, or the *Edit* button to edit the current keyboard file). **Note:** If the **CUA** keyboard is loaded, you must create a new one, as these shortcuts cannot be edited.

3. Select an item type from the *Item Types* list box (Figure 10-22).

4. Select an item (command) from the list (Figure 10-24).

If the selected item already has a keyboard shortcut applied to it, this will be indicated in the *Current Keystrokes* section of the dialog box of Figure 10-22.

5. Select a keyboard shortcut for the selected command, by entering the shortcut keys via the keyboard (Figures 10-25 and 10-26).

If the shortcut keys you enter have already been applied to another command, this will be reflected on the *Current* line within the *Change Assignment* section. In this case, you have the option of selecting the *Unassign* button to remove this shortcut key from this command (Figure 10-25).

To assign a shortcut key to a command, select the *Assign* button from the *Change Assignment* section of the dialog box (Figure 10-26).

6. Repeat for other commands or items as necessary.

7. You will be asked to save your changes as you exit the dialog box (Figure 10-29).

Speller

The WordPerfect *Speller* program is used to correct spelling mistakes (by offering alternate spellings of words it cannot locate within the current dictionary). It can be used in several ways and in this chapter, we look at these different options.

Starting the Speller

The WordPerfect *Speller* can be launched as a stand-alone application, or from within WordPerfect itself.

To launch *Speller* as a stand-alone application, you must double-click on the *Speller* icon within the *WordPerfect* group, in the *Windows Program Manager* (Figure 11-1).

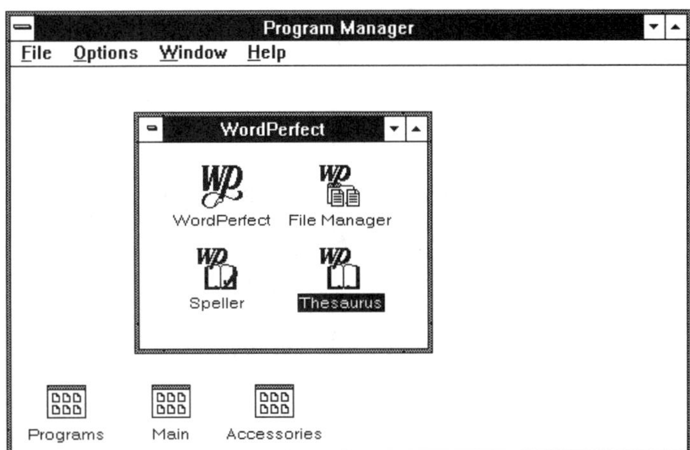

***Figure 11-1**. The Speller program can be launched directly from the WordPerfect group within the Program Manager.*

Speller can also be launched from within WordPerfect, using the *Speller* command from the **Tools** menu (Figure 11-2)—and in most cases this is how it will be used. When *Speller* is launched as a stand-alone program, it does not have the ability to spell-check entire documents—only single words.

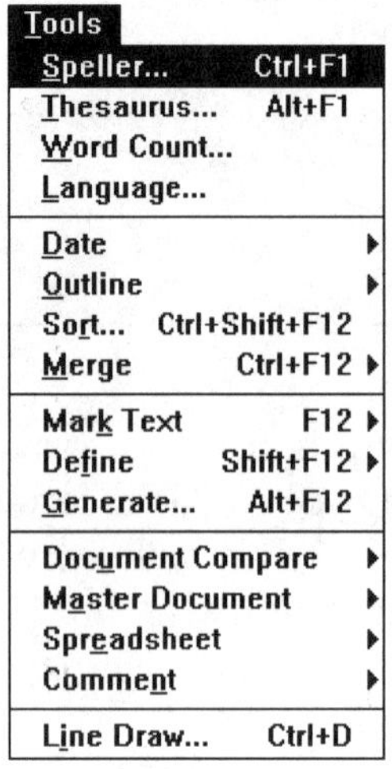

Figure 11-2. *The Speller command, from the* ***Tools*** *menu, is used to invoke the Speller from within WordPerfect.*

In this chapter, you will see how the *Speller* behaves in spell-checking a sample document (Figure 11-3). To spell check this document, all you need do is make sure the document is open prior to selecting the *Speller* command (Figure 11-2).

Figure 11-3. *The sample document we are using to demonstrate the options within Speller (we have inserted a few spelling mistakes).*

After selecting the *Speller* command from Figure 11-2, you are presented with the *Speller* window (Figure 11-4).

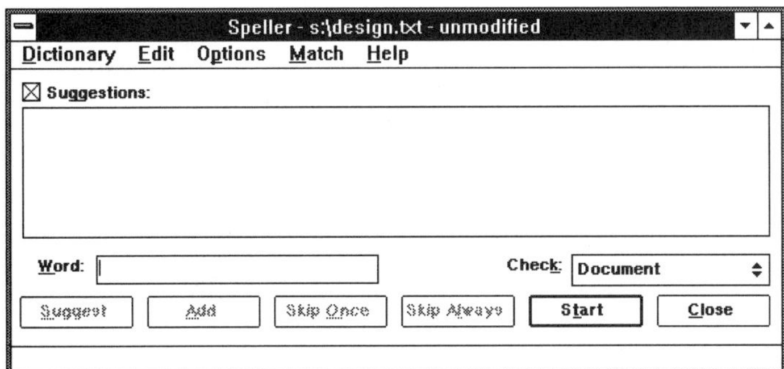

Figure 11-4. *The Speller window.*

The Speller window

Before performing any spell checking, first peruse the *Speller* window. For this example, we are assuming the *Speller* has been opened from within WordPerfect. If the *Speller* is opened from the *Windows Program Manager,* it has slightly different properties.

The Title bar of the *Speller* (Figure 11-5) displays the currently opened document name, which is the document that is about to be spell-checked.

Speller - s:\design.txt - unmodified 

Figure 11-5. *The Title bar of the Speller. Here, the Title bar reflects that the document about to be spell-checked is called* ***s:\design.txt.***

The Menu bar (Figure 11-6) is much like any Windows Menu bar—these menus contain some commands which control the way the *Speller* operates.

Dictionary Edit Options Match Help

Figure 11-6. *The Speller Menu bar. The Menu bar allows access to commands for altering Speller preferences.*

The *Suggestions* area of the *Speller* displays similar words to the one that has been selected as incorrect. It is from this area that you can make a choice of exactly which replacement word you want to select (Figure 11-7).

The *Suggestions* checkbox, if enabled, forces the *Speller* to automatically display alternate words, when it finds a word not in its dictionary. If disabled, you must perform an extra step if you want suggestions displayed for any word (Figure 11-7).

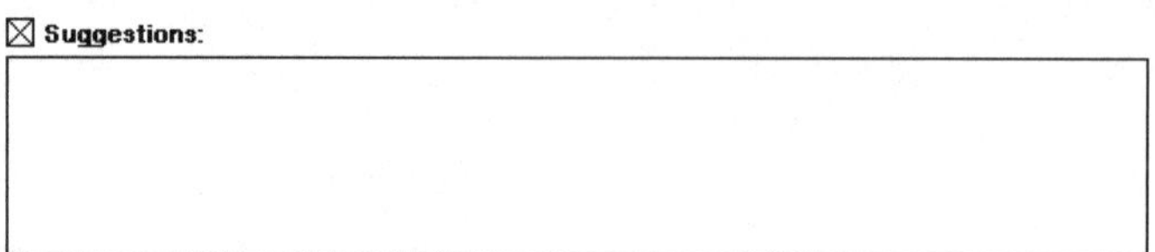

Figure 11-7. *The Suggestions checkbox and area. The usefulness of Suggestions will become more apparent as you actually start to use the Speller.*

The *Word* text box (Figure 11-8) can display different options — either a misspelled word, or the most likely replacement for a misspelled word. You may also edit a misspelled word in this area. See the **Using the Speller** section in this chapter for more details on how the *Word* text box is used by the *Speller*.

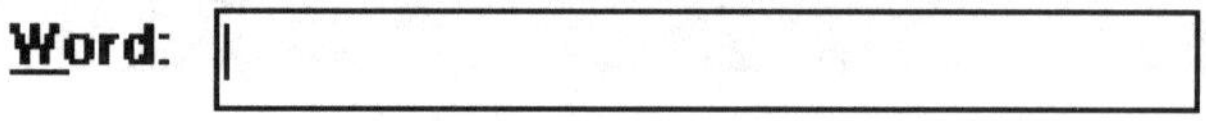

Word:

Figure 11-8. *The Word text box.*

The *Check* list box (Figure 11-9) determines exactly what group of words the *Speller* is to check. By default, if the *Speller* is started from within WordPerfect, the *Check* option will be *Document*, which means the entire document will be checked for spelling. However, you can make other selections here (see Figure 11-10) and a number of these choices will be explained later in this chapter.

Check: Document

Figure 11-9. *The Check option determines exactly which words will be spell-checked.*

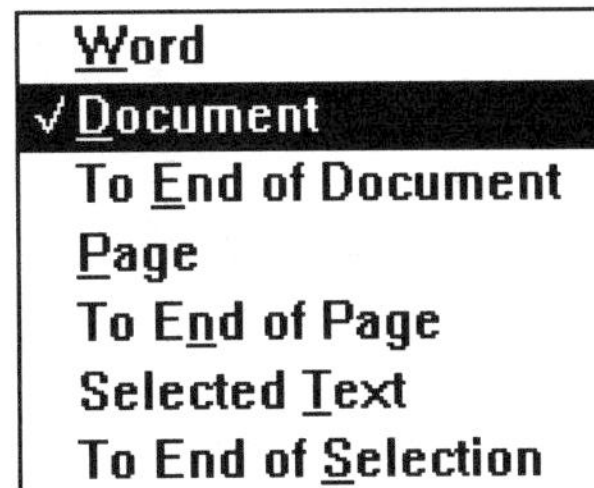

Figure 11-10. *By holding down the mouse button on the Check list box, you can select another option. These will be explained later in this chapter.*

The various option buttons at the bottom of the *Speller* window (Figure 11-11) will be explained in more detail as we get to them, however, here is a brief overview of the function of each button.

Figure 11-11. *The function of these options, along the bottom of the Speller window, will be explained in more detail later in this chapter.*

The *Suggest* button is used if the *Suggestions* check box of Figure 11-7 has been disabled. The *Speller* will search for suggestions based on the current word it has determined is misspelled.

The *Add* button can be used if WordPerfect finds a word which is not in its dictionary, but which you determine is correctly spelt. (This commonly happens with names.) Using *Add* will add the current word to a user dictionary, which the *Speller* will also check as it spell-checks a document.

The *Skip Once* button tells the *Speller* to ignore the word it has found just this time, and move on to the next mistake. If it finds this word again, it will display it again.

The *Skip Always* button tells the *Speller* to ignore this word for the remainder of the session.

The *Start* button is used to start the spell-check process. Once a misspelled word is found, this button changes to the *Replace* button.

The *Replace* button can be used to replace a misspelled word in the document with whatever word is currently in the *Word* text box (Figure 11-8).

The *Close* button closes the *Speller* program.

Using the Speller

In this example, the document in Figure 11-12 has been created and is currently open. The *Speller* command, from the **Tools** menu, is then selected (Figure 11-13).

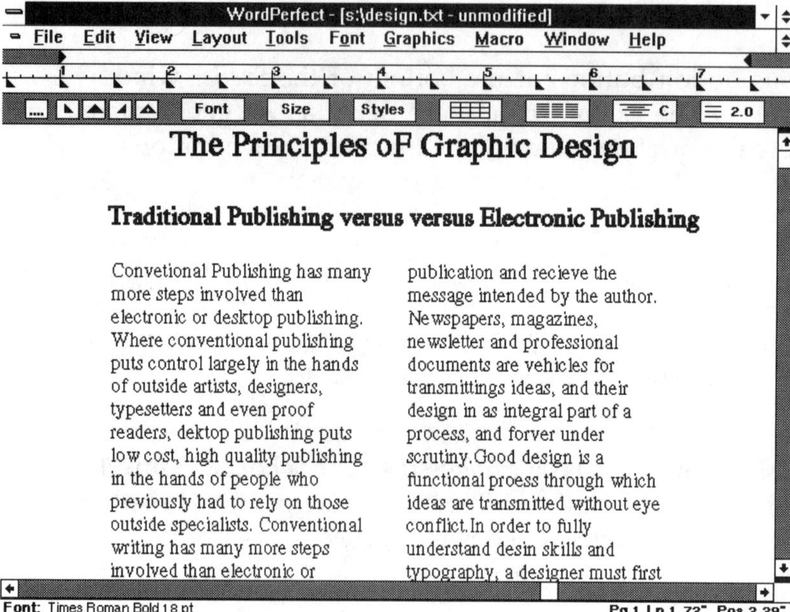

Figure 11-12. The sample document we are using to demonstrate the options within the Speller (we have inserted a few spelling mistakes).

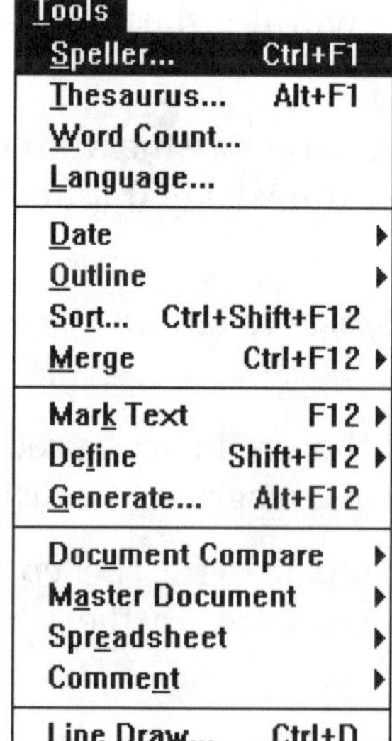

*Figure 11-13. The Speller command from the **Tools** menu is used to invoke the Speller from within WordPerfect.*

After selecting the *Speller* command from the **Tools** menu, the *Speller* window appears.

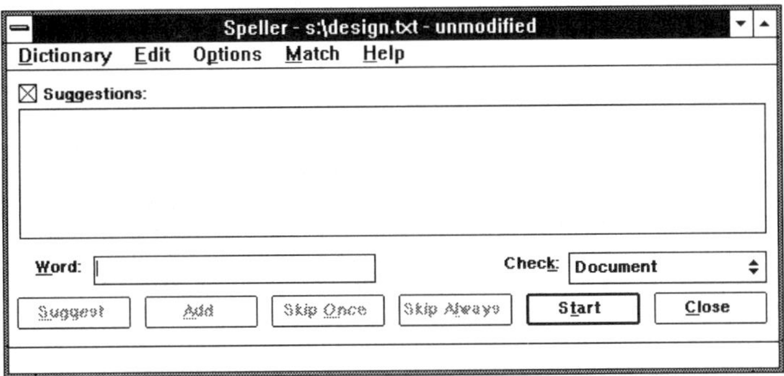

Figure 11-14. *The Speller window.*

By default, the Title bar of the *Speller* (Figure 11-14) displays the name of the currently open document (Figure 11-12).

The option in the *Check* list box indicates that the *Speller* is in *Document* mode (Figure 11-14).

To start the spell-checking process, you must click once on the *Start* button of Figure 11-14, highlighted below in Figure 11-15.

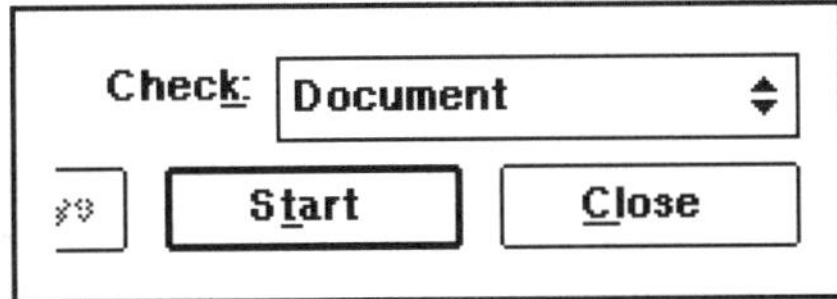

Figure 11-15. *The Start button is used to start the spell-checking process.*

When spell-checking has started, the *Speller* searches the current document for words not in its dictionary. Any words that do not appear in its dictionary are displayed as misspelled, and you are alerted as the words are found (Figure 11-16). In effect, the *Speller* stops and asks you what you want to do about this word.

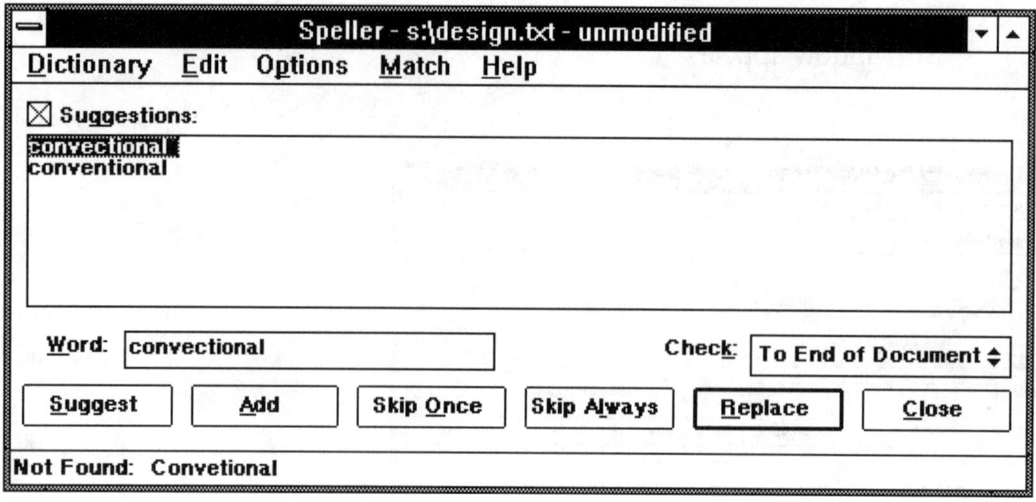

Figure 11-16. The Speller window, as it appears when a misspelled word has been found.

Note that in Figure 11-16, the word "Convetional" has been highlighted, indicated by the *Not Found: Convetional* note in the bottom left-hand corner of the window (Figure 11-17).

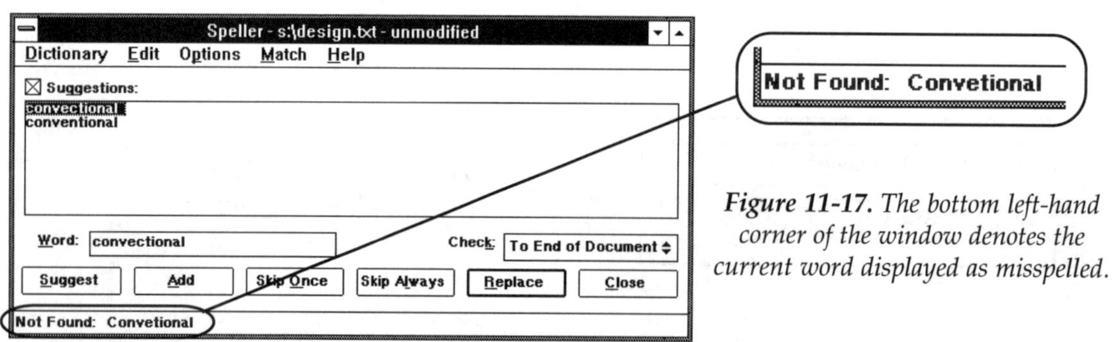

Figure 11-17. The bottom left-hand corner of the window denotes the current word displayed as misspelled.

In Figure 11-18, note that the *Speller* has also automatically made two suggestions as to how to correctly spell the current word, because the *Suggestions* option in this example is enabled.

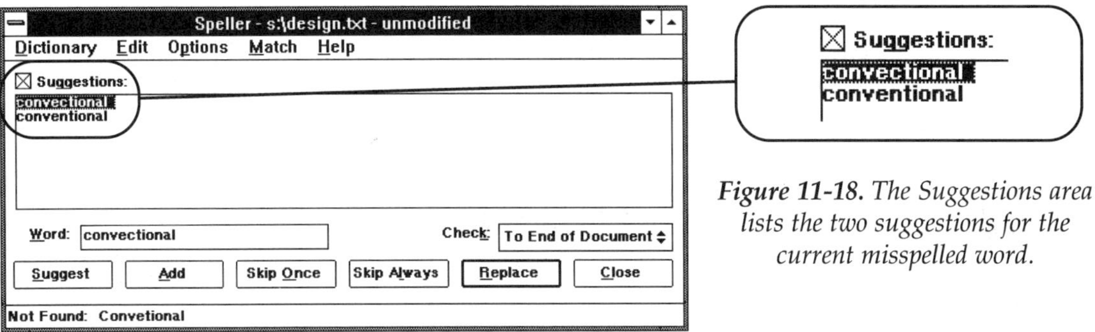

Figure 11-18. The Suggestions area lists the two suggestions for the current misspelled word.

It is now up to you to decide how to handle this word. First of all, you must decide if this word is actually misspelled, or if it is just not in WordPerfect's dictionary. In the Figure 11-18 case, you can safely assume that the word is misspelled.

Using Suggestions

Assuming that you agree that the word is misspelled, are any of the *Suggestions* correct? (If there are no suggestions, try clicking on the *Suggest* button.) If there are still no suggestions, stay tuned—this situation will be dealt with in a moment. In this example, the second suggestion, "conventional", is the correct replacement. To select this word, simply click on it in the list of suggestions (Figure 11-19) and it will appear in the *Word* text box.

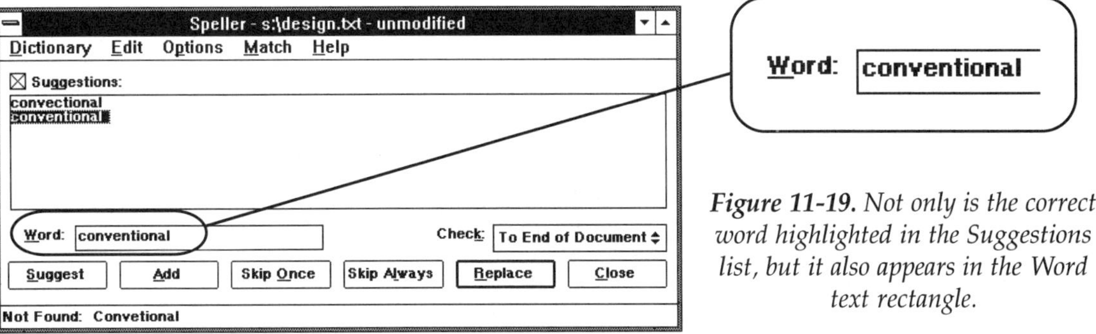

Figure 11-19. Not only is the correct word highlighted in the Suggestions list, but it also appears in the Word text rectangle.

Once the correct replacement appears in the *Word* text box, you are free to click on the *Replace* button. This will replace the word "convetional" (Figure 11-17) with the word "conventional" (Figure 11-19) in the document.

After the *Replace* button has been selected, the word is replaced in the document, and the *Speller* searches for the next incorrectly spelt word. In Figure 11-20, the word "dektop" has been picked up, and the *Speller* has found no alternative suggestions.

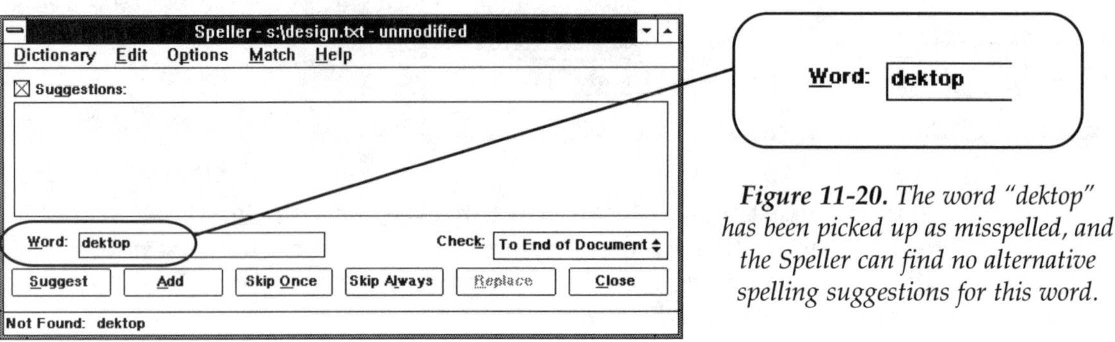

Figure 11-20. *The word "dektop" has been picked up as misspelled, and the Speller can find no alternative spelling suggestions for this word.*

Manual corrections

When no suggestions are offered by the *Speller*, it is up to you to determine how to correctly spell this word. To correct the word, you must edit the word as it appears in the *Word* text box (Figure 11-21).

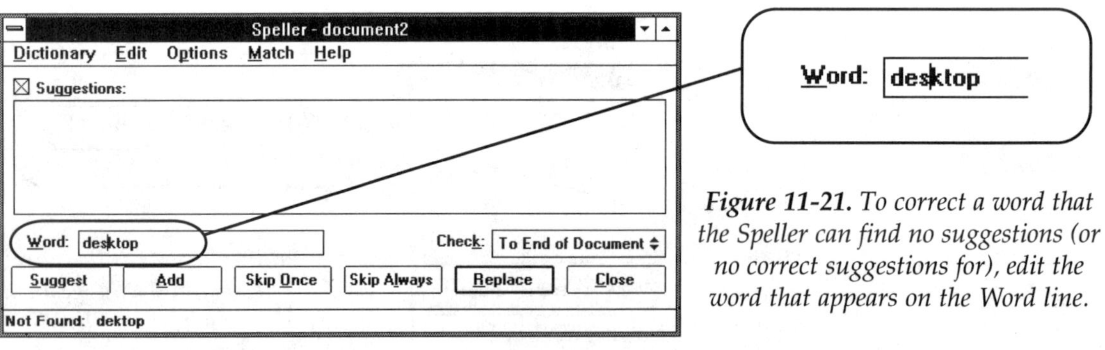

Figure 11-21. *To correct a word that the Speller can find no suggestions (or no correct suggestions for), edit the word that appears on the Word line.*

After correcting the word on the *Word* line (Figure 11-21), select the *Replace* button to replace the old word with the new one. The *Speller* then continues to spell-check the rest of the document.

Correctly spelt words

Occasionally, the *Speller* will detect a word as misspelled, when really it is spelt correctly. This situation happens commonly with proper names or technical terms. In Figure 11-22, the name "Meredith" is not recognized by WordPerfect, and hence it is listed as misspelled.

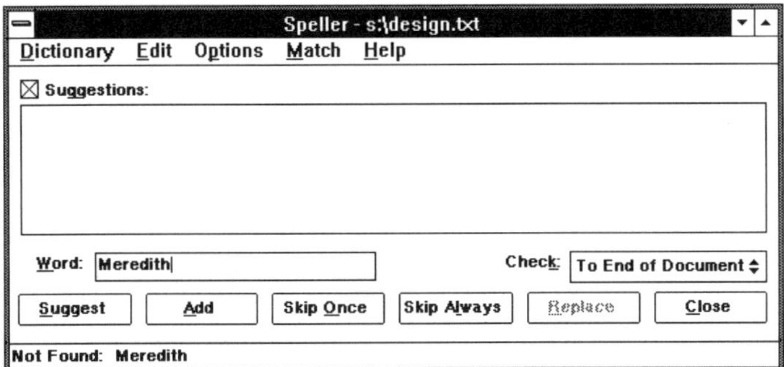

Figure 11-22. *The proper noun "Meredith" has been noted as misspelled by the Speller.*

When WordPerfect does not recognize a word that is in fact correctly spelt, you have several choices:

•Selecting the *Add* button tells the *Speller* to add this word to a user dictionary. The next time the *Speller* looks at this word, it will see it in the user dictionary and determine that it is correctly spelt.

•Selecting the *Skip Once* button will simply move onto the next incorrectly spelt word and ignore the current one.

•The *Skip Always* button will force the *Speller* to ignore this word for the remainder of this session. The next time you use the *Speller*, however, it will still list this word as incorrectly spelt.

Finishing a Speller session

A spell-checking session can be ended at any time by selecting the *Close* button from the *Speller* window.

When the *Speller* has completed checking a document, the words *Spell Check Completed* appear at the bottom left-hand corner of the window (Figure 11-23). When this happens, select *Close* to close the *Speller.*

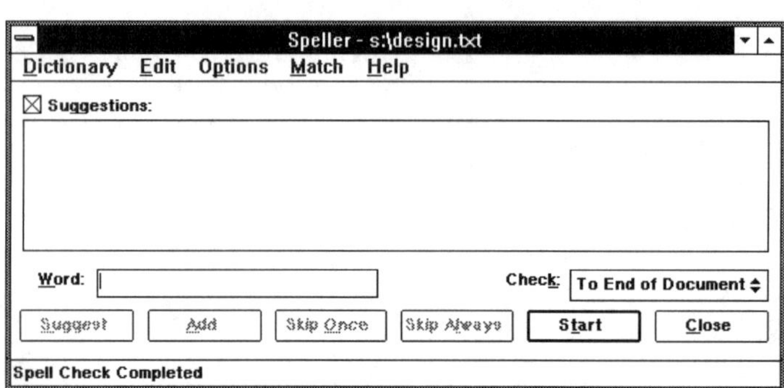

Figure 11-23. *When a spell-check is completed, this will be reflected in the bottom left-hand corner of the Speller window.*

Duplicate Words & Irregular Capitalization

The *Speller* can do more than just detecting spelling mistakes. It will, as an option, highlight duplicate words and also words that have suspicious capitalization. These two options can be enabled, or disabled, using the **Options** menu in the *Speller* window (Figure 11-24).

Options
√ Words with Numbers
√ Duplicate Words
√ Irregular Capitalization
Move to Bottom

Figure 11-24. *With the Duplicate Words and Irregular Capitalization options selected in the* ***Options*** *menu in the Speller, the Speller will also display problems in these areas.*

When a duplicate word, or a word with mixed capitalization, is found, another dialog box will appear (Figure 11-25).

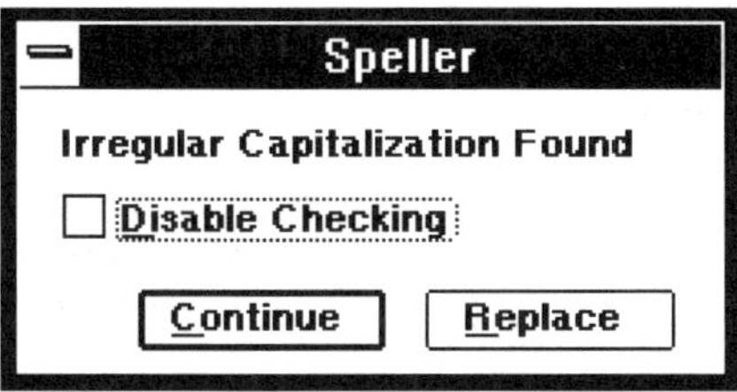

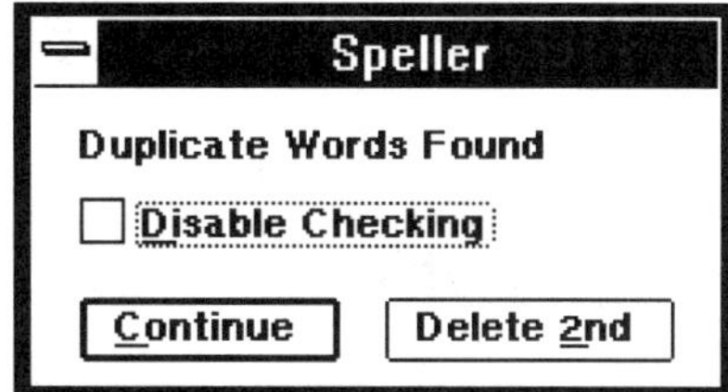

Figure 11-25. *The dialog boxes that appear when the speller has detected Irregular Capitalization (on the left) or Duplicate Words (on the right).*

When one of these dialog boxes appears, you can then choose to ignore (click on *Continue*) or correct the problem (click on *Replace* or *Delete 2nd*).

Loading a New Dictionary

It is possible with the WordPerfect *Speller* to use one of many main spelling dictionaries, as well as one of many user supplementary dictionaries. To alter the dictionary in use, you can select, from the **Dictionary** menu in the *Speller*, the *Main* or *Supplementary* commands and select a file from disk.

Supplementary or user spelling dictionaries have an SUP extension, while *Speller* main dictionaries have an LEX extension.

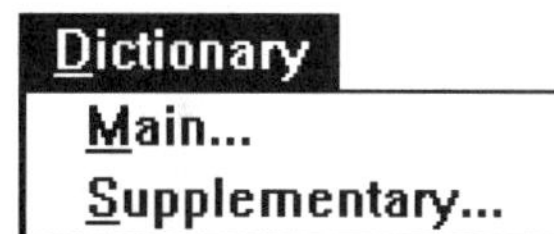

Checking words in context

It is often hard to determine whether in fact a word is incorrectly spelt, unless you can see that word as it appears in the text—in context. An easy way to ensure that you can see any errors in the text, as well as in the *Speller* window, is to select the *Move to Bottom* command from the **Options** menu (Figure 11-26).

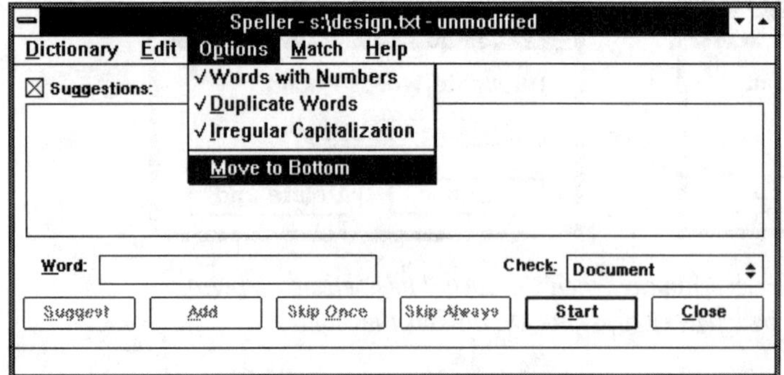

*Figure 11-26. The Move to Bottom command, from the **Options** menu in the Speller window, moves the Speller window to the bottom of the screen and displays errors highlighted in the text above the Speller window.*

In Figure 11-27, you can see the effect this option has—all errors are highlighted in the text above the *Speller* window—enabling you to check errors in context.

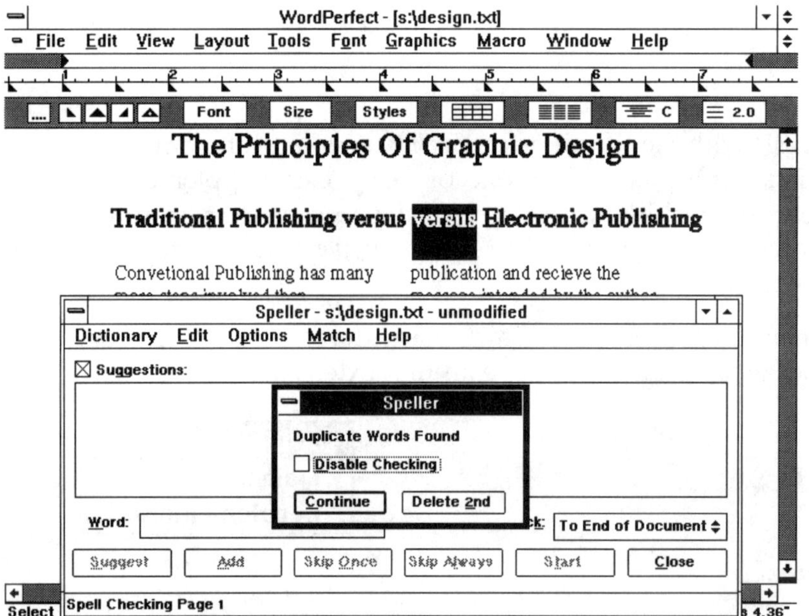

Figure 11-27. In this case, a duplicate word error has been found. Above the Speller window, in the text itself, the actual error is also highlighted.

Spell-checking selected text

The WordPerfect *Speller* can also spell-check only part of a document—the selected part.

As an example, we have selected some text from the document in Figure 11-28 before selecting the *Speller* command from the **Tools** menu.

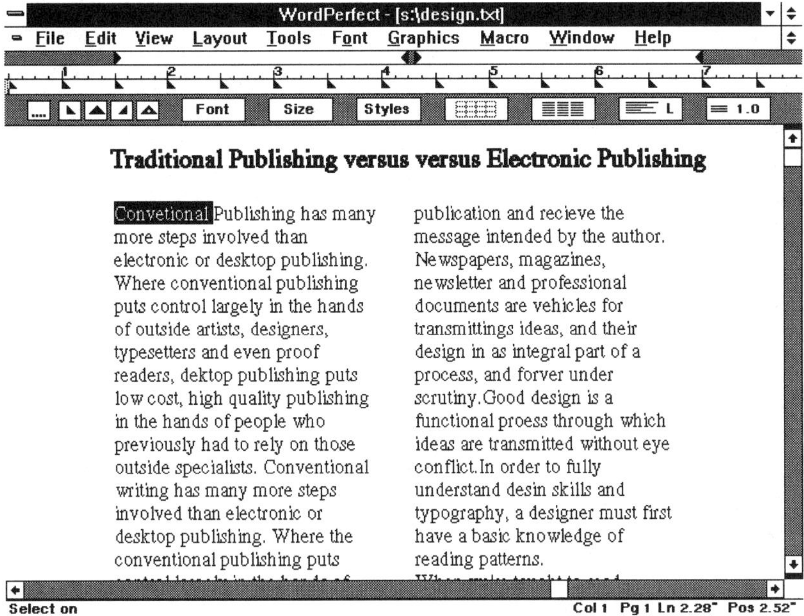

Figure 11-28. Here a single word has been selected prior to selecting the Speller command from the **Tools** *menu. This selected text could have been any length, from one word to many pages.*

If text is selected when the *Speller* command is activated, the *Speller* automatically defaults to *Selected Text* mode—indicated by the options listed in the *Check* list box (Figure 11-29).

If you wanted to spell-check the entire document, rather than just the selected text, you must select *Document* from the *Check* list box before selecting *Start* to start the checking.

Once the Speller has started in this mode, it operates in exactly the same fashion as already described.

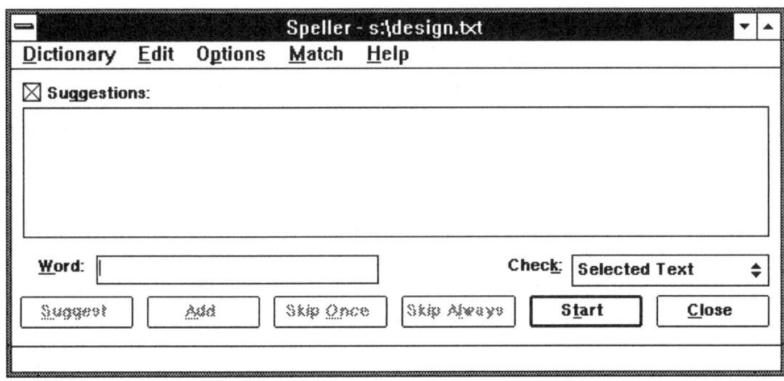

Figure 11-29. The Check option automatically defaults to Selected Text, if text has been selected within a document before the Speller is started.

Hints and Tips

Spell-checking words

The WordPerfect *Speller* can also check the spelling of single words of your choice, rather than entire documents at a time. This feature only operates when using the *Speller* in its stand-alone mode under Windows. With this approach, only the *Word* option from the *Check* list box in the *Speller* window (Figure 11-30) is selectable.

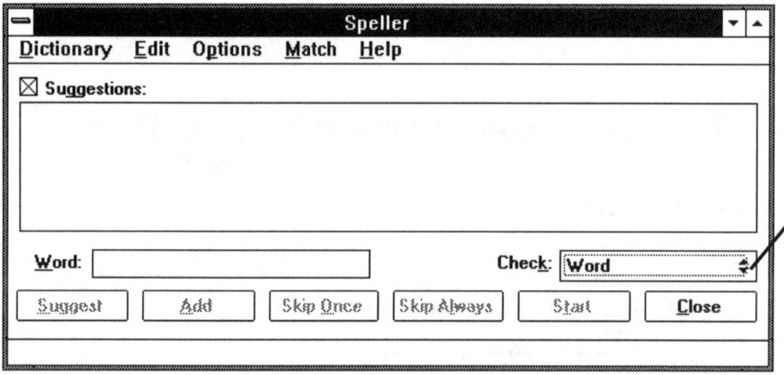

Figure 11-30. *Only the Word option in the Check list box is selectable when using the stand-alone speller.*

Insert your text cursor into the *Word* text box and key in the word you wish to spell-check (the word **'recieve'** in Figure 11-31).

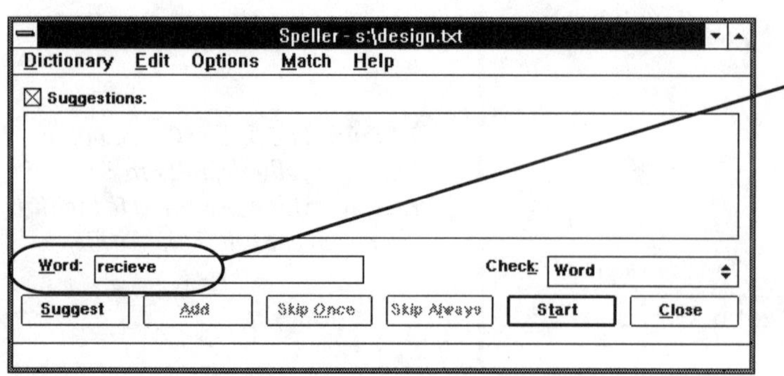

Figure 11-31. *Here the word 'recieve' has been entered into the Word text box for spell checking.*

After entering the word you wish to spell-check, click on the *Start* button (Figure 11-31). A list of alternative spellings (if any are found) will then be presented.

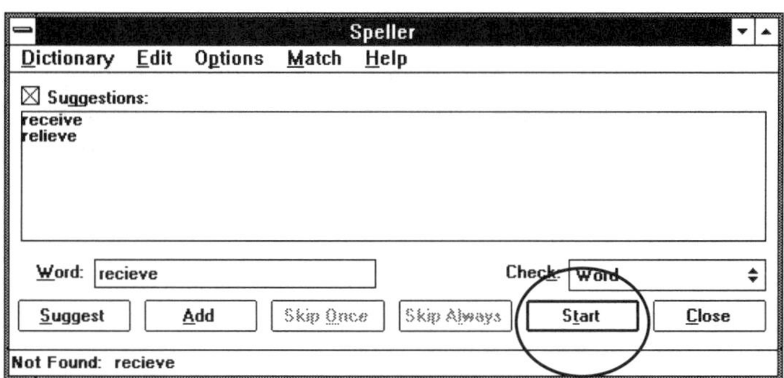

Figure 11-32. *After selecting the Start button, two suggestions have been made as to the correct or alternative spelling of this word.*

If a word is correctly spelt, the words *"Word Found: [correct word]"* will appear in the bottom left corner of the Figure 11-32 window. To check other words, backspace over the word already in the *Word* text box, enter another word, and press the *Start* button again.

Edit Menu

Using the **Edit** menu in the *Speller*, you can *Cut, Copy,* and *Paste* text contained in the *Word* text box to and from the Windows Clipboard. The *Undo* command affects the last editing change in the *Word* text box, and *Select All* selects all text, also from the *Word* text box.

Using wildcards in Word mode

When the *Speller* is operating in *Word* mode, you can, using the *Suggest* button, look up a word that matches a pattern. This pattern can use both text and wildcard symbols.

Wildcards are characters used to represent other characters. For example, question marks represent any single character, and the asterisk character, "*", represents any group of characters. These wildcards are the same that DOS and Windows use for file specifications. See Figure 11-33 for an example of using wildcard characters. These characters can be entered through the keyboard or selected through the **Match** menu within the *Speller*.

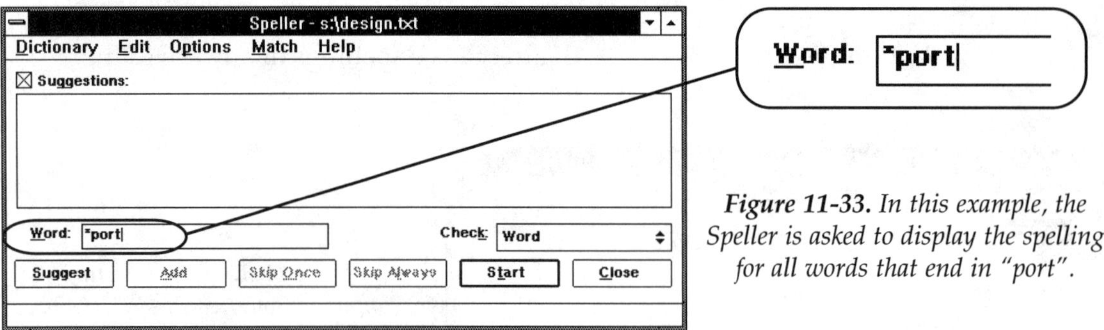

Figure 11-33. *In this example, the Speller is asked to display the spelling for all words that end in "port".*

In Figure 11-33, the string "*port" has been entered. As "*" is the wildcard character representing any number of any characters, this is the same as asking for all words that end in the characters "port".

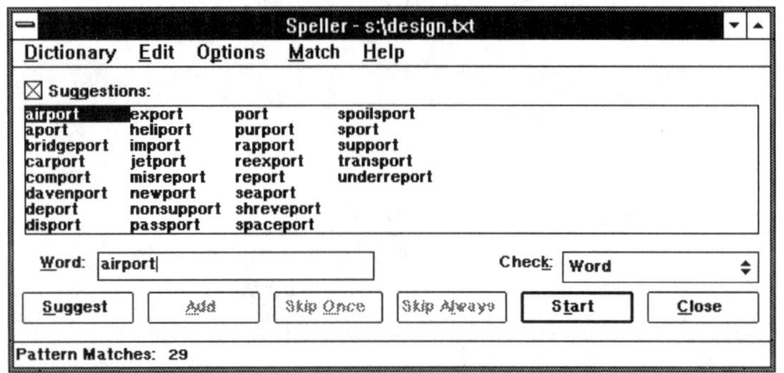

Figure 11-34. *Many matches are found for words ending in the text string "port".*

In Figure 11-34, you can see the results of clicking on the *Suggest* button. The *Speller* searches for all the words in its dictionary that end in "port", and displays them in the *Suggestions* area. If a wildcard option is not used when *Suggest* is chosen, then a list of phonetically similar words will appear in the *Suggestions* box.

Speller — Exercise

This training exercise is designed so that people of all levels of expertise with WordPerfect can use it to gain maximum benefit. In order to do this, the bare exercise is listed below this paragraph on just two pages, with no hints. The following pages contain the steps needed to complete this exercise for those who need additional prompting.

Steps in brief

1. *Start a new WordPerfect file.*
2. *Type in the following text exactly as it appears (with spelling mistakes included):*

Dear Ser,

I am riting to you in regard to the position you advertised in in saturday's newspaper.

I have had great experience in this field of work and was head of research at Dwyer Brothers Inc.

I hope to hear from you soon.

Yours faithfully,

Sigfreud.

---

3. *Activate the Speller and move the Speller window to the bottom of the screen using the appropriate command.*

4. *Start spell-checking the document.*
5. *Replace the first incorrect word, "Ser", with the correct word from the list of Suggestions, once the Speller has located it.*
6. *Replace the second incorrectly spelt word, "riting", with the correct word from the list of Suggestions, once the Speller has located it.*
7. *When the Speller prompts you that there are two of the same word, "in" appearing in succession, delete the second one.*
8. *Once the Speller halts at the company name, "Dwyer", continue checking without replacing the name or adding this name to the dictionary.*
9. *Add the person's name, "Sigfreud", to the dictionary, as it is highlighted by the Speller.*
10. *Once spell-checking is complete, close the Speller.*
11. *Key in the following text at the bottom of the letter.*

P.S. A prompt reply would be

---

12. *Reactivate the speller to search for an appropriate word for the end of this last sentence. You know the first four letters of the word, so ask the Speller to display all words in the dictionary that begin with "appr".*
13. *Find the appropriate word in the list of Suggestions, close the Speller, and key in this word.*

The details for completing these steps are on the following pages.

Steps in detail

1. *Start a new WordPerfect file.*

If you have just opened WordPerfect, you will be in a new WordPerfect file. If you are working on another WordPerfect document, select the *New* command from the **File** menu. If you are not in WordPerfect, start the program from Windows.

2. *Type in the following text exactly as it appears (with spelling mistakes included):*

Dear Ser,

I am riting to you in regard to the position you advertised in in saturday's newspaper.

I have had great experience in this field of work and was head of research at Dwyer Brothers Inc.

I hope to hear from you soon.

Yours faithfully,

Sigfreud.

Once you have opened a new WordPerfect file, key the text straight in, as shown in Figure 11x-1. For this exercise to work correctly, the keyed-in text must reflect the above text exactly.

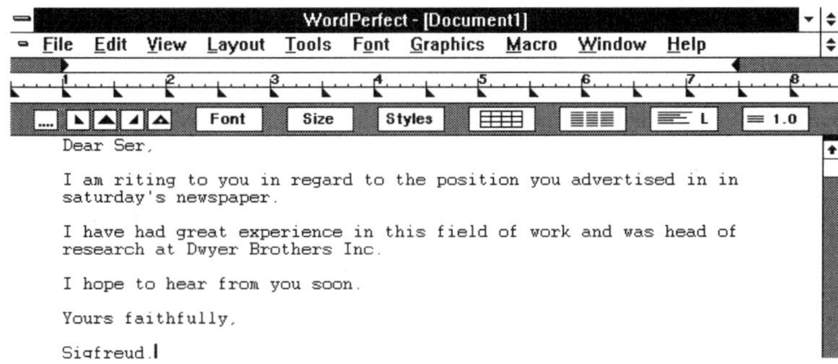

Figure 11x-1. *Type the required text into a new document.*

3. ***Activate the Speller and move the Speller window to the bottom of the screen using the appropriate command.***

To activate the *Speller*, select the *Speller* command from the **Tools** menu as in Figure11x-2.

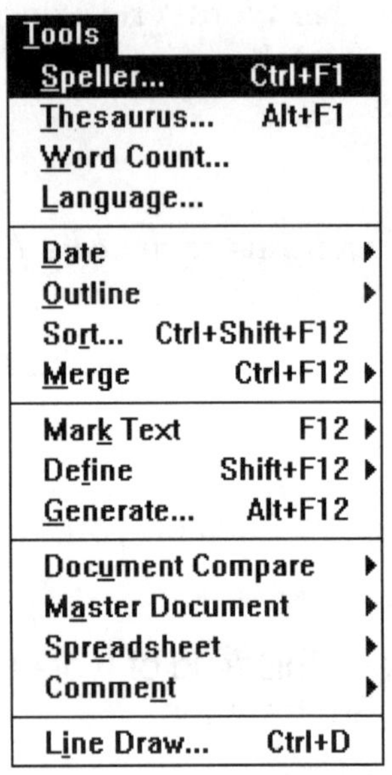

*Figure 11x-2. The Speller is activated by selecting the appropriate command from the **Tools** menu.*

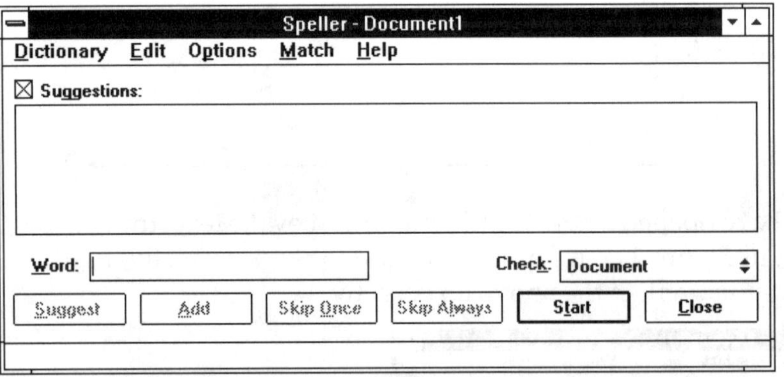

Figure 11x-3. The Speller window will appear after selecting the command of Figure 11x-2.

In order to see the document as it is being spell-checked, the *Speller* window can be moved to the bottom of the screen. This can be done in either of two ways. The first is to hold the mouse down on the Title bar of the *Speller* and drag it down, releasing the mouse when the window is at the bottom of the screen. The second way is through a menu command, which is requested for this exercise.

To move the *Speller* window automatically to the bottom of the screen, select the *Move to Bottom* command from the **Options** menu in the *Speller* Menu bar (Figure11x-4).

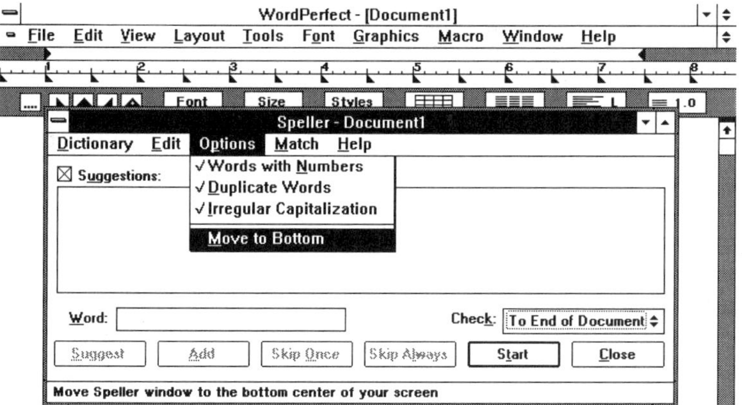

Figure 11x-4. *When the Speller window appears, it will usually cover the text in the document. The Move to Bottom command in the* ***Options*** *menu will reposition the Speller window to the bottom of the screen. It is then possible to see the text as it is being spell-checked.*

After selecting the command of Figure11x-4, you will see the *Speller* window move to the bottom of the screen as shown in Figure11x-5.

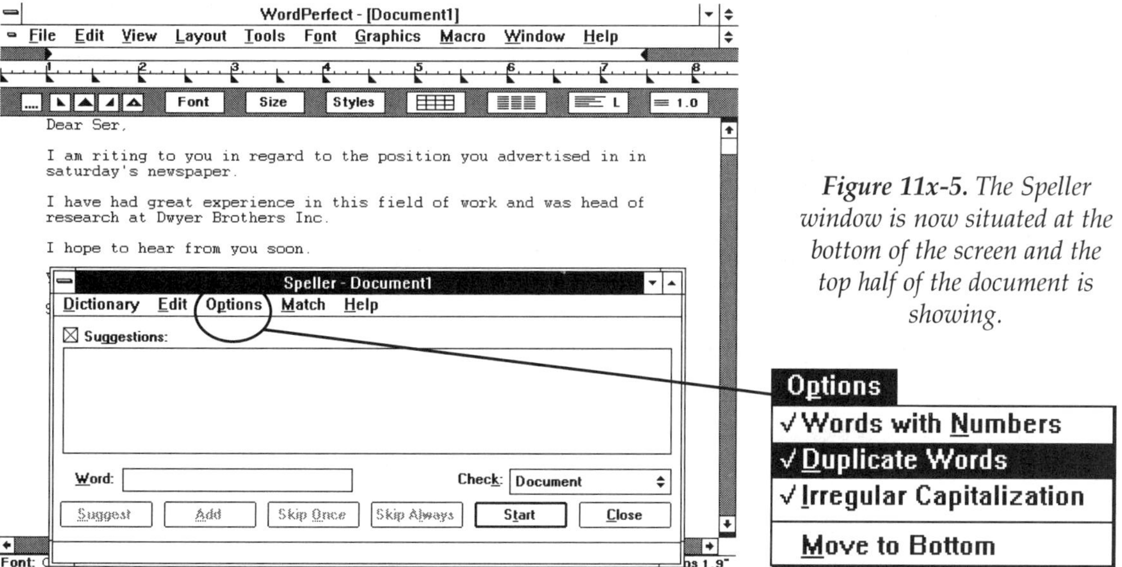

Figure 11x-5. *The Speller window is now situated at the bottom of the screen and the top half of the document is showing.*

Also perform one extra function which will be explained in step 7. Ensure that the *Duplicate Words* command in the *Speller* **Options** menu has a check mark next to it (Figure 11x-5).

4. ***Start spell-checking the document.***

Ensure that the option selected in the *Check* pop-up list reads *Document*. To start spell-checking, click on the *Start* button (Figure11x-6).

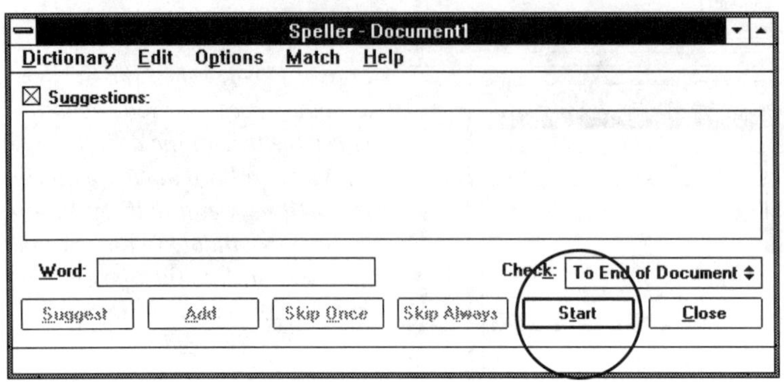

Figure 11x-6. Click on the Start button towards the bottom right of the Speller window to start the spell-checking procedure.

5. ***Replace the first incorrect word, "Ser", with the correct word from the list of Suggestions, once the Speller has located it.***

If you keyed in the text of step 1 correctly, the first mistake the *Speller* will pick up is the word "Ser" in the first line. The word will appear in the bottom left of the window, with the words *Not Found* before it. The *Suggestions* frame will include all words from the dictionary that *WordPerfect* finds similar to the incorrect word. The incorrect word is also highlighted in the text above the *Speller* window (see Figure 11x-7).

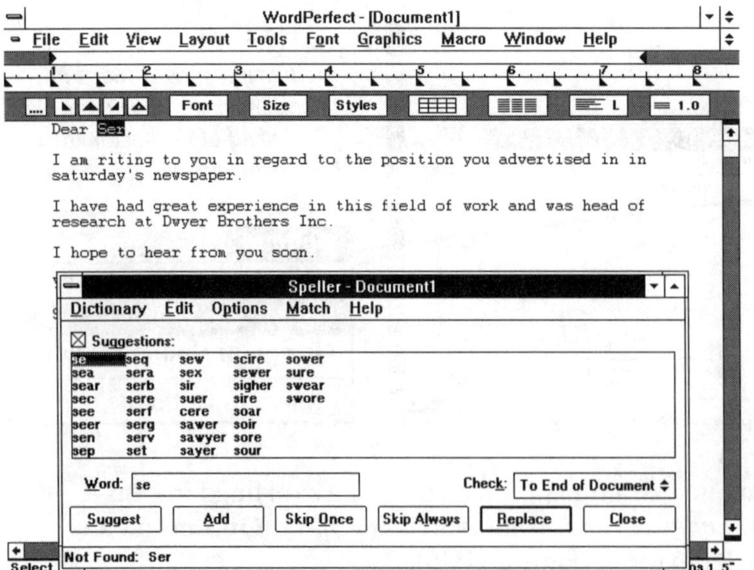

Figure 11x-7. The Speller has selected the word "Ser" in the first line as an incorrectly spelt word.

The correct word can now be selected from the list of suggested words. In this case, the correct word is "sir". Select it from the list and then click on the *Replace* button (Figure 11x-8).

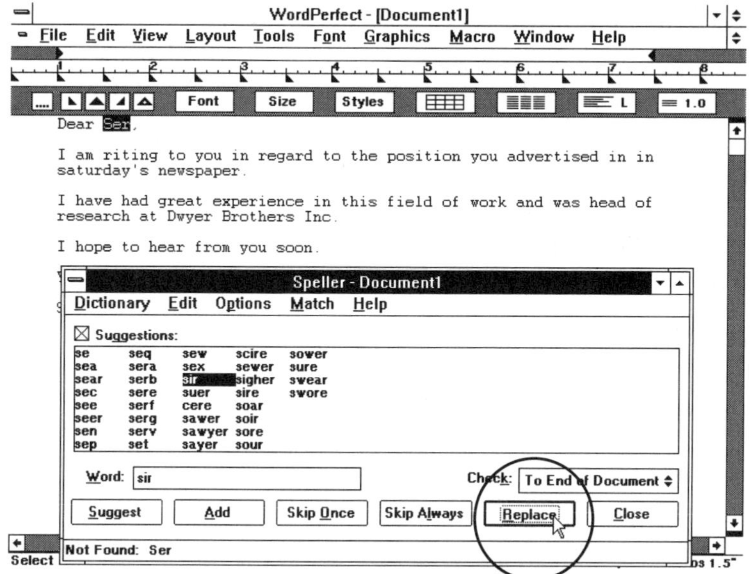

Figure 11x-8. Highlight the correct word from the list of suggested words and click on the Replace button. The text in the document will now compensate for this change and place the correct word in the proper place. It does not matter if the incorrect word had a first letter capital, as the new word will be replaced with the capitalization.

6. ***Replace the second incorrectly spelt word, "riting", with the correct word from the list of Suggestions, once the Speller has located it.***

The second incorrectly spelt word in the dummy letter is "riting". Once the *Speller* has located this word and displayed the list of suggestions, you then follow the same steps you did in step 5.

Find the correct word from the list of suggested words (in this case "writing"), highlight it and click on the *Replace* button (see Figure 11x-9). The word in the document will now be replaced with the word selected in the *Speller* window of Figure 11x-9.

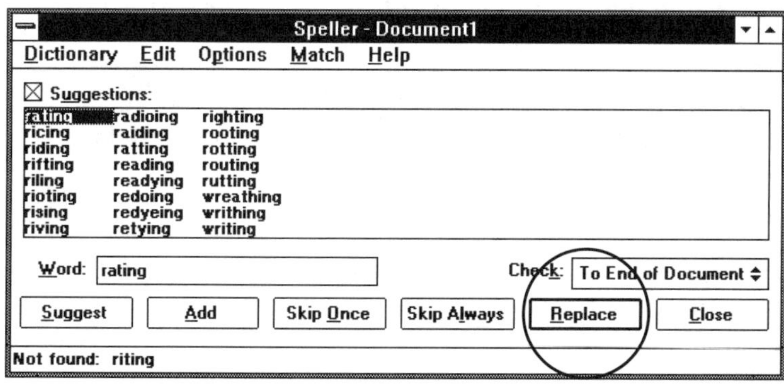

Figure 11x-9. The incorrect word is replaced with the correct one, by selecting the correct word from the list of Suggestions, and clicking on the Replace button.

7. ***When the Speller prompts you that there are two of the same word, "in", appearing in succession, delete the second one.***

In this exercise you keyed in the word "in" twice in the second paragraph. When *WordPerfect* locates these words, it will give you the option of continuing the spell checking or deleting the second word. For this exercise, you have been asked to delete the second one, so click on the *Delete 2nd* button as in Figure 11x-10.

Remember, at the end of Step 3, you selected the *Duplicate Words* command from the *Speller* **Options** menu. If this command is not activated, the *Speller* will not find duplicate words.

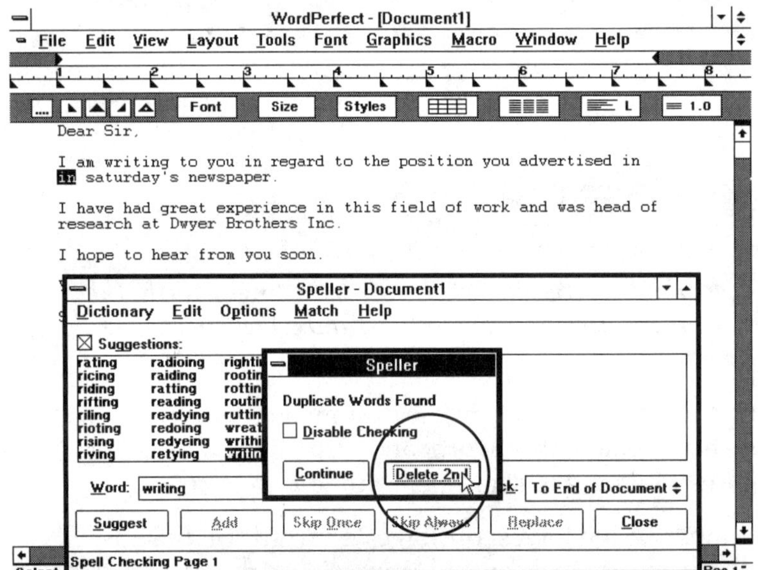

Figure 11x-10. *The Speller has highlighted the word "in" that appears twice in a row. For this exercise, you are deleting the second "in".*

8. ***Once the Speller halts at the company name, "Dwyer", continue spelling without replacing the name or adding this name to the dictionary.***

The word *Dwyer* is not in the *WordPerfect* dictionary, so it is highlighted as being incorrectly spelt. To leave this word as it is, without replacing it or adding it to the dictionary, you click on the *Skip Once* button as shown in Figure 11x-11.

If the word *Dwyer* appeared elsewhere in the document, you could select the *Skip Always* option, so the *Speller* will ignore it for the rest of this spell-check session.

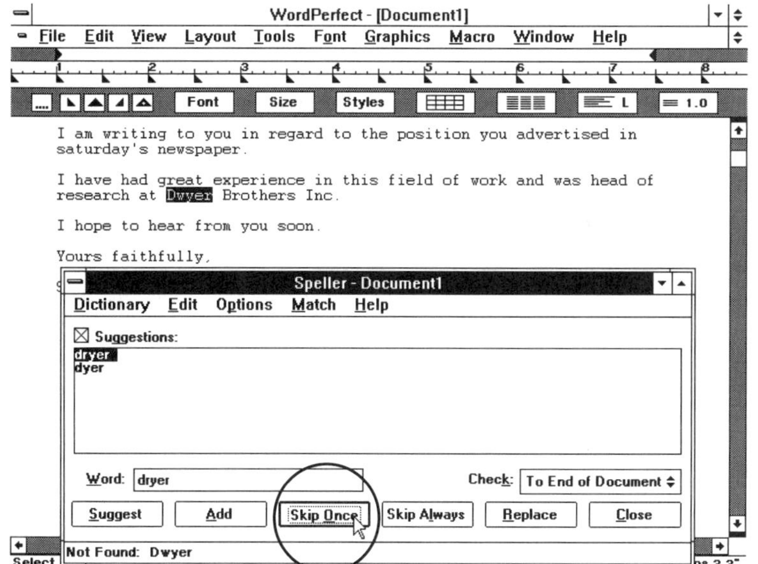

Figure 11x-11. Because the word Dwyer is not in the WordPerfect dictionary, it is selected as being an incorrectly spelt word. We know that it is correct, so select the Skip Once option allowing the Speller to bypass this word.

9. ***Add the person's name, "Sigfreud", to the dictionary, as it is highlighted by the Speller.***

The last word that the *Speller* will pick up in this document is the name at the end of the letter (Sigfreud). If this is your name, and you plan on writing many letters, it might be wise to add this word to the dictionary. To do this, click on the *Add* button once the *Speller* has highlighted the word (see Figure 11x-12). The word will now be added to the *Supplementary* dictionary.

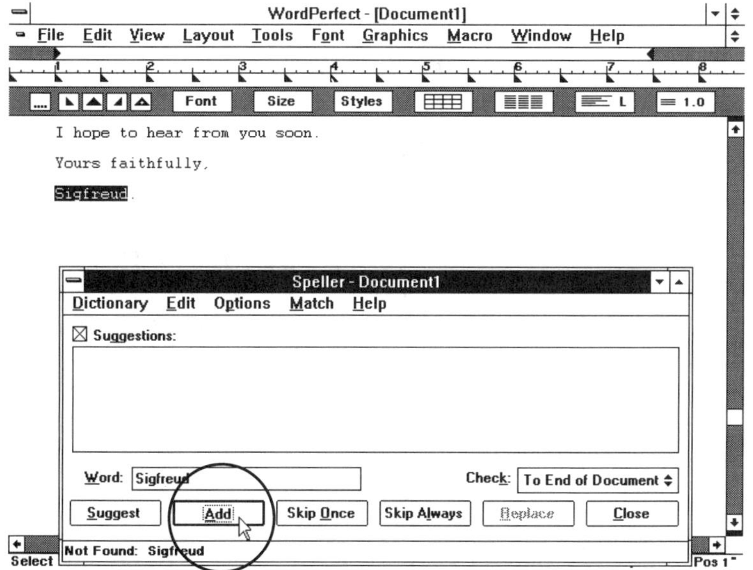

Figure 11x-12. The name at the bottom of the letter is being added to the dictionary.

10. Once spell-checking is complete, close the Speller.

When the *Speller* has finished spell-checking your document, the message in the bottom left of the window will read *Spell Check Completed*. The *Speller* is closed by clicking on the *Close* button at the bottom right of its window. This returns you to the document.

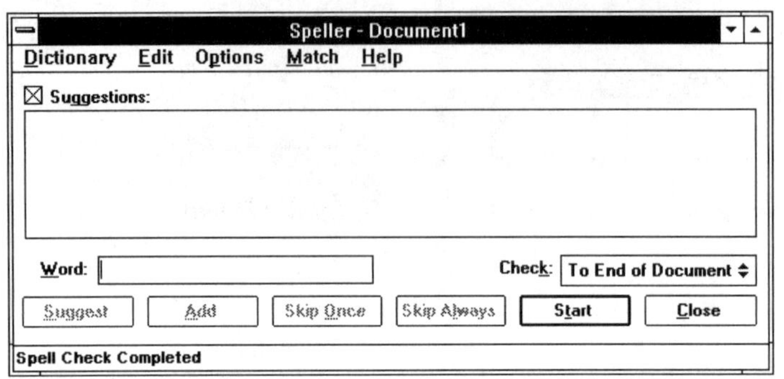

***Figure 11x-13**. The Speller has now completed spell checking the document, as indicated in the bottom left of the Speller window. Close the Speller by clicking on the Close button.*

11. Key in the following text at the bottom of the letter.

P.S. A prompt reply would be

To type in this text, place the cursor at the end of the letter and hit the Enter key twice. Then type the text as you did in step 1 (see Figure 11x-14).

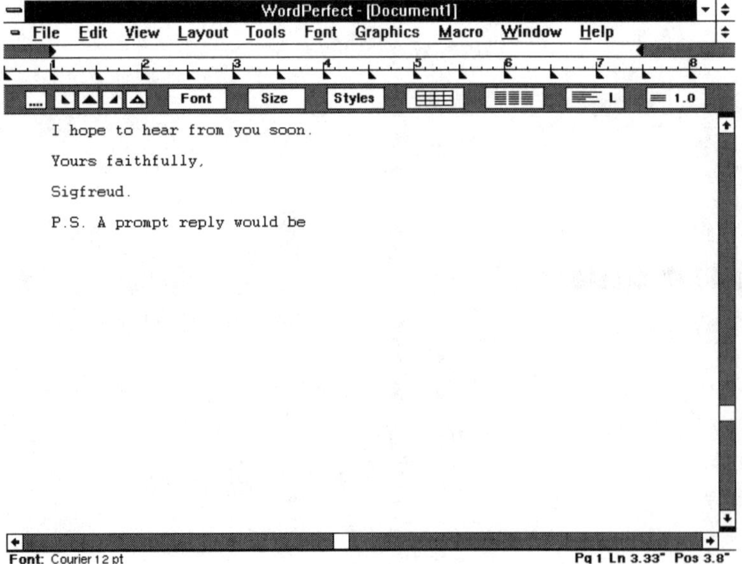

***Figure 11x-14**. The new line of text is keyed in at the bottom of the letter.*

12. ***Reactivate the Speller to search for an appropriate word for the end of this last sentence. You know the first four letters of the word, so ask the Speller to display all words in the dictionary that begin with "appr".***

Again, the *Speller* is activated by selecting the *Speller* command from the **Tools** menu (refer to Figure 11x-2). This time you are going to ask the *Speller* for a specific group of words.

Insert the cursor in the *Word* rectangle of the *Speller* window if it is not already there and key in the letters "appr" as in Figure 11x-15.

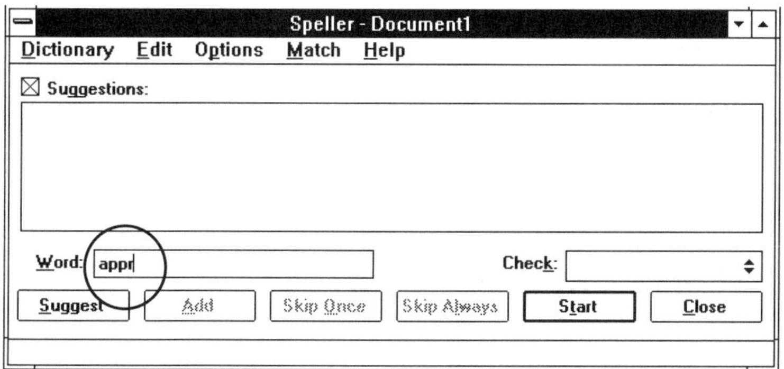

***Figure 11x-15**. You are going to ask the Speller to display all its words beginning with "appr". The first step in this procedure is to key these letters into the Word text box.*

Making sure your cursor is still in the *Word* text box after the letters, select the *Multiple Characters* option from the **Match** menu in the *Speller* (Figure 11x-16). This will place an asterisk ("*") symbol after the text (Figure 11x-17).

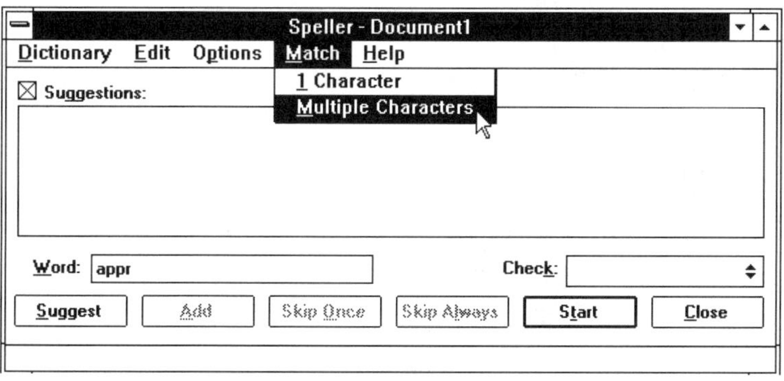

***Figure 11x-16**. After keying in the text, select the Multiple Characters option from the **Match** menu.*

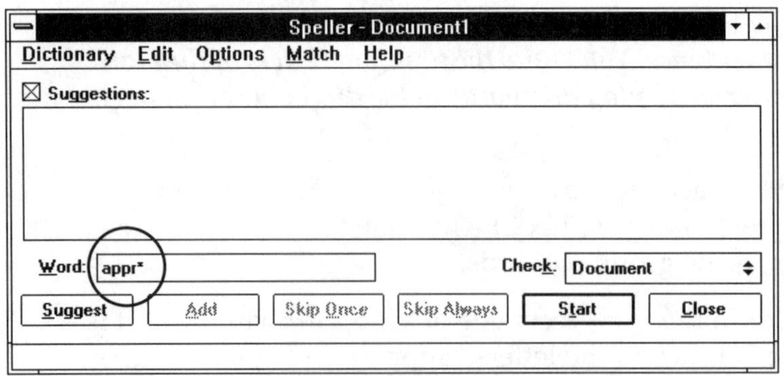

Figure 11x-17. *Selecting the Multiple Characters option from the* ***Match*** *menu places an "*" symbol in the Word text box after the text.*

If you now click on the *Suggest* button (Figure 11x-18), all words in the dictionary that begin with 'appr' will appear in the *Suggestions* frame as shown in Figure 11x-19.

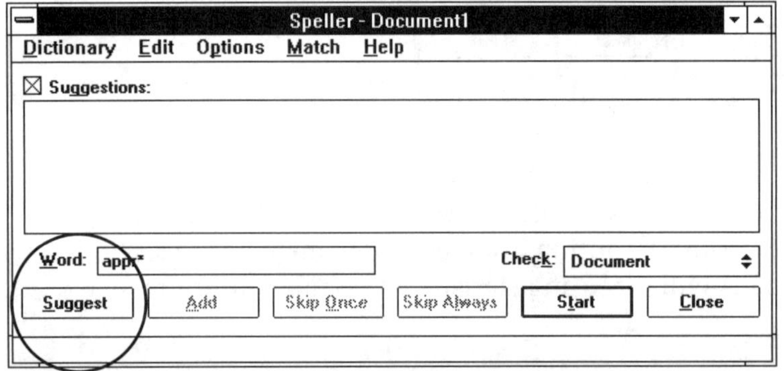

Figure 11x-18. *WordPerfect searches for all words that begin with 'appr', once you have clicked on the Suggest button.*

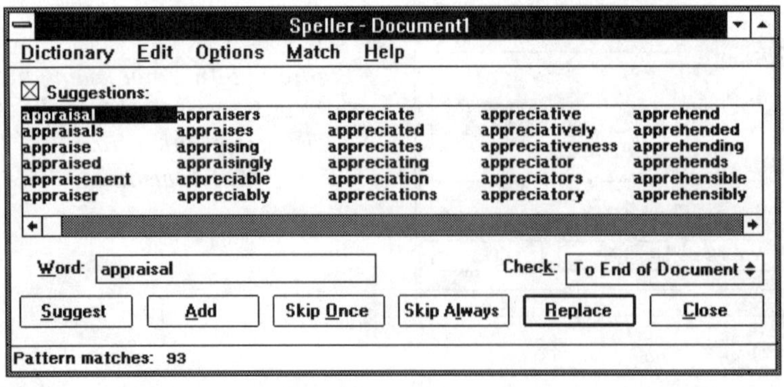

Figure 11x-19. *All words in the dictionary that begin with 'appr' are now listed in the Suggestions frame.*

13. Find the appropriate word in the list of Suggestions, close the Speller, and key in this word.

Now you can simply look for the word that you require, check how it is spelt, close the *Speller* and key in the correct word (Figure 11x-20). In this case the word is "appreciated".

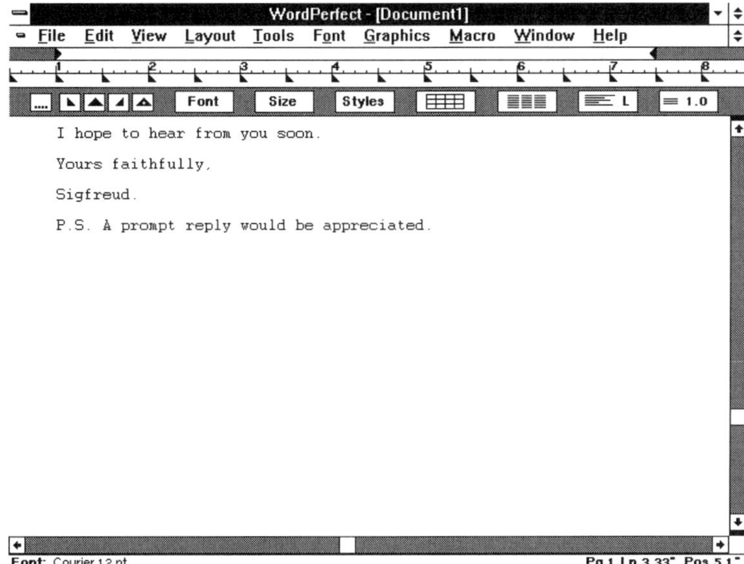

***Figure 11x-20**. Once the correct word has been located in the Speller window, close the Speller and key in the word.*

Thesaurus

The WordPerfect *Thesaurus* program operates like a traditional thesaurus by providing alternate words, of a similar (or opposite) meaning, for a given word. In other words, it provides synonyms and antonyms for selected words.

Starting the Thesaurus

Like the *Speller*, described in Chapter 11, the WordPerfect *Thesaurus* can be launched as a self running application, or from within WordPerfect itself.

To launch the *Thesaurus* as a stand-alone application, you locate and double-click on the *Thesaurus* icon, within the *WordPerfect* group in the *Windows Program Manager* (Figure 12-1).

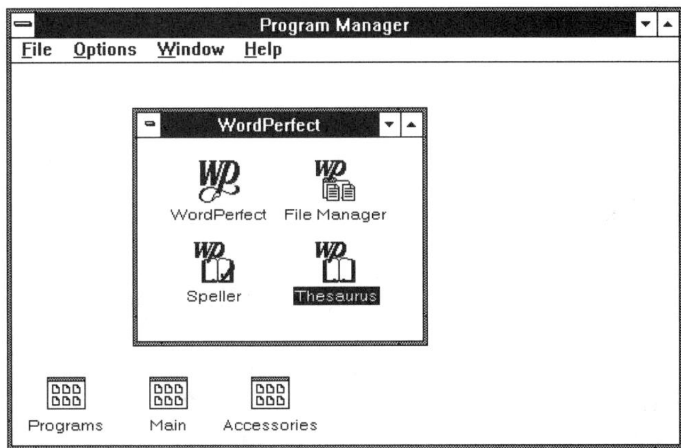

Figure 12-1*. The Thesaurus program can be launched directly from the WordPerfect group within the Program Manager.*

The *Thesaurus* can also be launched from within WordPerfect, using the *Thesaurus* command from the **Tools** menu (Figure 12-2)—in most cases this is where you will select it. When the *Thesaurus* is launched as a stand-alone program, it relies on the user to enter words, rather than providing a synonym (or antonym) for a selected word within a WordPerfect document.

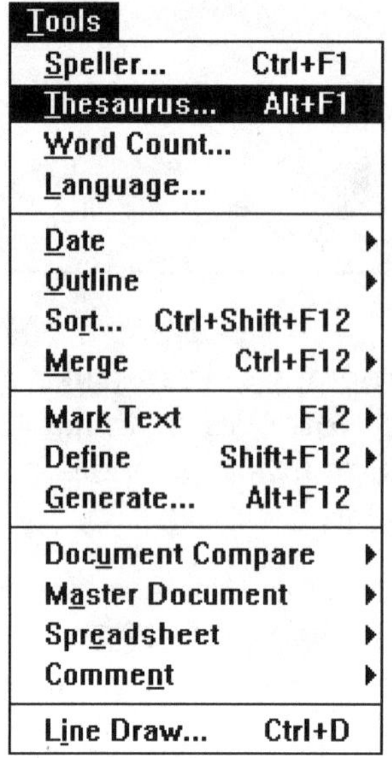

*Figure 12-2. The Thesaurus can also be started by selecting the Thesaurus command from the **Tools** menu within WordPerfect.*

In this chapter, the *Thesaurus* is looked at in detail. You study the *Thesaurus* window (Figure 12-3), the use of the *Thesaurus*, and the *Thesaurus* options.

The Thesaurus window

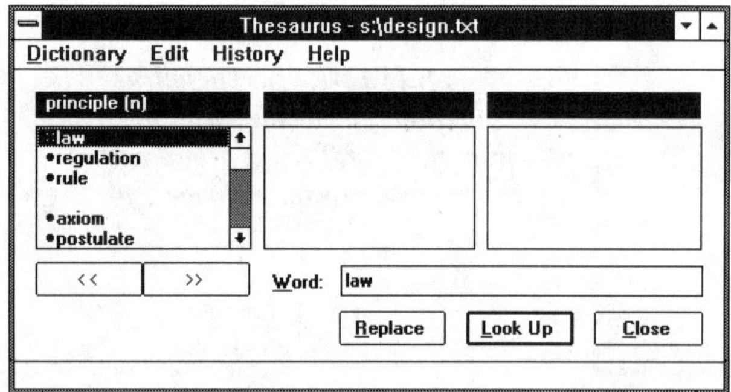

Figure 12-3. A sample Thesaurus window.

The Title bar of the *Thesaurus* (Figure 12-4) lists the currently open document. If the *Thesaurus* was started from the Program Manager as a stand-alone program, the Title bar would simply read "*Thesaurus*".

Thesaurus - s:\design.txt 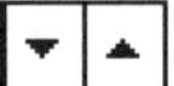

***Figure 12-4.** The Thesaurus Title bar—in this case started from within WordPerfect, using the Thesaurus command from the **Tools** menu. In this figure, the Thesaurus Title bar shows that the document **s:\design.txt** is currently open.*

The Menu bar (Figure 12-5) is much like the WordPerfect Menu bar—these menus contain commands which can control the way the *Thesaurus* operates.

Dictionary   Edit   History   Help

***Figure 12-5.** The Thesaurus Menu bar which allows access to commands for altering Thesaurus operation.*

The *Thesaurus* window contains three columns in its center window. In these three columns, synonyms and antonyms, for as many as three selected words, are displayed. In Figure 12-6, only the first column is being used and that column displays synonyms for the word "principle".

***Figure 12-6.** In the center of the Thesaurus window are three columns— used to display the synonyms for selected words.*

It is possible to search for more than three selected words in this window but only three can be displayed at one time. To gain access to additional words for display of synonyms and antonyms, you click on the left or right facing horizontal arrow buttons below column one (Figure 12-7).

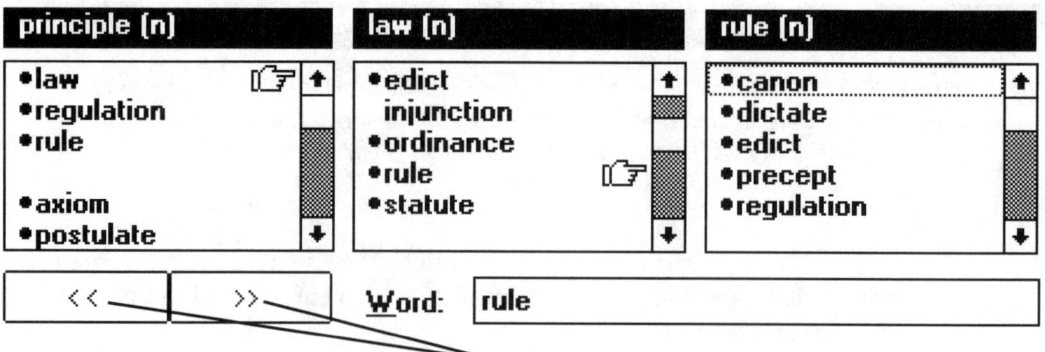

Figure 12-7. In this illustration, the three Thesaurus columns are filled with data. To allow you to see new columns of data, or to look over previous columns, you can use the left and right-hand arrow buttons, near the bottom left-hand corner of the window.

To the right of the arrow buttons is the *Word* text box (Figure 12-8). This text box displays the currently selected word and also provides a text entry area in which to enter new words for which you would like to obtain synonyms or antonyms.

Word: rule

Figure 12-8. The Word text box provides a display area for the currently selected word and also a text entry area for new words.

The various option buttons in the *Thesaurus* window (Figure 12-9) will be explained in more detail when you get to them; however, here is a brief overview of the operation of each of these buttons.

Figure 12-9. The options buttons within the Thesaurus dialog box.

The *Replace* button replaces the currently selected word in the *Word* text box—Figure 12-8—with the word which was originally selected on the WordPerfect page.

The *Look Up* button is used when you have manually entered or edited a word within the *Word* text box (Figure 12-8) and wish to look for synonyms or antonyms for that word.

The *Close* button is used to close down the *Thesaurus* program and return to the WP editing screen.

Using the Thesaurus

In this example, a document has been opened, as displayed in Figure 12-10. Selected words from this document will be used as examples of *Thesaurus* operation.

Figure 12-10. *Here the document* ***s:\design.txt*** *is opened before starting the Thesaurus.*

First, you select a word for which you wish to obtain a synonym or antonym. Once you have made your selection, click the mouse cursor within that word. In Figure 12-11, the text cursor has been inserted to the left of the word "Principles".

If you wish to work through with us in this chapter, create a new WordPerfect file and key in two words—"Principles" and "Traditional". These are the two words being used to illustrate Thesaurus operation.

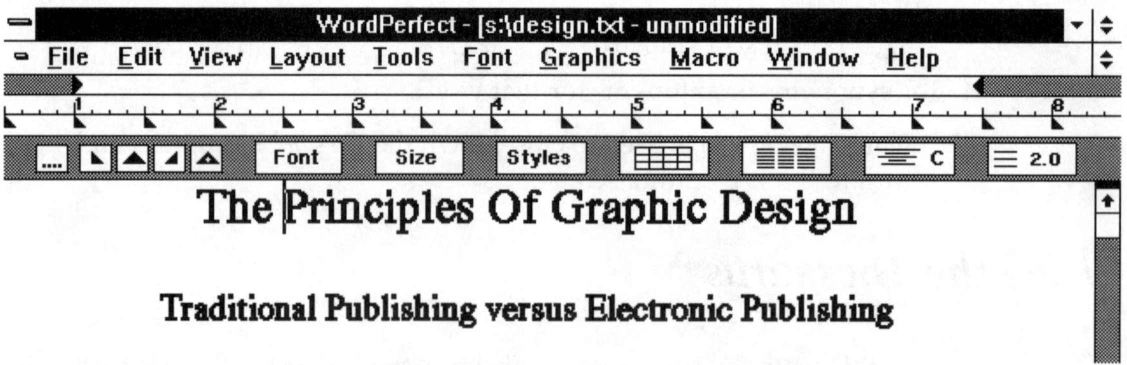

Figure 12-11. *In this case, the Thesaurus will be used to find a synonym for the word "Principles". Note that the text cursor has been embedded in this word, by clicking the mouse anywhere in the word.*

Your next step is to select the *Thesaurus* command from the **Tools** menu (Figure 12-12).

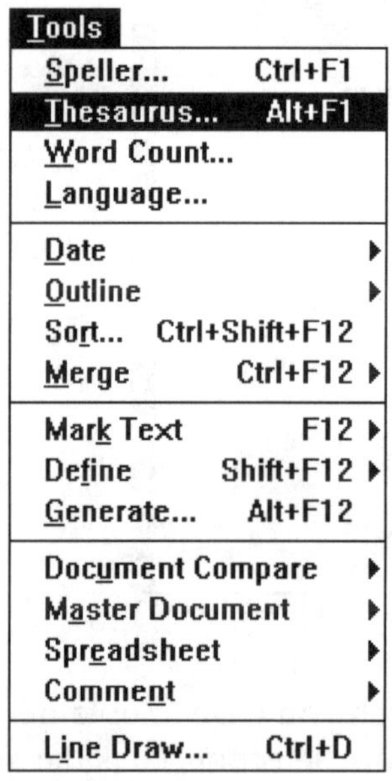

Figure 12-12. *The Thesaurus is started by selecting the Thesaurus command from the* ***Tools*** *menu.*

The *Thesaurus* window then appears and automatically searches for synonyms and antonyms for the selected word "Principles". The word "Principles" is highlighted in reverse video (Figure 12-13) and the result is displayed in the first column as shown in Figure 12-14.

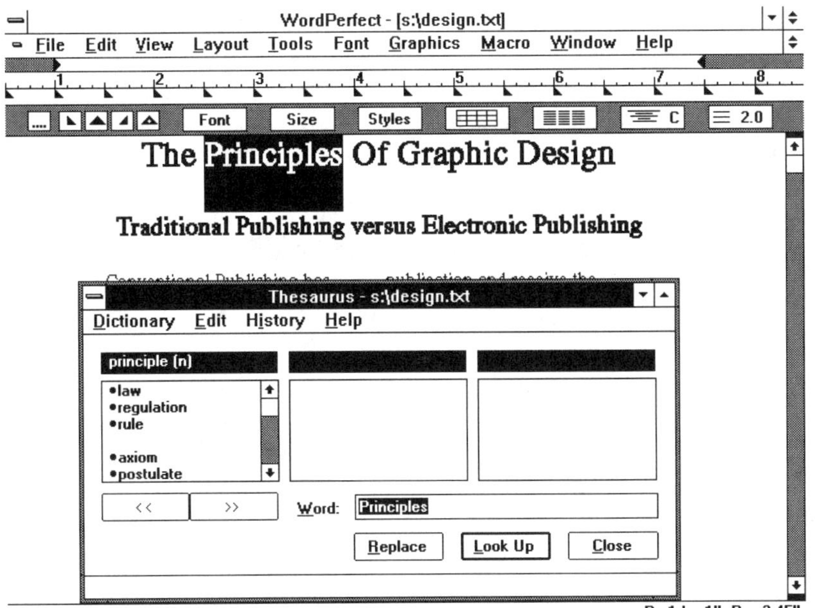

Figure 12-13. As the Thesaurus window appears, the word on screen ,"Principles", is automatically selected, and synonyms and antonyms are searched for this word.

If either a synonym or an antonym is found, the first column in the *Thesaurus* window lists these for the selected word (Figure 12-14).

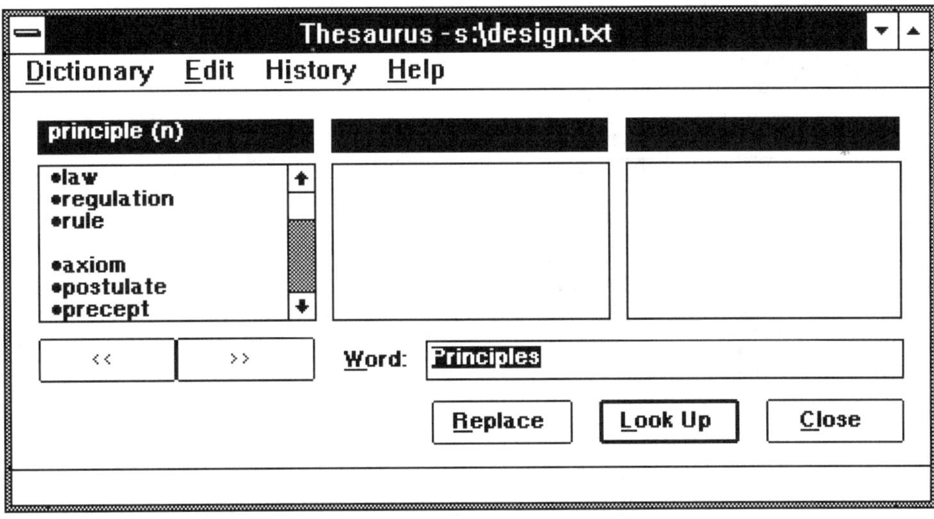

Figure 12-14. At the top of the first column is the selected word—"principle". This is known as the headword. In brackets next to this name is a letter indicating what part of speech this is. Below this word, synonyms and antonyms are displayed in a list.

In Figure 12-14, you can see that the selected word, or headword, "Principles", has been shortened to "principle" and is displayed in reverse video. As mentioned in the Figure 12-14 caption, the word is followed by a letter in brackets to the right. This letter is used to identify the word's part of speech.

The headword may be a noun (n), a verb (v), or an adjective, indicated by (a). In Figure 12-14, "principle" is a noun.

Finding synonyms

Underneath the headword, a list of synonyms, or words with meanings similar to the headword, is displayed. In Figure 12-14, these words are *law, regulation, rule, axiom,* and *postulate* which all have meanings similar to that of the headword, "principle". Other words can be seen by using the vertical scroll bar which has appeared within the first column.

Assume that in this current list of synonyms, there are no words that you consider a fit replacement for the word "principle" in the document. You can use many of the words within the list to start another search, by simply double-clicking on another word (Figure 12-15).

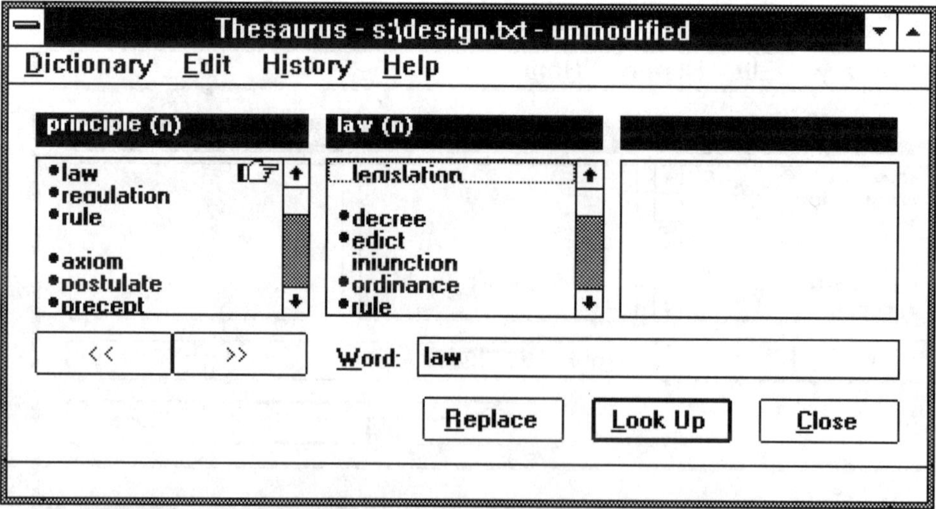

***Figure 12-15**. In this example, the word "law" was selected (double-clicked on) in the first column. The Thesaurus immediately performs another search, this time using "law" as the headword. The results are displayed in column two.*

In Figure 12-15, a small hand appears to the right of the selected word in the first column ("law"). This word then becomes the headword for the column to the right, in this case column two. The synonyms and antonyms for the word "law" are now displayed under that heading in column two.

Depending upon the word selected, you may find that the list of new synonyms (and antonyms) provides more useful suggestions than the original list in column one.

You are free to perform this feat as many times as you feel necessary —simply double-click on any word in any column and this word becomes the headword for the column immediately to its right. In Figure 12-16, the word "rule" from column two has been double-clicked on. The results are evident in column three.

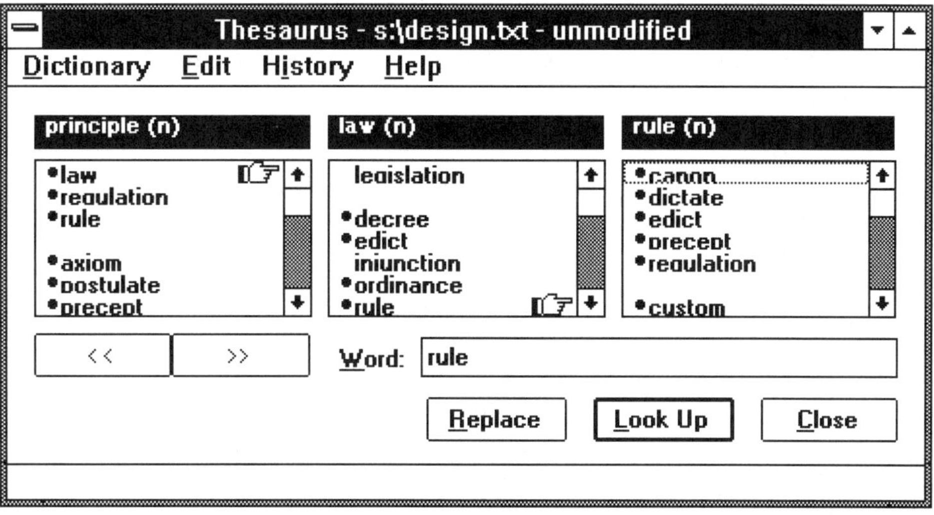

Figure 12-16. *The word "rule" has been double-clicked on in the second column. It becomes the headword, and the basis of a search for synonyms and antonyms, in column three.*

The above step can be performed more than three times—the columns simply scroll to the left as new headwords are selected. To move to the left and the right, if there are more than three full columns, you use the arrow buttons described in Figure 12-7 or, alternatively, the **History** menu. This latter option provides a list of all currently used headwords and lets you move back to the column for that headword by selecting it from the menu (Figure 12-17).

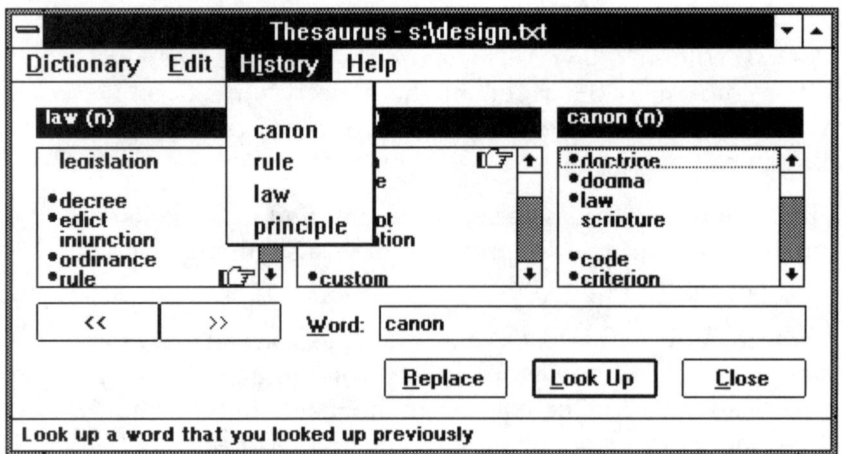

Figure 12-17. The **History** menu contains all of the headwords used in this session. The word canon at the top of column three in Figure 12-16 was also double-clicked before choosing the **History** menu.

If you decide not to use any synonyms offered here, you can return to the page by selecting the *Close* button.

Another word can be selected from within your document, as before, by clicking the mouse once in that word. In Figure 12-18, this word is "Traditional".

In Figure 12-18, a search is automatically performed for synonyms and antonyms for the selected word (the headword) "traditional".

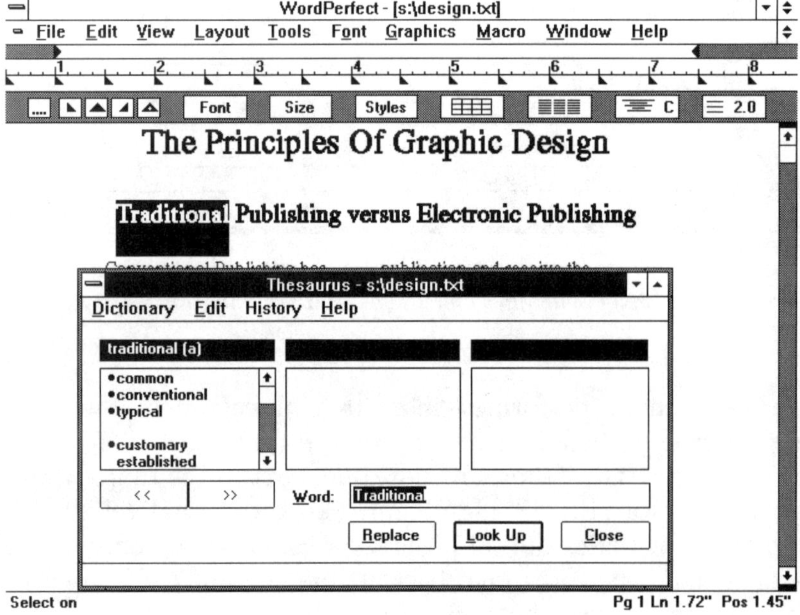

Figure 12-18. Select another word by clicking on it, before the Thesaurus command from the **Tools** menu is activated. In this case, the word is "Traditional".

Making replacements

In this case, assume that the word "conventional"—second down the list of synonyms under the headword "traditional"—is the word with which you wish to replace the originally selected word (Figure 12-18) "Traditional". Before the replacement can occur, the word must be selected from its column within the *Thesaurus* window (Figure 12-19).

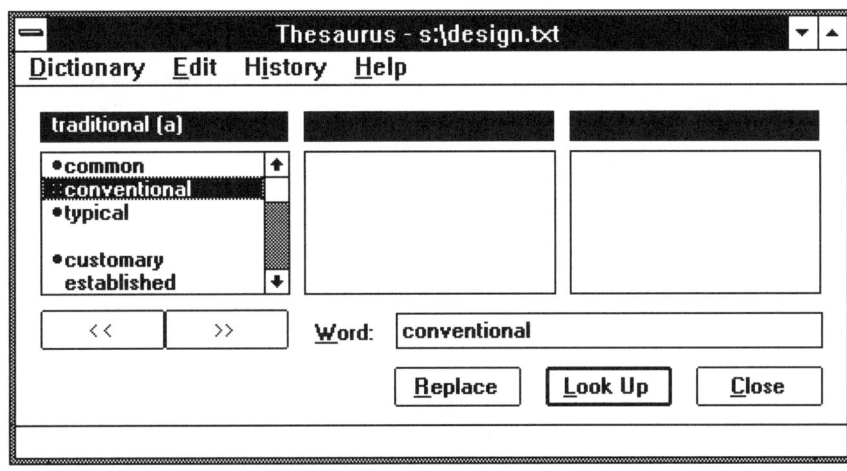

Figure 12-19. *The word "conventional" is selected as a suitable replacement for the originally selected word, "traditional", by clicking on it. Note that this selected word also appears as the word in the Word text box.*

After the desired word has been selected and appears in the Word text box (Figure 12-19), clicking on the *Replace* button replaces this word with the original word, back in the document (Figure 12-20).

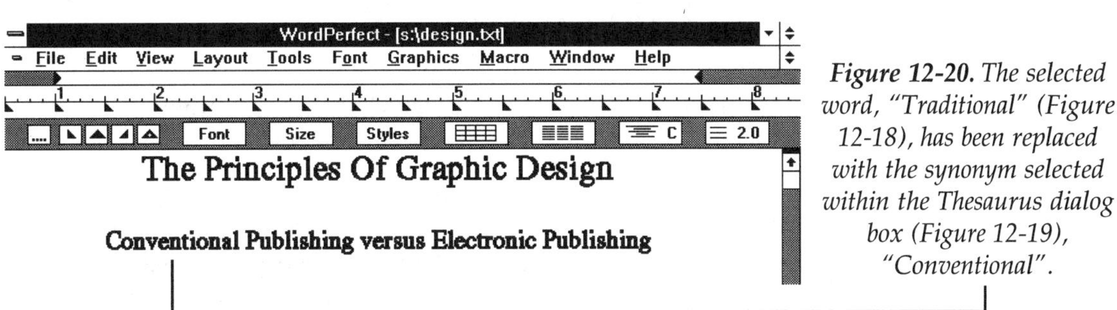

Figure 12-20. *The selected word, "Traditional" (Figure 12-18), has been replaced with the synonym selected within the Thesaurus dialog box (Figure 12-19), "Conventional".*

Finding antonyms

Antonyms (words of an opposite meaning) are listed after the synonyms at the bottom of the list. In Figure 12-21, the first column of Figure 12-14 was scrolled through until the headword, followed by the word "(ant)", was encountered. Underneath the "(ant)" heading are antonyms for the current headword.

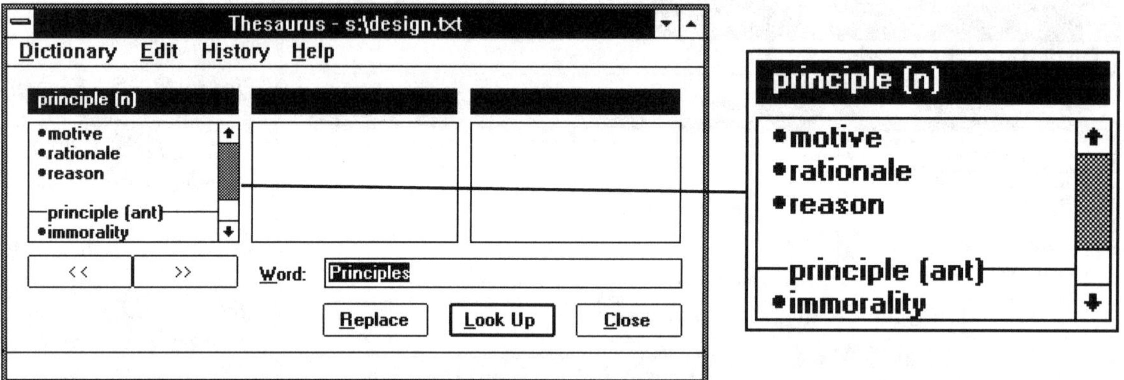

Figure 12-21. When the headword is found in the list with the string (ant) after it, this indicates that all the words that follow are antonyms of the headword. In this case, there is only one antonym listed—immorality.

Remember, it is quite possible that a particular word has no antonyms or that the *Thesaurus* cannot locate any from within the current dictionary.

Using the Thesaurus without WordPerfect

Using the *Thesaurus* outside of WordPerfect, as a stand-alone product, is similar to using the *Thesaurus* within WordPerfect.

When the *Thesaurus* is started as a stand-alone product (Figure 12-1), it is not linked to any document in any way, so it cannot tell whether any word has been selected in any document. It is therefore up to you to enter a word directly into this window (in the *Word* text box in Figure 12-8), and press the *Look Up* button (Figure 12-9).

Rather than having to type rather long words into the *Word* text box in the *Thesaurus* window, the *Thesaurus* provides full Clipboard functionality. Any word can be pasted into the *Word* text box by selecting the *Paste* command from the *Thesaurus* **Edit** menu (Figure 12-22).

Edit
Undo Alt+BkSp
Cut Shift+Del
Copy Ctrl+Ins
Paste Shift+Ins
Select All

Figure 12-22. *The Paste command from the Thesaurus* ***Edit*** *menu can be used to paste any words from the Clipboard directly into the Word text box of the Thesaurus window.*

By the same token, any replacement words that appear in the *Word* text box can, once selected, be copied to the Clipboard using the *Copy* command from the *Thesaurus* **Edit** menu. Remember, words appear automatically in the *Word* text box as they are selected from any column in the *Thesaurus* window—see Figure 12-19.

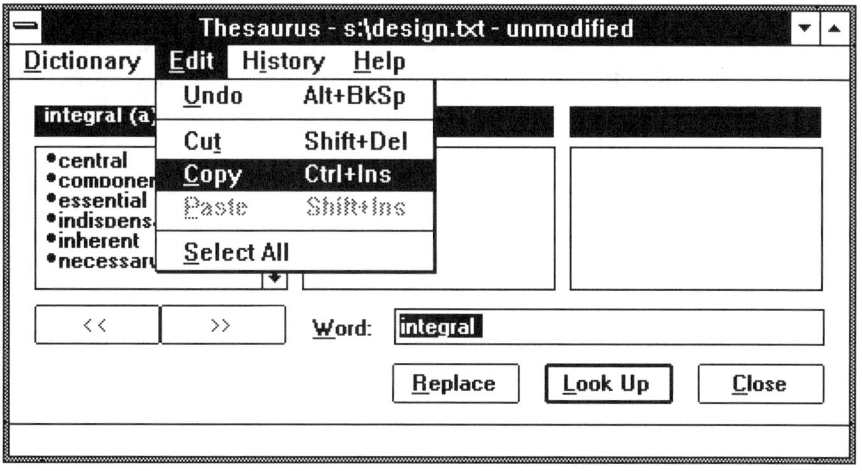

Figure 12-23. *Here the word "integral" is selected within the Word text box. The Cut or Copy commands from the Thesaurus* ***Edit*** *menu, can be used to copy this word to the Windows Clipboard.*

Errors

It is possible that the WordPerfect *Thesaurus* may not list any synonyms or antonyms for a word that you select. If this is the case, the bottom left-hand corner of the *Thesaurus* window will reflect the fact that the word was not found (Figure 12-24).

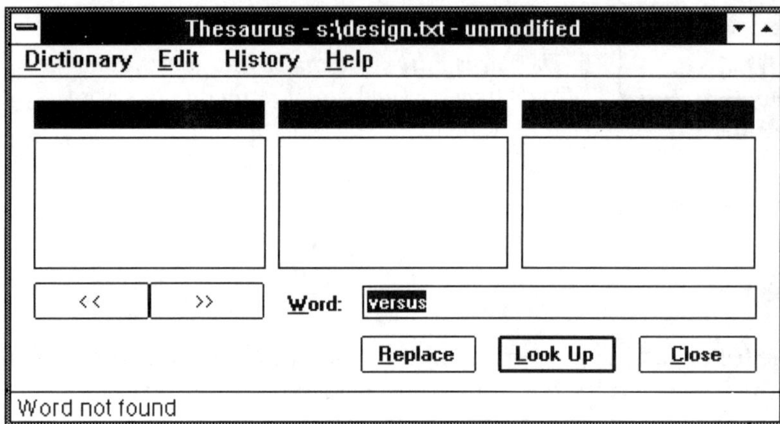

Figure 12-24. *The bottom left-hand corner of the Thesaurus window will let you know when a particular word cannot be found in the Thesaurus dictionary.*

Changing the Thesaurus dictionary

The *Change Dictionary* command in the **Dictionary** menu allows a dictionary other than the default *Thesaurus* dictionary to be used when searching for antonyms and synonyms.

Thesaurus — Exercise

This training exercise is designed so that people of all levels of expertise with WordPerfect can use it to gain maximum benefit. In order to do this, the bare exercise is listed below this paragraph on just one page, with no hints. The following pages contain the steps needed to complete this exercise for those who need additional prompting.

Steps in brief

1. *Open the Thesaurus as a stand-alone application.*
2. *Type the word "shape" into the Word text box.*
3. *Display all the synonyms and antonyms for this word in column one of the Thesaurus window.*
4. *Locate the word "outline" from the list of words under "shape". Make this word, "outline", the headword for column two of the Thesaurus window.*
5. *Highlight the word "substance" from column two and make it the headword of column one.*
6. *Using the appropriate menu command, make the word "shape" the headword of column one again.*
7. *Select the word "figure" from column one and copy it to the Clipboard. Close the Thesaurus, open a new WordPerfect file, and paste this word into the document.*
8. *Delete the word "figure" and retrieve the learn05.wkb file from the learn sub-directory.*
9. *Insert the text cursor into the word "Conference" and open the Thesaurus.*
10. *Select the word "seminar" from the list of synonyms.*
11. *Replace the word "Conference" with the word "Seminar".*

The details for completing these steps are on the following pages.

Steps in detail

1. Open the Thesaurus as a stand-alone application.

For the first part of this exercise you are going to use the *Thesaurus* outside of *WordPerfect*. As you do with any *Windows* program, the *Thesaurus* is activated by double-clicking on the relevant icon in the *Windows Program Manager* (Figure 12x-1).

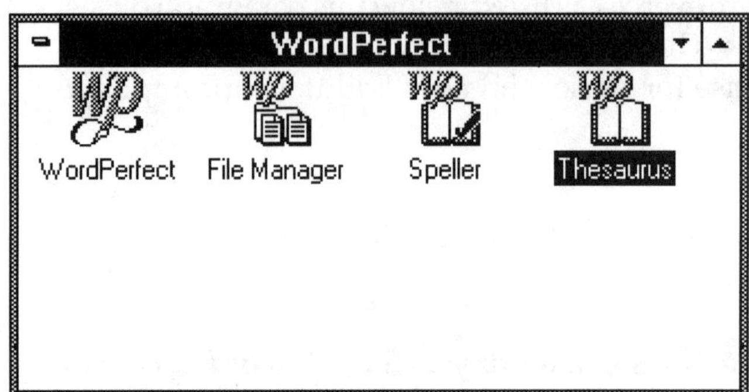

Figure 12x-1*. The Thesaurus is activated by double-clicking on the Thesaurus icon in the Windows Program Manager.*

After you have double-clicked on the icon, as shown in Figure 12x-1, the *Thesaurus* is activated (Figure 12x-2).

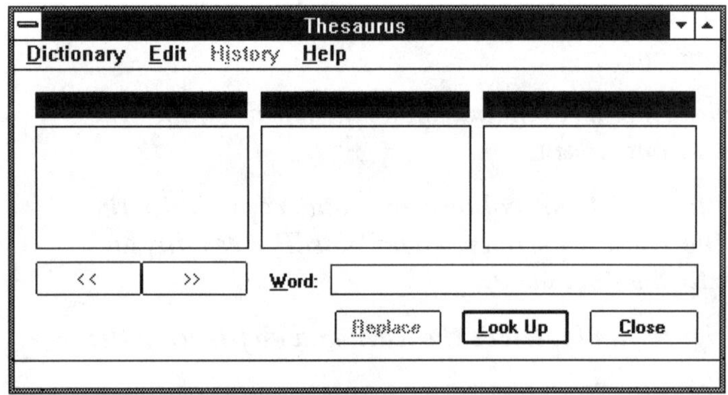

Figure 12x-2*. The Thesaurus is now open.*

2. Type the word "shape" into the Word text box.

Immediately after the *Thesaurus* is activated, the text cursor will be in the *Word* text box. Key the word "shape" directly into this rectangle (Figure 12x-3). If the flashing cursor is not in the *Word* text box, simply click inside it with the mouse, then key the text in.

3. Display all the synonyms and antonyms for this word in column one of the Thesaurus window.

Once the word "shape" has been keyed into the *Word* text box, click on the *Look Up* button (Figure 12x-3). This command will display all the synonyms and antonyms that the *Thesaurus* lists for this word (Figure 12x-4).

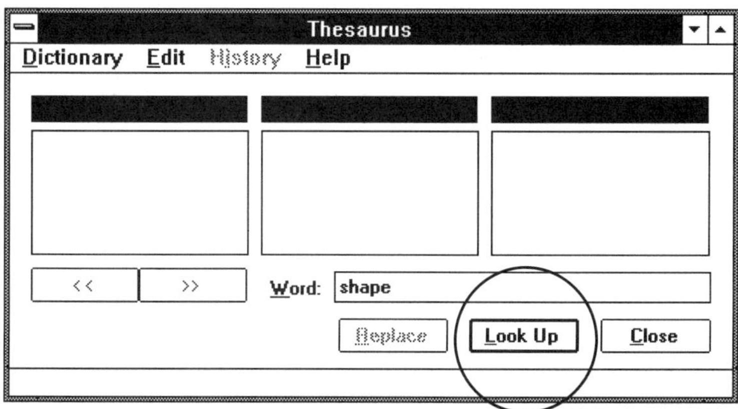

***Figure 12x-3**. Type the word "shape" into the Word text box and click on the Look Up button.*

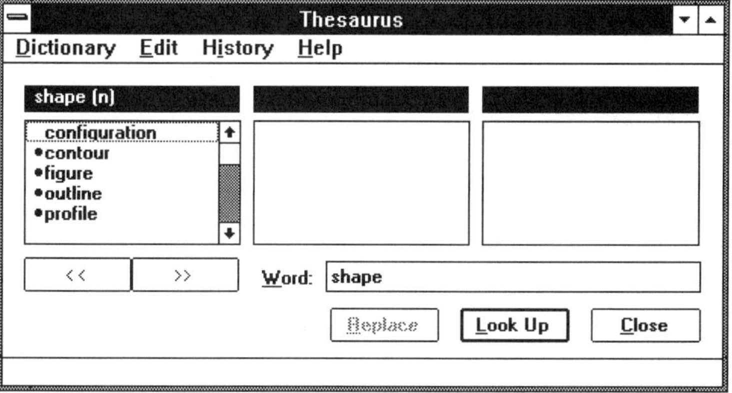

***Figure 12x-4**. Shape is now the first headword, with a list of synonyms below it.*

4. Locate the word "outline" from the list of words under "shape". Make this word, "outline", the headword for column two of the Thesaurus window.

The word "outline" is the fourth word down in the list of words under "shape". To make this the headword for the second column, double-click on it. Making "outline" the headword for column two will activate a list of synonyms (and antonyms) underneath the word, as happened with the word "shape" in column one. Figure 12x-5 illustrates the two headwords and their synonym lists.

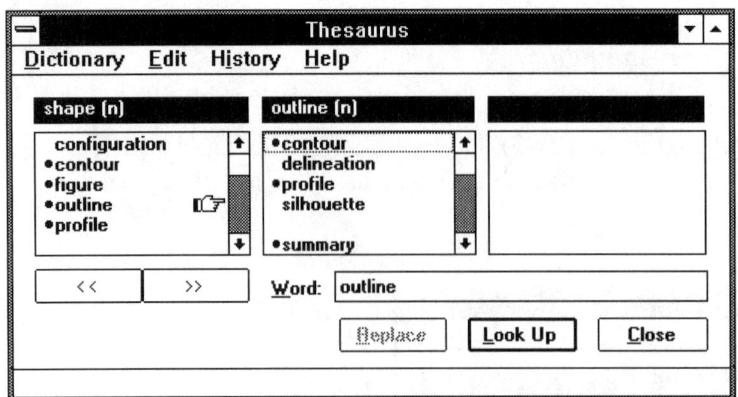

Figure 12x-5. The word "outline" is now the headword for column two. A list of synonyms and antonyms will appear in the column below the word.

5. ***Highlight the word "substance" from column two and make it the headword of column one.***

To find the word "substance" in the column two list, use the scroll bar (to the right of the column) to gain access to the words currently out of view (Figure 12x-6). "Substance", in this case, is an antonym and near the bottom of the list.

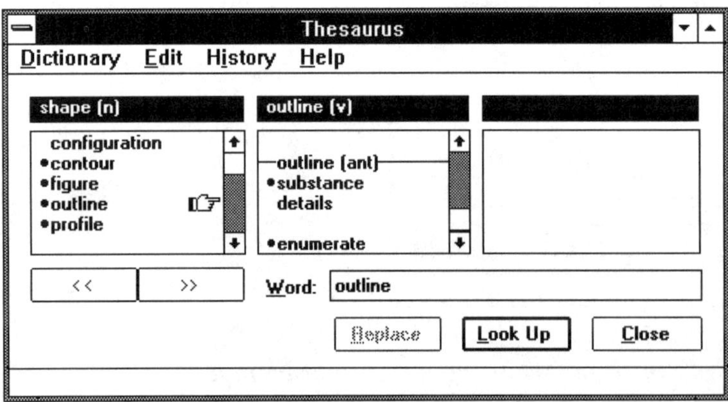

Figure 12x-6. Use the scroll bar, to the right of column two, to locate the word "substance" in the antonym section towards the bottom of the list.

Once you have located the word "substance", highlight the word by clicking on it with the mouse, as shown in Figure 12x-7.

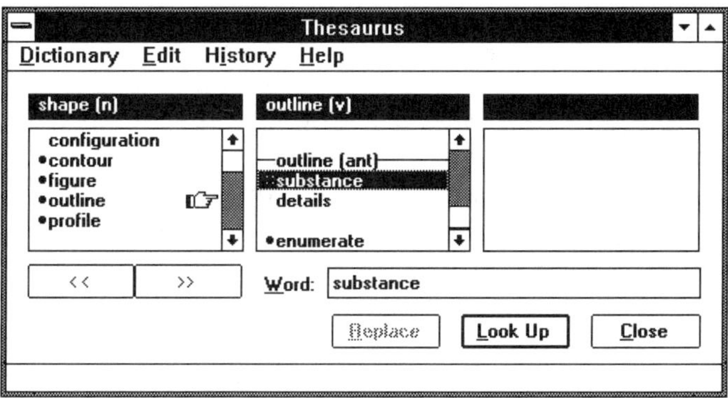

Figure 12x-7. Click on the appropriate word after locating it. Note how it appears in the Word text box after it is highlighted.

To make the highlighted word the headword for column one, click on the *Look Up* button (Figure 12x-8.) The headword previously in column one disappears and is replaced with the word "substance" (Figure 12x-9.)

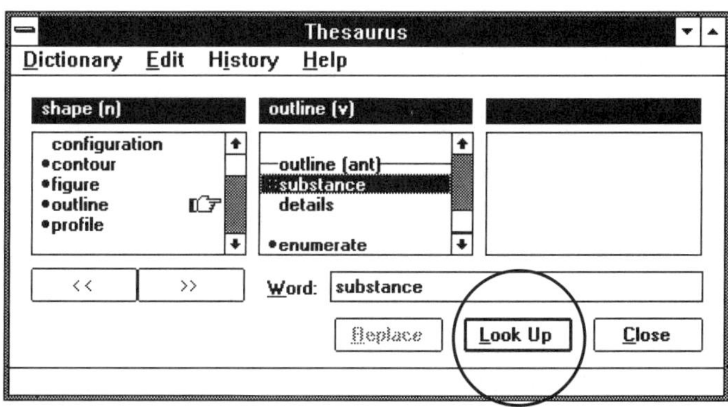

Figure 12x-8. After highlighting the word "substance", click on the Look Up button.

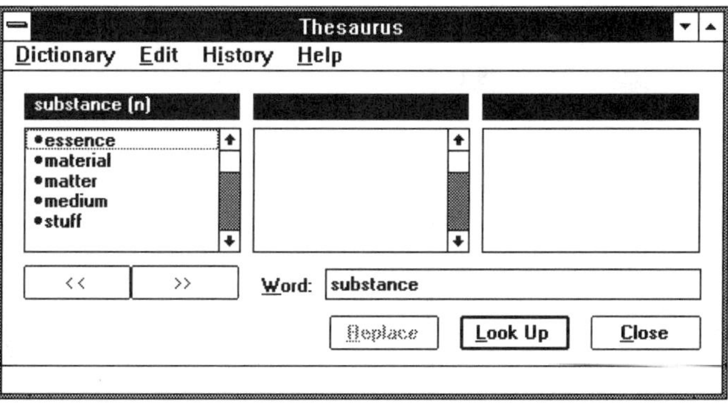

Figure 12x-9. The word "substance" is now the headword for column one.

6. ***Using the appropriate menu command, make the word "shape" the headword of column one again.***

Although the word you began with, "shape", no longer appears in any column, it is still possible to retrieve this word and its associated synonyms and antonyms. All words that were headwords since the *Thesaurus* was activated, are listed in the **History** menu. Select the word "shape" from the **History** menu (Figure 12x-10) and it will become the headword of column one again as displayed in Figure 12x-11.

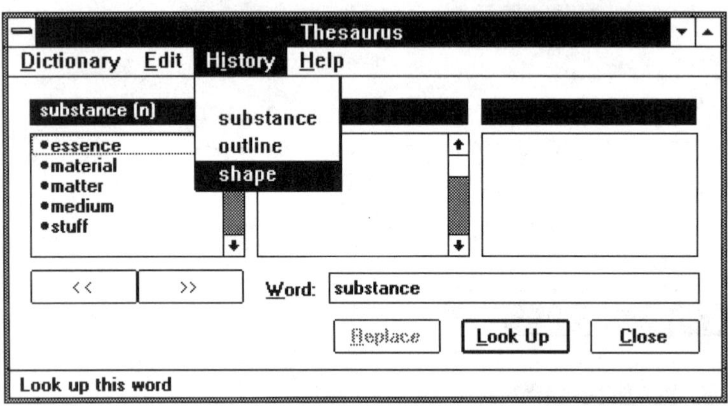

Figure 12x-10*. The* ***History*** *menu lists all words that were headwords since the Thesaurus was activated. A word selected from this menu becomes the headword of column one, taking the place of whatever word is currently there.*

7. ***Select the word "figure" from column one and copy it to the Clipboard. Close the Thesaurus, open a new WordPerfect file, and paste this word into the document.***

To *Copy* a word so that it appears in the Windows Clipboard, it must first appear in the *Word* text box. To put the word "figure" into the *Word* text box, you can type it in using the keyboard or, more easily, click on the word in column 1 as shown in Figure 12x-11.

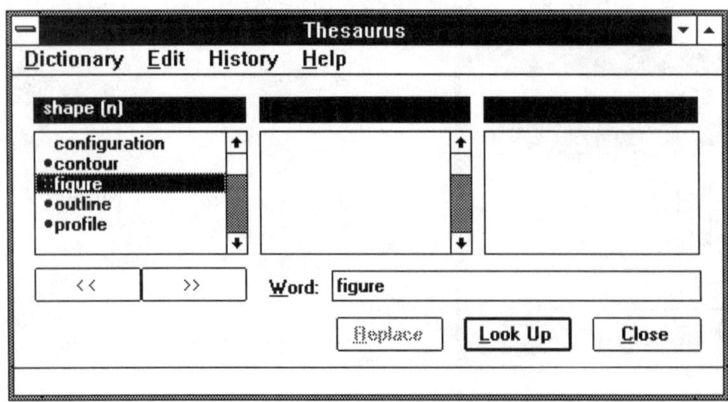

Figure 12x-11*. Click on the word "figure" in column one, so that it appears in the Word frame.*

Once the word "figure" is in the *Word* text box, it must be selected before you can *Copy* it. Select the word as you would in WordPerfect by holding the mouse down and dragging it over the word, releasing it at the end. Alternatively, place the mouse cursor over the word and double-click. The word is successfully selected when it appears in reverse video as in Figure 12x-12.

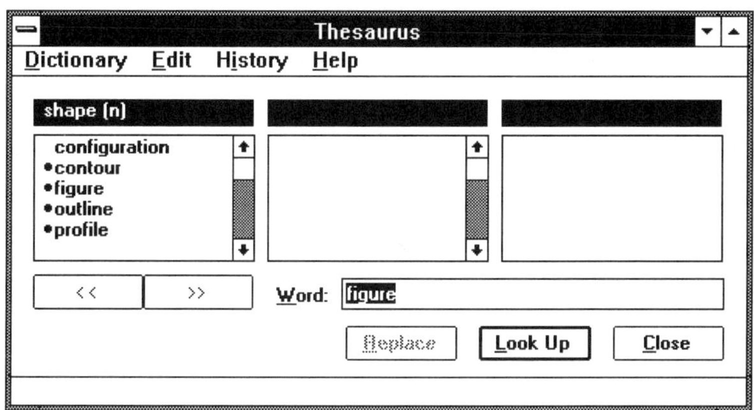

***Figure 12x-12**. Select the word "figure" in the Word text box.*

To make a copy of this word to the Windows Clipboard, select the *Copy* command from the **Edit** menu (Figure 12x-13).

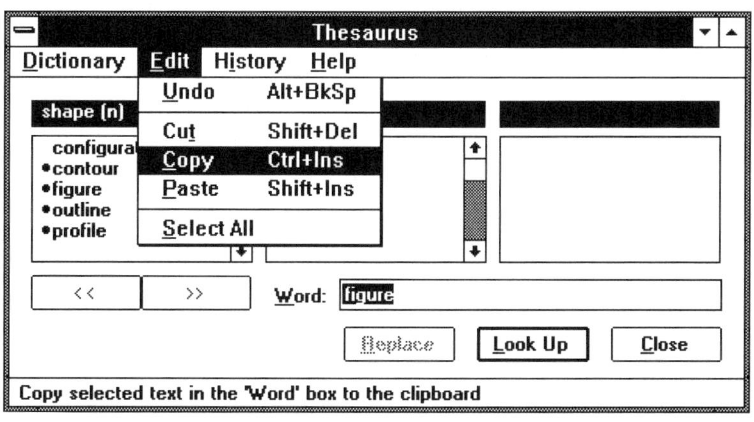

***Figure 12x-13**. The Copy command copies any selected text from the Word text box into the Windows Clipboard.*

Once you have copied the word, you can close the *Thesaurus* by clicking on the *Close* button (Figure 12x-14).

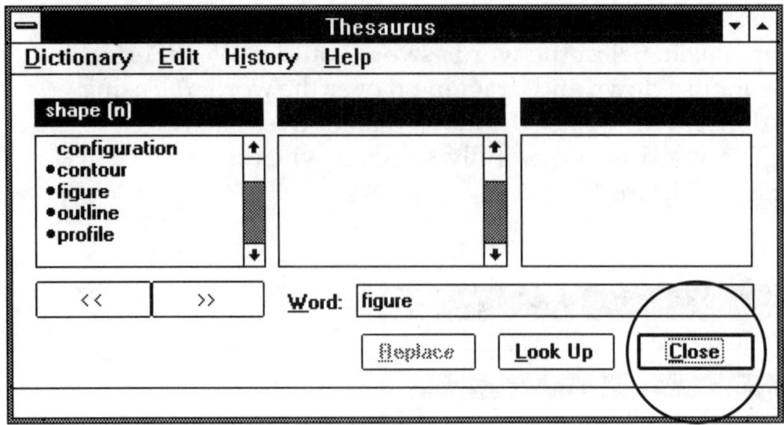

Figure 12x-14. Click on the Close button to close the Thesaurus.

To Open WordPerfect, double-click on the appropriate icon in the Windows Program Manager (Figure 12x-15).

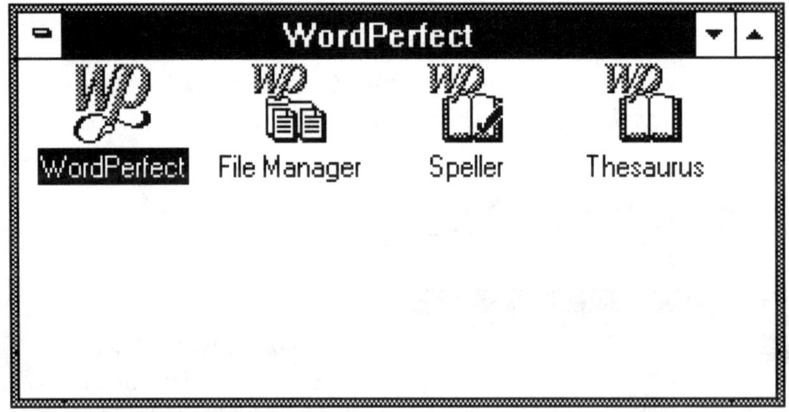

Figure 12x-15. Double-click on the WordPerfect icon to activate WordPerfect.

Once *WordPerfect* is open, you can *Paste* the word you copied from the *Thesaurus* directly into the new unmodified document. Do this by selecting the *Paste* command from the **Edit** menu (Figure 12x-16). The word will appear wherever the cursor is situated; in this case at the beginning of the document as shown in Figure 12x-17.

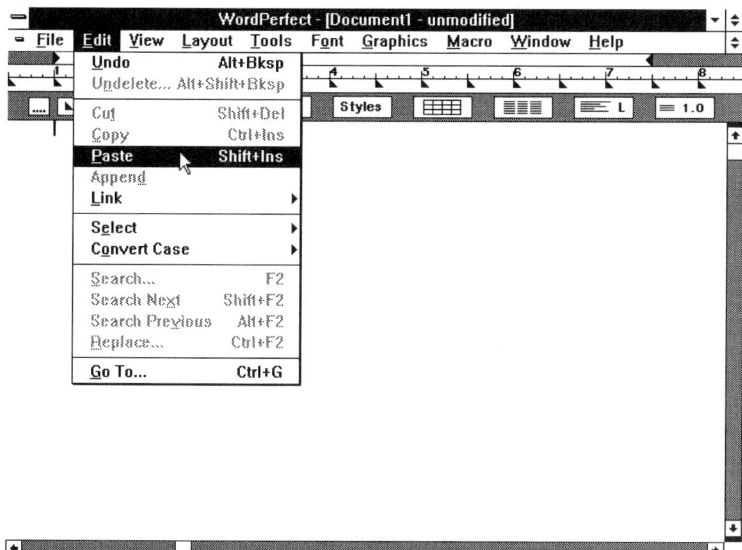

Figure 12x-16*. The Paste command will paste the Clipboard's contents into the current document. The last thing that was copied to the Clipboard was the word "figure" from the Thesaurus.*

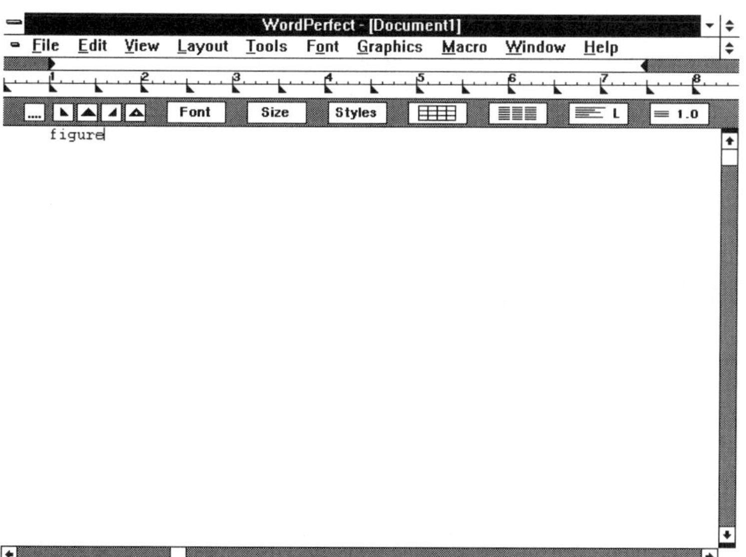

Figure 12x-17*. The word "figure" is now pasted into the current document.*

8. ***Delete the word "figure" and retrieve the learn05.wkb file from the learn sub-directory.***

If you have not moved the cursor since pasting the word "figure", you can delete the word directly, by pressing the *Backspace* key until the word disappears.

To retrieve the ***learn05.wkb*** file, first select the *Retrieve* command from the **File** menu (Figure 12x-18).

Figure 12x-18. *The Retrieve command will give you access to WordPerfect compatible files stored on your hard disk.*

After selecting the *Retrieve* command, the *Retrieve File* dialog box will appear. The ***learn05.wkb*** file is located in the ***learn*** sub-directory. To retrieve the file, simply double-click on the file name in the list of files (Figure 12x-19) or click on it once and then click on the *Retrieve* button.

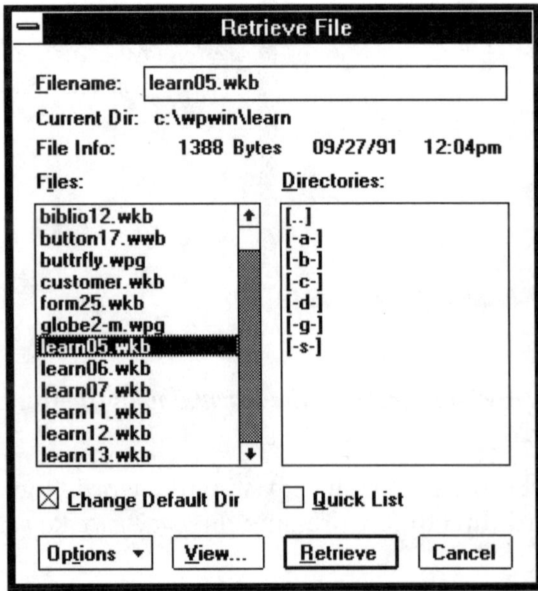

Figure 12x-19. *To retrieve the* ***learn05.wkb*** *file, double-click on it in the list of files, or click on it once and then click on the Retrieve button.*

Because you have made some changes to this new document (by pasting in the word from the Clipboard and then deleting it), you will be prompted, before the new file is retrieved, with the dialog box of Figure 12x-20. For this exercise, select *Yes*.

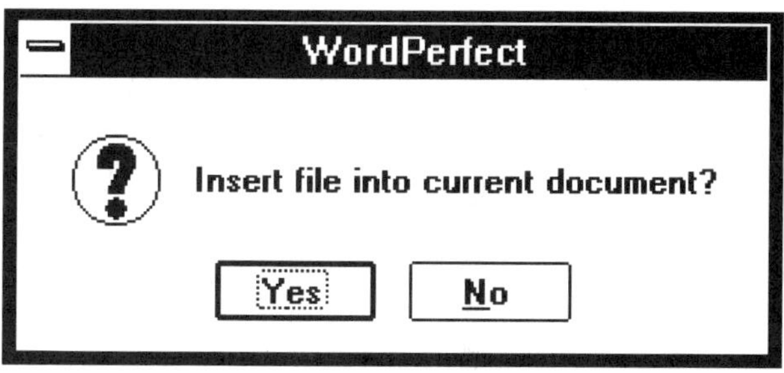

Figure 12x-20*. Select Yes to retrieve the* ***learn05.wkb*** *file into the current document.*

After selecting *Yes* in the Figure 12x-20 dialog box, the ***learn05.wkb*** file appears in the document displayed in Figure 12x-21.

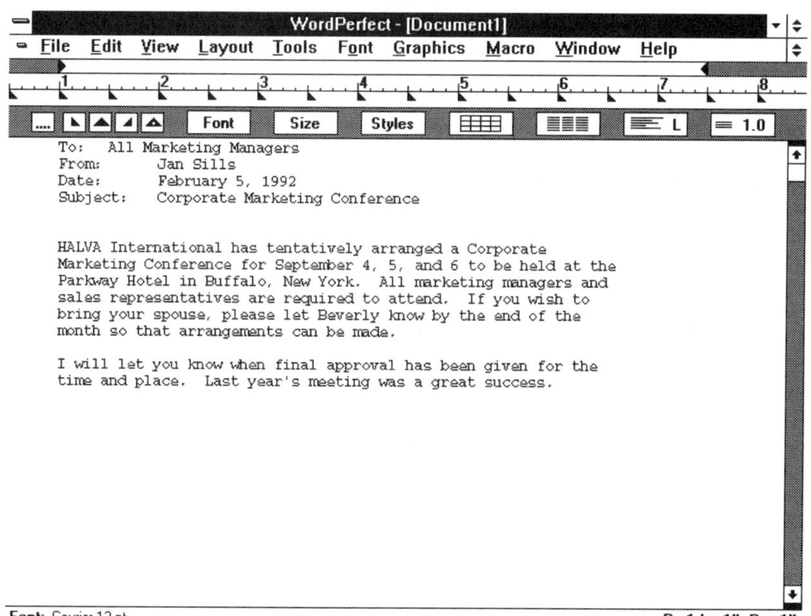

Figure 12x-21*. The* ***learn05.wkb*** *file has been retrieved into the current document.*

9. Insert the text cursor into the word "Conference" and open the Thesaurus.

Place the text cursor into the word "Conference", in the fourth line, by clicking on the word once with the mouse (Figure 12x-22).

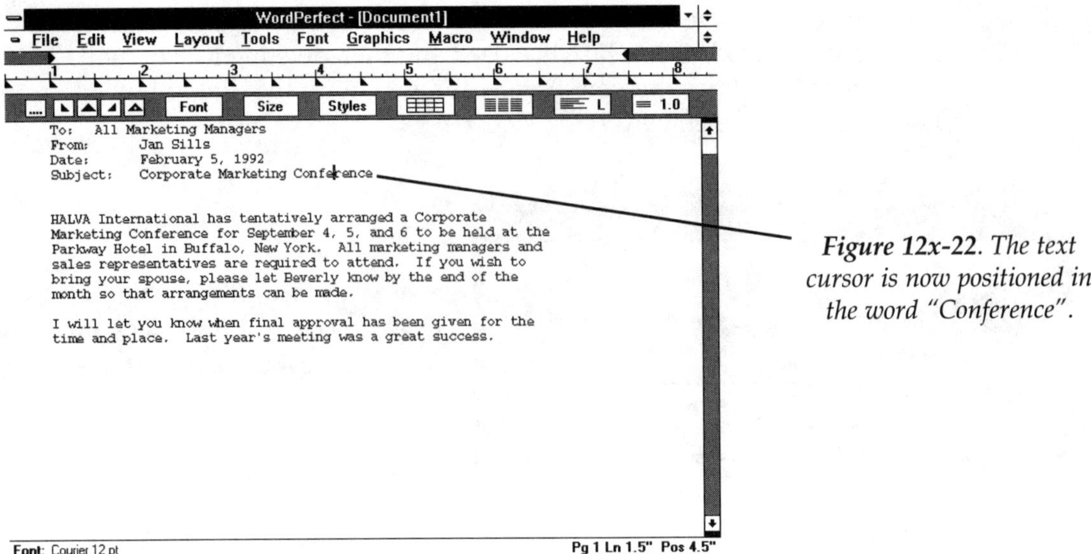

Figure 12x-22*. The text cursor is now positioned in the word "Conference".*

Once the cursor is positioned within the relevant word, activate the *Thesaurus* by selecting the *Thesaurus* command from the **Tools** menu (Figure 12x-23).

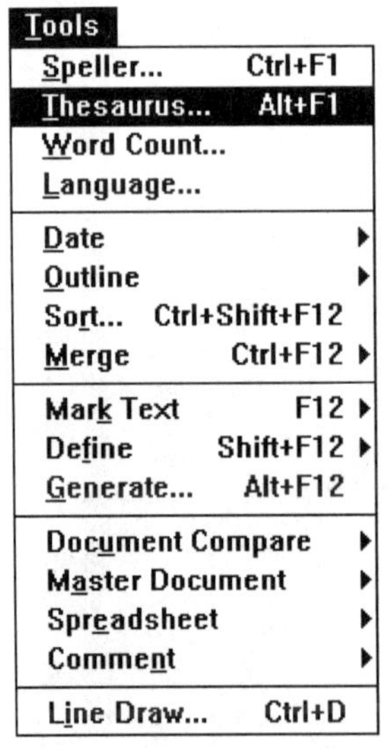

Figure 12x-23*. When you select the Thesaurus command from the* ***Tools*** *menu, the Thesaurus window appears.*

Because you activated the *Thesaurus* with the cursor inserted in a word, this word will automatically be the headword for column one, and a list of synonyms and antonyms will appear below it (Figure 12x-24).

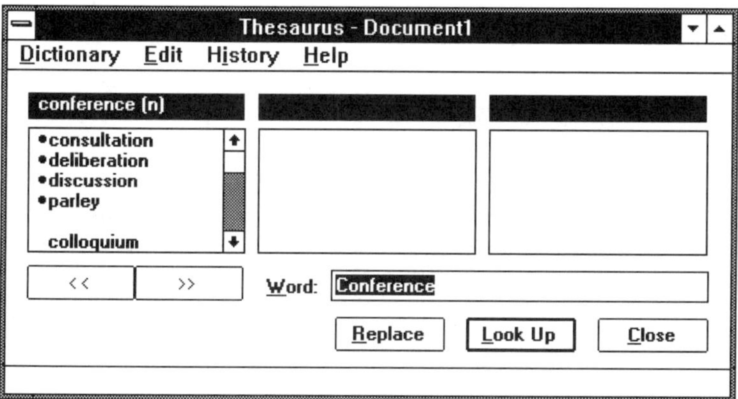

Figure 12x-24. The cursor was inserted into the word "Conference", in the document, and the Thesaurus was activated. The word with the cursor in it automatically becomes the headword of column one.

10. Select the word "seminar" from the list of synonyms.

Using the scroll bar, locate the word "seminar" in the list of words in column one (Figure 12x-25).

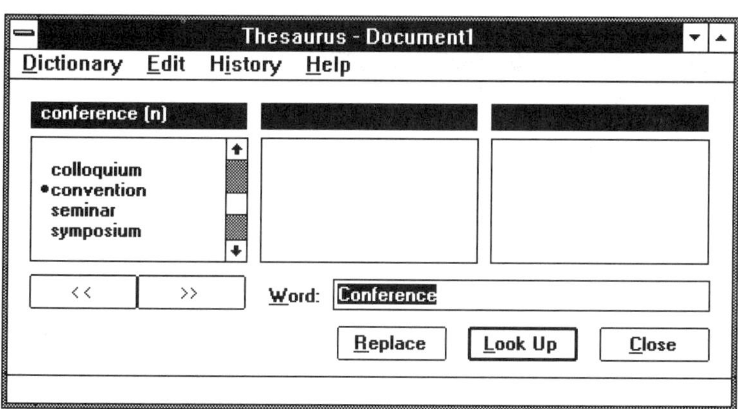

Figure 12x-25. Using the scroll bar to the right of column one, locate the word "seminar".

Once you have located the word "seminar", click on it once so that its name appears in the *Word* text box (Figure 12x-26).

11. Replace the word "Conference" with the word "Seminar".

Once the word "seminar" is in the *Word* frame, all you need to do is click on the *Replace* button (Figure 12x-26).

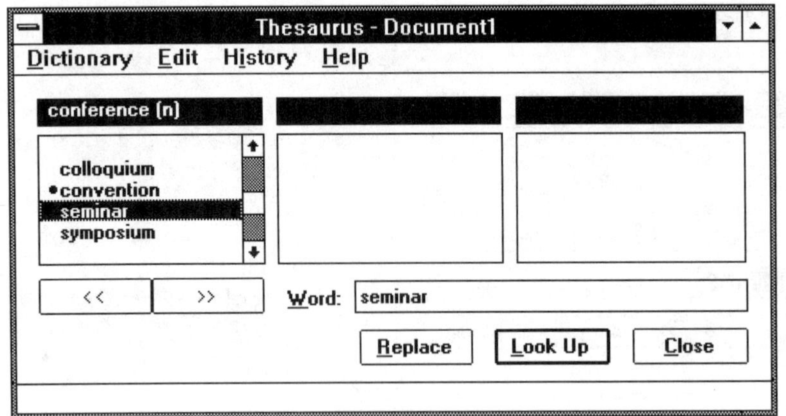

Figure 12x-26. *The word "Conference" is replaced with the word "seminar" by clicking on the Replace button.*

After clicking on the *Replace* button, the *Thesaurus* window disappears, and the word "Conference" is replaced with the word "Seminar" (Figure 12x-27).

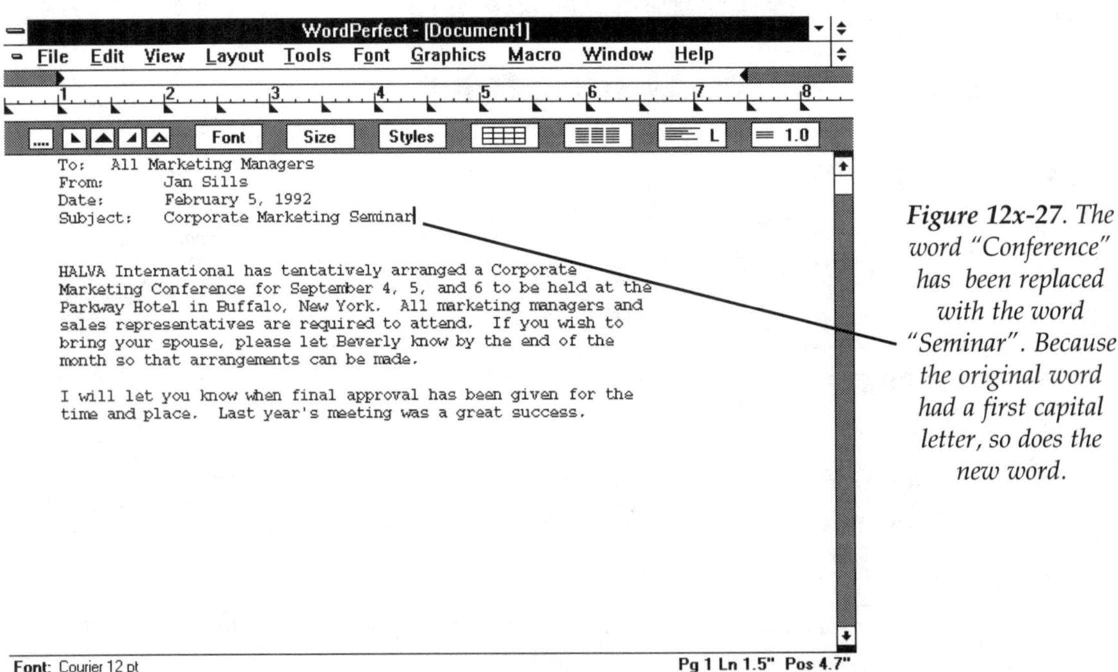

Figure 12x-27. *The word "Conference" has been replaced with the word "Seminar". Because the original word had a first capital letter, so does the new word.*

Preferences - (2)

As indicated in Chapter 10, setting *Preferences* in most software packages is important in determining exactly how a program operates and what settings it uses by default. Successfully setting defaults, or preferences, means the program runs the way you want it to run—it looks for files where you keep files, etc. Remember, preferences remain set even after you exit WordPerfect. These preferences only need be set once—unless of course you wish to modify them.

Chapter 10 described the first six *Preferences* commands of the **File** menu. This chapter looks at the remaining six.

Preferences/Initial Codes

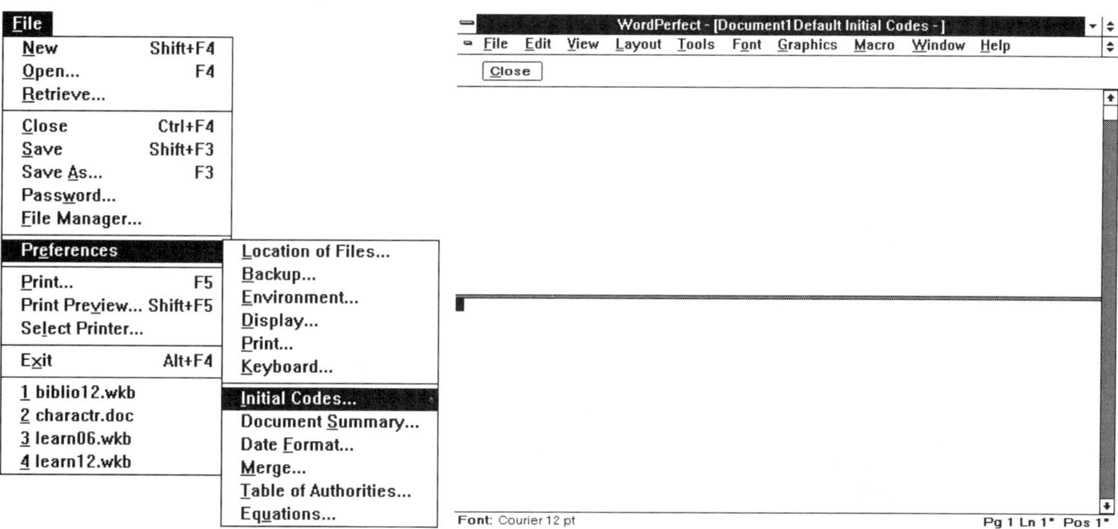

Figure 13-1. *The Preferences/Initial Codes command, and the effect this has on the WordPerfect editing screen.*

The *Initial Codes* command sets the default characteristics of all new documents, including, for example, the number of columns the document uses, the margin settings, the tab settings, the initial font and font size, and many other settings.

When *Initial Codes* is selected from the *Preferences* fly-out menu in the **File** menu (Figure 13-1), the screen splits, in much the same way as when the *Reveal Codes* command (see Chapter 5) is used. The *Initial Codes,* if any are set, will appear in the bottom half of the screen.

Let's say, for example, that you want all your new documents to initially have two columns and use the font Times Roman, 18pt. This can be achieved by simply selecting these commands while the *Initial Codes* screen is on.

In Figure 13-2, we used the *Columns/Define* command in the **Layout** menu and the *Font* command in the **Font** menu, to set the desired *Initial Codes.* In Figure 13-3, you can see the result this has on the screen.

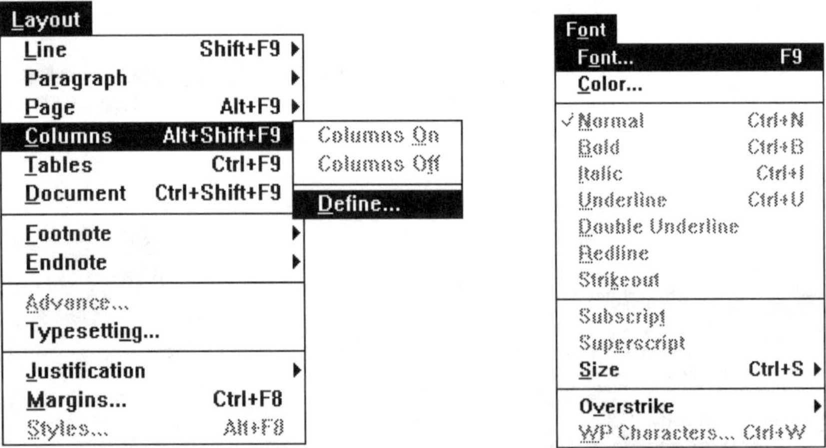

Figure 13-2. *After selecting Initial Codes, we used the Columns/ Define command to set up two columns and the Font command to set the font to Times Roman 18pt.*

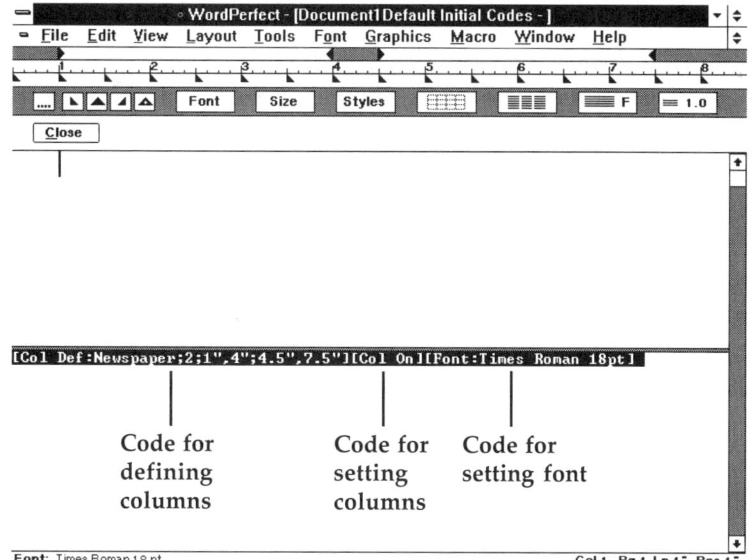

Figure 13-3. On the bottom half of the screen, you can see the Initial Codes selected from Figure 13-2. These particular codes set up two columns and the Times Roman 18pt font.

All codes defined as *Initial Codes* will be active for every document you create from now on. In the above example, every new document will use, as a default, two columns and the font Times Roman, 18pt.

Preferences/Document Summary

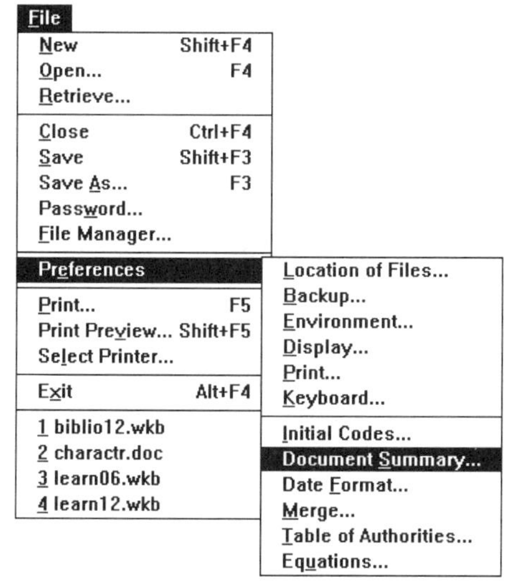

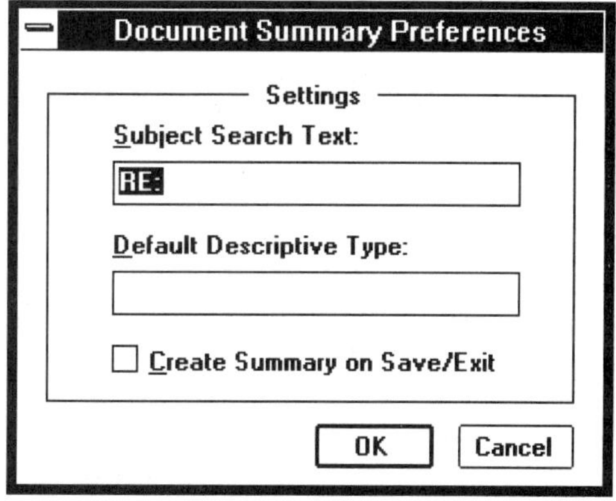

Figure 13-4. The Preferences/Document Summary command and dialog box.

A *Document Summary* is a brief overview about the subject matter of a document; a summary that can be used to categorize documents, or to search for specific types of documents. It can also be used by fellow WordPerfect users to quickly find out specific information on a particular file.

Before explaining the top parts of the *Preferences/Document Summary* dialog box, we will look at the last option within this dialog box —*Create Summary on Save/Exit*. With this option selected in Figure 13-4, you will be automatically asked to create a document summary as a document is initially saved (Figure 13-5). Alternatively, the dialog box of Figure 13-5 will appear if you select the *Document/Summary* command in the **Layout** menu.

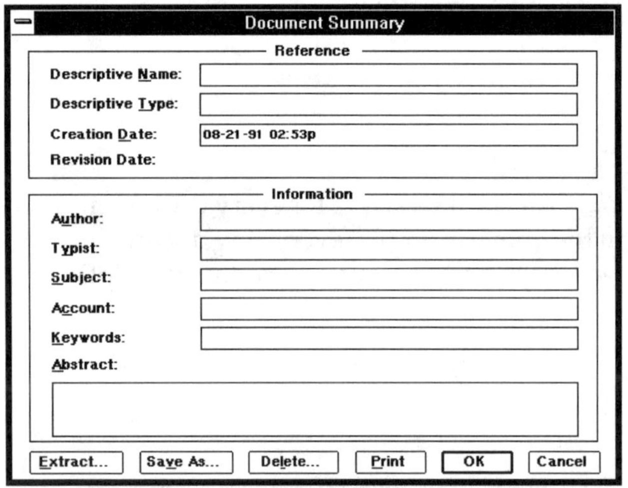

Figure 13-5. *The Document Summary dialog box. As you can see, most of the options in this dialog box are quite straightforward, and in fact some are filled out automatically (document creation and revision date, for example).*

If a *Document Summary* has been filled out for a particular document, you can view the details in that summary (as suggested above) by directly selecting the *Document/Summary* command from the **Layout** menu. If, on doing this, the dialog box of Figure 13-5 comes up empty (as in Figure 13-5), it means that there is no document summary for this document.

The *Subject Search Text* option, in the dialog box of Figure 13-4, allows WordPerfect to automatically determine the subject matter of a document. By default, it assumes that the subject matter in your documents will be placed after the words **"RE:"**. This assumes that your documents have a line in them reading, for example:

RE: Summer Sales Meeting

If this line exists, WordPerfect can search your documents for the line starting with **"RE:"**, and use the string after **"RE:"** as the document subject matter.

If you use a different string (e.g. **"Attn"**) to represent the subject matter of your documents, you can insert this string to replace **"RE:"** in the *Subject Search Text* area of the *Preferences/Document Summary* command dialog box.

When the *Subject Search Text* has been decided (be it "RE:" or a different text string), you can use the *Extract* button within the *Document/Summary* dialog box (Figure 13-5) to retrieve automatically a variety of information—including the *Subject* matter, the first 400 characters of the document, and the last *Author* and *Typist* entry made. Please refer to Figures 13-6 through 13-8 for examples of this feature.

25th December, 1999

RE: Summer Sales Meeting

It has been decided that the summer sales meeting for 1992 will be held at the Boris hotel in Cairns, Queensland, Australia. Please be there.

Regards,

Dwayne Dwyer

Executive Vice President

Figure 13-6. *A sample business letter.*

Information

Author:

Typist:

Subject:

Account:

Keywords:

Abstract:

Extract... | Save As... | Delete... | Print | OK | Cancel

Figure 13-7. *This is the bottom half of the Figure 13-5 Document/Summary dialog box for the sample letter in Figure 13-6, before any entries have been made.*

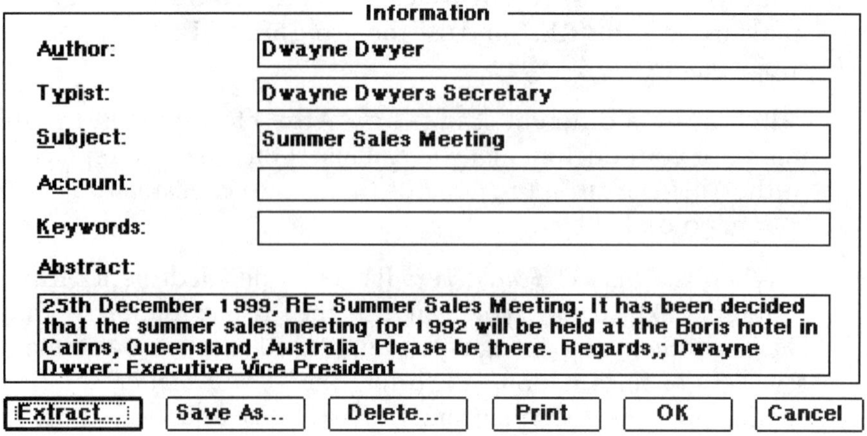

Information

Author: Dwayne Dwyer

Typist: Dwayne Dwyers Secretary

Subject: Summer Sales Meeting

Account:

Keywords:

Abstract:

25th December, 1999; RE: Summer Sales Meeting; It has been decided that the summer sales meeting for 1992 will be held at the Boris hotel in Cairns, Queensland, Australia. Please be there. Regards,; Dwayne Dwyer: Executive Vice President

Extract... | Save As... | Delete... | Print | OK | Cancel

Figure 13-8. *The bottom half of the Document/Summary dialog box after the Extract button (bottom left-hand corner) has been used.*
Note that the Author and Typist entries in this figure relate to the last ones manually entered on this WordPerfect System—they don't necessarily relate to the author of this document.

Figures 13-6, 13-7, and 13-8 tell the story of how the *Extract* feature can work with *Document Summaries.* Note in Figure 13-8 that the *Author* has been added (this is a copy of the last author entry manually entered in a document summary), the *Typist* has been added (as with *Author,* a copy of the last typist entry made in a document summary), the *Subject* has been added (the string after the current *Subject Search Text,* **"RE:"**), and in *Abstract,* the first 400 characters in the document have been inserted.

The entry in the *Default Descriptive Type* of the *Preferences/Document Summary* dialog box of Figure 13-4 is the default text that will appear on the *Descriptive Type* line of the *Document/Summary* dialog box of Figure 13-5. The *Default Descriptive Type* definition is up to you—it is a way of helping you categorize your documents. Key in whatever is appropriate—"letters", "memos", "faxes", etc.

Preferences/Date Format

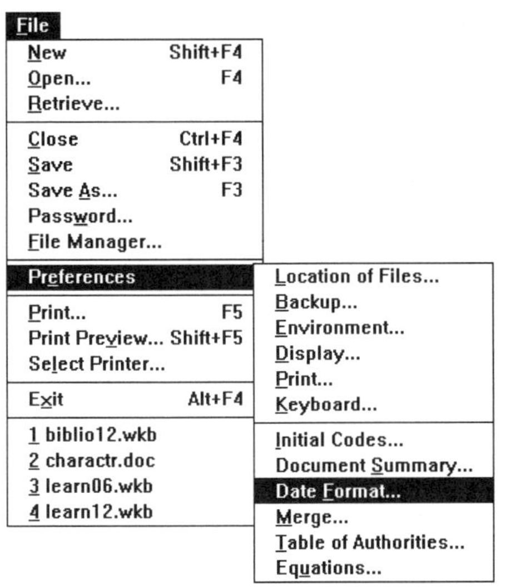

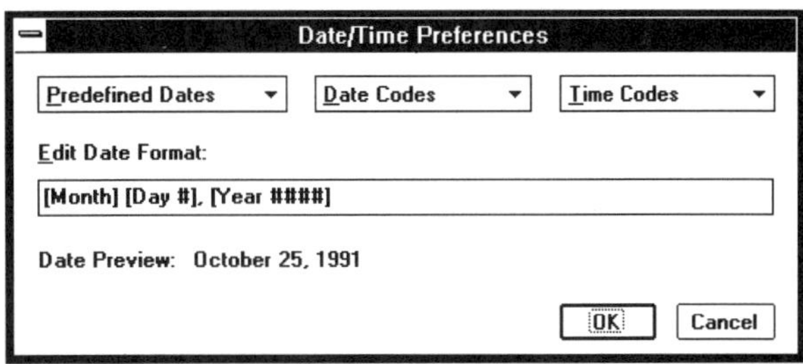

Figure 13-9. The Preferences/Date Format command and associated dialog box.

The settings of the *Preferences/Date Format* command determine the default date appearance when it is added automatically to your document.

As seen in Chapter 3, a date can be inserted into your document automatically using the *Date* command from the **Tools** menu (Figure 13-10).

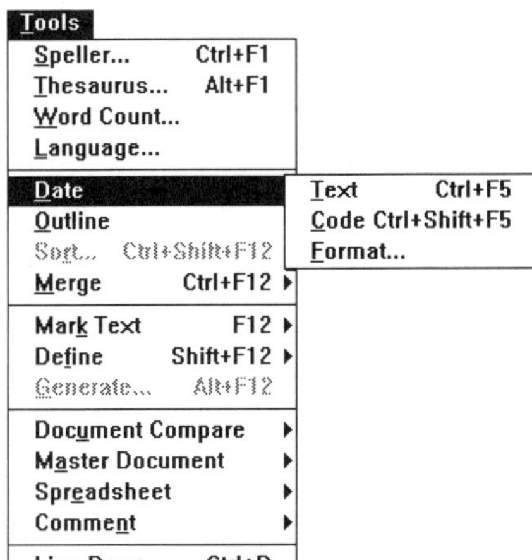

Figure 13-10. The Date command automatically inserts the date into a document. How the date appears in the document can be determined by the Preferences/Date Format command.

In the *Preferences/Date Format* dialog box (which actually reads *Date/Time Preferences*—Figure 13-9), is a line that reads: *Date Preview*. On this line, the current date will appear in the format of the current settings. This is how the date will appear when inserted into a document.

If you wish to alter the way the date appears, you can hold the mouse button down on the *Predefined Dates* list box and select a new date format from the sub-menu that appears (Figure 13-11).

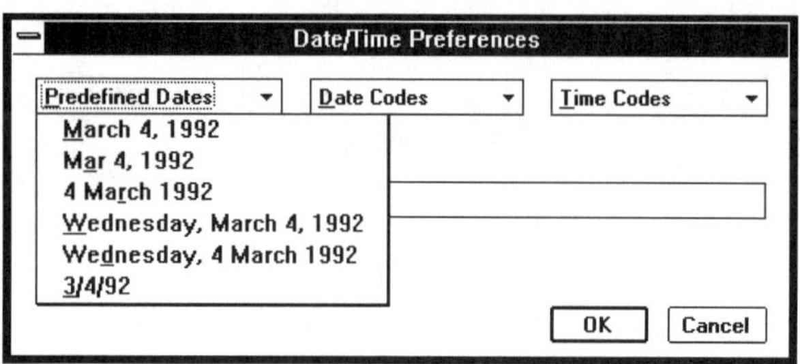

Figure 13-11. *Holding down the mouse button on the Predefined Dates sub-menu allows you to select a new date format.*

As a new date format is selected from the list in Figure 13-11, a new *Date Preview* appears, reflecting the new date format (compare the *Date Preview* of Figure 13-9 to the *Date Preview* of Figure 13-12).

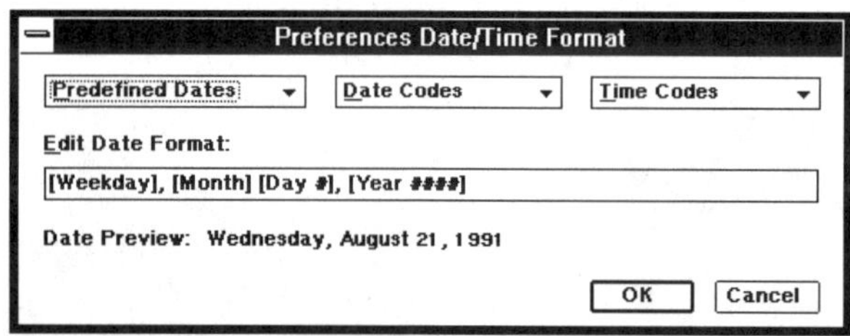

Figure 13-12. *Notice the new date preview in this dialog box, after a selection has been made from the list in Figure 13-11.*

Another method in which the date appearance can be altered is by editing the *Edit Date Format* line. This line reflects the current date format using a series of codes to represent months, days, etc.

In Figure 13-12, the current date code is **"[Weekday], [Month] [Day #], [Year ###]".** Each code corresponds to the *Date Preview* —**Wednesday, August 21, 1991.**

Rather than editing the *Edit Date Format* line directly, you can use preset codes from either the *Date Codes* list box (Figure 13-13) or the *Time Codes* list box (Figure 13-14).

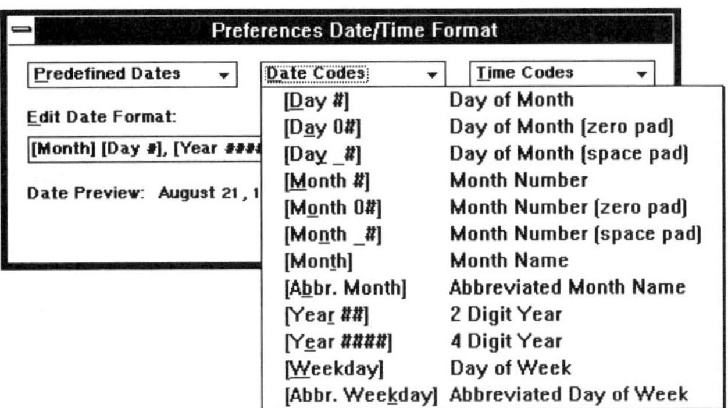

Figure 13-13. *This is a list of the various date codes that can be inserted on the Edit Date Format line, available by holding down the mouse button on the Date Codes list box.*

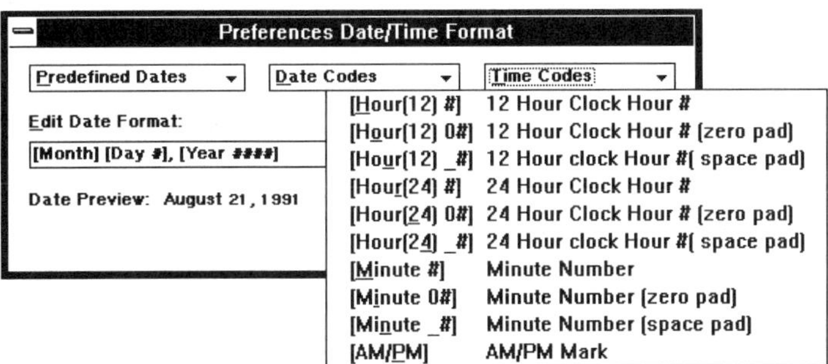

Figure 13-14. *These are the various time codes that can be inserted on the Edit Date Format line, available by holding down the mouse button on the Time Codes list box.*

As you can see from Figure 13-14, you can even add time codes to your date format, so that when you use the *Date* command of Figure 13-10, the date may conceivably appear in your document as:

Wednesday, August 21, 1991, 5:25 PM

Preferences/Merge

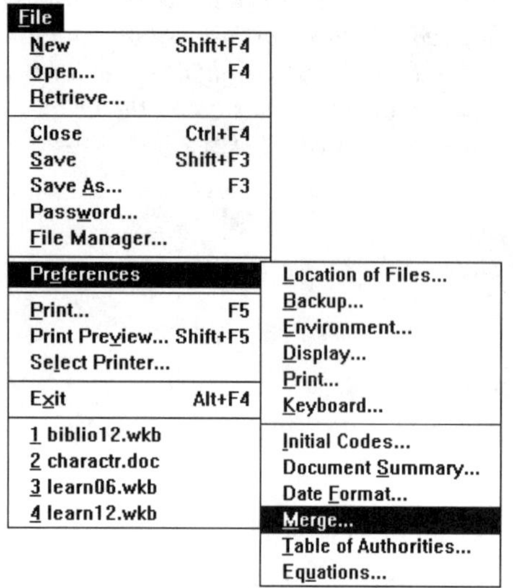

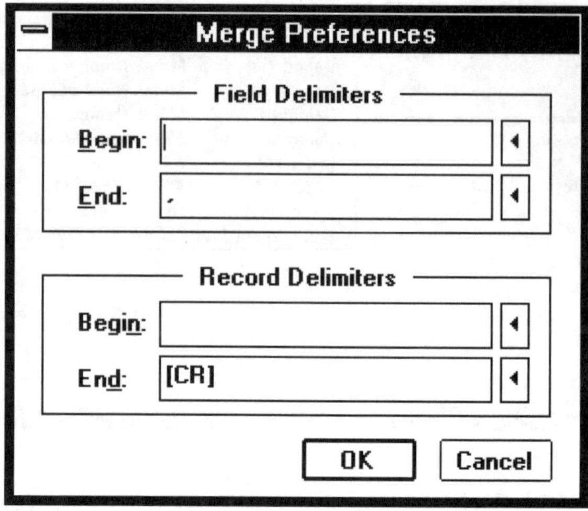

Figure 13-15. The Preferences/Merge command and associated dialog box.

The *Preferences/Merge* command determines the field and record delimiters used when DOS files, or merge files created by versions of WordPerfect earlier than WordPerfect 4.0, are merged with existing WordPerfect documents.

In most circumstances, the default merge settings will be suitable (most programs use commas to distinguish fields and carriage returns to distinguish records). However, if you do happen to create merge files in programs other than WordPerfect, you should check the format of these files and fill out the delimiters in this dialog box accordingly.

Preferences/Table of Authorities

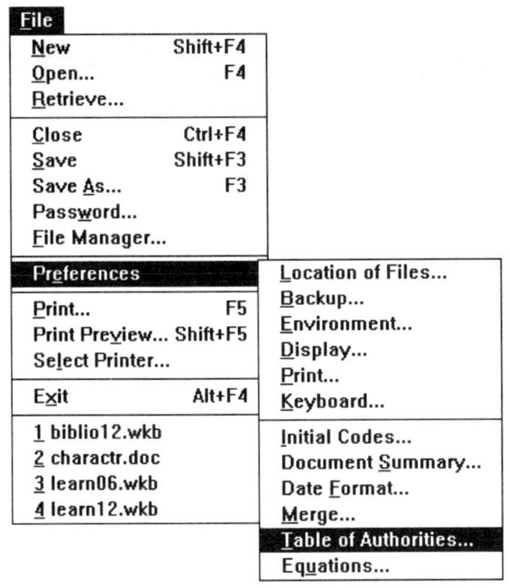

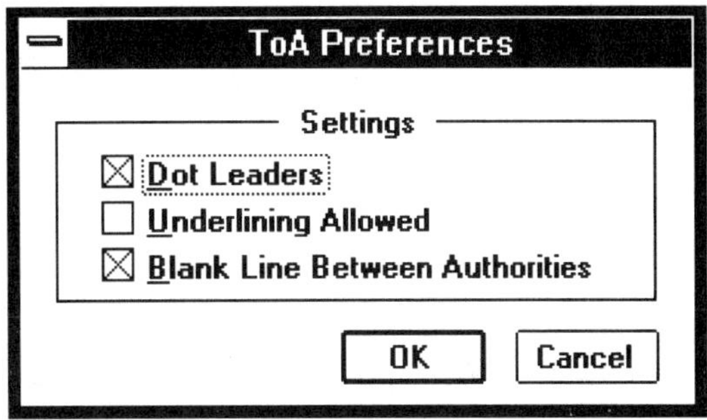

Figure 13-16. *The Preferences/Table of Authorities command and associated dialog box.*

A *Table of Authorities* is a table, formatted much in the fashion of a table of contents, that lists specific citations and statutes, and the pages on which they occur in the document.

The *Preferences/Table of Authorities* dialog box sets the default format of the table of authorities. The options (*Dot Leaders*, *Underlining Allowed*, and *Blank Line Between Authorities*) are quite straightforward, but may make more sense after looking at a sample Table of Authorities (Figure 13-17).

```
                  TABLE OF AUTHORITIES

Constitution, Statutes, and Regulations

Official Statutes Act:

   OSA 1911  (Intention to Commit) ..............4-5, 11
   OSA 1920  (Hearings in Camera) ..........546, 548, 654

Criminal Evidence Act:

   CEA 1898  (Evidence on Own Behalf) ..13, 15, 46-49, 51
   CEA 1965  (Submission of Records) .............20, 23
```

Figure 13-17. *An extract from a sample Table of Authorities, illustrating Dot Leaders, Blank Lines, and No Underlining Allowed.*

Preferences/Equations

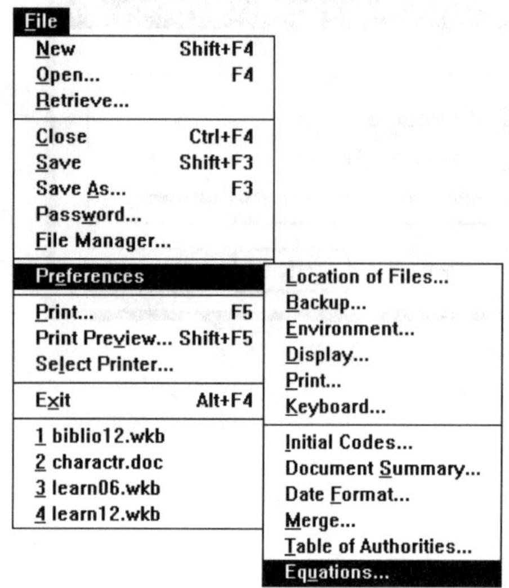

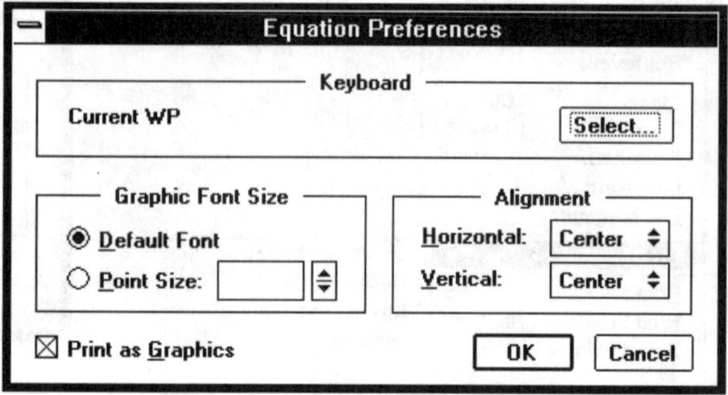

Figure 13-18. *The Preferences/Equations command and associated dialog box.*

WordPerfect allows the inclusion of scientific and mathematical equations in its documents, through its equation creation features. The options within the *Preferences/Equations* dialog box affect the default settings of equations—how they appear on screen, how they print, and how they are created.

$$a^2=\sqrt{b^2+c^2}$$

Figure 13-19. *A sample WordPerfect equation.*

The *Keyboard* loaded in this dialog box is the default keyboard layout used when equations are created in WordPerfect. (Equations are created using the *Graphics/Equation/Create* command.) If you *Select* the *Keyboard* button of Figure 13-18, you are presented with similar options as when you select the *Preferences/Keyboard* command (Chapter 10).

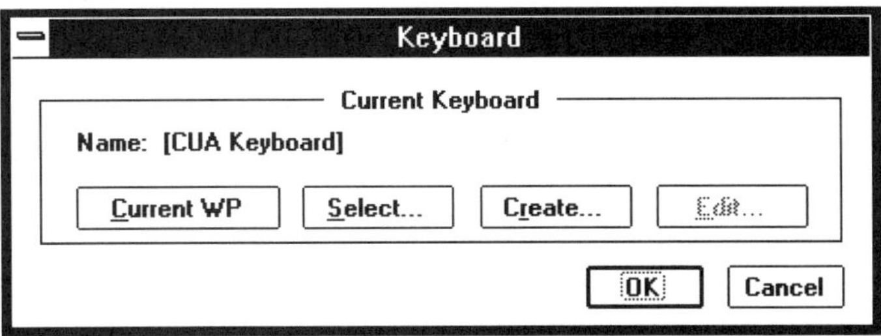

Figure 13-20. This dialog box appears when you click on the Keyboard Select button of Figure 13-18. To see how the options within this dialog box work, refer to the section in Chapter 10 on the Preferences/Keyboard command.

Within the *Graphic Font Size* section of the Figure 13-18 dialog box, you have two options on the appearance of an equation—*Default Font* or *Point Size*. When *Default Font* is selected, the size of the equation is determined by the surrounding text or the current font size.

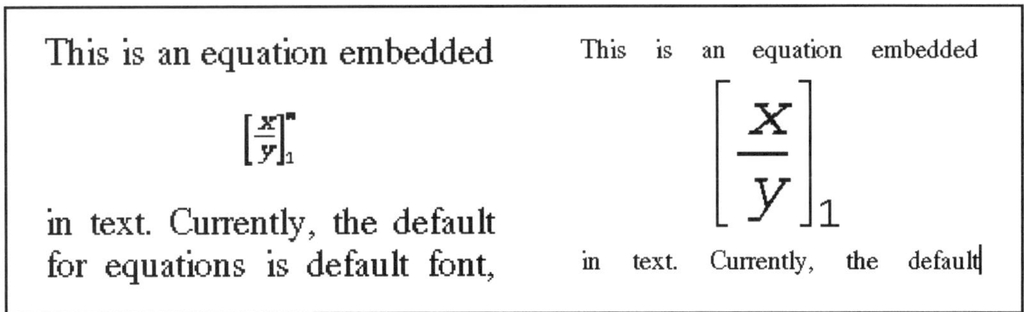

Figure 13-21. On the left, an equation created with the Default Font setting of Figure 13-18 enabled. On the right, the same equation with the Point Size option selected and set to 24 point.

Alignment

The *Alignment* options determine the *Horizontal* and *Vertical* positioning of equations on a line. The equations in Figure 13-21 were created with *Horizontal* and *Vertical Alignment* set to center.

Print as Graphics

The *Print as Graphics* option in Figure 13-18, if enabled, will send all equation characters to the printer as bitmaps. If disabled, WordPerfect will use a printer font for the equation characters (if they exist within a printer font). If the characters do not exist within a printer font, they will be sent to the printer as a bitmap, regardless of whether this option is enabled or disabled.

The Button Bar

The Button bar is a special WordPerfect feature that enables you to access commands quickly, without having to use the menus. The Button bar consists of a series of command buttons that is displayed above, below, or beside the editing screen in WordPerfect for Windows.

Each command that you can select using the menus has a corresponding command button that can be added to the Button bar.

Different situations may require Button bars which contain different commands. For this reason, WordPerfect allows you to create and save customized Button bars.

Macros, pre-programmed commands discussed in Chapter 20, can also be included as buttons on Button bars.

Selecting a Button bar

Selecting the *Button Bar* command from the **View** menu places the default Button bar at the top of the screen. Clicking on this command again will remove the Button bar from view. If the Button bar is not currently visible, select this command as shown in Figure 14-1. A Button bar, similar to that of Figure 14-2, will appear on screen.

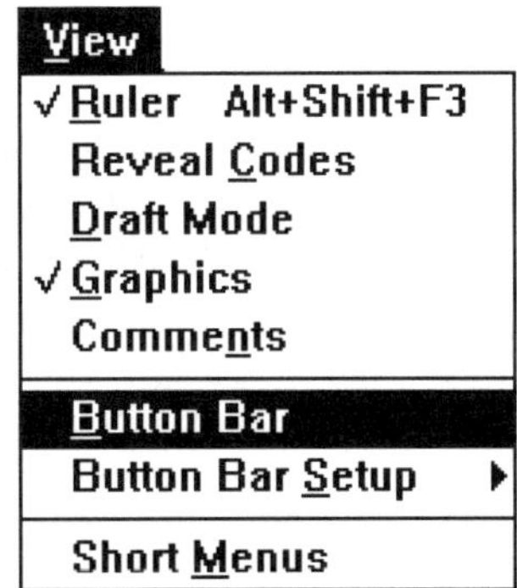

Figure 14-1. *To display the Button bar on the screen, select the Button Bar command from the* ***View*** *menu.*

WordPerfect includes a default Button bar file that defines a Button bar for general use in the editing screen. However, other Button bars for specialized use in graphics or tables are also available. These files are used to define the default Button bars when the relevant screens have been activated. Your Button bar may not necessarily be the same as the one shown below.

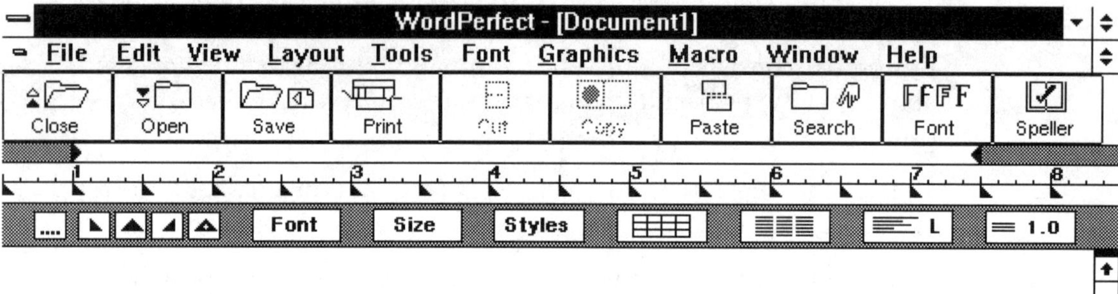

Figure 14-2. A WordPerfect for Windows Button bar.

Select the *Open* button from the Button bar. This action will invoke the same *Open File* dialog box that is activated using the *Open* or *Retrieve* commands in the **File** menu. In the *Open File* dialog box that is activated, select the ***learn06.wkb*** file from the ***learn*** sub-directory, as shown in Figure 14-3, and click on *Open*. The document on the editing screen will then look similar to the example of Figure 14-4.

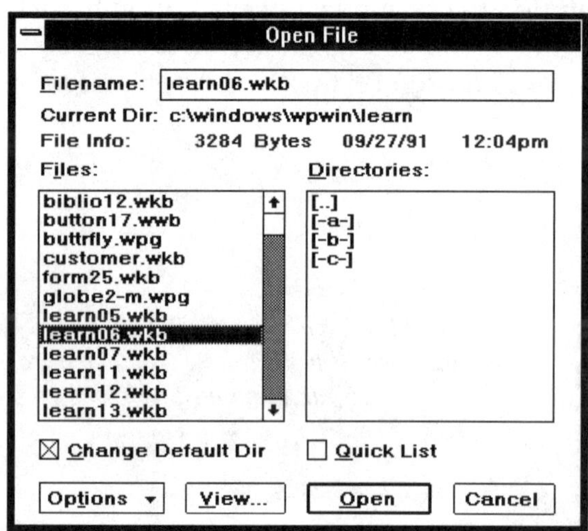

*Figure 14-3. Use the Open command in the **File** menu to load the file **learn06.wkb**.*

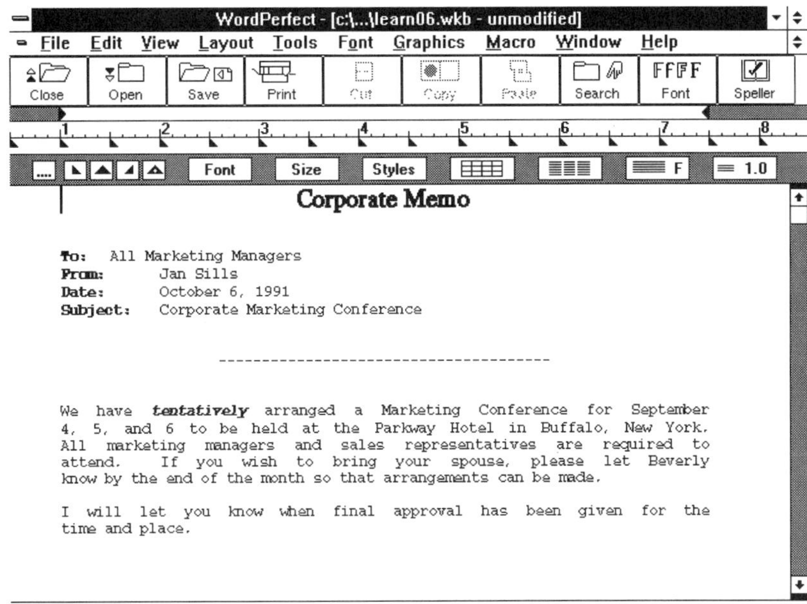

Figure 14-4. *The file* ***learn06.wkb****, a learning file which is included with WordPerfect for Windows, has been loaded into the editing screen.*

Select the words "Marketing" from the fifth line of text in the document, highlighting the words on the screen as seen in Figure 14-5. Now, select the *Cut* button from the Button bar. The selected text will now disappear as shown in Figure 14-6.

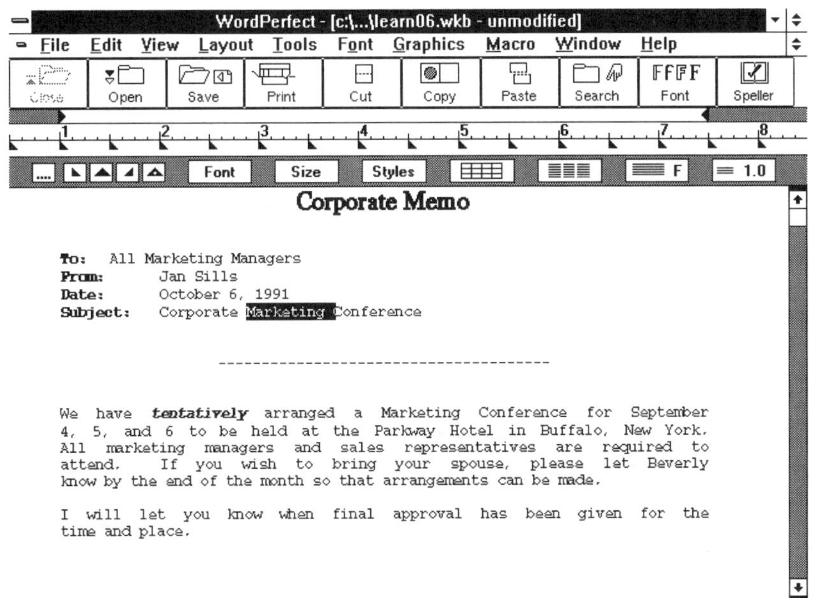

Figure 14-5. *Select the words "Marketing" on the screen as shown here.*

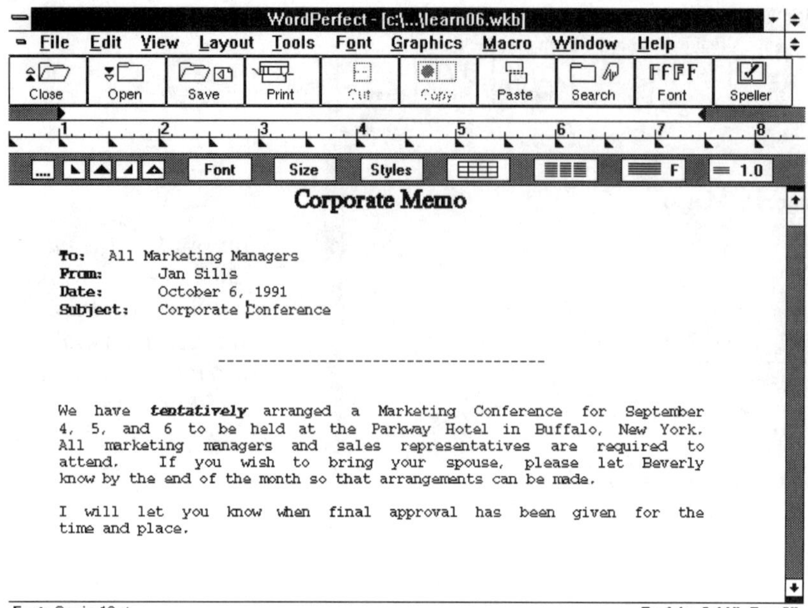

***Figure 14-6.** By clicking on the Cut button in the Button bar, the word "Marketing" has now been deleted from the document.*

Now choose the *Undo* command from the **Edit** menu to bring this text back onto the screen again.

Creating a Button bar

To create a customized Button bar that contains specific commands to which you want easy access, select the *Button Bar Setup* command from the **View** menu. From the fly-out menu that is activated, select the *New* command as seen in Figure 14-7.

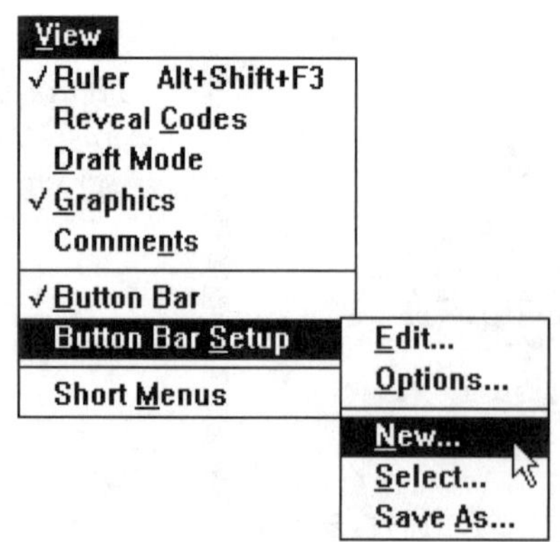

***Figure 14-7.** Use the New command in the Button Bar Setup fly-out menu from the **View** menu, to define a new Button bar.*

Notice that the default Button bar has been removed from the screen and that the *Edit Button Bar* dialog box is activated (Figure 14-8). As you move the cursor, notice that it has changed in appearance. The mouse now appears, as seen in Figure 14-8, as a hand holding a button.

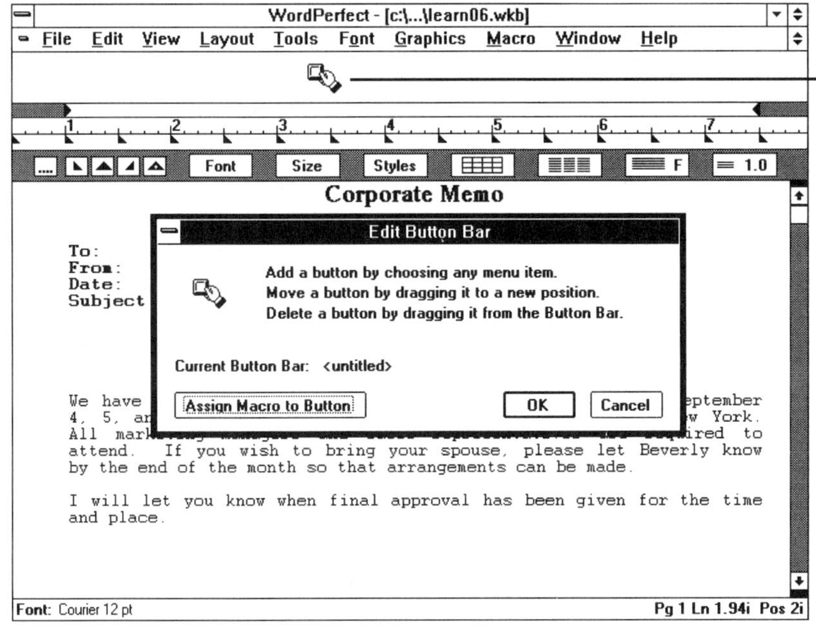

Figure 14-8. *The Edit Button Bar dialog box appears when the New command, shown in Figure 14-7, is selected. Note that the space below the Menu bar, where the Button bar is usually located, is empty. As a new Button bar is defined, this space will fill up with the newly selected command buttons. Note also that the mouse pointer has a special shape, to indicate that a Button bar is being edited.*

When the *Edit Button Bar* dialog box is activated, all commands in the menus are displayed in black and can be selected with the mouse pointer. To add a command button to the Button bar, simply choose any menu item as you would when ordinarily using WordPerfect.

For example, as seen in Figure 14-9, select the *Open* command from the **File** menu. Notice a new button, labeled *Open*, has been placed on the Button bar (Figure 14-10).

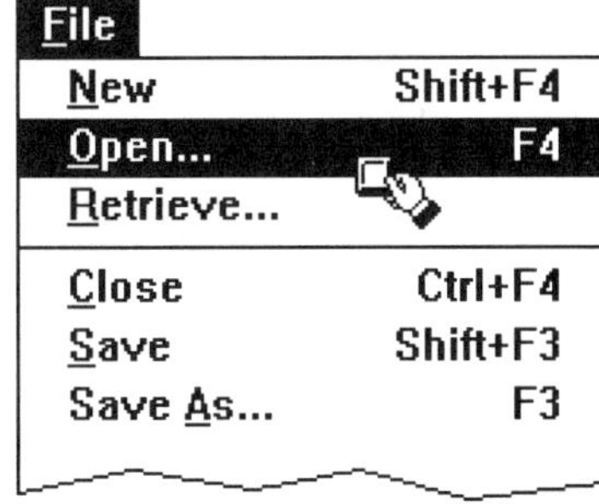

Figure 14-9. *The mouse cursor retains its special shape when you select commands from the menu. For each command selected from the menu, a button, representing that command, is added to the Button bar. In this example, the Open command is selected from the* ***File*** *menu.*

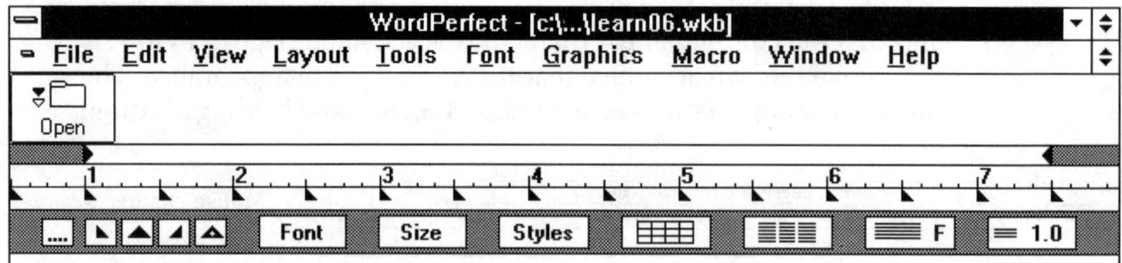

Figure 14-10. *Because the Open command was selected from the* ***File*** *menu, a command button representing the Open command has been added to the Button bar.*

Using the method described above, add, to the Button bar, the *New, Save As,* and *Print* commands from the **File** menu; the *Undo, Undelete, Cut, Copy,* and *Paste* commands from the **Edit** menu; the *Ruler* command from the **View** menu; and the *Normal, Bold, Italic,* and *Underline* commands from the **Font** menu.

Don't worry if you accidently add extra buttons to the Button bar. You will soon see how these mistakes can be corrected. The Button bar will now look like the one shown in Figure 14-11.

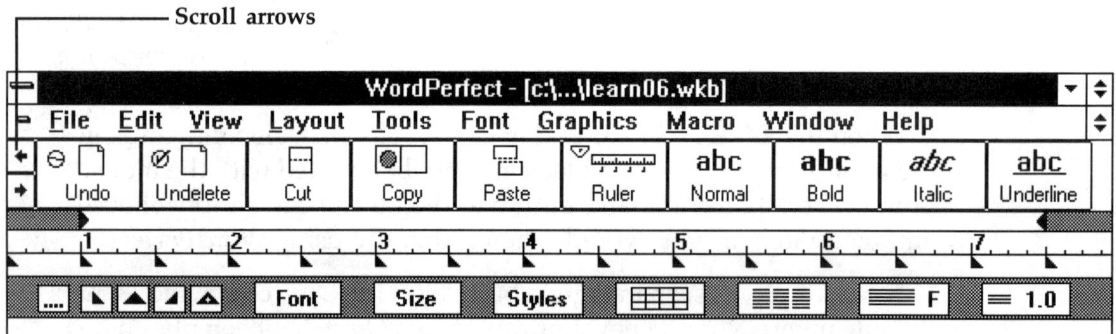

Figure 14-11. *After you have selected all the commands listed above, the Button bar will look like the example in this figure. Note the scroll arrows that let you access the buttons that are not currently visible on the screen.*

In this example (Figure 14-11), more buttons have been added to the Button bar than will fit on the screen at once. Notice the scroll arrows on the left of the Button bar, that let you move through buttons that are not displayed on the screen. These scroll arrows may or may not appear on your screen. Depending on the resolution of your screen, WordPerfect may or may not be able to display all these buttons at once.

Saving a Button bar

After you have finished adding buttons to the Button bar, as displayed in Figure 14-11, select the **OK** button in the *Edit Button Bar* dialog box. This command will activate the *Save Button Bar* dialog box shown in Figure 14-12.

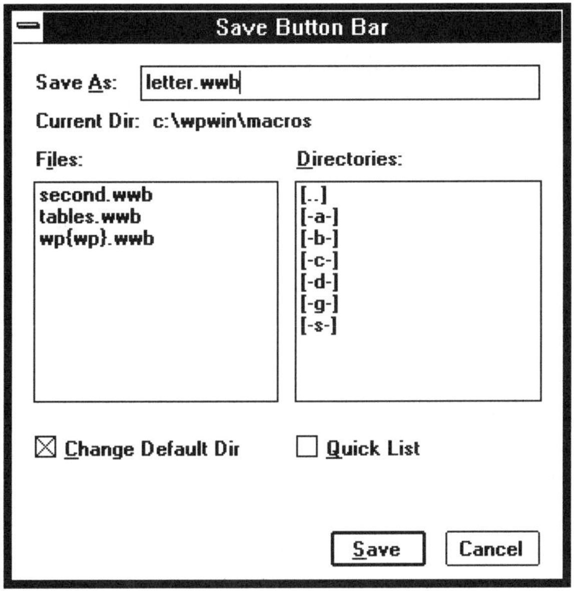

Figure 14-12. *The Save Button Bar dialog box allows you to give a name to the Button bar you have created and to save the information in a special Button Bar file with a **.wwb** extension.*

Button bar information is saved in special files with a "***wwb***" extension. The *Save Button Bar* dialog box, seen in Figure 14-12, works just like any other dialog box for saving files.

The flashing text cursor is automatically placed in the *Save As* text box. Type in the words "***letter.wwb***" and then click on the *Save* button. The newly created Button bar will be saved in a file called ***letter.wwb*** and WordPerfect will return to the editing screen.

Select the words "Marketing Conference" from the fifth line of text. Now click on the **Italic** button from the Button bar. This text will be italicized as shown in Figure 14-13.

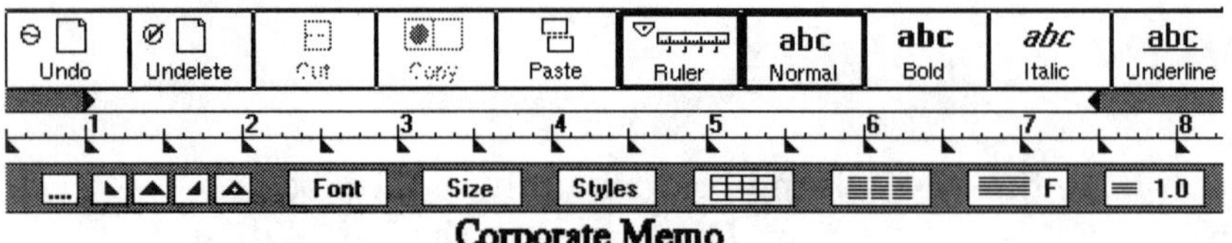

Corporate Memo

To: All Marketing Managers
From: Jan Sills
Date: October 6, 1991
Subject: Corporate *Marketing Conference*

We have **tentatively** arranged a Marketing Conference for September 4, 5, and 6 to be held at the Parkway Hotel in Buffalo, New York. All marketing managers and sales representatives are required to attend. If you wish to bring your spouse, please let Beverly know by the end of the month so that arrangements can be made.

***Figure 14-13.** The highlighted text has now become italicized.*

Editing a Button bar

Make sure that the Button bar you have just created is currently activated on the screen. If it is not, repeat the steps described previously in **Creating a Button bar** and **Saving a Button bar**. Select the *Button Bar Setup* option from the **View** menu. In the fly-out menu that is activated select the *Edit* command, as seen in Figure 14-14.

***Figure 14-14.** The Button Bar Setup/Edit command from the **View** menu, lets you modify the makeup of the currently active Button bar.*

As shown in Figure 14-15, the *Edit Button Bar* dialog box will appear on the screen and the mouse will once again take the form of a hand holding a button.

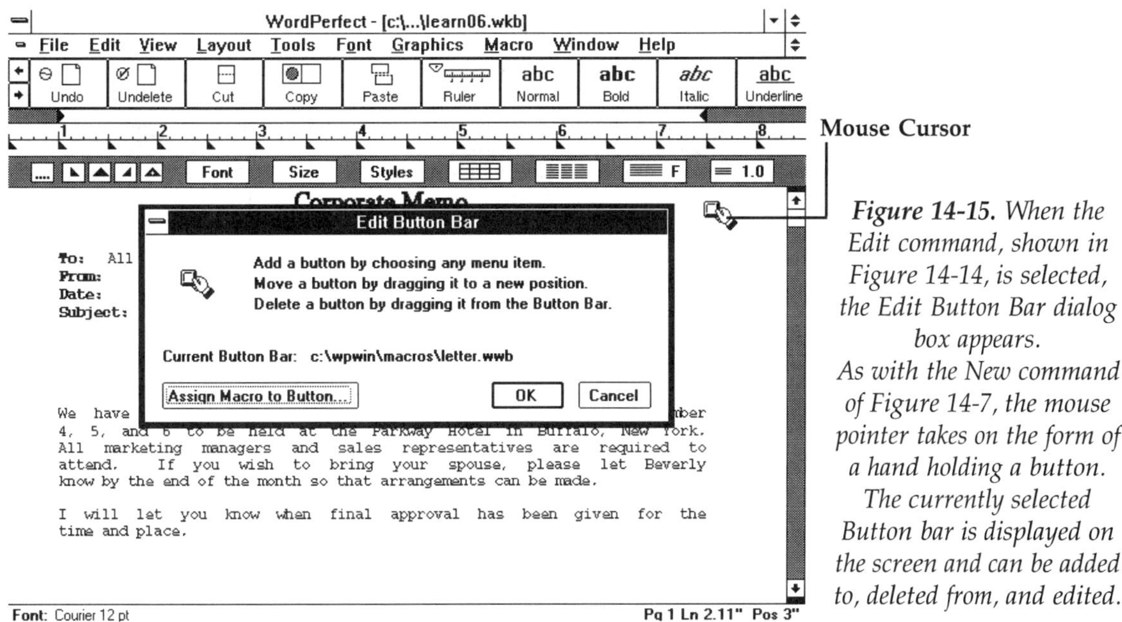

Figure 14-15. *When the Edit command, shown in Figure 14-14, is selected, the Edit Button Bar dialog box appears. As with the New command of Figure 14-7, the mouse pointer takes on the form of a hand holding a button. The currently selected Button bar is displayed on the screen and can be added to, deleted from, and edited.*

Add the *Font* command, from the **Font** menu, to the Button bar, using the method described above under **Creating a Button bar**. At this point you can add any other buttons you require for this Button bar.

To remove an unwanted command button from the Button bar, simply click and hold the mouse on that button and drag it from the Button bar, as demonstrated with the *Copy* command in Figure 14-16. When you release the mouse button, the command button will be removed from the Button bar.

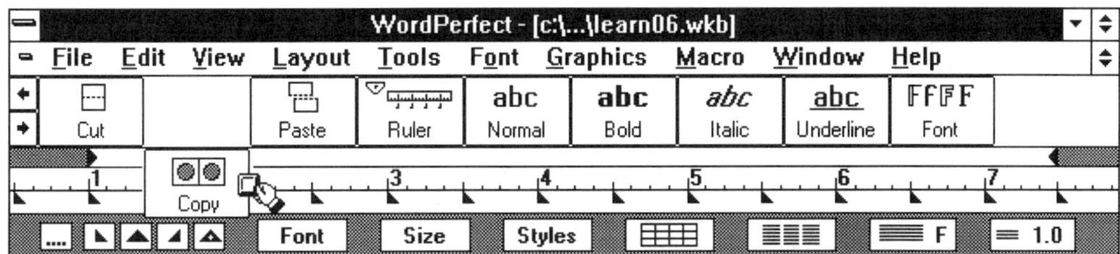

Figure 14-16. *To remove a command button from the Button bar, hold the mouse down on the desired button and drag it off the Button bar before releasing the mouse.*

Use this method to remove the *Undelete* command button from the Button bar. You may need to use the scroll arrows to the left of the Button bar to reach this command. The Button bar will now look like the example shown in Figure 14-17. To match yours with this figure, use the left or right-facing scroll arrows to align the *New* button as the first command, at the left side of the Button bar.

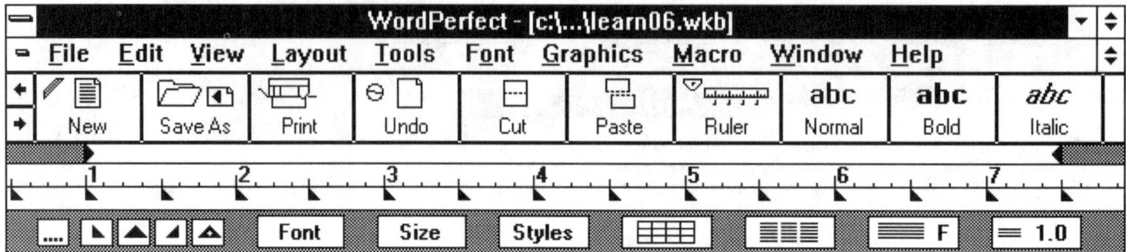

Figure 14-17. *After the indicated command buttons have been removed, the Button bar will look like the example shown here.*

To move a button, changing its position within the Button bar, hold the mouse down on the desired button and, without releasing it, drag the button to its new position on the Button bar. In the example in Figure 14-18, the *Bold* command button is being moved to the left-hand side of the Button bar.

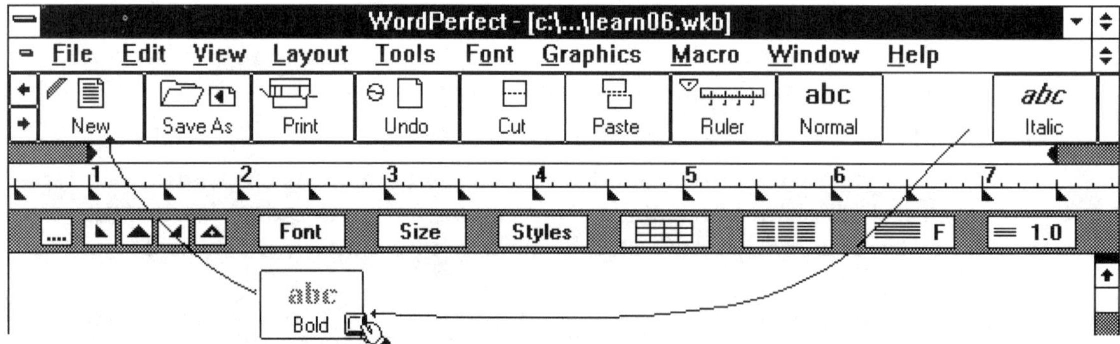

Figure 14-18. *To change a button's position in the Button bar, use the mouse pointer to select and drag the button to its new location. When you release the mouse button, the command button will be inserted into the button bar at its new position.*

When you have finished making changes to the Button bar, select **OK** in the *Edit Button Bar* dialog box to return to the editing screen. The changes you have made will automatically be added to the ***letter.wwb*** Button bar file you created earlier. The editing screen will now look like the example in Figure 14-19.

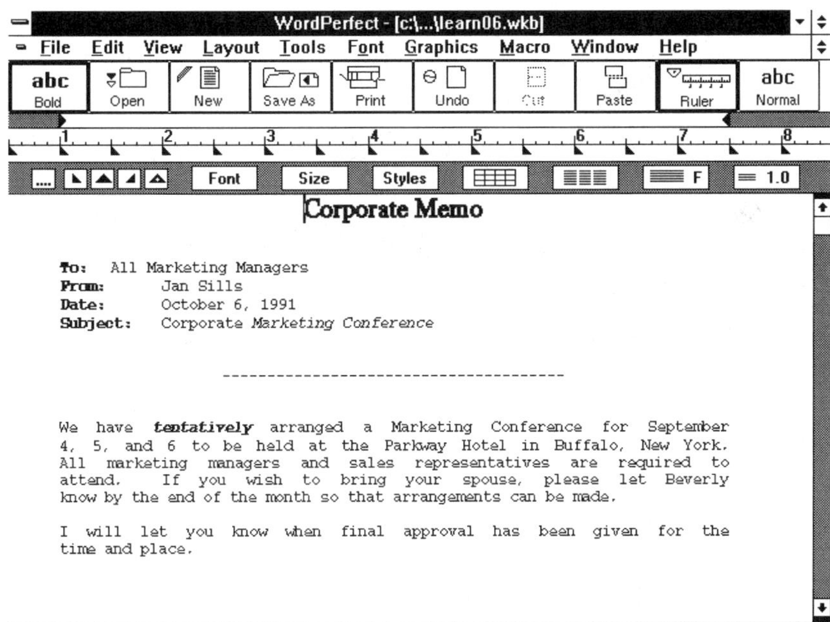

Figure 14-19. *The Button bar shown here should match the one on your computer. Note that the button representing the Bold command has been repositioned to the left-hand side of the Button bar.*

If you had selected the *Cancel* command, the changes you have just made would have been ignored and you would return to the editing screen with the original Button bar intact.

Button bar options

WordPerfect allows the position and style of the Button bar to be changed using the *Button Bar Options* dialog box, seen in Figure 14-20.

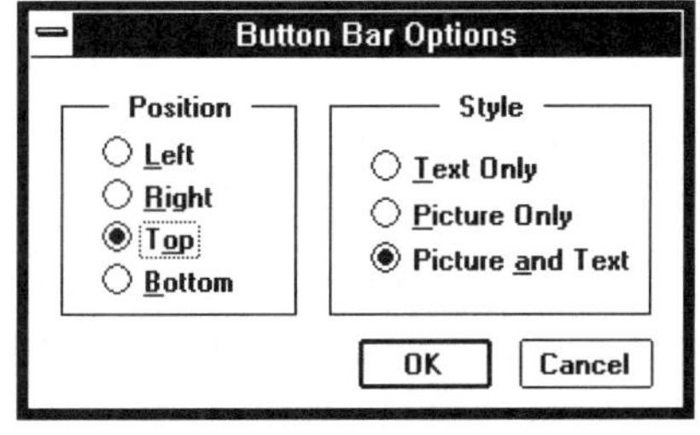

Figure 14-20. *The Button Bar Setup/Options command from the **View** menu invokes the Button Bar Options dialog box. This dialog box allows you to determine the position and style of the Button bar.*

The default setting is *Top* for the *Position* setting and *Picture and Text* for the *Style* setting. Using these default settings, the Button bar is positioned at the top of the screen, directly beneath the Menu bar, and its buttons display both a text description and a graphic representation of their functions.

Activate the *Button Bar Options* dialog box by selecting the *Button Bar Setup* command from the **View** menu. In the fly-out menu that is activated, select the *Options* command as seen in Figure 14-20.

Change the position and style of display for the Button bar you have created. Using the *Button Bar Options* dialog box, select the *Left* radio button in the *Position* section of the dialog box and the *Text Only* radio button in the *Style* section. Select **OK** to implement these changes. The editing screen will now look like the example in Figure 14-21.

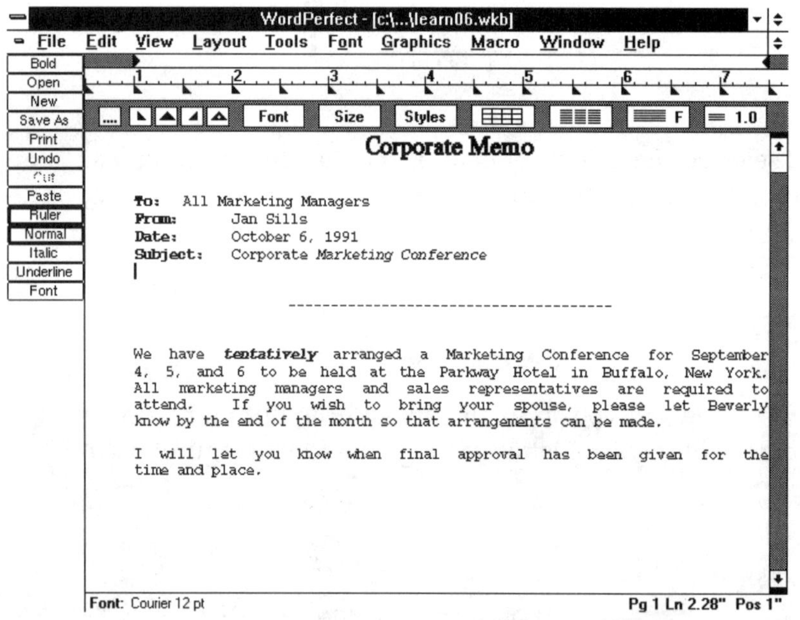

Figure 14-21. *When the Left option is selected for Position and the Text Only option is selected for Style in the Button Bar Options dialog box, the Button bar will take the form shown in this figure.*

Selections made in the *Button Bar Options* dialog box will affect how any Button bar, not just the current one, is displayed.

Position the Button bar back to the top of the screen, and display both pictures and text in its buttons, by using the *Button Bar Options* dialog box settings as shown in Figure 14-22.

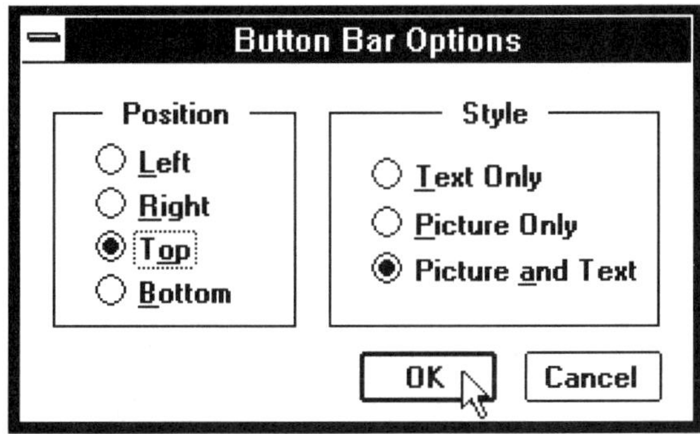

Figure 14-22. *Set the Button Bar Options dialog box as seen here, to return the Button bar to its usual position and style.*

Figure 14-23 shows the effects of some of the other options in the *Button Bar Options* dialog box.

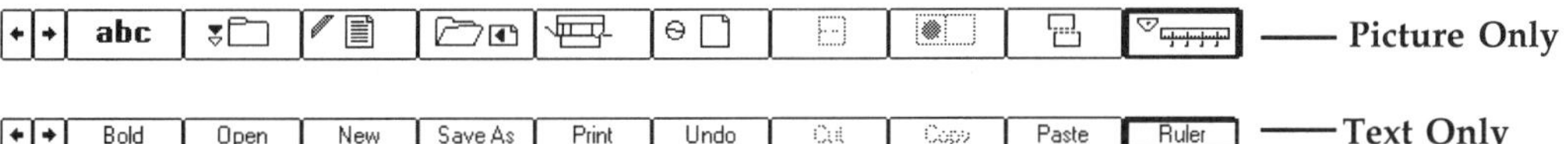

Figure 14-23. *The command buttons in the Button bar can display only pictures or only text, in addition to the usual display of both pictures and text.*

Changing Button bars

When you quit WordPerfect, the last Button bar that was in use becomes the new default Button bar, which will be displayed automatically when you choose the *Button Bar* command in the **View** menu.

To display a different Button bar, from one of the other Button bar files on your system, select the *Button Bar Setup* command in the **View** menu. In the fly-out menu that is activated (see Figure 14-14), click on the *Select* command.

The *Select Button Bar* dialog box, seen in Figure 14-24, will appear and display a list of available Button bar files. Highlight the file called: ***wp{wp}.wwb*** (which is WordPerfect's default Button bar file), then select the *Open* button. Notice that the Button bar has changed to the new arrangement shown in Figure 14-25.

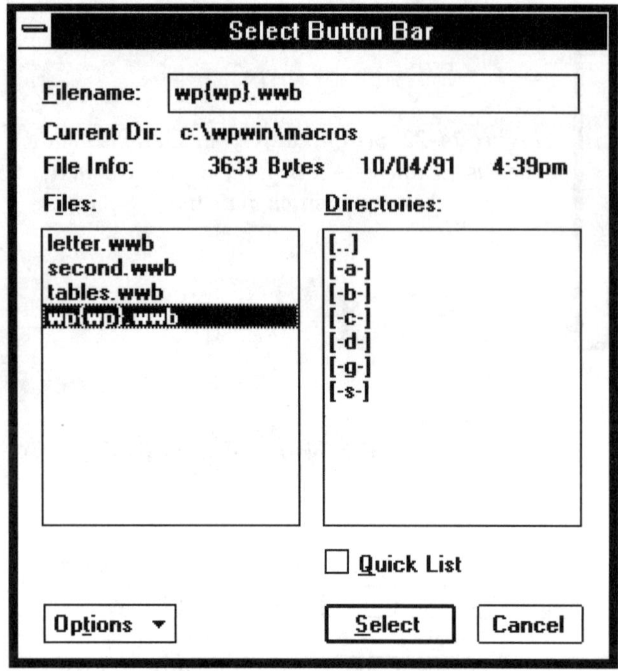

Figure 14-24. *Using the Select Button Bar dialog box, you can select any of the existing Button bar files. These files can be identified by their* ***wwb*** *extensions.*

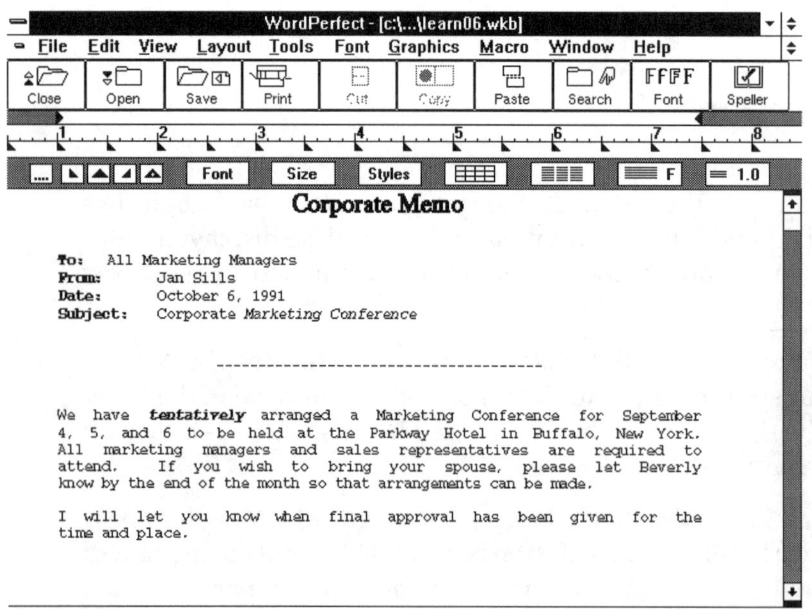

Figure 14-25. *The Button bar represented by the file called* ***wp{wp}.wwb*** *has now been displayed on screen. Notice that this Button bar is quite distinct from the one you created earlier in this chapter. It contains different command buttons and does not require scroll arrows. It is, in effect, the default button bar that appeared in Figure 14-2, when you first chose the Button Bar command from the* ***View*** *menu.*

The Save As command

The *Save As* command, in the *Button Bar Setup* fly-out menu (Figure 14-14), lets you save the current Button bar to a new file. Selecting this command will invoke the *Save Button Bar* dialog box shown in Figure 14-26.

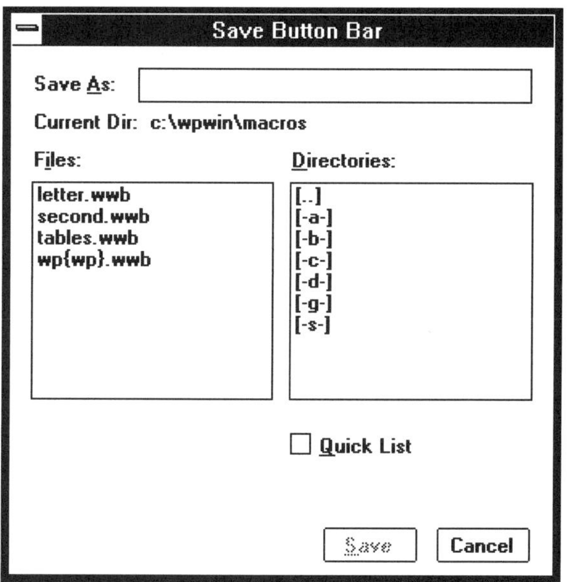

Figure 14-26. *The Save As command in the Button Bar Setup fly-out menu invokes the Save Button Bar dialog box. This command lets you save the currently active Button bar to a new .wwb file.*

This command is useful, because it lets you save an existing Button bar to a new file, before changing its configuration using the *Edit* command described earlier in the chapter.

Button Bar — Exercise

This training exercise is designed so that people of all levels of expertise with WordPerfect can use it to gain maximum benefit. In order to do this, the bare exercise is listed below this paragraph on just one page, with no hints. The following pages contain the steps needed to complete this exercise for those who need additional prompting.

Steps in brief

1. *Open the learn05.wkb file.*
2. *Activate the WordPerfect Button bar command.*
3. *Create a new Button bar which contains the Open, Close, Save As, Print, Center, Bold, and Italic command buttons.*
4. *Save the Button bar as learn05.wwb.*
5. *Using this Button bar, apply the Bold text attribute to the first four lines of text. Apply the Italic text attribute to the words "Corporate Marketing" in the fifth line of text.*
6. *Edit the Button bar by moving the Close command to the right end of the bar, and by also removing the Bold and Italic buttons.*
7. *Change the Button bar options so the Button bar is placed to the left of the screen with the buttons displaying text only.*
8. *Select the wp{wp}.wwb Button bar.*
9. *Reset the options so that the Button bar appears at the top of the screen with the buttons displaying both pictures and text.*
10. *Close the document, without saving changes.*
11. *Turn off the Button bar display.*

The details for completing these steps are on the following pages.

Steps in detail

1. *Open the learn05.wkb file.*

If you are already in WordPerfect, you do not have to close the current document, as WordPerfect can open multiple files at once. If you are not in WordPerfect, start the program from Windows.

To access the required file, select the *Open* command from the **File** menu. In the *Open File* dialog box that appears, select the file ***learn05.wkb*** from the ***learn*** sub-directory (Figure 14x-1) and click on *Open*.

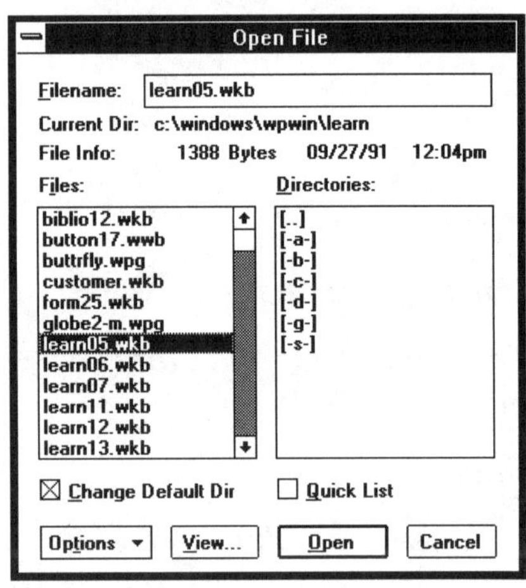

Figure 14x-1. *Select the* ***learn05.wkb*** *file from the Open File dialog box and click on Open.*

2. *Activate the WordPerfect Button bar command.*

Select the *Button Bar* command from the **View** menu as seen in Figure 14x-2.

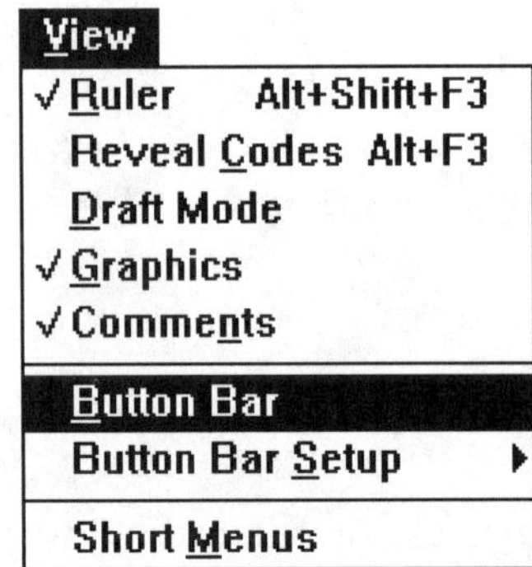

Figure 14x-2. *To make the Button bar appear on the screen, select the Button Bar command from the* ***View*** *menu. When the Button bar is activated, a check mark will be displayed alongside the Button Bar command in the menu.*

The previously loaded, or default, Button bar will be placed at the top of the screen directly beneath the Menu bar (Figure 14x-3).

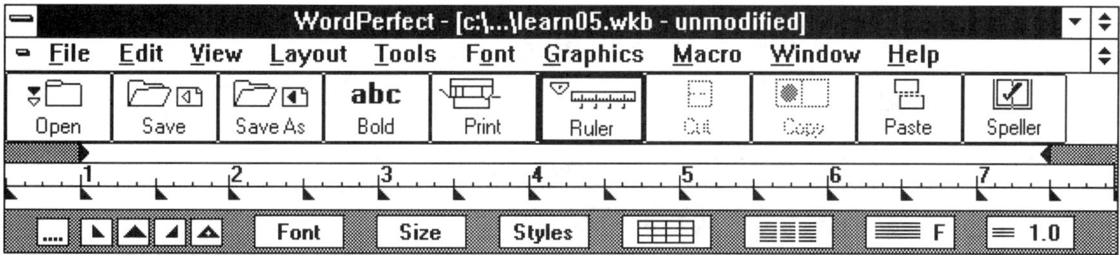

Figure 14x-3. *The last loaded, or default, Button bar appears when you activate the Button Bar command of Figure 14x-2. The Button bar on your screen may be different to this one.*

3. ***Create a new Button bar which contains the Open, Close, Save As, Print, Center, Bold, and Italic command buttons.***

Select the *Button Bar Setup* command from the **View** menu. In the fly-out menu that appears, select the *New* command (Figure 14x-4). The dialog box of Figure 14x-5 will appear.

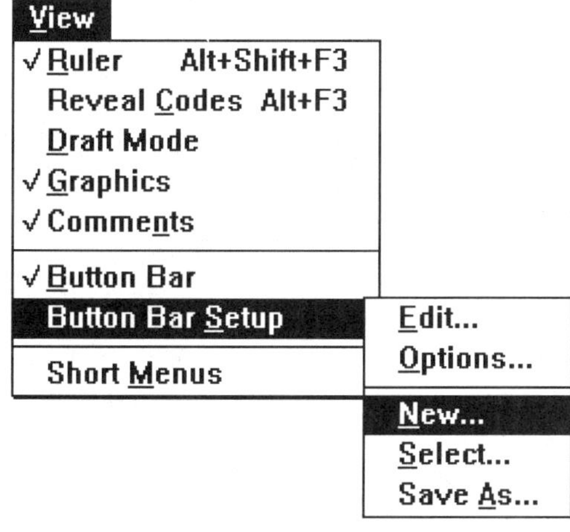

Figure 14x-4. *Use the Button Bar Setup/New command in the* ***View*** *menu to create a new Button bar.*

As seen in Figure 14x-5, the previous Button bar has been removed from the screen and the *Edit Button Bar* dialog box appears. The mouse pointer now takes on the appearance of a hand holding a button.

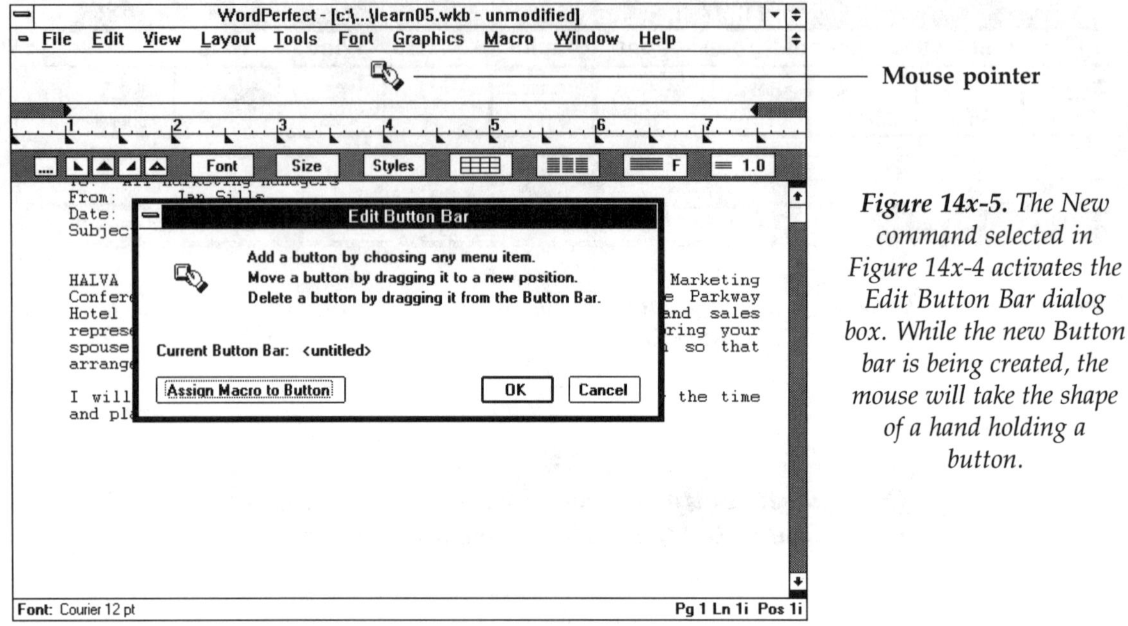

Figure 14x-5. *The New command selected in Figure 14x-4 activates the Edit Button Bar dialog box. While the new Button bar is being created, the mouse will take the shape of a hand holding a button.*

To add the *Open* button to the Button bar, select *Open* from the **File** menu using the mouse pointer. The *Open* button will now be placed on the Button bar as seen in Figure 14x-6.

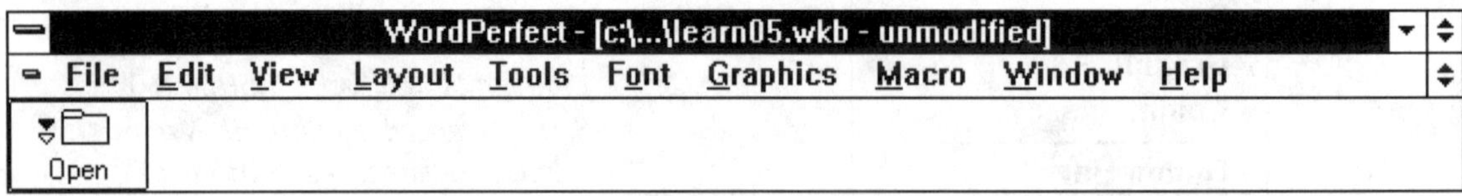

Figure 14x-6. *A command button representing the Open command is placed on the new Button bar after the Open command is selected from the* **File** *menu.*

Now, select *Close, Save As* and *Print,* one at a time from the **File** menu, which will place the corresponding buttons on the Button bar.

To place the *Center* button on the Button bar, select the *Line* command in the **Layout** menu and, in the fly-out menu that appears, select the *Center* command. A quicker and easier method is to simply press the Shift and F7 keys together—Shift+F7, and then the new button will appear.

To place the *Bold* and *Italic* buttons on the Button bar, select these commands from the **Font** menu or simply type in the shortcut key combinations (Control+B for Bold and Control+I for Italic). The Button bar will now look like the example in Figure 14x-7.

WordPerfect - [c:\...\learn05.wkb - unmodified]
File Edit View Layout Tools Font Graphics Macro Window Help
Open Close Save As Print Center Ln Bold Italic

Figure 14x-7. *After you have selected all of the required commands, the appropriate command buttons will be positioned in the Button bar.*

4. Save the Button bar as learn05.wwb.

Click on the **OK** button in the *Edit Button Bar* dialog box to activate the *Save Button Bar* dialog box (Figure 14x-8).

The text cursor is automatically placed in the *Save As* text box. Type in the file name ***learn05.wwb,*** and then select the *Save* button to return to the editing screen.

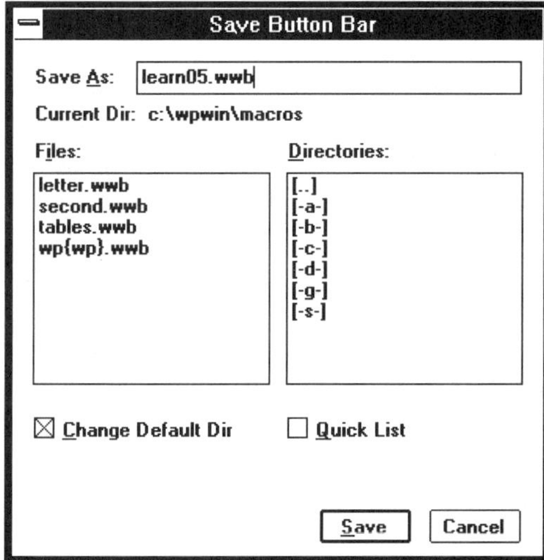

Figure 14x-8. *The Save Button Bar dialog box is activated when you select **OK** from the Edit Button Bar dialog box shown in Figure 14x-5. Use this dialog box, as shown here, to save the newly defined Button bar as a file called **learn05.wwb**.*

5. ***Using this Button bar, apply the Bold text attribute to the first four lines of text. Apply the Italic text attribute to the words "Corporate Marketing" in the fifth line of text.***

Select the first four lines of text making sure that all appear in reverse video as seen in Figure 14x-9.

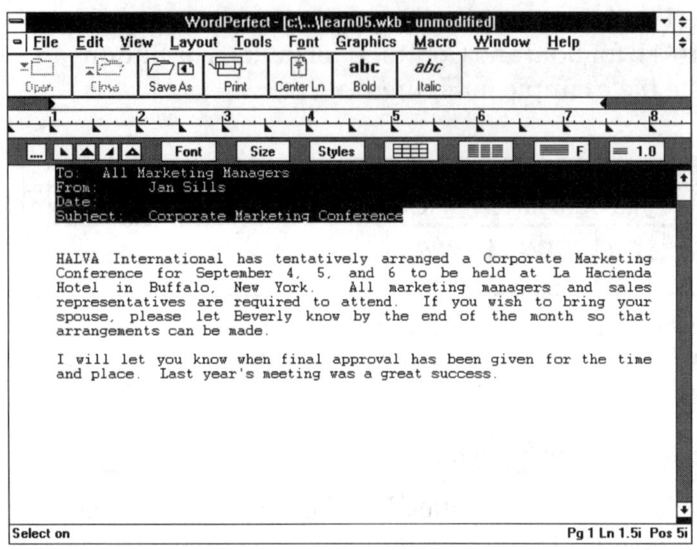

Figure 14x-9. *Select the first four lines in the document. Make sure that they are all highlighted (displayed in reverse video) as seen here.*

Now, click on the *Bold* button in the Button bar. The selected text, once deselected, now appears in bold faced letters, as seen in Figure 14x-10.

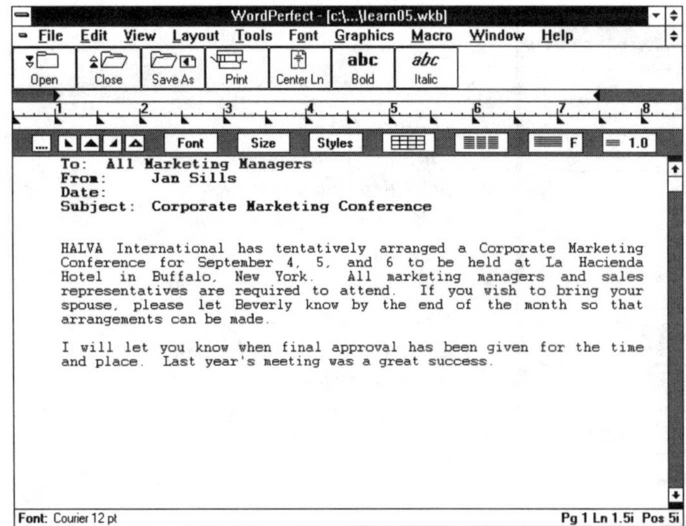

Figure 14x-10. *When the Bold command button is selected, the bold text attribute is assigned to the highlighted text. Clicking elsewhere on the editing screen to deselect the highlighted text, as has been done here, allows the bold attribute to be seen more easily.*

Select the words "Corporate Marketing" in the fifth line of text as illustrated in Figure 14x-11.

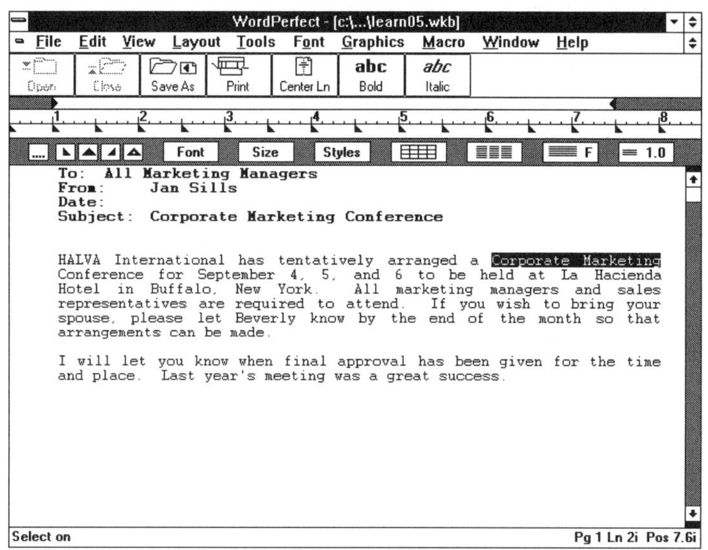

Figure 14x-11. *Select the words "Corporate Marketing" where they appear in the fifth line of text in the document.*

Next, select the *Italic* button in the Button bar. The selected text now appears italicized. The document will look like the example in Figure 14x-12, once the text has been deselected.

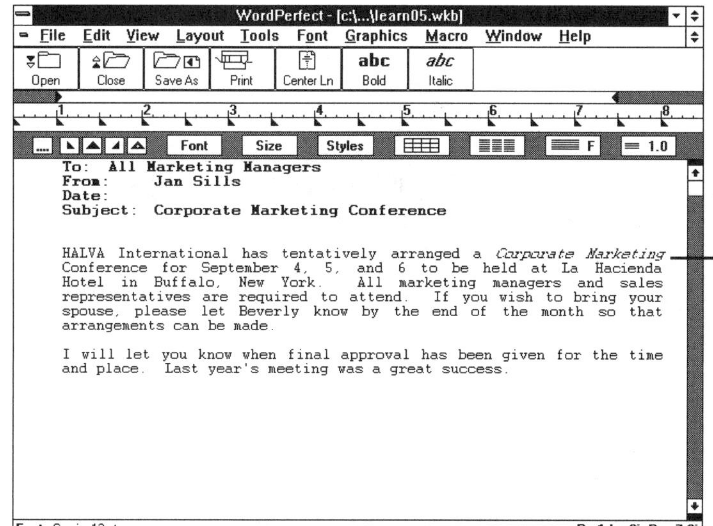

Figure 14x-12. *When the Italic command button is selected, the italic text attribute is assigned to the highlighted text.*

6. ***Edit the Button bar by moving the Close command to the right end of the bar, and by also removing the Bold and Italic buttons.***

Select the *Button Bar Setup* command from the **View** menu. In the fly-out menu that appears, select the *Edit* command (Figure 14x-13).

Figure 14x-13. *Use the Button Bar Setup/Edit command in the* ***View*** *menu to make changes to the currently selected Button bar.*

The *Edit Button Bar* dialog box will now appear on the screen and the current Button bar, saved in step 4 under the name ***learn05.wwb***, will remain in its place beneath the Menu bar.

To move the *Close* button to the right side of the Button bar, hold the mouse button down on the *Close* command button and, without releasing it, drag the button to the far right end of the Button bar (Figure 14x-14). Release the mouse button to place the *Close* button in its new position on the Button bar.

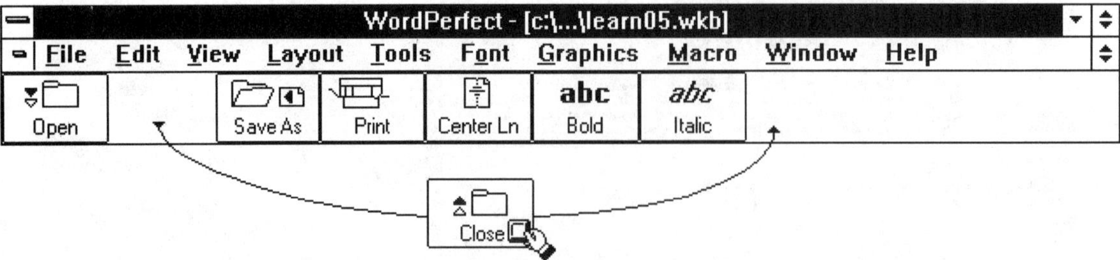

Figure 14x-14. *To move the Close button to the right-hand side of the Button bar, hold the mouse down on the Open command button and, without releasing the mouse, drag the Open button to its new position. When the Open button is positioned correctly, release the mouse button.*

To remove the *Bold* button from the Button bar, hold the mouse down on the *Bold* command button. Without releasing the mouse, drag the *Bold* button below the Button bar as demonstrated in Figure 14x-15 and then release the mouse. Repeat this operation to remove the *Italic* button from the Button bar.

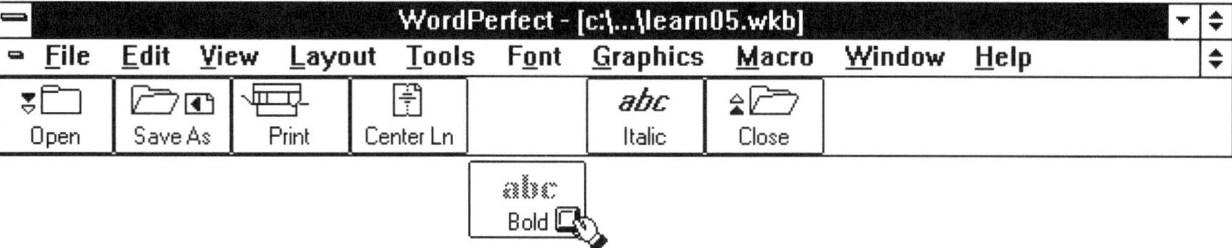

Figure 14x-15. *To remove a command button from the Button bar, use the mouse to drag the button off the Button bar and then release the mouse button. If the selected command button is not touching the Button bar, it will be deleted.*

Select the **OK** button in the *Edit Button Bar* dialog box to save the changes you have just made to the Button bar. These changes are automatically saved to the ***learn05.wwb*** file.

7. ***Change the Button bar options so the Button bar is placed to the left of the screen with the buttons displaying text only.***

To perform this step, select the *Button Bar Setup* command in the **View** menu. In the fly-out menu that appears, select the *Options* command (Figure 14x-16).

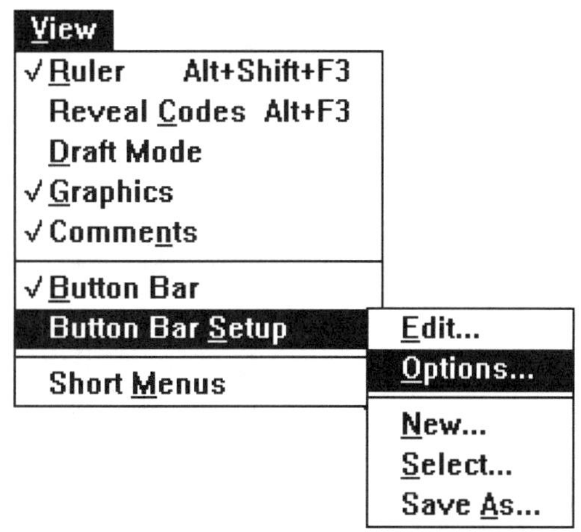

Figure 14x-16. *The Button Bar Setup/Options command in the* ***View*** *menu is used to modify the appearance and position of the Button bar.*

In the *Button Bar Options* dialog box, select the *Left* option from the *Position* box. Now, select the *Text Only* option from the *Style* box. The dialog box will now look like the one shown in Figure 14x-17.

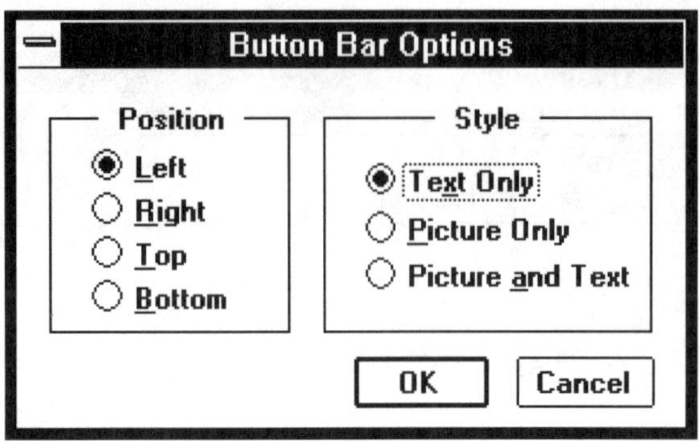

Figure 14x-17. *Make the Position and Style selections in the Button Bar Options as shown here, to display the Button bar without graphics and on the left side of the page. Click on* **OK** *when you have made the appropriate selections.*

Select **OK** to change the position and style of the Button bar. The Button bar will now look like the example in Figure 14x-18.

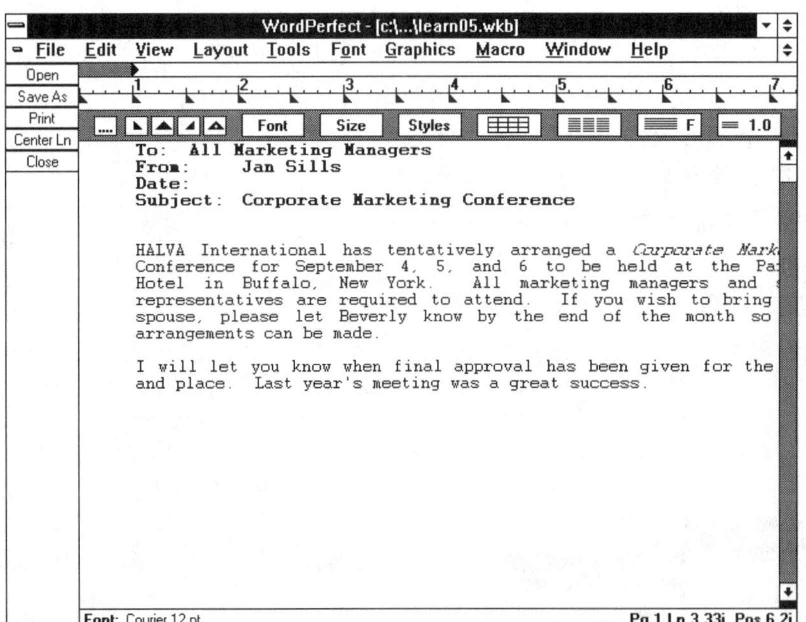

Figure 14x-18. *This figure shows the Button bar as it will appear after you have made the selections shown in Figure 14x-17.*

8. Select the wp{wp}.wwb Button bar.

Select the *Button Bar Setup* command from the **View** menu. In the fly-out menu that appears, choose the *Select* command (Figure 14x-19).

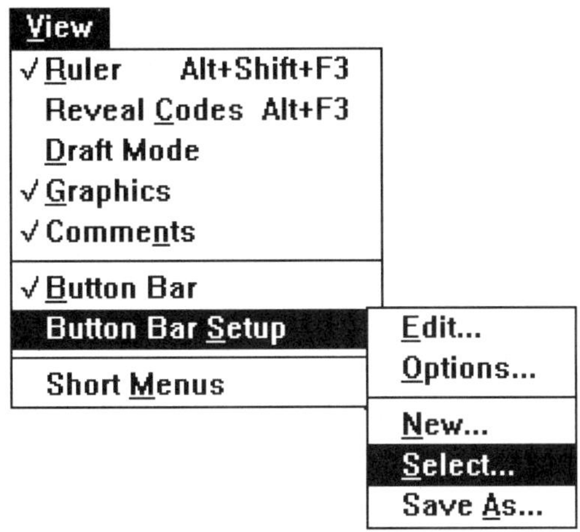

Figure 14x-19. *The Button Bar Setup/Select command in the **View** menu is used to select a Button bar from among the Button bar files already on disk.*

The *Select Button Bar* dialog box will be activated, as seen in Figure 14x-20. Highlight the file ***wp{wp}.wwb*** and click on the *Open* button. The Button bar you have just created is removed from the screen and a new one is now in its place.

Notice that the new Button bar maintains the same display options—text only and displayed on the left-hand side—as those you set in Figure 14x-17.

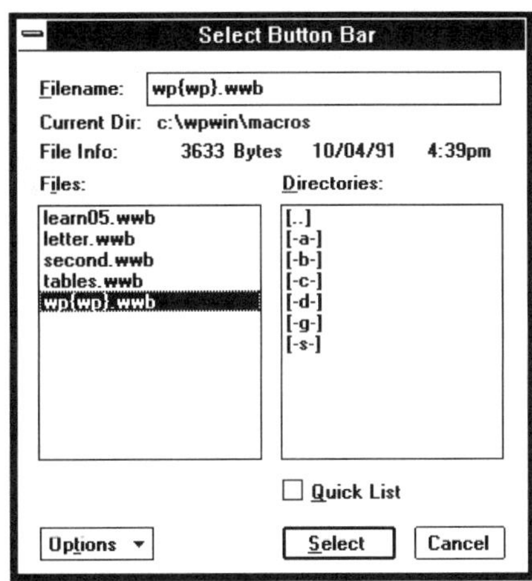

Figure 14x-20. *Using the Select Button Bar dialog box, select the Button bar file called **wp{wp}.wwb**.*

9. Reset the options so that the Button bar appears at the top of the screen, with the buttons displaying both pictures and text.

Select the *Button Bar Setup* command from the **View** menu again. In the fly-out menu that has been activated, select the *Options* command, as seen in Figure 14x-16 earlier in this exercise.

In the *Button Bar Options* dialog box that appears, select the *Top* option in the *Position* box and the *Picture and Text* option in the *Style* box, as shown in Figure 14x-21.

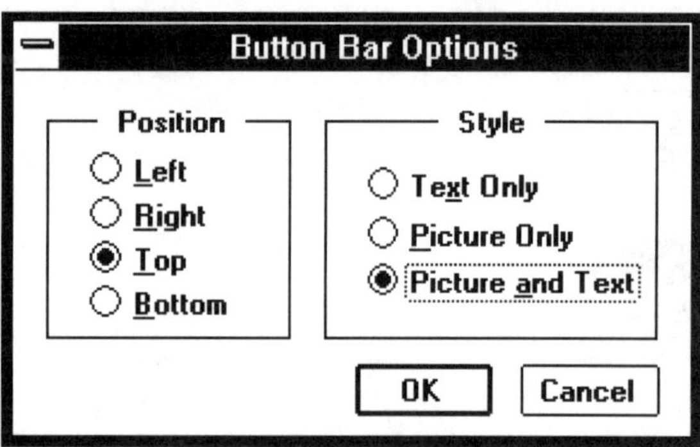

Figure 14x-21. *Use the Button Bar Options dialog box, as shown here, to reset the position and style of the Button bar to what it was before you began this exercise.*

Select **OK** to change both the position and display of the Button bar to match the one shown in Figure 14x-22.

Figure 14x-22. *After you have made the selection shown in Figure 14x-21, the Button bar will take on the appearance seen here and will be positioned at the top of the editing screen, below the Menu bar.*

10. Close the document, without saving changes.

Select the *Close* command from the **File** menu. Because changes have been made to the document since it was loaded, a warning dialog box, pictured in Figure 14x-23, will appear. Select *No* to not save changes.

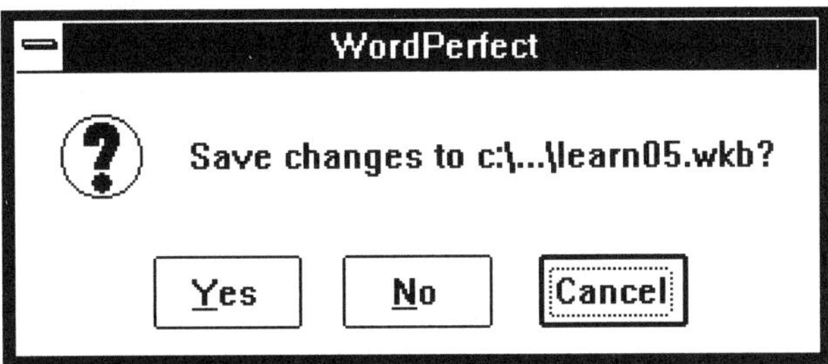

Figure 14x-23. *This warning dialog box appears when you try to close the document without saving the changes you have made. In this case, select the No option.*

The document ***lesson05.wkb*** is now removed from the screen.

11. Turn off the Button bar display.

The Button bar is active when there is a check mark next to the *Button Bar* command in the **View** menu (Figure 14x-24).

To turn off the Button bar display, simply select the *Button Bar* command in the **View** menu. This will remove the Button bar from the screen.

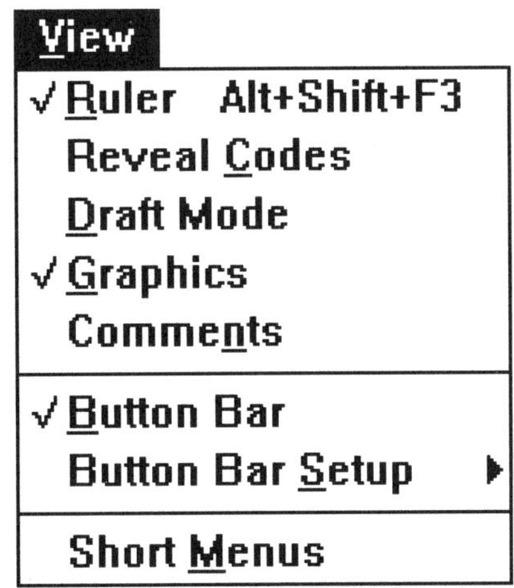

Figure 14x-24. *When the Button bar is active on the screen, a check mark appears beside its command in the **View** menu. When the Button bar is deactivated, by selecting the Button Bar command again, the check mark is removed.*

Styles

Styles created and edited in WordPerfect are designed to make document formatting faster and more consistent. A variety of formatting instructions are used to create each style and these formatting instructions can then be applied to a document, or selected text, in one operation.

There are two types of styles discussed in this chapter—*paired styles*, and *open styles*. WordPerfect also has an *outline styles* feature. This latter feature is briefly discussed in Chapter 22.

Paired styles

Paired styles are styles that affect only a small amount of text, and can be compared with a simple paired code. A code in the text turns the style on, and another code turns the style off. For example, you may have a paired style created for a heading—a style that automatically makes every heading use the font Times Roman, the size 24

Styles Defined

Styles created and edited in WordPerfect are designed to make the formatting a document consistent, and much quicker. Various formatting instructions go into creating each style, and these formatting instructions can be applied to a document, or selected text, as a whole.

There are two different types of styles--paired styles, and open styles.

Paired Styles

Paired styles are styles that affect only a small amount of text, and can be compared with a simple paired code. A code in the text turns the style on, and another code turns the style off. For example, you may have a paired style created for a heading--a style that automatically makes every heading use the font Times Roman, the size 24 point, uses centered justification, etc. You may have another paired style used for subheadings--this will force all subheadings to be perhaps Times Roman, 18 point, and left justified.

Figure 15-1. *On the left is some text that contains two subheadings, before a style has been applied to them. On the right, the same text is shown after a style has been applied to the subheadings. Both subheadings on the right look the same, and the formatting instructions (font, size, appearance, justification) were applied automatically, in one operation, through the use of a WordPerfect style.*

Styles Defined

Styles created and edited in WordPerfect are designed to make the formatting a document consistent, and much quicker. Various formatting instructions go into creating each style, and these formatting instructions can be applied to a document, or selected text, as a whole.

There are two different types of styles--paired styles, and open styles.

Paired Styles

Paired styles are styles that affect only a small amount of text, and can be compared with a simple paired code. A code in the text turns the style on, and another code turns the style off. For example, you may have a paired style created for a heading--a style that automatically makes every heading use the font Times Roman, the size 24 point, uses centered justification, etc. You may have another paired style used for subheadings--this will force all subheadings to be perhaps Times Roman, 18 point, and left justified.

point, and with centered justification. You may have another paired style, used for subheadings, which forces all subheadings to be, for example, Times Roman, 18 point, and left justified.

Open styles

Open styles are styles that are generally turned on for an entire document, or at least entire pages of a document, and control more the format of the page than the appearance of individual paragraphs on the page.

Normally, open styles contain such information as page size and margin settings. Open styles are generally created to make the initial formatting of documents quicker and easier.

Take, for example, a company that creates a periodic newsletter. This newsletter uses Letter size paper, has 0.5 of an inch margins all around the page, and uses three columns. All this information can be stored in a style, and applied to the document as a whole the next time a newsletter is created. This feature not only ensures that newsletters can be created more quickly but also that they retain the same look and feel.

Style files

Created styles are saved with, and can only be used in, the current document. If you wish to use styles created in one document in other documents, then they must be saved to a separate style file.

Any number of styles that are created in WordPerfect can be saved within a style file. These files should be saved on disk with an ***sty*** extension, making them easier to locate and use for future reference. In any one style file, there may be several WordPerfect styles.

By grouping a number of styles within a style file, WordPerfect allows you to create, for example, a ***newslet.sty*** file, which contains various styles pertaining to a monthly newsletter that your company may create.

When you next need to publish this newsletter, you can load in the style file ***newslet.sty***. You then have access to the WordPerfect styles within this style file.

Style defaults

You are now going to load a sample style file provided with WordPerfect: ***library.sty***. It is possible, however, that this style file may already be loaded.

Before you load this style file (***library.sty***), take a brief look at the *Location of Files* command from the *Preferences* fly-out menu in the **File** menu (Figure 15-2). This command contains controls which determine where WordPerfect looks for style files and which style file is loaded, by default, every time WordPerfect is started.

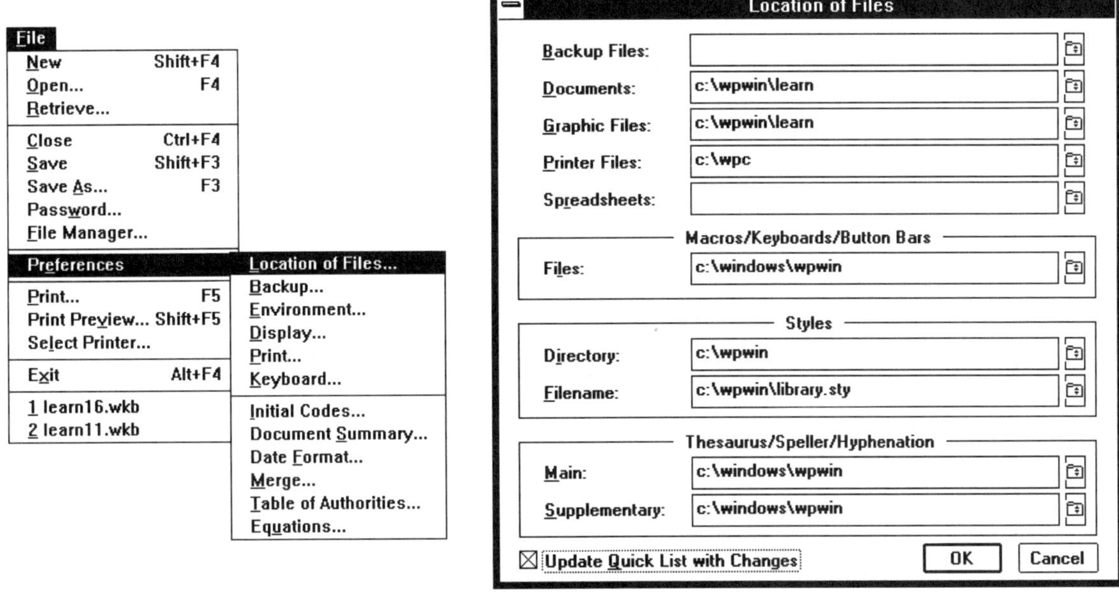

Figure 15-2. *The Preferences/Location of Files command in the* ***File*** *menu.*

The section within the Figure 15-2 dialog box that concerns the loading of style files is the *Styles* section (Figure 15-3).

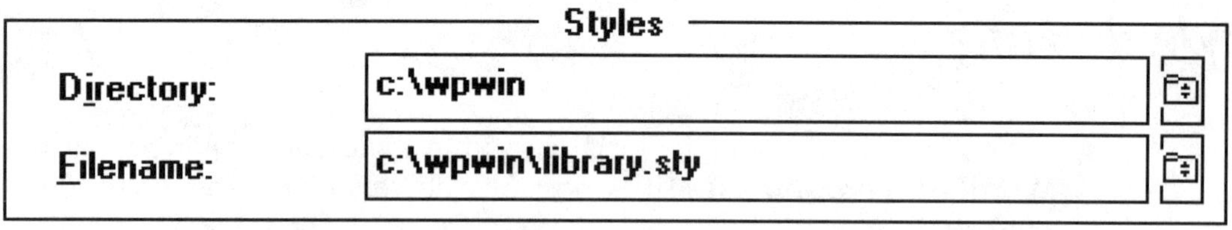

Styles

Directory: c:\wpwin

Filename: c:\wpwin\library.sty

Figure 15-3. The Directory and Filename text boxes, within the Styles section of the Figure 15-2 dialog box, determine where style files are located and which style file is loaded by default.

Figure 15-3 shows the two options within the *Styles* section of the Figure 15-2 dialog box.

The first option, *Directory*, determines the directory into which WordPerfect will initially look when asked to load a new style file. The directory name on this line should correspond to the directory where you intend to store your style files.

The second option, *Filename*, determines the name of the style file, that is loaded by default, whenever a new WordPerfect document is created or opened. In this case, the style file ***c:\wpwin\library.sty*** is loaded by default.

Ensure that the *Location of Files* dialog box has its *Styles* section set up as shown in Figure 15-3 and click on **OK**.

Loading style files

Regardless of the pathnames and filenames in the *Styles* section of the Figure 15-2 dialog box, you can choose any style file from any directory you wish. As mentioned earlier, you are now going to load the style file ***library.sty***.

To perform any sort of style file manipulation, you must select the *Styles* command from the **Layout** menu (Figure 15-4).

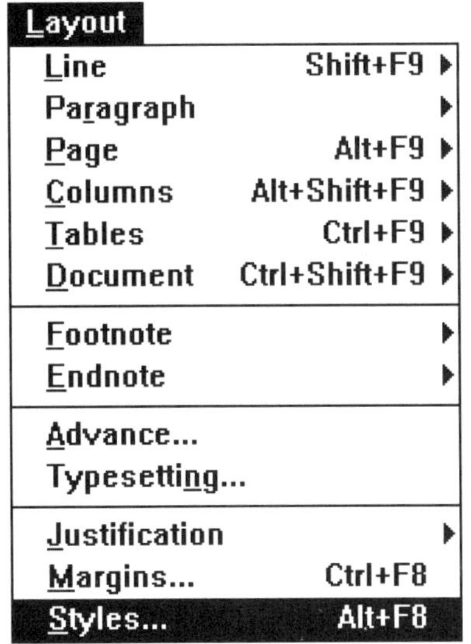

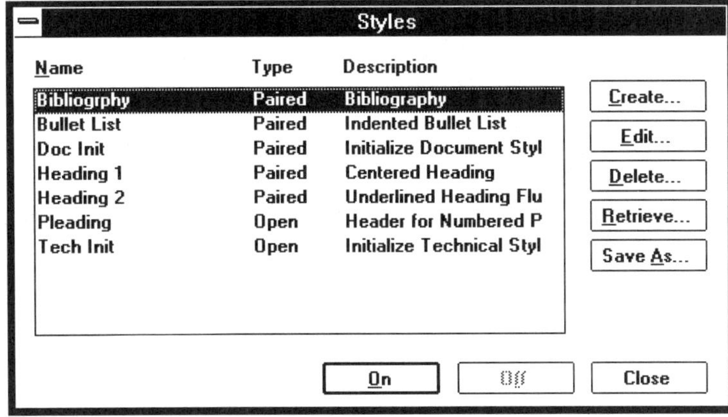

Figure 15-4. *The Styles command from the* ***Layout*** *menu is used to create, edit, delete, and manage styles.*

The *Styles* dialog box (Figure 15-4) lists the names of all styles that exist within the currently loaded style file. If your dialog box contains no style names, don't panic just yet. What has happened is that your *Styles* section of the *Location of Files* dialog box of Figures 15-2 and 15-3 has not been set up correctly. If the ***library.sty*** file name is not contained in the *Filename* section of Figure 15-3, you will not see the styles shown in Figure 15-4. Your ***library.sty*** file may be in a different directory than ours—search around your hard disk to find this file. In Figure 15-4, the style file ***library.sty*** has been loaded automatically.

As you can see, in Figure 15-4, there are several styles listed in this dialog box and, for each style, a *Name*, a *Type*, and a brief *Description* is provided. These listed styles are the styles to which you currently have access.

Along the right-hand side of the *Styles* dialog box (Figure 15-4) are the command buttons which allow you to *Create*, *Edit*, *Delete*, *Retrieve*, and *Save* styles and style files.

To load a new style file, select the *Retrieve* button from among the command buttons along the right-hand side of the dialog box. Select this button now and the *Retrieve Styles* dialog box of Figure 15-5 will appear. If your *Files* list box contains different files, make sure you are viewing the directory into which WordPerfect installs its sample style files.

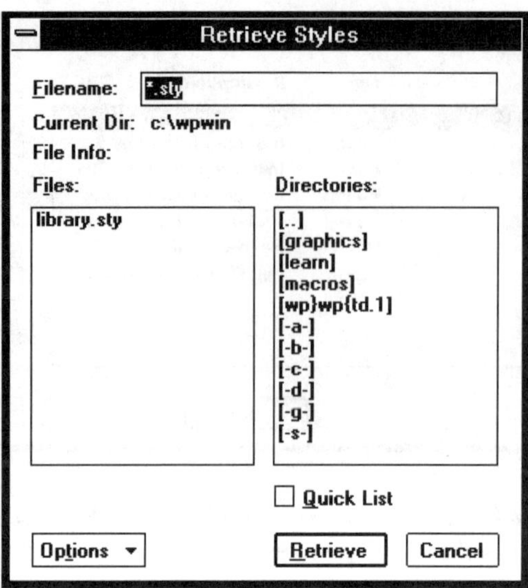

Figure 15-5. After selecting the Retrieve button from Figure 15-4, the Retrieve Styles dialog box will appear.

In Figure 15-5, the *Retrieve Styles* dialog box has appeared, asking you to select a style file to retrieve. If your dialog box of Figure 15-4 contains no style names, select the style file ***library.sty*** from your Figure 15-5 dialog box, and click on **OK**. (As suggested above, if ***library.sty*** is not listed in your Figure 15-5 dialog box, you may have to move to a different directory. By default, styles files are located in the ***wpwin*** directory.)

If your *Styles* dialog box looks the same as the one in Figure 15-4, listing the same style names, there is no need to load the style file ***library.sty*** again. However, if you happen to do this, you may see the Figure 15-6 dialog box. This is not a problem; it is just WordPerfect's way of saying that it is about to load in a style file that contains some style names that are the same as those already loaded. This message prevents you from accidentally overwriting styles when loading in different style files. However, in this case, you may just click on *Yes* or *No*—the result will be the same.

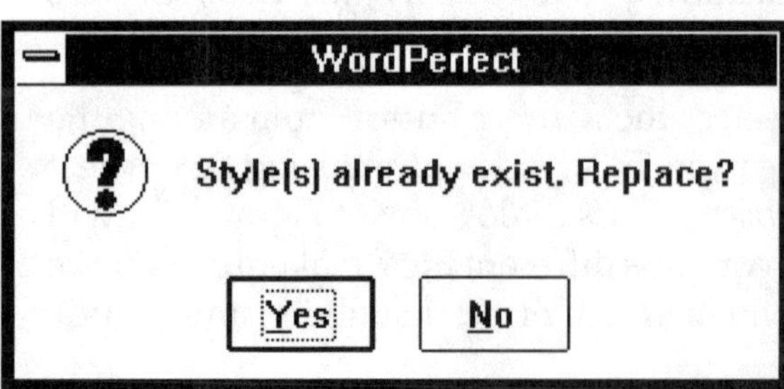

Figure 15-6. This dialog box appears when WordPerfect thinks you may be overwriting styles. However, in this case, it may occur if you accidentally loaded the same style file twice.

Whatever the case, your *Styles* dialog box should now look like the one shown in Figure 15-4.

When loading style files, a newly loaded style file does not replace the currently loaded style file. Any styles contained in the newly retrieved style file are added to the list of current styles.

In this manner, you can retrieve any number of style files using the *Retrieve* button and have access to all styles within these style files simultaneously.

If you do load several style files, it is quite possible that two totally different style files may well both have an identical style name, such as *Heading*. When this occurs, and you try to load both styles together, the dialog box of Figure 15-6 will appear. If you choose *Yes*, the style from the style file about to be loaded will overwrite the existing style. If you choose *No*, the existing style will remain, and the style of the same name will not be loaded from the style file still to be loaded.

Creating a paired style

The *Styles* dialog box will list all styles currently available for immediate use in WordPerfect. Each style is listed under three headings: the *Name* of the style, the *Type* of the style, and a brief *Description* of each style. As you create a new style, you will be asked to *Name* the style, define the style *Type*, and create a brief *Description* of the style for the benefit of you and other users.

In this chapter, you are going to create a style for a heading. The definition of this style will be:

Times Roman font

24 points

Bold

Centered

To create a new style, your first step is to select the *Create* button from the *Styles* dialog box of Figure 15-4. The *Style Properties* dialog box of Figure 15-7 will then appear.

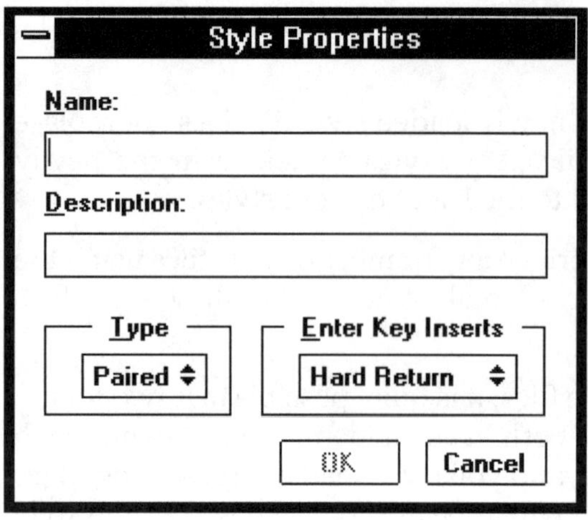

Figure 15-7. The Style Properties dialog box will first appear as you choose to create a new style.

The *Style Properties* dialog box (Figure 15-7) is used to define the style. In this dialog box, you enter the name, type, and description of the style.

As you are creating a style for a heading, call this style *Heading*. This name must be entered in the *Name* text box (Figure 15-8).

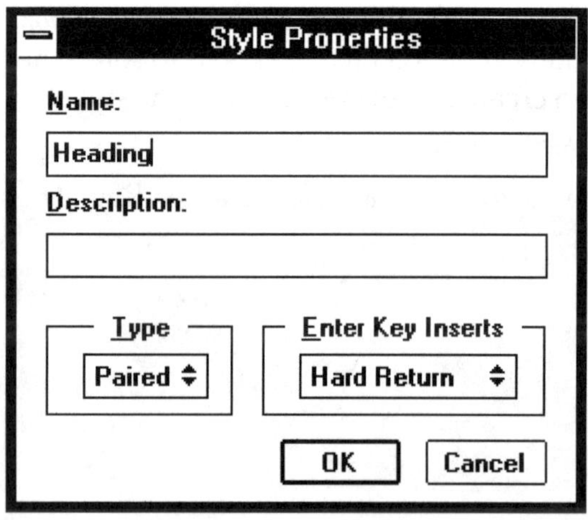

Figure 15-8. Enter the name of the style in the Name text box.

After entering the *Name* of the style, you should enter a brief description for this style, stating its purpose and its use. This description is entered in the *Description* text box (Figure 15-9).

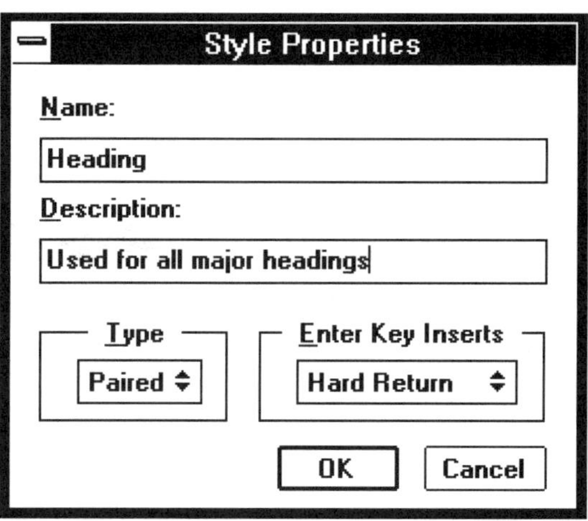

Figure 15-9. *Enter a brief description of the style in the Description text box.*

In Figure 15-9, a brief *Description* has been entered—in this case, the string "Used for all major headings". You are limited to 54 characters when creating a style description.

The style *Type* must then be defined—it is here that you determine whether this will be a *paired* style, or an *open* style. *Open* styles are generally used for document type formatting and *paired* styles are the type generally used for formatting small amounts, or paragraphs, of text. As you are creating a *Heading* style, make sure the pop-up list box under *Type* reads *Paired*.

Finally, as this is a *paired* style, you must define the *Enter Key Inserts* option. This lets you define how the Enter key, on your keyboard, affects a style.

If *Hard Return* is selected for *Enter Key Inserts*, the Enter key functions as normal. Keep this option selected.

If *Style Off* is selected for *Enter Key Inserts*, using the Enter key will automatically turn the style off. For styles such as the one you are creating, this is a handy option, as it frees you from having to turn the style off manually at the end of a paragraph. This option is best for styles that will rarely be used for more than one paragraph at a time.

If *Style Off/On* is selected for *Enter Key Inserts*, the Enter key will turn the style off, and then back on again. This makes each individual paragraph use a style on and a style off code.

After filling out the *Style Properties* dialog box, click on **OK** to actually create the style. The *Style Editor* screen, shown in Figure 15-10, will then appear.

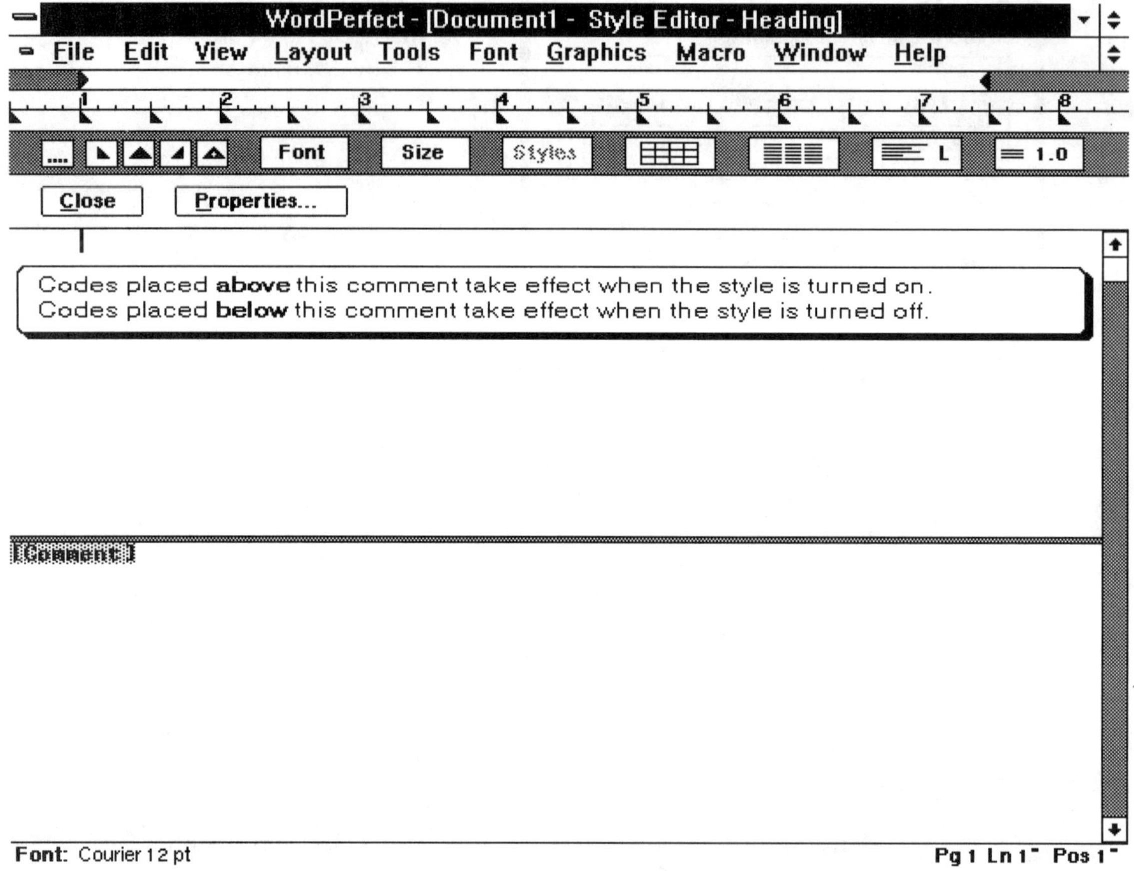

Figure 15-10. *The Style Editor screen.*

As you can see from Figure 15-10, the screen splits into two, with a *Reveal Codes* screen at the bottom.

When the screen reaches this stage, you are free to define the style, using standard WordPerfect commands. For example (remembering that the style you were asked to create is Times Roman, 24 point, bold, and centered), you can use the *Font* command in the **Font** menu to set the desired font and size for this style (Figures 15-11 and 15-12).

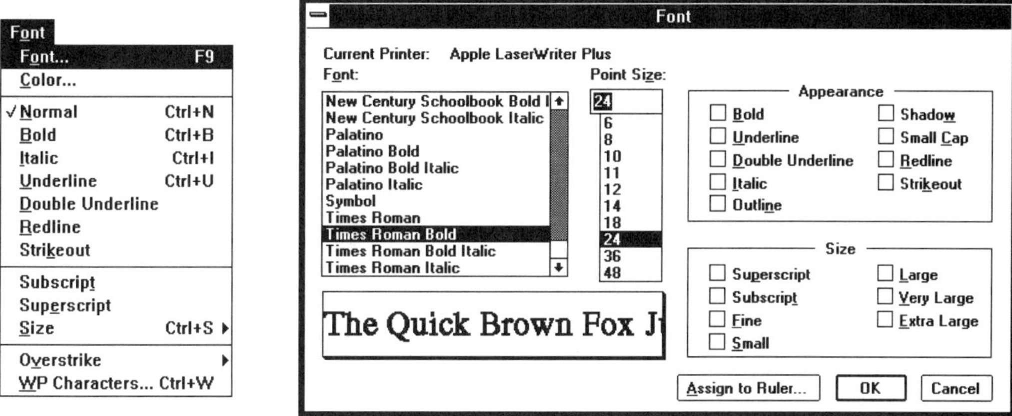

*Figure 15-11. The Font command in the **Font** menu is an example of one of the many commands that you can use to create formatting instructions for inclusion in a style.*

In Figure 15-11, the *Font* command from the **Font** menu was selected, and the font was set as per specifications—Times Roman, 24 point, bold. Once this has been selected, you can click on **OK**; the result is shown in Figure 15-12.

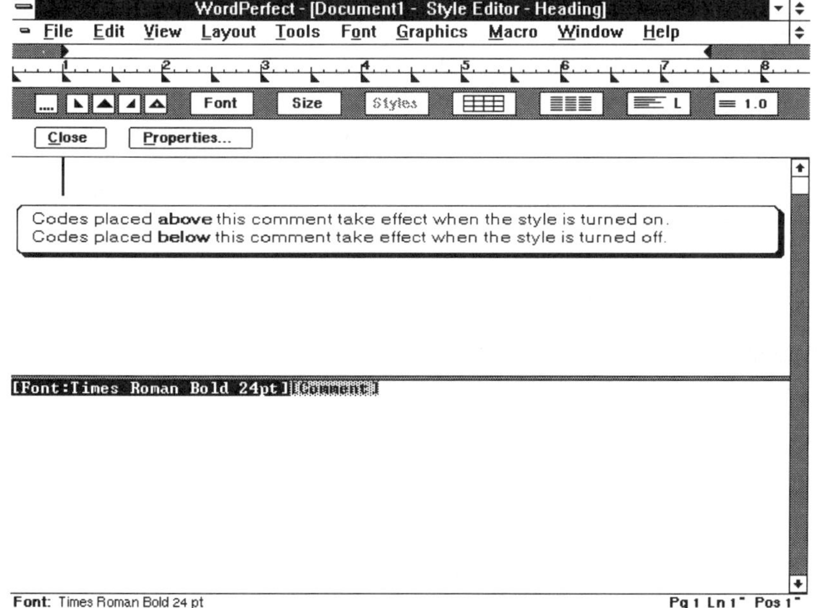

*Figure 15-12. After the font has been set using the Font command in the **Font** menu, the bottom half of the screen lists the codes which make up the current style.*

The other specification for this style was that it must be centered. To implement this attribute, select the *Center* command in the *Justification* fly-out menu in the **Layout** menu (Figure 15-13).

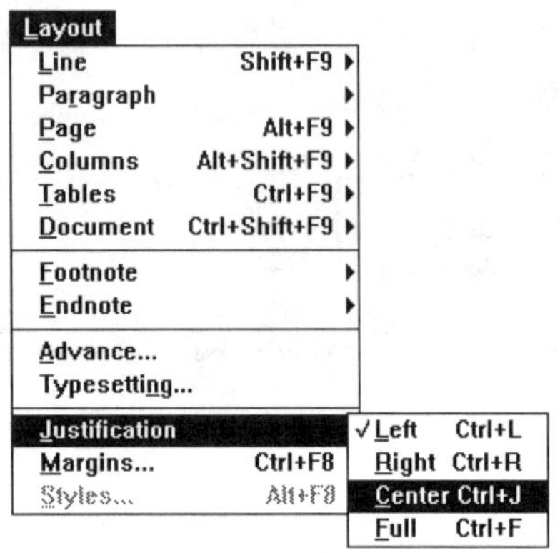

Figure 15-13. *Selecting a command, such as the one illustrated, will add this additional formatting instruction to the style being created.*

After selecting the *Justification/Center* command, the appropriate code is then added to the style definition as shown in Figure 15-14.

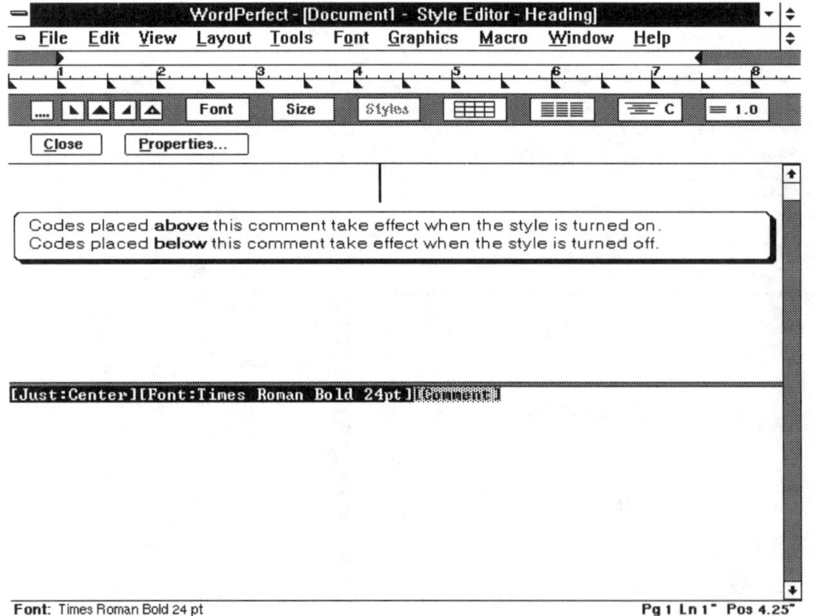

Figure 15-14. *The code for centering the paragraph is added to the other codes that define this style.*

This process is repeated, selecting any commands you wish, until such time as you have defined the style to your satisfaction.

You may have noticed that the top half of the *Style Editor* screen (Figure 15-14) is itself split in two halves (Figure 15-15).

Codes placed **above** this comment take effect when the style is turned on.
Codes placed **below** this comment take effect when the style is turned off.

Figure 15-15. *A comment is placed in the middle of the top half of the screen.*

The caption in this comment is quite self-explanatory. If the flashing text cursor appears above this comment (which it will by default), any commands you select will affect the style you are creating.

If the flashing text cursor appears below this comment (i.e. if you click the mouse button below it), any commands selected will affect text immediately after this style is turned off. This feature will make more sense as you start applying styles.

When you are satisfied with your style specifications, select the **Close** button of Figure 15-14 to return to the *Styles* dialog box of Figure 15-16. The style you just created—*Heading*—now appears in the list of styles.

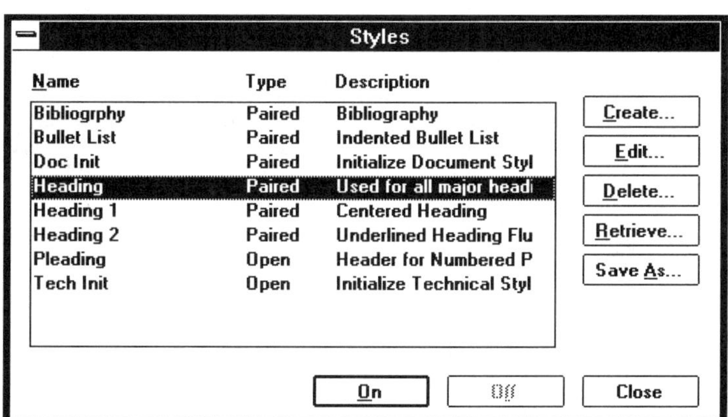

Figure 15-16. *The style you created, Heading, now appears in the list of styles, along with the style Type, and Description.*

If your *Styles* dialog box is the same as Figure 15-16, select the *Close* button to return to the editing screen.

Applying a paired style

To test how your newly created style works, you must have some text on the screen. Do not open a new file, as it is possible you may lose the style you just created. Rather, enter these two paragraphs on the screen (Figure 15-17).

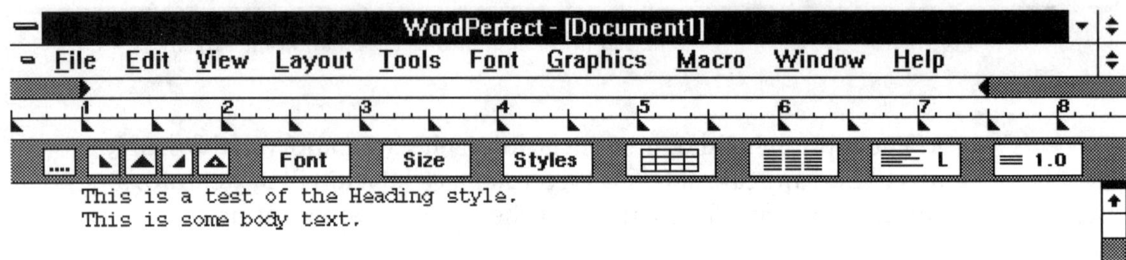

Figure 15-17. *To test the style you just created, type in these two paragraphs. Do not open a new file.*

Assume that you want to apply the style you just created—*Heading* —to the first paragraph on screen. To select this paragraph, quadruple-click the mouse on it, so that it becomes highlighted in reverse video (Figure 15-18).

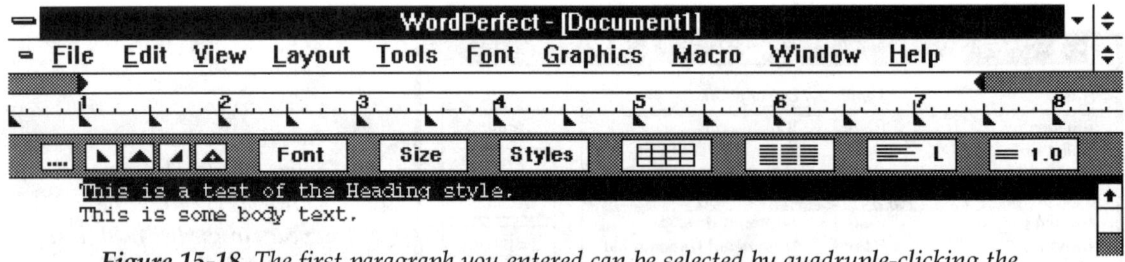

Figure 15-18. *The first paragraph you entered can be selected by quadruple-clicking the mouse on it. Alternatively, you can insert the mouse cursor in this paragraph, and choose the Select/Paragraph command from the* ***Edit*** *menu.*

Now, hold the mouse button down on the *Styles* button in the ruler (Figure 15-19). (If your ruler is not visible, select the *Ruler* command from the **View** menu.) You can see, in the list that appears, that all current styles are included. Release the mouse button on the style *Heading* to select that style (Figure 15-20).

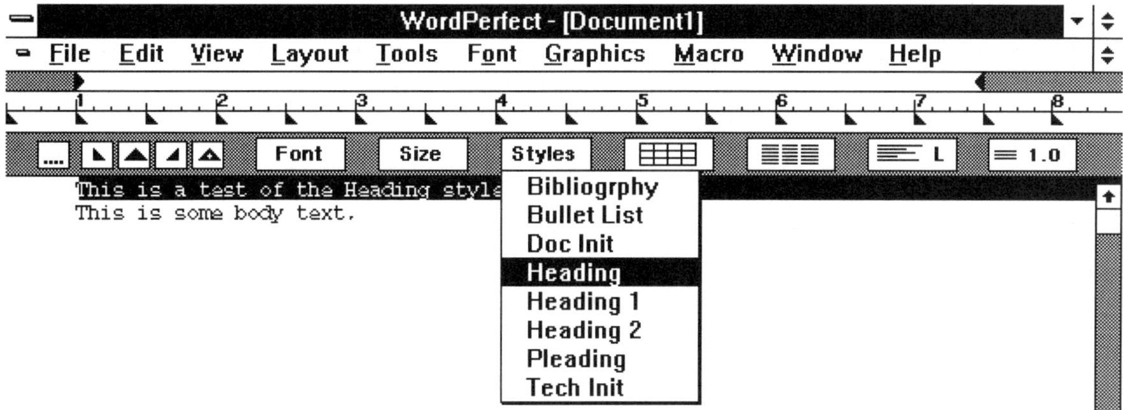

Figure 15-19. The Styles button in the ruler can be used to apply styles to selected text on screen.

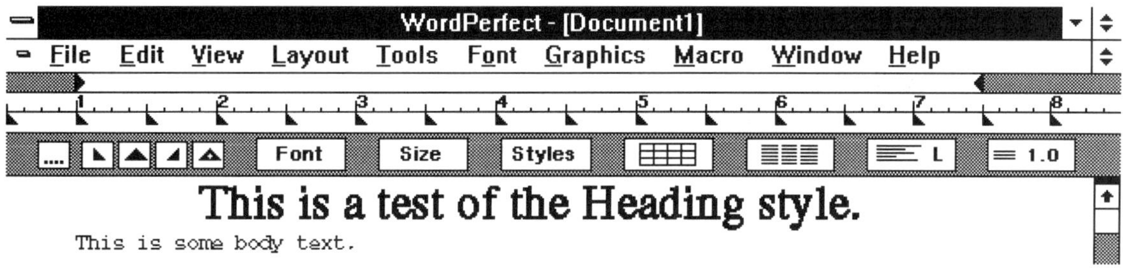

Figure 15-20. Here you see the result of selecting the style you created—the paragraph selected in Figure 15-18 now takes on the attributes as defined by the style, Heading.

In Figure 15-20, the style has been applied to the selected paragraph. *Paired styles* can be applied to any amount of selected text—from one word to several pages. However, depending on the formatting instructions, you may get undesirable results.

For this reason, it is best to apply any *paired styles* you create to entire paragraphs, rather than a few selected words, or parts of paragraphs.

Turning a paired style on/off

In the above example (**Applying a paired style**), a paragraph was selected, and the style applied to it.

As with any paired code, a *paired* style can be turned on (Figure 15-19) without having any text selected at all. If this is done, a code turning the style on, is placed into the document at the position of the text cursor. That style then formats the text following the *style on* code, until such time as a *style off* code is found. A *style off* code is inserted the same way as the *style on* code. With no text selected, select the style from the *Styles* button (Figure 15-19) that you wish to turn off.

Using open styles

In the last few pages, you have seen how to create and apply a *paired* style. Creating an *open* style is achieved in the same manner as creating a *paired* style, as long as you remember the fundamental differences between *open* styles and *paired* styles. The Figure 15-7 *Style Properties* dialog box is filled out the same way—except that the *Enter Key Inserts* section is not applicable and therefore cannot be selected. Clicking on **OK** in the Figure 15-9 dialog box provides the Figure 15-10 *Style Editor* screen with one difference—the *Codes placed above...* and *Codes placed below...* box (see below) is not required and does not appear.

Codes placed **above** this comment take effect when the style is turned on.
Codes placed **below** this comment take effect when the style is turned off.

This box does not appear on the Style Editor screen when creating open styles. It is not applicable to this type of style.

Applying an *open* style requires a little more thought, and a slightly different method, than does applying a *paired* style.

There is no point selecting text before applying an *open* style—it does not operate on the 'style on at the start of the selection, style off at the end of the selection' principle. An open code is turned on from where the text cursor is positioned in the document, and cannot be turned off.

Editing styles

To edit a style, select the *Styles* command in the **Layout** menu once again. Using the ruler, a shortcut method for selecting this command is to double-click the mouse on the *Styles* button in the ruler. The dialog box of Figure 15-21 will then appear.

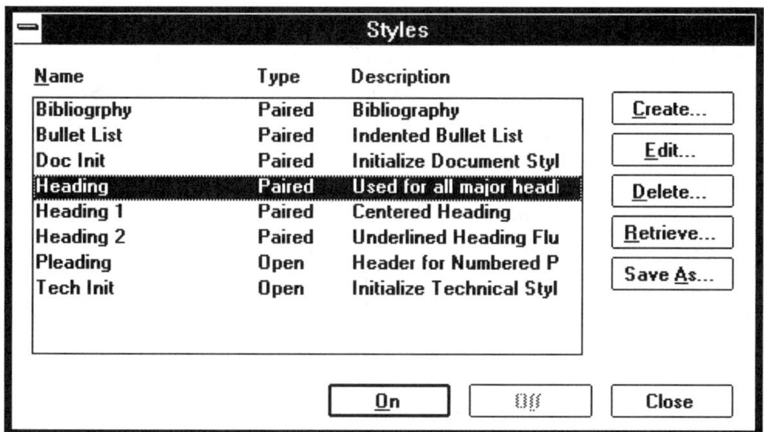

Figure 15-21. *The Styles dialog box.*

If you wish to edit any style—for example, change the typesize, the typestyle, or the margin that a particular style uses—you first select that style from the list of styles in the *Styles* dialog box (Figure 15-21). In this case, select the style you created: *Heading*.

After selecting the style you wish to edit, select the *Edit* button. The *Style Editor* screen will then re-appear (Figure 15-22).

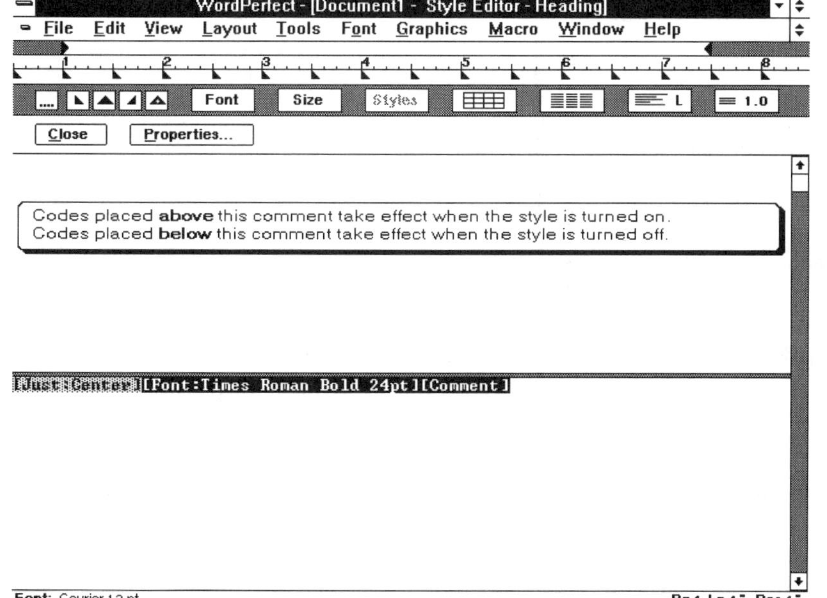

Figure 15-22. *The Style Editor screen re-appears when editing a style.*

To *add* formatting instructions to this style, you simply select the commands from the WordPerfect menus that contain these instructions, in exactly the same way as you did to create the style in the first place.

To *remove* formatting instructions from this style, you must use the bottom half of the screen—the *Reveal Codes* section. Every code that goes into making the current style is listed at the bottom of the screen. If you click the mouse on a particular code and press the Del key on the keyboard, that code will disappear.

To edit the style *Description*, style *Name*, or style *Type*, you can select the *Properties* button of Figure 15-22. The *Style Properties* dialog box that appeared after you initially selected the *Create* button (Figure 15-7) will re-appear, allowing you to edit any entries made in this dialog box (Figure 15-23). If you change the style name, WordPerfect will ask you for confirmation in a warning dialog box. Choose *Yes* or *No* as you require.

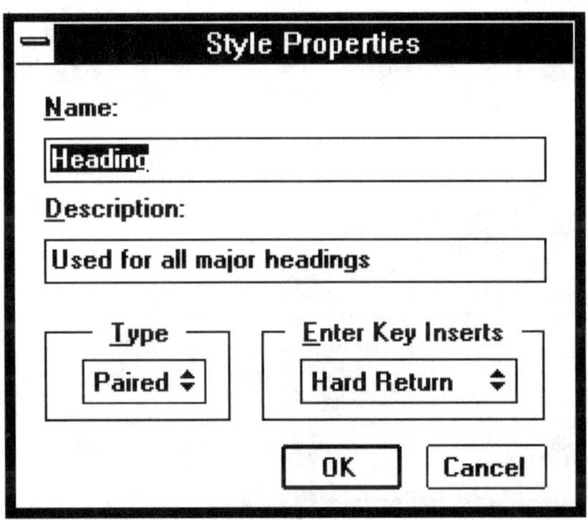

Figure 15-23. *The Style Properties dialog box can be edited after selecting the Properties button in Figure 15-22.*

After you have made any necessary changes to the dialog box of Figure 15-23, click on **OK** to save these changes and return to the *Style Editor* screen of Figure 15-22. To return to the *Styles* dialog box of Figure 15-21, after editing the style formatting instructions, click on the *Close* button of Figure 15-22.

Deleting styles

To delete a style from the *Styles* dialog box (Figure 15-21), select the style to be deleted from the list and click on the *Delete* button. The dialog box of Figure 15-24 will appear.

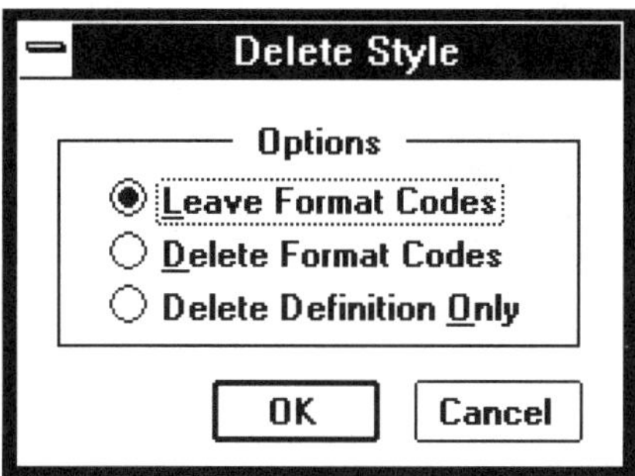

Figure 15-24. *The Delete style dialog box gives you several options.*

The options you have when deleting a style are quite simple:

Leave Format Codes will remove the style name from the list and the style name from the document (assuming that this style has been applied in the document somewhere). However, all the individual codes that go to make up the style will remain in the document as individual codes, not as part of a style.

Delete Format Codes will remove the style name from the list, and also all trace of any codes involved with this style (assuming this style has been applied somewhere in the text). In effect, it removes the style and all evidence and effect of the style from the document.

Delete Definition Only will only remove the style from this list. If the style has been applied in the text anywhere, the style remains in the text, as do all the codes related to that style.

From these options, you can make a selection, and click on **OK**. The appropriate action is then taken by WordPerfect.

Saving style files

After you have created styles, edited styles, and retrieved styles, you can save the list of current styles in the *Styles* dialog box in one file so that, in future, you only need to load that one file to gain this list of styles back.

Remember, as discussed earlier in this chapter, all styles created in the active document are saved with the document automatically—you do not have to create a file and save them to this file. Save styles to a file only if you wish to use them in other documents.

Saving a style file is quite easy; simply select the *Save* button. The *Save Styles* dialog box of Figure 15-25 will appear.

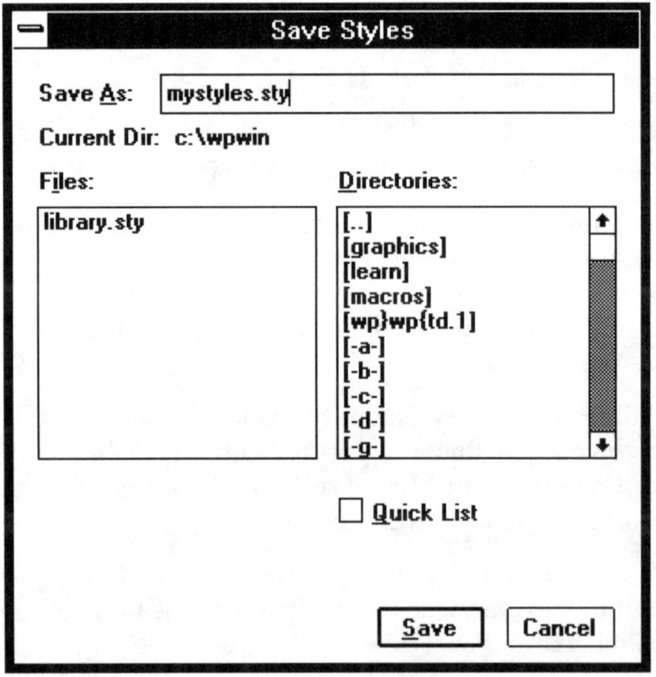

***Figure 15-25.** The Save Styles dialog box is much like any other Save dialog box in WordPerfect—enter the name of the style file in the Save As text box and click on Save.*

As with any other *Save* dialog box in WordPerfect (and all windows programs), you are free to determine into which drive and directory to save the file, using the *Directories* list box.

Once you have determined into which directory you wish to save the file, enter the desired file name in the *Save As* text box and click on *Save*. The style file is then saved to disk.

To load this style file in at any later stage, use the steps as described in the **Loading style files** earlier in this chapter.

To make a certain style file appear as the default style file when a new document is loaded, see the section earlier in this chapter on **Style defaults**.

Hints and Tips

What else can be included in a style?

Styles that you create using methods described in this chapter need not only contain codes. They may contain graphics, tables, or words. For example, follow these steps to create an open code, which includes a graphic:

Start a new document, by selecting the *New* command from the **File** menu.

Select the *Styles* command from the **Layout** menu.

Select the *Create* button from the *Styles* dialog box.

In the *Style Properties* dialog box that appears (Figure 15-26), make the style *Name* "Logo", edit the *Description* line to read "Logo, to appear at top of page", and make the *Type* of style *Open*. Then click on **OK**.

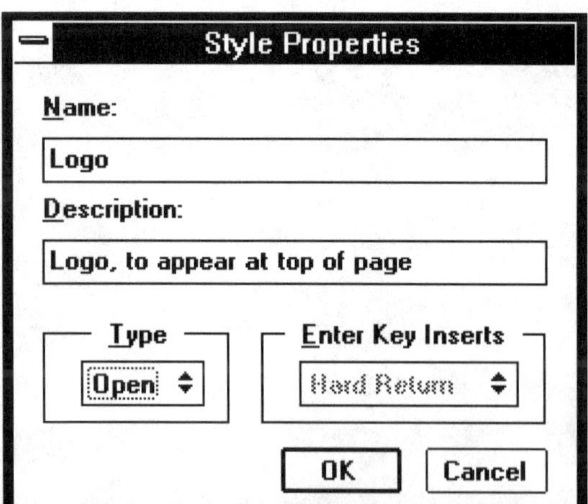

Figure 15-26. *Here is the Style Properties box, filled out as per instructions.*

You will now be at the *Style Editor* screen. Use the *Margins* command in the **Layout** menu to set the *Left* and *Right* margins in this style to 2 inches each (or equivalent) as shown in Figure 15-27.

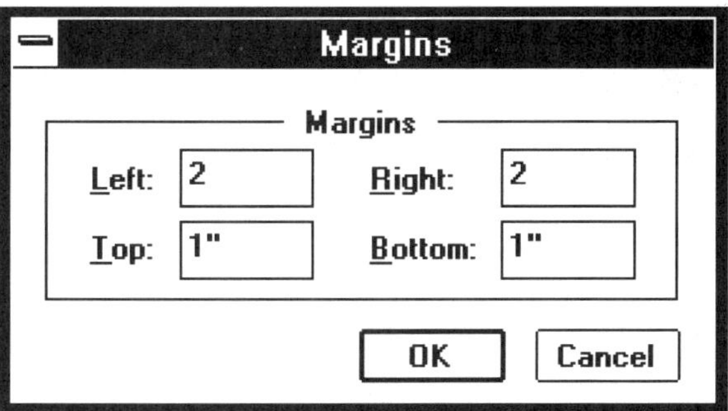

Figure 15-27. *Using the Margins command in the* **Layout** *menu, set the Left and Right margins to 2 inches each.*

Using the *Figure/Retrieve* command in the **Graphics** menu, load a sample graphics file (the actual file does not matter). If you wish to follow this example, we are loading the sample file from the ***learn*** sub-directory called ***globe2-m.wpg***. Click on this file, and click on *Retrieve* in Figure 15-28.

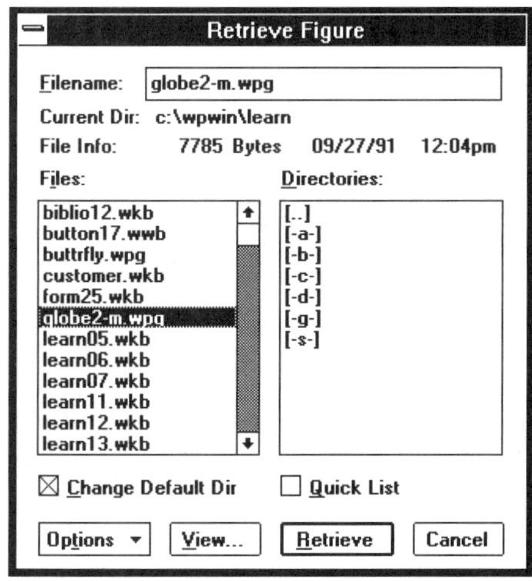

Figure 15-28. *Select the graphics file* ***globe2-m.wpg*** *for this example.*

The selected graphic will then be imported into the *Style Editor* screen (Figure 15-29).

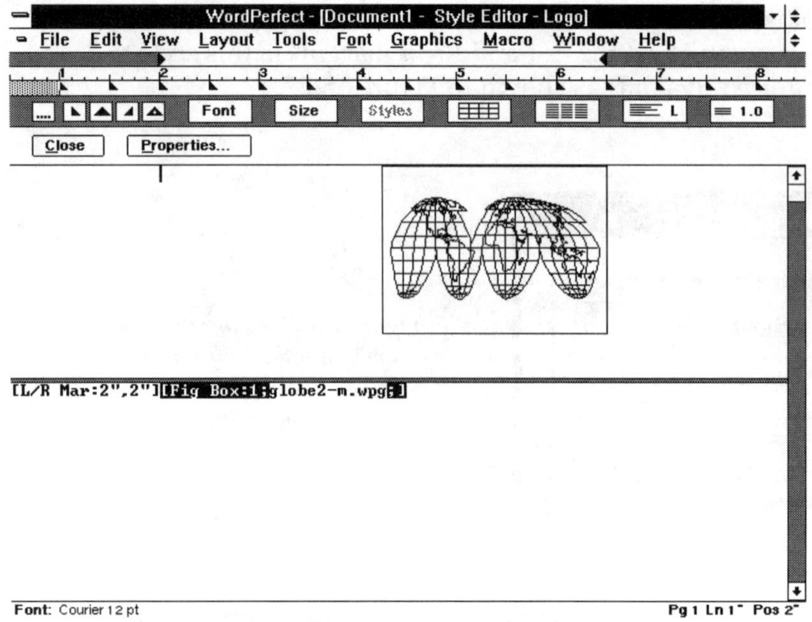

Figure 15-29. The imported graphic appears in the Style Editor screen.

The style is now completed—click on the *Close* button of Figure 15-29 to return to the *Styles* dialog box (Figure 15-30).

Styles

Name	Type	Description
Bibliogrphy	Paired	Bibliography
Bullet List	Paired	Indented Bullet List
Doc Init	Paired	Initialize Document Styl
Heading 1	Paired	Centered Heading
Heading 2	Paired	Underlined Heading Flu
Logo	Open	Logo, to appear at top
Pleading	Open	Header for Numbered P
Tech Init	Open	Initialize Technical Styl

Create... Edit... Delete... Retrieve... Save As...

On Off Close

Figure 15-30. The Styles dialog box lists the Logo open style you have just created.

Return to the WordPerfect screen by selecting the *Close* button in the *Styles* dialog box (Figure 15-30). As you started a new document before changing this style, you should currently have nothing on the screen except a text cursor.

Using the *Styles* button in the ruler (if your ruler is not showing, use the *Ruler* command from the **View** menu), select the style *Logo* (Figure 15-31).

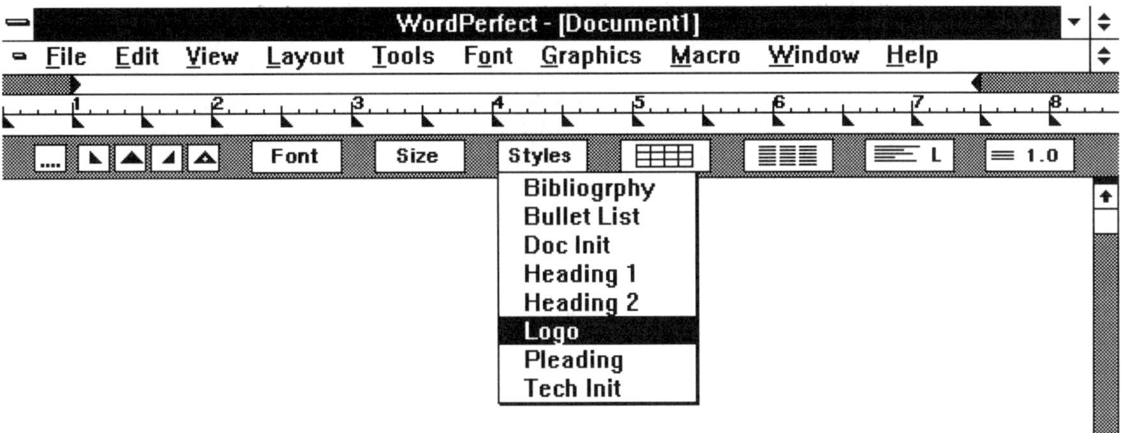

Figure 15-31. *Select the style Logo from the Styles button in the ruler.*

The style and the graphic that was added to it, appear on screen (Figure 15-32). Notice that, as well as the graphic appearing, the margins have also changed to 2 inches on the left and 6.5 inches (2 inches on 8.5 inch paper) on the right.

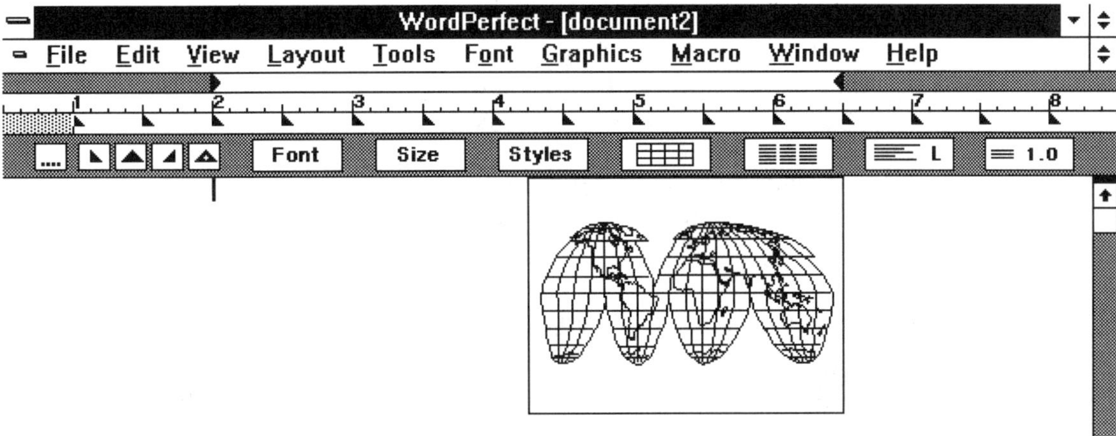

Figure 15-32. *The style Logo makes its appearance felt.*

In this case, you imported a graphic into a style. This graphic could be replaced by some text, a table, an equation, or even several graphics. Almost any WordPerfect feature can be included in a style.

How do styles appear in code?

Every time a style is applied to a document, or text in a document, a code is placed in the text. As usual, however, these codes are not visible until you use the *Reveal Codes* command from the **View** menu.

For example, take a look at some sample text which has had two styles applied to it—*Heading*, the paired code you created earlier in this chapter, and *Logo*, the *open* style you just created.

```
[Open Style:logo]This document has[SRt]
had an open style[SRt]
applied to it.[HRt]
[Style On:Heading]This[SRt]
paragraph[SRt]
has had a[SRt]
paired style[SRt]
applied to it.[HRt]
[Style Off:Heading]This paragraph is just a normal paragraph.
```

Figure 15-33. Styles as they appear in code.

Notice, in Figure 15-33, that the first code reads: [*Open Style: logo*]. This is how an open style appears in codes—always prefixed with the words "Open Style:".

The other style, *Heading*, is prefixed by *"Style On"*, and on the last line, by *"Style Off"*. This is indicative of a paired style—all text between the [*Style on:Heading*] and [*Style off:Heading*] is affected by the style *Heading*.

If you click on a code name in the *Reveal Codes* screen, the code expands to reveal all codes that went into defining that style (Figure 15-34).

```
[Open Style:logo]This document has[SRt]
had an open style[SRt]
applied to it.[HRt]
[Style On:Heading;[Just:Center][Font:Times Roman Bold 24pt]]This[SRt]
paragraph[SRt]
has had a[SRt]
paired style[SRt]
applied to it.[HRt]
[Style Off:Heading]This paragraph is just a normal paragraph.
```

***Figure 15-34.** Clicking on the code: [Style On: Heading] reveals what codes went into making this style.*

Styles — Exercise

This training exercise is designed so that people of all levels of expertise with WordPerfect can use it to gain maximum benefit. In order to do this, the bare exercise is listed below this paragraph on just one page, with no hints. The following pages contain the steps needed to complete this exercise for those who need additional prompting.

Steps in brief

1. *Start a new WordPerfect file.*
2. *Turn off the Auto Code Placement option in the Environment Settings dialog box.*
3. *Create an open style, called Page Format, with the following characteristics: a left margin at 0.75", right margin at 2", Left Justification and Times Roman, 12 point, text.*
4. *Create a paired style, called Text, with the following characteristics: Style Off/On Enter Key Insert option, 2.0 Line Spacing, Centered Justification and Helvetica Bold, 14 point, text.*
5. *Turn on the Page Format style.*
6. *Retrieve the learn18.wkb file.*
7. *Select the heading and apply the Text style to it.*
8. *Select the third paragraph of body text and apply the Text style to it.*
9. *Edit the Text style to have the following attributes: 1.5 Line Spacing, Right Justification, Helvetica, 12 point, Italic text. Also change the style name of Text to Text 2, while keeping the original Text style in the document.*
10. *Select the third paragraph of body text and apply the Text 2 style to it.*

The details for completing these steps are on the following pages.

Steps in detail

1. ***Start a new WordPerfect file.***

If you have just opened WordPerfect, you will be in a new WordPerfect file. If you are working on another WordPerfect document, select the *New* command from the **File** menu. If you are not in WordPerfect, start the program from Windows.

2. ***Turn off the Auto Code Placement option in the Environment Settings dialog box.***

For this exercise you are going to turn the *Auto Code Placement* option off, which by default will be on. This is so you can determine the order in which the codes are used in the styles. The *Auto Code Placement* option is located in the *Environment Settings* dialog box, which is activated by selecting the *Environment* command from the *Preferences* fly-out menu in the **File** menu (Figure 15x-1).

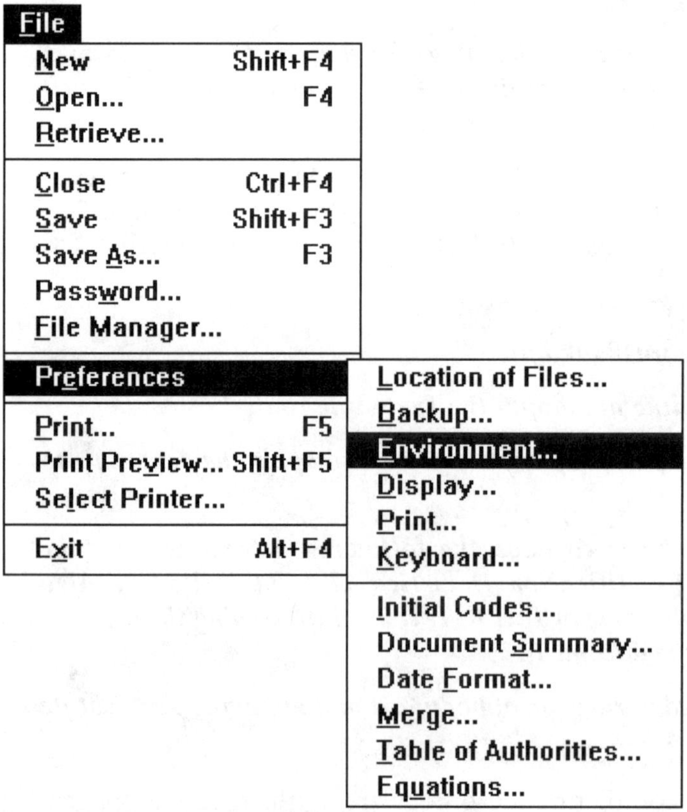

File
New Shift+F4
Open... F4
Retrieve...
Close Ctrl+F4
Save Shift+F3
Save As... F3
Password...
File Manager...
Preferences
Print... F5
Print Preview... Shift+F5
Select Printer...
Exit Alt+F4

Location of Files...
Backup...
Environment...
Display...
Print...
Keyboard...
Initial Codes...
Document Summary...
Date Format...
Merge...
Table of Authorities...
Equations...

***Figure 15x-1**. Select the Preferences/Environment command from the **File** menu.*

In the *Environment Settings* dialog box, deselect the *Auto Code Placement* option by clicking on it. This option is found at the top of the *Settings* section of Figure 15x-2. Then, click on **OK** to return to the editing screen.

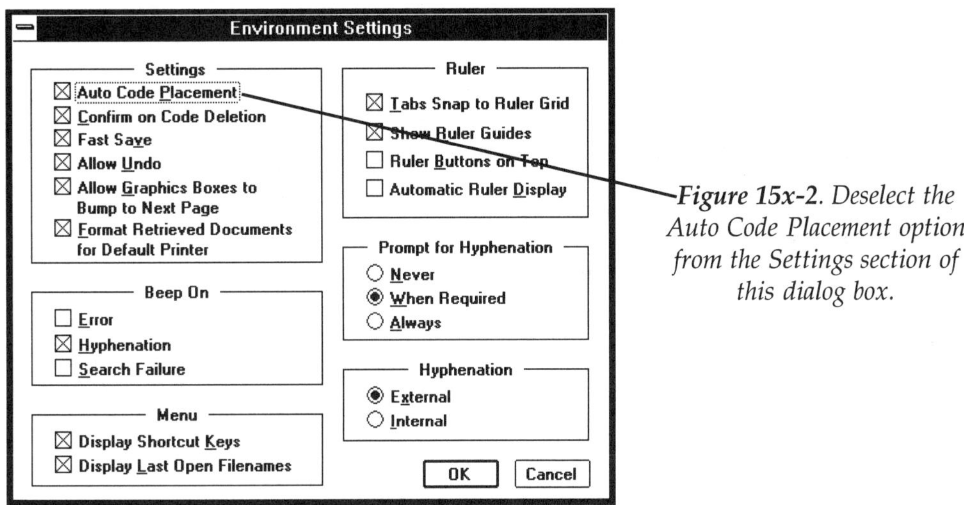

Figure 15x-2*. Deselect the Auto Code Placement option from the Settings section of this dialog box.*

3. ***Create an open style, called Page Format, with the following characteristics: a left margin at 0.75", right margin at 2", Left Justification and Times Roman, 12 point, text.***

You are now ready to start creating your own styles. To do this, select the *Styles* command from the **Layout** menu (Figure 15x-3).

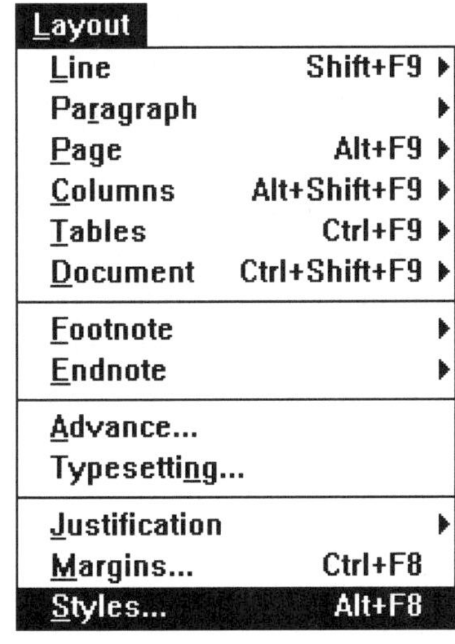

Figure 15x-3*. To create your own styles first select the Styles command from the* ***Layout*** *menu.*

Selecting the *Styles* command from the **Layout** menu, will activate the *Styles* dialog box of Figure 15x-4. If your dialog box is not similar to this, do not worry. The styles in the dialog box of Figure 15x-4 belong to a style file that is provided with WordPerfect. Depending on whether you have this file loaded, these styles may or may not appear.

To now create your own style, click on the *Create* button.

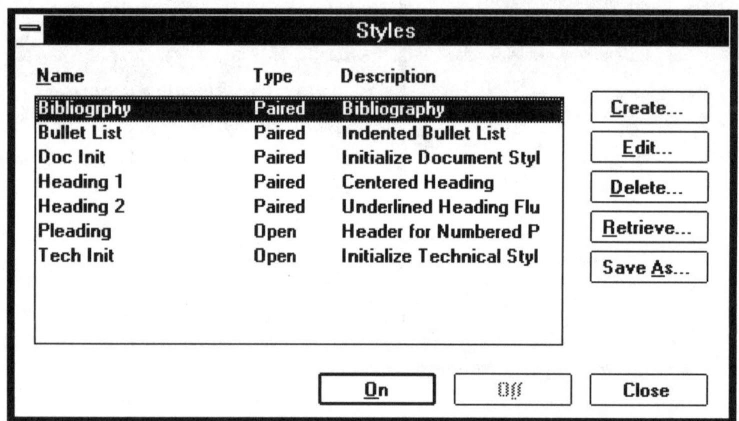

Figure 15x-4. *Once inside the Styles dialog box, click on the Create button.*

After clicking on the *Create* button in the *Styles* dialog box, the *Style Properties* dialog box of Figure 15x-5 is activated. This is the dialog box where you name and describe the style you are about to create. For this exercise, the name you are giving the style is Page Format. Key this name into the text box below the word *Name*. If you wish, you can also key in a description of the style in the text box below the word *Description*.

After keying in the name, hold the mouse down on the word *Paired* in the *Type* section of the dialog box. A small pop-up list appears allowing you to select the *Open* option. Set your dialog box up like that of Figure 15x-5, and click on **OK**. (Note that the *Enter Key Inserts* option is not selectable once you have chosen the *Open Type* of style. It only works with *Paired* styles.)

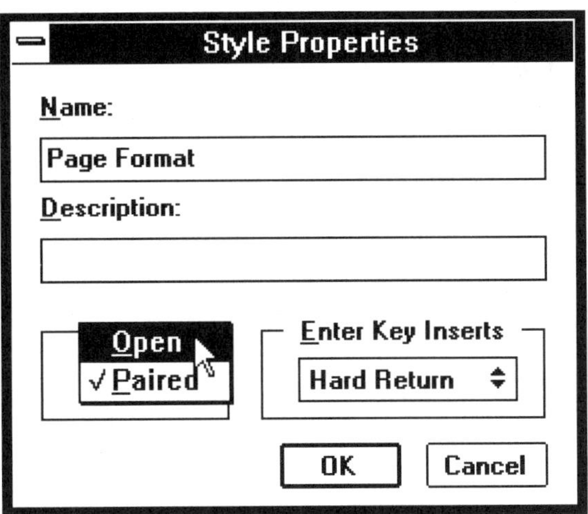

*Figure 15x-5. Key in Page Format in the Name text box, change the Type option to Open, and then click on **OK**.*

Once you have clicked on **OK** in the *Style Properties* dialog box, the *Style Editor* window of Figure 15x-6 is activated. Any commands you now select will be part of the style, and the codes associated with the commands will appear in the *Reveal Codes* window, at the bottom of the screen.

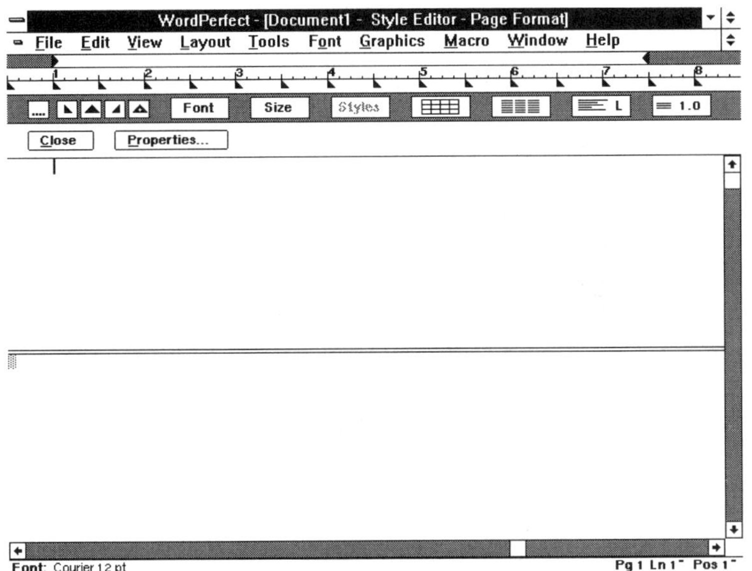

Figure 15x-6. Any commands you select with the Style Editor window active will be part of the style you are creating. The codes, relating to the commands you select, will appear in the Reveal Codes section of the window.

The first option you are setting for this style is the margins. To do this, select the *Margins* command from the **Layout** menu as shown in Figure 15x-7.

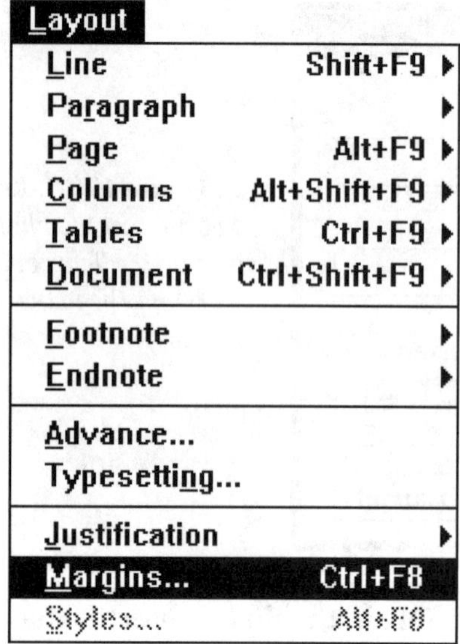

Figure 15x-7. To set the margins for your Page Format style, select the Margins command from the ***Layout*** *menu.*

In the *Margins* dialog box that appears, change the *Left* setting to 0.75 of an inch. Then select the setting in the *Right* box with the mouse (or alternatively, press the Tab key), and change the right margin setting to 2 inches (Figure 15x-8).

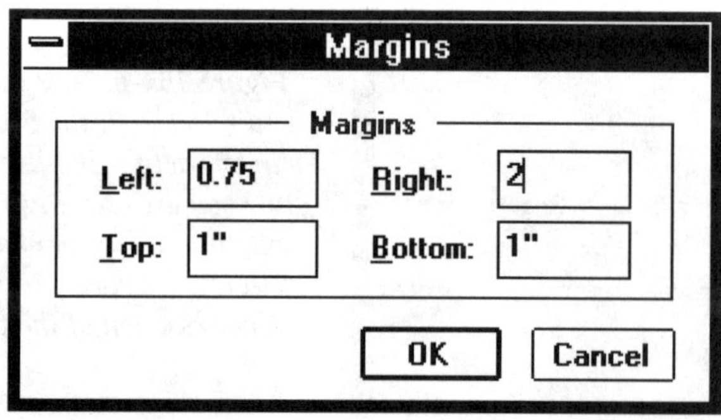

Figure 15x-8. Change the Left setting in the Margins dialog box to 0.75 and the Right setting to 2, then click on ***OK****.*

After clicking on **OK** in the *Margins* dialog box, a margin code will appear in the *Reveal Codes* section of the *Style Editor* window as shown in Figure 15x-9.

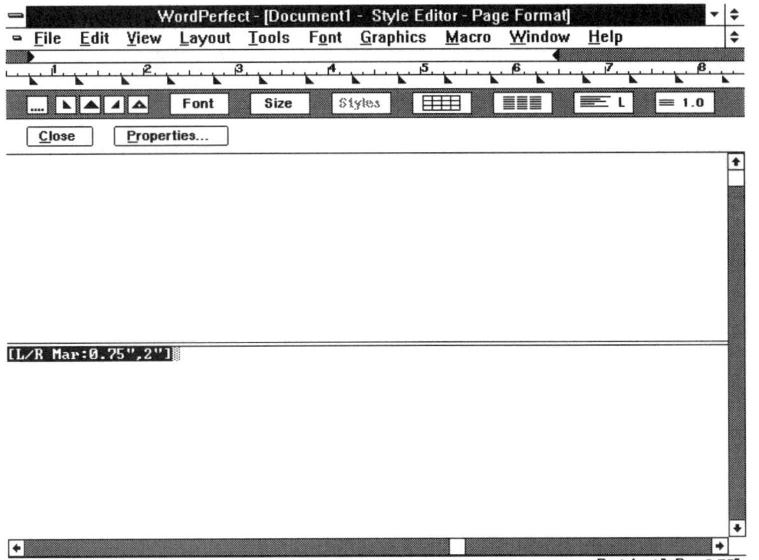

Figure 15x-9. The margin code in the Reveal Codes section of the screen reflects the changes you made in the Figure 15x-8 Margins dialog box.

The next option you will change is the *Justification* option, to *Left*. This can be done through the ruler or through a menu; in this example, use the menu. Select the *Left* option from the *Justification* fly-out menu in the **Layout** menu (Figure 15x-10).

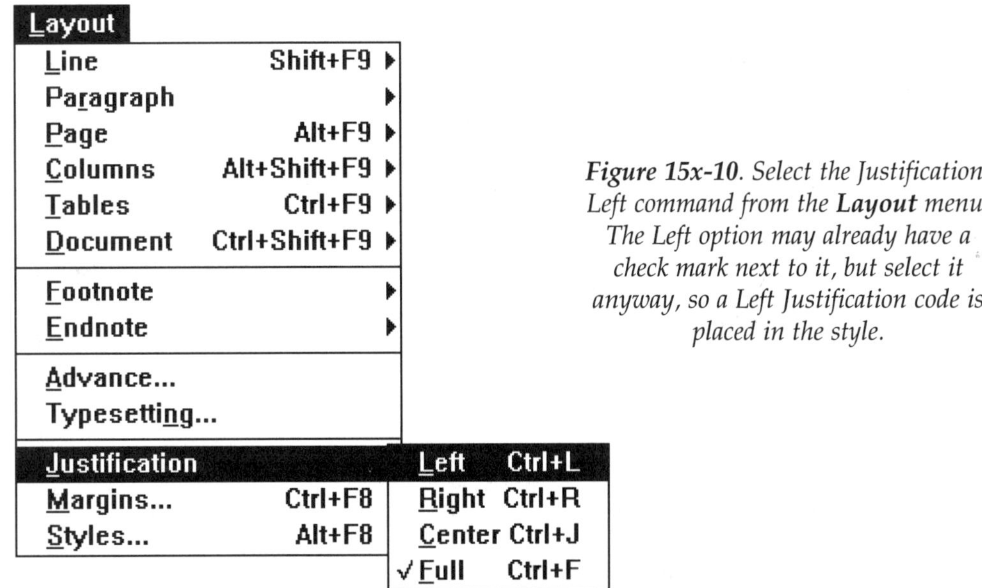

Figure 15x-10. Select the Justification/ Left command from the ***Layout*** *menu. The Left option may already have a check mark next to it, but select it anyway, so a Left Justification code is placed in the style.*

After selecting the *Left* option from the *Justification* fly-out menu, you will see a *Left Justification* code appear in the *Reveal Codes* window (Figure 15x-11).

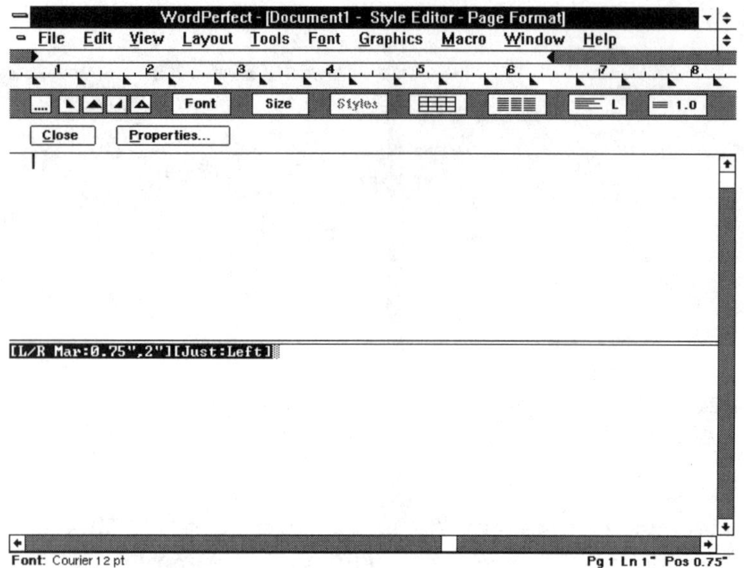

Figure 15x-11. Selecting the Left Justification option will place a Left Justification code in the Reveal Codes window.

The next part of this step is to select a font type and size. To do this, select the *Font* command from the **Font** menu (Figure 15x-12).

Font
Font... F9
Color...
√ Normal Ctrl+N
Bold Ctrl+B
Italic Ctrl+I
Underline Ctrl+U
Double Underline
Redline
Strikeout
Subscript
Superscript
Size Ctrl+S ▸
Overstrike ▸
WP Characters... Ctrl+W

Figure 15x-12. Select the Font command from the ***Font*** *menu in preparation for selecting a font and size for your style.*

The *Font* command activates the *Font* dialog box of Figure 15x-13. Use the scroll bar, in conjunction with the mouse, to locate the Times Roman typeface from the list of fonts available. Once you have located Times Roman, highlight it by clicking on it. Also, click on 12 in the *Point Size* list, if it is not already selected. After making these two changes in the *Font* dialog box, click on **OK**.

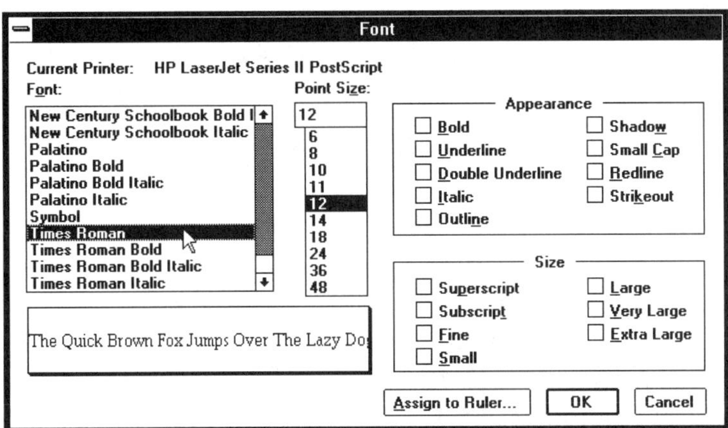

Figure 15x-13. Select the Times Roman option, from the list of available fonts, and then choose 12 from the Point Size list, before clicking on ***OK****.*

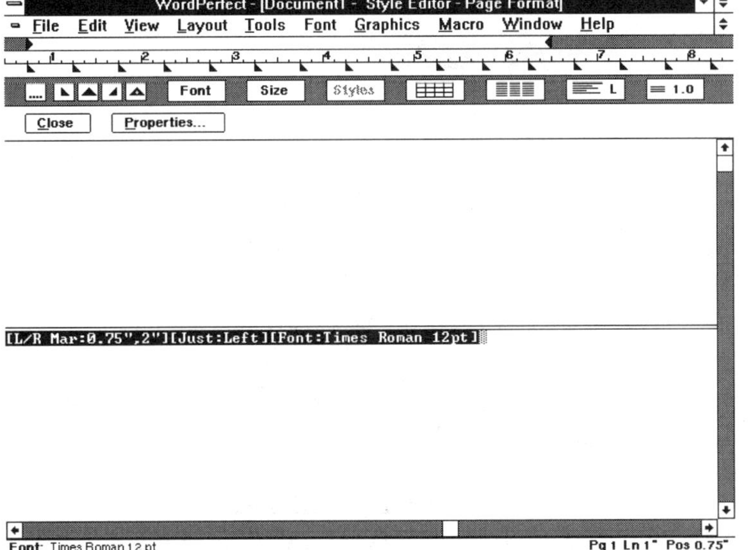

Figure 15x-14. *The changes you made in the Font dialog box are now reflected in the Reveal Codes window.*

Now that you have selected all the required options for the creation of this style, you can close the *Style Editor* window. Simply click on the *Close* button to achieve this (Figure 15x-15).

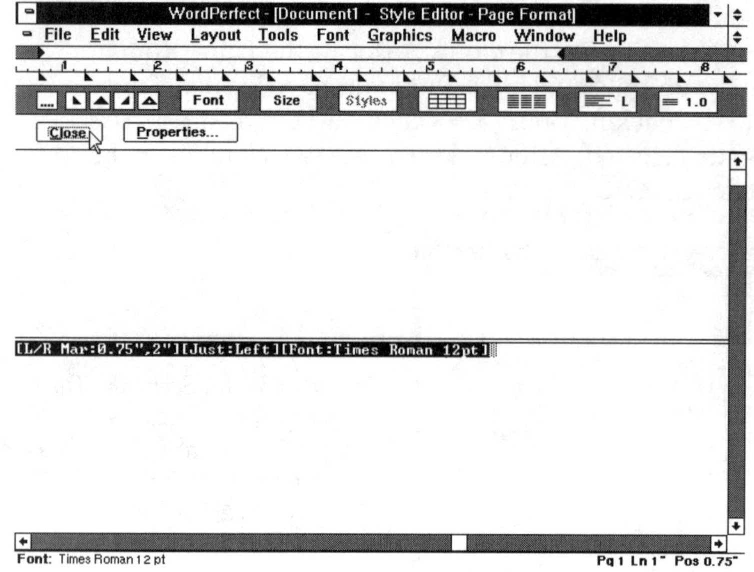

Figure 15x-15. Now that you have set up your style, click on the Close button to exit the Style Editor window.

Clicking on the *Close* button in the *Style Editor* window will return you to the *Styles* dialog box of Figure 15x-16. Do not exit this dialog box as the next step involves the creation of another style. However, in the list of styles, you will see the Page Format style you just created.

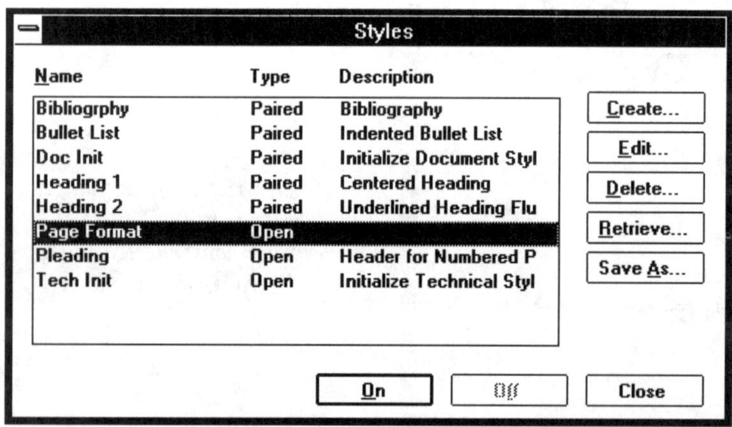

Figure 15x-16. On returning to the Styles dialog box, the style you have just created is included in the list.

4. ***Create a paired style, called Text, with the following characteristics: Style Off/On Enter Key Insert option, 2.0 Line Spacing, Centered Justification and Helvetica Bold, 14 point, text.***

At the end of the last step, you finished in the *Styles* dialog box of Figure 15x-16. Click on the *Create* button in preparation for step 4. This will activate the *Style Properties* dialog box again (Figure 15x-17).

This time, call the style you are about to create, Text. Key this word in the box below *Name*. If you like, you can put in a *Description* as well. This style is to be a *Paired* style, so do not change the *Type* option. Also, change the *Enter Key Inserts* option to *Style Off/On*. This means that, once back in your WordPerfect document, you can turn this style off and on by pressing the Enter key.

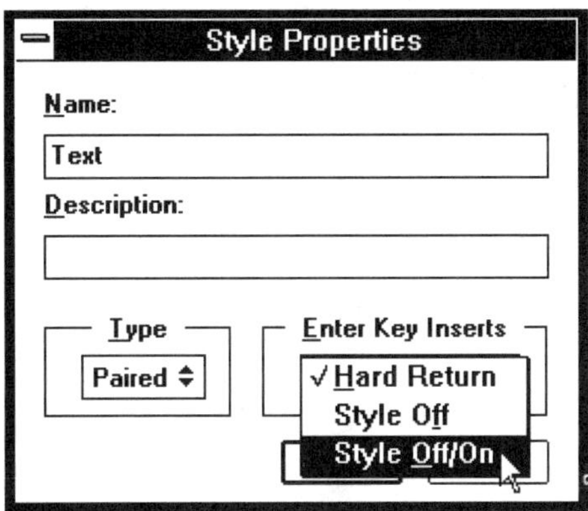

***Figure 15x-17**. Set your Style Properties dialog box up like this one and click on **OK**.*

After clicking on **OK** in the *Style Properties* dialog box, the *Style Editor* window appears again. The first option you are going to apply to this style is a 2.0 *Line Spacing*. If you have the ruler activated, select the 2.0 option from the *Line Spacing* button, at the right of the ruler (Figure 15x-18).

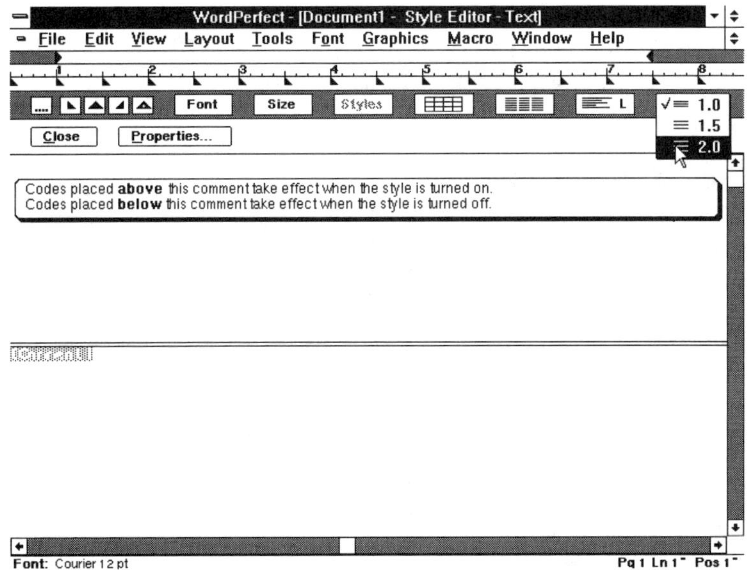

***Figure 15x-18.** Select the 2.0 option from the Line Spacing button in the ruler.*

If you are not currently displaying the ruler, select the *Spacing* command from the *Line* fly-out menu in the **Layout** menu. In the *Line Spacing* dialog box that appears, change the setting to 2.

Now, change the *Justification* option to *Center*. This can also be done through the ruler (Figure 15x-19).

If your ruler is not active, select the *Center* command from the *Justification* fly-out menu in the **Layout** menu.

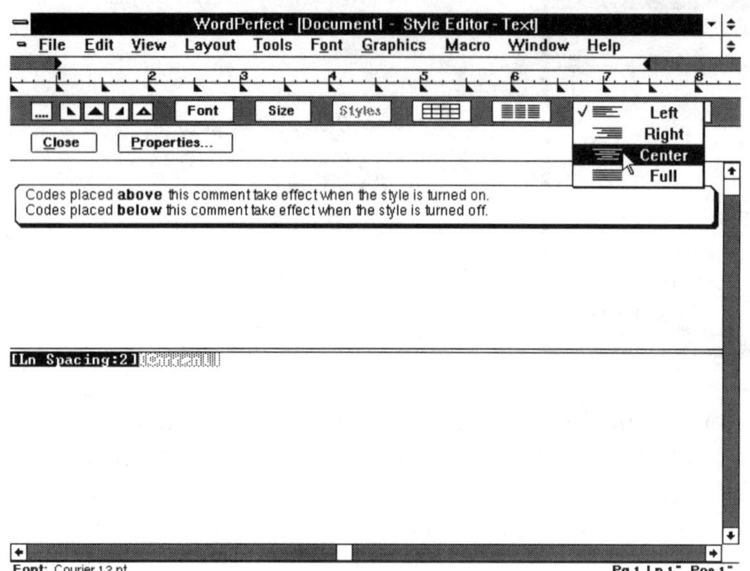

Figure 15x-19*. Change the Justification option to Center by selecting it from the Justification button in the ruler. Also, note the Line Spacing code in the Reveal Codes section of the screen, which appeared after the selection of Figure 15x-18.*

To change the typeface size and style, select the *Font* command from the **Font** menu to activate the *Font* dialog box of Figure 15x-20. Once in this dialog box, highlight the Helvetica Bold font from the list of fonts, and click on 14 in the *Point Size* list.

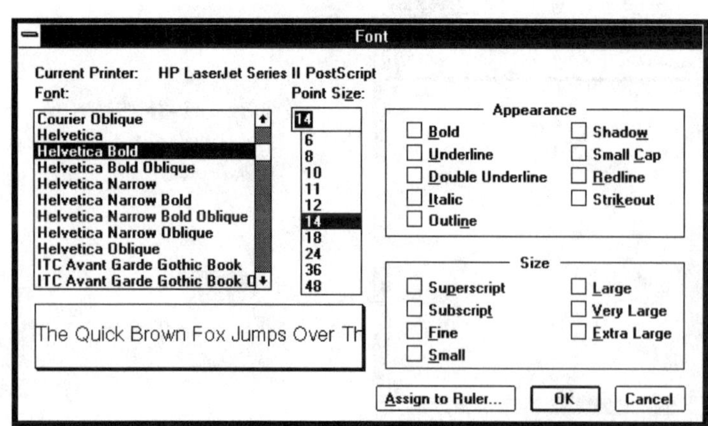

Figure 15x-20*. Locate and select Helvetica Bold from the list of fonts. Click on 14 from the Point Size list, and then click on* ***OK****.*

After clicking on **OK** in the *Font* dialog box of Figure 15x-20, you will see the codes for the changes made in this dialog box (Figure 15x-21). Now that you have finished setting up this style, click on the *Close* button in the *Style Editor* window. This will bring you back to the *Styles* dialog box where the Text style you just created will be in the list of styles.

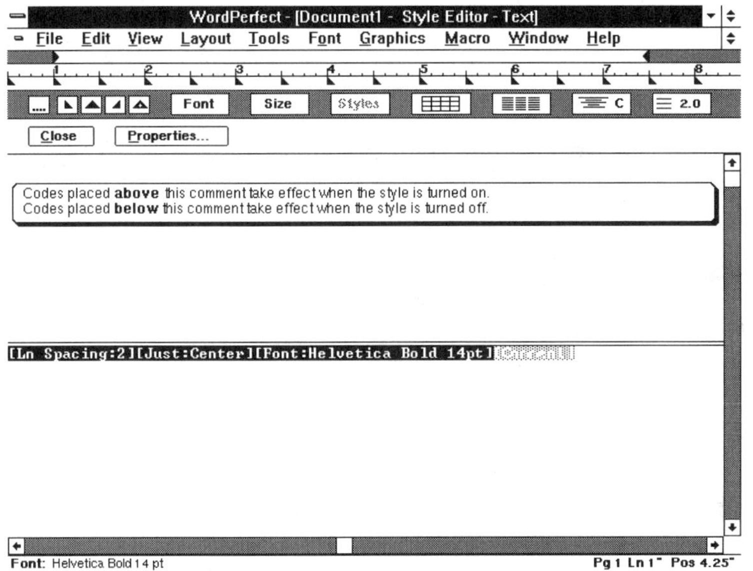

Figure 15x-21. *All the codes for the style you just created appear in the Reveal Codes section of the Style Editor window. Close the Style Editor window to return to the Styles dialog box.*

5. Turn on the Page Format style.

Before exiting the *Styles* dialog box, highlight the Page Format style by selecting it from the list of styles. Then, click on the *On* button (Figure 15x-22). This will return you to your document with the Page Format style active.

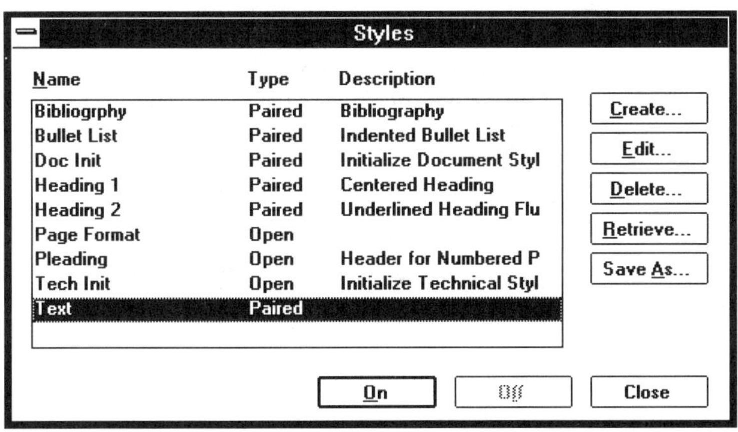

Figure 15x-22. *Select the Page Format style from the list of styles and then click on the On button. The Page Format style will now be active as you return to your document.*

6. Retrieve the learn18.wkb file.

To accomplish this step, first select the *Retrieve* command from the **File** menu to invoke the *Retrieve File* dialog box (Figure 15x-23). Locate the ***learn*** sub-directory in the ***wpwin*** sub-directory. Using the scroll bar to the right of the list of files, find and select the ***learn18.wkb*** file, and then click on the *Retrieve* button (Figure 15x-23).

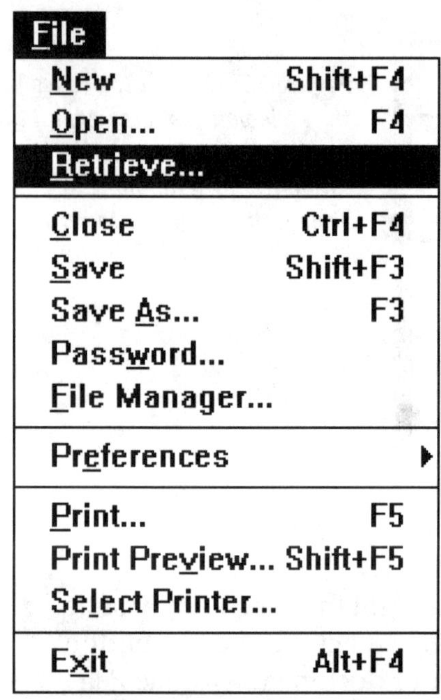

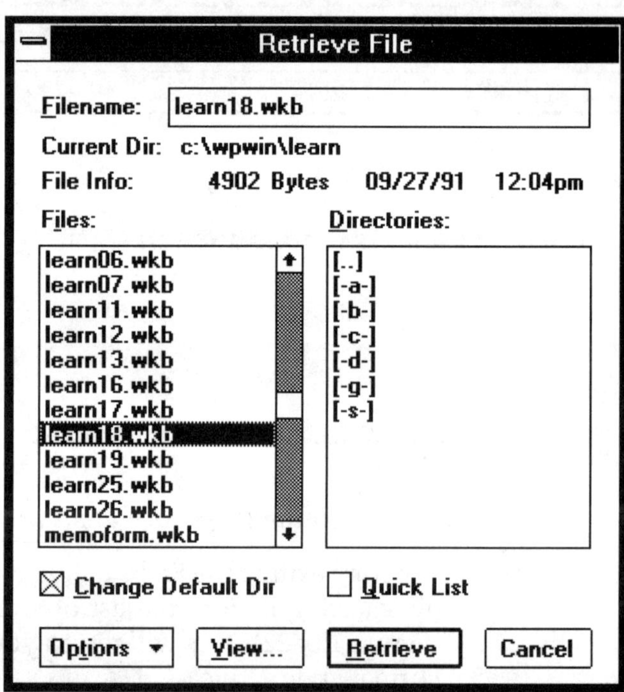

Figure 15x-23. Select the Retrieve command from the ***File*** *menu to gain access to the* ***learn18.wkb*** *file. After highlighting this file from the list of available files in the* ***learn*** *sub-directory, click on the Retrieve button. Alternatively, double-clicking on the filename will achieve the same result.*

Because you have made changes to the current document, you will be asked if you want to insert the selected file into the document (Figure 15x-24), after clicking on the *Retrieve* button. Click on the *Yes* option.

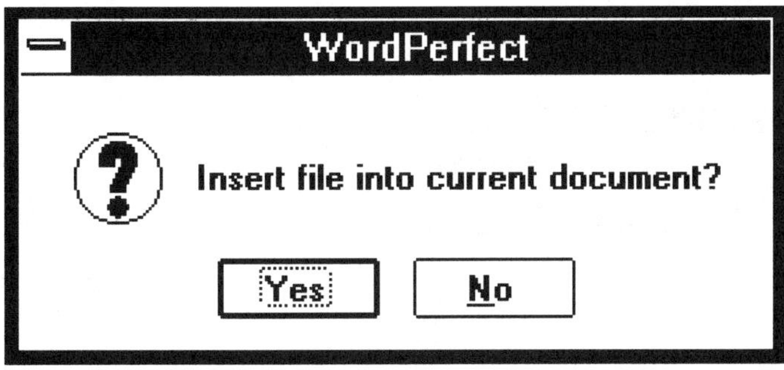

Figure 15x-24. Click on the Yes option when this screen prompt appears.

Because you turned the Page Format style on, the ***learn18.wkb*** file will be retrieved with the Page Format style's attributes now activated.

7. Select the heading and apply the Text style to it.

If your ruler is not active, select the *Ruler* command from the **View** menu, to make this step easier. Using the mouse, swipe the heading of the text so it becomes highlighted in reverse video. Now, when you select the Text style, it will only affect the selected text. Hold the mouse down on the *Styles* button in the ruler so that the list of available styles appears. Select the Text style (Figure 15x-25).

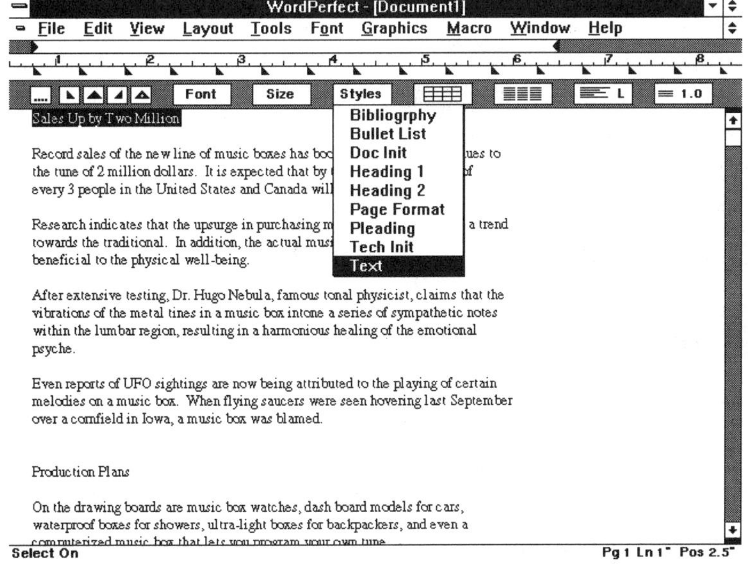

Figure 15x-25. After selecting the heading of the text, choose the Text option from the list of Styles available through the ruler.

The heading of the text has now changed to reflect the attributes of the Text style (Figure 15x-26).

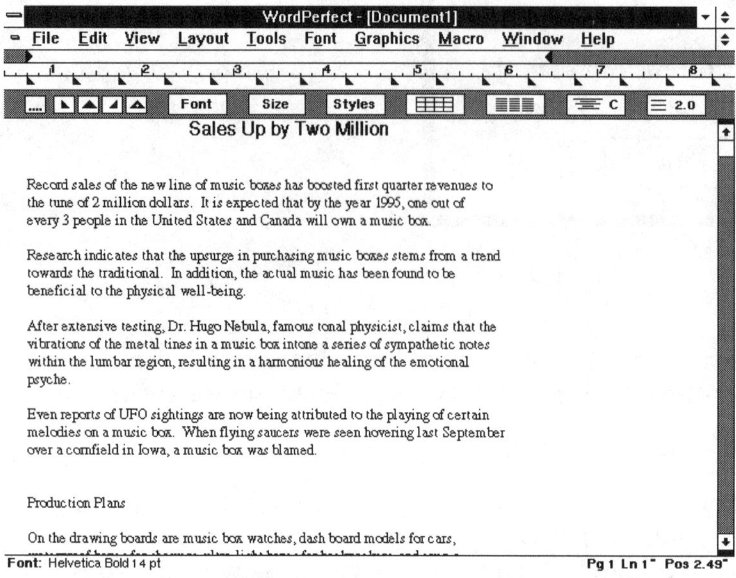

Figure 15x-26*. The text you selected, to which you applied the Text style, has now changed to reflect the attributes of this style.*

8. ***Select the third paragraph of body text and apply the Text style to it.***

The same procedure occurs when applying text to larger paragraphs. Select the third paragraph with the cursor, and choose the Text style from the list of styles in the ruler (Figure 15x-27).

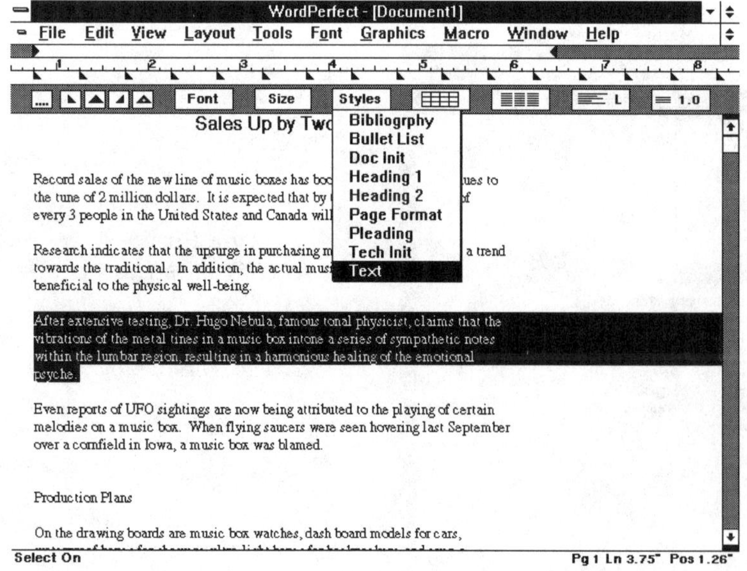

Figure 15x-27*. Select the third paragraph and then choose the Text style.*

The selected paragraph now reflects the Text style (Figure 15x-28).

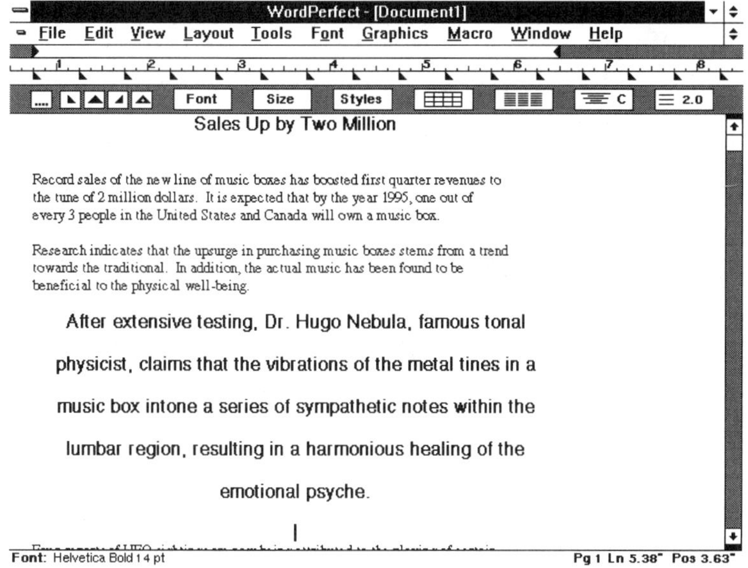

Figure 15x-28. From the actions of Figure 15x-27, the third paragraph now displays the Text style's attributes.

9. ***Edit the Text style to have the following attributes: 1.5 Line Spacing, Right Justification, Helvetica, 12 point, Italic text. Also change the style name of Text to Text 2, while keeping the original Text style in the document.***

Activate the *Styles* dialog box, by either selecting the *Styles* command from the **Layout** menu or by double-clicking on the *Styles* option in the ruler. Once this dialog box appears, highlight the Text style from the list of styles, and click on the *Edit* button (Figure 15x-29).

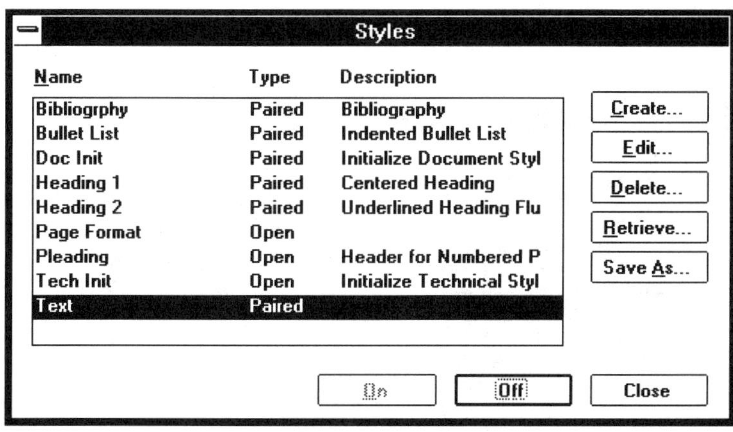

Figure 15x-29. In the Styles dialog box, select the Text style and click on the Edit button.

Clicking on the *Edit* button, with a style selected in the *Styles* dialog box, will bring you back to the *Style Editor* window for the selected style. It is now possible to change the attributes relating to this style. Before a new code can be inserted, any codes referring to the same option or command must be deleted first.

If you want to change the *Line Spacing* option, first select the *Line Spacing* code in the *Reveal Codes* window, by clicking on it once with the mouse (Figure 15x-30).

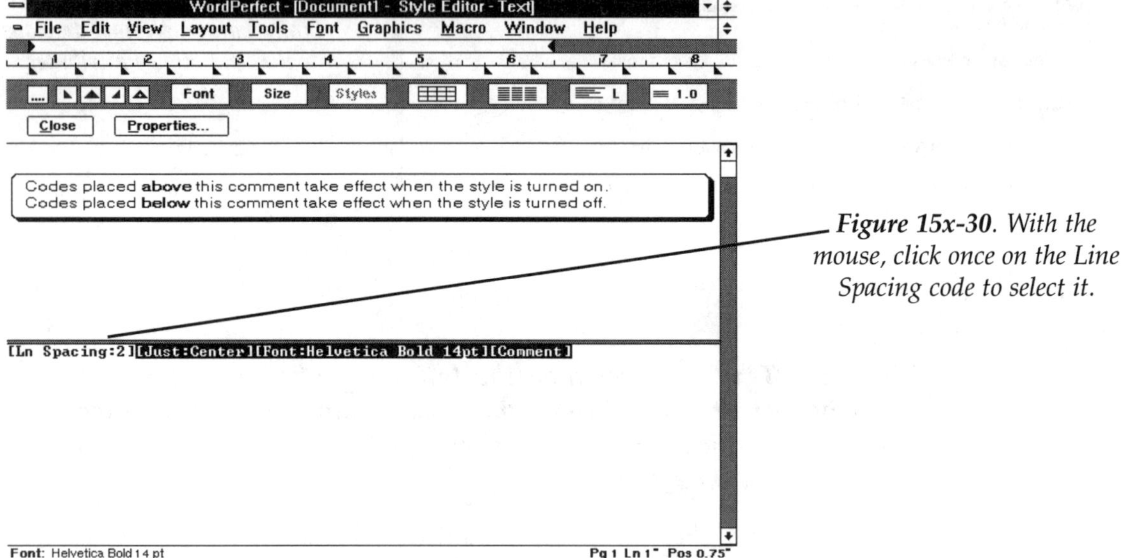

Figure 15x-30*. With the mouse, click once on the Line Spacing code to select it.*

Once you have selected the *Line Spacing* code in the *Reveal Codes* window, press the Delete key on your keyboard to remove this code. Now you can insert a new code by selecting the 1.5 option from the *Line Spacing* button on the ruler (Figure 15x-31). The new code will appear from where the old one was deleted.

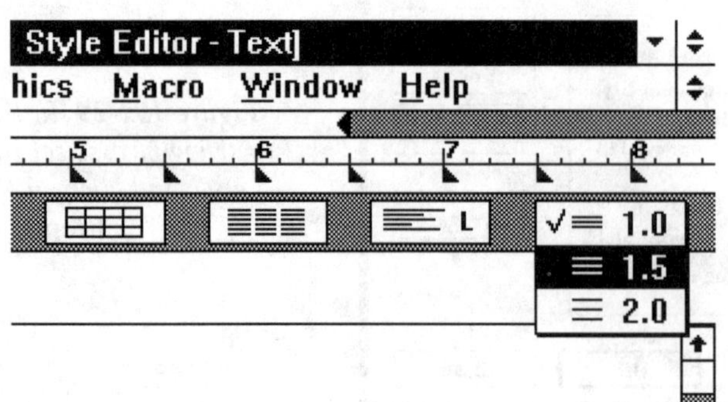

Figure 15x-31*. Selecting the 1.5 option from the Line Spacing menu will insert a new Line Spacing code in this style.*

Now, delete the *Justification* code the same way you deleted the *Line Spacing* code. You can then insert the new *Justification* code by either selecting *Right* from the *Justification* button in the ruler or by selecting the *Right* command from the *Justification* fly-out menu in the **Layout** menu, as shown in Figure 15x-32.

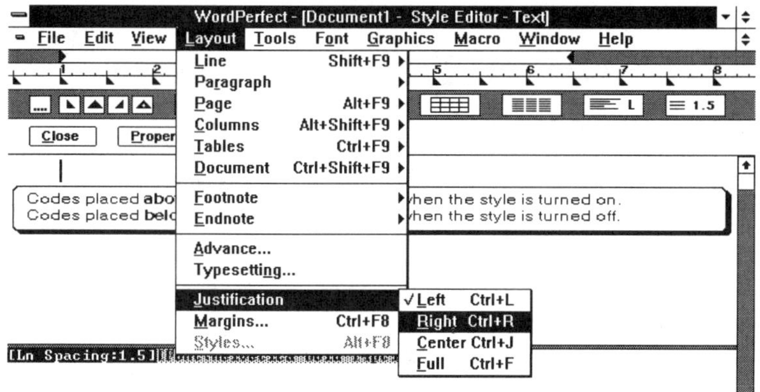

*Figure 15x-32. After deleting the Justification code, insert the new one by selecting the Justification/Right command in the **Layout** menu.*

Again, delete the *Font* code, and activate the *Font* dialog box from the *Font* command in the **Font** menu, to create a new font code.

Select the Helvetica option from the list of fonts, the 12 option from the *Point Size* list and the *Italic* option from the *Appearance* section of the *Font* dialog box (Figure 15x-33). Then click on **OK**.

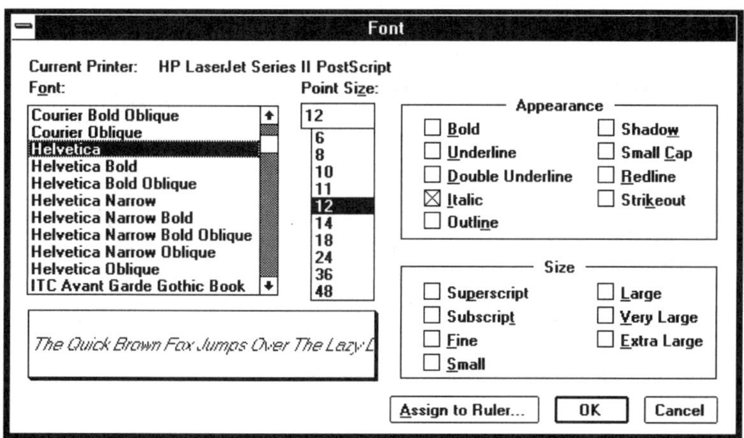

*Figure 15x-33. Set up your dialog box the same as this one, and click on **OK**.*

After making the necessary changes in the *Font* dialog box, you will see the *Reveal Codes* section of the *Style Editor* window displaying these changes (Figure 15x-34).

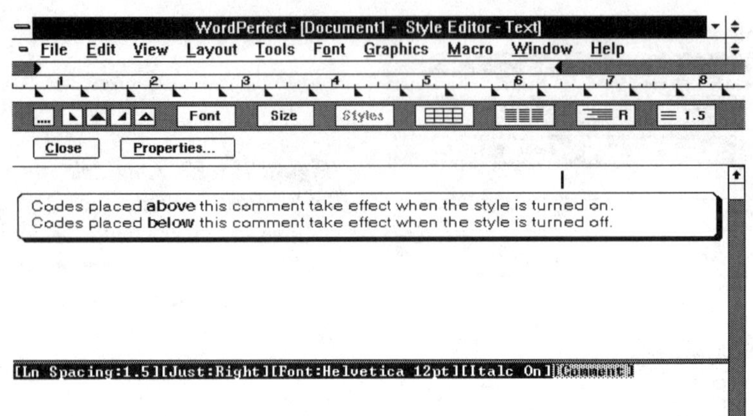

***Figure 15x-34.** The changes you made in the Font dialog box are reflected in the Reveal Codes section of the Style Editor window.*

To change the name of the style, click on the *Properties* button (Figure 15x-35). This will activate the *Style Properties* dialog box.

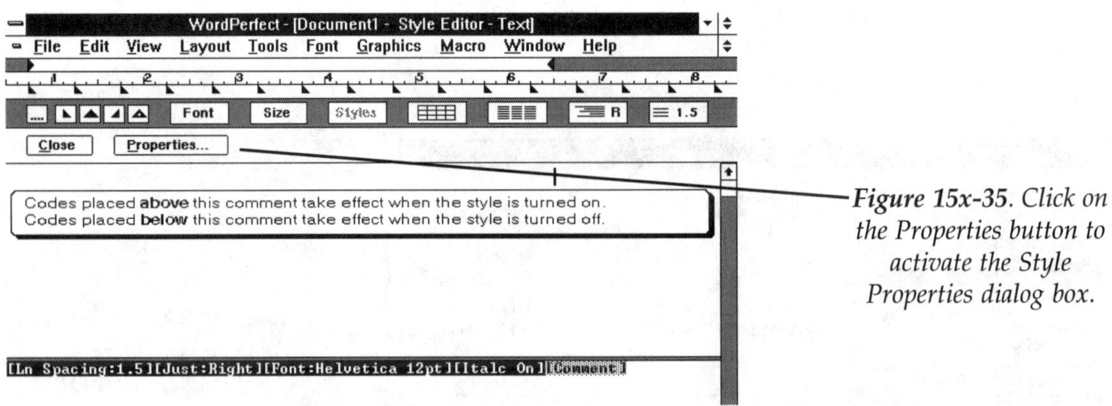

***Figure 15x-35**. Click on the Properties button to activate the Style Properties dialog box.*

Once inside the *Style Properties* dialog box, change the name to Text 2 (Figure 15x-36), and click on **OK**.

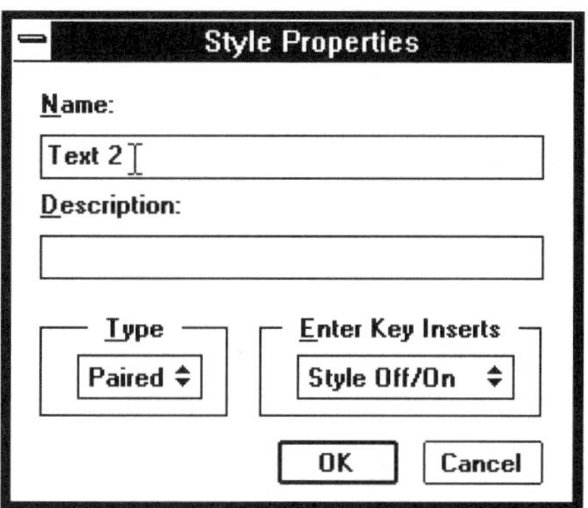

Figure 15x-36. Change the name of the style from Text to Text 2.

Clicking on **OK** in the *Style Properties* dialog box will return you to the *Style Editor* window. Now that you have done everything you need to do in the *Style Editor* window, you can exit by clicking on the *Close* button as you've done before. Because you changed the name of the style, the screen prompt of Figure 15x-37 will appear, after clicking on the *Close* button. If you click on the *Yes* option, the Text style will be changed to Text 2, wherever it appears in your document.

For this exercise, click on the *No* option. This will ensure that the Text option will remain available, as well as the newly created Text 2 style. This feature lets you base a style on another style, if they are going to be similar, without having to create the style from the beginning.

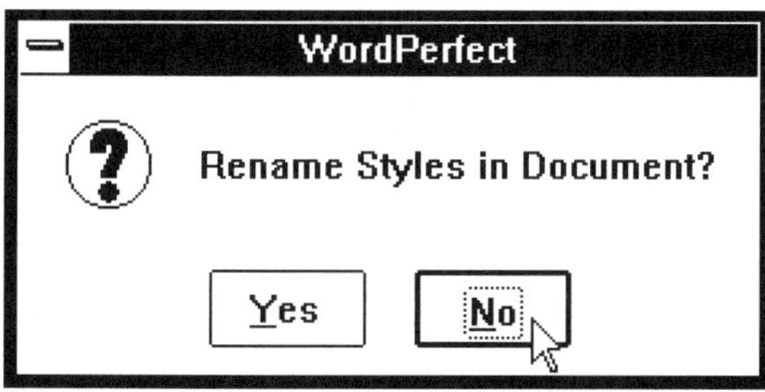

Figure 15x-37. Click on the No option so that both the Text and Text 2 styles are available within the document.

On returning to the *Styles* dialog box, click on the *Close* button to return to the document.

10. Select the third paragraph of body text and apply the Text 2 style to it.

Once you are back in the document, select the third paragraph again, and choose the Text 2 option from the *Styles* button in the ruler (Figure 15x-38).

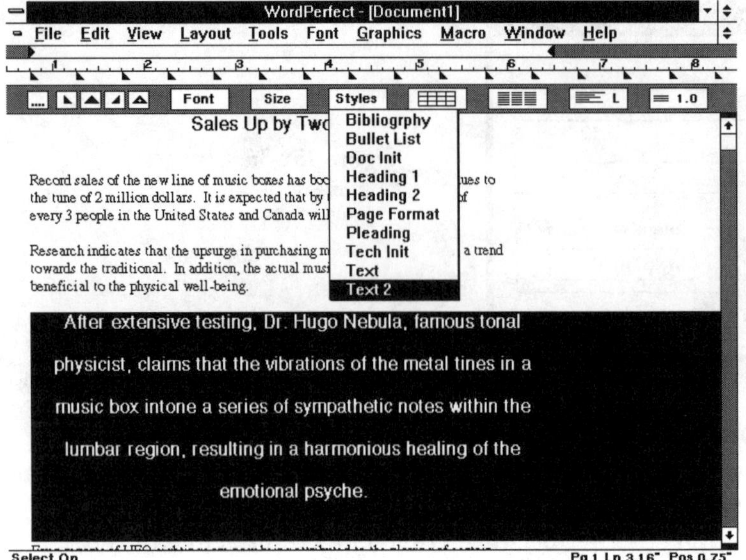

Figure 15x-38. Select the third paragraph again, and apply the newly created Text 2 style to it.

The third paragraph will then change to reflect the attributes of the Text 2 style (Figure 15x-39).

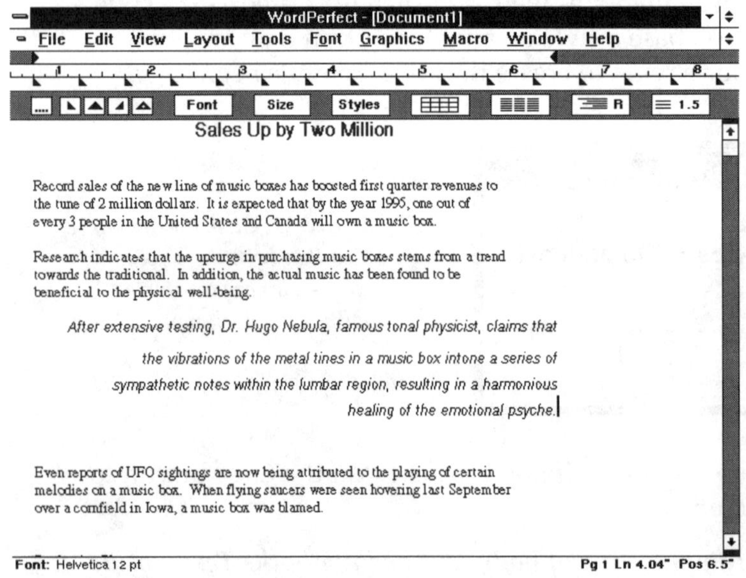

Figure 15x-39. The third paragraph has now changed after applying the Text 2 style to it.

Note: *It is advised that you turn the Auto Code Placement option in the Environment Settings dialog box on again. It was de-activated for this exercise so you could have control over the placement of codes.*

Quick Lists

In order to speed the process of opening, loading, and retrieving files, WordPerfect provides an option known as the *Quick List*.

A *Quick List* can be used to arrange different types of files into groups. When a group is selected, the files from that group can be viewed, opened, retrieved, or loaded. *Quick Lists* let you select a file from a list of file types, rather than from a list of directories. Figure 16-1 compares quick lists with directories.

Directories:	Quick List:
[document]	Documents
[fax]	Graphic Files
[letters]	Letters
[porder]	Outgoing faxes
[styles]	Purchase Orders
[-a-]	Style Libraries
[-b-]	
[-c-]	
[-d-]	
[-g-]	
[-s-]	

Figure 16-1. *On the left is the usual list of directories found in a file selection dialog box. This list is used to select the directory in which a file is located. When a Quick List (on the right) is used, files can be selected from Quick List categories without entering their directories.*

When a *Quick List* is in use, you cannot change directories to locate files; rather, you search through the entries in the *Quick List*. As a selection is made from the *Quick List*, the appropriate directory is automatically selected for you.

Using a Quick List

To demonstrate the use of the *Quick List*, select the *Open* command from the **File** menu (Figure 16-2).

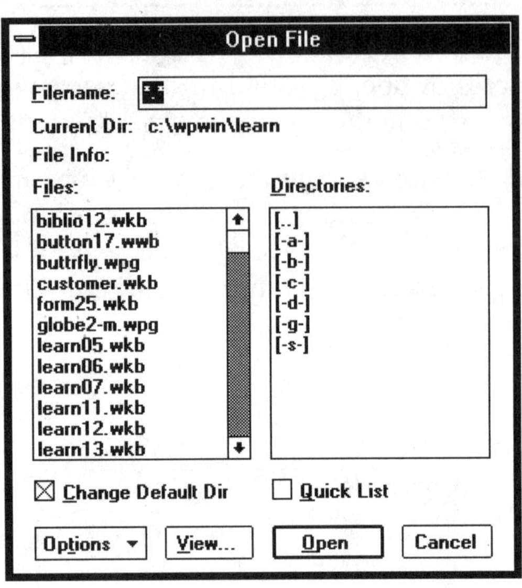

Figure 16-2. The Open File dialog box, as it appears by default. Yours may not necessarily list the same files as this one does. As usual, you may either select a file from the Files list, or select a new directory or drive from the Directories list.

In the *Open File* dialog box, note the *Quick List* check box near the bottom. Click on this check box once to select this option (Figure 16-3).

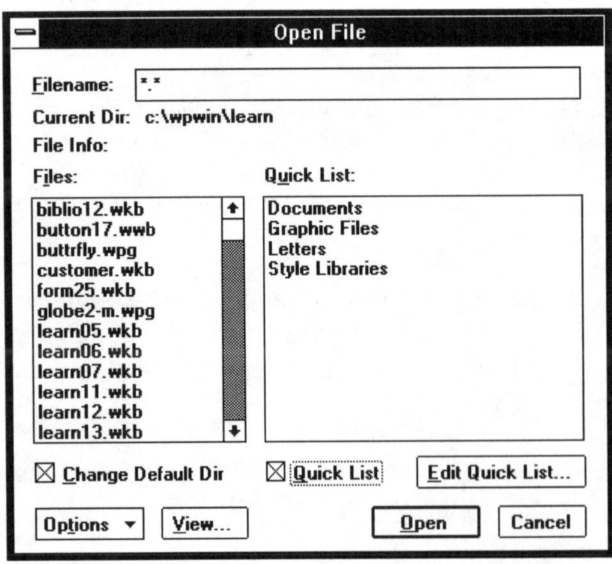

Figure 16-3. When the Quick List check box is selected, the Directories list disappears and is replaced by the Quick List.

The default Quick List

As seen in Figure 16-3, when the *Quick List* option is selected, the *Directories* list disappears, and the *Quick List* appears. The default *Quick List* will contain a number of entries depending upon the settings in the *Preferences/Location of Files* command from the **File** menu. This example will use the four entries listed below:

Documents

Graphic Files

Letters

Style Libraries

These four entries represent four different types of files that may be accessed. The *Quick List* can include a variety of file types (such as graphics and style files in this example), because the same *Quick List* is used by a range of file selection dialog boxes.

If, for example, you wanted to access a document, rather than a letter, double-click on the *Document* entry in the *Quick List* to automatically move to the directory where document files are located (as defined by the *Quick List*).

WordPerfect creates this default *Quick List* based on the entries made in the *Preferences/Location of Files* command from the **File** menu, as indicated above. This command tells WordPerfect the default directories for different types of files—WordPerfect uses these entries to decide which directory to open as a category is selected from the *Quick List*.

Imagine that the computer on which you are currently working is used by a variety of people. Different people tend to store their own data in their own sub-directories. When they return to use the machine again, they must locate their own sub-directory when they need to load a file. However, in using a *Quick List*, entries may be created for each user, so that the *Quick List* may appear as:

Joe's documents

Joe's graphics

Sarah's documents

Sarah's faxes

Carrie's documents

Paul's documents

The *Quick List* makes it easier for each person to locate his/her files. This feature also makes accessing files easier for users who are unfamiliar with the way sub-directories are organized on disk drives.

Editing the Quick List

To edit the *Quick List*, select the *Edit Quick List* button at the bottom right of the Figure 16-3 *Open File* dialog box. The *Edit Quick List* dialog box (Figure 16-4) will appear.

In the *Quick List* list box of Figure 16-4, the current file categories in the *Quick List* are displayed. As an entry from this list is selected (by clicking on it once), the sub-directory, or perhaps even individual filenames associated with that entry, are indicated towards the bottom of the dialog box, under the *Directory/Filename* line.

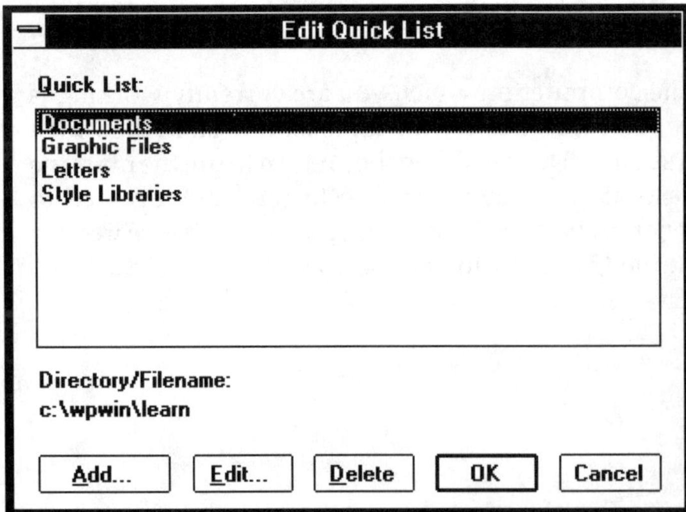

Figure 16-4. *The Edit Quick List dialog box.*

For example, in Figure 16-4, the *Quick List* item *Documents* is selected. Under the heading *Directory/Filename*, the sub-directory mentioned is ***c:\wpwin\learn***. The sub-directory listed on your system may, of course, be totally different; it depends on how the hard disk is organized.

Adding a Quick List item

You will now add an entry to the *Quick List* called "My Documents" (replace the word "*My*" with your name).

Select the *Add* button from the *Edit Quick List* dialog box of Figure 16-4. The *Add Quick List* dialog box appears as seen in Figure 16-5.

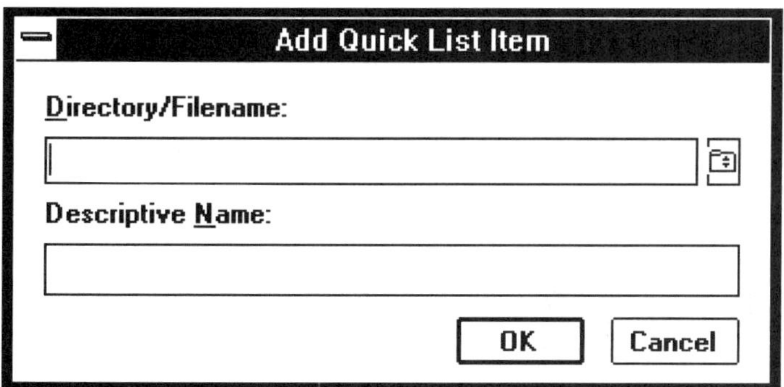

Figure 16-5. *The Add Quick List Item dialog box is used to add new file category items to the Quick List.*

Two parts of this dialog box must be filled out to add an item to the *Quick List*. First, move down to the bottom half of the dialog box, and enter "My Documents" (replacing "My" with your name) in the *Descriptive Name* text box (Figure 16-6).

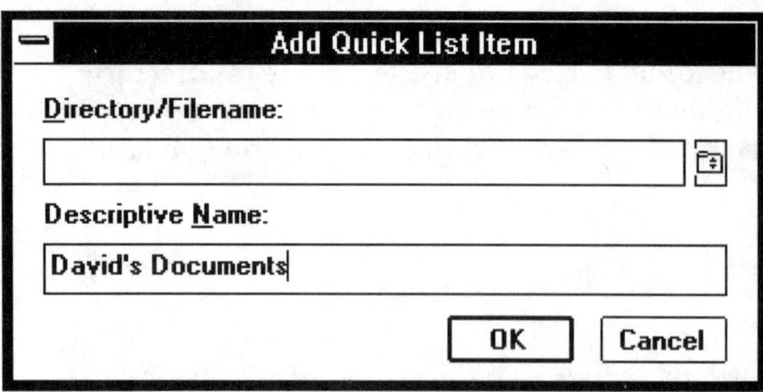

Figure 16-6. The string you insert in the Descriptive Name is the string that appears in the Quick List itself.

In Figure 16-6, "David's Documents" has been entered into the *Descriptive Name* text box. Whatever text appears in this text box will appear in the *Quick List* itself.

The next task is to associate a certain drive, directory, and perhaps even filename, with this *Quick List* entry. Enter a drive and directory path (and perhaps a filename) in the *Directory/Filename* text box. You may wish to click on the folder icon to the right of this text box, which will present you with a file selection dialog box as seen in Figure 16-7.

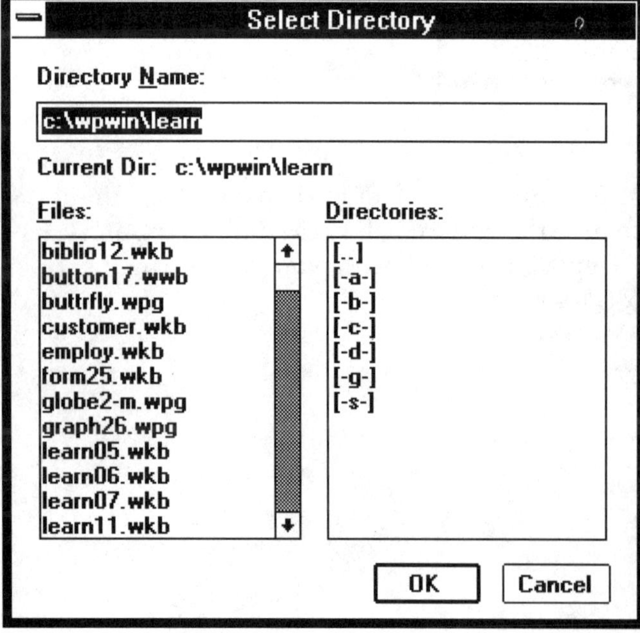

Figure 16-7. Selecting the folder icon next to the Directory/ Filename text box reveals a drive/ directory list. It is from this list that a directory can be selected.

If you are creating an item in a *Quick List* called "My Documents", use the Figure 16-7 *Select Directory* dialog box to locate the drive and directory in which your documents are located. If you currently have no documents on disk, you may wish to select the directory where you plan to store your files.

In this case, select any directory, but make a note of the directory selected. In Figure 16-8, the directory selected is ***c:\wpwin***, as listed in the *Directory/Filename* text box.

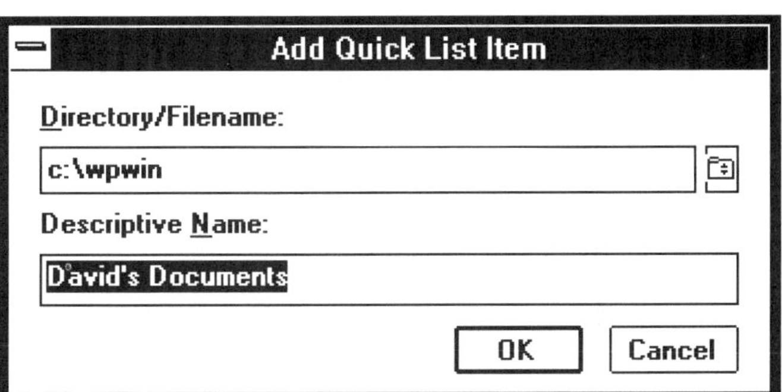

Figure 16-8. *The directory **c:\wpwin** has been selected as the directory to be associated with "David's Documents"*

Once you have filled in the two options as seen in the Figure 16-8 dialog box, click on the **OK** button to return to the *Edit Quick List* dialog box (Figure 16-9). The item you added to the *Quick List* now appears in the list of *Quick List* items.

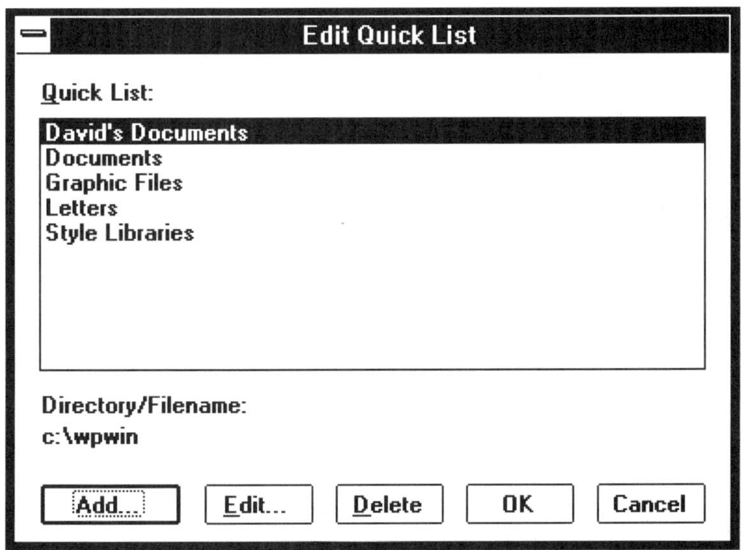

Figure 16-9. *The new Quick List item has been added to the Quick List.*

Click on **OK** in the *Edit Quick List* dialog box (Figure 16-9) to return to the *Open File* dialog box of Figure 16-10. The new *Quick List* item will now appear in this *Quick List* list box and can be selected if required.

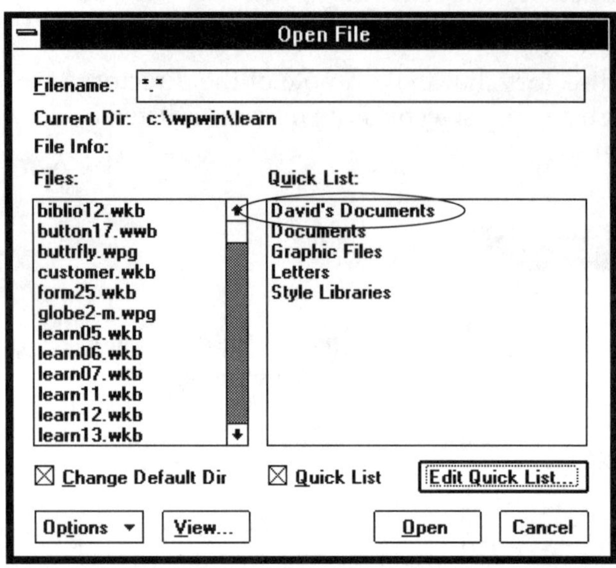

Figure 16-10. *"David's Documents" appears in the Quick List which is organized in alphabetical order.*

To check how this *Quick List* item works, select (by double-clicking) the *Quick List* item just created (in this case "*David's Documents*") as seen in Figure 16-11.

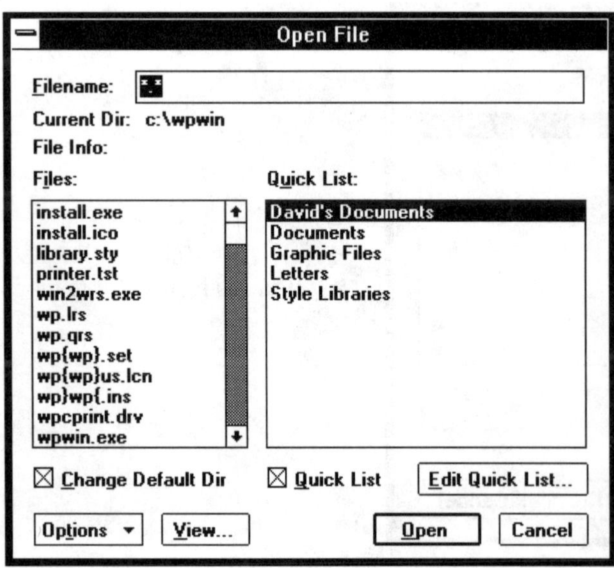

Figure 16-11. *Double-click on the David's Documents Quick List item to change the current sub-directory (note the Current Dir line near the top of the dialog box). The new sub-directory is the directory that was specified in the Add Quick List Item dialog box of Figure 16-8.*

In Figure 16-11, double-clicking on the new item from the *Quick List* caused the dialog box to display the contents of another directory (the ***c:\wpwin*** sub-directory—note the *Current Dir line*); this is the same sub-directory as specified in the *Add Quick List Item* dialog box (Figure 16-8). In Figure 16-10, before "David's Documents" was selected from the *Quick List*, the *Current Dir* was ***c:\wpwin\learn***.

Double-clicking on an item in a *Quick List* is really a simpler way of moving to another directory. Alternatively, you achieve the same result by selecting the *Quick List* item and then clicking on *Open*.

To demonstrate this idea further, double-click on the *Documents Quick List* item. The *Current Dir* line should change again and the files from the new sub-directory will be displayed in the *Files* list (Figure 16-12).

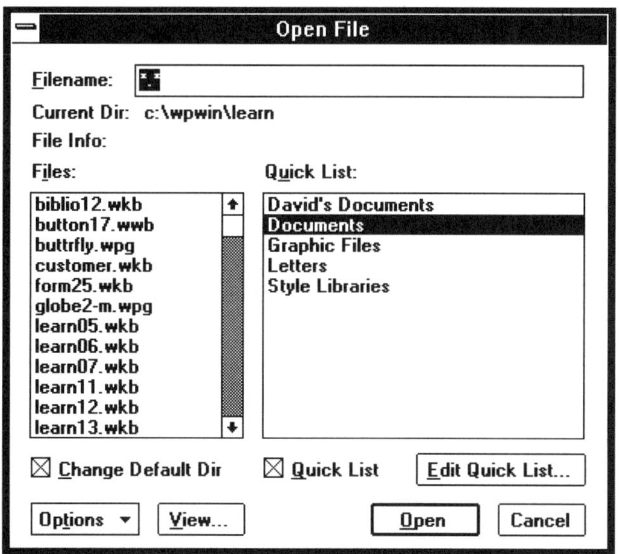

Figure 16-12. *After the Documents item is selected from the Quick List, the Current Dir changes again.*

Editing Quick List items

An item in a *Quick List* can be edited quite easily. Select the *Edit Quick List* button from the *Open File* dialog box seen above (Figure 16-12). The *Edit Quick List* dialog box appears as displayed in Figure 16-13.

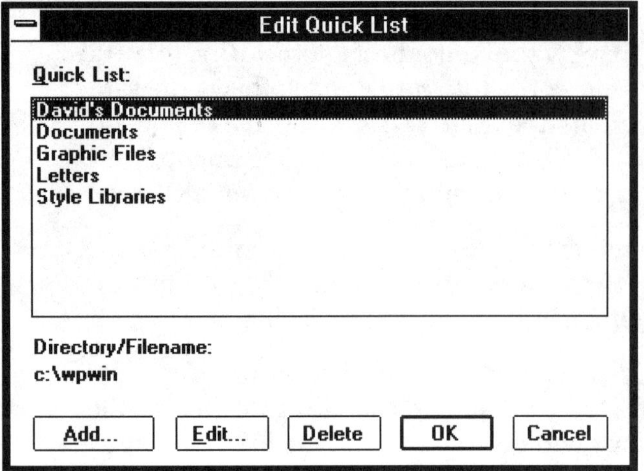

Figure 16-13. *The Edit Quick List dialog box.*

First, select the item in the *Quick List* that you would like to edit. In Figure 16-13, the *Letters* option from the *Quick List* was selected, and the *Edit* button at the bottom of the dialog box was clicked on to activate the *Edit Quick List Item* dialog box.

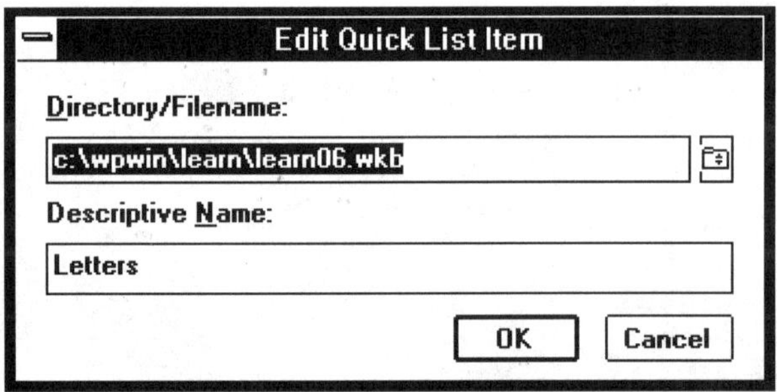

Figure 16-14. *The Edit Quick List Item dialog box appears; "Letters" appears in the Descriptive Name text box.*

When editing an entry, either the *Directory/Filename*, or the *Descriptive Name* of that item can be edited. Once either has been edited, click on **OK** to save these changes and return to the previous dialog box.

Before continuing, you may note something a little different about the *Directory/Filename* entry in Figure 16-14 and perhaps on your computer as well. It contains a drive name, a directory name, and also a file name. Previously, a *Quick List* entry was created using only a drive name and a directory name—not a file name.

The advantage of adding a file name to the *Directory/Filename* line is that when this particular item (*Letters*) is selected from the *Quick List*, it opens the actual file, rather than just changing directories.

Deleting a Quick List item

To remove an item from the *Quick List*, you must once again select the *Edit Quick List* button from the dialog box in Figure 16-12, to invoke the *Edit Quick List* dialog box of Figure 16-13.

To delete a particular item from this list, select that item and click on the *Delete* button from Figure 16-13. The warning dialog box of Figure 16-15 will appear.

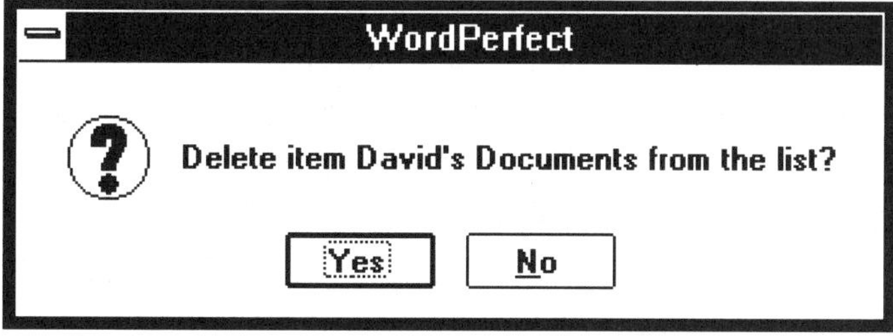

Figure 16-15. *Here, the item "David's Documents" was highlighted before the Delete button was selected. This dialog box requires confirmation before the item is deleted from the Quick List.*

Clicking on **YES** removes the item from the *Quick List*.

Hiding the Quick List

To hide the *Quick List*, and to resume a normal drive/directory method of locating files, click on the *Quick List* check box once more, so that it no longer includes a check mark.

Hints and Tips

As briefly mentioned earlier, the *Quick List* can be used to open or retrieve a file, by including the filename when the directory name is entered into the *Directory/Filename* text box in the *Edit Quick List Item* dialog box of Figure 16-14.

To illustrate this feature, select the *Open* command in the **File** menu. Make sure that the *Quick List* check box is selected and click on the *Edit Quick List* button.

In the *Edit Quick List* dialog box that is activated, click on the *Add* command button. In the *Descriptive Name* text box of the *Add Quick List Item* dialog box (Figure 16-16) type the words "Marketing Letter".

Select the sub-directory icon at the end of the *Directory/Filename* text box. In the *Select Directory* dialog box that appears, highlight the ***learn*** directory and select the **OK** button to return to the *Add Quick List Item* dialog box. Place your cursor at the end of the text in the *Directory/ Filename:* list box and type ***"\learn06.wkb".*** The dialog box will now look like Figure 16-16.

Add Quick List Item

Directory/Filename:

c:\wpwin\learn\learn06.wkb

Descriptive Name:

Marketing Letter

OK | Cancel

Figure 16-16. *The Add Quick List Item dialog box will now look like this.*

Select **OK** to return to the *Edit Quick List* dialog box, and select **OK** again, to return to the *Open File* dialog box. Select the *Cancel* command button to close the *Open File* dialog box and return to the document screen.

Now, select the *Open* command from the **File** menu, once again. In the *Open File* dialog box, select the *Marketing Letter* item in the *Quick List* list box (Figure 16-17). Select the *Open* command button to open this file and place it in the active window.

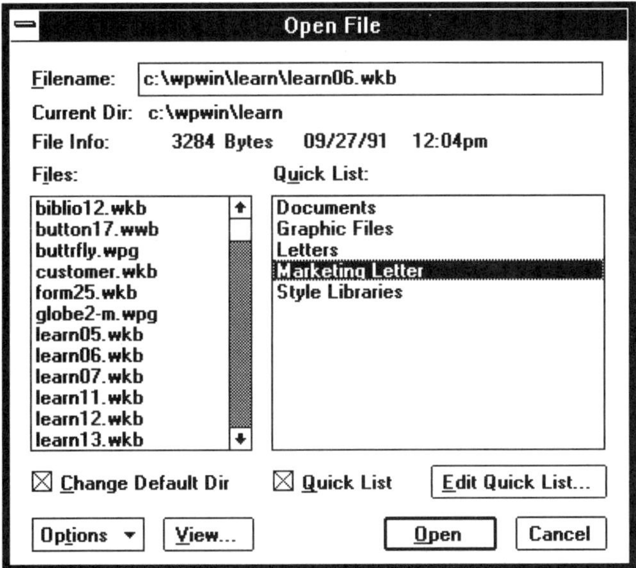

Figure 16-17. *The Marketing Letter Quick List item highlighted in the Quick List list box in the Open File dialog box.*

Name search

If there are numerous items in a *Quick List*, a quick keyboard shortcut can be used to select items. To use this shortcut, press the Alt and the U keys together (Alt+U) on the keyboard. Now, enter some text and a small rectangle will appear at the top of the *Quick List*. WordPerfect then attempts to determine what item name you are entering, and endeavors to select that item.

For example, a *Quick List* item called "Style Libraries", could be selected by pressing the Alt and U keys together (to invoke the shortcut capability) and then entering the letter "S". The first item in the *Quick List* starting with an S would then be highlighted automatically. As you progressively type more letters, a different item may be selected in the *Quick List* (i.e., the first entry starting with "St", then the first entry starting with "Sty", etc).

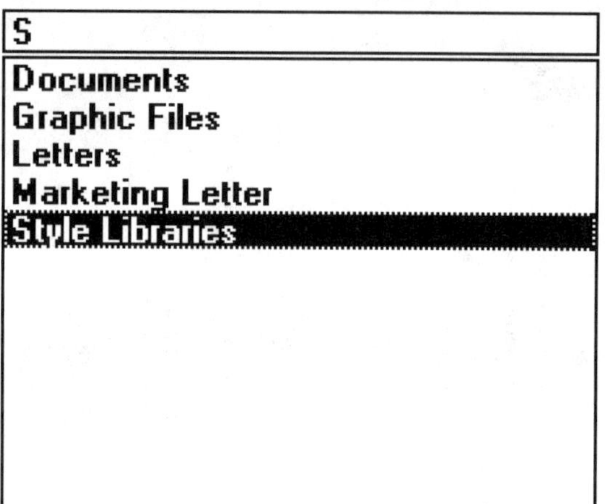

Figure 16-18. *After typing the Alt+U key combination and then any other letter (in this case, an "S"), WordPerfect attempts to select the Quick List item you are indicating. The only option in the list starting with S has now been selected.*

Wild cards

Wild cards can be used as replacements for other characters in a directory when adding *Quick List* items. For example, the asterisk (*) can be used to represent multiple characters in the file name. Creating a *Quick List* item with the entry in the *Directory/Filename* text box of **c:\learn*.txt** would, if selected, display all files with the extension of ***txt*** in the learn directory.

Using the question mark (?) in a filename will represent any single character in that filename. For example, creating a *Quick List* item with the entry in the *Directory/Filename* text box of **c:\learn\web??.wp** would, when selected, display all documents beginning with "***web***" followed by any two characters and a ***wp*** extension.

Advanced Text Editing

In Chapter 3, **Editing Text**, many text editing features of WordPerfect are described in detail. In this chapter, more complex editing features are discussed and illustrated.

Using such features as *Redline*, *Overstrike*, *Strikeout*, *WP Characters*, *Center Text*, *Date Code* and *Format*, *Superscript* and *Subscript*, and *Color*, documents can become more professional looking and far easier to manage.

Redline and Strikeout

Both *Redline* and *Strikeout* are font attributes that can be used when editing documents to aid in the correction of those documents.

The *Redline* attribute is commonly used to mark newly added text in a document and thus distinguish this text from the original text. *Strikeout* is used to mark text that can, or should, be deleted from a document. Both commands are found in the **Font** menu (Figure 17-1).

Font
Font... F9
Color...
✓ Normal Ctrl+N
Bold Ctrl+B
Italic Ctrl+I
Underline Ctrl+U
Double Underline
Redline
Strikeout
Subscript
Superscript
Size Ctrl+S ▸
Overstrike ▸
WP Characters... Ctrl+W

Figure 17-1. The Redline and Strikeout commands are found in the ***Font*** *menu, and are applied as are any other commands from this menu.*

The screen appearance of *Redline* text in documents depends on the type of monitor used. On a color monitor, *Redline* text appears as red colored text. On a monochrome monitor, *Redline* text is only visible when viewing a document in *Draft* mode.

To decide the method in which *Redline* will be displayed in *Draft* mode, use the *Preferences/Display* command, from the **File** menu. Within this command, the *Draft Mode Colors* command button can be used to alter the appearance of a range of text attributes including *Redline*. This command is discussed in Chapter 10, **Preferences - (1).**

In this chapter, the WordPerfect document used for all examples is called ***learn13.wkb*** and is found in the ***learn*** sub-directory.

Applying the Redline and Strikeout attributes

To apply either the *Redline* or *Strikeout* attribute to text, select the appropriate command in the **Font** menu.

Place the text cursor before the first character in the line "The First Fifty Years", and select the *Redline* command from the **Font** menu (Figure 17-2).

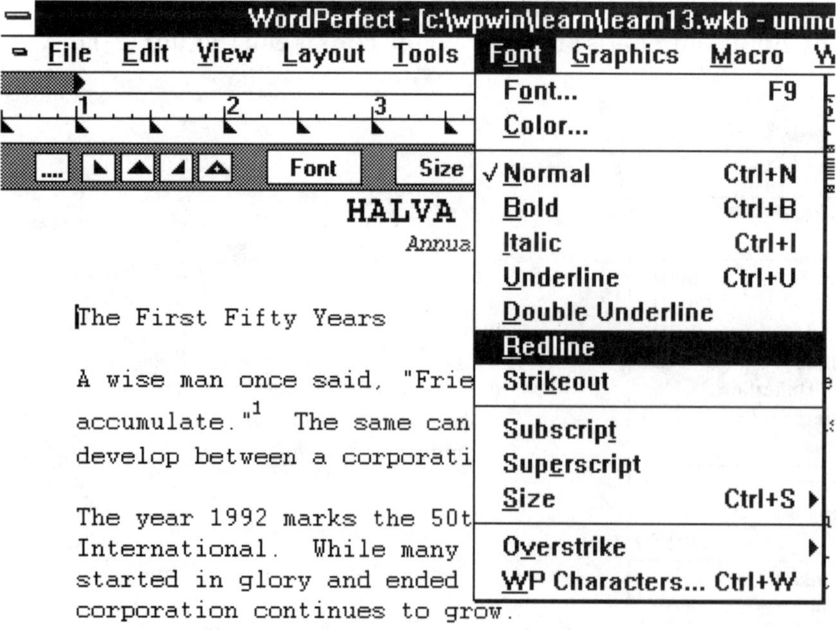

Figure 17-2. In this example, the text cursor has been inserted before the paragraph beginning "The First Fifty Years", and the Redline command from the menu has been selected.

Now enter the words "For liberal delegates only", and press the Enter key to insert a line break (Figure 17-3).

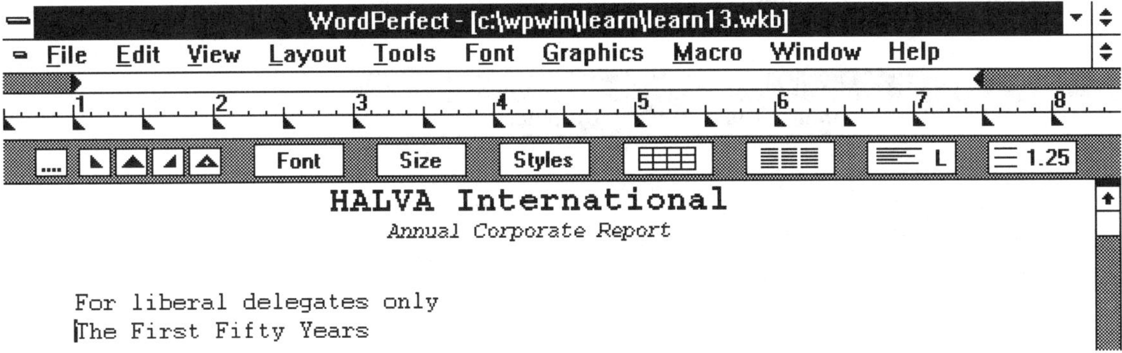

Figure 17-3. Any text inserted after the Redline command of Figure 17-2 (in this case, "For liberal delegates only" followed by the Enter key) has the Redline text attribute.

If a color monitor is used, the text just entered will appear in red. If a monochrome monitor is used, the *Redline* text appearance will be no different from that of ordinary text—only by selecting *Draft Mode*, or *Reveal Codes* from the **View** menu, will the *Redline* attribute be apparent (Figure 17-4).

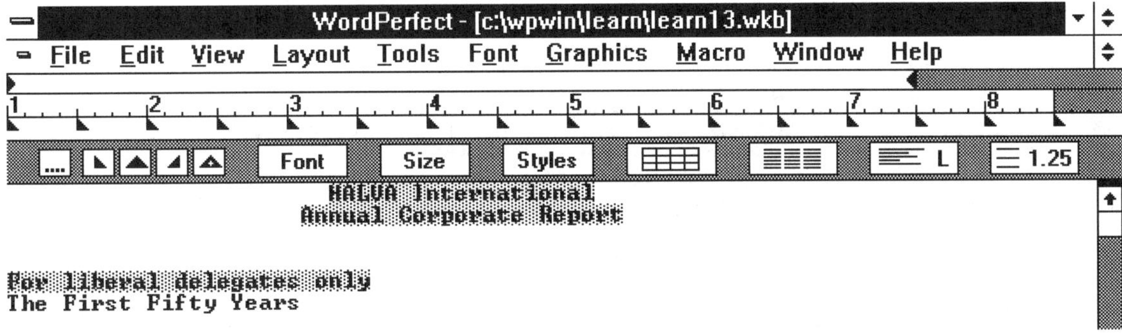

Figure 17-4. This screen illustrates how Redline text appears while in Draft mode. This display may look a little different on your screen, as the appearance of Redline text in Draft mode can be altered using the Draft Mode Colors option, in the ***File****/Preferences/Display command.*

Strikeout text appears on all screens as regular text with a horizontal line through the middle of it. Assigning the *Strikeout* text attribute to text is achieved using the same method as applying *Redline* or any other attribute from the **Font** menu.

Both the *Redline* and *Strikeout* attributes can also be applied to selected text. Select the text reading "A wise man once said", and select the *Strikeout* command from the **Font** menu. All selected text is applied the *Strikeout* attribute (Figure 17-5).

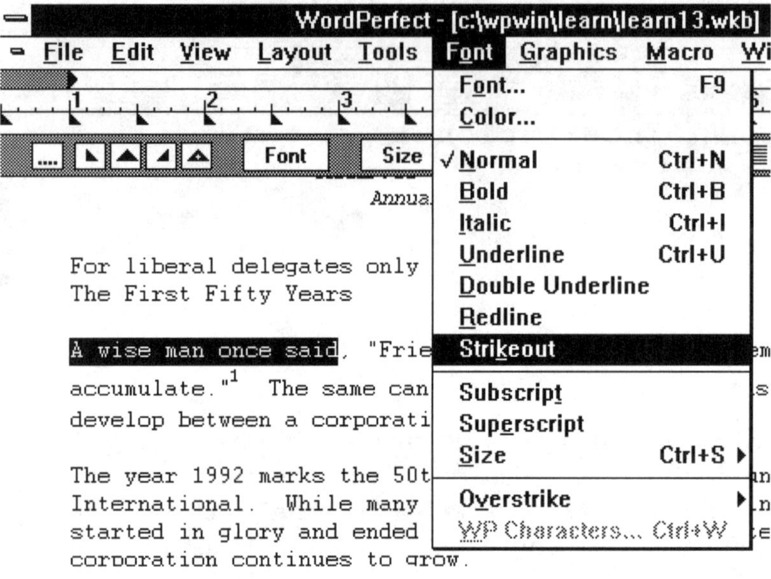

Figure 17-5. The first five words in the fifth paragraph have been selected and the Strikeout command from the ***Font*** *menu then applied.*

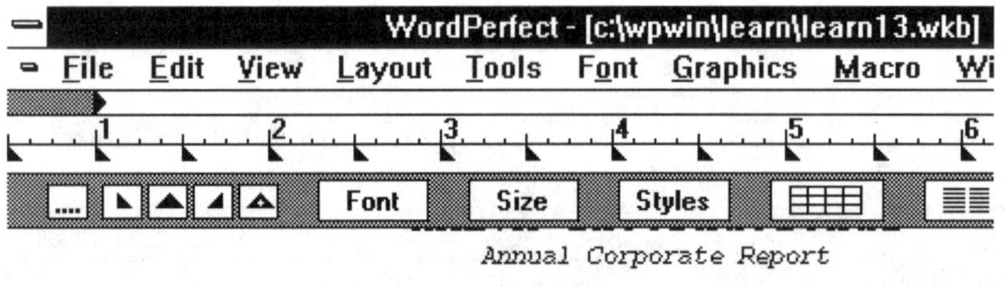

Figure 17-6. The result of Figure 17-5—the selected text now has a horizontal line running through it.

Depending on the capabilities of your printer, text assigned the *Strikeout* attribute will print as displayed on screen. However, the printed appearance of text marked with *Redline* depends on the *Redline* method selected (Figure 17-7) and the printer's capabilities.

As a default, most laser printers print *Redline* text with a shaded background.

You can decide the way Redline text appears when printed, using the *Redline Method* command from the *Document* fly-out menu in the **Layout** menu (Figure 17-7).

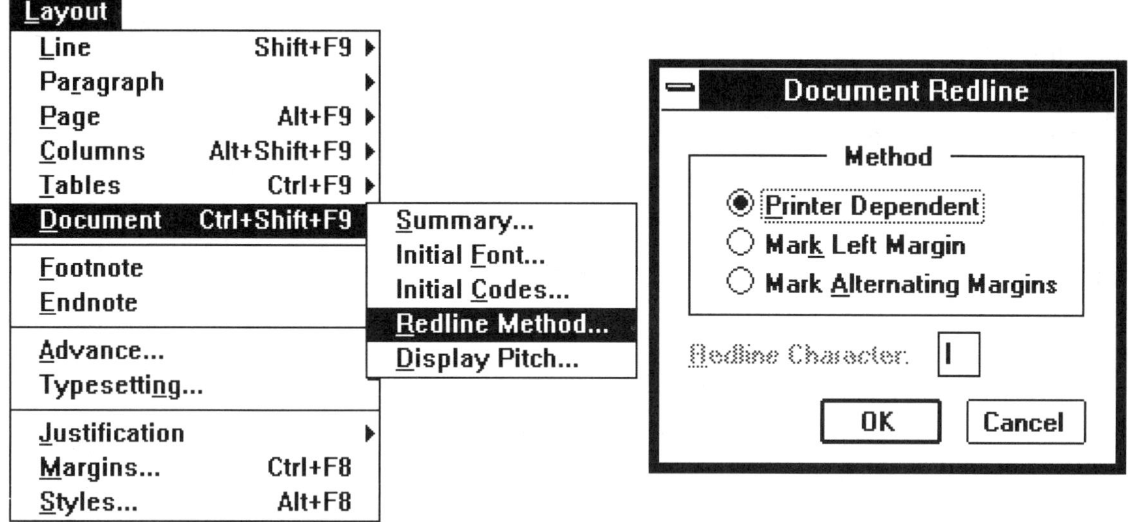

Figure 17-7. The Redline Method command and dialog box.

The *Redline Method* determines the way *Redline* text is printed on the page. The default *Redline Method* used by WordPerfect is a vertical bar in the margin (|). Other characters can be used if desired.

Figure 17-8. This illustration shows how redline text may appear on a laser printer when Printer Dependent is selected from the Figure 17-7 dialog box.

If either the *Mark Left Margin* or *Mark Alternating Margins* radio button is selected, the *Redline Character* text box will become active. If you would like a different character to denote printed *Redline* characters, delete the vertical bar and then type the character desired.

Halva International

Annual Corporate Report

* For Liberal delegates only
The First Fifty years

~~A wise man once said~~, “Friends come and go, but enemies

Figure 17-9. *This illustration shows how Redline text may appear on a laser printer when Mark Left Margin is selected from the Figure 17-7 dialog box, and the Redline Character changed to an asterisk.*

Removing Redline codes and Strikeout text

Redline codes can be removed from a document (without deleting the text within the codes) while, simultaneously, all text marked with the *Strikeout* attribute can be deleted.

This function is normally performed in the final phase of editing. In the currently open document, the text marked with *Strikeout* will be removed while, simultaneously, the *Redline* text attribute (not the *Redline* text) will be removed from the document.

Select the *Remove Markings* command from the *Document Compare* fly-out menu in the **Tools** menu and then select **OK**, as shown in Figure 17-10.

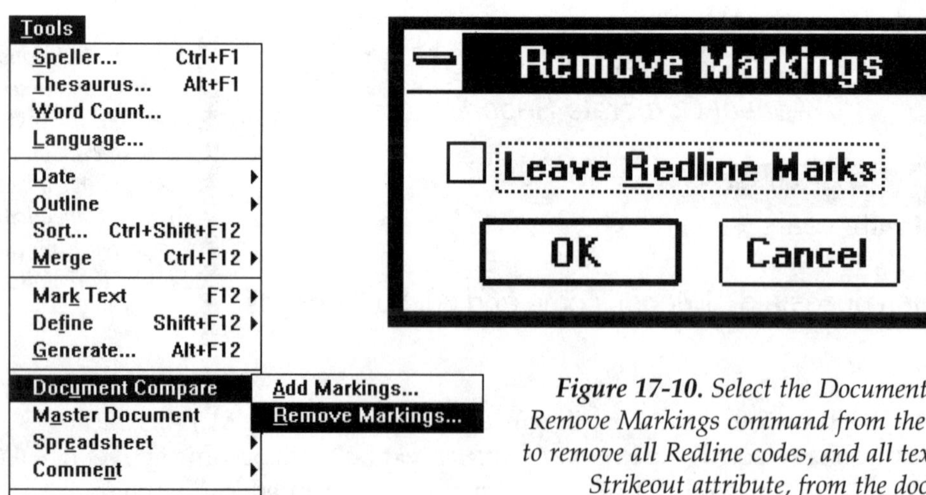

Figure 17-10. *Select the Document Compare/ Remove Markings command from the **Tools** menu to remove all Redline codes, and all text that has the Strikeout attribute, from the document.*

Check your document to see that the *Redline* codes have been removed (the text between the codes remains), and that the text marked with the *Strikeout* attribute has been removed (Figure 17-11).

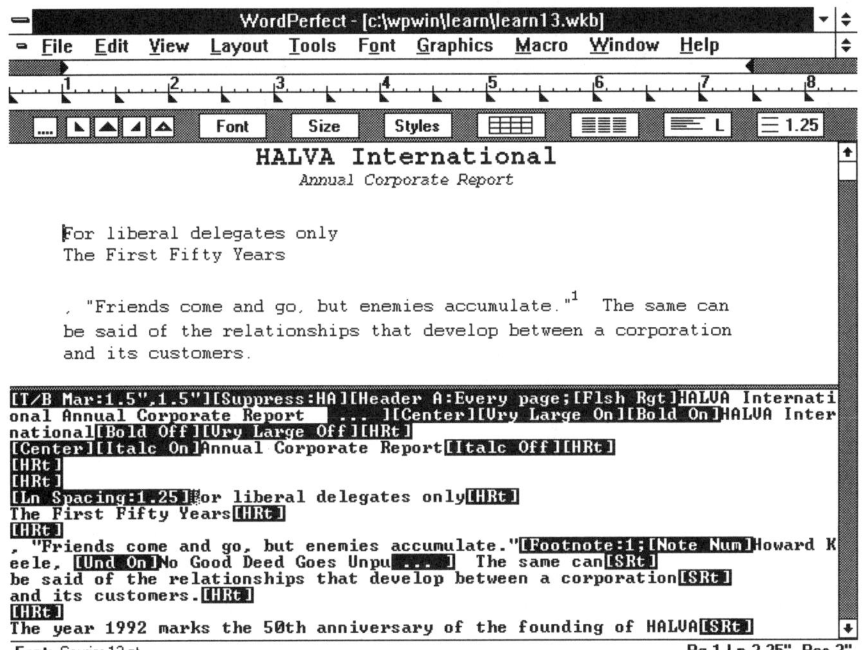

***Figure 17-11.** Redline codes have disappeared, as has the Strikeout text.*

The Superscript and Subscript commands

Superscript text is text which is positioned slightly above the normal line of text in a document. *Subscript* text is positioned slightly underneath the normal line of text in a document.

To insert *Superscript* or *Subscript* text in a document, position the text cursor in the document and select the required command from the **Font** menu (Figure 17-12). Turn either command off by selecting the *Normal* command from the **Font** menu.

In Figure 17-12, the example is taken from the document open at the moment, ***learn13.wkb,*** using the third paragraph of the document. To perform the same task yourself, select the word "liberal", and select the command *Subscript* from the **Font** menu. Then select the word "only", and select the *Superscript* command from the **Font** menu.

In the *Preferences/Print* command, from the **File** menu, an option within the *Size Attribute Ratio* allows you to decide what percentage the size of the text is reduced each time the *Superscript*, or *Subscript* attributes are applied to text. This is discussed briefly in Chapter 10 - **Preferences - (1).**

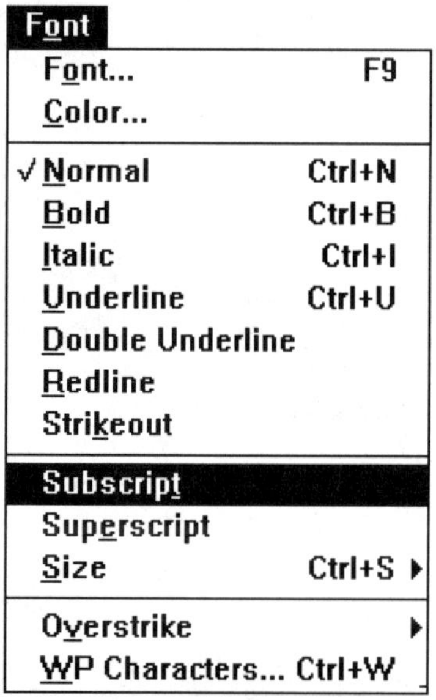

Font
Font... F9
Color...
✓Normal Ctrl+N
Bold Ctrl+B
Italic Ctrl+I
Underline Ctrl+U
Double Underline
Redline
Strikeout
Subscript
Superscript
Size Ctrl+S ▸
Overstrike ▸
WP Characters... Ctrl+W

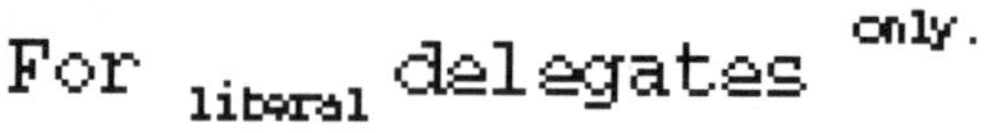

For $_{\text{liberal}}$ delegates ^{only}.

Figure 17-12. *The Subscript and Superscript commands are found in the* **Font** *menu. Above is an example of subscript (the word "Liberal", and superscript (the word "only").*

WordPerfect characters

In WordPerfect, there are 12 character sets containing more than 1500 characters that cannot be accessed using a standard keyboard. If your printer is capable of printing graphics, these characters may be used.

To insert a WordPerfect character into a document, position the cursor where the character is to be inserted. Select *WP Characters* from the **Font** menu to activate the *WordPerfect Characters* dialog box seen in Figure 17-13.

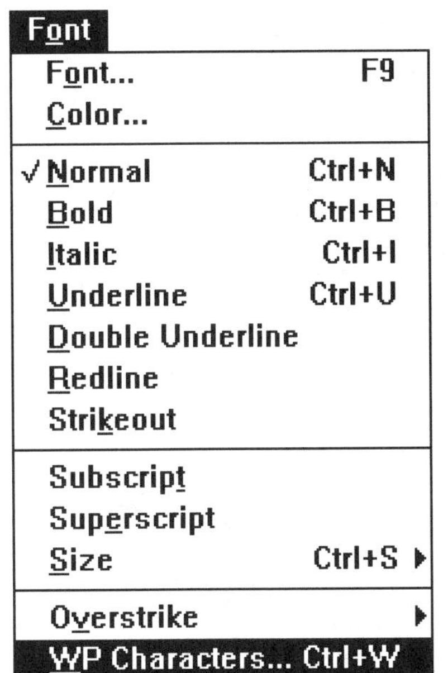

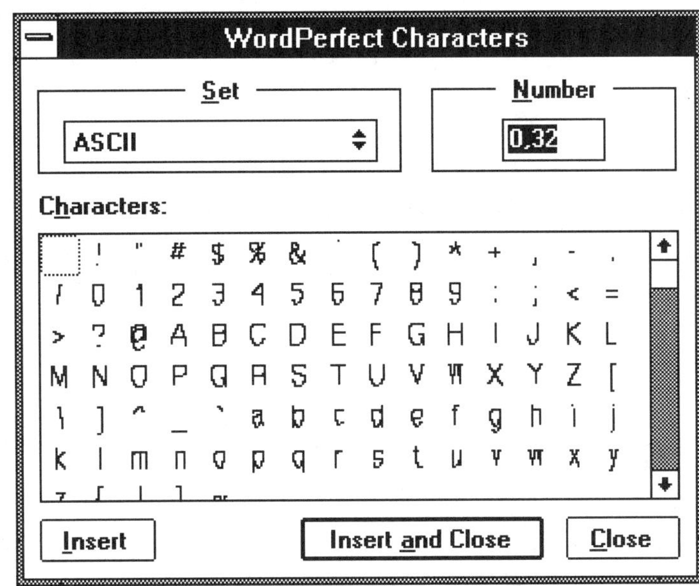

*Figure 17-13. The WP Characters command from the **Font** menu provides access to a wide range of special characters that do not appear on the average keyboard.*

Select a character set from the *Set* pop-up list box. As an illustration, select the *Japanese* set and click on any one of the characters that appears in the *Characters* list box. As a character is selected, its character number is reflected in the *Number* list box (Figure 17-14).

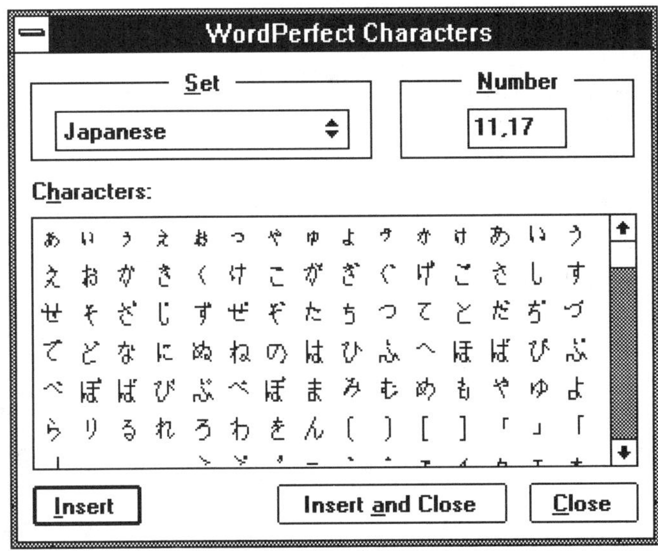

Figure 17-14. Here the Japanese set has been selected from one of the many character sets. One of the characters can be selected by clicking once on it. The number of that character is then reflected in the Number text box.

Character combinations can also be typed into the *Number* box to compose digraphs, symbols, and diacritics. Typing the letters "ro," for example, without a space or a comma, will create the ® symbol.

To insert the chosen characters into a document (Figure 17-15) at the flashing cursor position, select the *Insert* command button from Figure 17-14. To insert a character and close the dialog box in one move, select the *Insert and Close* command button. To close the dialog box without inserting any characters, simply select the *Close* command button.

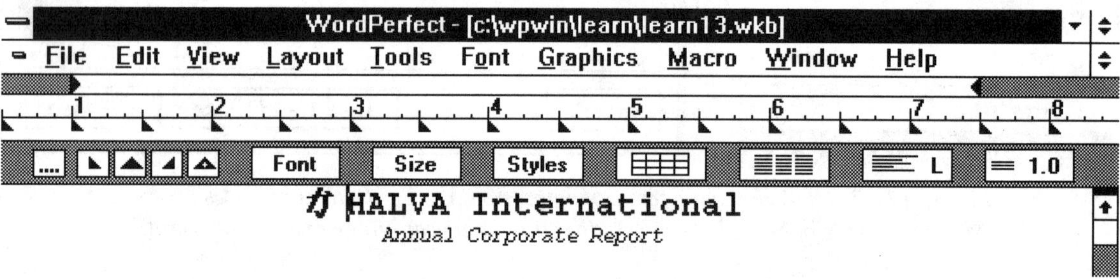

Figure 17-15. *This Japanese character was created by inserting the cursor before the first character in the heading, selecting the WP Characters command from the* **Font** *menu, selecting the Japanese set, choosing the desired character, and, finally clicking on the Insert and Close command button.*

To make the *WordPerfect Characters* dialog inactive, click once in the document area (outside the dialog box). The dialog box will remain on the screen, however, as an inactive window. To activate the dialog box again, click in it.

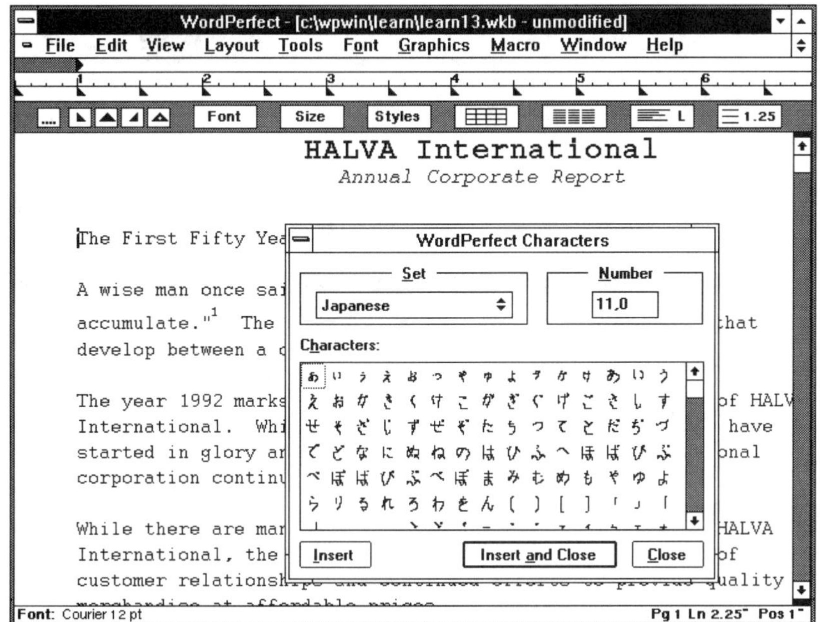

Figure 17-16. The WP Characters dialog box is now inactive, and the text behind the dialog box can be edited as normal. The dialog box can be activated again by clicking on it once.

The Overstrike command

The *Overstrike* option in WordPerfect combines characters to create new characters not found on the keyboard. Remember that many character combinations, including international characters, are already provided in the WordPerfect character sets.

To create an *Overstrike* character, position the flashing cursor in the document where the character is to be inserted. Select the *Create* command from the *Overstrike* fly-out menu in the **Font** menu (Figure 17-17).

In the *Create/Edit Overstrike* dialog box, type in the characters needed to create the new *Overstrike* character. For example, to create the symbol shown below, type in the letters "-" and "t".

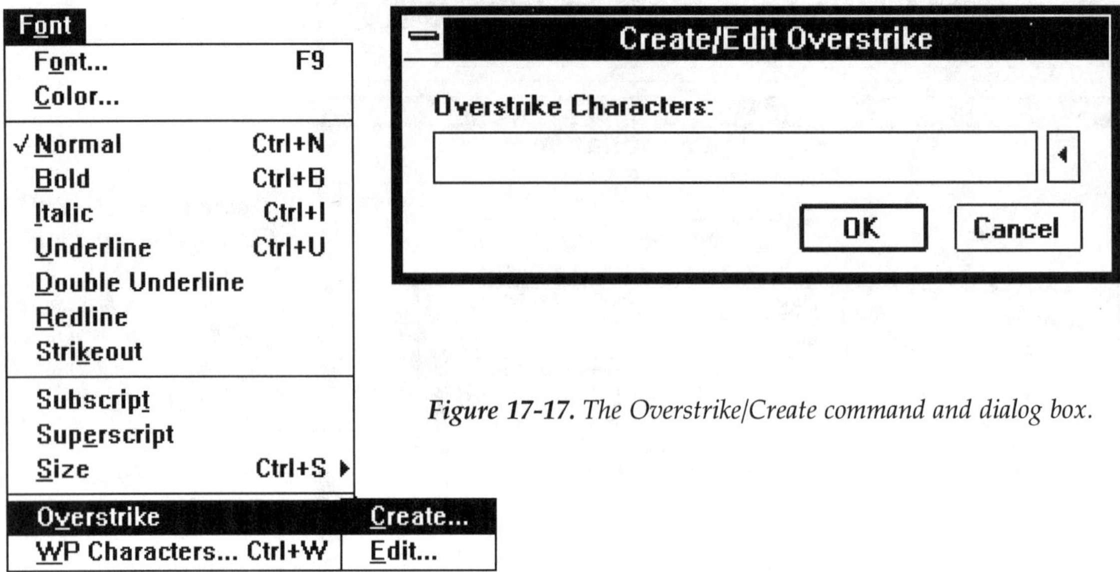

Figure 17-17. The Overstrike/Create command and dialog box.

Size and appearance attributes can be assigned to any created *Overstrike* character by selecting the button with the left facing arrow at the end of the *Create/Edit Overstrike* text box (Figure 17-18). In the sub-menu activated, select the attribute that is required.

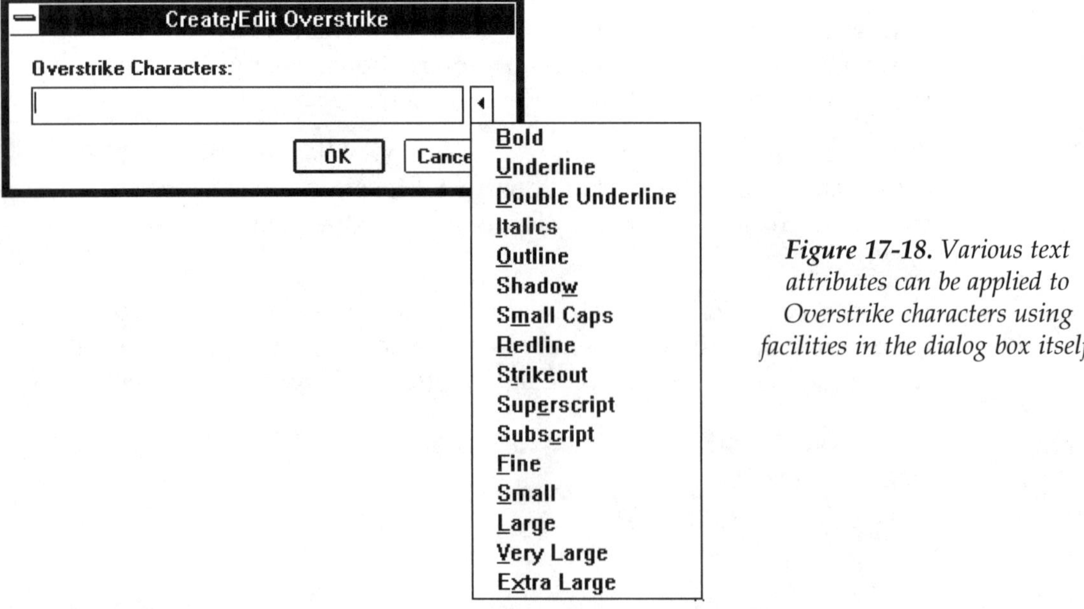

Figure 17-18. Various text attributes can be applied to Overstrike characters using facilities in the dialog box itself.

Select **OK** to close the dialog box and insert the created *Overstrike* character into the document at the current cursor position.

Any *Overstrike* character that is created can be edited by positioning the cursor after that character and selecting the *Edit* command from the *Overstrike* fly-out menu in the **Font** menu.

To edit the character, change the characters in the *Overstrike Characters* text box of the *Create/Edit Overstrike* dialog box (Figure 17-19).

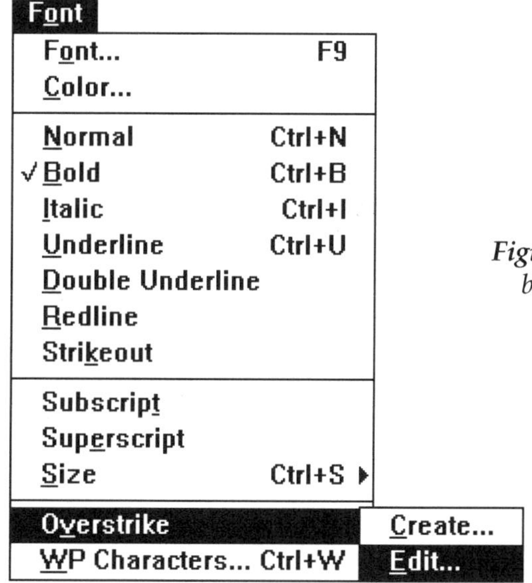

Figure 17-19*. The Overstrike/Edit command can be used to edit single or multiple Overstrike characters in a document.*

To make changes to numerous *Overstrike* characters in a document, place the cursor anywhere in the document and select the *Overstrike/ Edit* command.

WordPerfect will search, from the cursor position, backwards through the document. When an *Overstrike* is encountered, it will be displayed in the *Create/Edit Overstrike* dialog box, ready for editing. If no *Overstrike* is found during a backwards search, WordPerfect will search forwards. If no overstrike exists in the document, WordPerfect will report an error.

The Center Page command

This command centers a page of text vertically between the top and bottom margins on a page.

Move to page five of the ***learn13.wkb*** document, insert the text cursor, and select the *Center Page* command from the *Page* fly-out menu in the **Layout** menu (Figure 17-20).

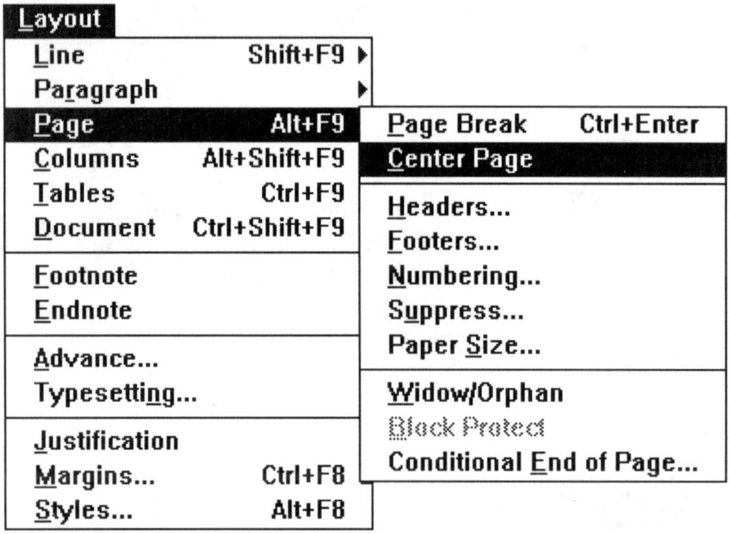

Layout
Line Shift+F9
Paragraph
Page Alt+F9
Columns Alt+Shift+F9
Tables Ctrl+F9
Document Ctrl+Shift+F9
Footnote
Endnote
Advance...
Typesetting...
Justification
Margins... Ctrl+F8
Styles... Alt+F8

Page Break Ctrl+Enter
Center Page
Headers...
Footers...
Numbering...
Suppress...
Paper Size...
Widow/Orphan
Block Protect
Conditional End of Page...

Figure 17-20. *The Page/Center Page command is used to vertically center a page of text on the page.*

Selecting the *Center Page* command does not change the way text is displayed on the screen, it only affects the way it is printed.

When *Center Page* is active, a check mark appears beside the *Center Page* command in the menu (Figure 17-21).

Figure 17-22 illustrates how page five is centered, using the *Print Preview* command from the **File** menu.

To turn off this command, click on *Center Page* again, to remove the check mark.

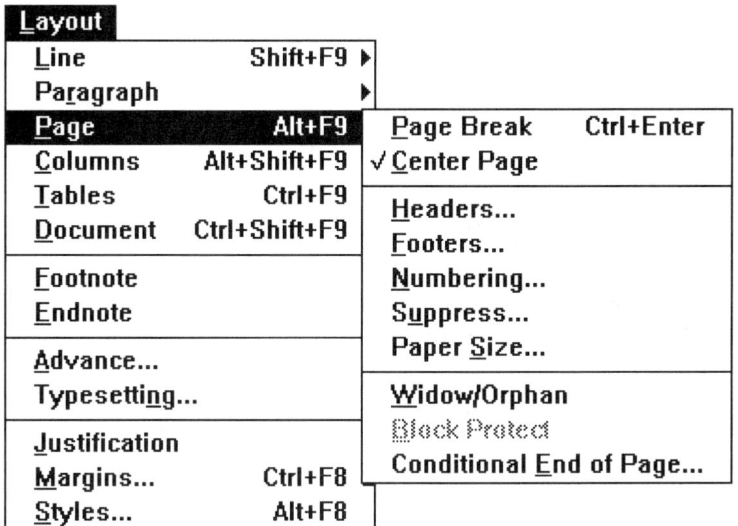

Figure 17-21. *The check mark next to the Page/Center Page command indicates that this page is currently centered (vertically).*

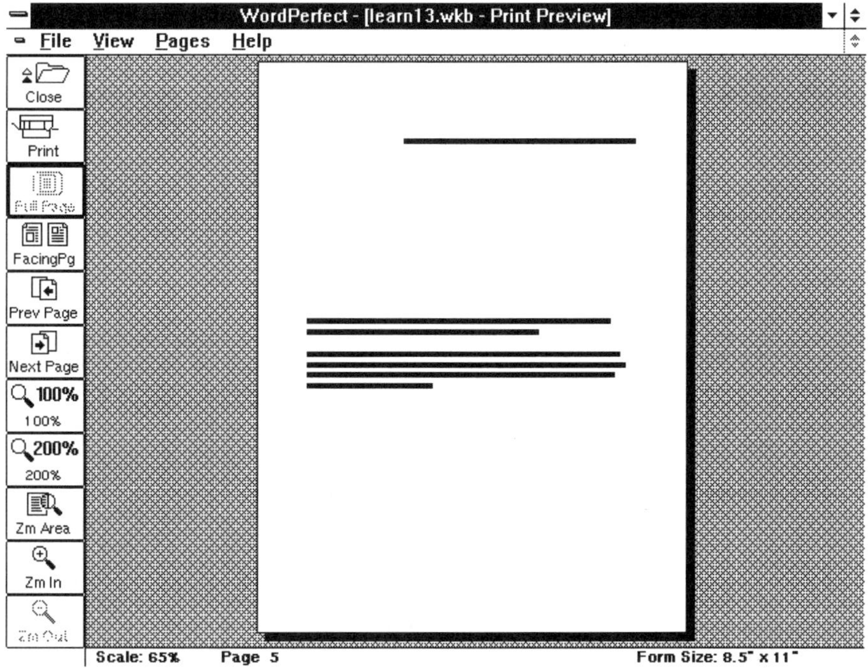

Figure 17-22. *Page five is centered vertically, as seen by selecting the Print Preview command from the* ***File*** *menu.*

Date code and format

In Chapter 3 - **Editing Text**, the insertion of the current date into a document is discussed in detail. However, the manner in which the date is placed and its appearance in a document can vary.

Before using this command, insert the text cursor just before the fifth paragraph on the page (if you have been following this chapter from the start, this paragraph may look a little different than if you have just joined). The fifth paragraph is the paragraph below the one that reads "The First Fifty years".

Selecting *Date* in the **Tools** menu activates a fly-out menu that lists three commands (Figure 17-23). The *Date/Text* command has already been discussed in Chapter 3.

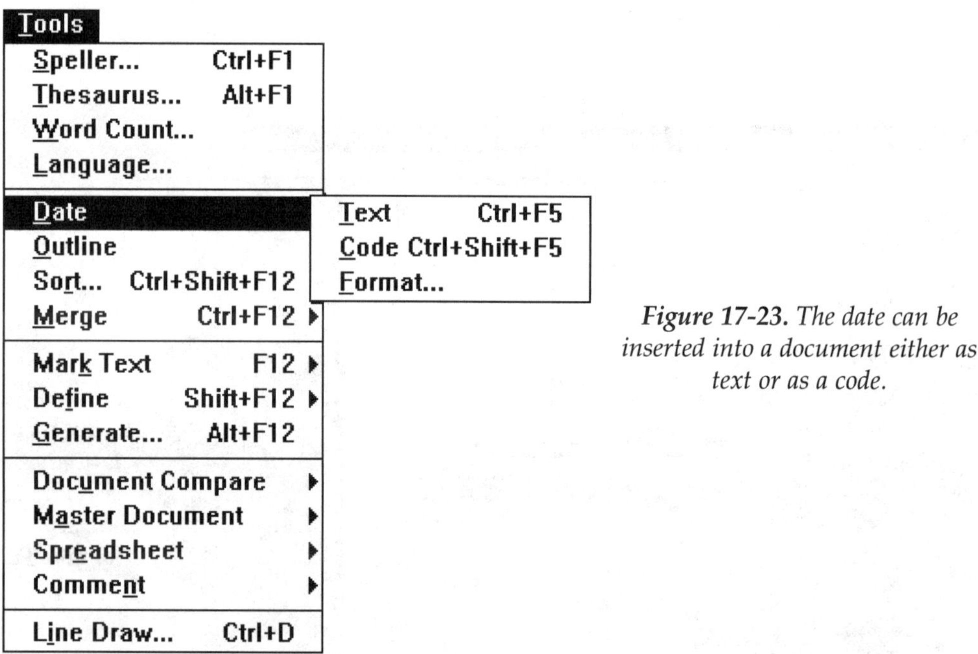

***Figure 17-23.** The date can be inserted into a document either as text or as a code.*

Selecting *Code* in the *Date* fly-out menu places a date code into the document at the current cursor position (select this command now). Inserting the date as a code, rather than actual text, allows this date to be updated every time the document is opened, or printed. The only way to tell the difference between the *Text* date and the *Code* date in a document is to view it in the *Reveal Codes* screen (Figure 17-24).

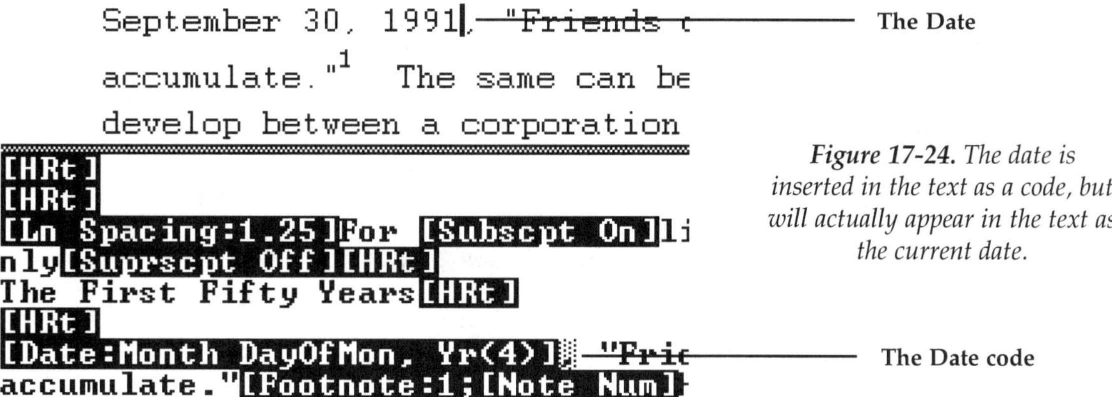

Figure 17-24. The date is inserted in the text as a code, but will actually appear in the text as the current date.

The manner in which the date is displayed by default may depend on the language version of WordPerfect being used. Despite the version, however, you do have a good deal of control over how this date may be displayed.

To change the date format, select the *Date/Format* command (Figure 17-25).

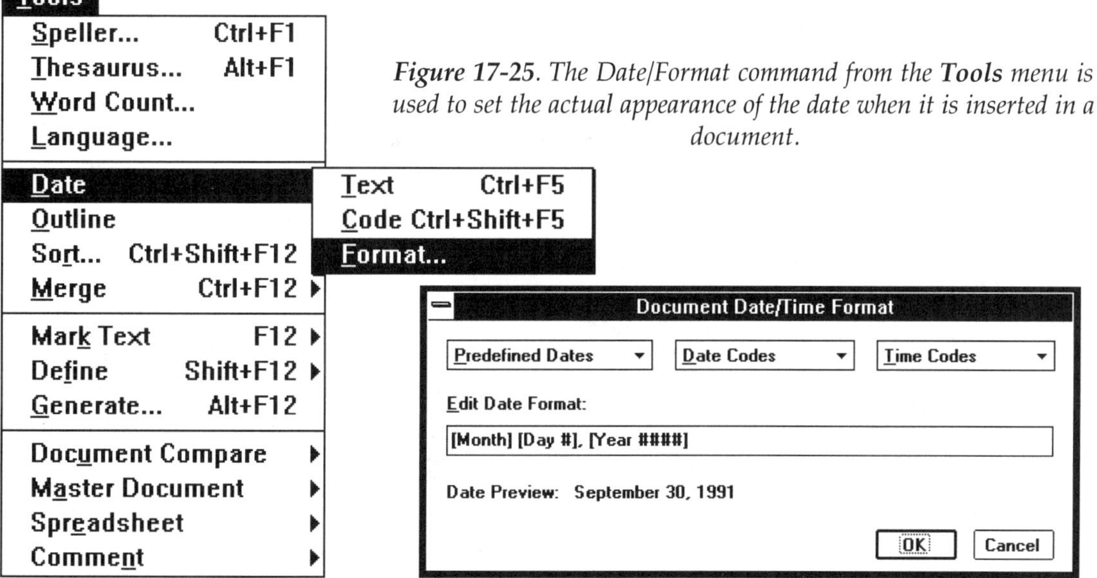

*Figure 17-25. The Date/Format command from the **Tools** menu is used to set the actual appearance of the date when it is inserted in a document.*

In the *Document Date/Time Format* dialog box, select the *Predefined Dates* list box to activate the sub-menu of predefined date formats from which you may make a selection (Figure 17-26). As a selection is made from this list, it is reflected in the *Date Preview* (bottom of dialog box), and the *Edit Date Format* lines.

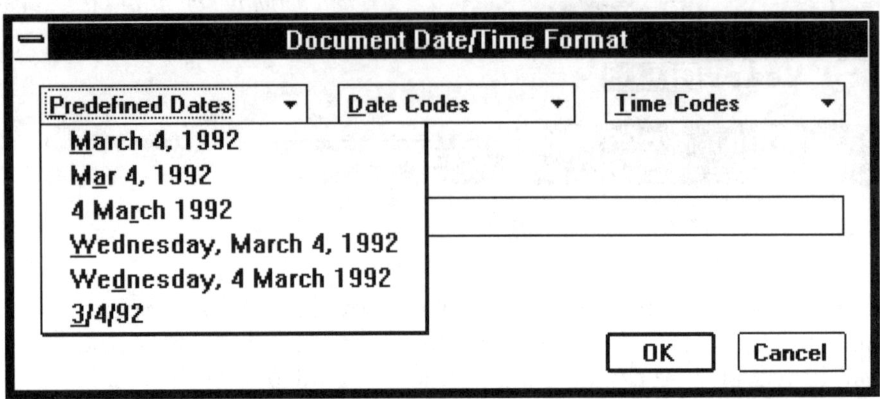

Figure 17-26. *Any of the various predefined date formats can be selected from the Predefined Dates sub-menu in this dialog box.*

Custom date formats can also be created, using the *Document Date/Time Format* dialog box. To create a custom date format, clear the text that appears in the *Edit Date Format* text box (Figure 17-27).

Edit Date Format:

[Month] [Day #], [Year ####]

Figure 17-27. *The Edit Date Format text box reflects in code the current date format. Editing this code will affect how the date will appear in your documents.*

Select options from either the *Date Codes* (Figure 17-28), or *Time Codes* (Figure 17-29) lists, by clicking on either of these buttons. These options will then appear in the *Edit Date Format* text box. Using various options in the lists under these buttons, build a custom date and time appearance (regular keyboard characters can also be added to the *Edit Date Format* text box). Numbers, the dollar sign, or the percent sign, cannot be used in this text box.

Date Codes

[Day #]	Day of Month
[Day 0#]	Day of Month (zero pad)
[Day _#]	Day of Month (space pad)
[Month #]	Month Number
[Month 0#]	Month Number (zero pad)
[Month _#]	Month Number (space pad)
[Month]	Month Name
[Abbr. Month]	Abbreviated Month Name
[Year ##]	2 Digit Year
[Year ####]	4 Digit Year
[Weekday]	Day of Week
[Abbr. Weekday]	Abbreviated Day of Week

Figure 17-28. *The predefined Date Codes.*

Time Codes

[Hour(12) #]	12 Hour Clock Hour #
[Hour(12) 0#]	12 Hour Clock Hour # (zero pad)
[Hour(12) _#]	12 Hour clock Hour #(space pad)
[Hour(24) #]	24 Hour Clock Hour #
[Hour(24) 0#]	24 Hour Clock Hour # (zero pad)
[Hour(24) _#]	24 Hour clock Hour #(space pad)
[Minute #]	Minute Number
[Minute 0#]	Minute Number (zero pad)
[Minute _#]	Minute Number (space pad)
[AM/PM]	AM/PM Mark

Figure 17-29. *The predefined Time Codes.*

The *Date Preview* line (Figure 17-30), shows how the date will appear when it is inserted into a document.

Date Preview: September 30, 1991

Figure 17-30. *The Date Preview line shows how the date will appear, using the current date.*

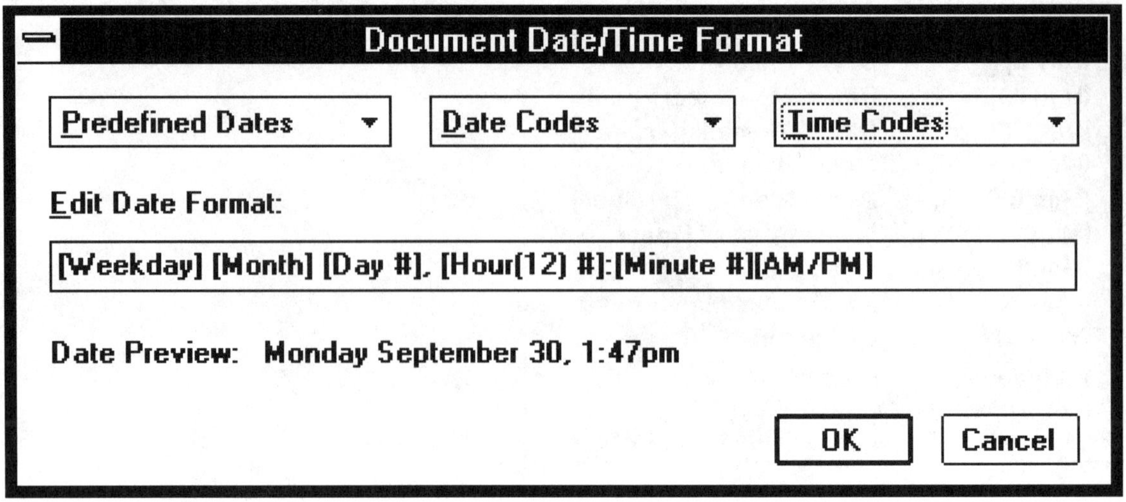

Document Date/Time Format

Predefined Dates ▾ Date Codes ▾ Time Codes ▾

Edit Date Format:

[Weekday] [Month] [Day #], [Hour(12) #]:[Minute #][AM/PM]

Date Preview: Monday September 30, 1:47pm

OK Cancel

Figure 17-31. *A Custom Date Format.*

Figure 17-31 illustrates a custom date. Look closely at the codes in the *Edit Date Format* text box, they correspond to selections in the *Date Codes* and *Time Codes* sub-menus. The Spacebar has been used to pad the codes out (by clicking the mouse in the *Edit Date Format* line, and pressing the Spacebar) and some keyboard characters such as a comma and a colon have been manually added to this line. See if you can emulate this format in your dialog box. The *Date Preview* line might be an easier way to visualize exactly the custom date format created.

The Color command

Within the **Font** menu, a command called *Color* can be used to change the color of text (either of selected text, or text from the current cursor position onwards). Colors can be created or selected from a range of predefined colors. Results are displayed on screen (on color monitors) and can be printed on any of a range of color printers supported by Windows or WordPerfect.

To use this command, either select the text you wish to alter or insert the text cursor into the document at some point. Then select the *Color* command from the **Font** menu (Figure 17-32).

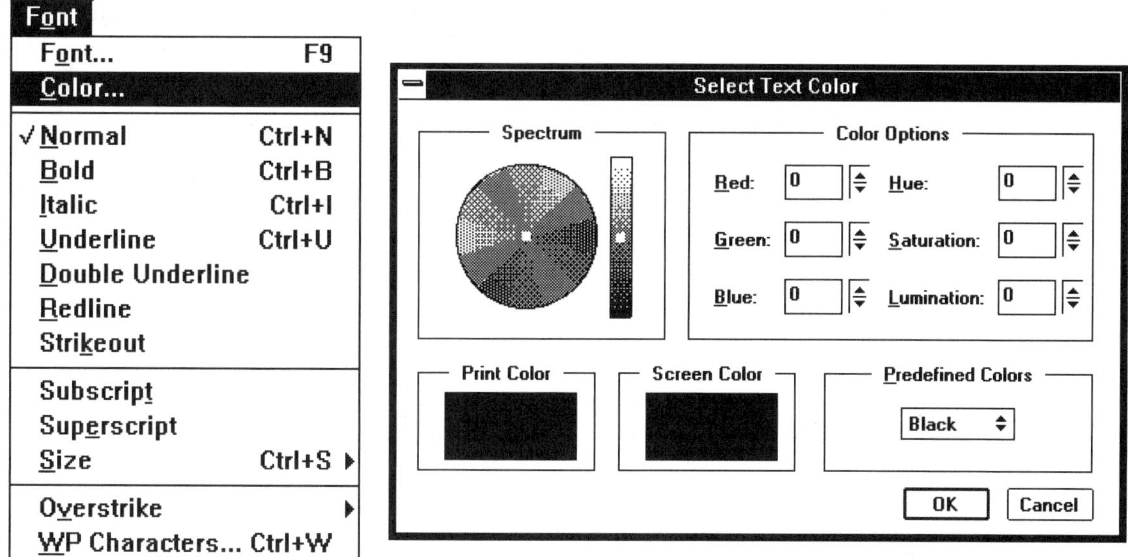

*Figure 17-32. Selecting the Color command from the **Font** menu activates the Select Text Color dialog box.*

The easiest way to select a color for text is to select one of the predefined colors, available from the *Predefined Colors* pop-up list box.

As any of the *Predefined Colors* are selected, note that other settings in the dialog box change to reflect the selection made (Figure 17-33).

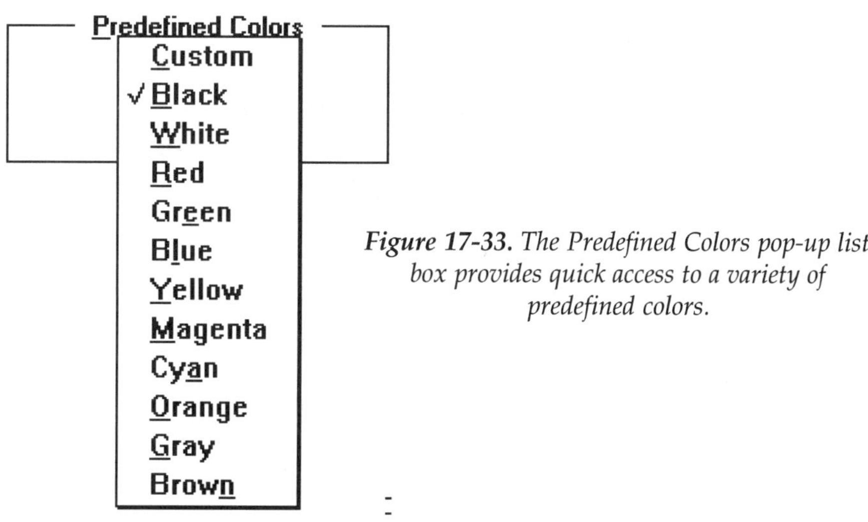

Figure 17-33. The Predefined Colors pop-up list box provides quick access to a variety of predefined colors.

Above the *Predefined Colors* pop-up list box is the *Color Options* area. Within this area, any selected color is reflected in two ways—using the *Red, Green* and *Blue*, and the *Hue, Saturation,* and *Lumination* methods. Any particular color can be described using a mixture of values in these settings.

For example, the color *Orange* is made up of a value of 170 for *Red*, a value of 63 for *Green*, and a value of 0 for *Blue*. The same color, *Orange*, can also be defined using a value of 22 for *Hue*, 100 for *Saturation*, and 33 for *Lumination* (illustrated in Figure 17-32).

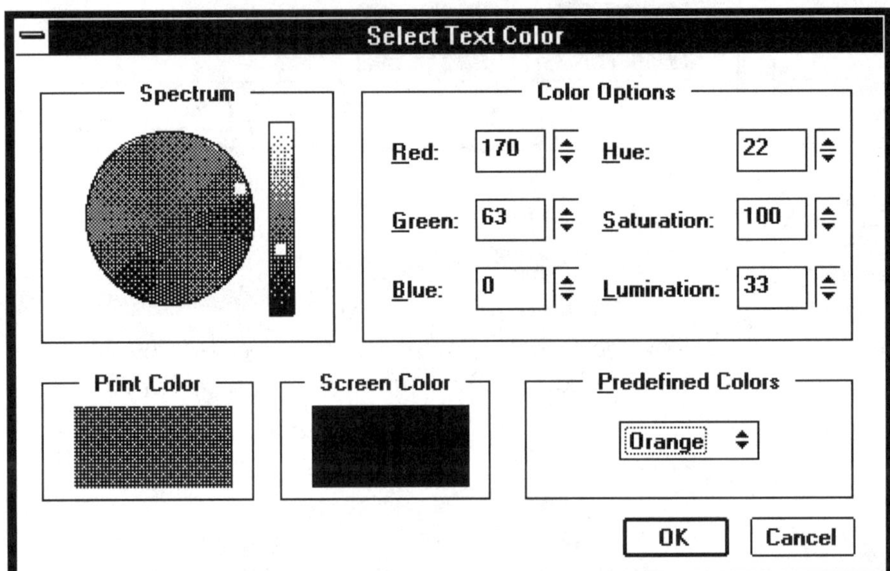

***Figure 17-32.** The color Orange has been selected from the Predefined Colors pop-up list box. The definition of the color Orange, using the two available methods described above, is illustrated in the Color Options section of the dialog box.*

Using the *Red, Green* and *Blue* text boxes, enter values to create your own colors using a mix of these three primary colors. Valid settings for each of these colors range from 0 through to 255. If each color was set to 255, the resultant color would be white; if each was set to 0, the resultant color would be black.

To the right of the *Red, Green* and *Blue* gauges are the *Hue, Saturation,* and *Lumination* text boxes. As with the *Red-Green-Blue* method, values can be entered into these text boxes. *Hue* may run from 0 to 360, while *Saturation* and *Lumination* run from 0 to 100 each.

Altering the color using either method will result in the values in the other method changing to reflect the new color.

The *Spectrum* circle may also be used either to select a color, or to reflect the currently defined color. Clicking the mouse button down anywhere in the circle will select the color displayed under the mouse pointer. As a color is selected in this manner, the values for *Red-Green-Blue* and *Hue-Saturation-Lumination* also change.

By selecting a vertical position in the vertical bar to the right of the *Spectrum* circle, the *Lumination* of the circle is altered (Figure 17-33).

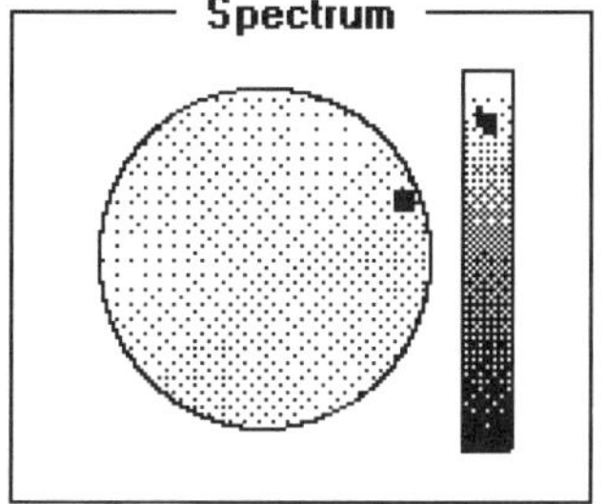

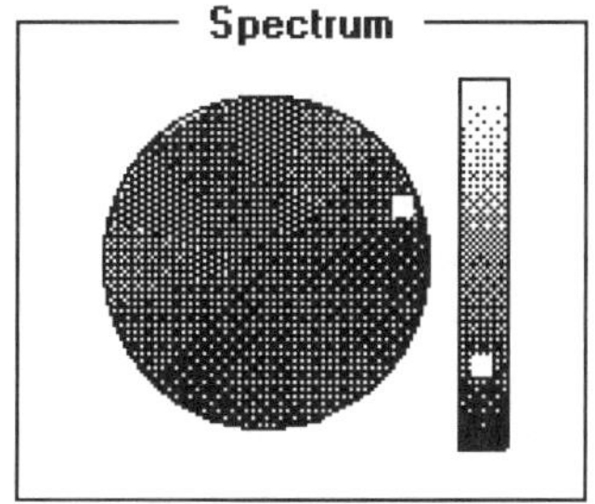

Figure 17-33. *Note the position of the dot in each of the vertical bars, and how the brightness of the corresponding Spectrum circle changes. The higher the dot is to the top of the bar, the brighter the circle.*

This dialog box also reflects (as accurately as the screen will allow) the currently selected color as it will print (in the *Print Color* box), and how this color will appear on screen (in the *Screen Color* box) (Figure 17-34).

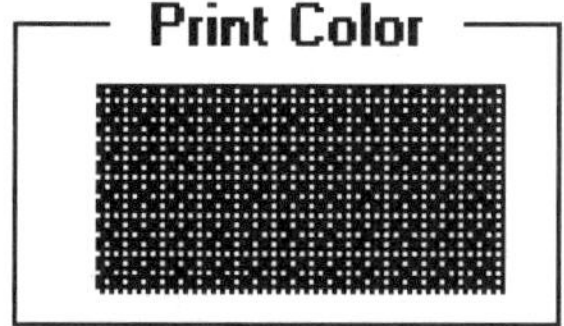

Figure 17-34. *The Print Color (as accurately as the screen will allow) and Screen Color of the selected color are reflected in this dialog box.*

Select any one of the *Predefined Colors* or customize your own and then select **OK.** This color will now display on screen for the text you selected before activating the *Select Text Color* dialog box.

Searching and replacing

WordPerfect provides *Search*, *Search Next*, *Search Previous*, and *Replace* commands, which enable the location and modification of any string or code within a document.

The Search command

Searching for any string of text, or code, in a document is achieved using the *Search* command, from the **Edit** menu (Figure 17-35).

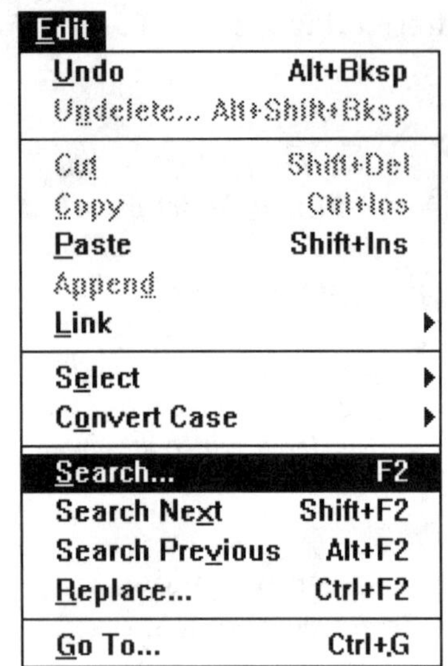

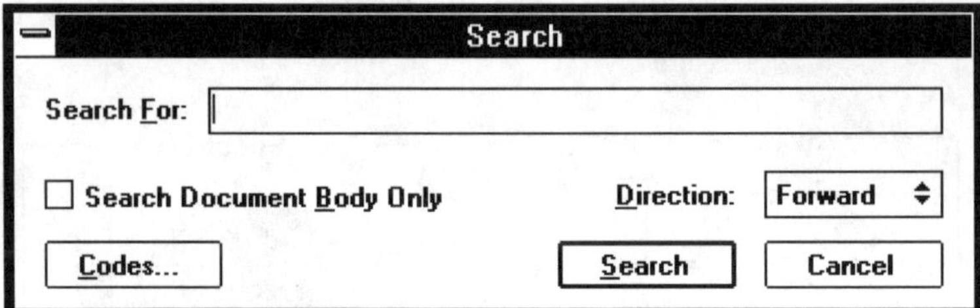

*Figure 17-35. The Search command from the **Edit** menu and its dialog box.*

Once the *Search* dialog box has been invoked, enter the string for which to search in the *Search For* text box and click on the *Search* button. WordPerfect will then find the first occurrence of the specified string in the document. However, there are other options.

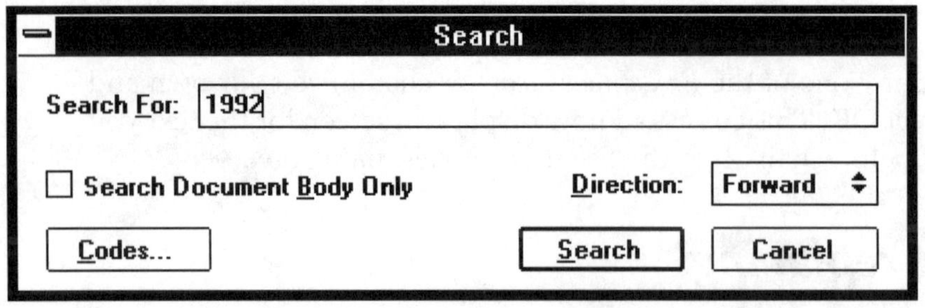

Figure 17-36. Enter the string 1992 in the Search dialog box. This is what WordPerfect will locate in the current document.

The *Search Document Body Only* check box, if checked, will force WordPerfect to ignore such things as headers, footers, footnotes, endnotes, figure box captions, and text boxes.

The search direction may also be specified using the *Direction* pop-up list box, which contains two entries: *Forward*, and *Backward*. If *Forward* is selected, WordPerfect will search from the current cursor position to the end of the document. If *Backward* is selected, WordPerfect will search from the current cursor position to the start of the document.

Searching for codes

Figure 17-37 shows the dialog box that appears when the *Codes* command button is selected from the *Search* dialog box. It lists every code that may be found in a WordPerfect document. Using selections made from this list (to insert a selection from this list into the *Search For* text box, select the code, and click on the *Insert* button), WordPerfect can search for specific situations including hyphens, hard returns, and underlined text.

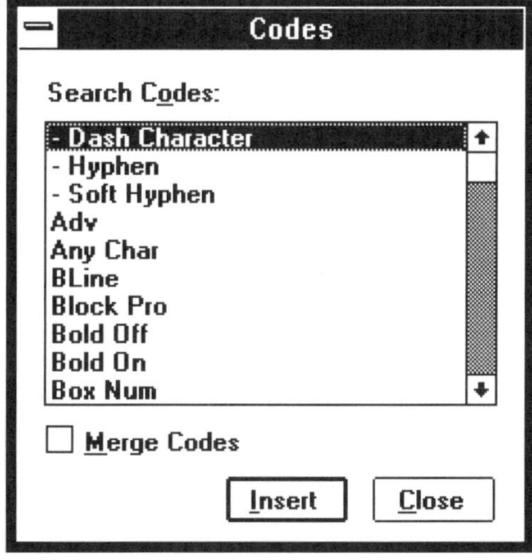

Figure 17-37. *The Codes dialog box lists every code that can be found in a WordPerfect document and these codes can be inserted into the Search dialog box .*

Using wildcards

Codes may be mixed with text in the *Search For* text box. The code *Any Char*, for example, can be used to signify any character in a string. For example, "Word[Any Char]erfect" will search for the word "WordPerfect", where in fact the fifth letter may be any letter, or character, at all (not just "P").

The codes facility is discussed in more detail in Chapter 5 - **Codes**.

When the *Search* button is selected, WordPerfect will search for the first occurrence of the text in the *Search For* text box. If this text is found, the text cursor is placed after its occurrence in the document and the *Search* dialog box disappears (Figure 17-38).

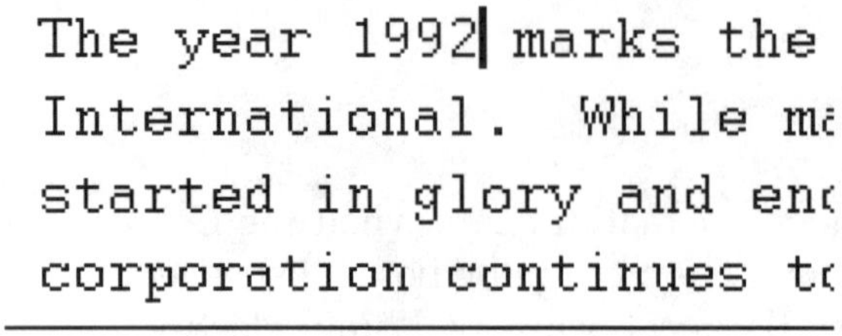

The year 1992| marks the
International. While m
started in glory and en
corporation continues t

Figure 17-38. *In this example, the string "1992" has been found, and the text cursor placed after this string.*

If the *Search For* text is not found, WordPerfect will report an error message, using the Status bar (Figure 17-39).

String Not Found:"1992"

Figure 17-39. *The Status Bar will report when a search string is not found. This message will only remain in the Status bar for a few seconds.*

The Search Next command

Once WordPerfect has located the first occurrence of a string of text, you may wish to search for the next occurrence of this same string. If this is the case, do not select the *Search* command again. Select either the *Search Next* (to search forwards through the text), *or Search Previous* (to search backwards through the text) commands (Figure 17-40), from the **Edit** menu. These commands will now search for the next occurrence of the string last inserted in the *Search* dialog box (Figure 17-36).

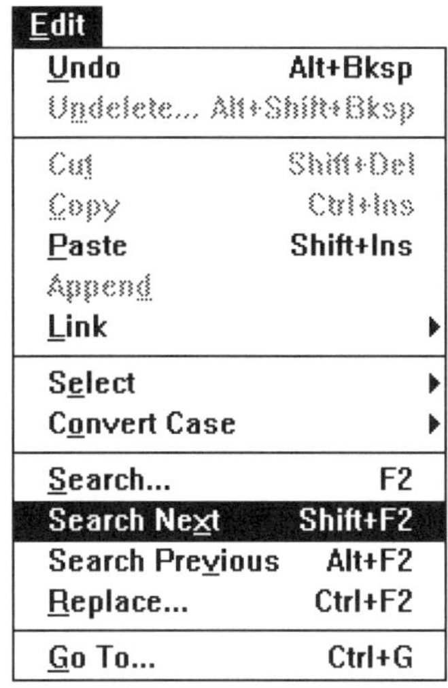

Figure 17-40. *The Search Next command searches forward through the text to search for the next occurrence of the string last inserted in the Search dialog box. The Search Previous command searches backwards through the text for the same thing.*

Replacing text

Before looking at the *Replace* command, insert the cursor at the very start of the document, before the very first character in the file. Now select the *Replace* command from the **Edit** menu (Figure 17-41).

Quite often the reason to locate a string of text is to replace it with another string. This process can be carried out automatically, using the *Replace* command.

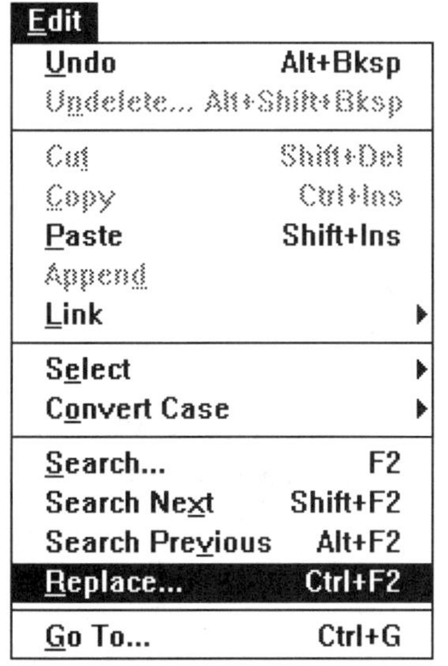

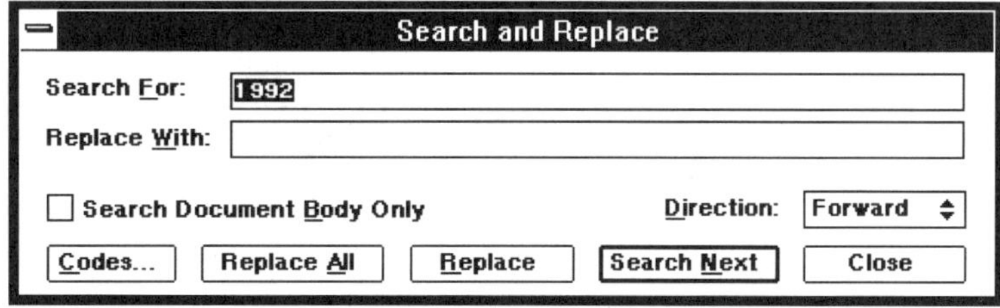

Figure 17-41. *The Replace command and dialog box.*

The *Replace* command is closely linked with the *Search* command. So much so, in fact, that the string last inserted in the *Search* dialog box appears in the *Replace* dialog box automatically ("1992" in Figure 17-41).

In this case, enter the string "HALVA" in the *Search For* text box. This is the text that will be replaced. Insert the string "ACME" in the *Replace With* text box. This is the text that will replace the text in the *Search For* text box.

The *Search Document Body Only* check box, the *Direction* pop-up list, and the *Codes* button, work as they did with the *Search* command.

Once *Search For* and *Replace With* strings have been entered, make a selection from the buttons along the bottom of the dialog box (Figure 17-42).

Figure 17-42. *The Replace options along the bottom of the Replace dialog box.*

Selecting the *Replace All* button causes WordPerfect to make replacements to all text that matches the text in the *Search For* text box, without pausing for confirmation of any of these changes.

The *Search Next* button finds the next occurrence of the text in the *Search For* text box and highlights it in the document. You may then choose either the *Search Next* or the *Replace* button, depending on whether you would actually like to replace the text selected or move on. If you select *Search Next*, WordPerfect searches for and highlights the next occurrence of the text. If you choose *Replace*, WordPerfect replaces the currently highlighted text and moves on to the next occurrence of the text.

Choose *Search Next* to find the first occurrence of the word "HALVA", and select *Replace* to replace the selected word with "ACME". After this, select the *Replace All* button to replace all occurrences of the word "HALVA" with "ACME" automatically.

Capitalization

When entering text into a *Search For* text box (using either the *Search* or *Replace* commands), lowercase characters will match with either lowercase or uppercase characters in the document. If you enter uppercase characters in this text box, only uppercase characters will be matched.

Advanced Text Editing — Exercise

This training exercise is designed so that people of all levels of expertise with WordPerfect can use it to gain maximum benefit. In order to do this, the bare exercise is listed below this paragraph on just one page, with no hints. The following pages contain the steps needed to complete this exercise for those who need additional prompting.

Steps in brief

1. *Open the learn16.wkb file from the learn sub-directory.*
2. *On the line under "The First Fifty Years", insert the current date as a code.*
3. *Replace every occurrence of the string "HALVA International" with a bolded version of "HALVA International".*
4. *Locate the first occurrence of the string "HALVA International", and insert a trademark sign after it.*
5. *Superscript the trademark.*

The details for completing these steps are on the following pages.

Steps in detail

1. Open the learn16.wkb file from the learn directory.

Use the *Open* command from the **File** menu (Figure 17x-1) to open ***learn16.wkb***, which will be found in the ***learn*** sub-directory on your computer (Figure 17x-1).

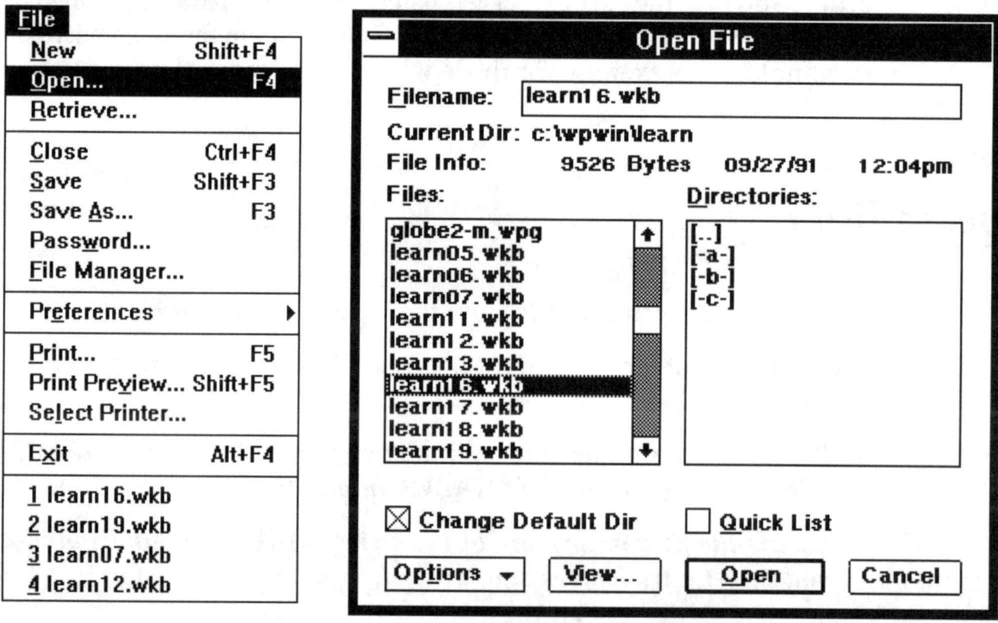

*Figure 17x-1. Use the Open command from the **File** menu, to activate the Open File dialog box. From here, select the file **learn16.wkb** from the **learn** sub-directory, and click on Open.*

2. On the line under "The First Fifty Years", insert the current date as a code.

Insert the text cursor on the line under the paragraph that reads "The First Fifty Years" (Figure 17x-2).

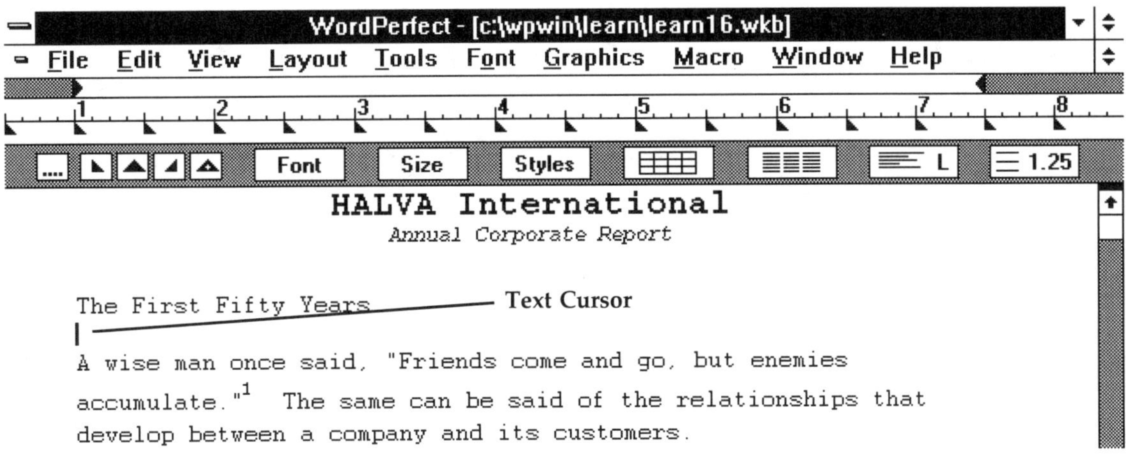

Figure 17x-2. Note where the text cursor has been inserted here—insert the text cursor in the same place in your document.

To insert the current date as a code, select the *Date/Code* command from the **Tools** menu (Figure 17x-3).

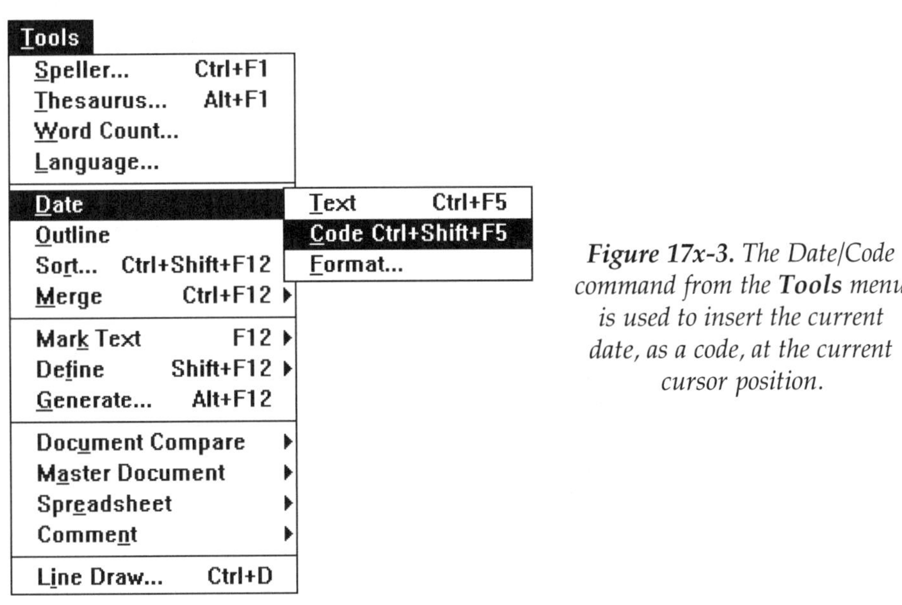

*Figure 17x-3. The Date/Code command from the **Tools** menu is used to insert the current date, as a code, at the current cursor position.*

The current date is then inserted into the document (Figure 17x-4).

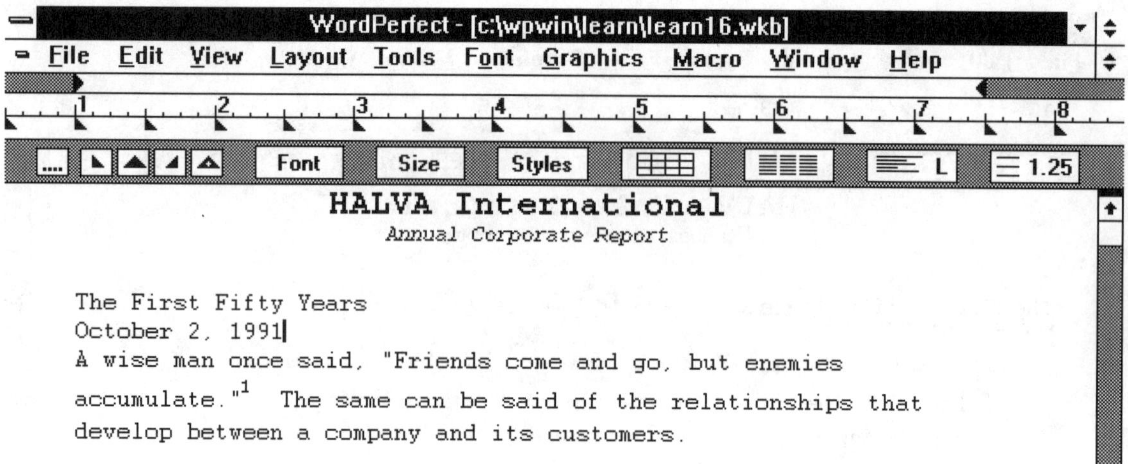

Figure 17x-4. *The current date is inserted at the text cursor location of Figure 17x-2.*

3. ***Replace every occurrence of the string "HALVA International" with a bolded version of "HALVA International".***

Before you start this step, you should insert the text cursor before the very first character in the document, so that the search and replace operation can be performed in one move.

To replace any string of text, you must select the *Replace* command from the **Edit** menu (Figure 17x-5).

Edit	
Undo	Alt+Bksp
Undelete...	Alt+Shift+Bksp
Cut	Shift+Del
Copy	Ctrl+Ins
Paste	Shift+Ins
Append	
Link	▸
Select	▸
Convert Case	▸
Search...	F2
Search Next	Shift+F2
Search Previous	Alt+F2
Replace...	Ctrl+F2
Go To...	Ctrl+G

Figure 17x-5. *The Replace command, from the* ***Edit*** *menu, is used to replace a string of text with another.*

In the *Replace* dialog box that appears, enter the string "HALVA International" on the *Search For* line (Figure 17x-6).

Search and Replace

Search For: HALVA International

Replace With:

Search Document Body Only

Direction: Forward

Codes... Replace All Replace Search Next Close

Figure 17x-6. *Enter the string "HALVA International" on the Search For line.*

Insert the text cursor on the *Replace With* line and select the *Codes* button (Figure 17x-7). This is necessary, as you need to insert a bold code in the *Replace With* text box.

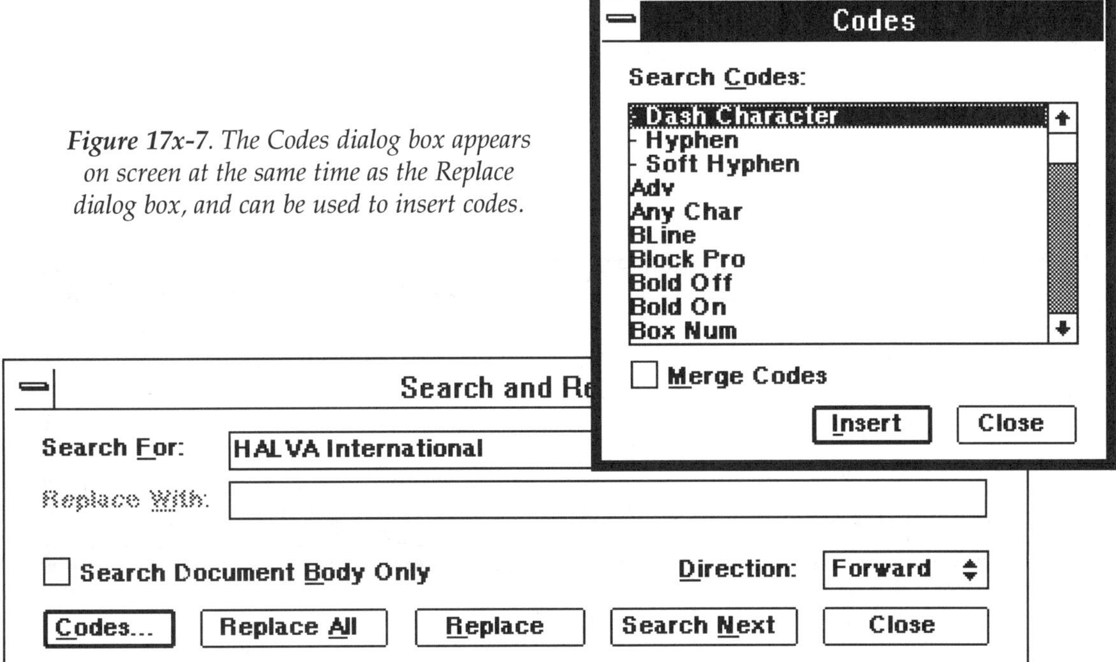

Figure 17x-7*. The Codes dialog box appears on screen at the same time as the Replace dialog box, and can be used to insert codes.*

Locate the *Bold On* code from the *Replace Codes* list and select it. Then, click on the *Insert* button, and the code will appear automatically in the *Replace With* line (Figure 17x-8).

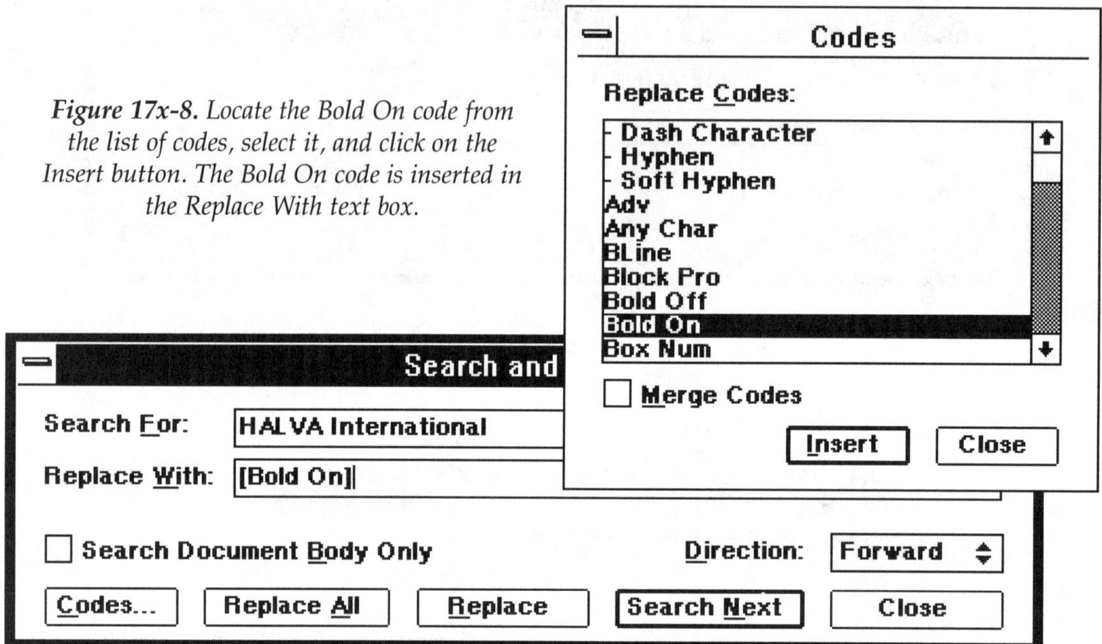

Figure 17x-8. Locate the Bold On code from the list of codes, select it, and click on the Insert button. The Bold On code is inserted in the Replace With text box.

After the *Bold On* code, enter the string "HALVA International" on the *Replace With* line (Figure 17x-9).

Search and Replace
Search For: HALVA International
Replace With: [Bold On]HALVA International
Search Document Body Only
Direction: Forward
Codes... Replace All Replace Search Next Close

Figure 17x-9. Insert the string "HALVA International" after the Bold On code in the Replace With text box.

Move back to the *Codes* dialog box and locate the *Bold Off* code. Select this code, click on the *Insert* button, and then the *Close* button (Figure 17x-10). The *Bold Off* code is inserted on the *Replace With* line and the *Codes* dialog box disappears (Figure 17x-11).

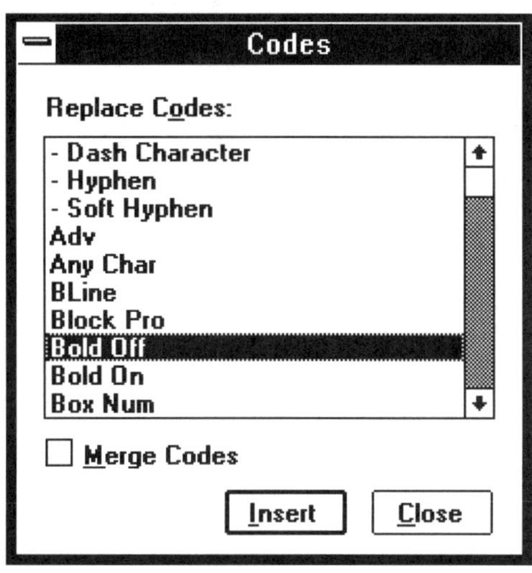

Figure 17x-10. *After entering the string in Figure 17x-9, locate the Bold Off code in the Codes list, select it, and then click on the Insert button, followed by the Close button.*

Figure 17x-11*. The code is now inserted into the Replace With text box.*

To replace all occurrences automatically, select the *Replace All* button. WordPerfect will then spend a few seconds replacing the string in the text. Click on the *Close* button to exit the *Search and Replace* dialog box.

Assuming the *Search For* string entered in Figure 17x-6 was correctly spelt, your editing screen will look like Figure 17x-12. In Figure 17x-12, the *Search and Replace* dialog box has been closed, and the top of the file is being viewed. (The *Replace* operation may leave you looking at the bottom of the file.)

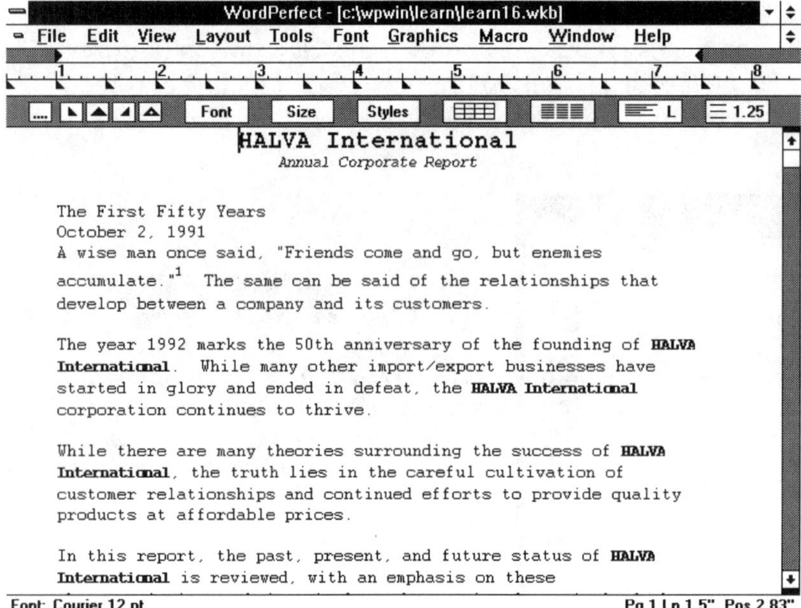

Figure 17x-12. *Every occurrence of the string "HALVA International" in the document has been bolded. Use the scroll bar to move back to the beginning of your document.*

4. ***Locate the first occurrence of the string "HALVA International", and insert a trademark sign after it.***

The first occurrence of this string is in the heading. Insert the text cursor after this string (Figure 17x-13).

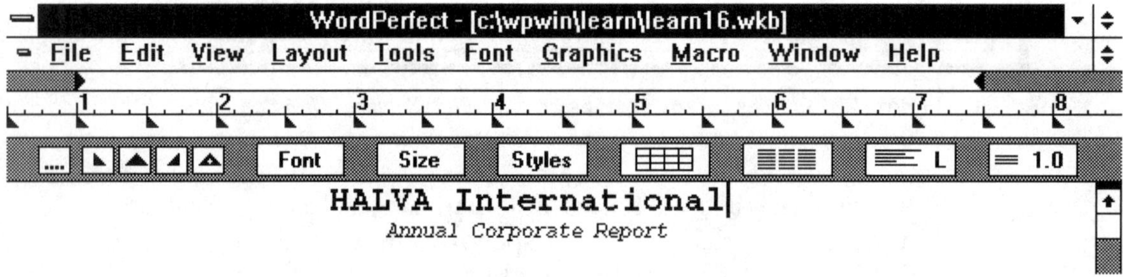

Figure 17x-13. *Insert the text cursor after the first line of text.*

The trademark character is a WordPerfect symbol. To access this symbol, select the *WP Characters* command in the **Font** menu (Figure 17x-14). The *WordPerfect Characters* dialog box is then activated.

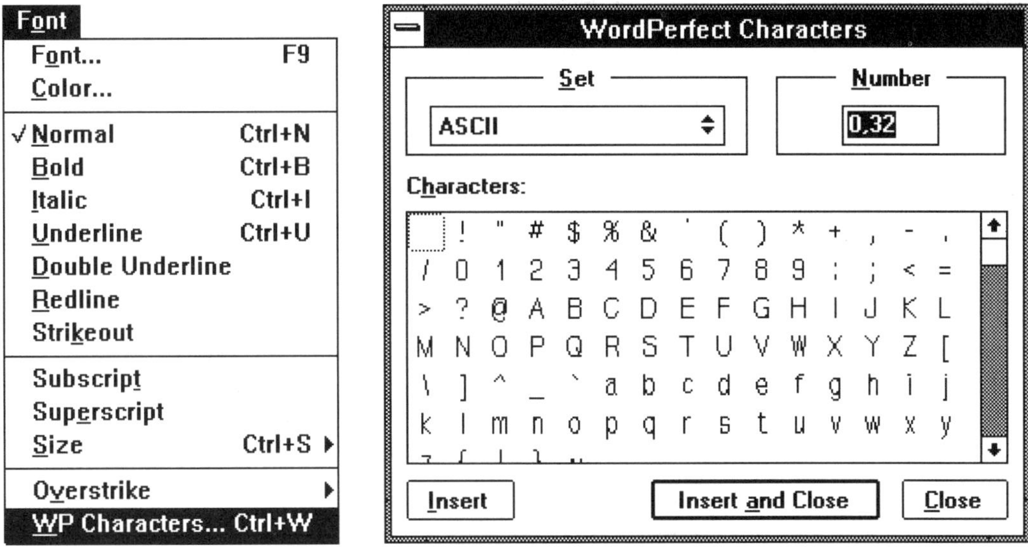

Figure 17x-14. *To insert special characters into a document, select the WP Characters command from the* **Font** *menu.*

From the *Set* pop-up list of Figure 17x-14, select the *Typographic Symbols* set (Figure 17x-15).

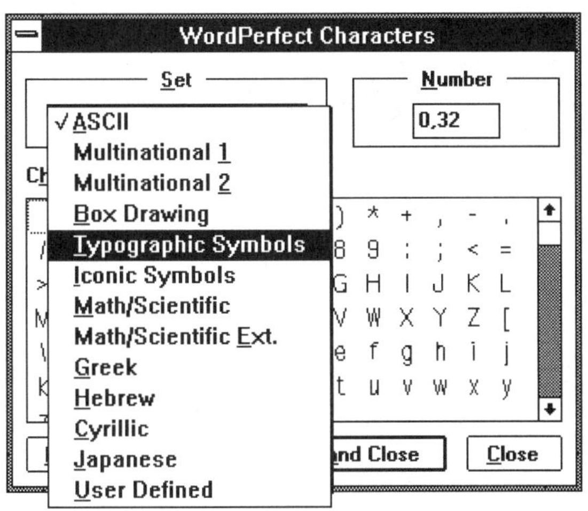

Figure 17x-15. *Select the Typographic Symbols character set from the Set pop-up list in this dialog box.*

Character number 4,41 is the trademark symbol. Select this symbol and click on the *Insert and Close* button (Figure 17x-16).

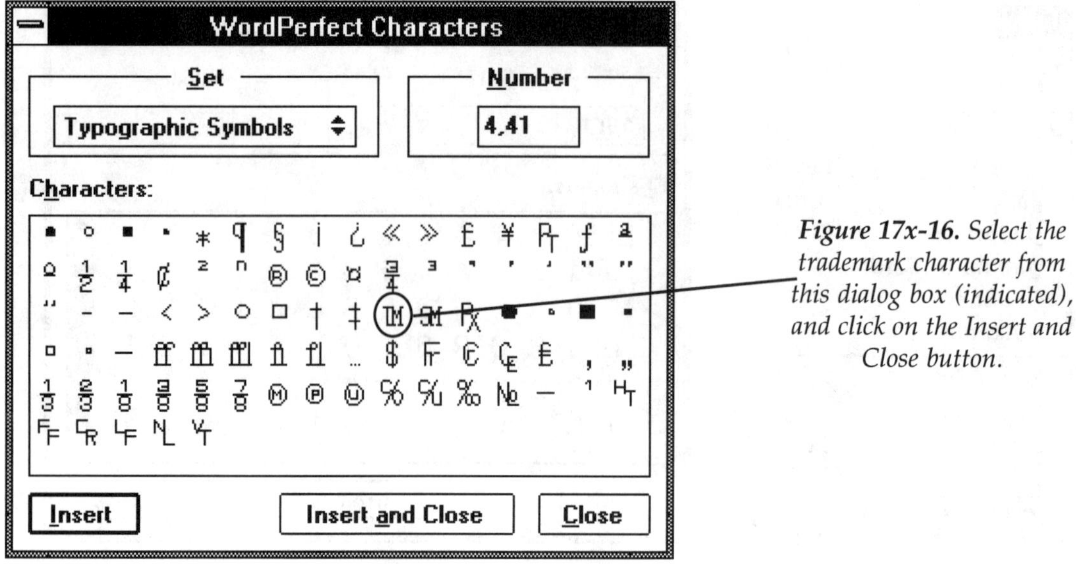

Figure 17x-16. *Select the trademark character from this dialog box (indicated), and click on the Insert and Close button.*

The trademark symbol is then inserted in the text at the cursor position (Figure 17x-17).

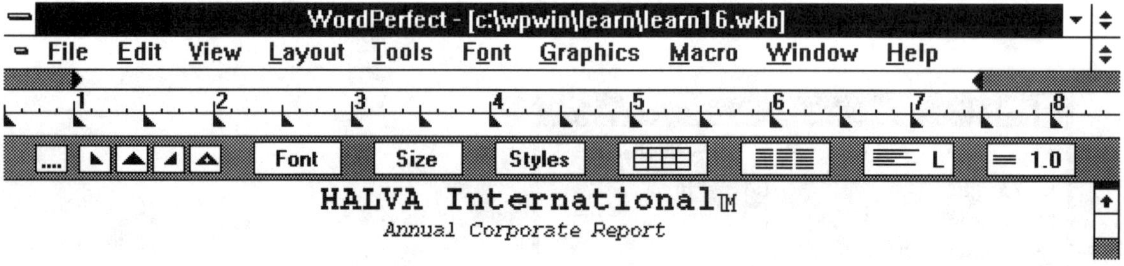

Figure 17x-17. *The trademark symbol is inserted in the text.*

5. ***Superscript the trademark.***

Select the trademark symbol by swiping it (Figure 17x-18).

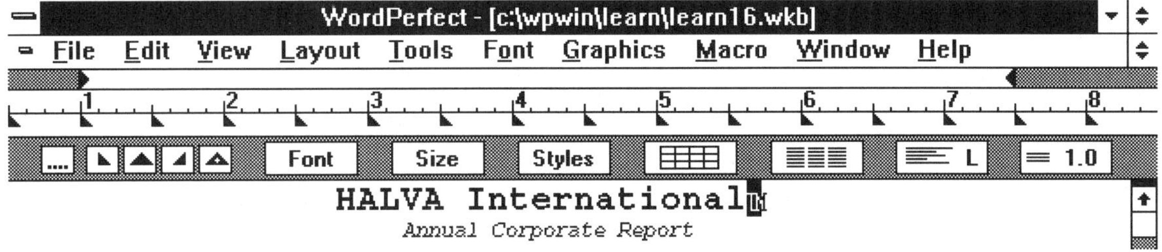

Figure 17x-18. Select the trademark symbol by "swiping" it.

Select the *Superscript* command from the **Font** menu as shown in Figure 17x-19.

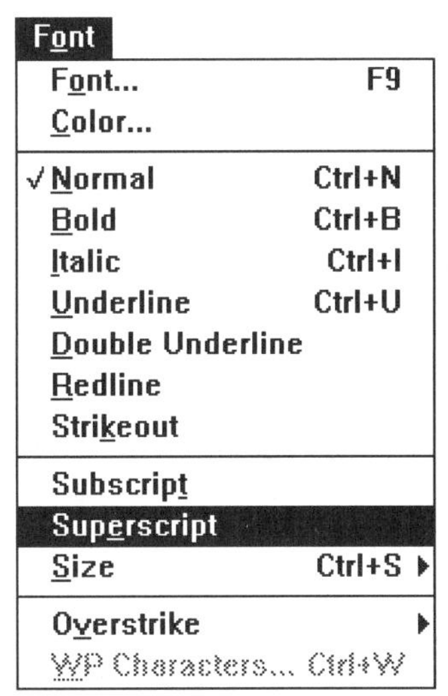

*Figure 17x-19. Select the Superscript command from the **Font** menu.*

The trademark character is now superscripted (Figure 17x-20).

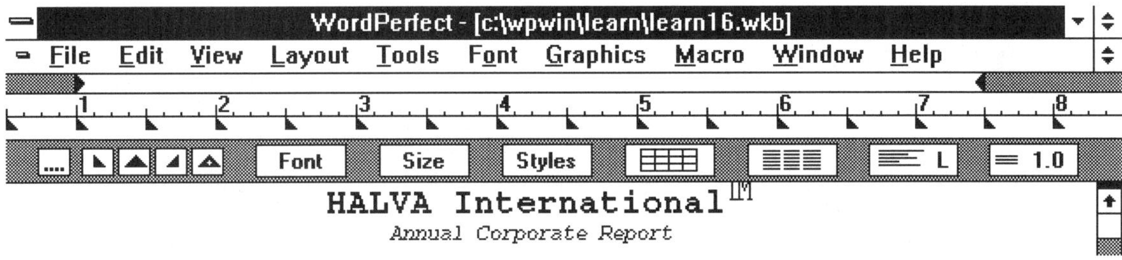

Figure 17x-20. The trademark character is now superscripted on screen (it may be a little obscured by the ruler).

Merging

WordPerfect provides a merge facility (often referred to as a mail merge) that allows you to create multiple documents based on a main, or primary, document and a secondary document containing a series of variables.

One of the main applications for this feature is a standard business letter which is to be sent, personally addressed, to many customers. Rather than typing out each letter individually, only one letter need be created. A second file is then created, containing only the names and addresses of the customers to whom the letter will be sent. After merging these two files, a third file is generated, containing one personally addressed letter for each customer listed in the second file.

To create a merged file is quite simple. It consists of two main steps—creating a *primary* file (this is the main file—in the above example, the letter), and a *secondary* file (this is the file that contains the variables—in the above example, the names and addresses of all the customers). In this chapter you will be creating secondary and primary file examples and then performing a merge operation to produce multiple letters.

Creating a secondary file

Before creating a secondary file, you must determine how many different variables are required. For example, in a business letter the information required might be:

Full Name of Customer

Company Name

Address

First Name of Customer (for salutation)

Every piece of variable information is known as a *field*. In this example, there are four variables which translates to four fields when merging.

Having decided on the number of fields and their contents, you then create the secondary file. The secondary file will contain one record for each customer. Each of these records will be made up of the four fields mentioned above.

Start a new WordPerfect file for this purpose (you may need to select the *New* command from the **File** menu).

Creating records in the secondary file

To create a record, you must enter the details of the customer, in four different fields—full name, company name, company address, and first name. In real life you may already have a list of all your customers—in this example you will work from this list of five companies:

Brett Smith
Widget & Company
23 Morning Street
Jonestown

Meredith Flake
Flakey Pastry
123 Baker Street
Cooktown

Betty Dickie
Pilliga Arts & Crafts
2 Main Street
Pilliga

Dr. Dwayne Dwyer
Smithtown 24 Hour Surgery
12 Smith Street
Smithtown

Carrie Barnes
Mok Art
630 Belmont Parade
Bellevue Hill

On the first line of the secondary file, type the full name of the first customer (Figure 18-1).

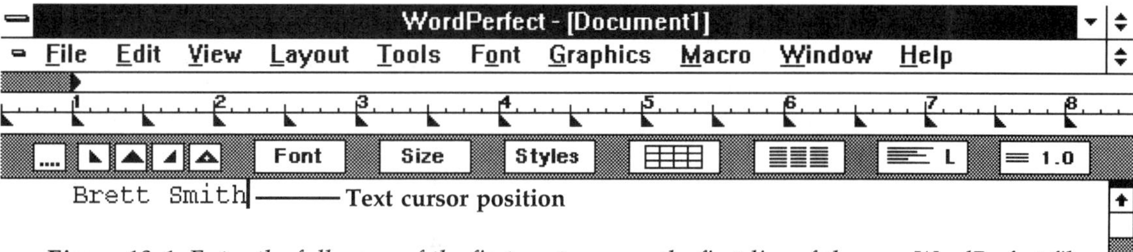

Figure 18-1. *Enter the full name of the first customer on the first line of the new WordPerfect file.*

The first field (full name) has now been entered. To let WordPerfect know that a field has ended, select the *End Field* command from the *Merge* fly-out menu in the **Tools** menu (Figure 18-2). Make sure you do this without moving the cursor from its position, as shown in Figure 18-1.

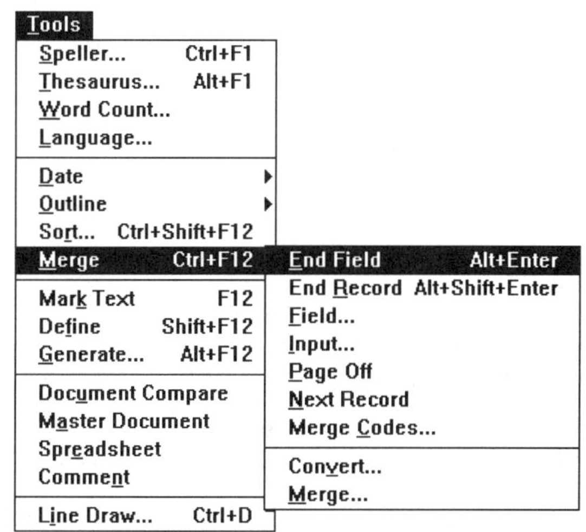

Figure 18-2. *The Merge/End Field command from the* ***Tools*** *menu is used to let WordPerfect know that a field has been entered.*

When the *Merge/End Field* command is selected, an *END FIELD* code appears on the editing screen to the right of the text (Figure 18-3), and the cursor automatically moves to the beginning of the next line.

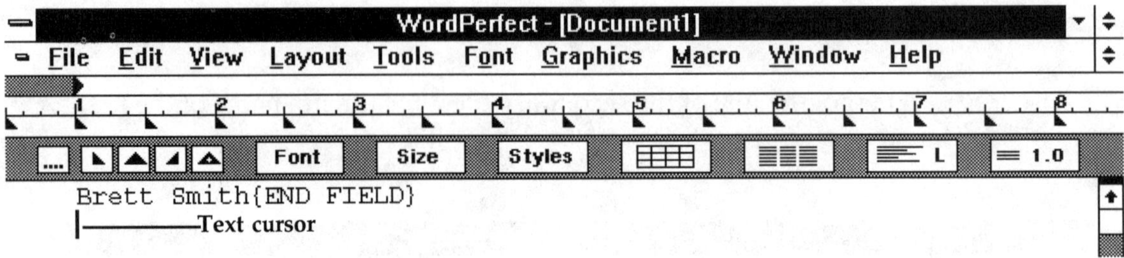

Figure 18-3. An END FIELD code appears on the editing screen, and the cursor moves down to the next line, after the command of Figure 18-2 is selected.

Having entered the first field, enter the second field, which is the company name (Figure 18-4). Remember to check the list from the earlier pages.

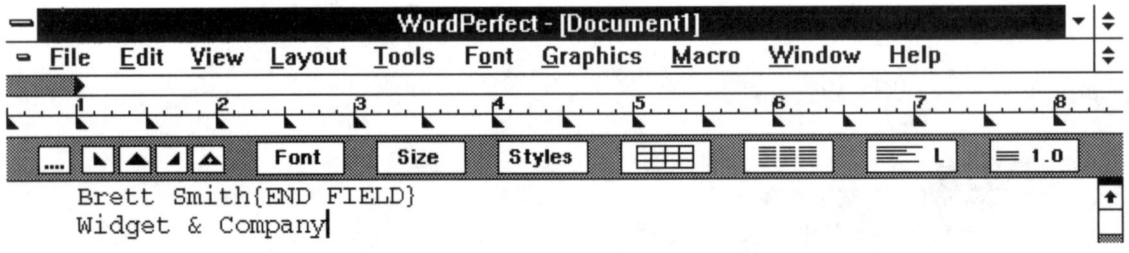

Figure 18-4. The second field, the company name, has now been entered.

As the second field consists purely of the company name, it too has now been entered. Again, select the *Merge/End Field* command to let WordPerfect know that a field has been entered. Alternatively, you may select the shortcut command for ending a field: hold down the Alt key, and press the Enter key. Either way, the screen then appears as shown in Figure 18-5.

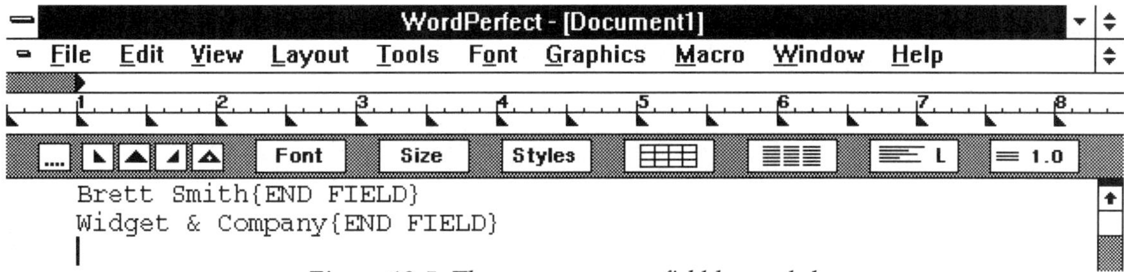

Figure 18-5. The company name field has ended.

Now move on to enter the third field, which is the company address. Enter the address of the first customer listed. The address will span over two lines—at the end of the first line, use the normal Enter key—there is no need to use an *END FIELD* code until the entire address has been entered as displayed in Figure 18-6.

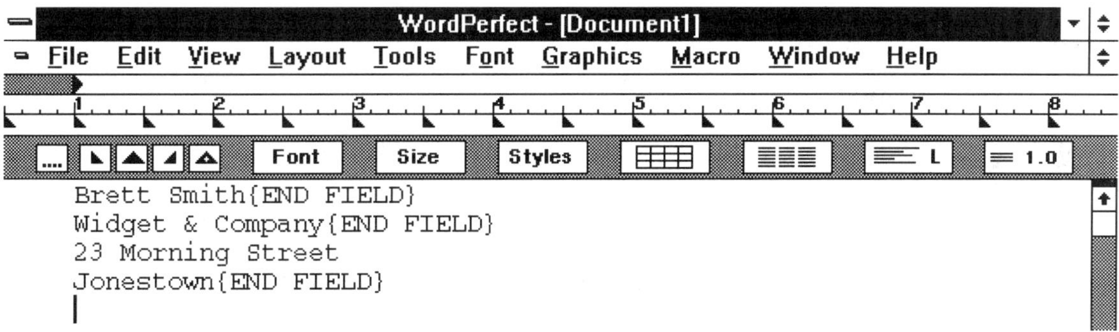

*Figure 18-6. The address has been entered and the Merge/End Field command, from the **Tools** menu (Figure 18-2), has been selected again.*

The third field in Figure 18-6 spanned two lines—it is quite possible for a field to span any size, from one letter to several pages.

Finally, the fourth field is the customer's first name—which in this case is "Brett". Enter this name and, once again, select the *Merge/End Field* command from the **Tools** menu (Figure 18-7).

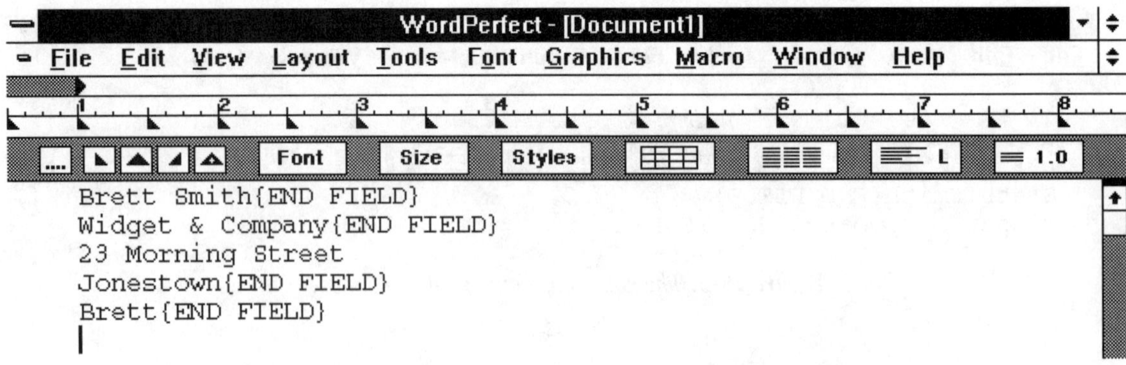

***Figure 18-7.** The fourth and final field in this example has been entered: the customer's first name.*

At this stage, all four fields have been entered. This means that you have entered the entire *record*. When this happens, you must let WordPerfect know, by selecting the *End Record* command from the *Merge* fly-out menu in the **Tools** menu (Figure 18-8).

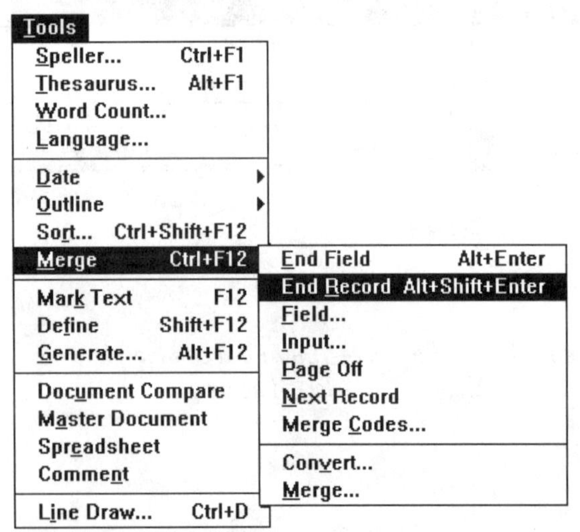

***Figure 18-8.** The Merge/End Record command from the **Tools** menu is used to end a record when creating a secondary file.*

Figure 18-9 illustrates the *END RECORD* code that is inserted in the text. As well as this code, two vertical lines (similar to a page break) are inserted under the first record. The cursor automatically moves to the start of a new record.

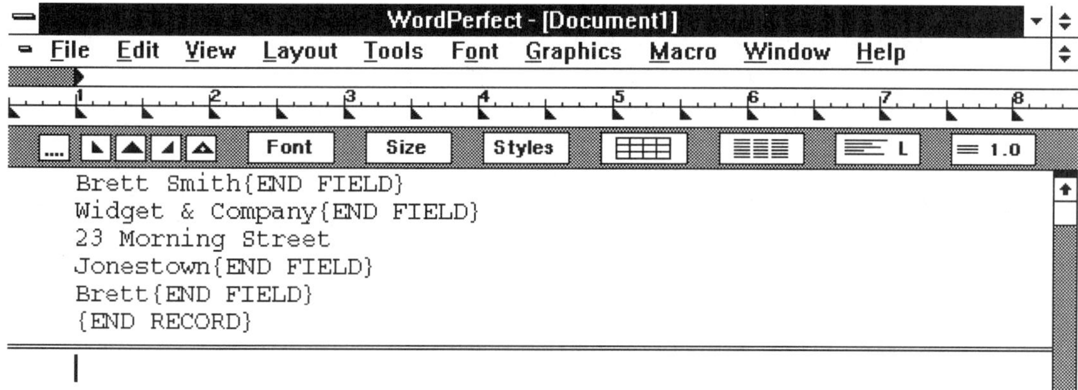

Figure 18-9. *The End Record code appears much like a page break in text. You may wish to use the shortcut combination to end a record, Alt+Shift+Enter.*

All other records can be entered into this document in the same manner as this record was entered. Repeat the process until all five records have been entered.

Figure 18-10 illustrates how the screen will look after some more records from the list of names earlier in this chapter have been entered.

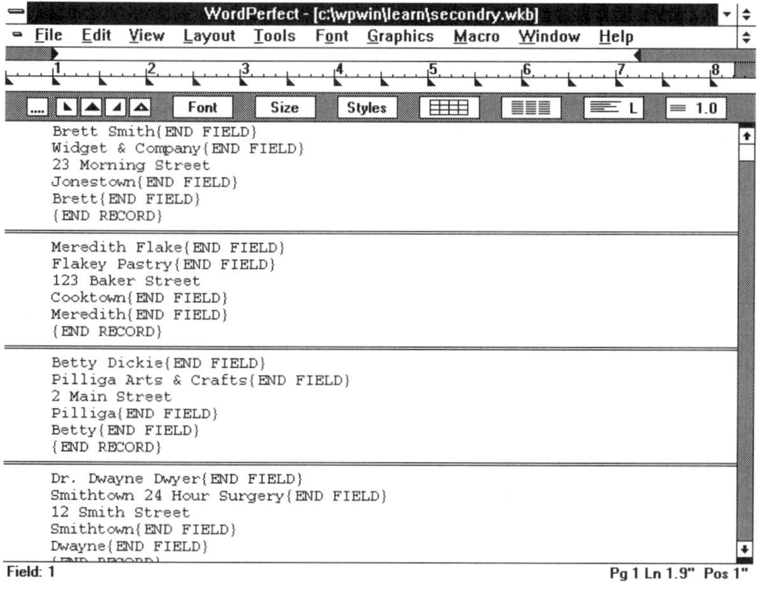

Figure 18-10. *Note that every record looks very similar—each contains four fields.*

Once all the customer names have been entered in this fashion, the secondary file is complete. Save this file, using the name ***secondry.wkb*** (Figure 18-11). You can, of course, call this file anything you like once you start using the merge operation for real applications.

WordPerfect - [c:\wpwin\learn\secondry.wkb - unmodified]

Figure 18-11. *Save the file you have created under the name **secondry.wkb**.*

Notes about creating secondary files:

- A secondary file can contain as many records as you like.
- A record in a secondary file can contain as many fields as you like.
- A field can be any length, from one character, to several pages.
- Every record in the same secondary file MUST contain the same number of fields, even if a field is empty.

A field in one record can be of a different size to the same field in another record in the same secondary file—i.e., the address of one company may be two lines long, while the address for another company may be either longer or shorter.

Creating a primary file

The primary file contains the standardized letter with which the names in the secondary file will be merged.

Once again, in WordPerfect, start a new file by selecting the *New* command from the **File** menu.

This file will contain the text that makes up the bulk of every letter. In addition, this file will include special codes that tell WordPerfect where the data from the secondary file is to be inserted.

In normal circumstances, the date is always included at the top of a letter. It is possible that the actual merge operation will be carried out at a later date. Therefore, you cannot insert today's date at the top of the letter.

WordPerfect provides a facility that allows you to add merge codes to a primary file. The date at the time of the merge, rather than today's date, is one of these codes. To insert a merge code in a document, select the *Merge Codes* command from the *Merge* fly-out menu in the **Tools** menu (Figure 18-12).

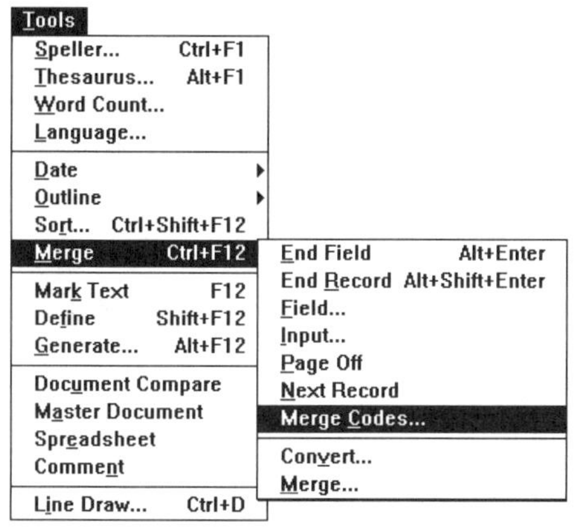

Figure 18-12. *The Merge/Merge Codes command from the **Tools** menu is used to add special codes, such as the date, to a primary file.*

The *Insert Merge Codes* dialog box (Figure 18-13) then appears. Scroll down the entries in this list to find the date code as shown in Figure 18-13.

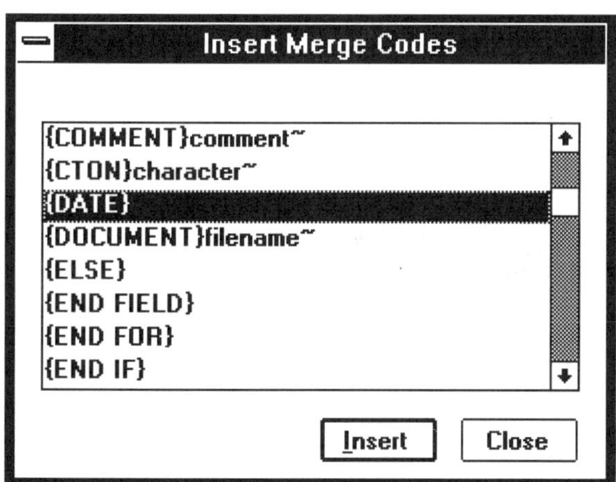

Figure 18-13. *Select the DATE code from the Insert Merge Codes dialog box.*

After selecting the *DATE* code, click on the *Insert* button from this dialog box, then the *Close* button. The *DATE* code is inserted in the document, at the text cursor position (Figure 18-14).

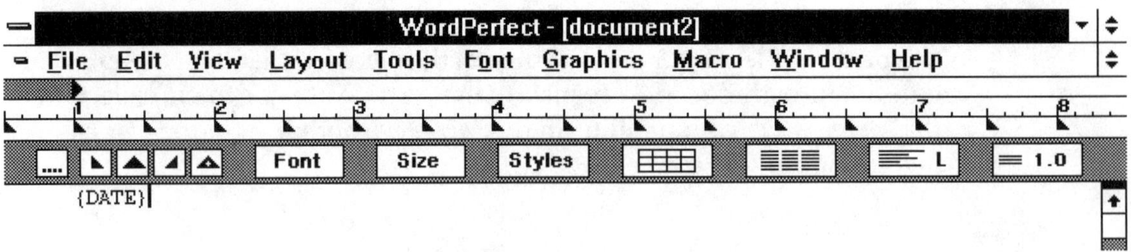

Figure 18-14. The Merge Code DATE is inserted into the document.

After inserting the *DATE* code, press the Enter key three times on your keyboard to move the text cursor down the page a little.

Under the date of this letter, the customer's name, the customer's company and the company address will appear. These three variables are all fields in the secondary file created earlier in this chapter. The customer name was the first field, the company name was the second, and the company address was the third.

To let WordPerfect know that it must insert a field from the secondary document into the place where the text cursor is currently located, select the *Field* command from the *Merge* fly-out menu in the **Tools** menu (Figure 18-15).

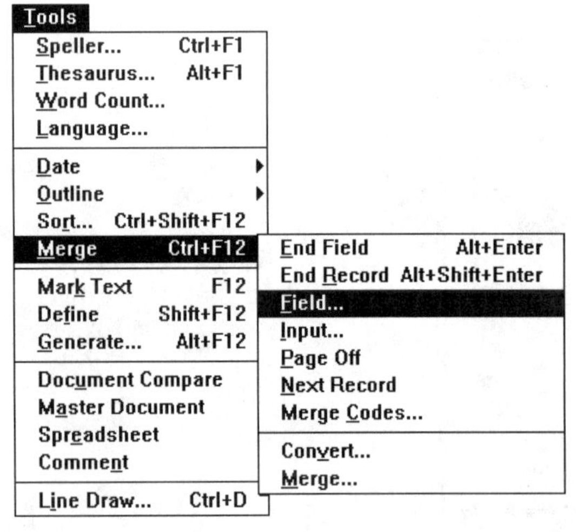

*Figure 18-15. The Merge/Field command from the **Tools** menu is used to let WordPerfect know that a field from a secondary file will be inserted where the text cursor is currently positioned.*

The *Merge/Field* command causes the *Insert Merge Code* dialog box of Figure 18-16 to appear.

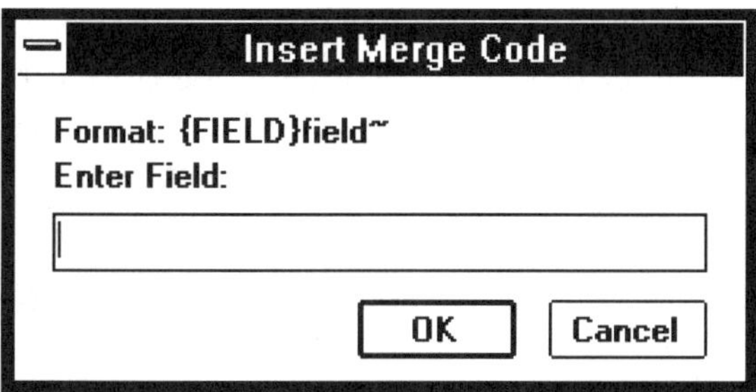

Figure 18-16. *The Insert Merge Code dialog box lets you determine which field from the secondary file should be inserted at the text cursor.*

In the *Insert Merge Code* dialog box of Figure 18-16, enter the number of the field from the secondary file, that should appear at the current position of the text cursor. In this case, the name of the customer is to appear here and this was the first field created in the secondary file. Thus, enter the number "1" in the *Enter Field* text box as shown in Figure 18-17.

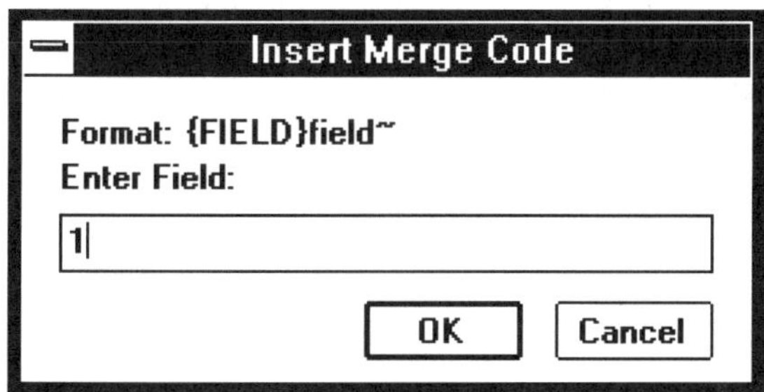

Figure 18-17. *Enter the number of the field from the secondary file that should appear at the text cursor position.*

After the **OK** button has been clicked, WordPerfect will insert a code into the document noting that *FIELD* number 1 will be inserted at this point (Figure 18-18).

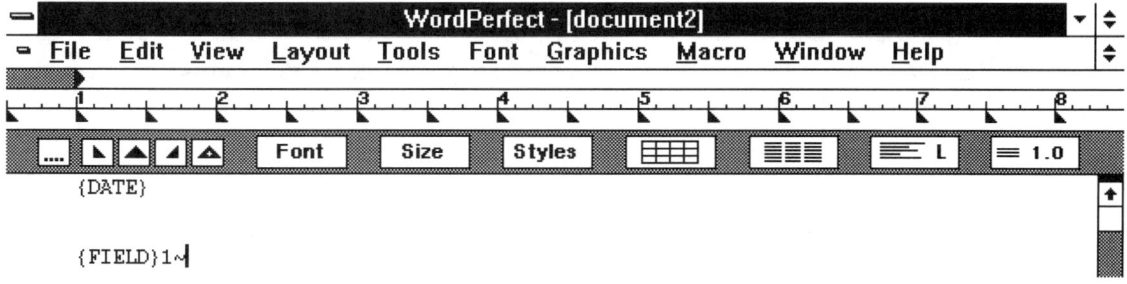

Figure 18-18. *A {FIELD}1~ code is inserted in the text, indicating that field number 1 from the secondary file will be inserted at this point.*

When the editing screen looks like the example in Figure 18-18, press the Enter key once to move the text cursor one line down the screen, to the position in the letter where the name of the company will appear. The company name was the second field created in the secondary file.

Select the *Merge/Field* command from the **Tools** menu to let WordPerfect know that the company field (the second field) from the secondary file will be merged at this position. The dialog box of Figure 18-16 will appear again. This time, enter the number "2" into this dialog box (Figure 18-19).

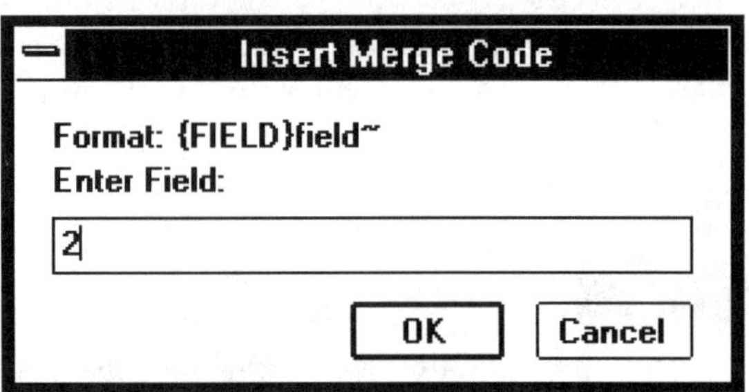

Figure 18-19. *Entering the number "2" in this dialog box indicates that the second field created in the secondary file is the one to be merged at this position.*

Once again, click on **OK**, and WordPerfect will insert a merge code into the text indicating that field number 2 will be inserted at this position (Figure 18-20).

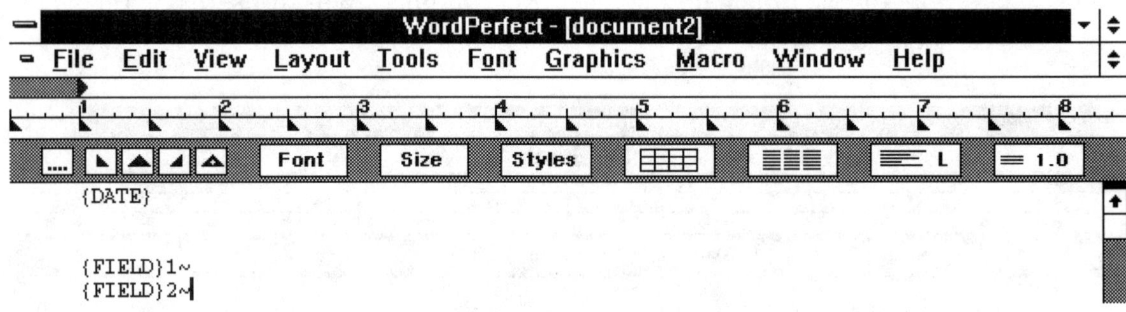

Figure 18-20. *Codes now exist in the text indicating that both field number 1 and field number 2 will be merged into the primary document.*

Press the Enter key once to move the cursor down to a new line. On this line, the company address is to appear. The company address was the third field created in the secondary file.

Select the *Merge/Field* command from the **Tools** menu again, and insert the number "3" in the resulting dialog box (Figure 18-21).

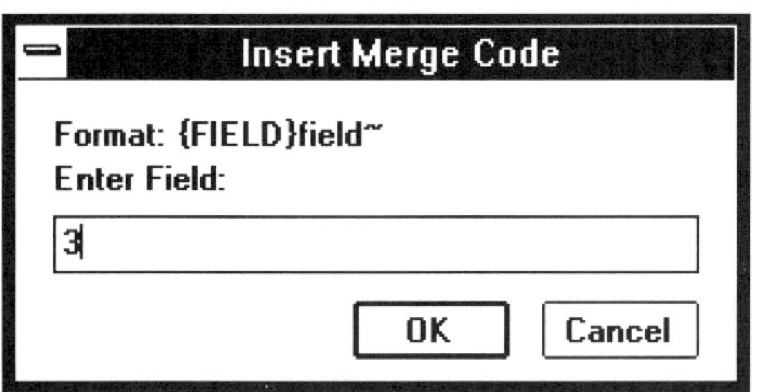

Figure 18-21. *Insert the number 3 in this dialog box to represent the third field in the secondary file.*

Again, the appropriate code is inserted into the text (Figure 18-22).

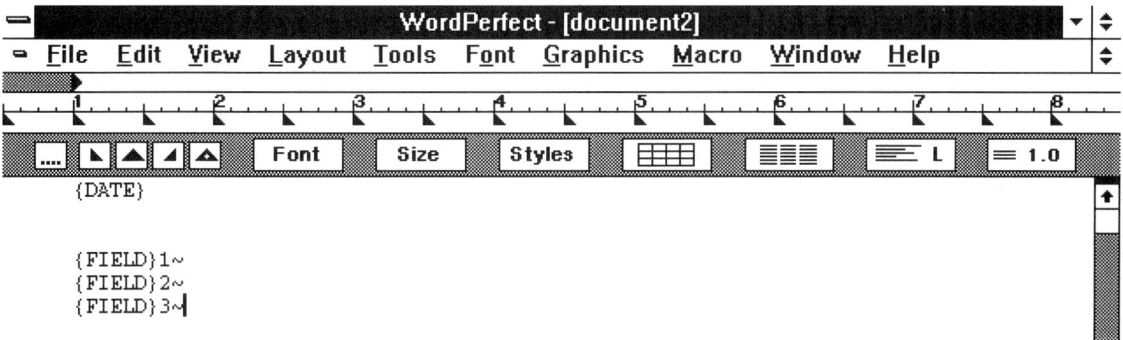

Figure 18-22. *Another merge code is inserted into the text.*

After the code for the company address has been entered (Figure 18-22), press the Enter key three times, to move the text cursor down to a point where the letter will actually begin (Figure 18-23).

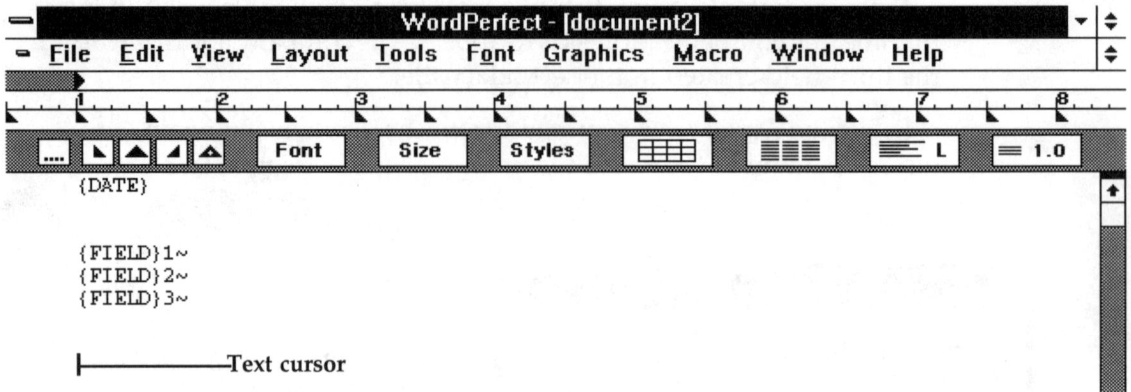

Figure 18-23. *Press the Enter key three times to move the text cursor down a few lines to where the body of the letter will begin.*

It is at this point in the document that the main body of the letter will actually begin. To start the letter, enter the word "Dear", and press the Spacebar once (Figure 18-24).

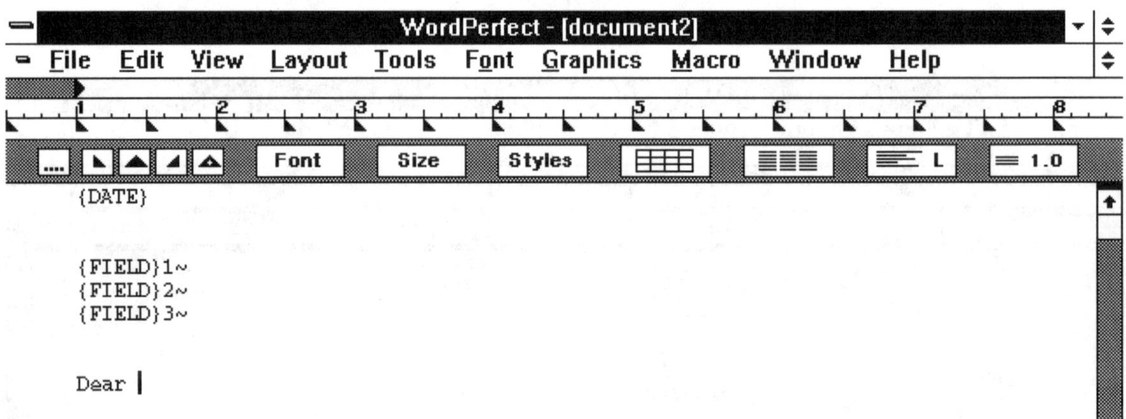

Figure 18-24. *Enter the word "Dear", and press the Spacebar once, to begin the letter.*

Remember, as the secondary file was created, the fourth and final field in each record was the first name of the customer. Insert this field at this point, to call the customer by name (i.e., "Dear Brett,").

Select the *Merge/Field* command from the **Tools** menu once again and enter the number "4" in the resultant dialog box (Figure 18-25).

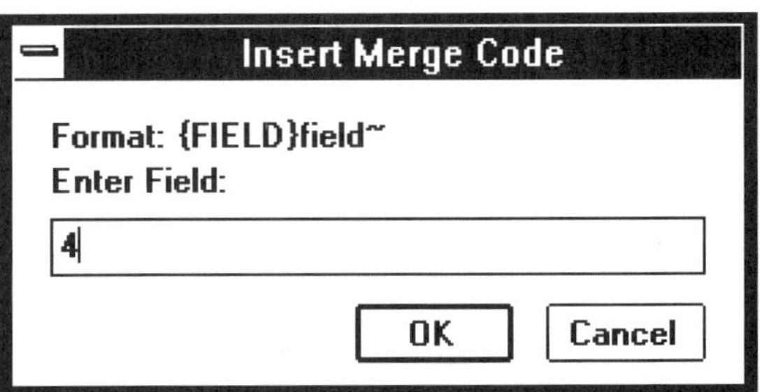

Figure 18-25. Enter the number "4" to indicate the fourth and final field created earlier in the secondary file.

After the **OK** button is clicked, the screen will appear as shown in Figure 18-26.

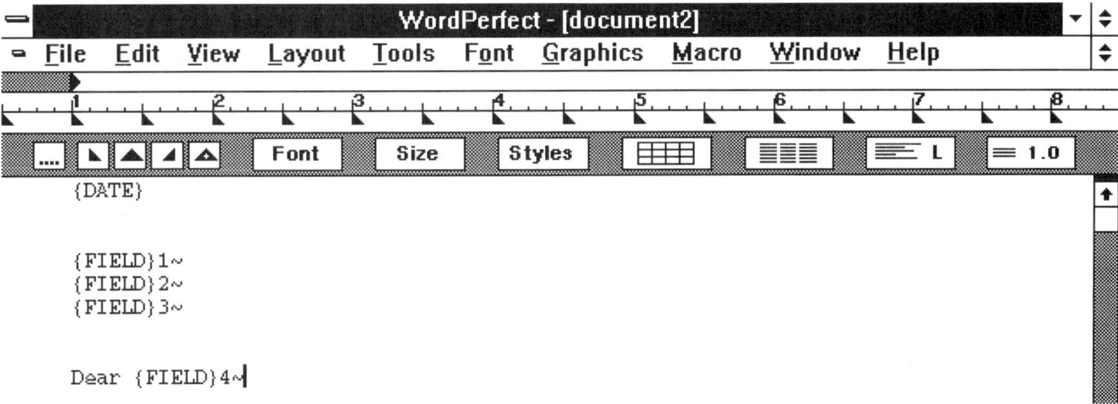

Figure 18-26. The merge code representing field number 4 is inserted into the text.

Type in a comma, after the code for field number 4, and press the Enter key twice (Figure 18-27) to position the text cursor for keying in the main body of the letter.

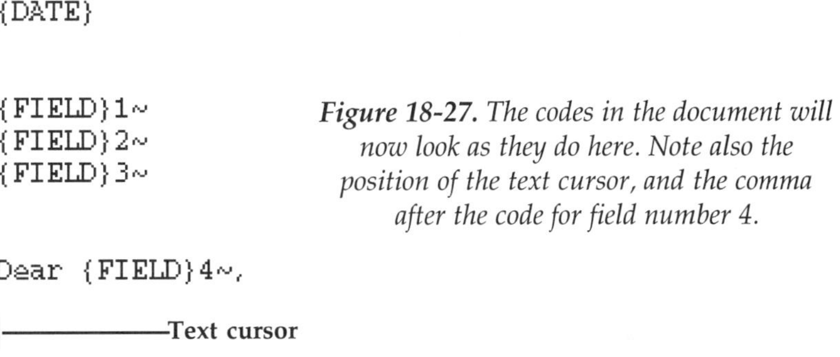

Figure 18-27. The codes in the document will now look as they do here. Note also the position of the text cursor, and the comma after the code for field number 4.

Now the main body of the letter can be entered. Enter the following paragraphs of text:

Widget Wobblers Inc. are pleased to be able to offer you three great specials for a short time only.

The Mighty Widget, the Wonder Widget, and the Deluxe Widget are all on sale for less than two-thirds their normal price.

Stocks are limited, so get your orders in now.

Regards,

Dan Widget
Chairman, Widget Wobblers Inc.

The screen will appear as depicted in Figure 18-28.

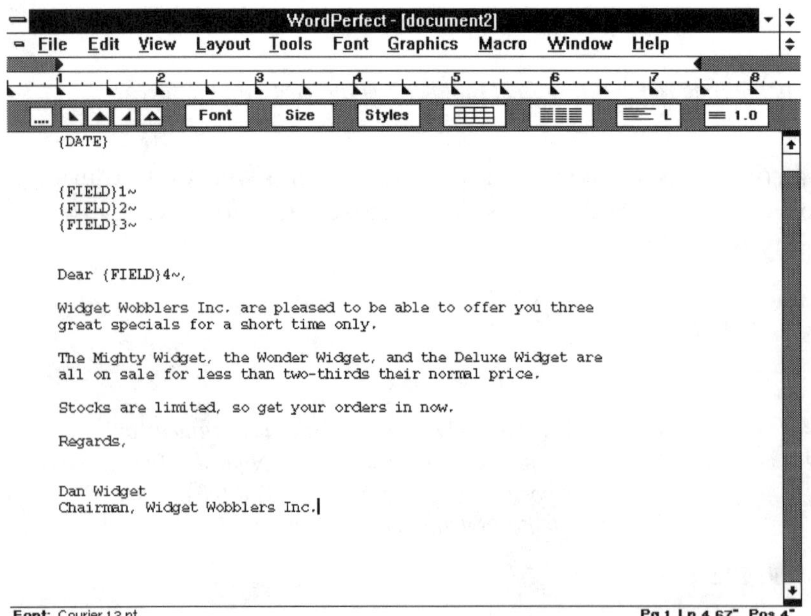

Figure 18-28. *The primary file (the letter) has now been completed.*

The primary file has now been completed. Save this file, using the name ***primary.wkb*** (Figure 18-29).

WordPerfect - [c:\wpwin\learn\primary.wkb - unmodified]

Figure 18-29. *Save the primary file using the filename* ***primary.wkb.***

Performing the merge operation

Once the primary and secondary files have been created, they do not have to be open within WordPerfect to perform the merge operation. Select the *New* command from the **File** menu to open a new WordPerfect file. This file will be used to contain the results of the merge operation.

To perform the merge, select the *Merge* command from the *Merge* fly-out menu in the **Tools** menu (Figure 18-30).

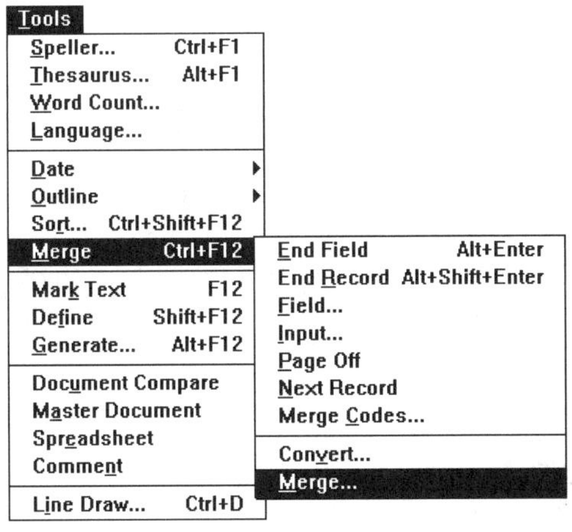

Figure 18-30. *The Merge/Merge command from the* ***Tools*** *menu is used to begin the merge operation.*

When the *Merge/Merge* command is selected, the *Merge* dialog box of Figure 18-31 appears, asking for the name of the primary and secondary files.

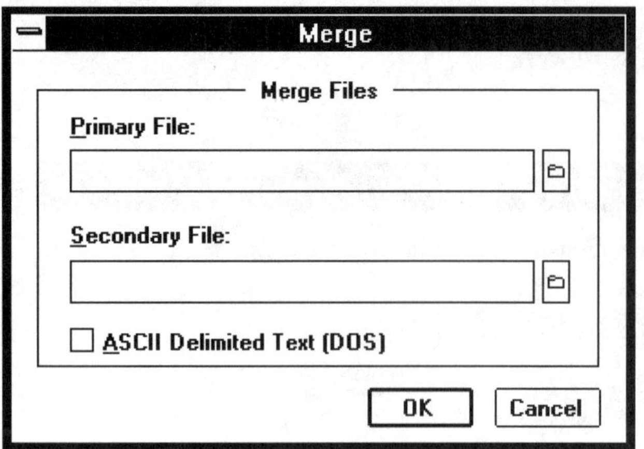

Figure 18-31. The Merge dialog box requests the name of the primary and secondary files to be used in the merge operation.

Under the heading *Primary File*, enter the name and location of the primary file created for this merge (Figure 18-32). In this case, the name of the file is ***primary.wkb***. If you not remember the name of the file, or do not wish to type it in the directory, click on the file-folder shaped button to the right of the *Primary File* text box. This button will cause a file selection dialog box to appear, from which you can select the desired file.

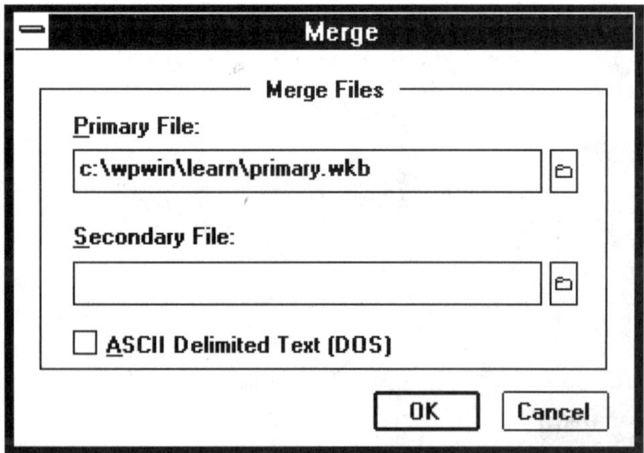

Figure 18-32. The name of the primary file and sub-directory location have been entered into the Primary File text box of the Merge dialog box.

In the *Secondary File* text box, you must enter the name and location of the secondary file created for this merge. In this case, this is the file ***secondry.wkb*** (Figure 18-33).

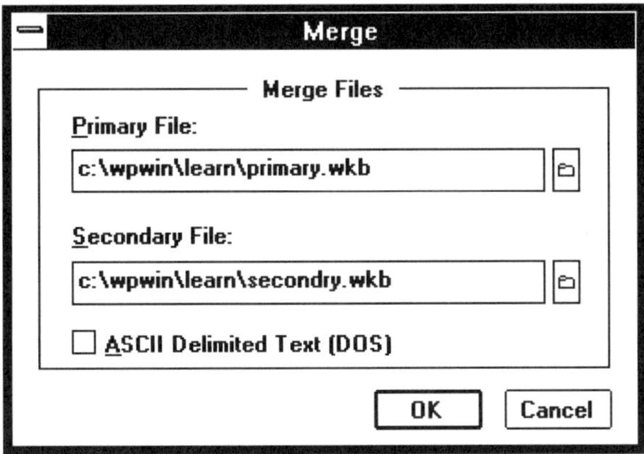

Figure 18-33. *The name and location of the primary and secondary files have now been entered into this dialog box.*

To start the merge operation, select the **OK** button. The merged files are added to the currently open window—which is the new file you just created. Figure 18-34 shows, as an example, the very first page in the file.

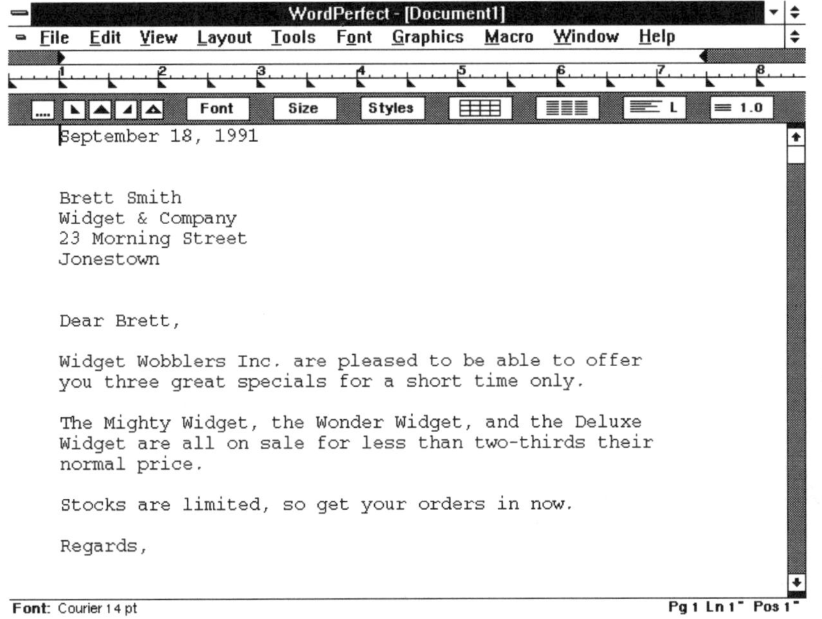

Figure 18-34. *The name, company name, and address of the first record in the secondary file have been merged with the information in the primary file.*

A merge operation can be canceled by pressing the ESC button during the merge.

The document containing this merged information can be treated like any other WordPerfect document. You may now print or save this document if you wish.

Hints and Tips

When a merge doesn't work

There are several things to check when a merge operation fails.

Were the *End Field* and *End Record* codes inserted correctly into the secondary file?

```
Meredith Flake{END FIELD}
Flakey Pastry{END FIELD}
123 Baker Street
Cooktown{END FIELD}
{END RECORD}
```

Figure 18-35. *An End Field code must appear at the end of each field and an End Record code at the end of each record, for each record in the secondary file.*

Does every record in the secondary file contain the same number of fields?

Were merge codes inserted correctly into the primary file?

Were the primary and secondary files correctly identified before the merge operation started?

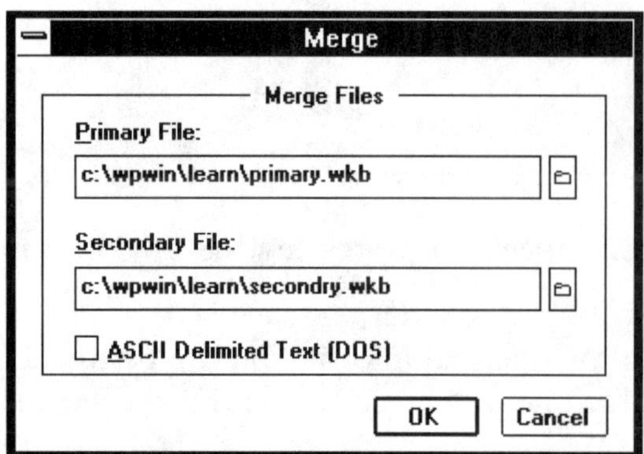

Figure 18-36. *Both the secondary and primary files must be correctly identified in this dialog box for the merge operation to work successfully.*

Were any hard returns inserted between fields in the secondary file? If so, they should be removed. The *End Field* code will automatically move the text cursor to the start of a new line.

Other merge options and tips

Merge programming codes and variables

The types of merge codes that can be inserted into a document to control a merge are quite extraordinary. See the WordPerfect Reference manual Appendices titled **Merge Programming Commands** and **Merge Variables** for more details.

Including graphics and codes in a primary file

You must remember that as a merge file is created, all of the information in the primary file is repeated for every record in the secondary file. As a secondary file is normally a list of customers, it can grow quite large, perhaps into many thousands of records. Therefore, if a graphic was included in a primary file, it may be repeated thousands of times after a merge, as will any codes at the start of a primary file. If a complex graphic was used, the resulting file could be prohibitively large.

You can use the *Graphic on Disk* function when loading a graphic into a primary file to counter this problem. This function forces WordPerfect not to take a copy of the file into the document but to use the graphic as it appears on disk. This method speeds the merge operation and saves on disk space.

Any codes that appear at the start of a document (page size, margins, and tab stops in particular) will be repeated for every page in the merged file. Rather than inserting these codes directly into the primary file, you may wish to use the *Initial Codes* command from the *Document* fly-out menu in the **Layout** menu, which has the same effect but does not insert codes in the document.

Merging — Exercise

This training exercise is designed so that people of all levels of expertise with WordPerfect can use it to gain maximum benefit. In order to do this, the bare exercise is listed below this paragraph on just two pages, with no hints. The following pages contain the steps needed to complete this exercise for those who need additional prompting.

Steps in brief

1. *Create the following secondary merge file using the merge field inserts where indicated:*

Craig Wilson{END FIELD}
Sally{END FIELD}
12 Ridge Road, Enfield{END FIELD}
Exercise Bike{END FIELD}
{END RECORD}

Jenny Oak{END FIELD}
Sean{END FIELD}
39 Taylor Street, Manly{END FIELD}
Hydraulic Bench Press{END FIELD}
{END RECORD}

Andrew Watt{END FIELD}
Sean{END FIELD}
73 Ocean Parade, Fairlight{END FIELD}
Dumb bells{END FIELD}
{END RECORD}

---

2. *Save the file as second.wkb.*

3. ***Create a primary merge file by typing in the following text and inserting the date and field merge codes.***

{DATE}

Dear {FIELD}1~,

Our sales representative, {FIELD}2~, visited your premises at {FIELD}3~ recently to demonstrate our products to you. As you showed interest in our {FIELD}4~, enclosed is some detailed information on this product.

Regards

Wally Roo
Director

---

4. ***Save the file as first.wkb.***
5. ***Open a new document and merge the two files together.***

The details for completing these steps are on the following pages.

Steps in detail

1. *Create the following secondary merge file using the merge field inserts where indicated:*

Craig Wilson{END FIELD}
Sally{END FIELD}
12 Ridge Road, Enfield{END FIELD}
Exercise Bike{END FIELD}
{END RECORD}

Jenny Oak{END FIELD}
Sean{END FIELD}
39 Taylor Street, Manly{END FIELD}
Hydraulic Bench Press{END FIELD}
{END RECORD}

Andrew Watt{END FIELD}
Sean{END FIELD}
73 Ocean Parade, Fairlight{END FIELD}
Dumb bells{END FIELD}
{END RECORD}

In a new WordPerfect file, start typing in the required text. Key in the first name on the list (Figure 18x-1).

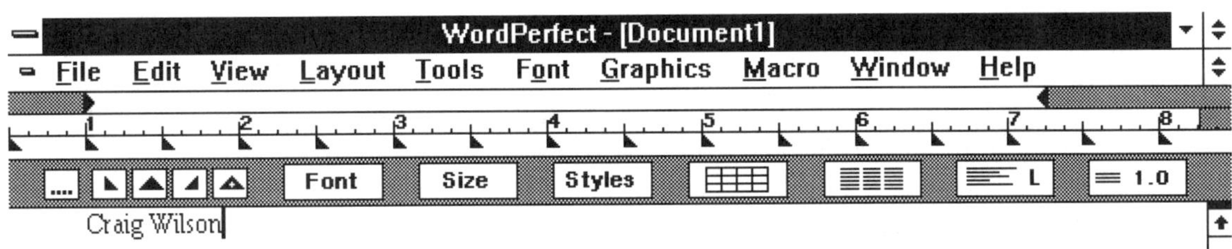

Figure 18x-1. Start typing in the secondary text file as shown here.

After typing in the name, "Craig Wilson", select the *Merge/End Field* command from the **Tools** menu (Figure 18x-2) to insert the field code at the end of the first line (Figure 18x-3).

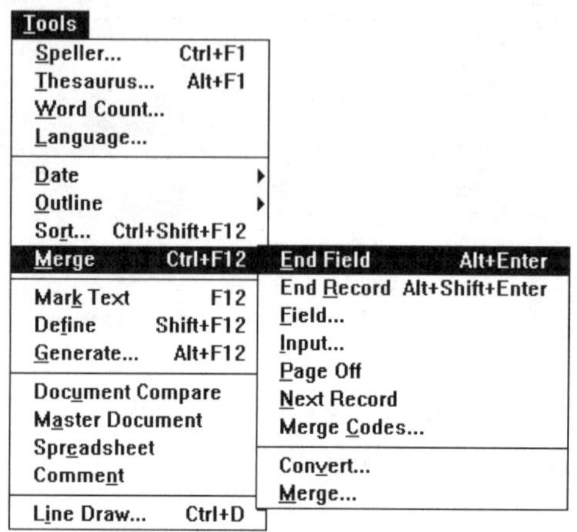

Figure 18x-2. *Select the Merge/End Field command when you have typed in the first line of text.*

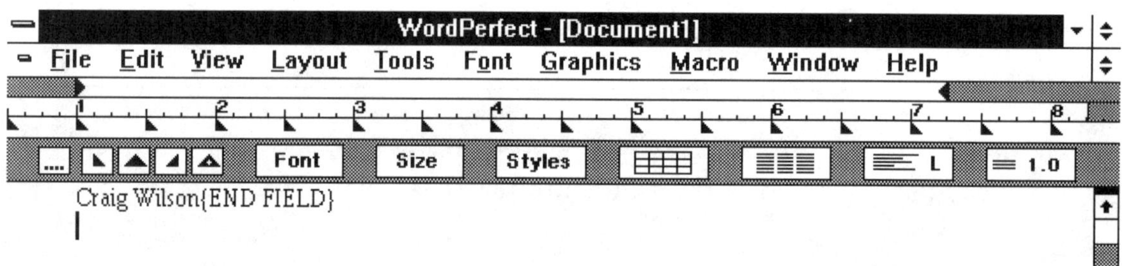

Figure 18x-3. *This is how the End Field command looks when inserted in the text.*

Type in the next line of text, "Sally", and again select the *End Field* command from the *Merge* fly-out menu (Figure 18x-4).

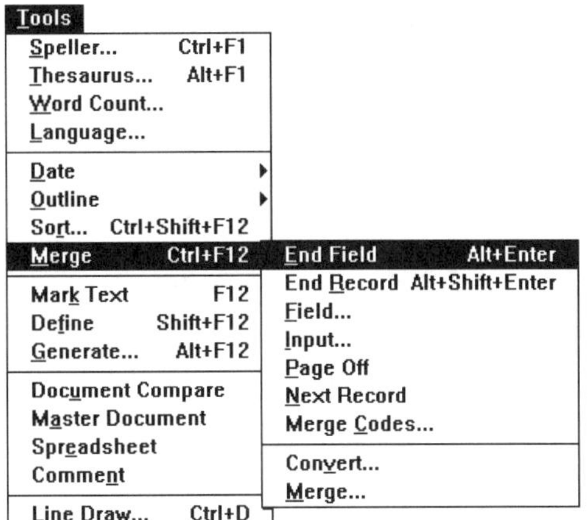

Figure 18x-4. After typing in the second line of text, select the Merge/End Field command once more.

Repeat this same procedure for the third and fourth lines of text. When you have finished, the text will look like that shown in Figure 18x-5.

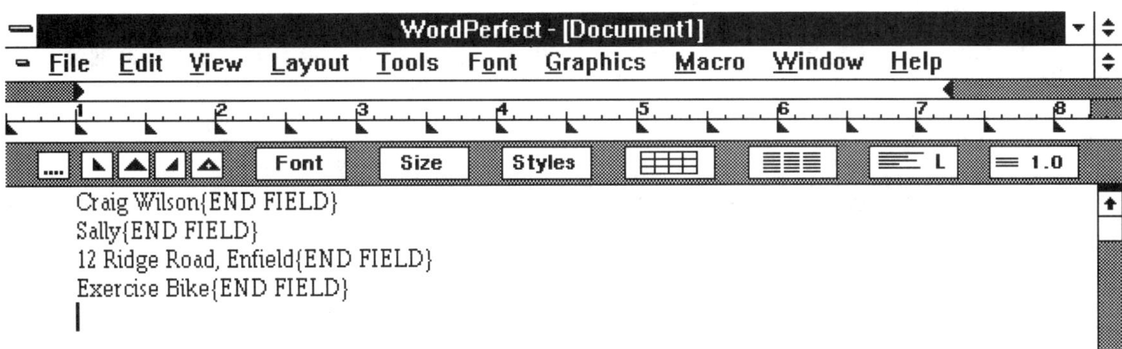

Figure 18x-5. *This is how the first section of text will appear after typing in the fourth line of text.*

The next step you need to perform is to select the *Merge/End Record* command from the **Tools** menu (Figure 18x-6). This inserts a code to end this particular record.

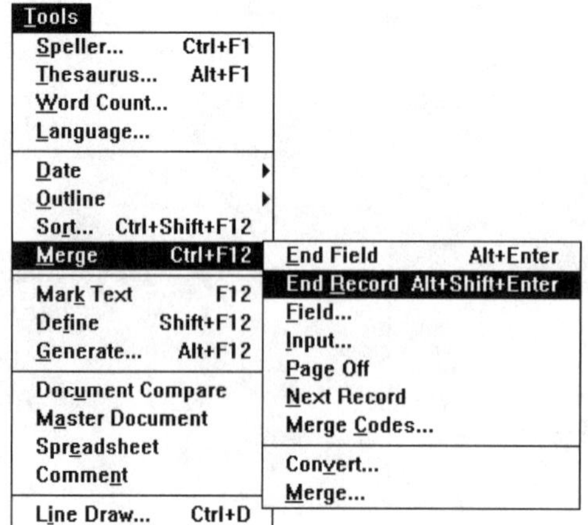

Figure 18x-6. *Select the End Record command from the Merge fly-out menu in the* ***Tools*** *menu.*

Figure 18x-7 displays the result of inserting the *End Record* code for this section. Note the double line that is also inserted, which is actually a page break. The cursor is now positioned for typing in the next record.

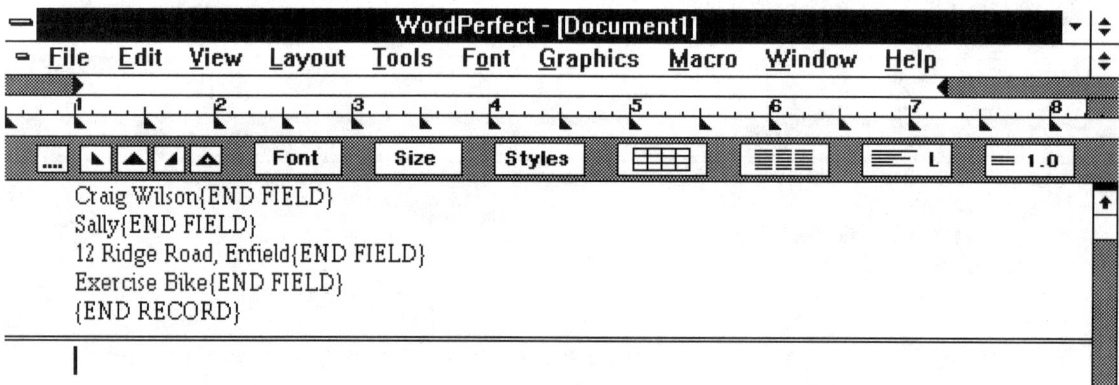

Figure 18x-7. *The result of inserting an End Record code from Figure 18x-6.*

Type in the next two records of text following the same procedure as described for the first one. On completion, compare your result with Figure 18x-8.

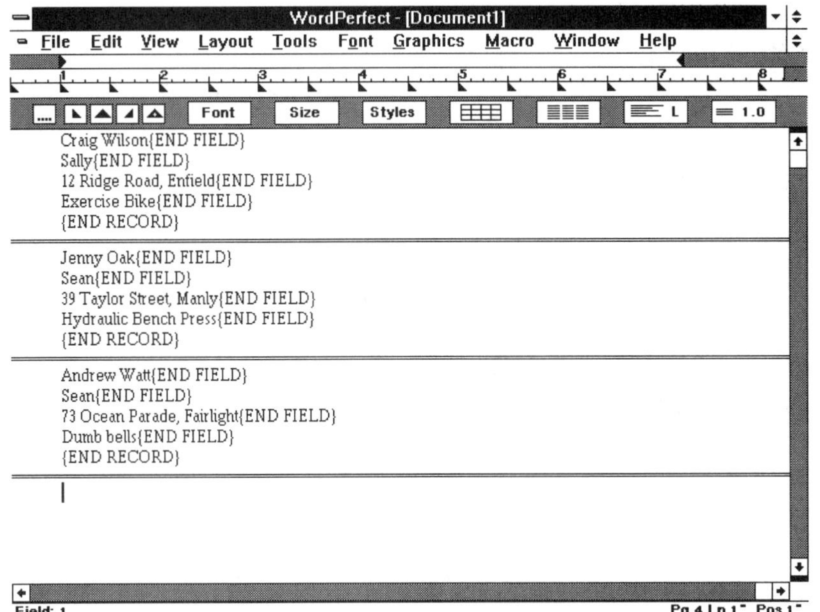

Figure 18x-8. This is how the secondary text file looks on completion.

2. *Save the file as second.wkb.*

Select the *Save* command from the **File** menu to activate the *Save As* dialog box. In the *Save As* text box, type in the name of the file as ***second.wkb*** and then click on *Save* (Figure 18x-9). For this exercise, the file was saved in the ***learn*** sub-directory. You may prefer to save it elsewhere.

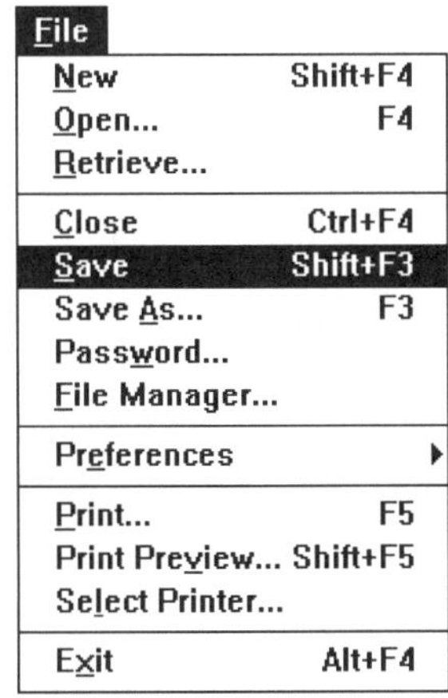

*Figure 18x-9. Select the Save command and save the file as **second.wkb**.*

3. ***Create a primary merge file by typing in the following text and inserting the date and field merge codes.***

{DATE}

Dear {FIELD}1~,

Our sales representative, {FIELD}2~, visited your premises at {FIELD}3~ recently to demonstrate our products to you. As you showed interest in our {FIELD}4~, enclosed is some detailed information on this product.

Regards

Wally Roo
Director

Create a new WordPerfect file by selecting *New* from the **File** menu. You are now ready to type in the primary merge file. The first thing needed is to insert a merge date code into the document. To do this, select the *Merge/Merge Codes* command from the **Tools** menu (Figure 18x-10).

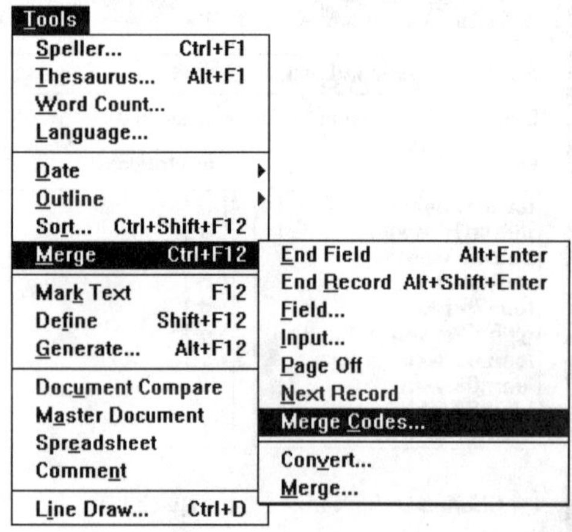

Figure 18x-10. *To insert the merge date code, select the Merge/Merge Codes command from the **Tools** menu.*

The *Insert Merge Codes* dialog box is activated after selecting the *Merge Codes* command. In this box, locate the *DATE* code and highlight it with the mouse (Figure 18x-11). Click on the *Insert* button, which inserts the code on the page, but does not close the dialog box. This allows you to insert a series of codes onto the page without reselecting the command each time. To close the dialog box, click on *Close.*

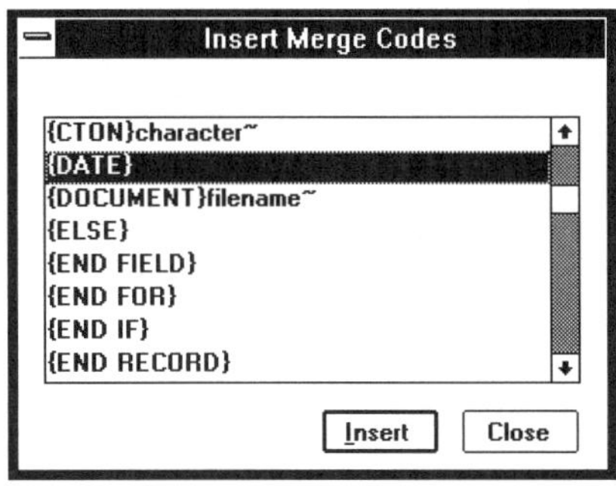

Figure 18x-11. *Highlight the DATE code, click on the Insert button, and then click on the Close button.*

Now, press the *Enter* key twice and type in the word "Dear ". Next, select the *Merge/Field* command from the **Tools** menu to insert the first field code (Figure 18x-12). When the dialog box of Figure 18x-13 appears, type in "1" and select **OK**. Figure 18x-14 shows the result.

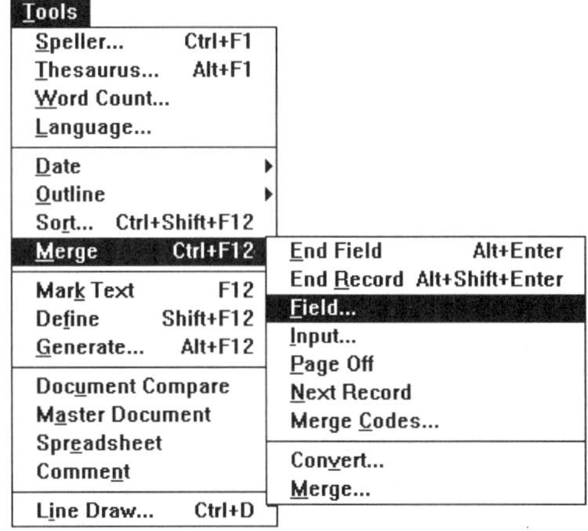

Figure 18x-12. *Type in the text as shown here and then select the Merge/Field command.*

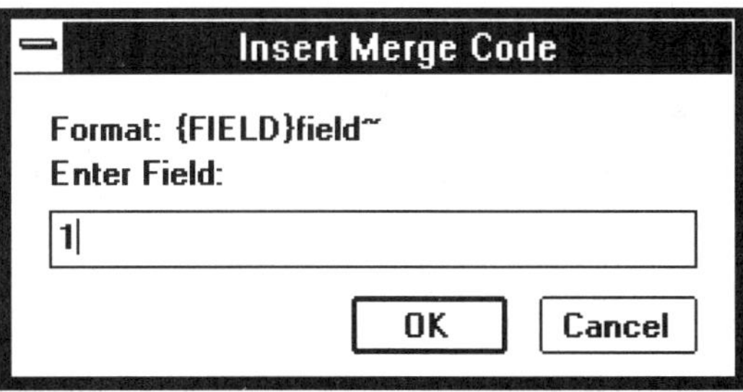

Figure 18x-13. *In the Insert Merge Code dialog box, type in 1 and select* ***OK.***

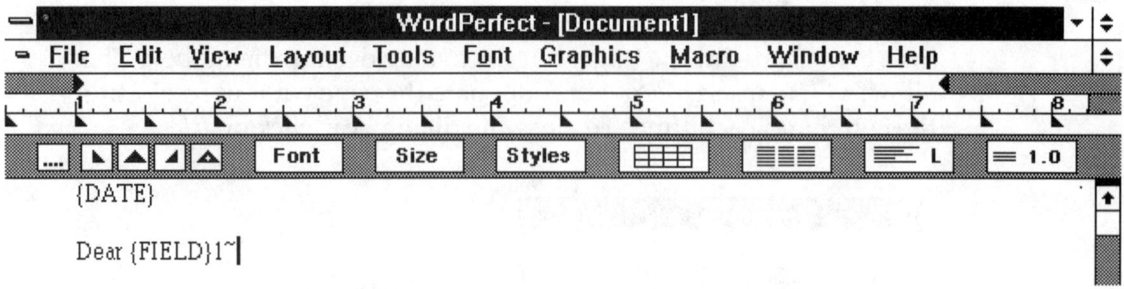

Figure 18x-14. *This is how the primary file looks so far.*

Type in the text of the letter as detailed above, making sure to enter the field merge codes as you go along, following the same procedure just demonstrated, but increasing the number each time. When you have finished, there will be four field codes and the file will look like the example of Figure 18x-15.

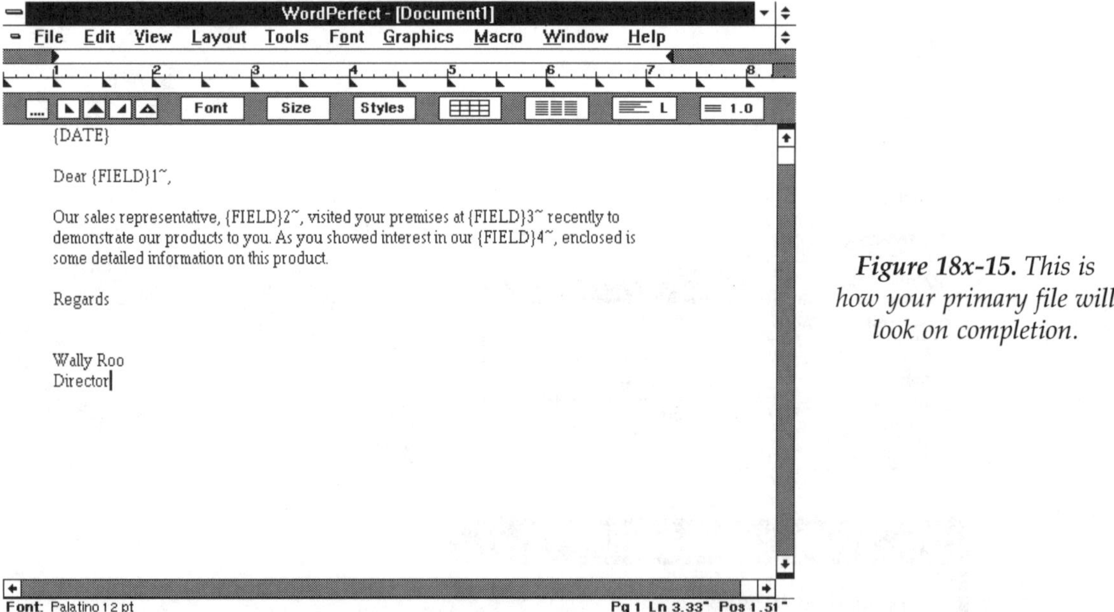

Figure 18x-15. *This is how your primary file will look on completion.*

4. Save the file as first.wkb.

Select the *Save* command from the **File** menu and save the file as ***first.wkb*** (Figure 18x-16).

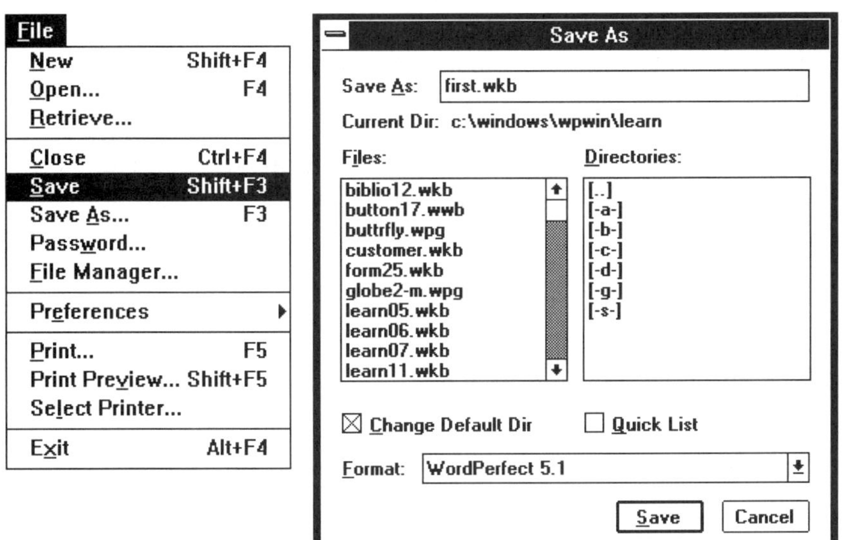

Figure 18x-16. *Save the file as* ***first.wkb.***

5. Open a new document and merge the two files together.

Select *New* from the **File** menu to start a new document. Once in the new document, go straight to the **Tools** menu and select the *Merge/ Merge* command as shown in Figure 18x-17.

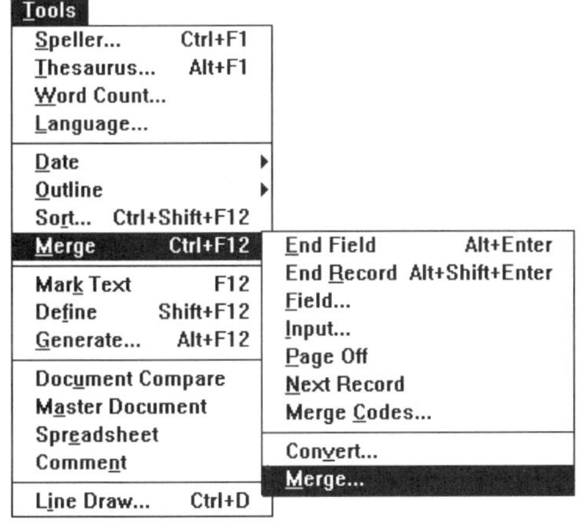

Figure 18x-17. *In the new document, select the Merge/Merge command.*

In the *Merge* dialog box that appears, you insert the primary and secondary file names, plus their path, into the appropriate text boxes (Figure 18x-18). The best way of doing this, to ensure that you do not make a typing error, is to click on the small rectangle to the right of the text boxes to activate the *Select File* dialog box (Figure 18x-19). Here you can locate the correct file name, highlight it with the mouse, and click on the *Select* button.

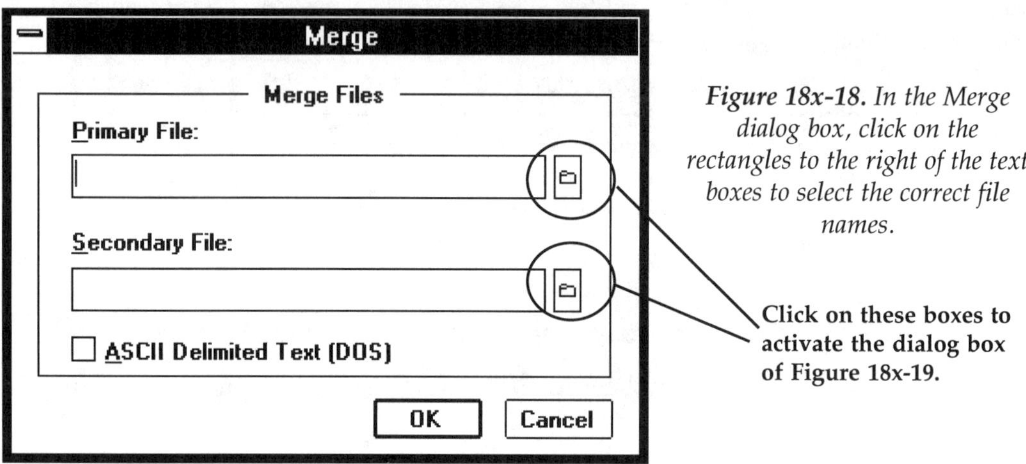

Figure 18x-18. *In the Merge dialog box, click on the rectangles to the right of the text boxes to select the correct file names.*

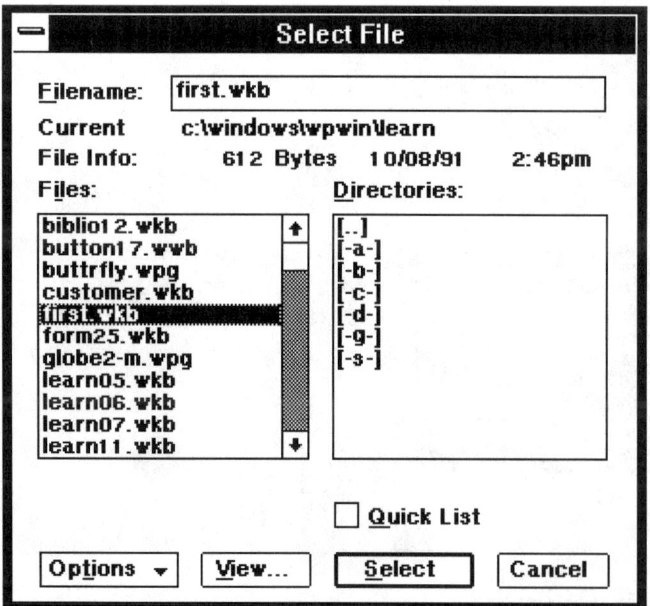

Figure 18x-19. *In the Select File dialog box, highlight the appropriate file and click on the Select button.*

Repeat this procedure to select both file names so that your dialog box is identical to the one in Figure 18x-20. Select **OK** to commence the merge operation. In a few moments, WordPerfect will have merged both files and provided the form letters as shown in Figure 18x-21.

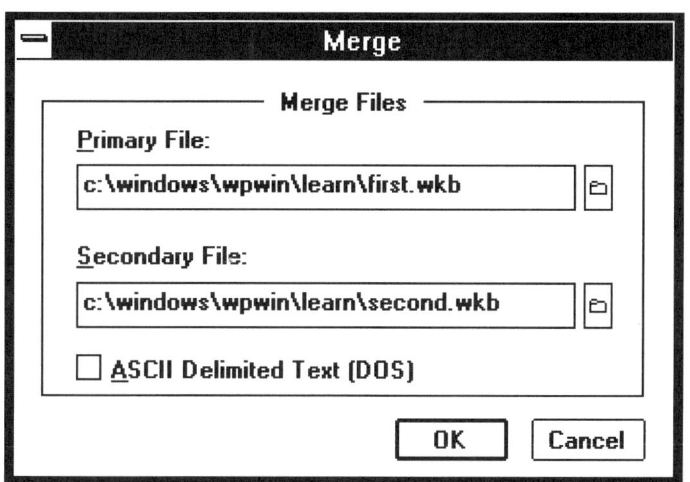

Figure 18x-20. *The completed Merge dialog box, with primary and secondary files included. Click on* ***OK****.*

In Figure 18x-19, this file has been saved as ***merge.wp5***.

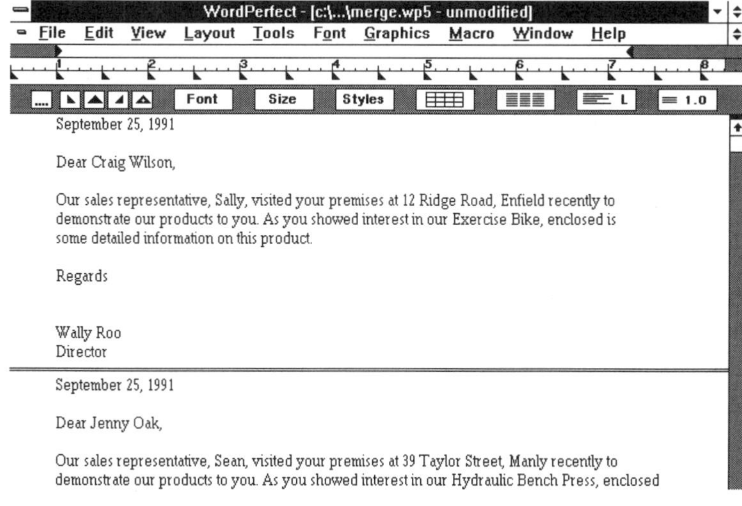

Figure 18x-21. *This figure shows the results of the merge operation. This screen shot is displaying the beginning of the document.*

Graphics

There are two types of graphics that are used in WordPerfect; imported graphics and internal graphics. Imported graphics are graphics that are brought into a WordPerfect document but have been created using other graphics programs. Internal graphics are graphics that are created using WordPerfect's own graphic features. This chapter looks at both of these types of graphics.

Boxes

WordPerfect uses 'boxes' to hold all types of graphics (except for internally created lines and rectangles). Boxes can hold text, equations, or imported graphics.

All of these boxes can be moved around the screen and can be edited. The boxes differ in how their contents are edited. An imported graphic, for example, must be edited differently than an equation.

This chapter looks mainly at boxes that contain an imported graphic. However, toward the end of the chapter, some of the other types of boxes that can be created are discussed as well.

Imported graphics

WordPerfect is capable of importing graphic files created in a wide range of graphic programs. Some of the programs with whose files WordPerfect is compatible, include CorelDRAW!, PC Paintbrush, Harvard Graphics, Lotus 1-2-3, and AutoCad. Nearly all graphics programs are now capable of producing common file formats, such as ***pcx*** or ***eps***. There are very few graphics programs that cannot produce a file format compatible with WordPerfect.

Many graphics programs are capable of creating graphics in the WordPerfect graphic, *wpg,* format. Graphics imported in *wpg* format are more flexible for modifying in WordPerfect.

Importing a graphic

To import a graphic into a WordPerfect document, position the cursor in the approximate position in the text where the graphic is to be placed in its figure box. For this example, open the file: ***learn12.wkb*** (Figure 19-1) and place the cursor after the third line.

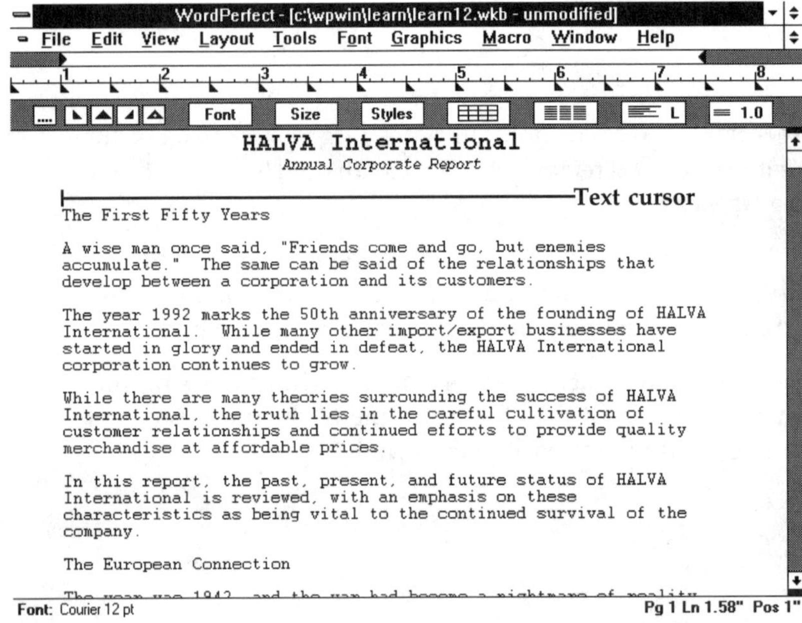

Figure 19-1. *The* ***learn12.wkb*** *file has been opened and the text cursor positioned after the third line.*

To load a graphic at the text cursor, select the *Retrieve* command from the *Figure* fly-out menu in the **Graphics** menu. This command activates the *Retrieve Figure* dialog box of Figure 19-2.

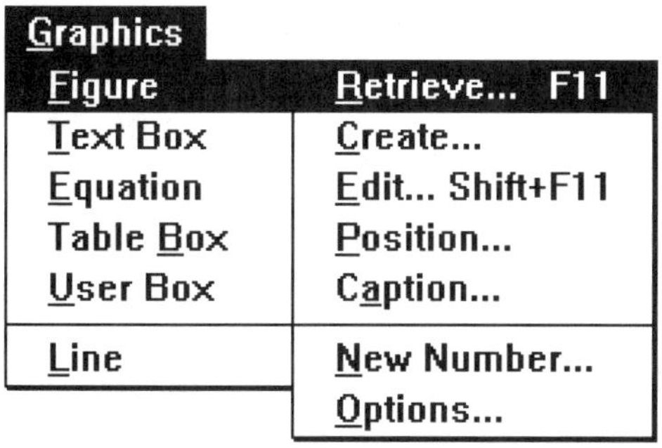

Graphics
Figure | Retrieve... F11
Text Box | Create...
Equation | Edit... Shift+F11
Table Box | Position...
User Box | Caption...
Line | New Number...
Options...

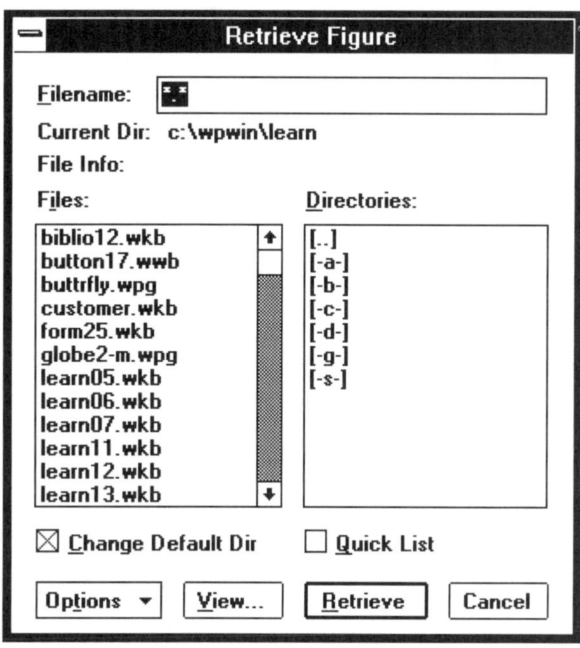

Figure 19-2. *After selecting the Retrieve command from the Figure fly-out menu, the Retrieve Figure dialog box appears. Move to the learn sub-directory as shown here.*

Some sample graphic files provided with WordPerfect.

The *Retrieve Figure* dialog box provides access to any graphic file in your computer system. In this example, the dialog box lists all the files that are in the ***learn*** sub-directory. In this directory, graphics can be identified by their ***wpg*** (WordPerfect Graphic) file extension.

To view a graphic, before loading it, you highlight the file name in the *Files* list and click on the *View* button.

For this example, view the graphic ***buttrfly.wpg,*** as shown in Figure 19-3. Locate this file in the list of file names, highlight it with the mouse, and click on the *View* button. Now, click on *Retrieve* to import this file into your document.

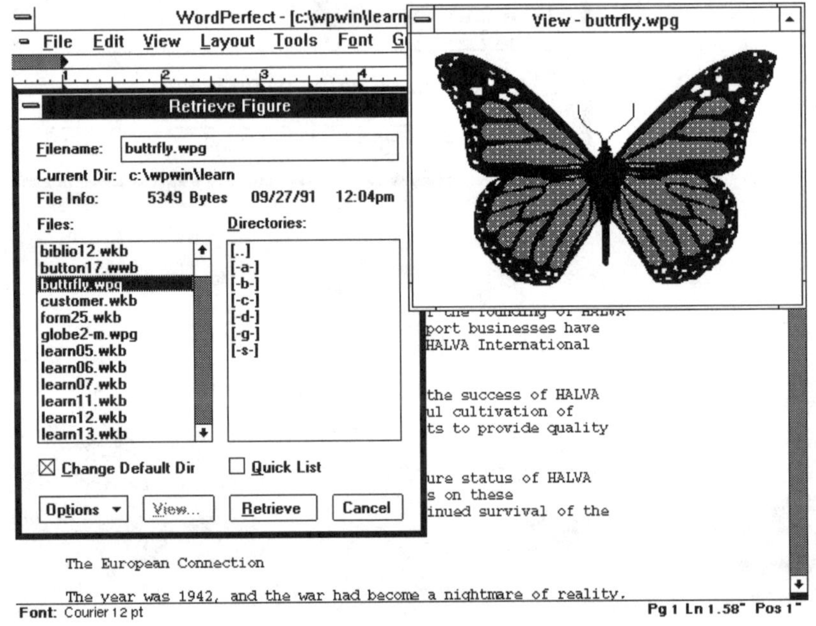

Figure 19-3. *To view a graphic file before loading it into WordPerfect, highlight the file name (in this case* ***buttrfly.wpg)*** *and click on the View button.*

After *Retrieve* is selected, the graphic will be inserted into the document automatically (Figure 19-4). The top of the 'figure box' that contains the graphic will be aligned with the line that held the text cursor, prior to selecting the *Retrieve* command. The default position for a figure box is on the right-hand side of the page.

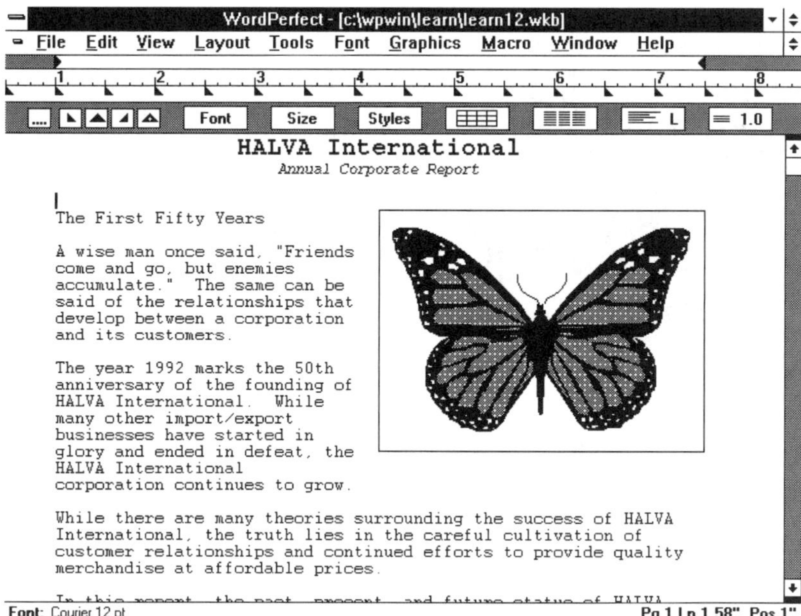

***Figure 19-4**. The graphic is loaded into the document in a figure box. By default, the figure box is positioned on the right-hand side of the page.*

Note that the text has automatically run around the figure box without overlapping or obscuring it.

Using the mouse with graphics

Moving a figure box

The easiest way to reposition a figure box is to use the mouse. Notice that when the mouse is positioned inside the borders of a figure box, its shape changes to an arrow-head. When the left mouse button is held down within a figure box, the figure box can be dragged to a new position on the screen (Figure 19-5). When the mouse button is released, the figure box moves to the new position in the text and the text reflows around the figure box (Figure 19-6).

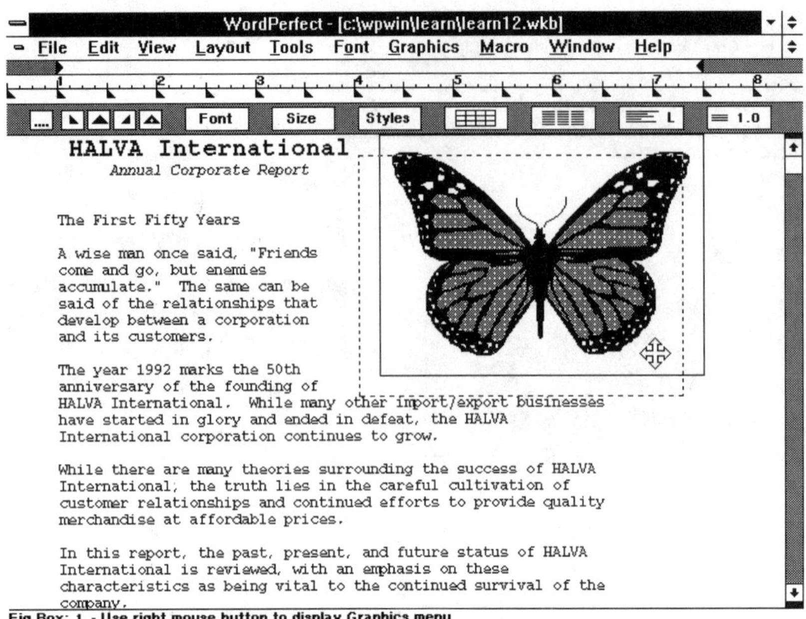

Figure 19-5. To move a figure box, hold the left mouse button down on that figure box and move the mouse to a new position on the page. A dotted outline of the figure box will follow the mouse as it moves.

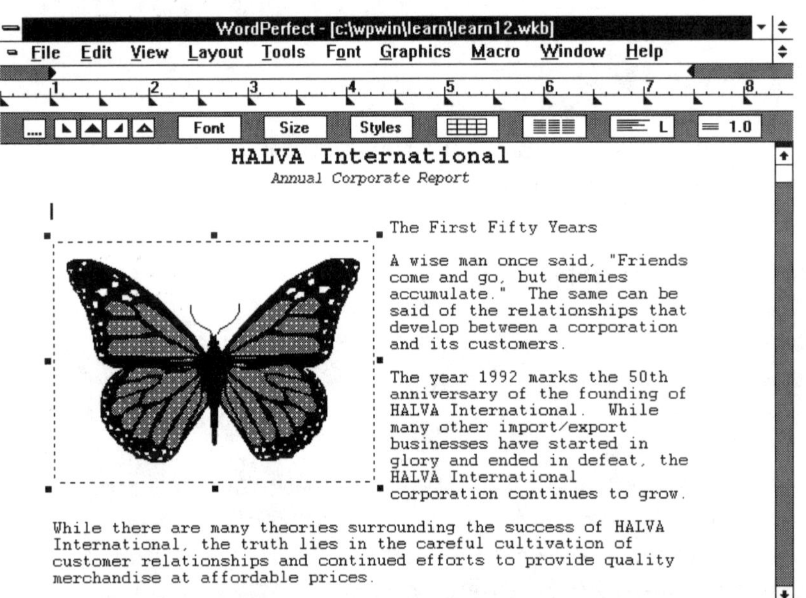

Figure 19-6. When the mouse button is released, the figure box is redrawn at its new position and the text reflows around the figure box.

Resizing a figure box

The mouse can also be employed to quickly enlarge or reduce the size of a figure box.

Clicking on a figure box with the left mouse button displays eight black boxes, or 'handles', around it (Figure 19-7). These handles are used to resize a figure box.

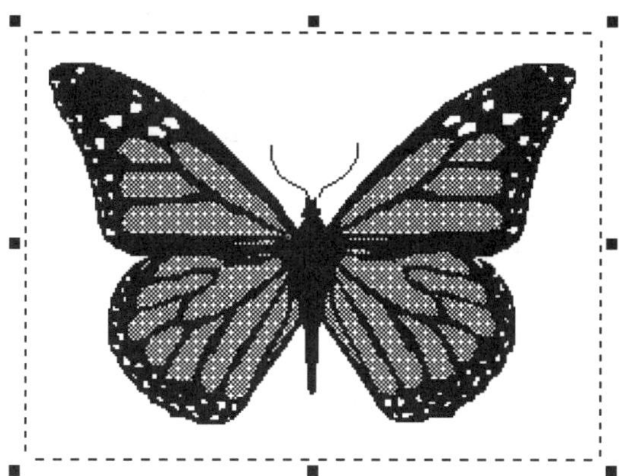

Figure 19-7. *When a figure box is selected, by clicking on it once, eight black rectangles, or handles, appear around it. These handles can be used to resize the figure box.*

To resize the figure box, hold the mouse button on one of these handles. When a handle is dragged, the sides of the figure box adjacent to that handle can be repositioned. For example, if the mouse button was held on the handle in the bottom center of the figure box, only the bottom side of the box could be repositioned, as seen in Figure 19-8.

Figure 19-8. *Hold the mouse button down on any handle and move the mouse to resize the figure box. On the left, the bottom center handle has been used to resize this figure box, to the diagram on the right.*

To resize the figure box horizontally, hold the mouse button down on one of the side handles and move the mouse to the left or right before releasing the mouse button.

If the mouse button is held on one of the corner handles, both sides adjacent to that corner can be adjusted at once.

An imported graphic inside a figure box will, by default, resize with the figure box; however, it will always maintain its aspect ratio, or relative scale.

As a figure box is resized, it will always be redrawn when the mouse button is released, and the text will always reflow around it.

Adding a caption to a figure box

To add a caption to a figure box, click on the figure box with the right mouse button (Figure 19-9). Do this to your figure box now.

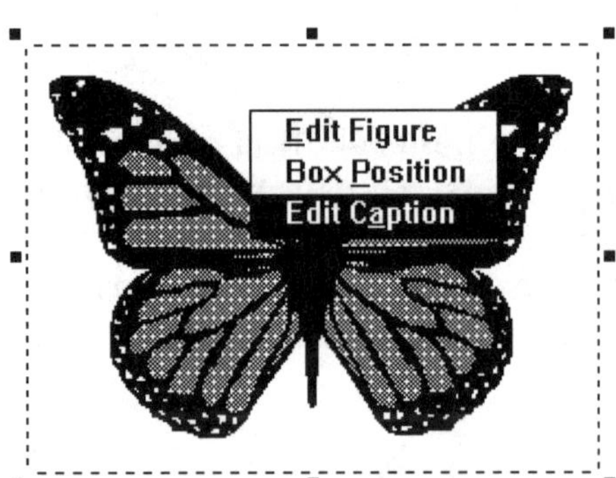

Figure 19-9. *Clicking on a figure box with the right mouse button invokes the* ***Graphic*** *menu, from which commands can be selected to further edit the figure box or the graphic within it.*

The **Graphic** menu appears when the right mouse button is clicked in a figure box. The third option in this menu (selections, as always, are made with the left mouse button) is the *Edit Caption* command. The *Caption Editor* (Figure 19-10) appears when this command is selected.

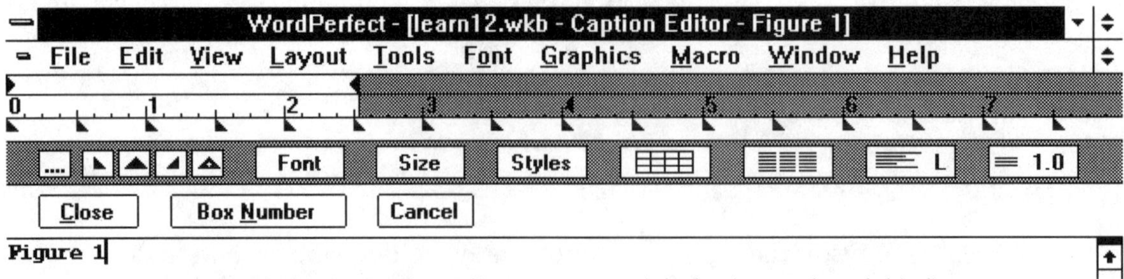

Figure 19-10. *The Caption Editor screen. By default, the number of this figure will appear as the first part of the caption.*

In the *Caption Editor*, you enter the text which is to appear in the caption. The *Box Number*, "Figure 1", which is automatically inserted, may be deleted if desired. If you then wish to re-insert it, click on the *Box Number* button to add the words "Figure X" (Where "X" represents the number of this figure box). Now, enter the text ": The Butterfly" (Figure 19-11).

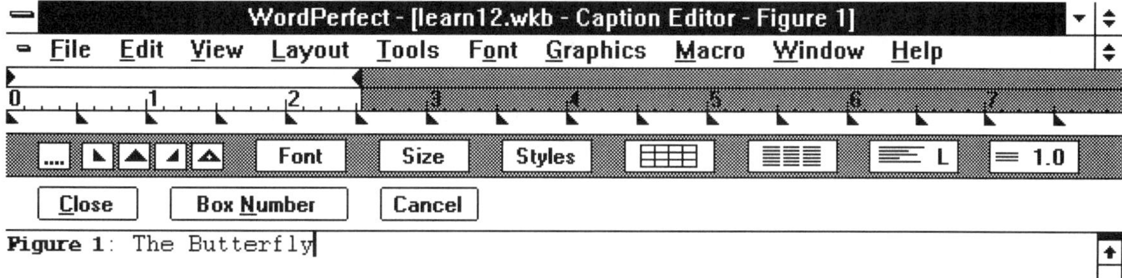

***Figure 19-11**. Add the figure caption text in this Caption Editor screen.*

When the caption text is complete, click on *Close*, to add the caption to the Figure box (Figure 19-12).

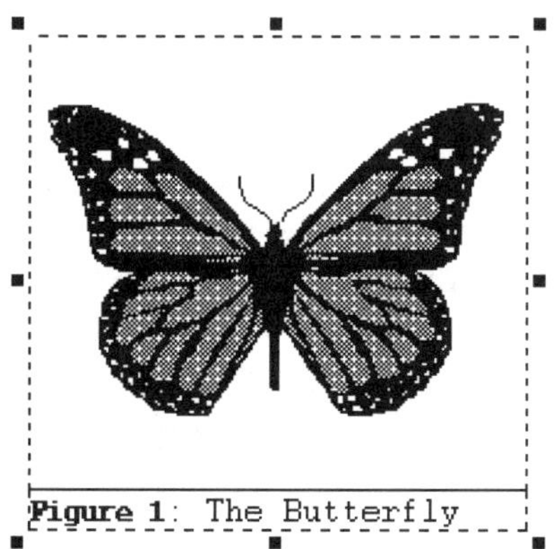

***Figure 19-12**. The caption appears below the figure box. Later in this chapter, you will see how the position of this caption can be moved.*

This caption will move around with the figure box and can only be edited by following the same steps you took to create the caption in the first place.

The caption of a figure box can also be created and edited using the *Caption* command from the *Figure* fly-out menu in the **Graphics** menu.

The Figure Editor

To edit a graphic (most editing can only be performed and viewed on screen when a WordPerfect Graphic—a file with a ***wpg*** extension—is used), click once on the figure box with the right mouse button. This action once again invokes the **Graphic** menu. From this menu, select the *Edit Figure* command (Figure 19-13).

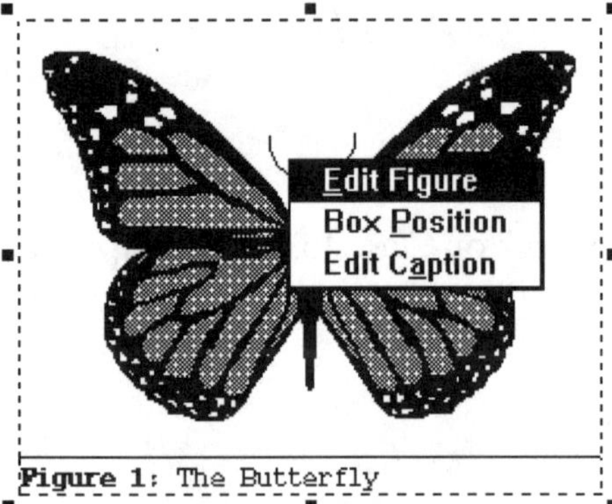

Figure 19-13. *To edit the graphic within a figure box, click on the figure box containing the graphic with the right mouse button and select the Edit Figure command from the* ***Graphic*** *menu that appears. Alternatively, you may double-click on the figure box with the left mouse button.*

The *Figure Editor* that appears (Figure 19-14) provides a range of commands and facilities that allow the graphic to be edited. All of these commands affect only the graphic within the box—they have no power over the appearance or position of the figure box in which the graphic is located.

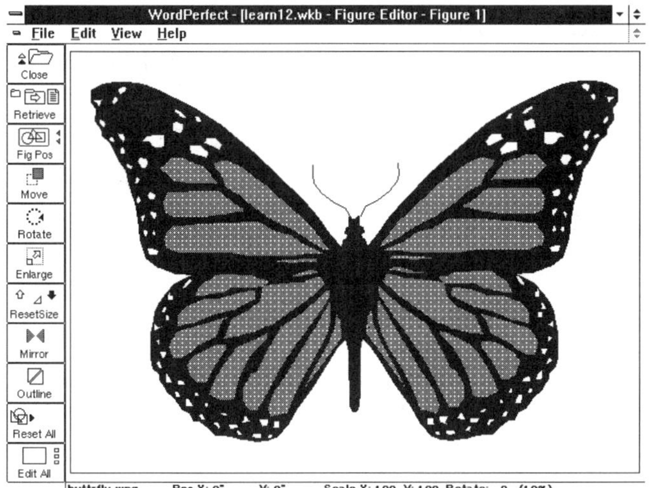

Figure 19-14. *The Figure Editor provides an enlarged view of the graphic that is being edited.*

The *Figure Editor* includes commands for enlarging the graphic, rotating the graphic, mirror-imaging the graphic, and outlining the graphic.

The use of most of these commands is quite self-explanatory. Note that the commands listed below can be selected from the menu or, if available, also from the Button bar.

Moving a graphic

Select the *Move* command from the **Edit** menu to move the graphic within the box. Hold down the mouse button on the picture, drag the mouse to the graphic's new position, and release the mouse. The graphic will now occupy this new position (Figure 19-15). Reselect the *Move* command to disable moving the graphic.

Rotating a graphic

Select the *Rotate* command from the **Edit** menu; a crosshair now appears on the graphic (Figure 19-16).

Hold down the mouse button on an edge of the crosshair and move the mouse around in the direction in which the graphic is to be rotated (Figure 19-17). Repeat as necessary, then reselect the *Rotate* command to disable further rotation.

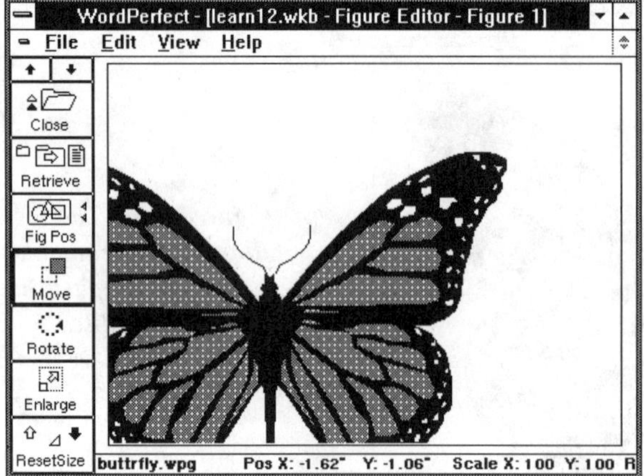

***Figure 19-15.** A moved graphic.*

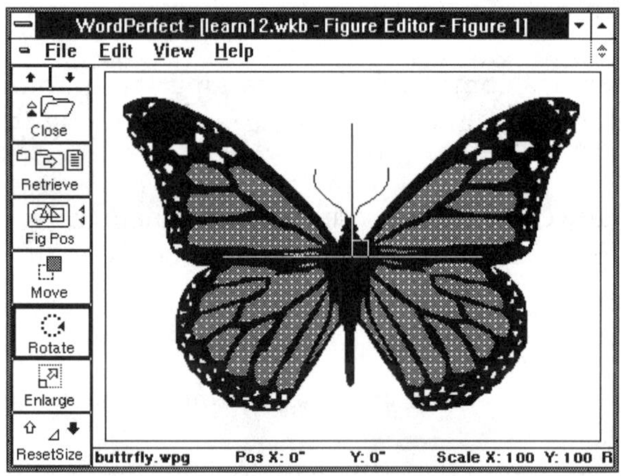

***Figure 19-16.** A crosshair appears on the graphic when the Rotate command is selected. This crosshair helps with the rotation of the graphic.*

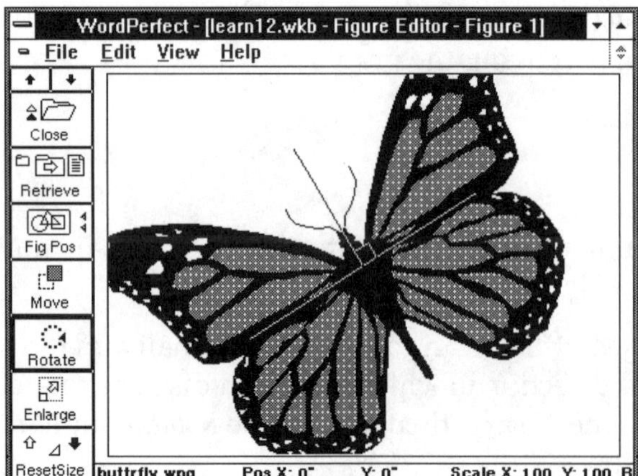

***Figure 19-17**. A rotated graphic.*

To scale a graphic

The graphic can be scaled in a variety of ways using the *Scale* command from the **Edit** menu (Figure 19-18).

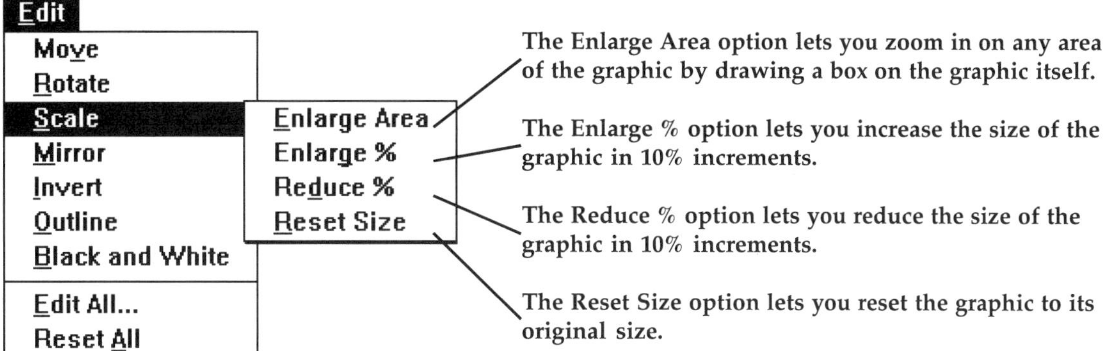

Figure 19-18. *The graphic scaling options.*

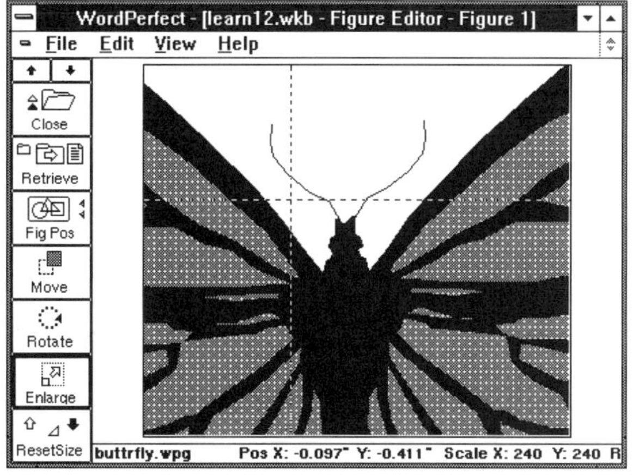

Figure 19-19. *This graphic has been enlarged using the Enlarge Area option. Once you do this, deselect the Scale/Enlarge Area command.*

Making a mirror image of a graphic

Select the *Mirror* command from the **Edit** menu. The graphic will instantly mirror itself horizontally; now deselect this command.

To invert the graphic

Select the *Invert* command from the **Edit** menu. The graphic will instantly invert. Dark areas will turn light and light areas dark; much like a negative.

Outlining (removing the color and shades from) a graphic

Select the *Outline* command from the **Edit** menu. All color in the figure turns white leaving a black and white image only (Figure 19-20). Deselect this command to return to a color image.

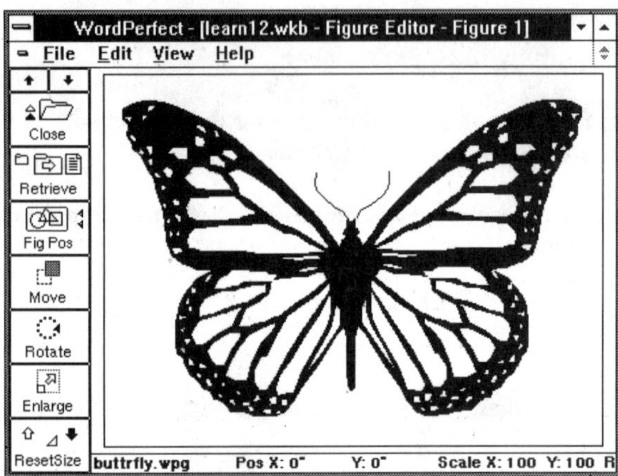

Figure 19-20. *This graphic has had the Outline command used on it.*

Black and White command

When you select this command from the **Edit** menu, all colors in the figure change to black. Deselect this command to return the figure to normal.

Editing all imported graphics

The *Edit All* command, from the **Edit** menu, allows the above editing commands to be applied at one time to the graphic in the *Figure Editor* box.

In the *Edit All* dialog box (Figure 19-21), almost all commands listed in the *Figure Editor* **Edit** menu can be applied, either by filling out text boxes or by selecting check boxes.

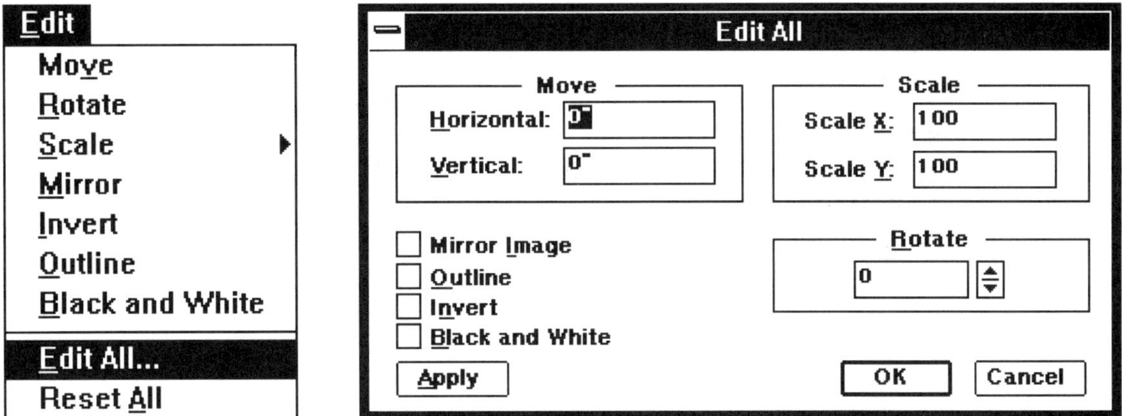

***Figure 19-21. The** Edit All command in the **Edit** menu allows multiple edit options to be applied at one time to the selected graphic. Clicking on the Apply button lets you see the results without closing the dialog box.*

The *Reset All* command, at the bottom of the **Edit** menu, can be used to undo all changes made to any graphic in a document.

Save As command

Once changes have been made to a graphic in the *Figure Editor*, the *Save As* command from the **File** menu can be used to save this graphic under a new name, leaving the original graphic in its unchanged form.

Graphic on Disk command

When a graphic is loaded into a WordPerfect document, WordPerfect makes a copy of the graphic to store as part of the document. The original graphic on disk can then be deleted or changed and it will not affect the graphic imported into the WordPerfect file.

You can also create a link to the original graphic on disk so that, as the graphic on disk is edited (perhaps by a dedicated graphics package), the changes will be reflected in the WordPerfect document. To do this, select the *Graphic on Disk* command from the **File** menu of the *Figure Editor* screen (Figure 19-20). You will be asked to supply a file name under which this graphic is to be saved and, from here on in, linked.

The Figure Editor Button bar

By default, the *Figure Editor* Button bar appears on the *Figure Editor* screen. This Button bar contains many of the commands found in the various *Figure Editor* menus. It may be turned off using the *Button Bar* command in the *Figure Editor* **View** menu or edited using the *Button Bar Setup/Edit* command from the same menu.

The Status bar

Along the bottom of the *Figure Editor*, various details of the graphic are listed, including its name, size, rotation angle, and position (Figure 19-22). This part of the screen is called the Status bar.

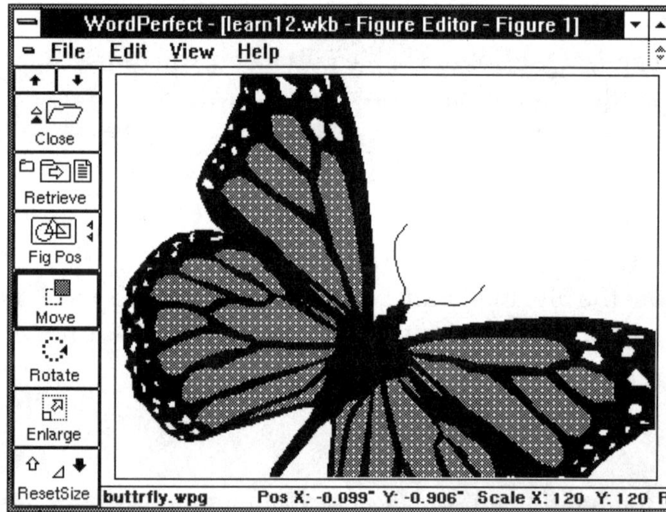

Figure 19-22. *The Status bar along the bottom of the screen indicates some of the many ways that the graphic may have been edited.*

Exiting the Figure Editor

To return to the WordPerfect editing screen, select the *Close* command from the *Figure Editor* **File** menu. The graphic will appear in the editing screen along with any changes made in the *Figure Editor* (Figure 19-23).

The *Cancel* command in the **File** menu will return you to the Editing screen without saving any changes made to the graphic.

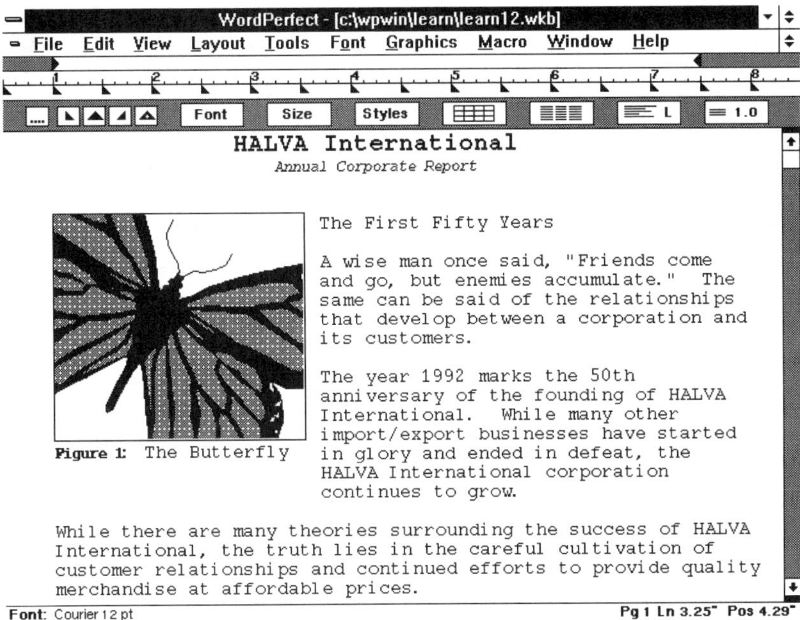

***Figure 19-23.** The graphic appears on screen reflecting all changes made to it in the Figure Editor.*

The *Figure Editor* can also be invoked by double-clicking on a figure box, or by selecting the graphic and choosing the *Figure/Edit* command from the **Graphics** menu.

Positioning a Figure box

Earlier in this chapter, the method for moving and resizing a figure box, using the mouse, was discussed. Now a method for more precisely moving and resizing a figure box is described.

To invoke the **Graphic** menu once more, click again on the figure box with the right mouse button. Select the *Box Position* command from the **Graphic** menu that pops up, to invoke the *Box Position and Size* dialog box of Figure 19-24.

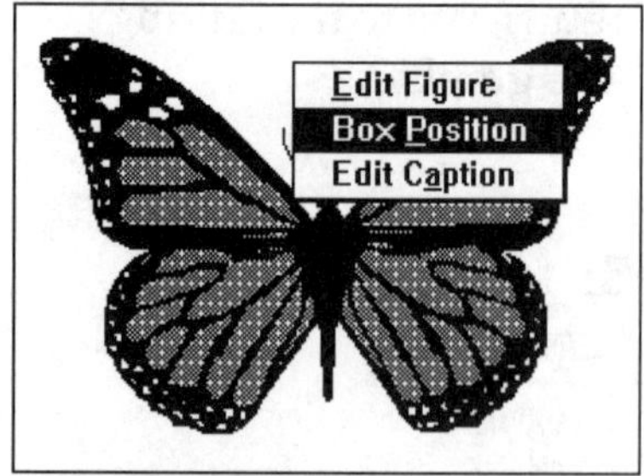

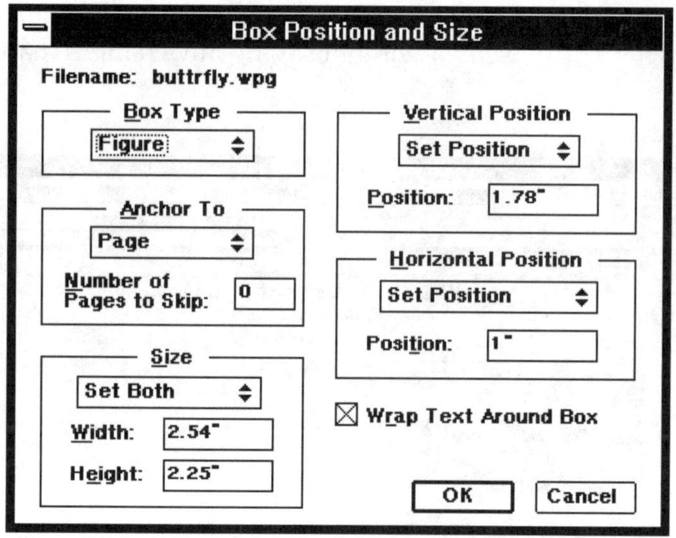

Figure 19-24. *Click on the figure box once with the right mouse button, to reveal the* ***Graphic*** *menu, and select the Box Position command from this menu.*

At the top of the *Box Position and Size* dialog box (Figure 19-24), the name of the imported graphic is listed next to the heading: *Filename.*

The following comments all refer to the *Box Position and Size* dialog box of Figure 19-24.

In the *Box Type* pop-up list box, the current *Box Type* is reflected. When dealing with imported graphics, this option will normally be set to *Figure*. Other box types can be created, with very similar properties to a *Figure* box. If a new *Box Type* is selected, then the box, or the graphic inside the box, is not altered in any way. However, the box will thereafter be treated as the new box type selected. This fact becomes important later, because different box types are numbered separately, and are affected by different codes in the text (see **Editing a figure box** later in this chapter).

A figure box can be anchored, or tied, to the current *page*, current *paragraph*, or even current *character*, by selecting one of these options from the *Anchor To* pop-up list box.

If *Page* is selected from *Anchor To*, this figure box will remain on the same position on the page, regardless of how the text around this figure box moves.

If *Paragraph* is selected, this figure box will move with the paragraph in which it is currently positioned. The code representing the figure box is moved to the first character position in the paragraph.

If *Character* is selected, the figure box becomes part of a text line. The code appears as a single character in the line and moves along with the surrounding text.

The *Size* pop up list box (Figure 19-25), provides a number of ways to adjust the size of the figure box.

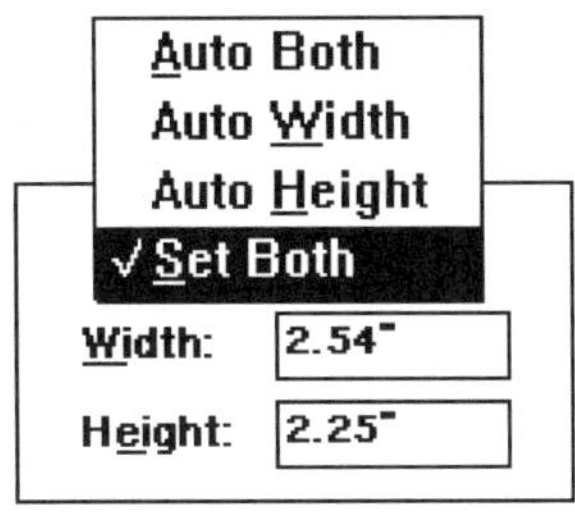

Figure 19-25. *The Size pop-up list box provides a variety of ways to resize the figure box.*

Depending on the option selected from the *Size* pop-up list box, an exact height, or width, for the selected figure box can be specified. If *Set Both* is selected from this pop-up list, both a width and a height for the figure box can be entered.

Figure 19-26. *If Auto Height is selected for the Size pop-up list, only a Width can be entered manually for this figure box. The height will be determined automatically by WordPerfect.*

Using the *Vertical Position* pop-up list box (Figure 19-27), the position of the figure box, relative to the top of the page, paragraph, or line in which it is anchored, can be set. The effect these options have on the box depends on how the box is anchored (see *Anchor To* above).

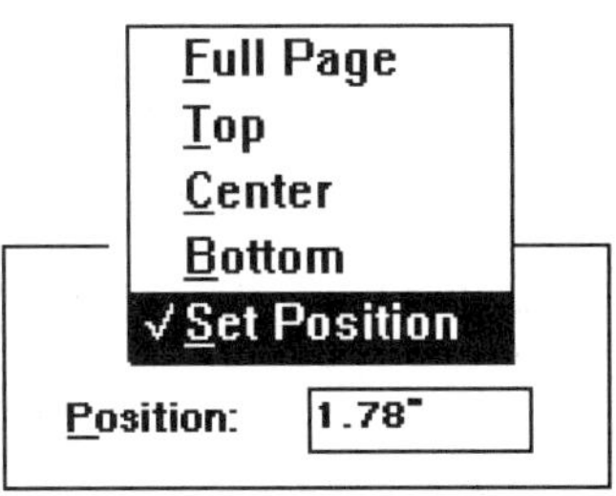

Figure 19-27. *The Vertical Position dialog box allows you to determine where the graphic will appear on the page, paragraph, or line (depending on how the figure box is anchored).*

If *Page* is selected for *Anchor To* above, then selecting *Top* from the *Vertical Position* pop-up list box moves the figure box to the top of the page. *Center* will center the box vertically on the page. *Full Page* stretches the box to reach from the top to the bottom of the page. *Bottom* moves the figure box to the bottom of the page. *Set Position* lets a distance from the top of the page be specified, in the *Position* text box.

If *Paragraph* is selected for *Anchor To*, then the selections for *Vertical Position* are relative to the paragraph in which the figure box is located, rather than the entire page. For example, selecting *Bottom* will align the bottom of the figure box with the bottom line in the paragraph.

If *Character* is selected for *Anchor To*, then the selections for *Vertical Position* are relative to the baseline of the line in which the figure box code is placed.

The *Horizontal Position* pop-up list box (Figure 19-28) works in a very similar manner, but it refers to the horizontal position, rather than the vertical position, of the figure box.

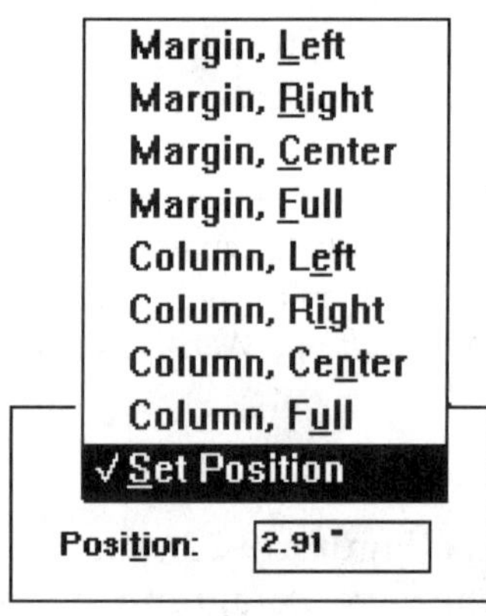

Figure 19-28. *The Horizontal Position pop-up list box lets you specify how the figure box appears on the page in relation to the current margin, or column.*

Finally, the *Wrap Text Around Box* check box option enables, or disables, the facility to run the text automatically around the figure box.

The *Box Position and Size* dialog box can also be invoked by selecting the graphic and choosing the *Position* command from the *Figure* fly-out menu in the **Graphics** menu, or by selecting the *Box Position* command from the *Figure Editor* **File** menu.

Click on *Close* to return to the Editing screen.

Renumbering boxes

Every figure box in a document is assigned a number by WordPerfect. This is the number which is assigned to that figure when a caption is applied to it.

To start the figure numbering at any number other than one, or to number figures manually, you need to insert the cursor before the code denoting the figure box and select the *New Number* command from the *Figure* fly-out menu in the **Graphics** menu. (You may need to use the *Reveal Codes* screen to select the correct cursor location.)

From the dialog box that appears (Figure 19-29), select a new number for the following figure box.

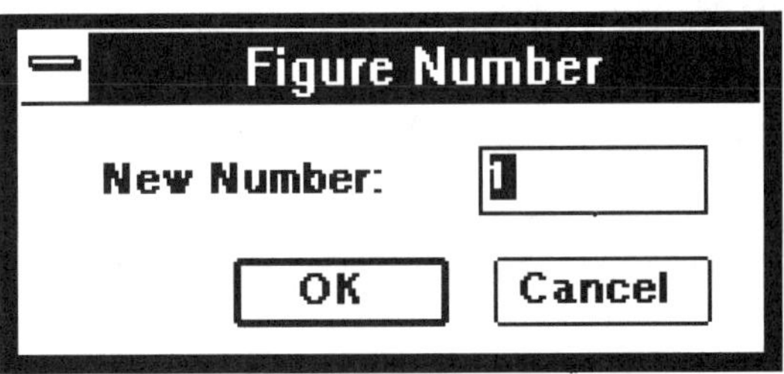

Figure 19-29. *The number assigned to a figure box can be edited using this dialog box.*

Editing a figure box

By default, each figure box appears with a thin single outline around it. WordPerfect allows the appearance of figure boxes to be changed in a number of ways.

A single figure box cannot be edited simply by highlighting that box and selecting a command. The text cursor must be inserted somewhere in the document before the figure box to be edited, so that a code, that will affect all future boxes of this type, is inserted into the text.

Once the text cursor is inserted as described, select the *Options* command from the *Figure* fly-out menu in the **Graphics** menu to invoke the *Figure Options* dialog box of Figure 19-30.

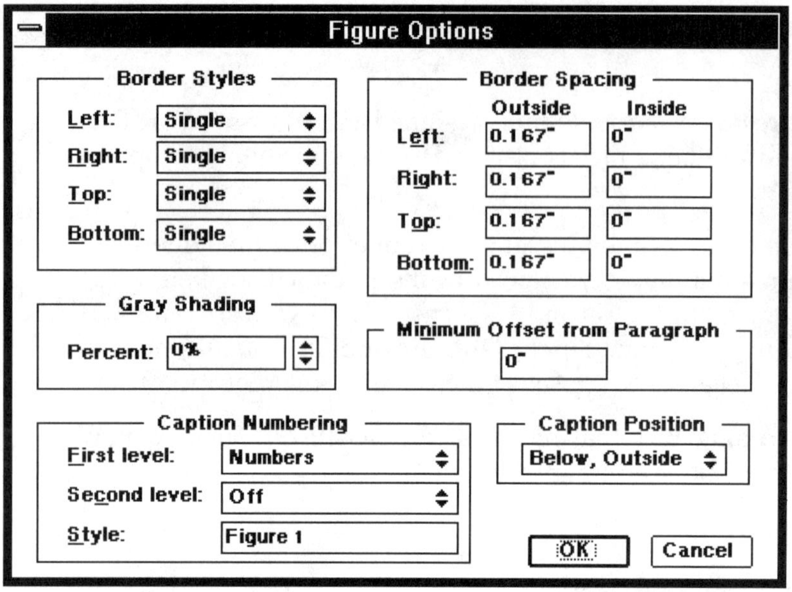

Figure Options

Border Styles
Left: Single
Right: Single
Top: Single
Bottom: Single

Border Spacing
Outside Inside
Left: 0.167" 0"
Right: 0.167" 0"
Top: 0.167" 0"
Bottom: 0.167" 0"

Gray Shading
Percent: 0%

Minimum Offset from Paragraph
0"

Caption Numbering
First level: Numbers
Second level: Off
Style: Figure 1

Caption Position
Below, Outside

OK Cancel

Figure 19-30. *The Figure Options dialog box lets you edit the appearance of the actual figure box. To use this command, you need to insert the cursor in the text somewhere before the location of the figure box code.*

The following comments refer to the *Figure Options* dialog box of Figure 19-30.

The *Border Styles* section of this dialog box lets a border style for each edge of the figure box be specified. Each pop-up list box in this section lets a single, double, thick, dashed, dotted, or extra thick border style, be selected.

The *Gray Shading* section of this dialog box lets you specify a percentage of gray for a figure box background. 50%, for example, will cause figure boxes from this point on in your document to have a 50% gray background.

The *Border Spacing* section of the dialog box lets a margin for both the inside and outside of a figure box be specified. A margin, in a figure box, is an area of white space, in which text or graphics may not infringe.

The *Minimum Offset from Paragraph* figure refers to the minimum distance a figure box may appear from the top of a paragraph, assuming that the box is anchored to the paragraph using the *Anchor To* setting in the *Box Position* dialog box, when the figure box and paragraph appear at the bottom of the page. This feature is aimed at preventing, as much as possible, the separation of a figure box from the paragraph to which it is anchored.

The *Caption Position* pop-up list box allows the position of a caption, related to a figure box, to be specified. Earlier, the caption created appeared below the figure box—using this option, this caption can be made to appear anywhere around the figure. The different options in this list box are shown in Figure 19-32.

The *Caption Numbering* section allow several options to be specified. The *First Level* and *Second Level* pop-up list boxes determine the figure numbering method—whether it be *Numbers*, *Letters*, or *Roman Numerals.* Two level numbering is generally disabled—figures are numbered sequentially by default. Selecting a style for *Second Level* numbering enables two level numbering, so that boxes are numbered 1.1, 1.2, 1.3, etc. When second level numbering reaches the number 31, numbering is restarted (i.e. 1.31 is followed by 2.1).

By default, captions always contain the words "Figure X" (where "X" represents the figure number). To change this default text to, for example, "Table X" or "Graphic X", enter the appropriate words in the *Style* text box.

Figure 19-33 illustrates an edited figure box. The settings in the *Figure Options* dialog box used to edit this figure box are illustrated in Figure 19-31.

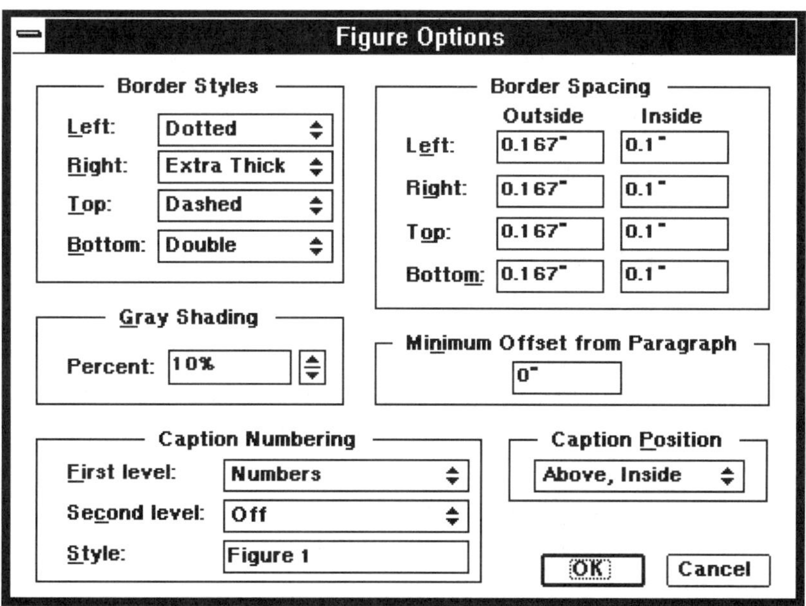

Figure 19-31. *This Figure Options dialog box has now had several options edited. Figure 19-33 illustrates the affect of these changes.*

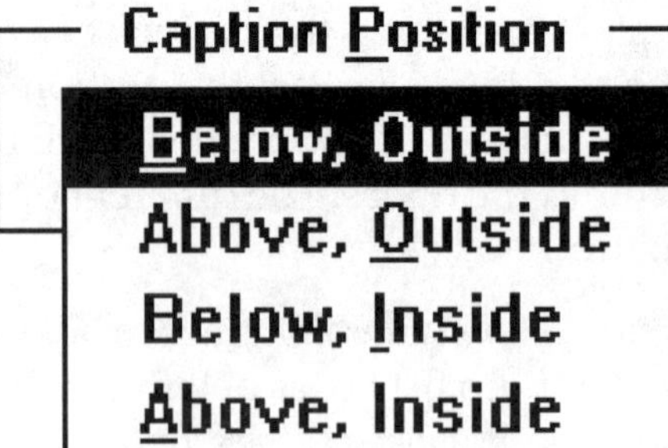

Figure 19-32. These are the different options available for positioning captions with figures.

***Figure 19-33.** To see how this figure box was set up, check the options in the Figure Options dialog box of Figure 19-31.*

More about the different types of boxes

As mentioned at the start of this chapter, there are several types of graphic boxes that can be created and used in WordPerfect. So far, this chapter has dealt almost exclusively with figure boxes, which are used to hold imported graphics.

There are five different type of boxes that can be created within WordPerfect. These boxes correspond to the five menu commands at the top of the **Graphics** menu—*Figure, Text Box, Equation, Table Box,* and *User Box* (Figure 19-34).

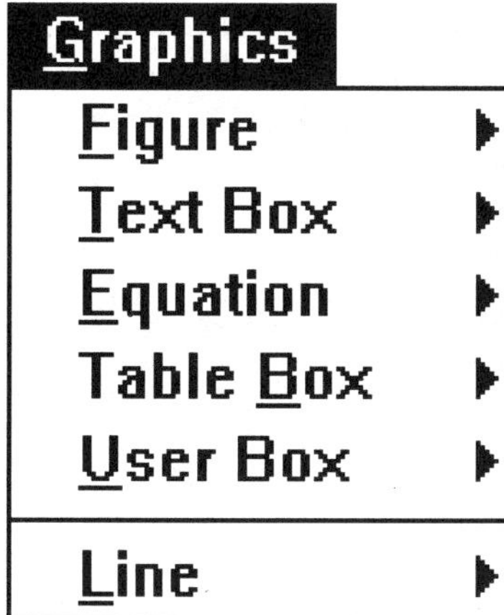

Figure 19-34. *Each of the first five commands in the **Graphics** menu lets you create a graphics box of some kind. Each command has a fly-out menu very similar to the one pictured on the right—illustrating how alike these boxes are.*

Each type of box is basically the same, although each is designed to hold different kinds of graphics. Each can be moved, edited, positioned, be given captions, and renumbered, in the ways already described for figure boxes. There are, however, are few minor differences between these boxes.

Each different type of box is numbered separately. If you create ten figure boxes and then one text box, then it is text box number 1, not number 11.

An earlier section of this chapter looked at how a figure box is edited and mentioned that the changes made using the *Figure/Options* command inserts codes into the text which affect all future figure boxes. This fact remains true—text boxes will not be affected at all by figure box codes and vice versa. Each different type of box is affected only by codes inserted using the *Options* command from its own fly-out menu.

Text boxes

A text box, in almost all cases, is exactly the same as a figure box, but it contains text, rather than an imported graphic.

It is created and edited in exactly the same manner as a figure box. It uses the *Text Box* fly-out menu, however, rather than the *Figure* fly-out menu, from the **Graphics** menu.

To create a text box, use the *Text Box/Create* command from the **Graphics** menu. The *Text Box Editor* screen appears (Figure 19-35), allowing you to enter text which is to appear in the text box.

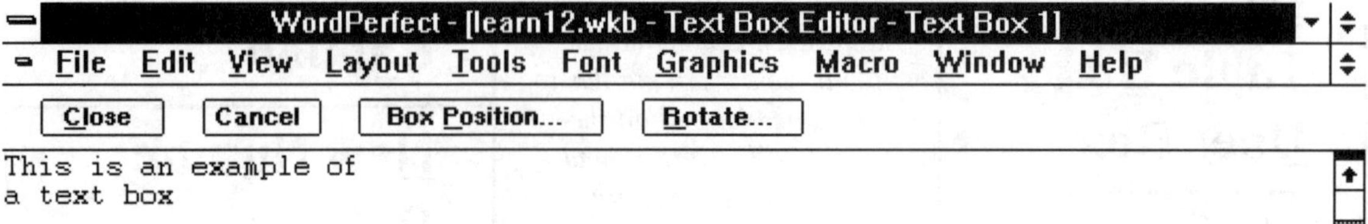

Figure 19-35. *The Text Box Editor screen is used to enter text that is to appear inside a text box.*

Moving, resizing, positioning and editing this text box work the same way as described for figure boxes. Simply replace the references to the *Figure* fly-out menu with the *Text Box* fly-out menu from the **Graphics** menu. Of course, when editing the contents of a text box, the *Text Box Editor* is invoked rather than the *Graphics Editor*.

Figure 19-36 illustrates a text box as it may appear in the WordPerfect editing screen.

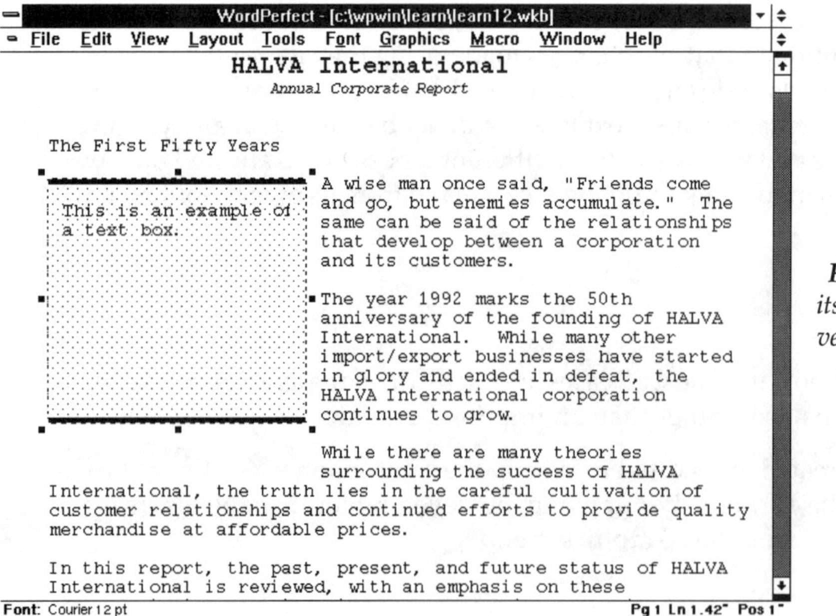

Figure 19-36. *Apart from its contents, a text box looks very similar, and behaves in a very similar way, to a figure box.*

Equations

Equations, like figures and text, can appear in boxes and, once again, have almost all the same properties as these other boxes.

However, the *Equation Editor* (Figure 19-37) is different than the figure and text box editors. This dialog box is invoked through the *Equation/Create* command from the **Graphics** menu.

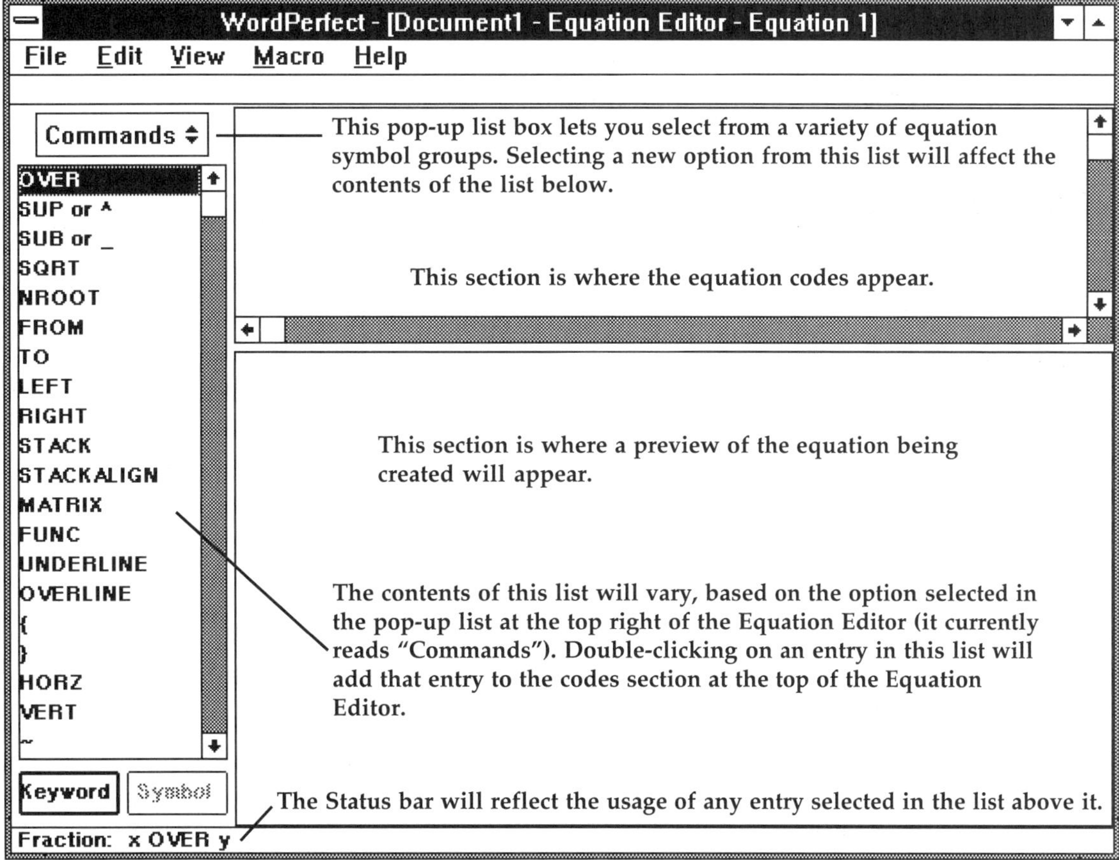

Figure 19-37. *The Equation Editor.*

The following figures (Figure 19-38 and Figure 19-39) illustrate some equation examples.

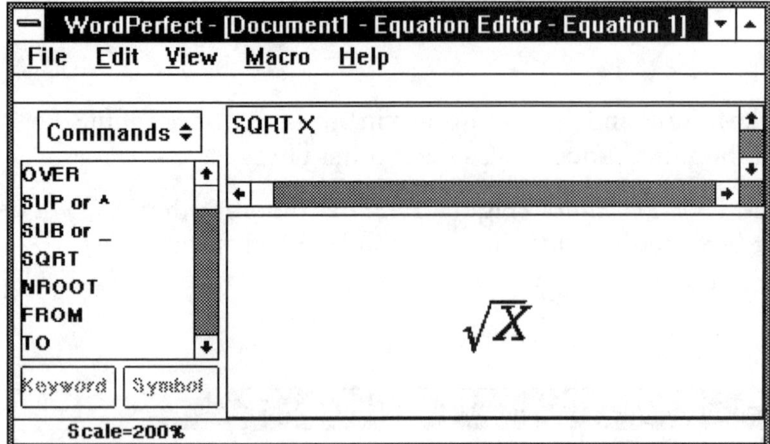

Figure 19-38. The code appears at the top part of the Equation Editor, and the Preview at the bottom. The code is selected from the list to the left of the Equation Editor and the Keyword button is then clicked on.

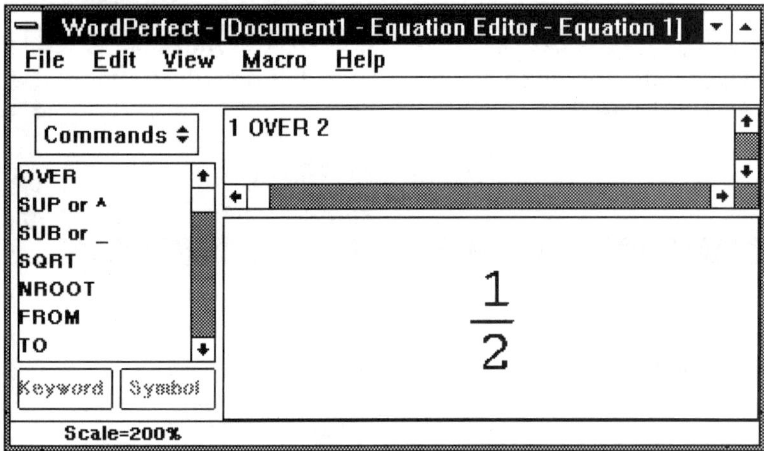

Figure 19-39. Once again, both the code and the preview appear in this screen. Select the Redisplay command from the ***View*** *menu to ensure that your equation appears in the Preview screen.*

Table boxes

Table boxes allow the creation of generic graphics boxes that do not conform to any of the other box types described above.

For example, this option could be use to hold an imported graphic that is not intended to be numbered in sequence with the other figure boxes. In addition, the display options set for figure boxes in the *Figure Options* dialog box (Figure 19-31) would not apply to imported graphics in table boxes.

The *Select Editor* dialog box of Figure 19-40 lets you select the type of table box through a choice of any of the three graphics box editors described above. This dialog box is activated through the *Create* command from the *Table Box* fly-out menu in the **Graphics** menu.

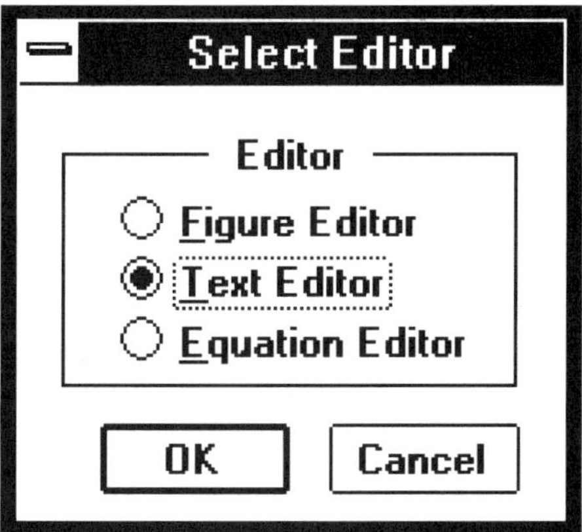

Figure 19-40. When you wish to create a Table Box, you are asked what Editor you would like to use to create the contents of this box.

User boxes

Creating a user box is the same as creating a table box—it becomes merely another box that may be numbered separately, and be assigned different properties to other boxes.

Internal graphics

WordPerfect provides the facility to create graphics without having to use a separate, dedicated graphics package. You are, however, restricted to a few simple shapes—lines and boxes. These shapes are, however, useful for many purposes.

Creating horizontal or vertical lines in WordPerfect is essentially the same (they both use the same dialog box). The only real difference is that a horizontal line is created using the *Line/Horizontal* command from the **Graphics** menu and a vertical line is created using the *Line/Vertical* command in the **Graphics** menu. In this chapter, the line drawing featured is demonstrated with the *Line/Horizontal* command (Figure 19-41).

Before creating a line on the page, it is a good idea to insert the text cursor into the document at a point where the line should appear (although this move is not strictly necessary). For example, in the document currently open (which was ***learn12.wkb*** opened in Figure 19-1), insert the text cursor before the very first character in the file.

To create a horizontal line, select the *Line/Horizontal* command from the **Graphics** menu (Figure 19-41).

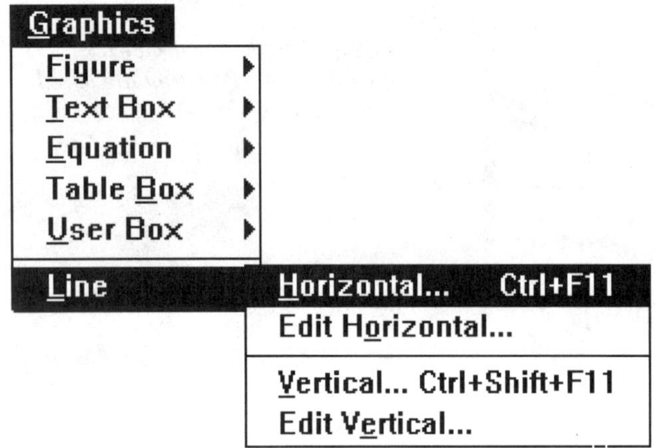

Figure 19-41. *The Line/Horizontal command is used to add a horizontal line to a document.*

The *Create Horizontal Line* dialog box (Figure 19-42) allows you to design a line and position it on the page.

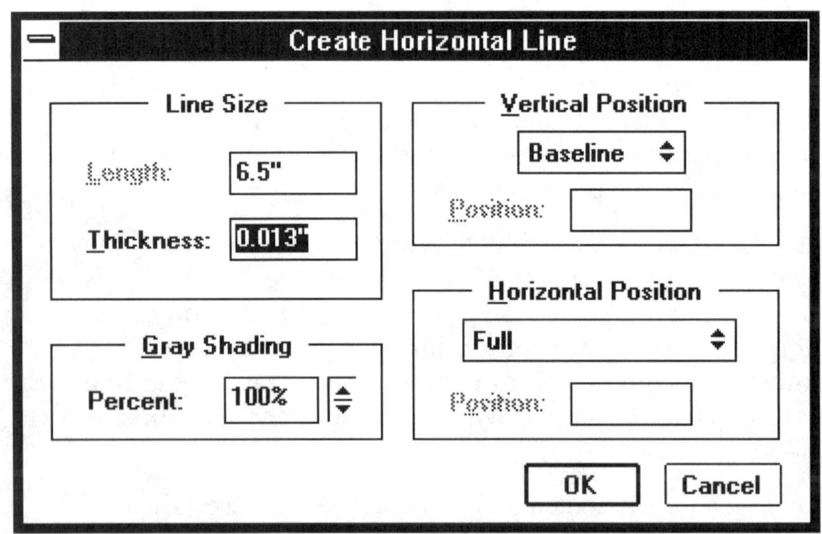

Figure 19-42. *The Create Horizontal Line dialog box.*

In the *Line Size* section, specify both the *Length* and *Thickness* of the line being created. If the length option is grayed, this value will have to be filled in at a later date.

Under the *Gray Shading* section, specify the shade of this line as a percentage of black in the *Percent* text box.

The *Vertical Position* pop-up list box contains two choices: *Baseline,* which means the horizontal line will appear on the baseline of the line on which the cursor is currently inserted, or *Specify,* which allows you to enter the distance from the top of the page that this line will appear in the *Position* text box. For this example, make sure *Baseline* is selected.

The *Horizontal Position* allows the line to be justified. If *Full* is selected for *Horizontal Position,* the line will run from the left to the right margin, across the page. If *Left, Right,* or *Center* is selected, the *Length* of the line, under the *Line Size* section, can be specified

If *Specify* is selected for *Horizontal Position,* enter a value into the *Position* text box below this option. This figure will represent the left most point of the line (i.e., if "2" is inserted in this text box, the line will start two inches from the left of the page).

Fill out the *Create Horizontal Line* dialog box as shown in Figure 19-43. Select **OK**, and a line will appear in the document as shown in Figure 19-44.

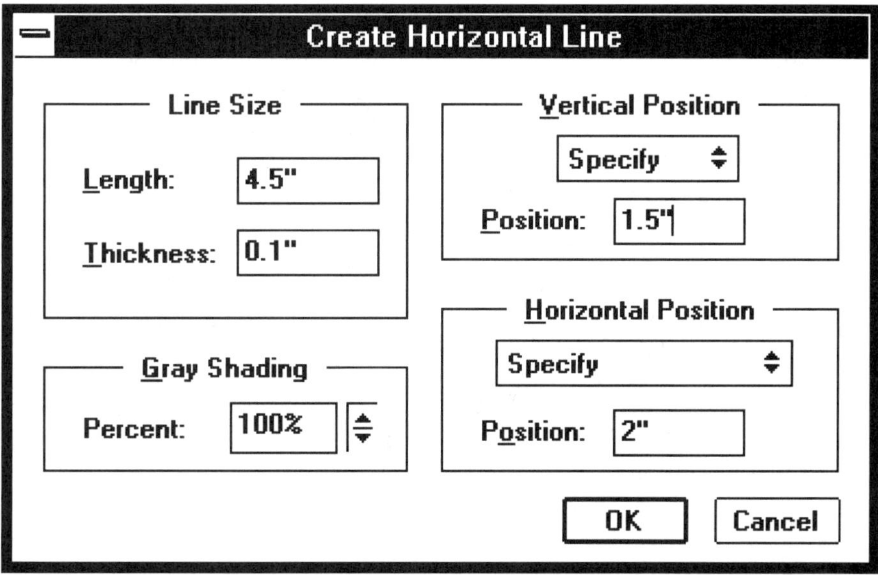

Figure 19-43. *Fill out your dialog box as illustrated here, to provide the result as shown in Figure 19-44.*

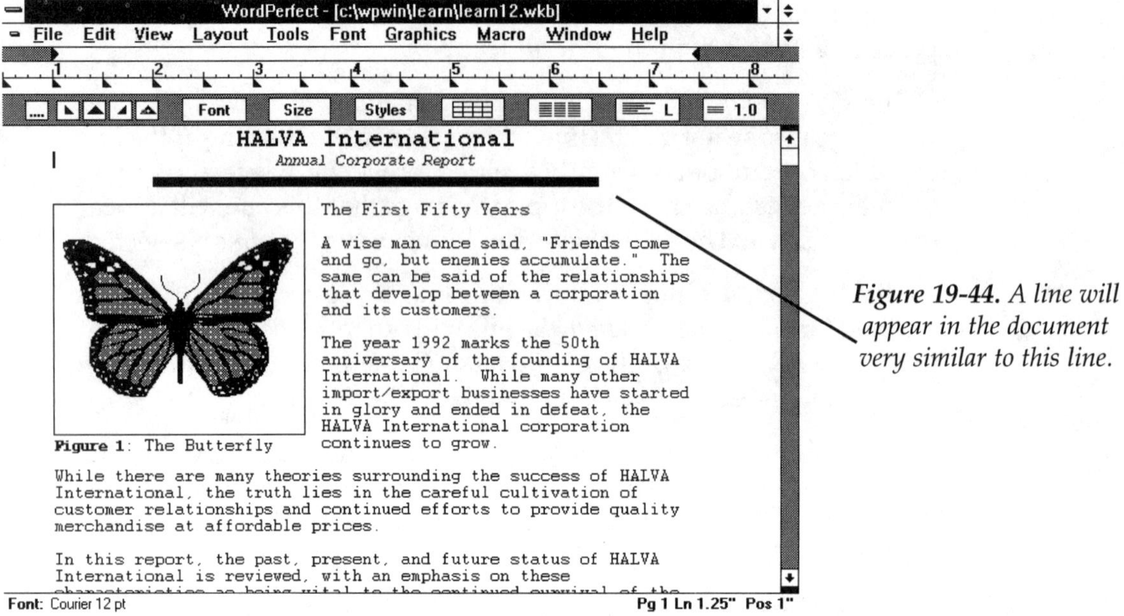

Figure 19-44. *A line will appear in the document very similar to this line.*

Editing an internal graphic

In many ways, an internally created line can be edited in much the same way as the figure boxes created earlier in the chapter. Clicking the mouse on an internal graphic causes handles to appear around the edge of the graphic. An internal graphic's size and position can then be edited in the same way as figure boxes (see **Using the mouse with graphics** earlier in this chapter).

To edit an internally created line using a dialog box, click on the graphic with the right mouse button. A small sub-menu appears, listing one command—*Edit Horizontal Line* for a horizontal line, and *Edit Vertical Line* for a vertical line.

Alternatively, select the graphic by clicking on it once, and selecting either the *Line/Edit Horizontal* or *Line/Edit Vertical* commands from the **Graphics** menu.

Graphics — Exercise

This training exercise is designed so that people of all levels of expertise with WordPerfect can use it to gain maximum benefit. In order to do this, the bare exercise is listed below this paragraph on just one page, with no hints. The following pages contain the steps needed to complete this exercise for those who need additional prompting.

Steps in brief

1. *Start a new WordPerfect Document.*
2. *Before loading a graphic, use the Figure/Options command to set up all figure boxes with a Thick outline and a 10% background tint.*
3. *Retrieve the graphic globe2-m.wpg from the learn sub-directory.*
4. *Size the figure box so that it stretches from the left margin to the right, but keep the same height.*
5. *Retrieve the text file learn05.wkb from the learn sub-directory.*
6. *Insert the text cursor at the start of the fifth line in the document (which is blank), and create a horizontal line using the default settings.*
7. *Move the figure box so that the first four lines of text appear above the figure box, and the rest below.*
8. *Insert a caption below the figure box reading "The new corporate logo".*

The details for completing these steps are on the following pages.

Steps in detail

1. ***Start a new WordPerfect Document.***

If you have just opened WordPerfect, you will be in a new WordPerfect file. If you are working on another WordPerfect document, select the *New* command from the **File** menu. If you are not in WordPerfect, start it from Windows.

2. ***Before loading a graphic, use the Figure/Options command to set up all figure boxes with a Thick outline and a 10% background tint.***

Any changes you make using the *Figure/Options* command from the **Graphics** menu will affect all following figure boxes. As the text cursor is already at the start of the file, this is an ideal place to use the *Figure/Options* command. Select this command, as shown in Figure 19x-1, to activate the associated dialog box.

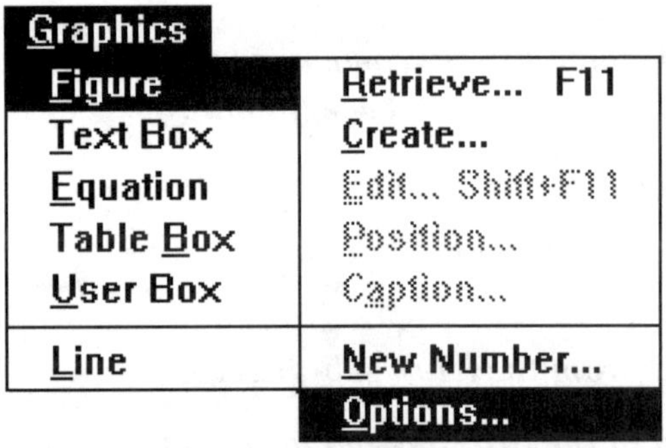

Figure 19x-1. *To set the appearance of figure boxes in this document, select the Figure/Options command from the* **Graphics** *menu.*

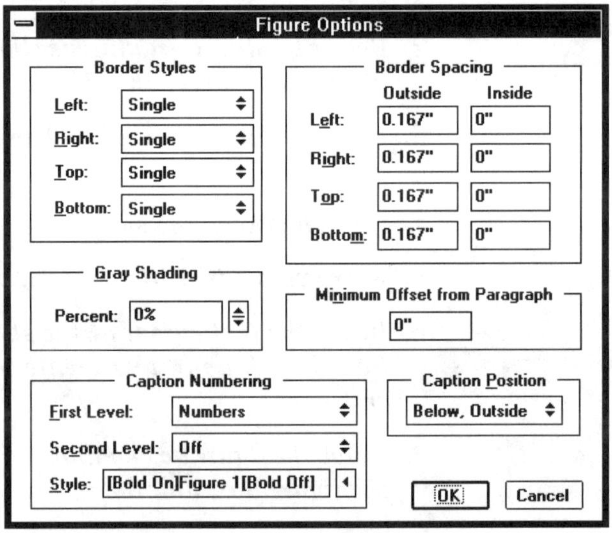

This step requires that you set all sides of the figure box at the "Thick" option. To achieve this, select the *Thick* option from the *Left*, *Right*, *Top* and *Bottom* pop-up lists in the *Figure Options* dialog box (Figure 19x-2).

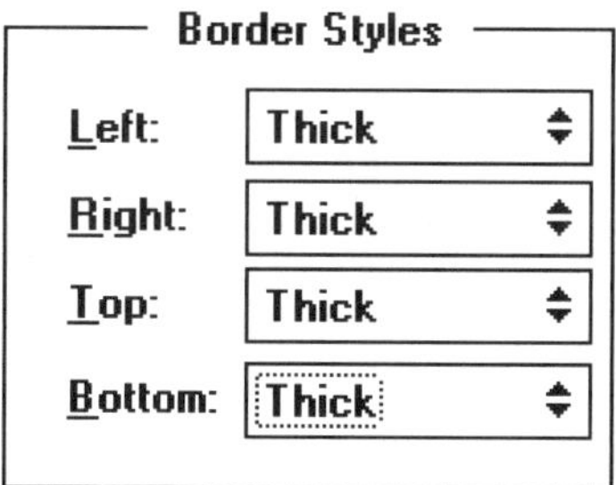

Figure 19x-2. *To ensure that the border of future figure boxes in this document are "Thick", select the "Thick" option from all pop-up lists in the Border Styles section of the Figure 19x-1 dialog box.*

To ensure that the figure box has a background tint of 10%, select 10% for the *Gray Shading* option (Figure 19x-3).

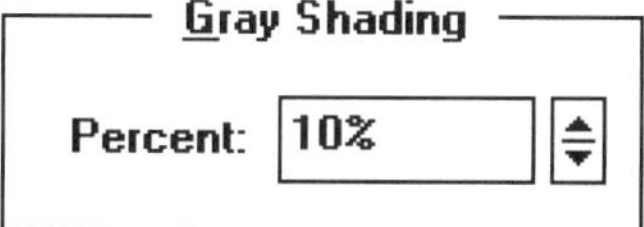

Figure 19x-3. *Select 10% as the entry for the Gray Shading text box to ensure that future figure boxes have a background tint of 10% black.*

Click on **OK** to save these settings in this document.

3. Retrieve the graphic globe2-m.wpg from the learn sub-directory.

This step is achieved by selecting the *Figure/Retrieve* command from the **Graphics** menu (Figure 19x-4).

Graphics	
Figure	Retrieve... F11
Text Box	Create...
Equation	Edit... Shift+F11
Table Box	Position...
User Box	Caption...
Line	New Number...
	Options...

Figure 19x-4. *To import a graphic into WordPerfect, you select the Figure/Retrieve command from the* ***Graphics*** *menu.*

In the dialog box that appears, select the file ***globe2-m.wpg*** from the *learn* sub-directory (Figure 19x-5) and click on *Retrieve*. Your screen will now look like Figure 19x-6.

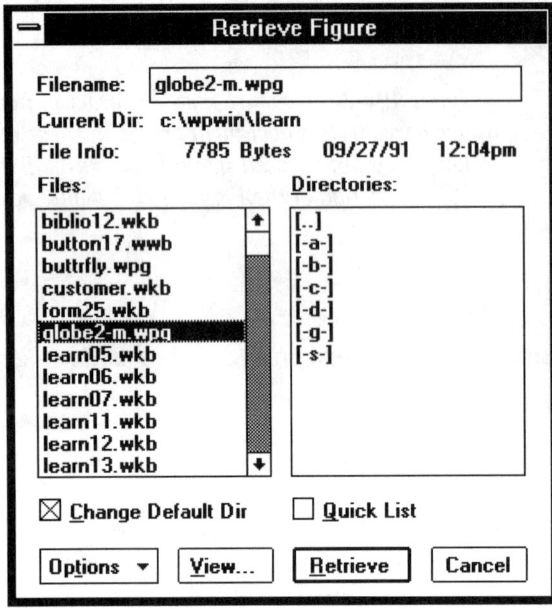

Figure 19x-5. Select the graphic **globe2-m.wpg** from the **learn** sub-directory on your computer. Click on Retrieve to actually load the selected graphic.

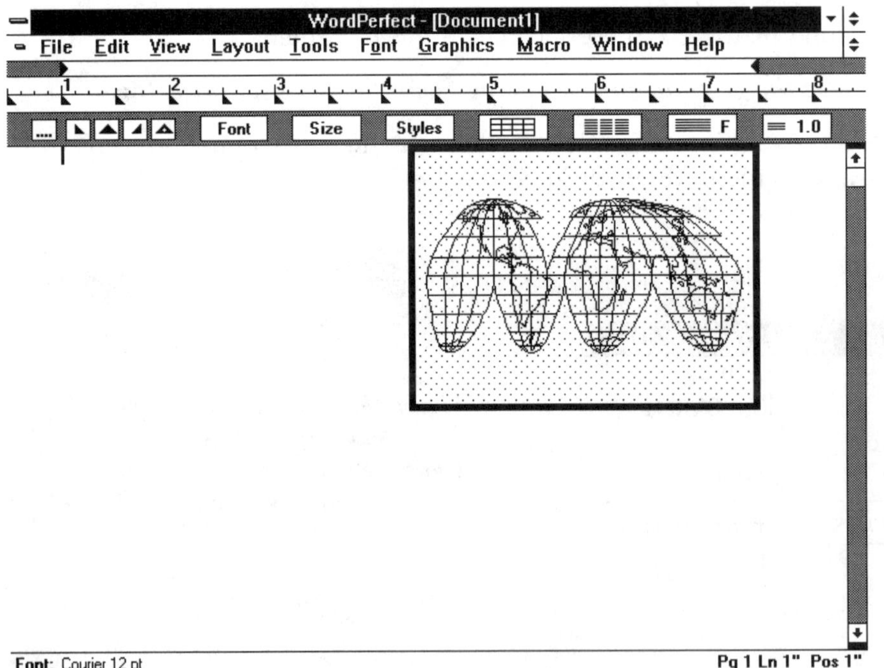

Figure 19x-6. The graphic is loaded onto the page. Note the appearance of the figure box—it uses the settings performed in step 2 of this exercise.

4. ***Size the figure box so that it stretches from the left margin to the right, but keep the same height.***

The simple way to stretch the figure box across the top of the page is to select the figure box once, by clicking on it with the left mouse button. Handles will appear around the edge of the box as shown in Figure 19x-7.

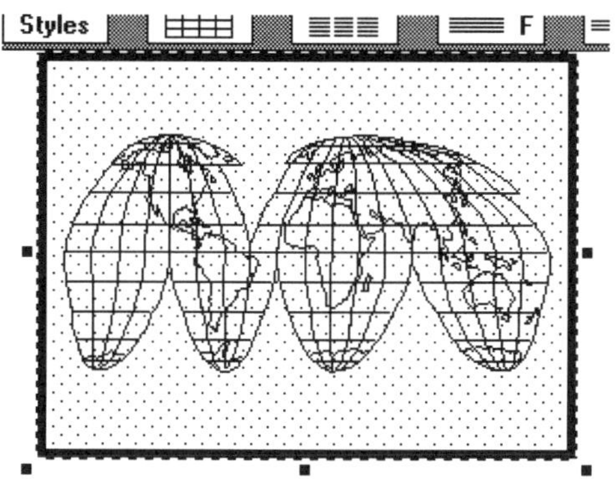

Figure 19x-7. *Clicking on a figure box (or any type of box) once will display the selection handles around that box. These handles are used to resize the figure box.*

Hold the mouse button down on the left hand, center, handle of the figure box, and move the mouse across to the left-hand margin and release (Figure 19x-8). If you are using the ruler, this step is much easier, as it is quite simple to align the mouse with the margin marker in the ruler (Figure 19x-8).

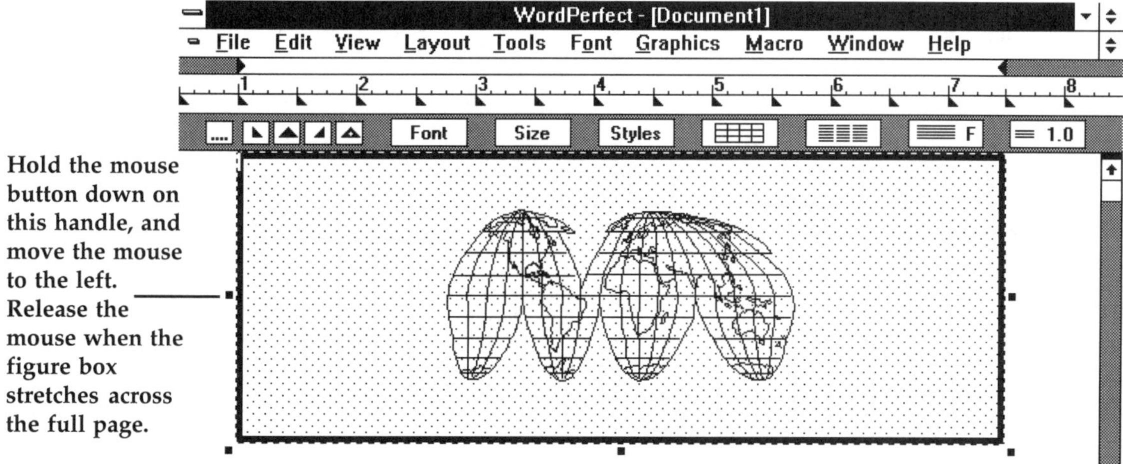

Figure 19x-8. *The resized figure box.*

5. Retrieve the text file learn05.wkb from the learn sub-directory.

To perform this step, you can leave the text cursor where it is. Text will flow around this figure box and, as the figure box is at the very top of the page, will simply appear below the box.

Use the *Retrieve* command from the **File** menu (Figure 19x-9) to locate the file ***learn05.wkb***. Select this file from the ***learn*** sub-directory (Figure 19x-10), and click on *Retrieve*. A WordPerfect dialog box will now appear on the screen asking if you wish to insert this file into the current document. Click on the *Yes* option.

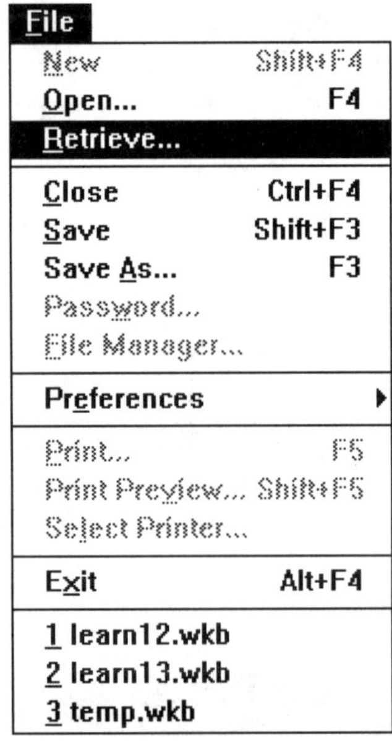

Figure 19x-9. *To retrieve a text file, click on the Retrieve command from the* ***File*** *menu.*

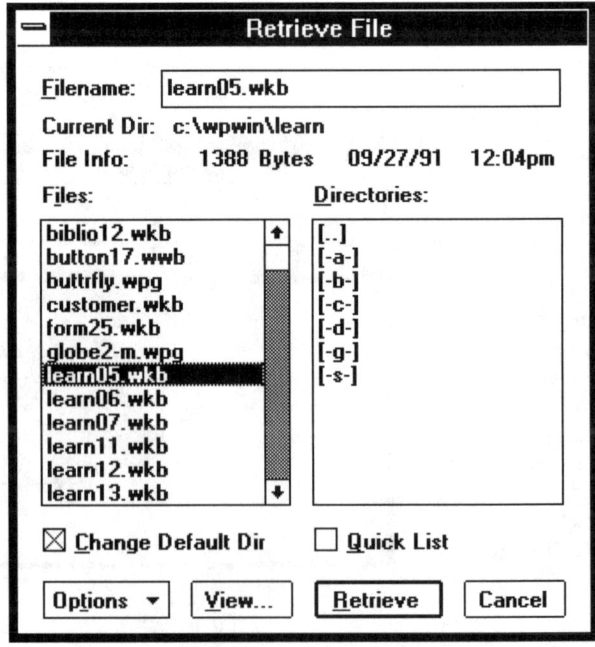

Figure 19x-10. *Select the file* ***learn05.wkb*** *from the* ***learn*** *sub-directory, and retrieve it by clicking on the Retrieve command.*

The text will flow onto the page, below the figure box, as shown in Figure 19x-11. If text has run down the side of your box, you may have to resize the figure box, to make it extend a little further past the page margins.

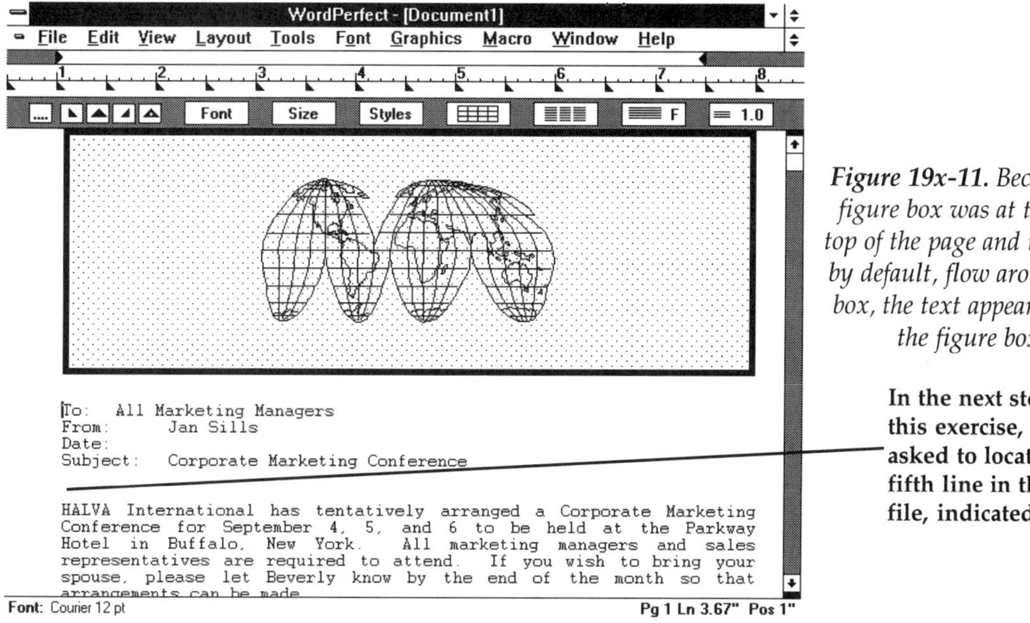

Figure 19x-11. *Because the figure box was at the very top of the page and text will, by default, flow around this box, the text appears below the figure box.*

In the next step of this exercise, you are asked to locate the fifth line in the text file, indicated here.

6. ***Insert the text cursor at the start of the fifth line in the document (which is blank), and create a horizontal line using the default settings.***

Locate the fifth line in the text (Figure 19x-11), and insert the text cursor.

Select the *Line/Horizontal* command from the **Graphics** menu (Figure 19x-12). As you have been asked to create a line using default settings, simply click on **OK** from the dialog box that appears (Figure 19x-12).

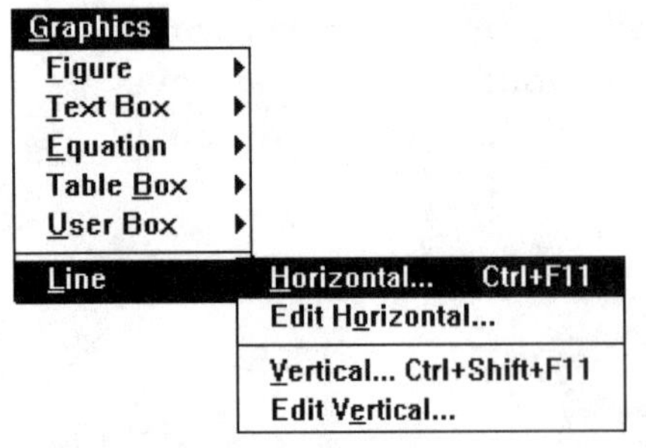

Figure 19x-12. *The Line/Horizontal command from the* ***Graphics*** *menu is used to create horizontal lines in your documents.*

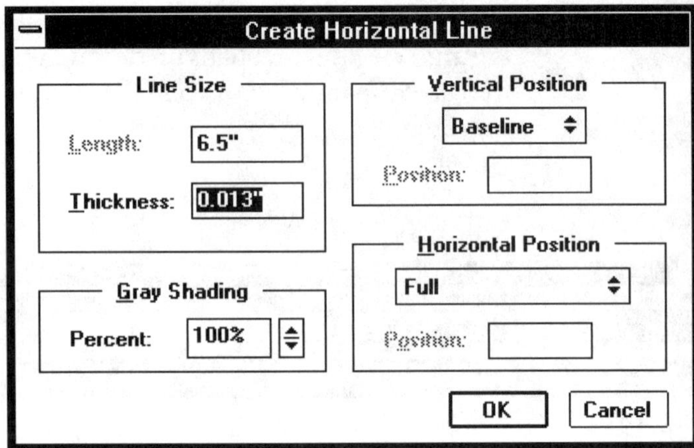

Your screen will appear as in Figure 19x-13.

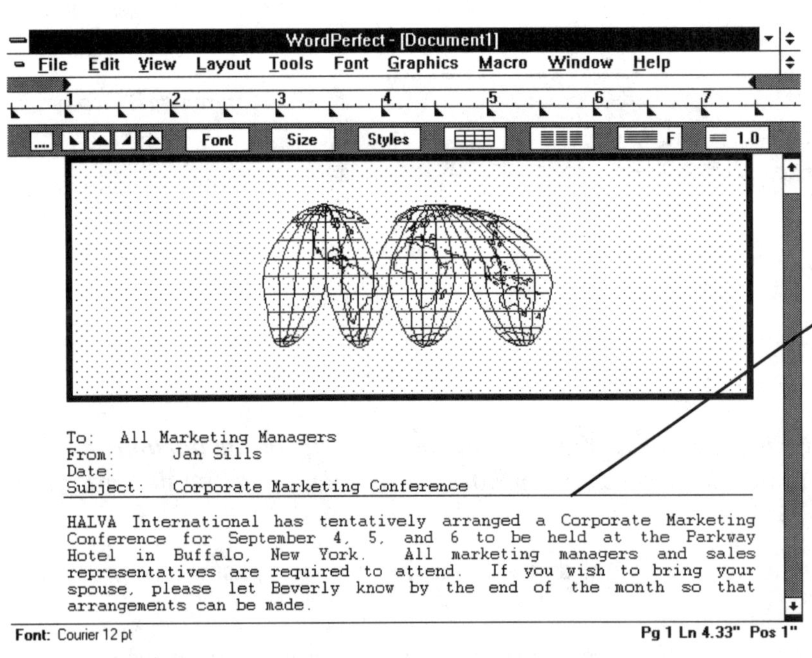

Figure 19x-13*. Using the default settings in the dialog box of Figure 19x-13, a horizontal line will appear in your document on the same line as the text cursor was inserted.*

7. ***Move the figure box so that the first four lines of text appear above this box, and the rest below.***

To move the figure box down the page, hold the left mouse button down on this box, and move it down the page a couple of inches, and release the mouse. You may have to move it up or down several times to position it as shown in Figure 19x-14.

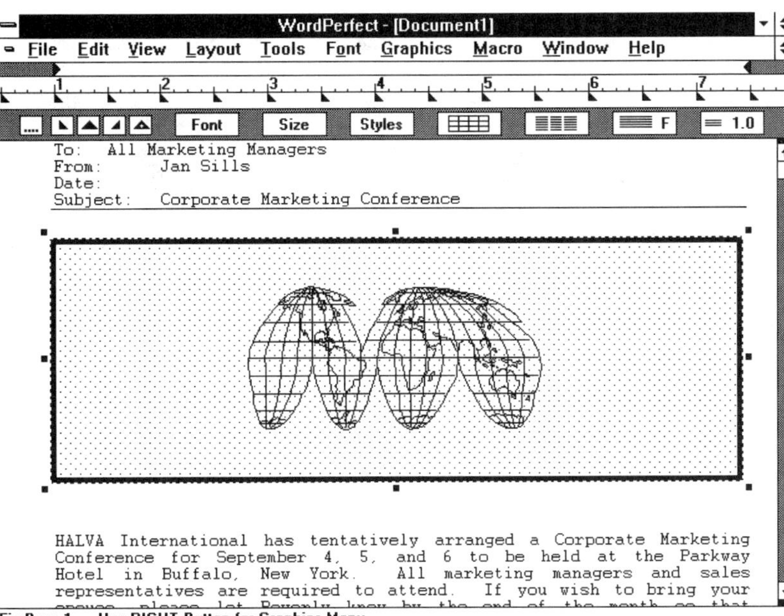

Figure 19x-14. *Here the figure box has been moved down the page, using the mouse, so that the first four lines of text appear above the box.*

8. Insert a caption below the figure box reading "The new corporate logo.".

To insert a caption under this figure box, click on the figure once with the right mouse button. From the small menu that appears (Figure 19x-15), select the *Edit Caption* command by clicking on it with the left mouse button. The *Caption Editor* screen will appear (Figure 19x-16).

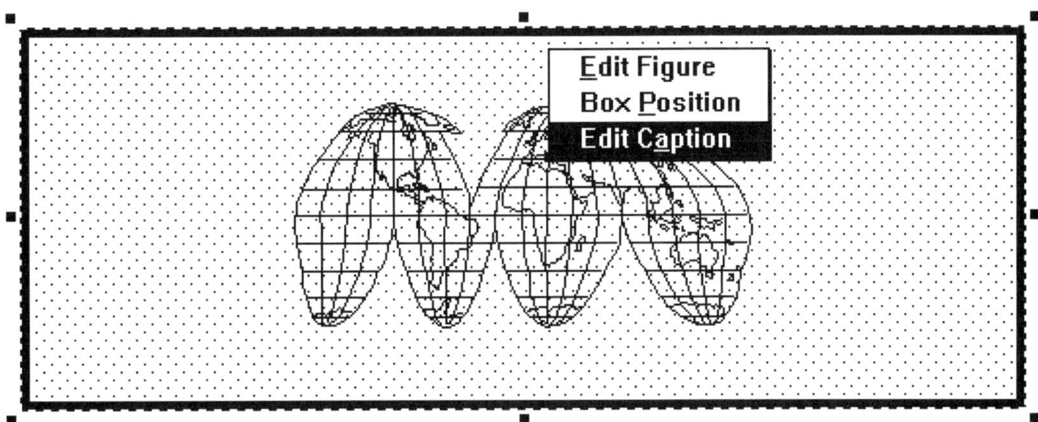

Figure 19x-15. *To add a caption to a figure box, you first click on the figure with the right mouse button, and select the Edit Caption command, with the left mouse button, from the small menu that then appears.*

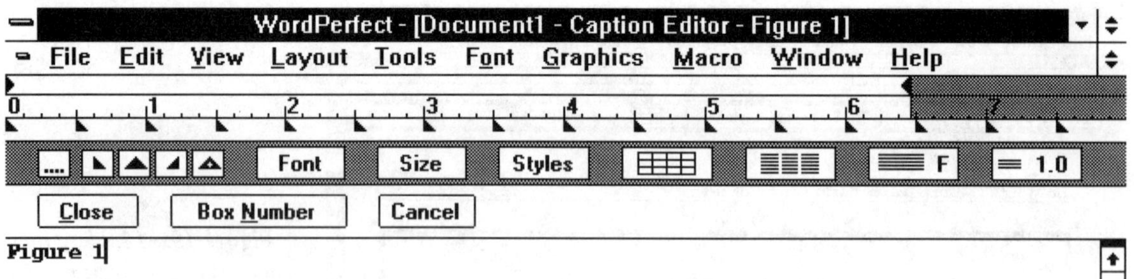

***Figure 19x-16.** The Caption Editor screen.*

In the *Caption Editor* screen, delete the letters "Figure 1" by using the backspace key. Enter the text "The new corporate logo." as shown in Figure 19x-17.

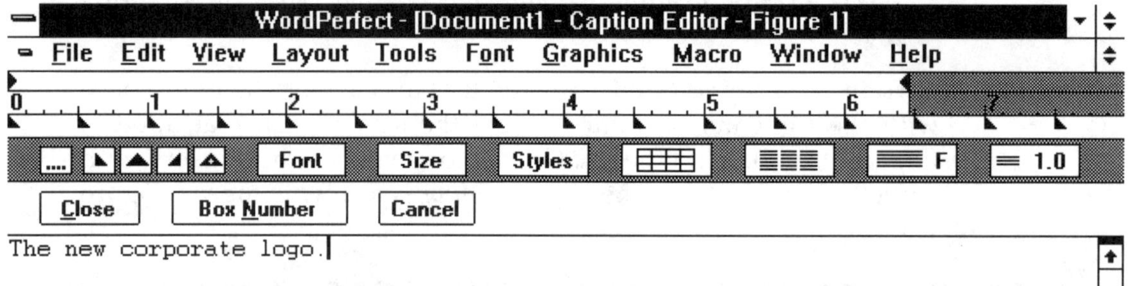

***Figure 19x-17.** Backspace the words "Figure 1" from the Caption Editor screen (this will only require one backspace), and enter the words "The new corporate logo.".*

Click on the *Close* button to return to the editing screen. Your screen will appear as shown in Figure 19x-18.

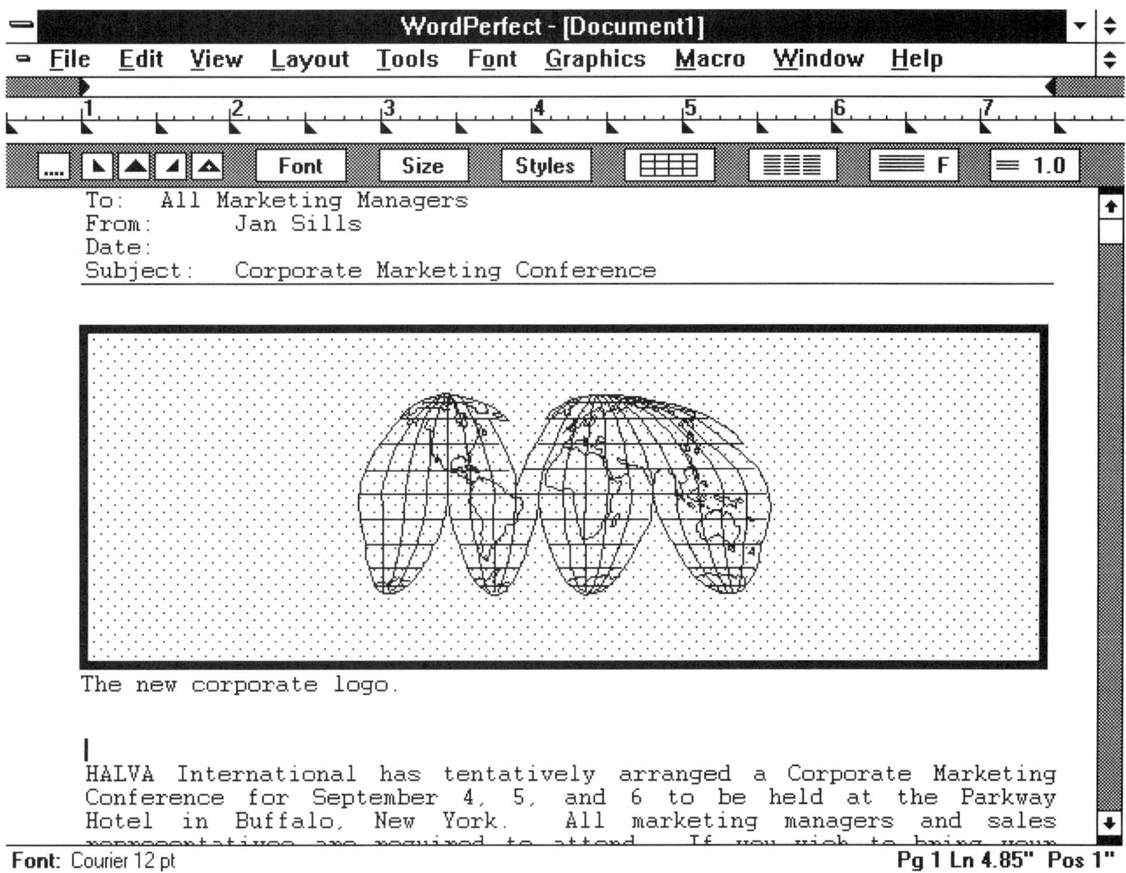

Figure 19x-18. *The finished product!*

Macros

Macros are created in WordPerfect to perform a series of tasks in one operation. By using a macro, you alleviate the need to repeat certain steps that you find yourself doing frequently.

Creating a simple macro

Take, for example, letter writing—at the bottom of every letter, you generally type something similar to the following paragraphs:

Warmest Regards,

Fred Smith
Chairman of the Board

Rather than having to type in this information every time you create a letter, you can create a macro that does this for you, and simply play (or run) that macro when the letter ends.

To follow the examples in this chapter, make sure you have a new WordPerfect document window open—achieved by selecting the *New* command from the **File** menu.

To create a macro, you first select the *Record* command from the **Macro** menu (Figure 20-1).

*Figure 20-1. The Record command from the **Macro** menu is used to create macros.*

After selecting the *Record* command in Figure 20-1, you are presented with the *Record Macro* dialog box of Figure 20-2. This dialog box allows you to name and describe macros.

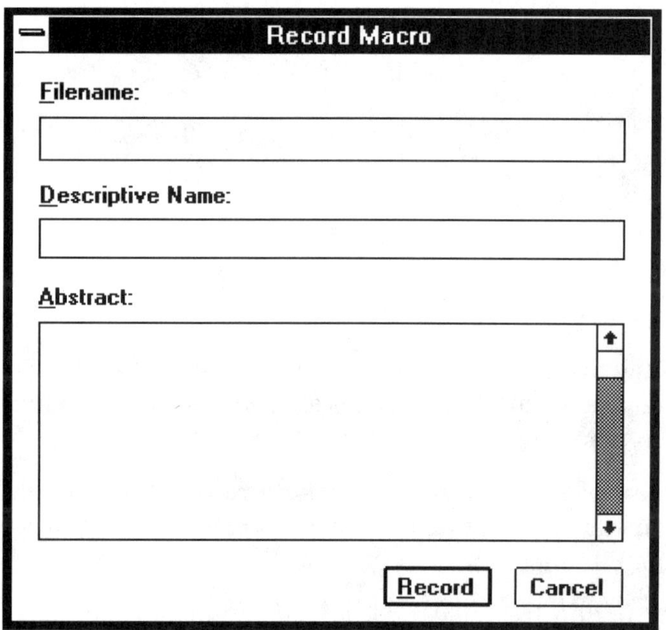

Figure 20-2. The Record Macro dialog box.

On the first line, in the *Filename* text box, you name the file that will hold this macro. Every macro you create is stored in its own individual file with the extension ***wcm***. In this case, enter the name ***signoff*** (Figure 20-3). WordPerfect will automatically apply the extension ***wcm***.

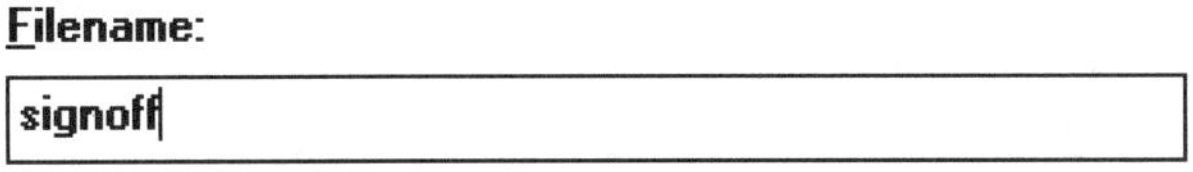

Filename:

signoff

Figure 20-3. Every macro is stored in its own file—a file you name by inserting a name in the Filename text box of the Record Macro dialog box.

In the *Descriptive Name* text box, insert a brief description of this macro. In Figure 20-4, "Sign Off From Business Letter" has been entered.

Descriptive Name:

Sign Off From Business Letter

Figure 20-4. The Descriptive Name text box is used to provide a brief description of this macro.

At this stage, the macro can be recorded by selecting the *Record* button of Figure 20-2. After clicking on this button, you are returned to the normal WordPerfect editing screen, with the words *"Recording Macro"* displayed in the Status bar, at the bottom left-hand corner of the screen (Figure 20-5).

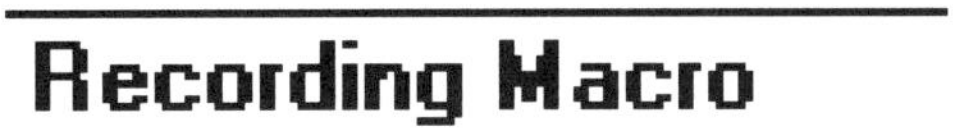

Recording Macro

Figure 20-5. The bottom left-hand corner of the screen lets you know when you are recording a macro.

Recording a macro from here is basically a question of selecting the commands, importing the graphics, and entering the text that you wish to be associated with this macro.

In this example, you were asked to make a macro that will automatically enter the following words:

```
Warmest Regards,


Fred Smith
Chairman of the Board
```

To create this macro, enter these words on the screen while the macro is being recorded. Enter the first line, then press the Enter key three times. (This gives the space between the first and second lines as shown in Figure 20-6.)

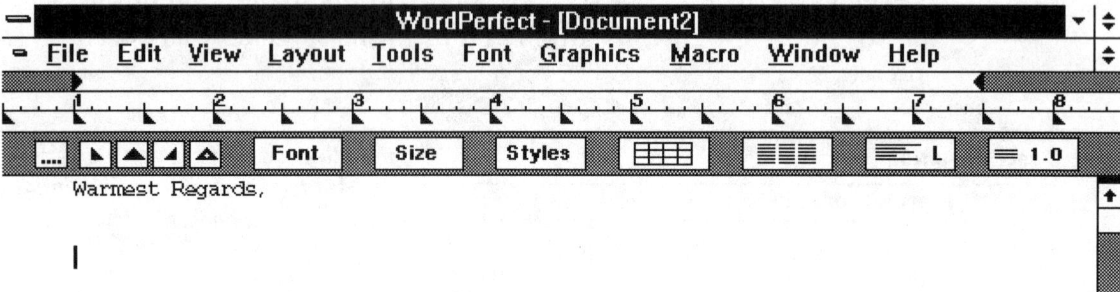

Figure 20-6. The first line of text has been entered, and the Enter key pressed three times. (Note the position of the flashing text cursor.)

The next line in these paragraphs has been bolded. Therefore, you should select the *Bold* command in the **Font** menu before you enter the next line of text (Figure 20-7).

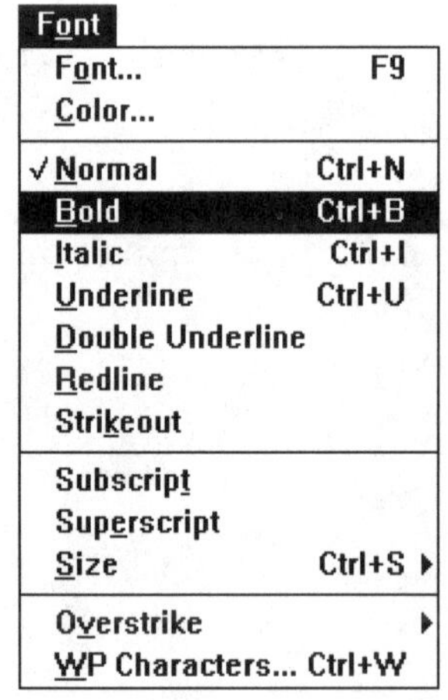

*Figure 20-7. To bold the next line of text that you enter, select the Bold command from the **Font** menu.*

Now you can enter the next line of text (Figure 20-8). Remember to hit the Enter key only once after typing this line.

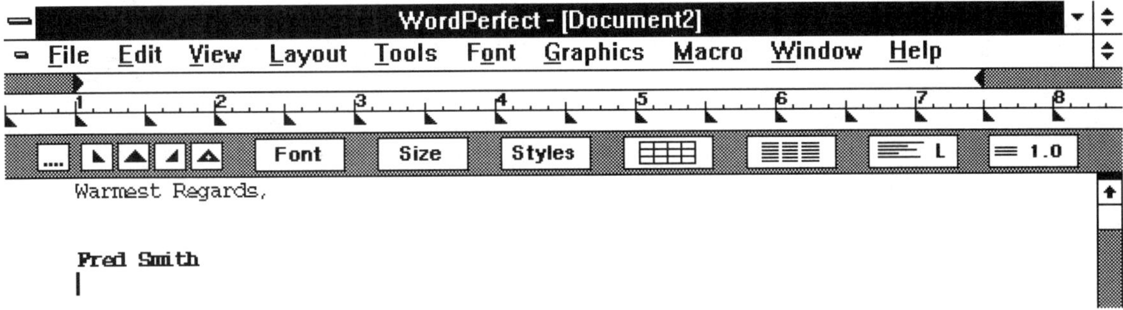

Figure 20-8. The next line of text appears in bold, as you selected that command (Figure 20-7) before entering the text.

The next line of text is in italics only. The bold attribute is still activated from the previous line. Therefore, deactivate the bold code by selecting the *Bold* command once more (Figure 20-7).

Next, select the *Italic* command from the **Font** menu (Figure 20-9). This command imports the italic attribute in the text typed next.

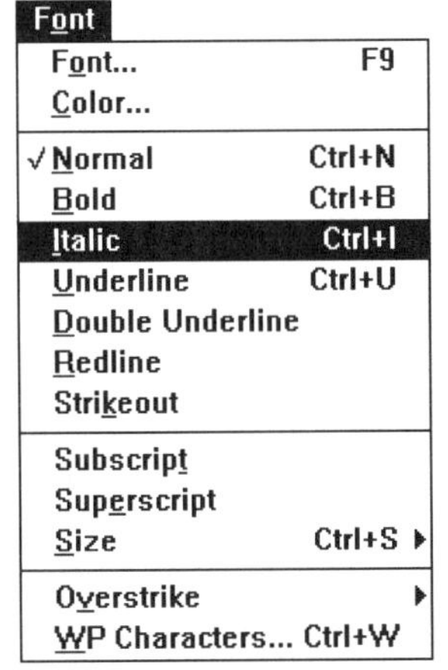

*Figure 20-9. Select the Italic command from the **Font** menu, to ensure that the last line of text you enter is in italics.*

Now you can enter the last line of text (Figure 20-10).

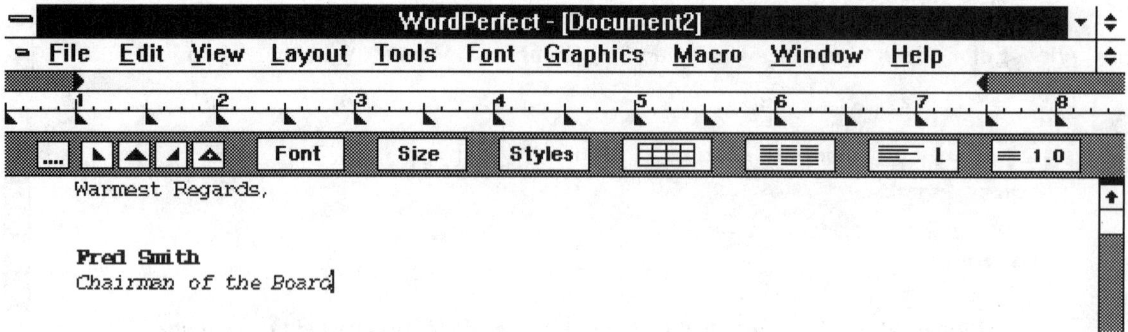

Figure 20-10. The last line of text will now appear in italics.

The macro has now been completed—all that remains is to finish recording the macro. This is achieved via the *Stop* command in the **Macro** menu (Figure 20-11).

Figure 20-11. Selecting the Stop command from the **Macro** *menu immediately ceases the recording of the macro, and saves all information to the macro file.*

Although this was a simple macro, with only a few commands and some text involved, much more complex macros can be created if you wish. If you are interested in creating extremely complex macros (macros can become almost a programming language), WordPerfect has a manual known as the WordPerfect Macros manual, which you may wish to purchase.

Mice and macros

You must be very careful when using the mouse on the WordPerfect screen when recording a macro. Not all mouse movements (including scrolling and selecting of text), can be recorded within a macro. Menu commands can, however, be selected using the mouse. In fact, when recording a macro, the mouse cursor will change to the Windows "no-entry" icon when it passes over the editing screen, indicating that no mouse actions can be recorded directly on the editing screen.

As much as possible, use the keyboard to navigate around WordPerfect and its dialog boxes. Windows provides an adequate, if clumsy, method of using the keyboard to move through menus, commands, and dialog boxes.

When opening or using files within a macro, try to refer to the file by name, rather than scrolling through a list to find a file.

Pausing during macro recording

While recording a macro, you may want to determine where a certain command or file that you want to incorporate into this macro is located. If this is the case, there is no need to stop recording the macro, you can select the *Pause* command from the **Macro** menu as shown in Figure 20-12.

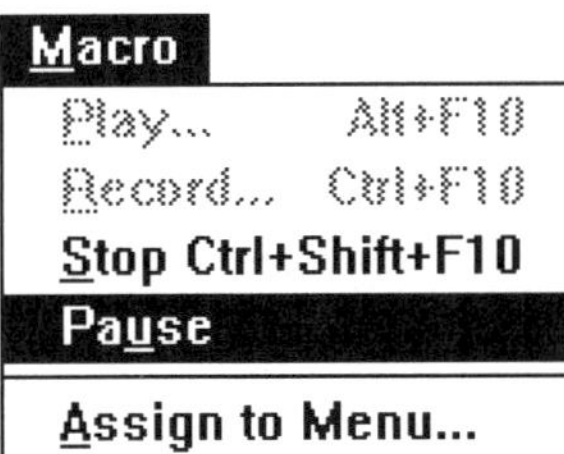

Figure 20-12. *Selecting the Pause command from the **Macro** menu will suspend the recording of the macro until such time as the command is reselected. While a macro recording is paused, the Pause command in the **Macro** menu will have a check mark next to it (Figure 20-13).*

Macro
Play... Alt+F10
Record... Ctrl+F10
Stop Ctrl+Shift+F10
√ Pause
Assign to Menu...

Figure 20-13. *A check mark next to the Pause command indicates that the current macro recording has been paused. You must reselect this command to restart recording.*

Any actions performed on screen, after the *Pause* command is selected from the **Macro** menu, are ignored while the *Pause* command remains selected (Figure 20-13). When the *Pause* command is clicked on again, recording will resume from where it was stopped.

Playing a macro

Recording a macro is of no use unless you can also play that macro back whenever you wish.

Before playing back the macro just created, make sure you have a clear document window in front of you, either by deleting all the text in the current window, or selecting the *New* command from the **File** menu.

To play back a macro, select the *Play* command from the **Macro** menu (Figure 20-14).

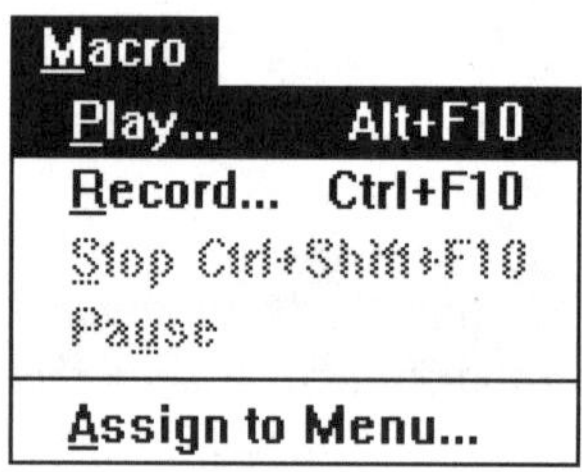

Figure 20-14. *To play back a pre-recorded macro, select the Play command from the* ***Macro*** *menu.*

After the *Play* command is selected, the *Play Macro* dialog box appears, asking you to select a macro to play (Figure 20-15).

This dialog box lists the different macros currently saved on your system. In the case of Figure 20-15, there are several—including the ***signoff.wcm*** macro file you have created in this chapter. This method of playing a macro—choosing it from the *Play Macro* dialog box is only one of a number of ways to run macros. Other methods are discussed later in this chapter.

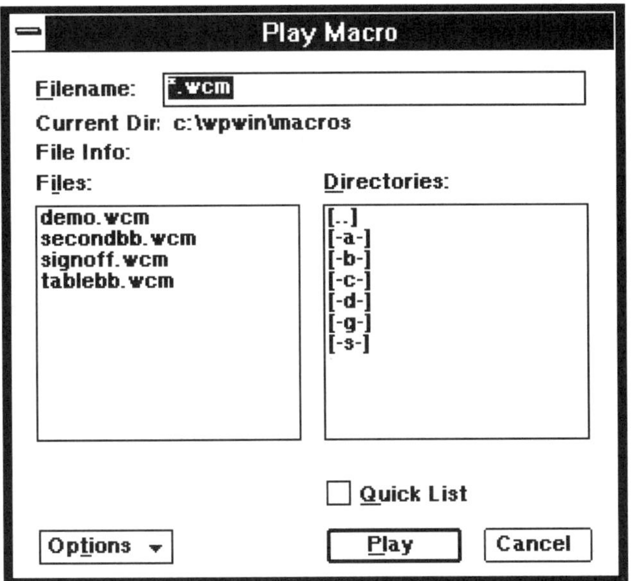

Figure 20-15. The Play Macro dialog box asks you what macro you would like to play. In the Files list, you can see the macro you recently created— ***signoff.wcm.***

To play the macro, select it from the list and click on *Play*, or double-click on the macro name. Your *Play Macro* dialog box (Figure 20-15) may contain several macro files, or it may contain only one. Locate the macro with the name ***signoff.wcm***; then double-click on it with the mouse to cause it to be played. The result is shown in Figure 20-16.

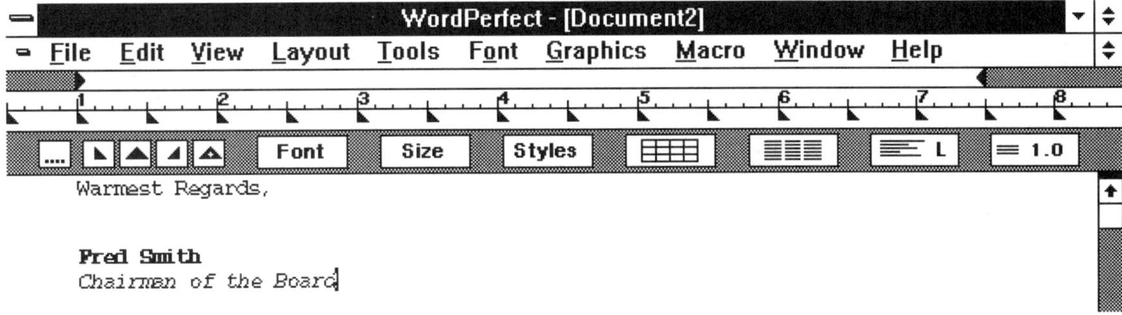

Figure 20-16. *The macro is played and automatically enters the text and formatting on the screen. The text is entered from where the flashing text cursor was, before the Play command was selected.*

Adding a macro to the Macro menu

For a macro to be really beneficial, it must be easy to play. To make it very easy to play, WordPerfect allows you to add your macros to the **Macro** menu, where they can be selected like a normal command.

Select the *Assign to Menu* command in the **Macro** menu (Figure 20-17).

Figure 20-17. *The Assign to Menu command allows you to add a macro to the* ***Macro*** *menu.*

The Figure 20-18 dialog box then appears.

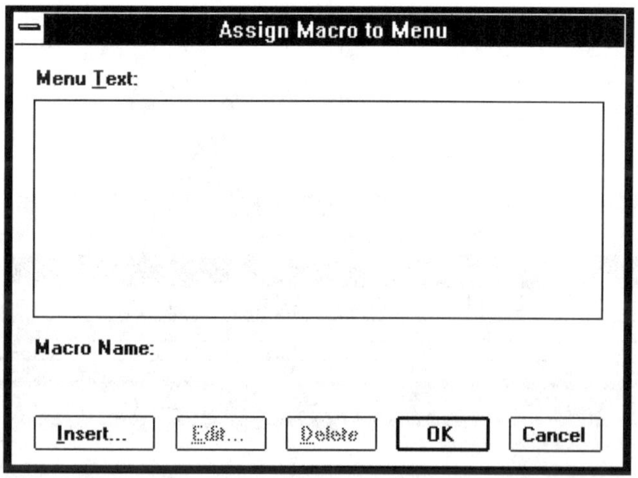

Figure 20-18. *The Assign Macro to Menu dialog box.*

To add a macro to the menu, select the desired macro files by clicking on the *Insert* button of Figure 20-18. The *Insert Macro Menu Item* dialog box will then appear, as shown in Figure 20-19.

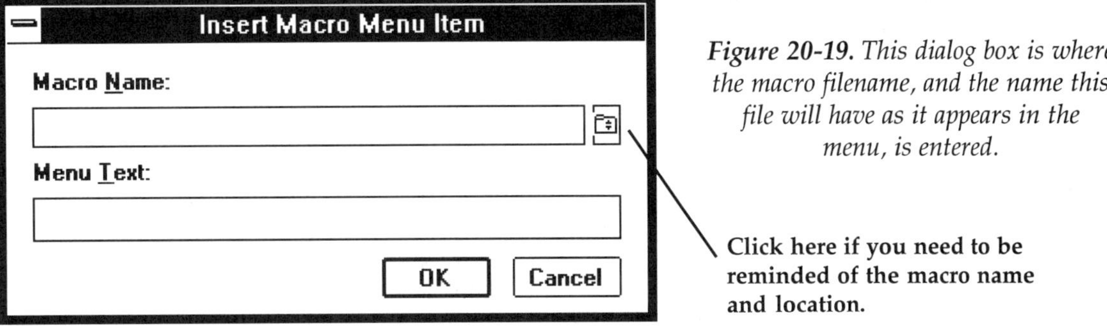

Figure 20-19. *This dialog box is where the macro filename, and the name this file will have as it appears in the menu, is entered.*

The *Macro Name* text box, in the *Insert Macro Menu Item* dialog box, is where the name of the macro file you wish to add to the menu is entered. If you cannot remember the name of the file and its directory, click on the small folder icon to the right of this text box, which brings up the *Select File* dialog box of Figure 20-20.

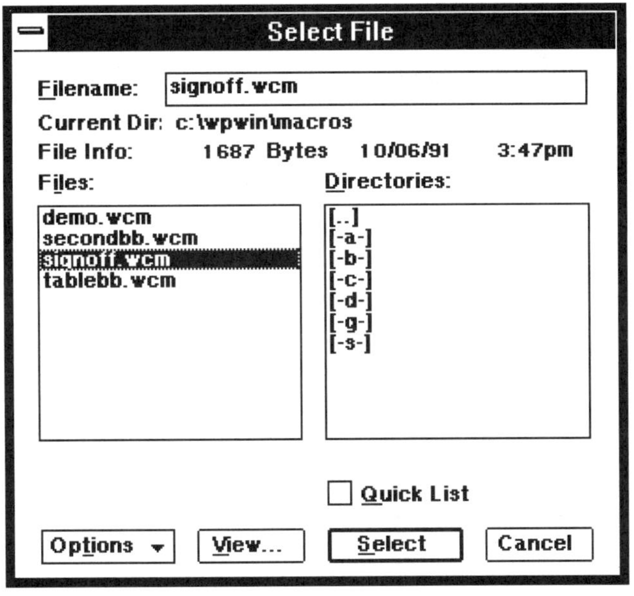

Figure 20-20. *From this dialog box, you can select which macro file you would like to add to the* **Macro** *menu. In this example, there are several macro files from which to choose.*

In the *Select File* dialog box for this example (Figure 20-20), there are several filenames—including the macro you created: ***signoff.wcm***. A macro can be selected from this dialog box by double-clicking (or by clicking once and then choosing *Select*). It then appears as shown in Figure 20-21 in the *Insert Macro Menu Item* dialog box.

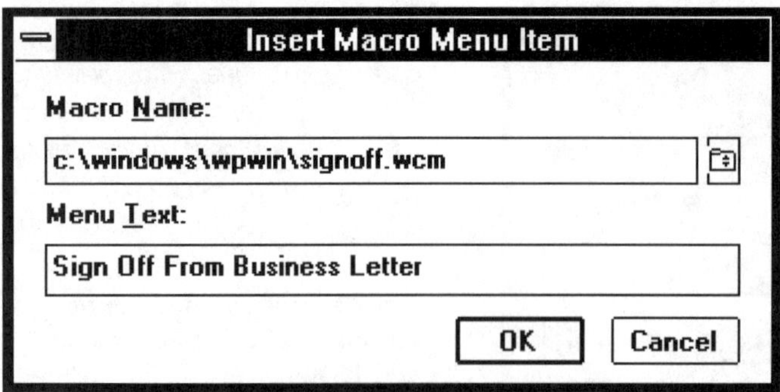

Figure 20-21. The macro filename selected in the Figure 20-20 dialog box is automatically added to the Macro Name text box.

Note also what has happened in Figure 20-21. The *Descriptive Name* you entered into the Figure 20-4 text box, when originally naming the macro, has now appeared in the *Menu Text* text box. This is the actual text which will appear in the **Macro** menu.

You can now click on **OK**, to return to the Figure 20-22 *Assign Macro to Menu* dialog box.

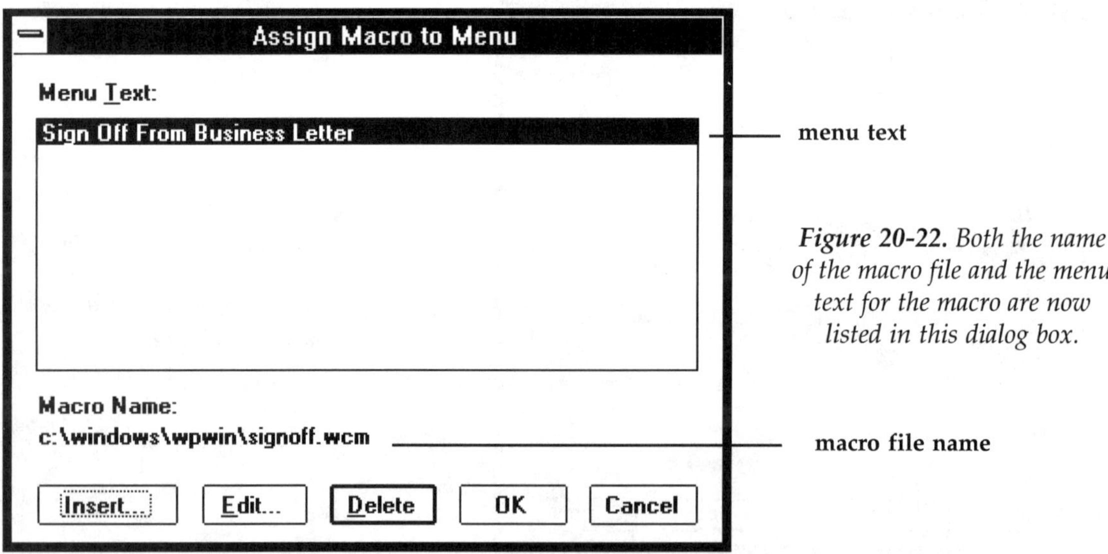

Figure 20-22. Both the name of the macro file and the menu text for the macro are now listed in this dialog box.

The steps you followed to add this macro name to the **Macro** menu can be repeated as often as is necessary to add other macros to this list.

A selected macro can also be deleted from this list by selecting the *Delete* button.

Click on **OK** from Figure 20-22 to see if this procedure has worked. After returning to the editing screen, select the **Macro** menu—it will now appear as shown in Figure 20-23.

Selecting the *1 Sign Off From Business Letter* command from the **Macro** menu is now the equivalent of playing the macro using the *Play* command in the **Macro** menu.

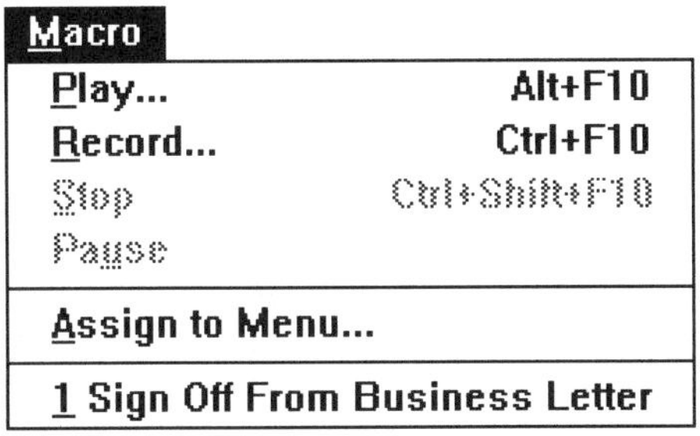

Macro

Play... Alt+F10

Record... Ctrl+F10

Stop Ctrl+Shift+F10

Pause

Assign to Menu...

1 Sign Off From Business Letter

Figure 20-23. *The macro has now been added to the* ***Macro*** *menu. It appears with a 1 in front of it—future macros added to this menu will also be numbered.*

Making macros easier to play

Macros can also be played from the Button bar, where a button can be created to represent a macro, or through a shortcut key combination of your own choosing. To create a shortcut key for a macro, use the *Preferences/Keyboard* command, from the **File** menu—please see Chapter 10, **Preferences - (1),** for more information.

Macros — Exercise

20ex

This training exercise is designed so that people of all levels of expertise with WordPerfect can use it to gain maximum benefit. In order to do this, the bare exercise is listed below this paragraph on just one page, with no hints. The following pages contain the steps needed to complete this exercise for those who need additional prompting.

Steps in brief

1. *In a new file, create a macro for a letterhead with the following specifications:*

   Type in your company name and address in Helvetica bold, 14 point, and center it. Leave two line spaces.

   Enter the current date, through the Date command, in Helvetica bold, 12 point, centered. Leave two line spaces.

   Type in "Dear Sir/Madam," in Times 10 point, left aligned.

Webster and Associates
Unit 2/ 25 Frenchs Forest Road
Frenchs Forest NSW 2086

Current Date

Dear Sir/Madam,

---

2. *Assign the macro to the menu.*
3. *Play the macro in a new WordPerfect file.*

The details for completing these steps are on the following pages.

Steps in detail

1. *In a new file, create a macro for a letterhead with the following specifications:*

   Type in your company name and address in Helvetica bold, 14 point, and center it. Leave two line spaces.

   Enter the current date, through the Date command, in Helvetica bold, 12 point, centered. Leave two line spaces.

   Type in "Dear Sir/Madam," in Times 10 point, left aligned.

Webster and Associates
Unit 2/ 25 Frenchs Forest Road
Frenchs Forest NSW 2086

Current Date

Dear Sir/Madam,

Select *New* from the **File** menu to create a new document. In this new WordPerfect file, select *Record* from the **Macro** menu, which is the first step in creating a macro.

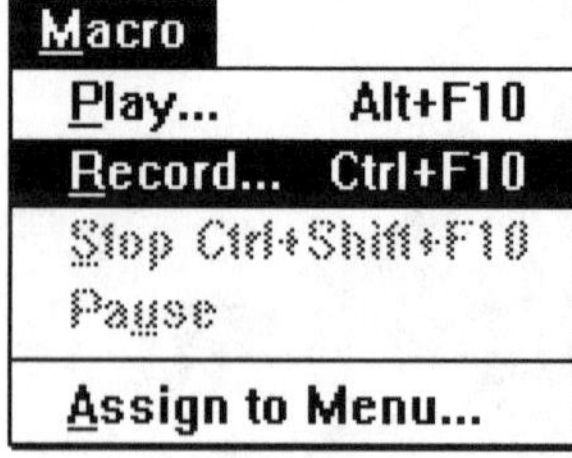

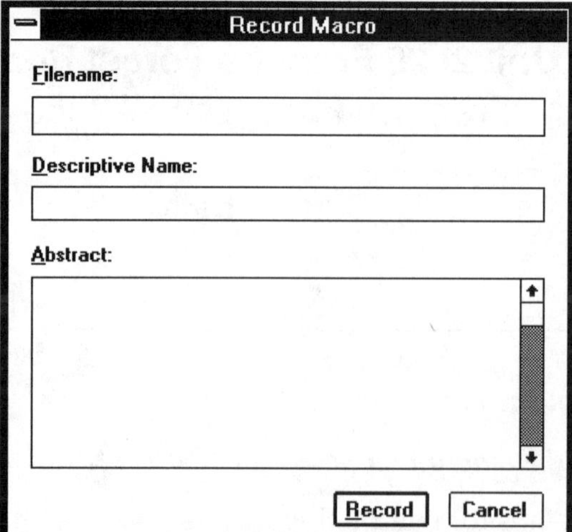

Figure 20x-1. Select Record from the ***Macro*** *menu to activate the Record Macro dialog box.*

Inside the *Record Macro* dialog box, key in the file name for the macro you are creating—in this case, ***lethead***. In the *Descriptive Name* text box, type in "Letterhead with date" as a description for the macro (Figure 20x-2). When you have done this, click the mouse on the *Record* button to return you to the screen.

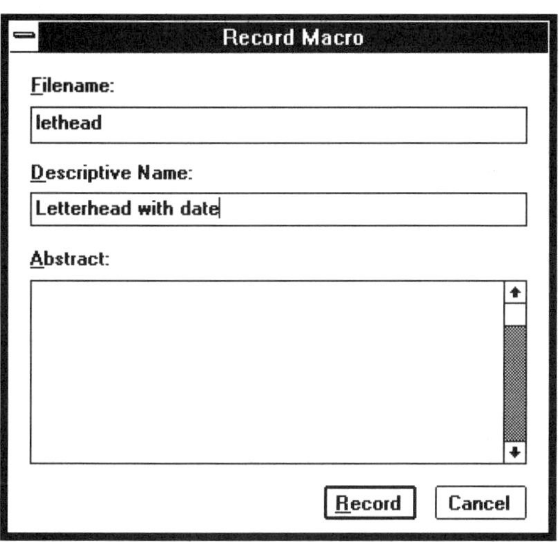

Figure 20x-2. *Type file name in as **"lethead"** and the Descriptive Name as "Letterhead with date". Then select the Record button to return you to the editing screen.*

You are now ready to type and format the required text, which will be recorded as part of the macro. Before typing in your company name and address, you will need to select Helvetica bold, 14 point, and center alignment from the appropriate menu commands. Follow Figures 20x-3 and 20x-4 to see how this is done.

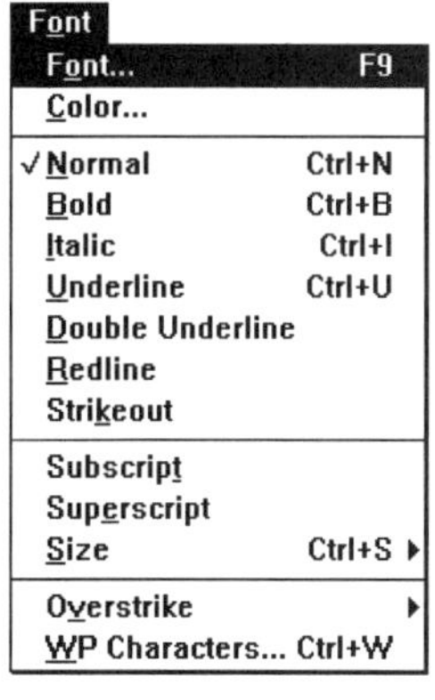

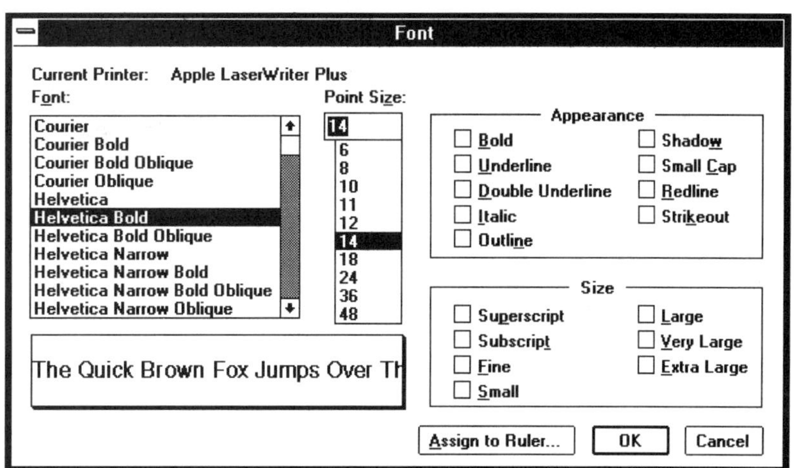

Figure 20x-3. *Activate the Font dialog box through the* ***Font*** *command, select Helvetica Bold, 14 point, and click on* ***OK****.*

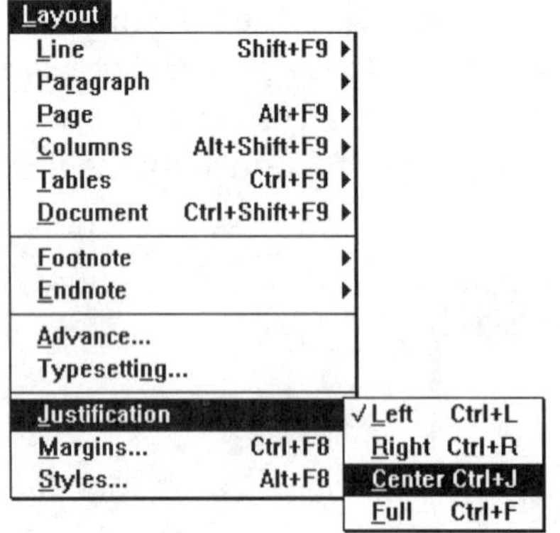

Figure 20x-4. Next, go to the **Layout** menu and select Center from the Justification fly-out menu.

You are now ready to key in the text. Type in your company name and address as illustrated in Figure 20x-5, and then press the Enter key twice.

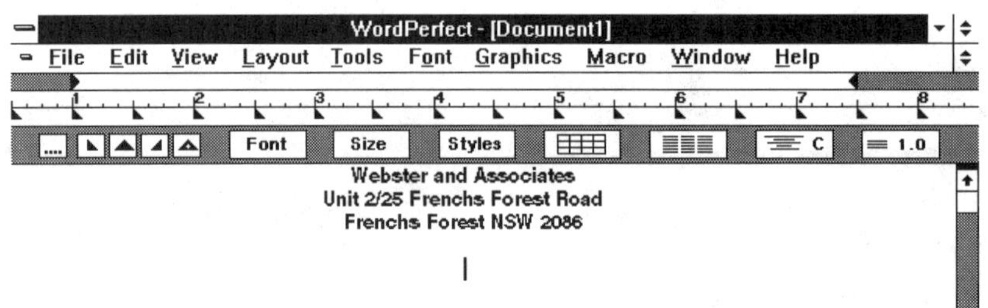

Figure 20x-5. Type in your company name and address as shown here. Press the Enter key twice after doing this.

The next step is to enter the date. Before doing this, you need to change the point size to 12 (all other attributes remain the same). Go to the **Font** menu again, select the *Font* command, and change the point size to 12 (Figure 20x-6).

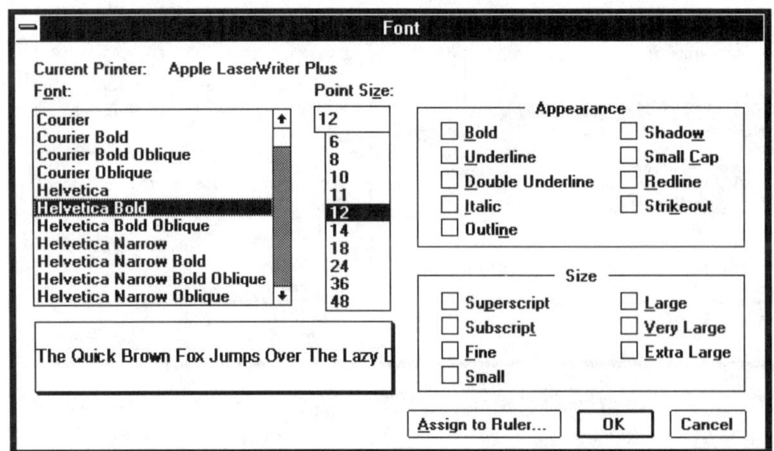

Figure 20x-6. Change the point size to 12.

You are now ready to enter the date. To insert the current date, select the *Date/Text* command in the **Tools** menu (Figure 20x-7). The date will appear to the left of the cursor (see Figure 20x-8). Then press the Enter key twice, ready to key in the last line of your macro.

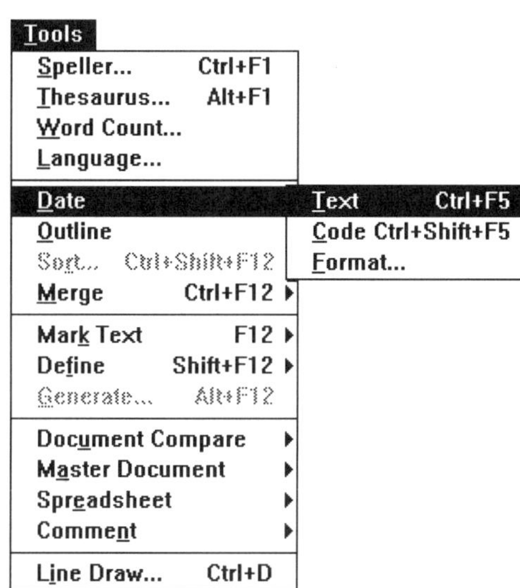

Figure 20x-7. *Insert the date using the Text command from the Date fly-out menu, in the* ***Tools*** *menu.*

Check Figure 20x-8 to see how the date looks on your page. Whenever you use this macro, once completed, the current date will always appear in this position because you used the date insertion feature. The date format may be different, depending on the date format settings on your machine.

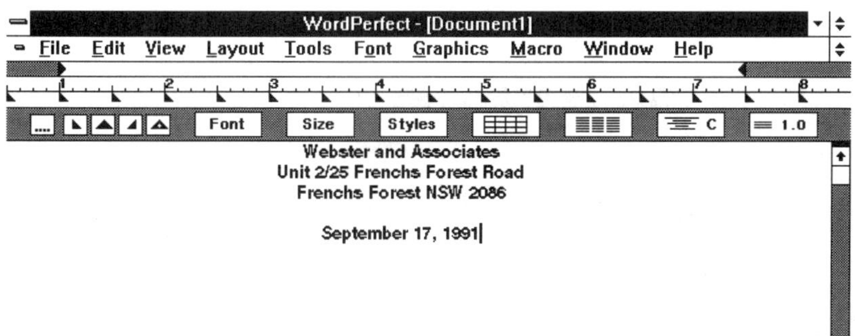

Figure 20x-8. *This is how the date will look on your page. Press the Enter key twice, after the date line.*

The last thing to type in is "Dear Sir/Madam," in the specified font, point size and alignment. Follow Figures 20x-9 through 20x-11 for further instructions.

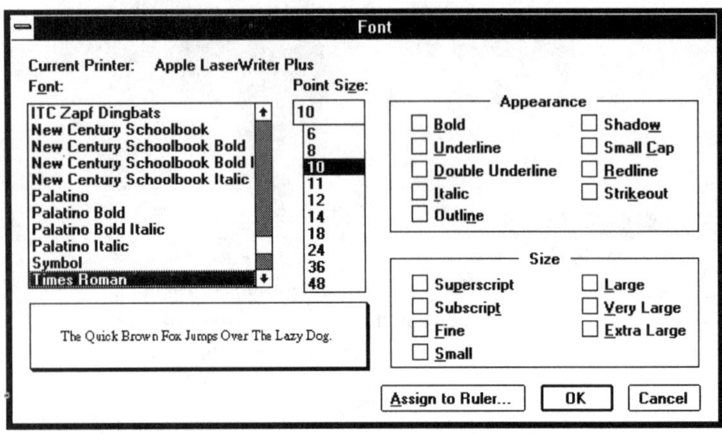

Figure 20x-9. Select the Font command from the ***Font*** menu to activate this dialog box. Change the font to Times Roman and the point size to 10, as shown here. Now select ***OK***.

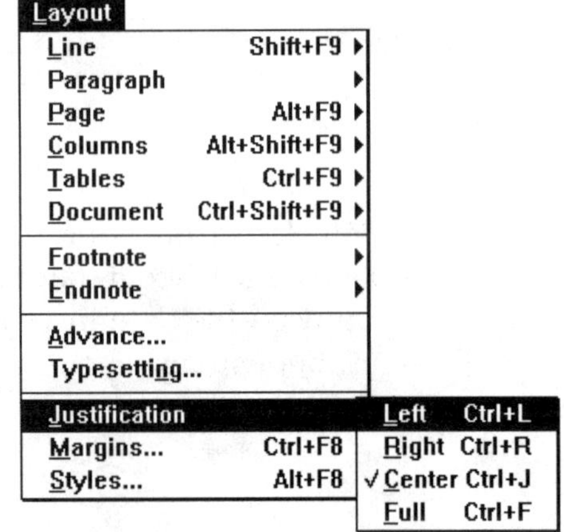

Figure 20x-10. Change the Justification to Left by selecting the Justification/Left command from the ***Layout*** menu.

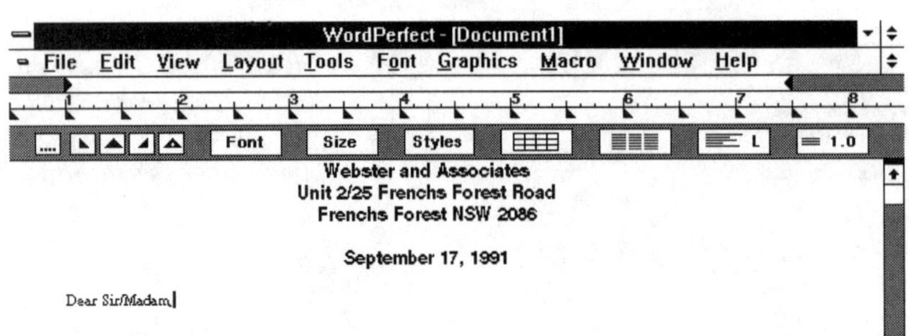

Figure 20x-11. Now type in the required text.

You have now finished the macro. The last thing that remains to be done is to select the *Stop* command from the **Macro** menu (Figure 20x-12), which will stop any further actions being recorded.

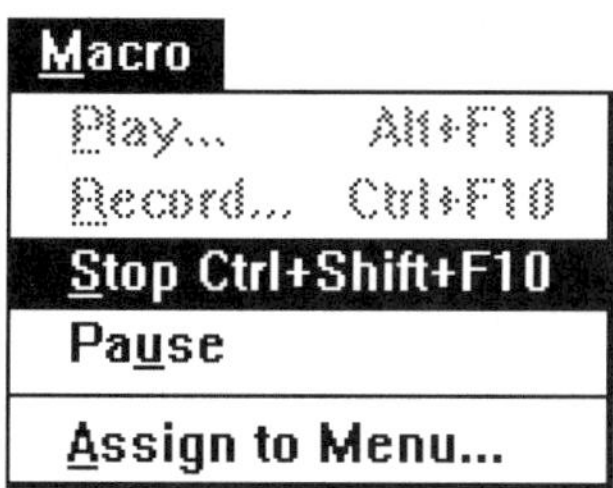

Figure 20x-12. *To complete the macro, select the Stop command from the **Macro** menu.*

2. *Assign the macro to the menu.*

You are now to assign this macro to the menu, so it can be easily selected as a menu command. From the **Macro** menu, select the *Assign to Menu* command (Figure 20x-13), to activate the dialog box of Figure 20x-14. See the captions of Figures 20x-14 and 20x-15 for more details.

Figure 20x-13. *Select the Assign to Menu command from the **Macro** menu, to activate the dialog box of Figure 20x-14.*

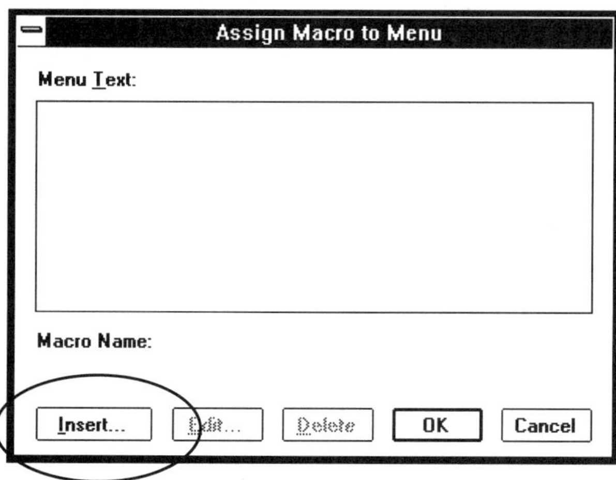

Figure 20x-14. *In the Assign Macro to Menu dialog box, click on the Insert button to activate the dialog box of Figure 20x-15.*

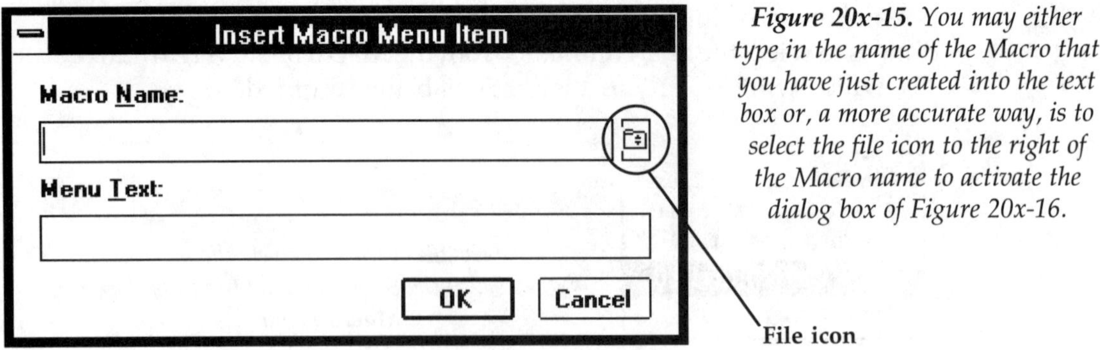

Figure 20x-15. *You may either type in the name of the Macro that you have just created into the text box or, a more accurate way, is to select the file icon to the right of the Macro name to activate the dialog box of Figure 20x-16.*

In Figure 20x-16, you can select the macro file of your choice by highlighting it with the mouse and clicking on *Select*. This figure includes a number of macros as well as the one you just created. You may have more or less macros in your list.

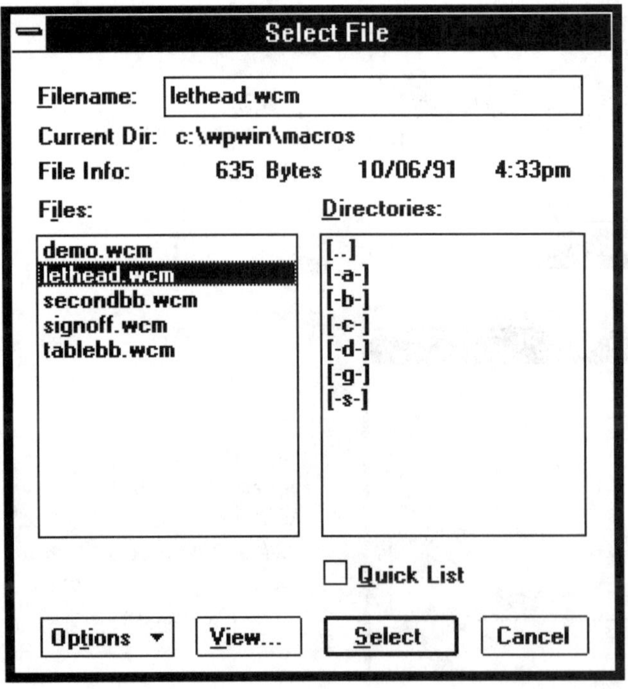

Figure 20x-16. *Highlight the file* ***lethead.wcm*** *and click on Select. The dialog box of Figure 20x-17 now appears.*

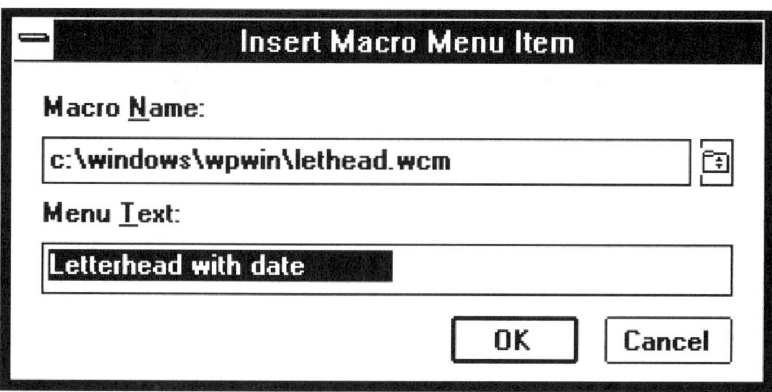

Figure 20x-17. *Note that the macro file name and also text entered into the Descriptive Name of the Figure 20x-2 dialog box now appear. Select* ***OK*** *to invoke the Figure 20x-18 dialog box.*

After clicking on **OK**, the next dialog box lets you view the information you have just entered (Figure 20x-18). Note that there are *Edit* and also *Delete* buttons, which can be used to modify the information here. After selecting **OK**, check the **Macro** menu, as shown in Figure 20x-19, to confirm that the macro name does appear.

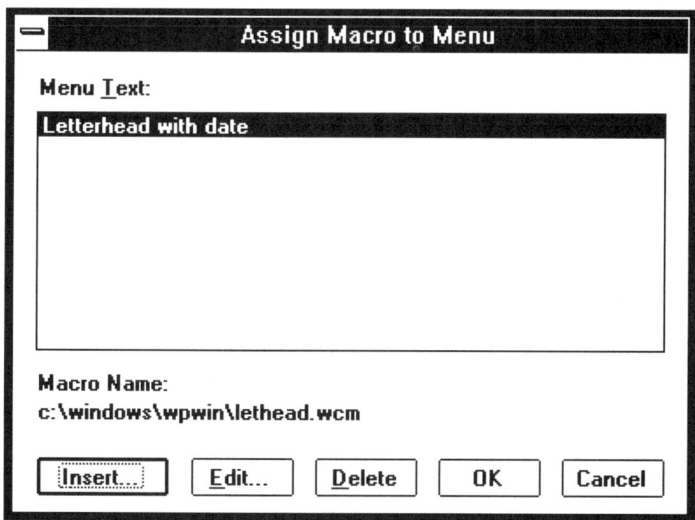

Figure 20x-18. *This is how the command will appear in the menu. The macro file name is also displayed in the bottom left of the dialog box. Select* ***OK*** *once more to bring you back to the editing screen.*

Figure 20x-19. *Check the* ***Macro*** *menu to see that the new menu command appears at the end of the list, as it does here.*

3. Play the macro in a new WordPerfect file.

It is now time to try your macro out to see if it has worked. Select *New* from the **File** menu to start a new WordPerfect document. Then select the macro name from the **Macro** menu (Figure 20x-21). The result is shown in Figure 20x-22.

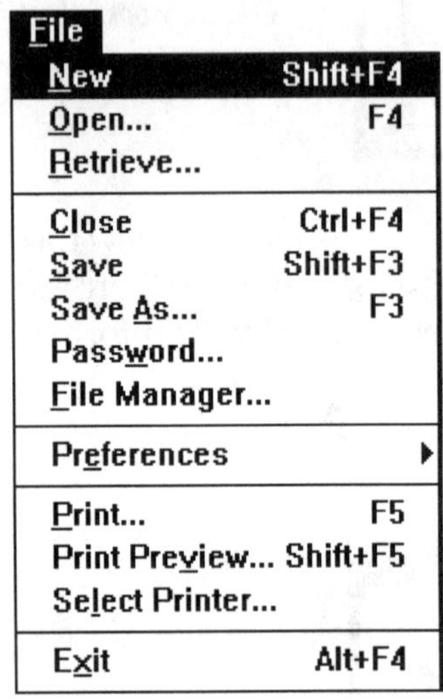

Figure 20x-20. *Select New from the* ***File*** *menu to start a new file.*

Figure 20x-21. *Select the new macro command in the* ***Macro*** *menu.*

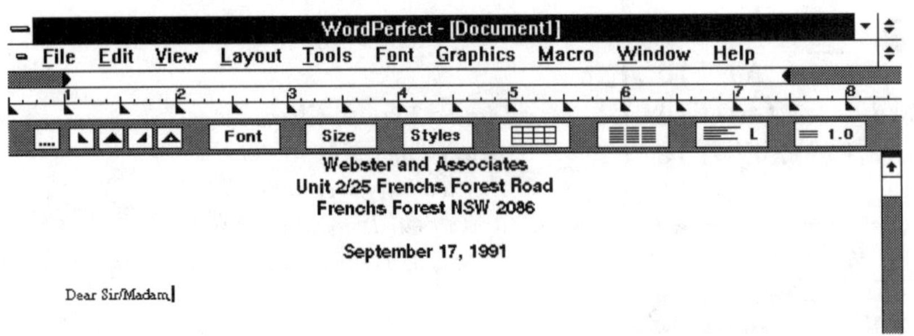

Figure 20x-22. *The macro is now played out into a new WordPerfect file. If you have followed the steps correctly, it will appear as displayed here.*

Tables

Table basics

Tables are used with WordPerfect for a variety of reasons—for collating and adding tabular data, for form creation, or to enhance a document. Some sample tables are seen below. As you can see, a table (in its most basic form) is really a kind of grid, in which you can enter data.

Using a table makes some information much easier to handle in a document—particularly data that previously involved tricky and complex tab settings.

	Monday	*Tuesday*	*Wednesda*	*Thursday*	*Friday*	*Saturday*	*Sunday*
9.00AM							
10.00AM							
11.00AM							
12.00AM							

Figure 21-1. *Tables can be created in all shapes and sizes, to handle all types of information. This may involve simple text data, as in this table...*

Sales Figures By Year					
Year / Quarter	*1st*	*2nd*	*3rd*	*4th*	***Total***
1989	$424,040.00	$456,032.00	$498,000.00	$487.00.00	**$1,378,559.00**
1990	$666,897.00	$598,000.00	$758,000.00	$987,012.00	**$3,009,909.00**
1991	$1,045,234.00	$1,534,567.00	$2,245,789.00	$2,234,666.00 (projected)	**$7,060,256.00**
1992 (projected)	$3,000,000.00	$3,250,000.00	$3,999,000.00	$4,500,000.00	**$14,749,000.0**

Figure 21-2. *...or numeric data, as in this table. WordPerfect tables can also perform spreadsheet-like functions, performing calculations on the numbers within the cells of a table.*

Sales Figures By Year					
Year / Quarter	*1st*	*2nd*	*3rd*	*4th*	***Total***
1989	$424,040.00	$456,032.00	$498,000.00	$487.00.00	**$1,378,559.00**
1990	$666,897.00	$598,000.00	$758,000.00	$987,012.00	**$3,009,909.00**
1991	$1,045,234.00	$1,534,567.00	$2,245,789.00	$2,234,666.00 (projected)	**$7,060,256.00**
1992 (projected)	$3,000,000.00	$3,250,000.00	$3,999,000.00	$4,500,000.00	**$14,749,000.0**

Figure 21-3. *Tables created in WordPerfect need not necessarily look like tables—you have full control over the appearance of the outline and the vertical and horizontal lines within the table. In this example, all lines have been made invisible.*

A table defined

In this chapter, reference is made to the several parts that make up a table—namely cells, columns, and rows. Figure 21-4 defines each of these terms.

A *column* refers to a vertical line of data. This table is made up of 9 columns. Columns are named and referred to by a letter. The first column is A, the second B, and so on.

	A	B	C	D	E	F	G	H
1		*Monday*	*Tuesday*	*Wednesda*	*Thursday*	*Friday*	*Saturday*	*Sunday*
2	*9.00AM*							
3	*10.00AM*							
4	*11.00AM*							
5	*12.00AM*							

A *row* refers to a horizontal line of data. This table is made up of 5 rows. Rows are named and referred to by a number. The first row is 1, the second 2, and so on.

A *cell* is the smallest component of a table—it refers to the area in which text can be entered. In this table, the words Monday, Tuesday, etc., occupy one cell each.

Note that cells are labeled by their column/row position. If the cell occurs in Column B, and in Row 3, it is referred to as Cell B3.

Figure 21-4. *Cells, columns, and rows within tables.*

Creating tables

Tables can be created in one of two methods: through a menu command or through the ruler. In Figure 21-5, the *Tables/Create* command, from the **Layout** menu, is used to create a table.

The only initial decision you need make when creating a table is the number of rows and columns—however, these values can easily be altered at a later date.

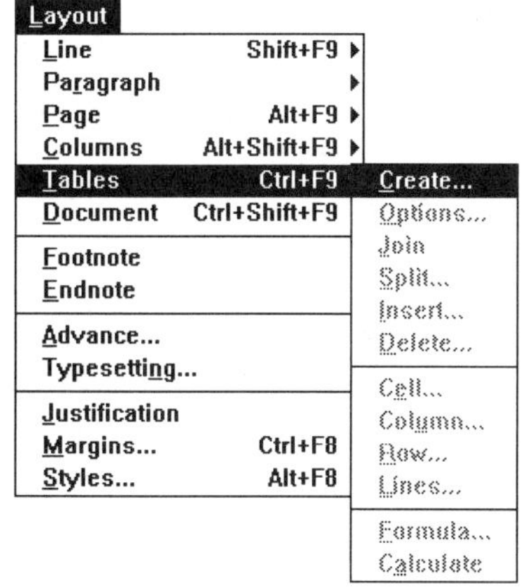

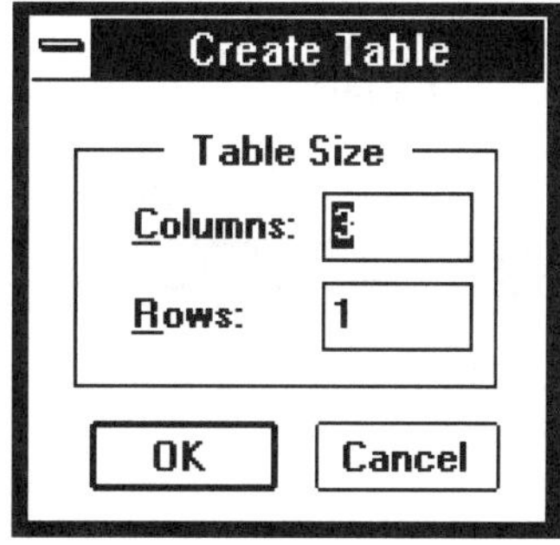

Figure 21-5. The Tables/Create command, from the ***Layout*** *menu, is used to create a table. Initially, the only information you must provide is the amount of columns and rows you want within this table.*

The other method by which a table can be created is through the ruler. Although this method initially seems a little more involved, it is actually a quicker, and more intuitive method of creating tables.

To create a table, you first locate the *Table* button on the ruler (Figure 21-6). If you double-click on this button, the dialog box of Figure 21-5 will appear. However, this button can also be used in a slightly different fashion to create tables.

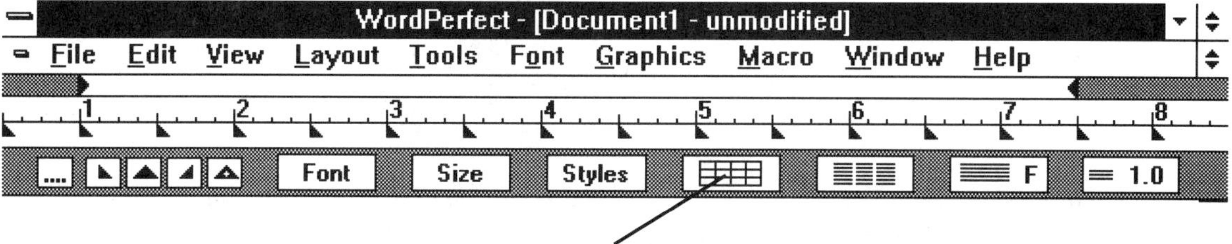

Figure 21-6. *The Table button appears just to the right of the Styles button in the ruler.*

If you hold the mouse down on this button, a small table or grid will appear on screen (Figure 21-7).

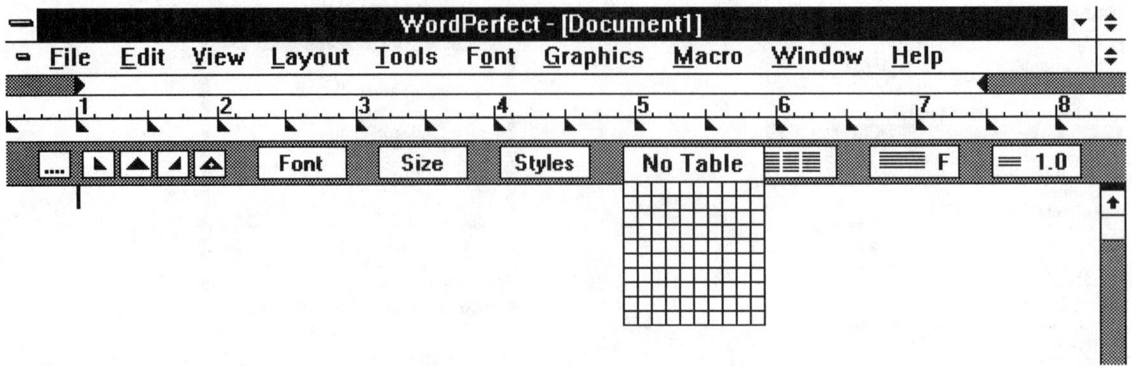

Figure 21-7. *When the mouse is held down on the Table button from the ruler, this pop-up table appears.*

As you can see from Figure 21-7, this pop-up table appears as a grid, which can be used to create your table.

As the mouse is dragged over the grid, the words "No Table" change to reflect the mouse position on the pop-up grid. Squares in the grid also begin to highlight (Figure 21-8).

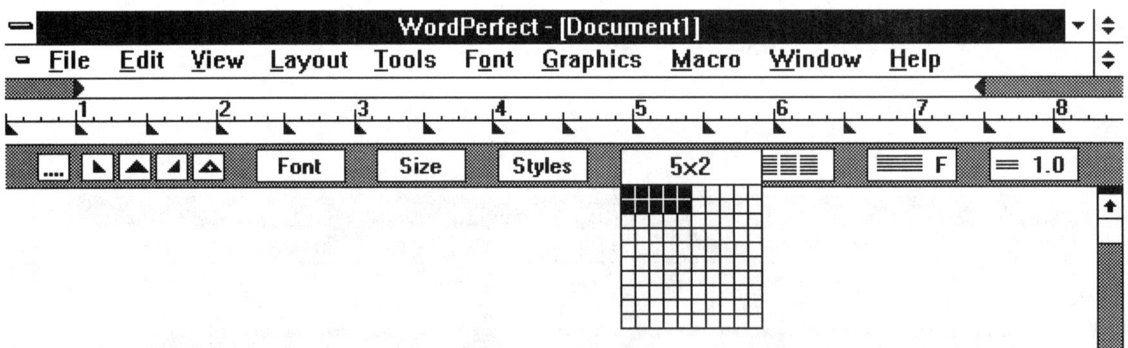

Figure 21-8. *Here the mouse is dragged down over the grid of the pop-up option. As this is done, two figures appear above the grid—these figures represent the columns and rows in the created table.*

If the mouse button was released in Figure 21-8, a table would be created with the dimension of 5 columns by 2 rows (hence the 5x2 in the pop-up option heading). This also relates to the number of squares highlighted—5 columns wide by 2 rows long.

This pop-up grid will expand as you move the mouse down and to the right, allowing you to create large tables. In Figure 21-9, a table would be created made up of 32 columns and 43 rows.

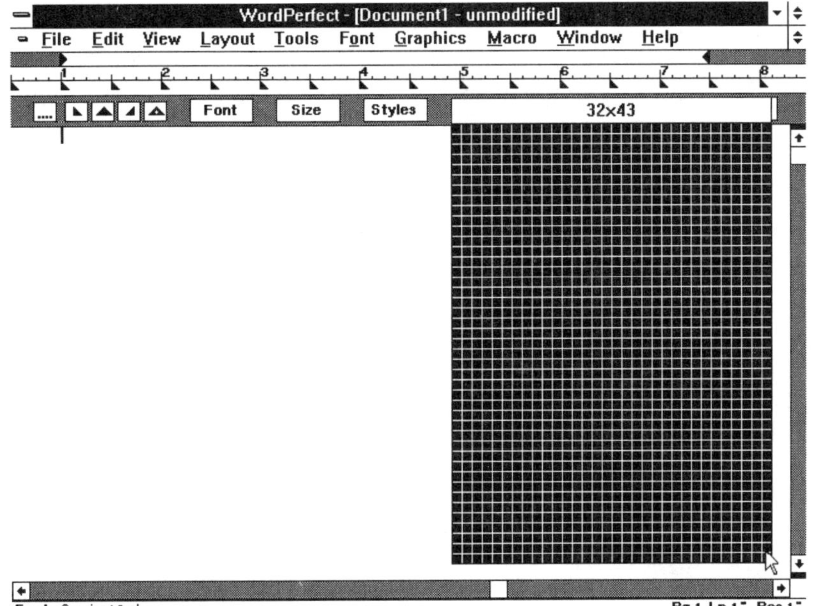

Figure 21-9. *The table pop-up grid will expand if you wish to create larger tables.*

In this example, create a table consisting of 8 columns and 5 rows, by releasing the mouse button when it appears as shown in Figure 21-10. Figure 21-11 shows the table that results from this action.

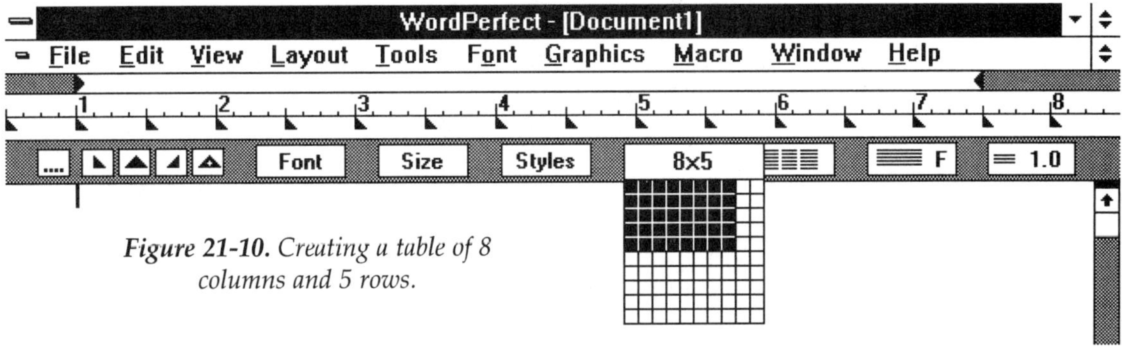

Figure 21-10. *Creating a table of 8 columns and 5 rows.*

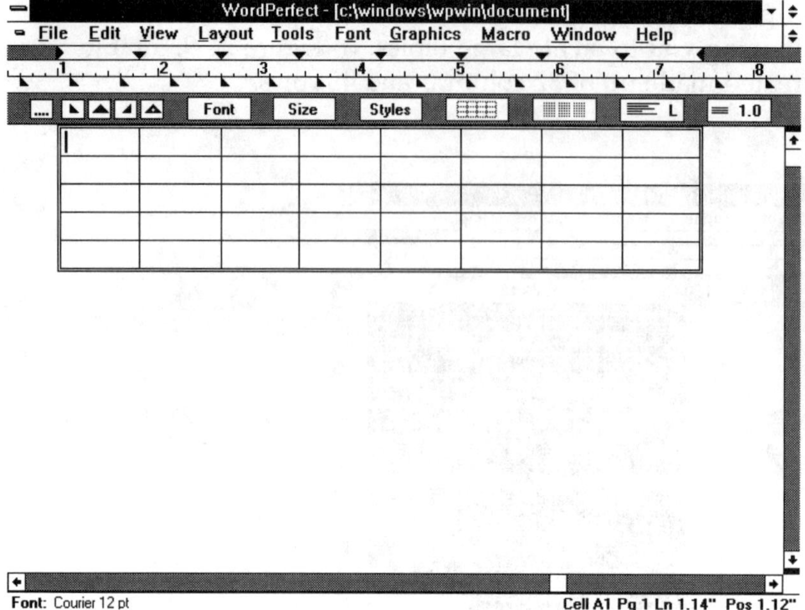

Figure 21-11. The table, 8 columns by 5 rows, as it initially appears on the WordPerfect screen.

Entering text into a table

When a table is created, the text cursor appears in the top left-hand corner cell—or cell A1. The Status bar in the bottom right-hand corner of the screen (Figure 21-12) shows the current cursor position, including the cell.

Figure 21-12. The Status bar (bottom right-hand corner of the screen) reflects the current cell position of the text cursor—in this case, cell A1 (the top left-hand corner of the table).

Text can be entered into this cell, or any cell, exactly as it is done in other parts of WordPerfect. Simply move to the cell into which you wish to enter text, and type away. Any cell will expand automatically to accommodate extra text (Figure 21-13). Enter the text shown in Figure 21-13.

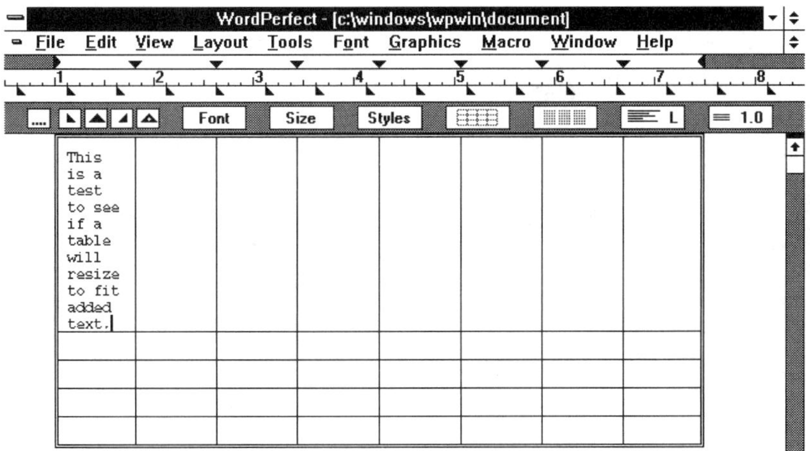

Figure 21-13. Cell A1 has expanded vertically to contain the extra text entered. Any cell will expand in this fashion to contain extra text.

As a cell expands vertically, all cells in that same row also expand, as shown in Figure 21-13.

Applying attributes to text in tables

All text in tables can be edited in the normal fashion—by selecting the text, and applying whatever font, justification, or type style you wish to that text.

In a later section in this chapter (starting from **Cell formatting**), options can be applied to certain cells, rows, or columns that will also affect text size, justification and text style. Generally, text formatting instructions applied using normal text editing features will override text formatting applied using commands discussed in the **Cell formatting** and **Column formatting** sections later in this chapter.

Moving around in a table

You can insert the text cursor into any cell, simply by moving the mouse pointer over that cell and clicking once. The flashing text cursor will then appear in that cell. The Status bar (Figure 21-12) will reflect the cell into which you have moved.

You may find it easier to move from cell to cell using the keyboard. Move to the next cell by pressing the Tab key and the previous cell using the Shift+Tab key. Alternatively, the arrow keys will move you to any cell, indicated by the direction of the arrow (Figure 21-14).

Figure 21-14. The arrow keys can be used to move to any cell, in any direction indicated by the arrow. The Tab key can also be used to move you to the next cell along, while the Shift+Tab key combination will move you back one cell.

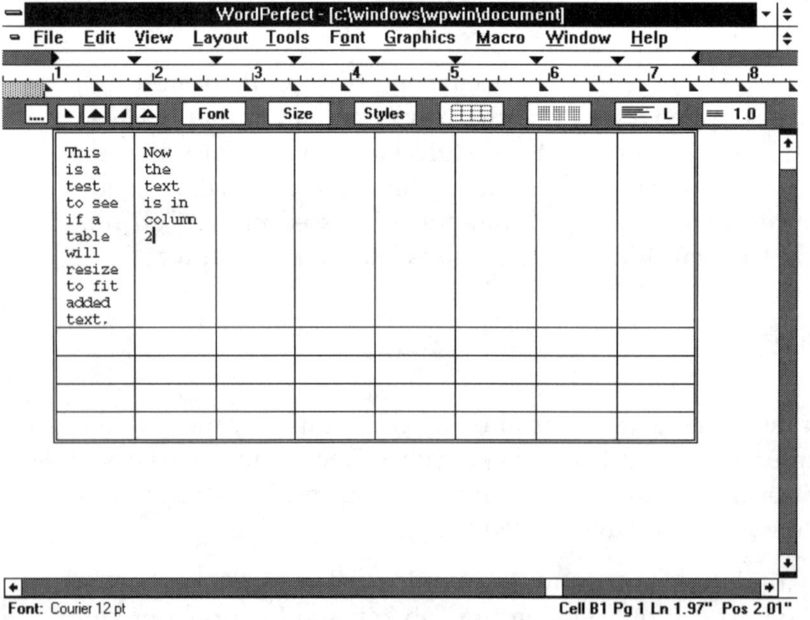

Figure 21-15. In this illustration, the Tab key was pressed once after completing the text in the first cell. The text cursor then appeared in the second cell, where more text was entered.

Editing table appearance

Once a table is created, you may be a little more specific as to the appearance of that table, by selecting the *Options* command from the *Tables* fly-out menu in the **Layout** menu (Figure 21-16).

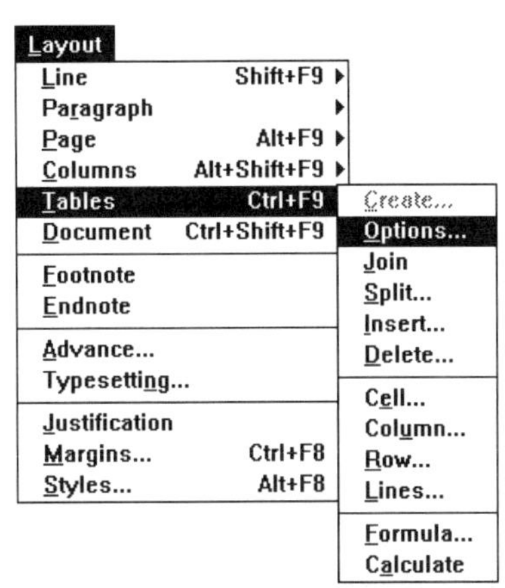

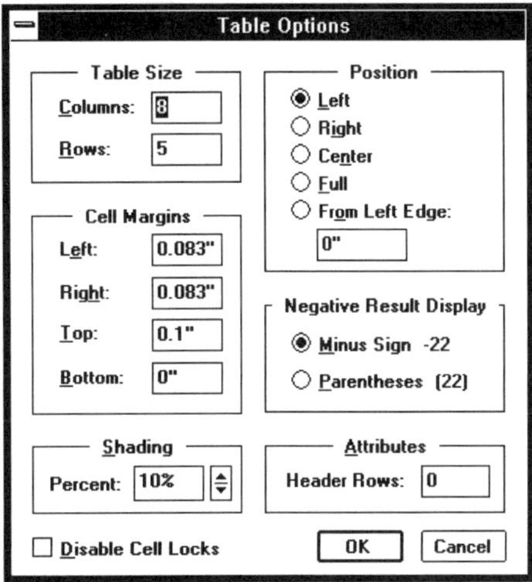

Figure 21-16. *The Tables/Options command from the* ***Layout*** *menu and the associated dialog box.*

The *Table Size* section of Figure 21-16 allows you to alter the number of *columns* and *rows* in the current table—simply enter the new number for either item. Initially, this section will show the current number of *rows* and *columns* (Figure 21-17). New rows/columns are added or deleted at the bottom and right of the table, respectively.

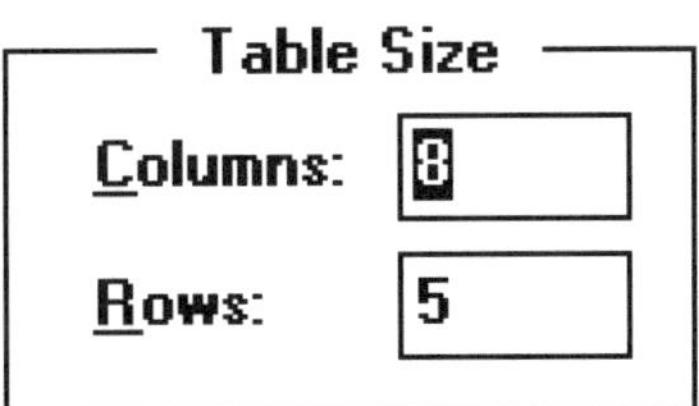

Figure 21-17. *Using the Table Size section of the Table Options dialog box (Figure 21-16), you can alter the current number of rows and/or columns in the current table.*

The settings within the various options of the *Cell Margins* section list the inside margins of each cell in the table—the white space around the inside of the cell between text and the cell border. There is a separate setting, which you can alter if you wish, for each side of a cell —*Left*, *Right*, *Top*, and *Bottom* (Figure 21-18).

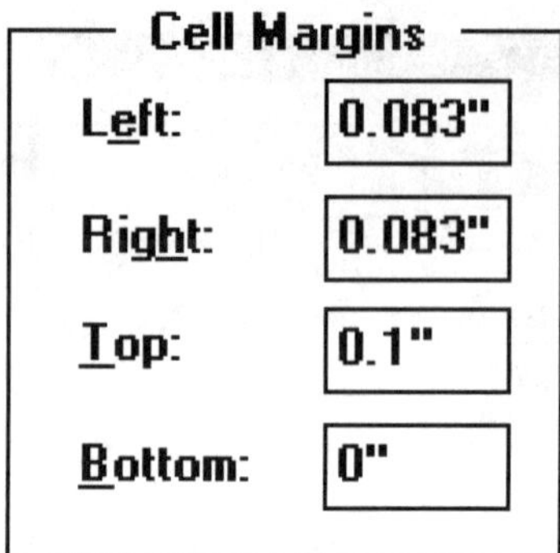

Figure 21-18. *The settings within the Cell Margins section of the Figure 21-16 dialog box reflect the inside margin of each cell—the white area around the inside of each cell.*

Later in this chapter, you look at how individual cells can be shaded, using an option in another dialog box. However, the figure in the *Shading* option within the Figure 21-16 dialog box determines the percentage to which cells can be shaded. It does not, at this stage, cause any cells to become shaded. For more details, see the **Cell formatting** section.

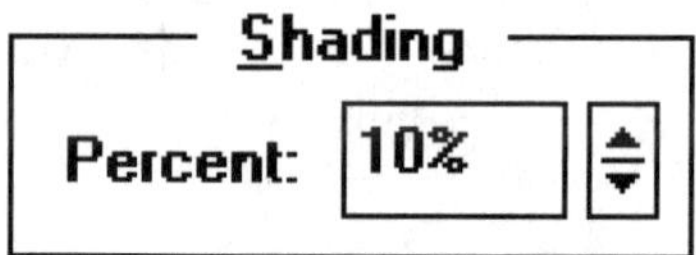

Figure 21-19. *The figure in the Shading section determines the percentage cells will be shaded should shading be turned on for these cells.*

By default, tables extend from the left to the right margin on the page. As columns and cells are added, deleted, and resized, the width of the table may well change. If this occurs, the *Position* section in this dialog box (Figure 21-20) determines the horizontal position of the table within a page. (One way to reduce the size of a table is to decrease the width of one or more columns. See Figure 21-51 for more details.)

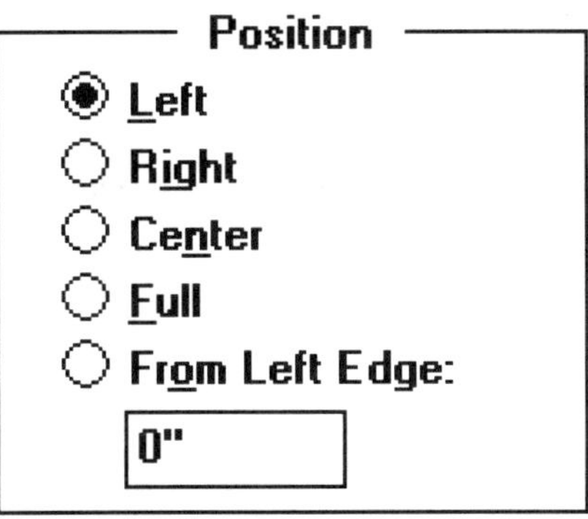

Figure 21-20. *The Position section in this dialog box determines the horizontal position of a table within the left and right margins of the page.*

Tables may be aligned much as text can be aligned—*Left* (Figure 21-21), *Right* (Figure 21-22), *Center* (Figure 21-23), *Full* (Figure 21-24), or a specific distance from the left margin (*Left Edge*). The specific distance from the left is entered in the text box under the *From Left Edge* radio button (Figure 21-20).

Sales Figures By Year					
Year / Quarter	*1st*	*2nd*	*3rd*	*4th*	***Total***
1989	$424,040.00	$456,032.00	$498,000.00	$487.00.00	**$1,378,559.00**
1990	$666,897.00	$598,000.00	$758,000.00	$987,012.00	**$3,009,909.00**
1991	$1,045,234.00	$1,534,567.00	$2,245,789.00	$2,234,666.00 (projected)	**$7,060,256.00**
1992 (projected)	$3,000,000.00	$3,250,000.00	$3,999,000.00	$4,500,000.00	**$14,749,000.0**

Figure 21-21. *This table uses the Left setting from Figure 21-20.*

Figure 21-22. *This table uses the Right setting from Figure 21-20.*

Sales Figures By Year					
Year / Quarter	*1st*	*2nd*	*3rd*	*4th*	***Total***
1989	$424,040.00	$456,032.00	$498,000.00	$487.00.00	**$1,378,559.00**
1990	$666,897.00	$598,000.00	$758,000.00	$987,012.00	**$3,009,909.00**
1991	$1,045,234.00	$1,534,567.00	$2,245,789.00	$2,234,666.00 (projected)	**$7,060,256.00**
1992 (projected)	$3,000,000.00	$3,250,000.00	$3,999,000.00	$4,500,000.00	**$14,749,000.0**

Sales Figures By Year					
Year / Quarter	*1st*	*2nd*	*3rd*	*4th*	***Total***
1989	$424,040.00	$456,032.00	$498,000.00	$487.00.00	**$1,378,559.00**
1990	$666,897.00	$598,000.00	$758,000.00	$987,012.00	**$3,009,909.00**
1991	$1,045,234.00	$1,534,567.00	$2,245,789.00	$2,234,666.00 (projected)	**$7,060,256.00**
1992 (projected)	$3,000,000.00	$3,250,000.00	$3,999,000.00	$4,500,000.00	**$14,749,000.0**

Figure 21-23. *This table uses the Center setting from Figure 21-20.*

Sales Figures By Year					
Year / Quarter	*1st*	*2nd*	*3rd*	*4th*	***Total***
1989	$424,040.00	$456,032.00	$498,000.00	$487.00.00	**$1,378,559.00**
1990	$666,897.00	$598,000.00	$758,000.00	$987,012.00	**$3,009,909.00**
1991	$1,045,234.00	$1,534,567.00	$2,245,789.00	$2,234,666.00 (projected)	**$7,060,256.00**
1992 (projected)	$3,000,000.00	$3,250,000.00	$3,999,000.00	$4,500,000.00	**$14,749,000.0**

Figure 21-24. *This table uses the Full setting from Figure 21-20.*

Later in this chapter, you will see how to perform calculations on numbers within cells. At times, the results of these calculations may be negative numbers. The *Negative Result Display* option (Figure 21-25) determines how negative numbers are displayed within a cell (if it is the result of a calculation). Calculations and Formulae are discussed in the **Formulae and calculations** section of this chapter.

Negative Result Display

◉ Minus Sign -22

○ Parentheses (22)

Figure 21-25. *The Negative Result Display determines the appearance of negative numbers in cells when they are the result of a calculation.*

If a table is very long (i.e., has a large number of rows), or begins towards the bottom of a page, it is possible that this table may continue on a new page.

In this case, it is wise to repeat the heading information at the top of the table, so that the table can be understood without having to refer back to previous pages.

For example, in Figure 21-24, there are two rows that should be repeated if the table is split across two or more pages (Figure 21-26). The first row, which reads "Sales Figures By Year" is the description of the table—it should certainly be repeated on subsequent pages. The second row, which explains the data in each column (i.e. 1st, 2nd, 3rd etc.) should also be repeated on subsequent pages.

Sales Figures By Year					
Year / Quarter	*1st*	*2nd*	*3rd*	*4th*	***Total***

Figure 21-26. *These are the 'header rows' from the table of Figure 21-24.*

The number specified in the *Attributes* section of the *Table Options* dialog box of Figure 21-16, in the *Header Rows* option (Figure 21-27), determines how many rows of a table WordPerfect will automatically repeat at the top of a page, should a table be split across two or more pages.

Attributes

Header Rows: 2

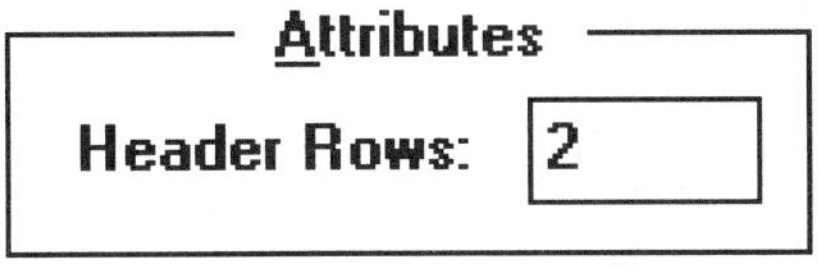

Figure 21-27. *The number in this option determines the number of rows on the top of a table automatically repeated on the following pages with the table. For this sample table, the value would be 2.*

Selecting cells

In explaining the previous steps, we looked at table settings and appearance as a whole. WordPerfect also provides facilities that allow you to alter the appearance, or properties, of individual cells within a table.

The first step in altering cells within a table is to select them. Cells are selected in much the same fashion as is text.

Before looking at selecting cells, you may notice one thing—as the mouse is moved over the cells in a table, the mouse cursor may change from the text editing cursor, the I-bar, to one of two shapes (Figures 21-28 and 21-29).

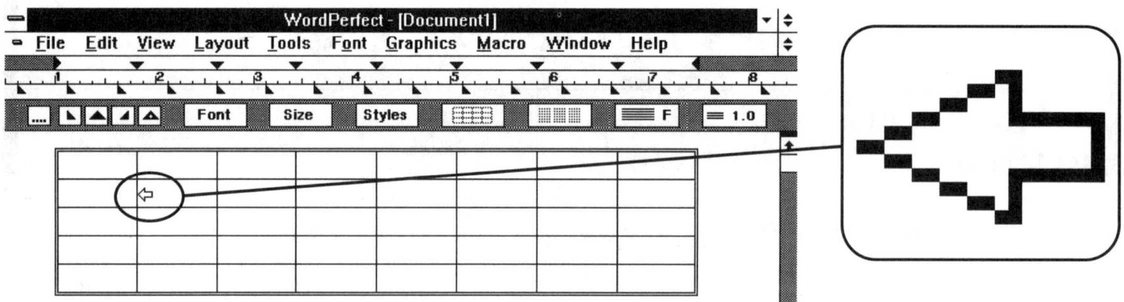

Figure 21-28. *The mouse cursor will take on this appearance as it is passed over a vertical line within a table.*

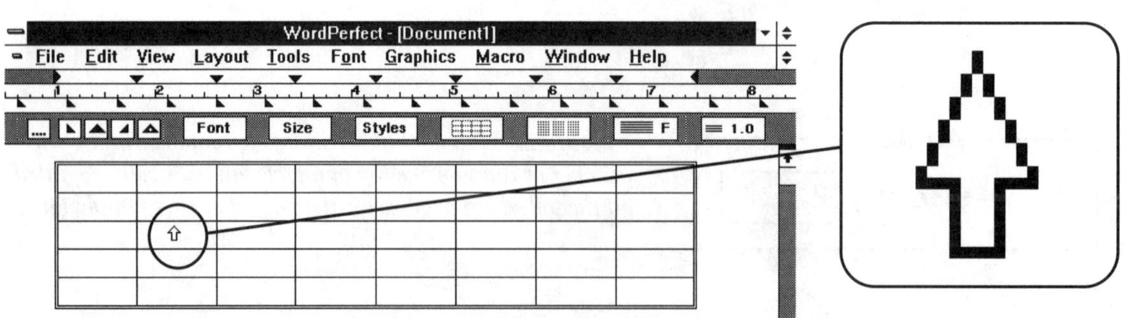

Figure 21-29. *The mouse cursor will take on this appearance as it is passed over a horizontal line within a table.*

Selecting a single cell

When a mouse cursor changes to either that of Figure 21-28 or Figure 21-29, clicking the mouse once will select the cell in which the mouse cursor is currently positioned. A cell is 'selected' when it appears in reverse video (Figure 21-30).

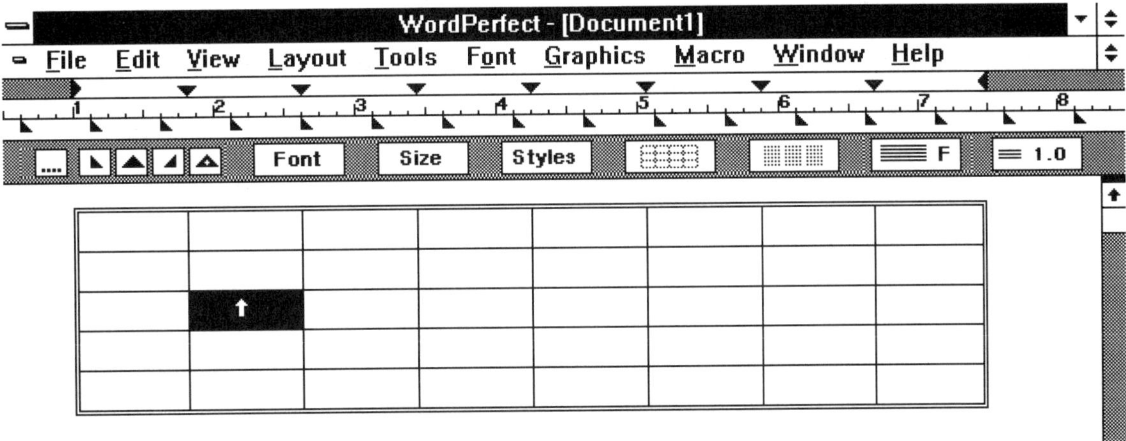

Figure 21-30. *Once the mouse cursor takes on the appearance as described in Figures 21-28 or 21-29, the mouse can be clicked once to select the cell over which the mouse is currently placed.*

Selecting an entire row or column

To select an entire row, you first move the mouse over a vertical line in a table, so that the mouse cursor takes on the appearance as described in Figure 21-28.

To select an entire column, you first move the mouse over a horizontal line in a table, so that the mouse cursor takes on the appearance as described in Figure 21-29.

Once the mouse cursor has changed to the horizontal or vertical arrow, double-clicking the mouse will select that row or column, respectively (Figure 21-31).

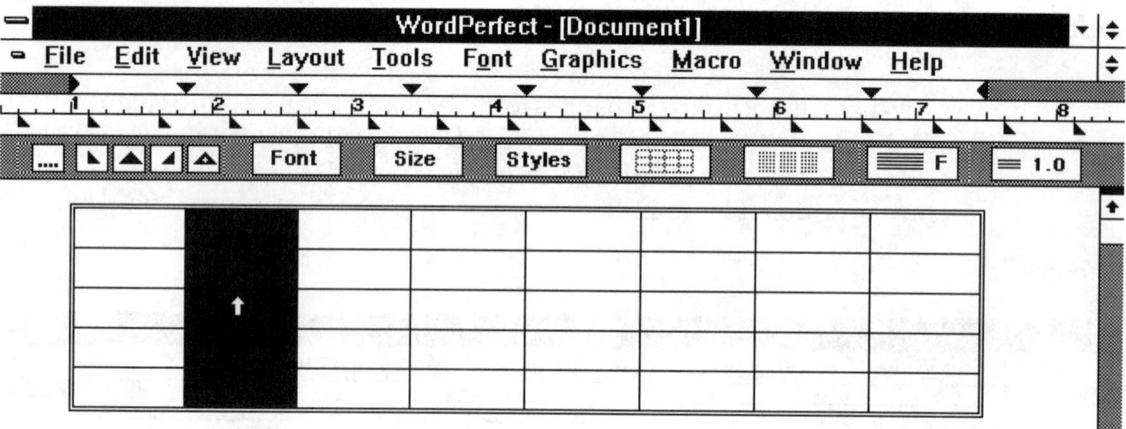

Figure 21-31. Once the mouse cursor takes on the horizontal or vertical arrow appearance, it can be double-clicked to select either the row or column (depending on the cursor shape) in which the mouse is currently placed.

Selecting an entire table

To select an entire table, follow the steps as described in **Selecting an entire row or column**. However, instead of double-clicking the mouse, triple-click the mouse.

Selecting any number of cells

In many cases, it is not just a cell, or exactly one column or row, that you would like to select. Many times it may be two or three cells, or half of two columns. In these cases, you can select cells in a different way.

To select any number of cells as shown in Figure 21-32:

Position the mouse cursor in the top left-hand corner of the range of cells you would like to select.

Hold down the mouse button, and drag the mouse cursor across to the bottom right-hand corner of the range of cells you would like to select.

Release the mouse button.

All cells between the cell in which you clicked, and the cell to which the mouse was dragged, are now selected (Figure 21-32).

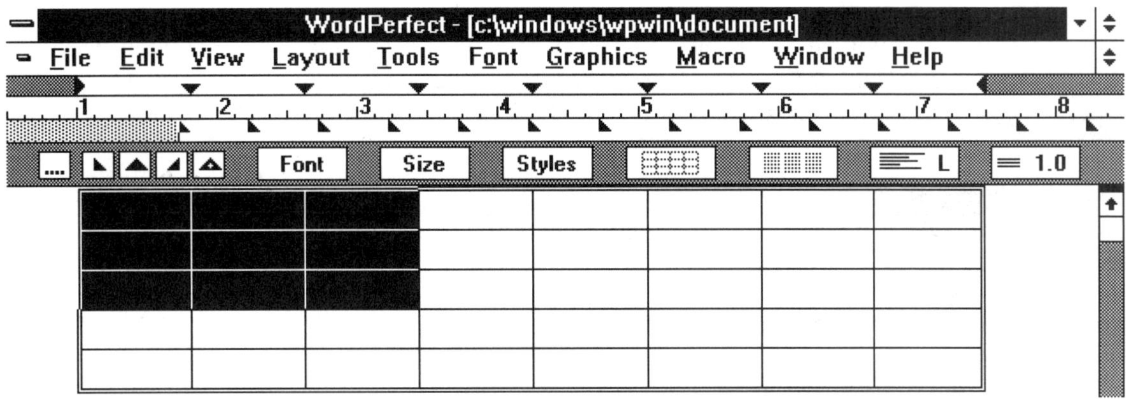

Figure 21-32. *In this table, nine cells are selected—using the method described in* ***Selecting any number of cells****.*

Joining cells

Consider the difference between the tables in Figures 21-33 and 21-34.

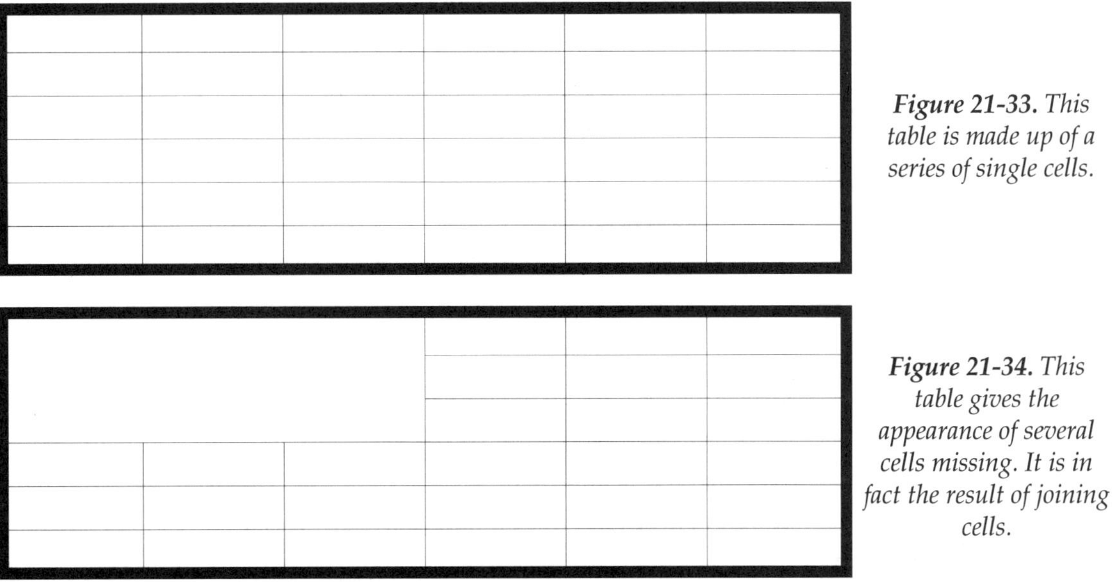

Figure 21-33. *This table is made up of a series of single cells.*

Figure 21-34. *This table gives the appearance of several cells missing. It is in fact the result of joining cells.*

In Figure 21-34, several cells have been joined. You may wish to join cells for several reasons—creating header rows, for example. Before any cells can be joined, they must be selected. In Figure 21-35, nine cells have been selected.

If your initial table, created in Figure 21-11, is a little messy by now, start a new file and create it again, as discussed earlier. Now select the nine cells, as shown in Figure 21-35.

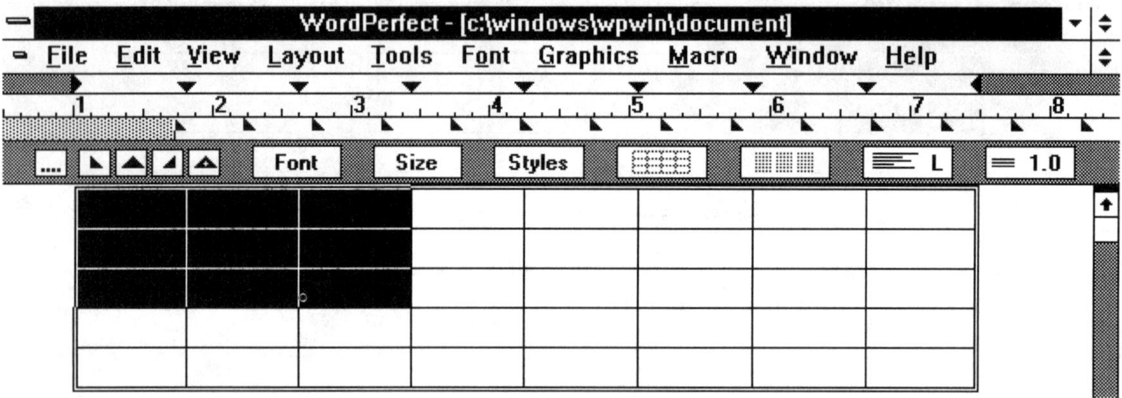

Figure 21-35. *Currently, the table in this diagram appears much like the table initially created in Figure 21-11. Nine cells have been selected from this table.*

After selecting the cells you wish to join, select the *Join* command from the *Tables* fly-out menu in the **Layout** menu (Figure 21-36).

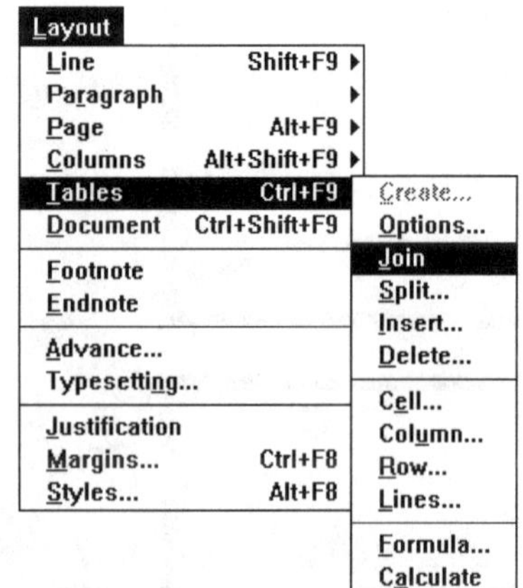

Figure 21-36. *Selecting the Tables/Join command from the Layout menu will join all selected cells.*

All selected cells in the table on screen then become one cell as shown in Figure 21-37.

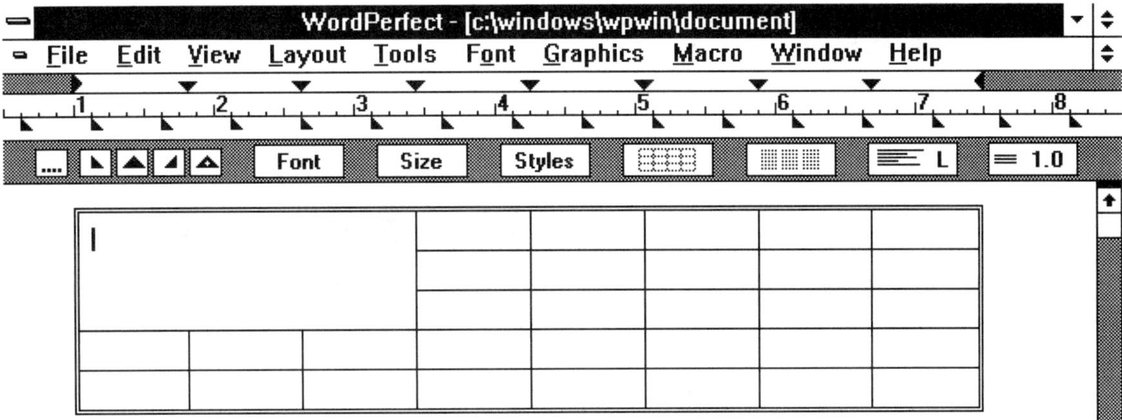

Figure 21-37. The cells that were selected in Figure 21-35 have now joined to become one large cell.

Once cells have been joined, the new large cell acts as a single cell—it is selected in the same way—and text is entered into that cell in the same way as it is for other cells.

Splitting cells

Splitting cells involves creating smaller cells within cells or 'unjoining' cells that have been joined using the *Tables/Join* command as shown in Figure 21-36.

Figure 21-38. The top left hand cell in this table (Cell A1) has been split into five smaller cells.

Cells can be split in two ways—you may select many cells and split them all, or split only the cell in which the text cursor is currently positioned.

To split a cell, you select the *Split* command from the *Tables* fly-out menu in the **Layout** menu (Figure 21-39).

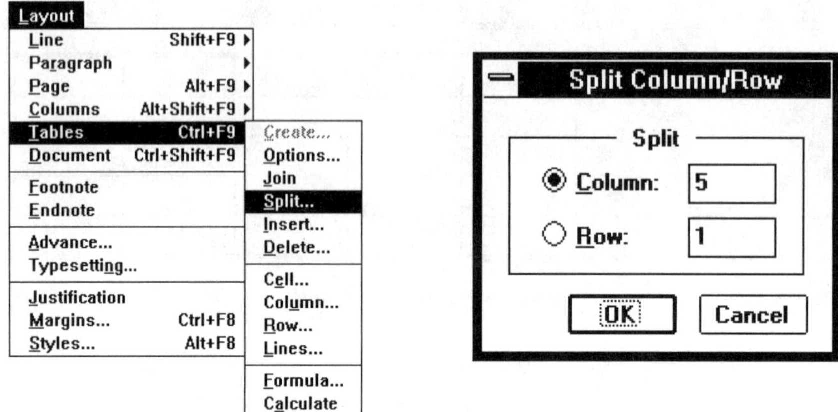

Figure 21-39. *The Tables/Split command splits cells into smaller cells—either vertically (columns), or horizontally (rows).*

As you can see from the dialog box in Figure 21-39, a cell, or cells, (if multiple cells were selected before selecting this command), can be split into either *Columns*, or *Rows*. The choice you make here (you must make a choice, you cannot split cells into columns and rows at the same time) determines the shape of the new cells.

Simply enter the number of rows or columns into which you would like to split the selected cells. In Figure 21-38, Cell A1 was split into five columns.

If the splitting of cells produces an undesirable result, you can select the newly created multiple cells and use the *Tables/Join* command from the **Layout menu** (see the previous section on **Joining cells**) to return to a single cell.

Table editing

Inserting rows and columns

New rows and columns can be inserted into any position within a table by selecting the *Insert* command from the *Tables* fly-out menu in the **Layout** menu (Figure 21-40).

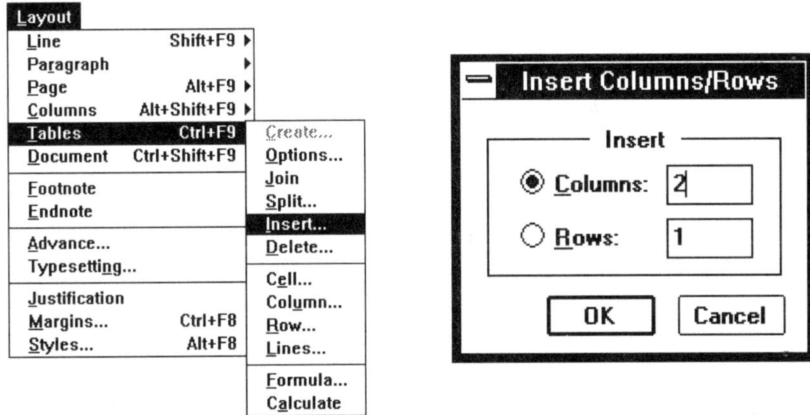

Figure 21-40. The Tables/Insert command is used to add new columns and/or rows to a table.

When inserting rows or columns, it is important to remember the following:

If you are adding a column to a table, that column will be added to the *left* of the column in which the text cursor is currently positioned.

If you are adding a row to a table, that row will be added *above* the row in which the text cursor is currently positioned.

Deleting rows and columns

Rows and columns can be deleted from any position within a table by inserting the cursor in the table and selecting the *Delete* command from the *Tables* fly-out menu in the **Layout** menu (Figure 21-41).

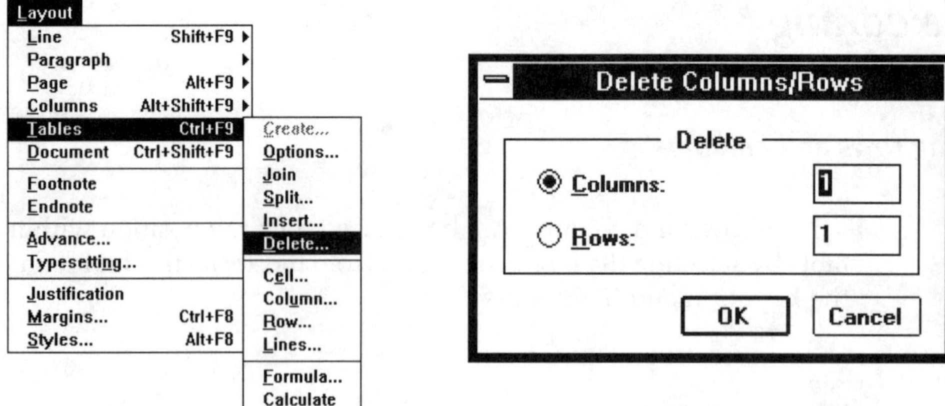

Figure 21-41. *Deleting rows or columns is achieved by selecting the Tables/Delete command in the* ***Layout*** *menu.*

You can delete selected *Rows* or *Columns*, but rows and columns cannot be deleted together. By inserting a number after the *Columns* or *Rows* selection in the *Delete Columns/Rows* dialog box in Figure 21-41, multiple columns or rows may be deleted.

Any data contained within deleted rows and columns is also deleted.

If multiple rows or columns, or parts thereof, are selected in the table before the *Tables/Delete* command is selected, these are the rows or columns that will be affected by this command.

In Figure 21-42, only part of the first three columns is selected. However, if the *Tables/Delete* command is invoked, and *Columns* selected from the resulting dialog box, all of the first three columns (not just the parts selected) would be deleted.

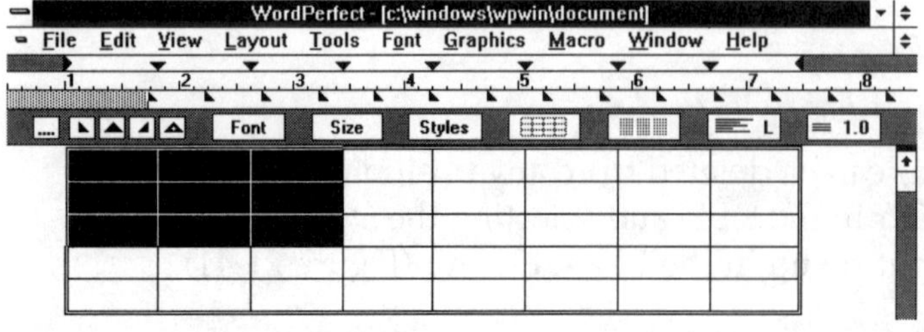

Figure 21-42. *Although only part of the first three columns is selected, these columns can be deleted entirely using the Tables/Delete command from the* ***Layout*** *menu.*

Deleting entire tables

Tables can be deleted if they are entirely selected (see **Selecting an entire table** section), by pressing the Delete key on the keyboard. This action will invoke the dialog box of Figure 21-43.

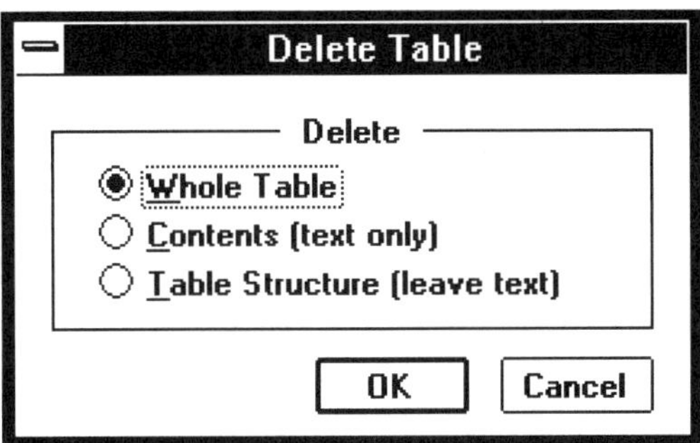

Figure 21-43. *Pressing the Delete (Del) key on the keyboard, when an entire table is selected, will invoke this dialog box.*

You then have the option of deleting the entire table, *Whole Table*; just the contents of the table, *Contents (text only)*; or the table itself minus the contents of the table, *Table Structure (leave text).*

Cutting/copying/pasting rows and/or columns

Selected cells can be *Cut, Copied,* or *Pasted* using the *Cut, Copy,* and *Paste* commands in the **Edit** menu. If you just select text within a single cell, then only that text is cut or copied, not the cell structure. If you drag the mouse through to an adjacent cell, you are selecting both the text and the cell structure.

The dialog box in Figure 21-44 will appear when the *Cut* or *Copy* commands are selected. If you choose *Selection,* only the text within the cells you have selected will be cut or copied. Choosing *Row(s)* or *Column(s)* will delete the entire row or column selected, including text.

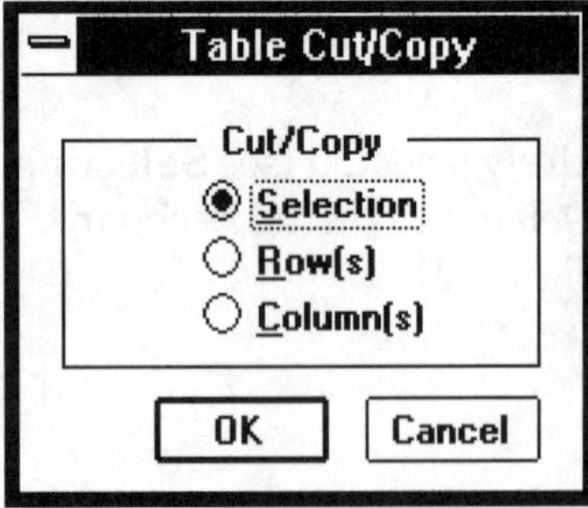

Figure 21-44. The dialog box that appears as you cut or copy selected rows or columns from a table.

Cell formatting

The properties of individual cells can be altered using the *Cell* command from the *Tables* fly-out menu in the **Layout** menu. This command affects the cells that are already selected.

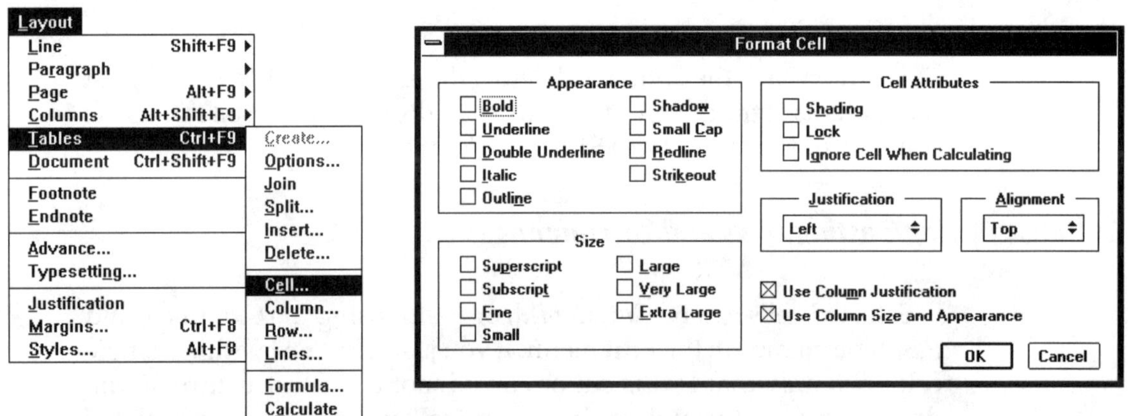

*Figure 21-45. The Tables/Cell command from the **Layout** menu can be used to alter the properties of individual or selected cells.*

Most options within this command control how text appears within a cell—its appearance, justification and general size. If empty cells are formatted using this command, text will automatically take on the appropriate attributes when it is later entered into these cells.

In the *Appearance* section of this dialog box (Figure 21-46) are options that control the appearance of text in the selected cells but not the appearance of the cells themselves. Any of these styles applied to cells using this dialog box override styles that have been applied to the text in the cell.

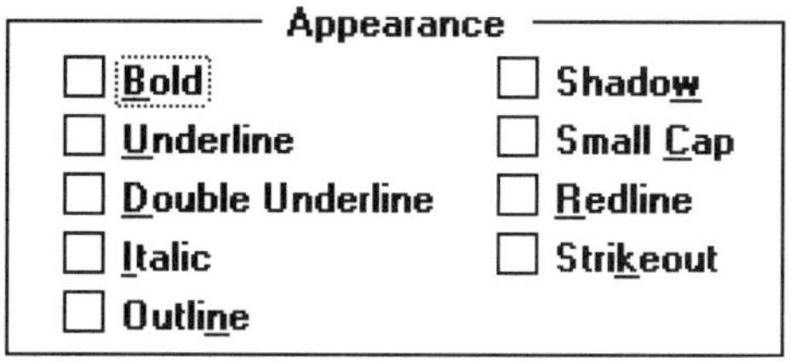

Appearance

- ☐ Bold
- ☐ Underline
- ☐ Double Underline
- ☐ Italic
- ☐ Outline
- ☐ Shadow
- ☐ Small Cap
- ☐ Redline
- ☐ Strikeout

Figure 21-46. *The options selected within the Appearance section of this dialog box are forced upon the text in the selected cells.*

Similar to the *Appearance* section of this dialog box, the *Size* section will alter the size of any text (or future text) in the selected cells (Figure 21-47). Once again, it will override the current size of the text. The options in this section are similar to the options within the **Font** menu, discussed in Chapter 3.

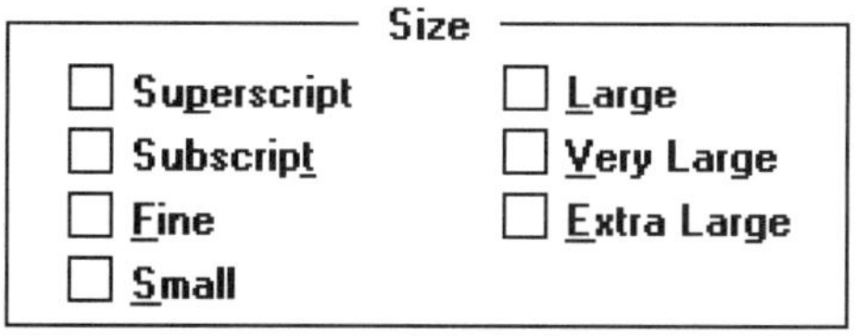

Size

- ☐ Superscript
- ☐ Subscript
- ☐ Fine
- ☐ Small
- ☐ Large
- ☐ Very Large
- ☐ Extra Large

Figure 21-47. *The options selected within the Size section of this dialog box are forced upon the text in the selected cells.*

The *Cell Attributes* options (Figure 21-48) are slightly different from the other options within this dialog box—these options affect the cell itself, rather than the appearance of text inside the cells.

The *Shading* option, if enabled, will cause the selected cells to take on a shade of gray. The actual amount of shading is determined by the figure set for *Shading* in the *Table Options* dialog box (see Figures 21-16 and 21-19 earlier in this chapter under **Editing table appearance**).

The *Lock* option, if enabled, prevents anyone from changing the information in a cell.

Later in this chapter, you will see how to perform calculations on certain selected cells within a table. Normally, when WordPerfect is asked to perform a calculation, it considers all cells in the formula. You can select certain cells, however, and check the *Ignore Cell When Calculating* option. The numbers within the selected cell(s) will then be left out of any calculation.

Cell Attributes
☐ Shading
☐ Lock
☐ Ignore Cell When Calculating

Figure 21-48. *The options within Cell Attributes control some properties of the cell itself.*

Justification and *Alignment* (Figure 21-49) are two related options within the *Format Cell* dialog box. *Justification* controls the justification of text in the selected cells—your choices are *Left, Full, Right, Center,* or *Decimal Align.*

The *Alignment* command performs a similar function to the *Justification* option, although alignment refers to vertical justification. Your options here—*Top, Bottom,* or *Center,* control where the text appears vertically within a cell.

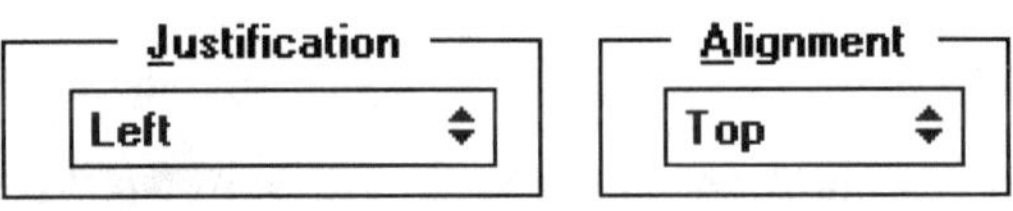

Figure 21-49. *The Justification and Alignment options control the position of text in a cell.*

Two options in the bottom right-hand side of the *Format Cell* dialog box (Figure 21-45) control which command has precedence over the appearance of text in the selected cells—the *Cell* command in the *Tables* fly-out menu or the *Column* command in the *Tables* fly-out menu (explained next).

If either the *Use Column Justification,* or *Use Column Size and Appearance* options are selected, then the options you set in the *Column* command in the *Tables* fly-out menu (using the *Appearance, Size,* or *Justification* sections) will override the options set in this dialog box.

☒ Use Column Justification
☒ Use Column Size and Appearance

Figure 21-50. *The Use Column Justification and Use Column Size and Appearance options determine which formatting commands take precedence —the Tables/Cell options, or the Tables/Column options.*

Column formatting

A column within a table can be formatted using the *Column* command in the *Tables* fly-out menu in the **Layout** menu (Figure 21-51).

Before this command can be selected, you do not need to select an entire column of cells. If no cells are selected, this command affects the entire column in which the text cursor is currently located. If multiple cells are selected, this command will affect every column in which a cell has been selected.

This command will affect an entire table if the entire table is selected before selecting this command (see **Selecting an entire table** earlier in this chapter).

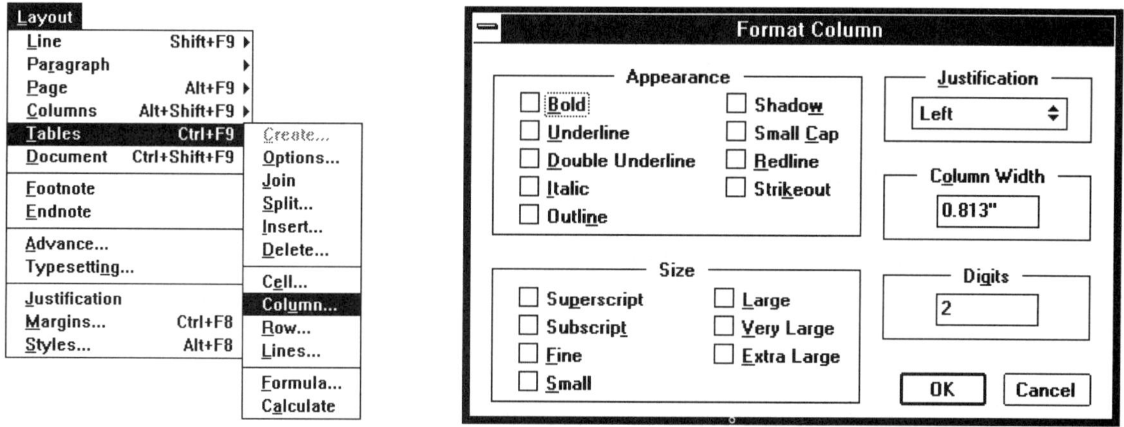

Figure 21-51. The Tables/Column command and the associated dialog box.

The *Format Column* dialog box (Figure 21-51) is similar, in many ways, to the *Format Cell* dialog box (Figure 21-45). It contains many options which control the way text appears within cells in selected columns.

The *Appearance*, *Size*, and *Justification* sections of this dialog box are exactly as described within the **Cell formatting** section of this chapter, except that using this command, selected columns are affected, rather than selected cells.

To determine which command has precedence over the formatting of text in a particular cell, refer to the *Use Column Justification* and *Use Column Size and Appearance* options in the previous section on **Cell formatting** (Figure 21-50).

The setting in the *Column Width* text box (Figure 21-52) determines the width of the currently selected columns. Initially, it will display the width of the current column (but will be empty if several columns of different widths are currently selected).

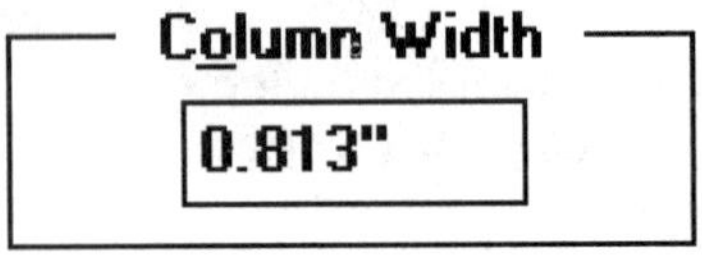

Column Width

0.813"

Figure 21-52. *The figure inserted in the Column Width text box determines the width of the currently selected column(s).*

In the *Digits* text box (Figure 21-53), you can insert a figure representing the maximum number of decimal points involved in a calculation. This relates to a later section in this chapter: **Formulae and calculations.**

A simple calculation may involve adding the numbers in certain cells, and placing the answer in another cell. The *Digits* option, controls, for the selected columns, how many digits appear after the decimal point resulting from a calculation.

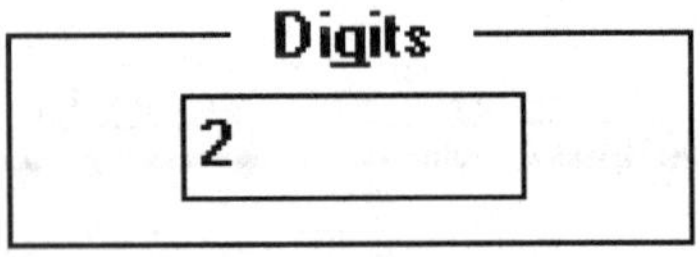

Digits

2

Figure 21-53. *Insert the number of digits in this text box that you would like to appear after the decimal point.*

Row formatting

A row within a table can be formatted using the *Row* command from the *Tables* fly-out menu in the **Layout** menu (Figure 21-54).

Before this command can be selected, you do not need to select an entire row of cells. If no cells are selected, this command affects the entire row in which the text cursor is currently located. If multiple cells are selected, this command will affect all rows in which a cell is selected.

This command will affect an entire table if the entire table is selected before selecting this command (see **Selecting an entire table** earlier in this chapter).

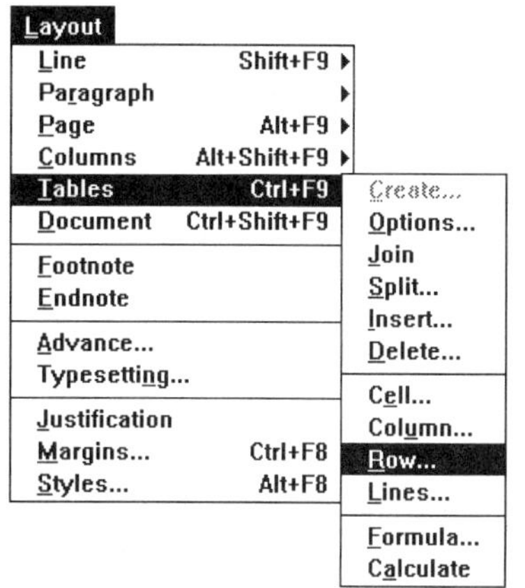

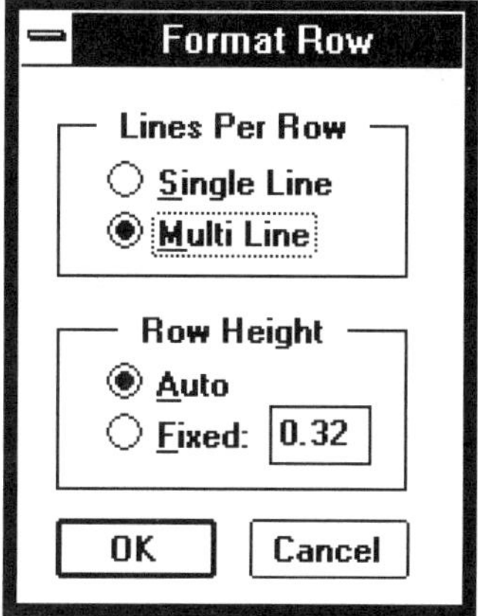

Figure 21-54. *The Tables/ Row command and associated dialog box.*

The *Format Row* dialog box (Figure 21-54) controls two things about selected rows—the maximum number of lines in a row and the height of a row.

In the *Lines Per Row* option (Figure 21-55), you can select either *Single Line*, or *Multi Line*. *Multi Line* allows text in a cell to continue over several lines, whereas *Single Line* limits the text in any of the cells in the selected row to a single line. Figure 21-13, earlier in this chapter, shows a good example of a multi line cell.

Figure 21-55. *The Lines Per Row option in the Format Row dialog box.*

The *Row Height* option (Figure 21-56) determines whether the selected rows are set to a specific height—entered in the *Fixed* text box—or are allowed to expand as the length of text is increased (*Auto*). If you select the *Fixed* option and enter a measurement size, in the text box to its right, then all text entered larger than this size (either because of point size or multiple lines) will not print and will not show in the *Print Preview* window.

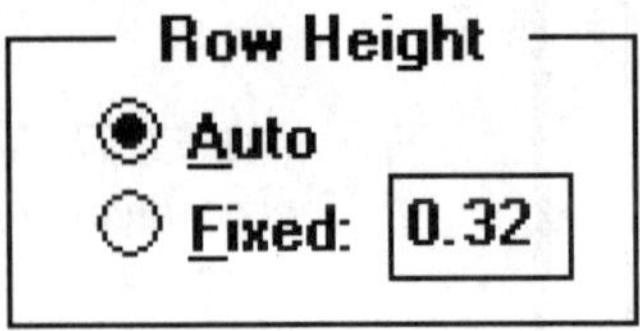

Figure 21-56. *The Row Height option.*

Table line formatting

To control the appearance of all lines forming the grid of a table, including the border and the interior vertical and horizontal lines, you must use the *Lines* command from the *Tables* fly-out menu in the **Layout** menu (Figure 21-57).

This command affects either the cell in which the text cursor is currently positioned, or the selected cells. If you wish to edit all the lines within a table, you must select the entire table (see **Selecting an entire table** earlier in this chapter).

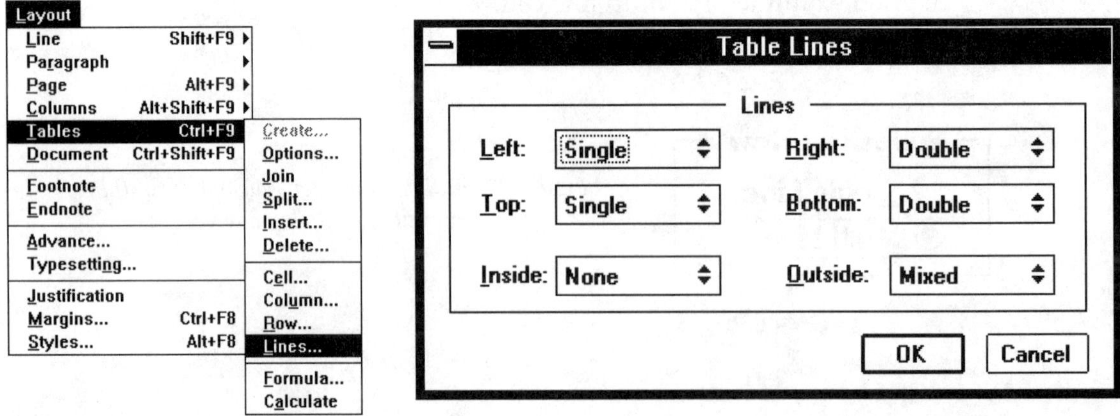

Figure 21-57. *The Tables/Lines command controls the appearance of all lines related to a table.*

Within the *Table Lines* dialog box of Figure 21-57 are six pop-up lists, which relate to different, fairly self-explanatory parts of a table or selected cells.

For example, the *Left* pop-up list box controls the appearance of the left-hand side of the selected cells. The *Right* pop-up list box controls the right-hand side, etc. For each of these six pop-up list boxes, you have a number of choices as indicated in Figure 21-58.

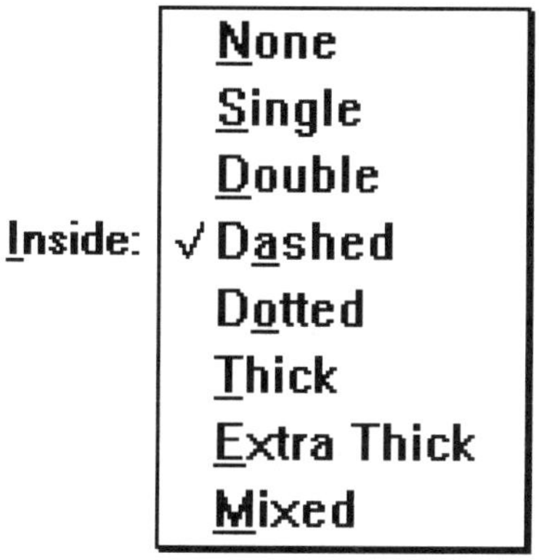

Inside:
- None
- Single
- Double
- √ Dashed
- Dotted
- Thick
- Extra Thick
- Mixed

Figure 21-58. *For each line in and around selected cells, you can select one of several line styles.*

Formulae and calculations

WordPerfect provides a feature whereby calculations can be performed on numbers within selected cells and the results placed in another cell. This is very much like a spreadsheet function.

Take, for example, this table (Figure 21-59):

Sales Figures By Year					
Year / Quarter	*1st*	*2nd*	*3rd*	*4th*	***Total***
1989	$424,040.00	$456,032.00	$498,000.00	$487.00.00	
1990	$666,897.00	$598,000.00	$758,000.00	$987,012.00	
1991	$1,045,234.00	$1,534,567.00	$2,245,789.00	$2,234,666.00 (projected)	
1992 (projected)	$3,000,000.00	$3,250,000.00	$3,999,000.00	$4,500,000.00	

Figure 21-59. *This table involves a series of numbers (representing sales per quarter) and a series of cells under the Total heading. WordPerfect provides a facility that allows you to automatically add the contents of selected cells (each quarter) and display the results in another cell (Total).*

To perform automatic calculations, you must first determine which cells are going to be involved in this calculation.

In Figure 21-59, there are actually four calculations that can take place, so let's look at the first one, which involves the cells in the row labeled "1989". First of all, this is the third row. The cells that you need to actually add together are in the 2nd, 3rd, 4th and 5th columns, or as columns are referred to by letter, columns B, C, D, and E. Hence, the cells you have to add together are cells B3, C3, D3 and E3.

The sum of cells B3, C3, D3 and E3 should be displayed in F3. Refer back to Figure 21-4 at the beginning of this chapter if you are having trouble with cell identification.

Once you have identified the cells in which you would like to perform a calculation, you can select the *Formula* command from the *Tables* fly-out menu in the **Layout** menu (Figure 21-60). No particular cell or cells need be selected before you select this command. It is useful, however, to insert the cursor in the cell where the result is to be calculated.

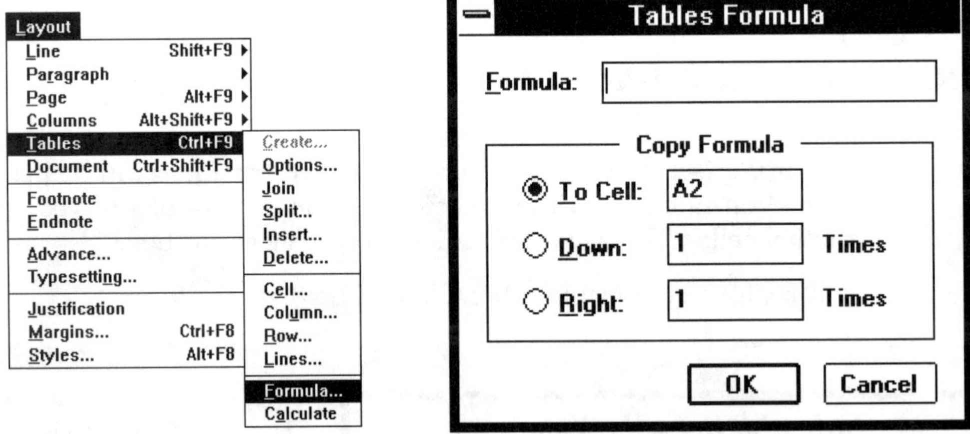

Figure 21-60. The Tables/Formula command and associated dialog box.

In the *Formula* line, insert the names of the cells that you would like to add, subtract, multiply, or divide. Note:

A1+A2 adds the values in cells A1 and A2

*A1*A2 multiplies the value in cell A1 by the value in cell A2*

A1-A3 subtracts the value in cell A3 from the value in cell A1

A1/A2 divides the value in cell A1 by the value in cell A2

The above operators can be mixed on one line. For example, a formula may take the form:

*A1+A2*A3*

In our example (Figure 21-59), the formula is quite simple—B3+C3+D3+E3. This is inserted in the *Formula* text box (Figure 21-61).

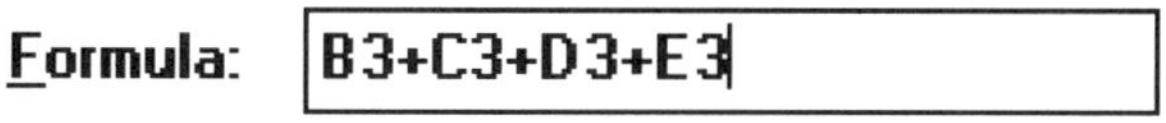

Formula: B3+C3+D3+E3

Figure 21-61. *On the Formula line, type a formula involving the cells in the table. General mathematical rules apply when creating this formula.*

The cell in which you would like the result displayed is entered in the *To Cell* text box, under the *Copy Formula* section (Figure 21-62). It initially said A2 in Figure 21-60—this is because the cursor was in cell A2 as we entered the dialog box. If the cursor is placed directly into the cell where the result should be displayed—in this case F3—before choosing the *Formula* command in the *Tables* fly-out menu, then you would not need to perform the operation of Figure 21-62.

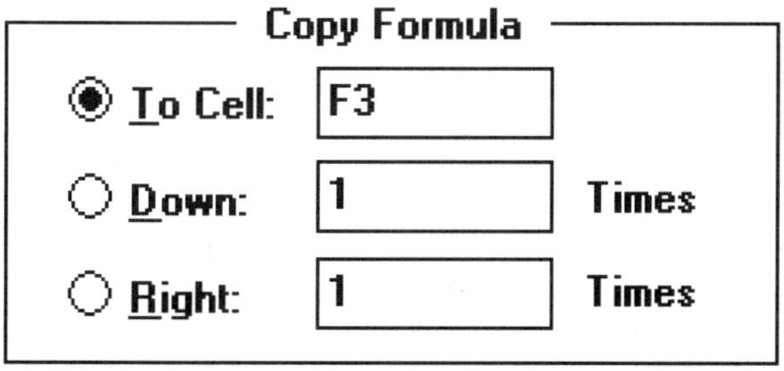

Copy Formula
To Cell: F3
Down: 1 Times
Right: 1 Times

Figure 21-62. *Enter in the To Cell box, the cell where the result of the Figure 21-61 formula should be displayed. In this case the cell is F3.*

The options, *Down* and *Right*, will copy the formula to another cell —as many cells to the right of, or as many below, the cell named in the *To Cell* line. For example, if you wanted F4 to display the result of B4 + C4 + D4 + E4, you only need to click on the *Down* button and this formula will be assigned to cell F4. Entering the value "2" in the *Down* box would do the same thing for F5.

After clicking on **OK** to exit this dialog box (Figure 21-60), WordPerfect will perform the calculation based on the entries in this dialog box.

If, as generally happens, a table is edited, it may be that a figure involved in a formula is changed. To make sure that all formulae have been updated (i.e., recalculated to include all recent changes), you would select the *Calculate* command from the *Tables* fly-out menu from the **Layout** menu (Figure 21-63).

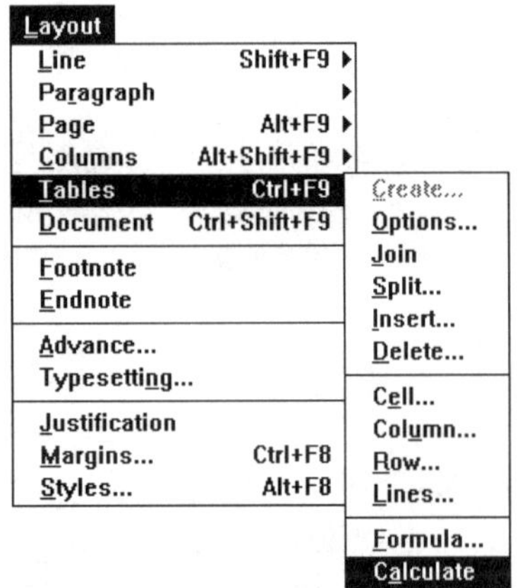

Figure 21-63. *The Tables/Calculate command will recalculate, and update, all formulae within a table.*

Upon selecting this command, all formulae in the current table are recalculated and updated.

Other formula features

It is also possible to perform the following additional features with the *Table Math* option:

- Copy the formula result to a different cell. Insert the cursor in the cell that contains the formula (say F3 from Figure 21-62), select the *Formula* command from the *Tables* fly-out menu and, in the Figure 21-62 dialog box, change the *To Cell* figure from F3 to the required new cell.

- Ignore certain cells when calculating. Figure 21-48 in the **Cell formatting** section of this chapter showed how to set up a cell to be ignored during calculations.
- Use *Subtotal* "(+)", *Total* "(=)" and *Grand Total* "(*)" functions to calculate numbers within columns. Functions are just abbreviated formulae. You insert these functions into cells the same way you do formulae. The *Subtotal* function adds numbers in the column above it. The *Total* function adds Subtotals directly above it and the *Grand Total* adds *Totals* directly above it.
- Delete a formula in a table. Select the cell that contains the formula to be deleted and choose the *Cut* command from the **Edit** menu.
- Calculate formulae in locked cells. Figure 21-48 under **Cell formatting** in this chapter showed how to lock cells. WordPerfect will still use this locked cell as part of its calculation.
- Use *Tables Formula* dialog box as a calculator. Any cell can be used to hold the result of a numeric calculation. Insert the cursor in the required cell, choose the *Formula* command from the *Tables* fly-out menu, define the numeric calculation in the *Formula* box (Figure 21-61) and click on **OK**. The result will then appear in the selected cell. See Figure 21-64 for an example.

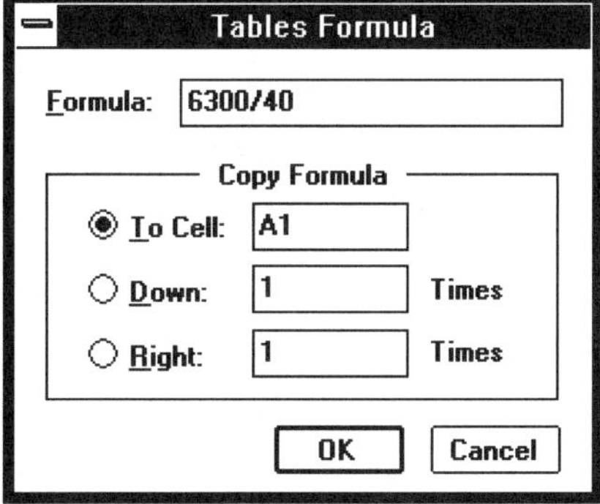

157.50	

Figure 21-64. *The calculation is entered into the Formula text box, and after selecting OK, the result is displayed in the table cell in which the text cursor had been inserted.*

Hints and Tips

Using the ruler to resize columns

You may have noticed, if you are using the ruler while creating and working with tables, that the ruler displays the total width and the column widths of the selected table (Figure 21-65).

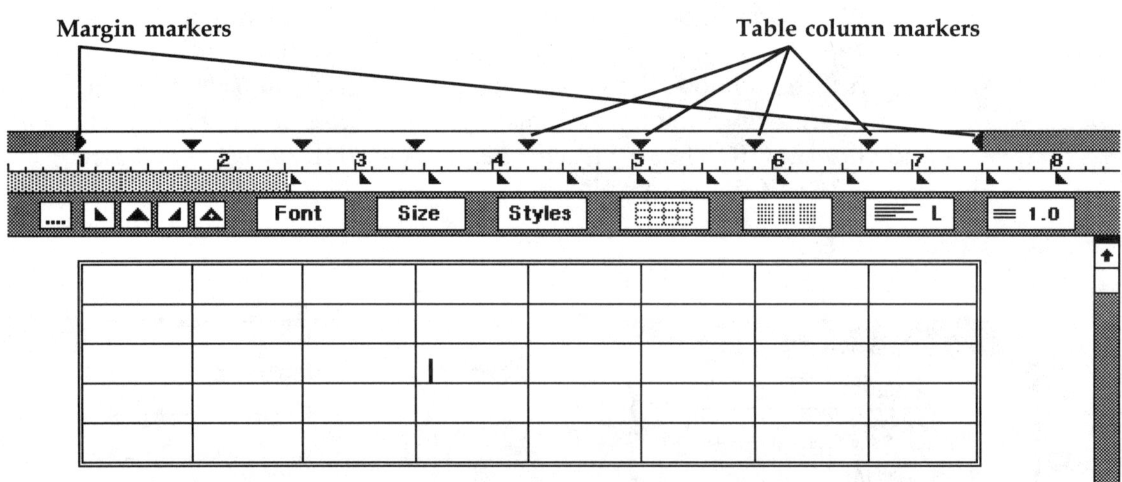

Figure 21-65. The ruler reflects table and column widths for an entire table. When the text cursor appears in any cell within a table, the table margins, and a triangular marker representing each column in the table, appear in the ruler.

Above each of the interior column lines in a table, a marker appears in the ruler. A margin marker also appears which reflects the left and right margins for the table.

These table margin and column indicators (Figure 21-65) can be used to alter the width of the columns in a table.

To alter the width of a table column, hold the mouse button down on the marker above the column and drag the marker to the left or the right (Figure 21-66). When the mouse is released, the size of the column is altered (Figure 21-67).

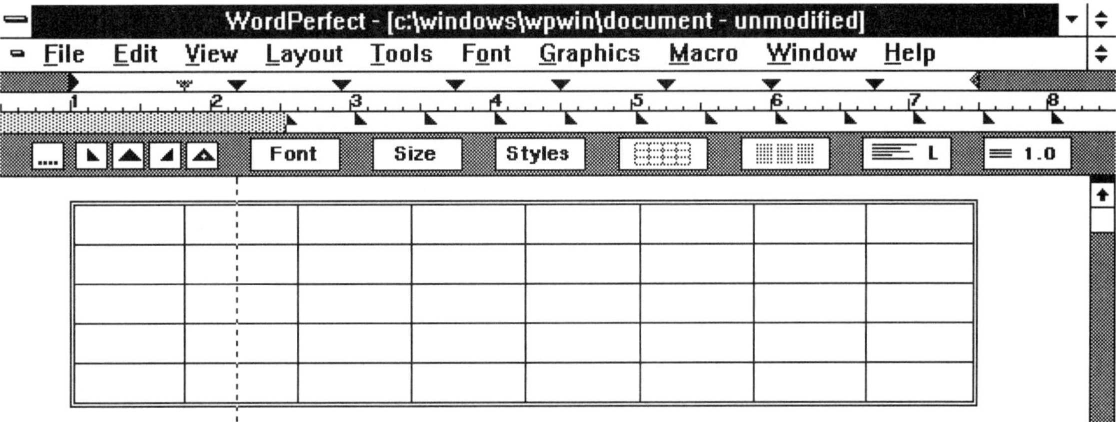

Figure 21-66. *The process of dragging a marker in the ruler to alter column width. Here the width of the first column in the table is being increased—the dotted line dragged along the ruler represents the new width of the column as the column marker is moved.*

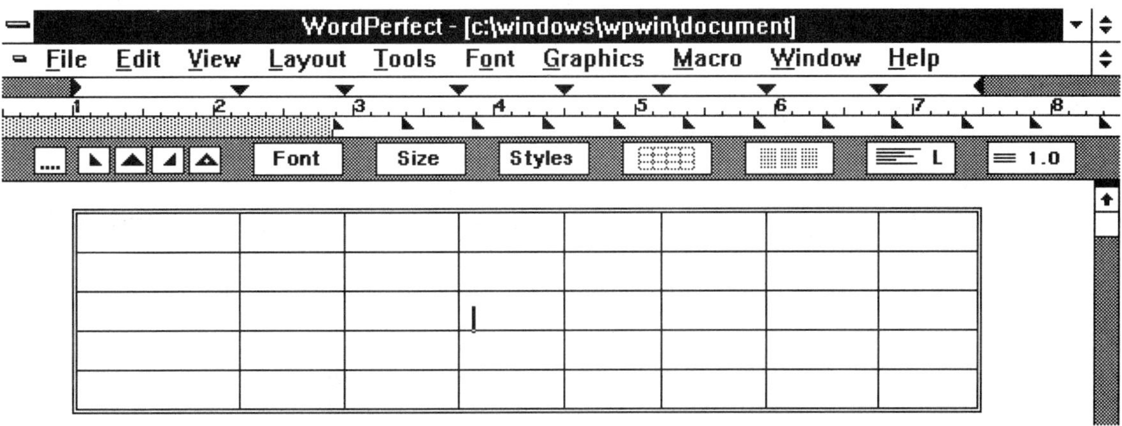

Figure 21-67. *As the mouse is released, the width of the column has changed. The column marker in the ruler now reflects the new width of the first column in the table.*

If you hold down the Ctrl key on the keyboard as you drag a column marker around, not only does the column in question resize, but all columns to the right of the column you are resizing move, to compensate for the new size of the column, and retain their original width.

Using the ruler to move a table

By holding the mouse button and dragging the margin markers in the ruler, shown in Figure 21-65, for a particular table, you can alter the position of the table horizontally on the page. This process will also alter its width.

Figures and tables

WordPerfect features, such as importing graphics and creating equations, can all be performed within a table. As long as the text cursor is within a table, it acts in much the same way as when it is outside a table—files can be retrieved, graphics can be retrieved, and equations can be created.

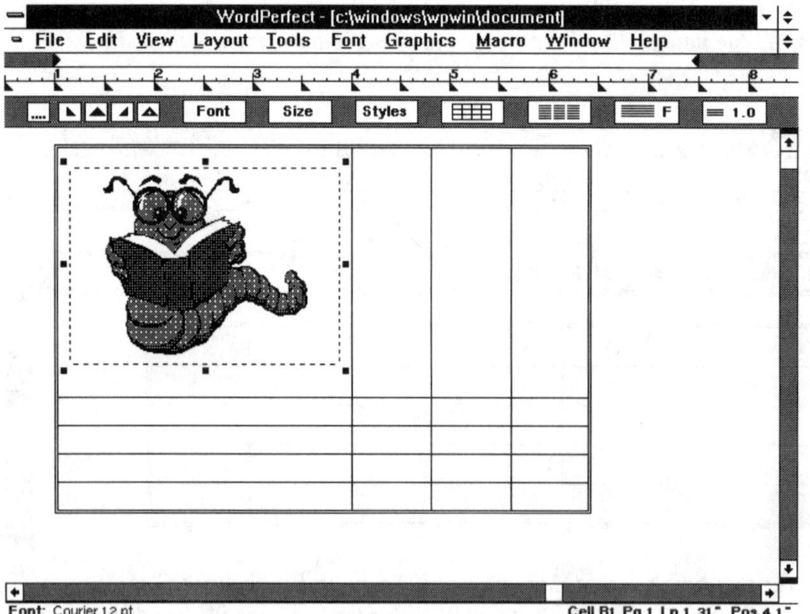

Figure 21-68. A retrieved graphic within a table.

Tables — Exercise

This training exercise is designed so that people of all levels of expertise with WordPerfect can use it to gain maximum benefit. In order to do this, the bare exercise is listed below this paragraph on just one page, with no hints. The following pages contain the steps needed to complete this exercise for those who need additional prompting.

Steps in brief

1. ***Start a new WordPerfect file.***
2. ***Recreate the table shown in Figure 21x-1. Use the Formula command to calculate the total number of boxes.***

COOKIE SALE		
	Saturday	**Sunday**
Bill	50 boxes	20 boxes
Peggy	10 boxes	35 boxes
		Total 115 boxes

Figure 21x-1. *Creating this table is the objective of this exercise.*

The details for completing these steps are on the following pages.

Steps in detail

1. *Start a new WordPerfect file.*

If you have just opened WordPerfect, you will be in a new Wordperfect file. If you are working on another WordPerfect document, select the *New* command from the **File** menu. If you are not in WordPerfect, start the program from Windows.

2. ***Recreate the table shown in Figure 21x-1. Use the Formula command to calculate the total number of boxes.***

There are two ways you can create the initial table. One way is to select the *Create* command from the *Tables* fly-out menu in the **Layout** menu. For this exercise, however, you will create the table from the ruler. If you do not currently have the ruler active, select the *Ruler* command from the **View** menu.

Once the ruler has been activated, hold the mouse down on the button in the ruler that represents the table. Drag the mouse down and across, and do not release the button until the figures above the table read 3x5 (Figure 21x-2). This expression means the table will be 3 columns wide by 5 rows down, which is the size required for this exercise.

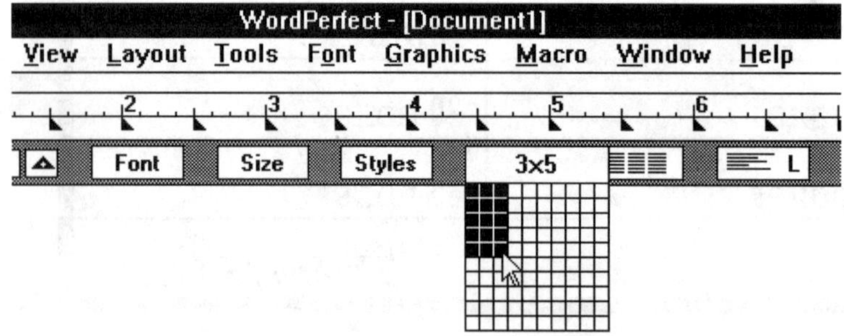

Figure 21x-2. *To create a table 3 columns wide by 5 rows down, hold the mouse down on the table button in the ruler, and drag it down and across until the figures above this grid read 3x5.*

Once you have released the mouse button, the table will appear on screen as displayed in Figure 21x-3.

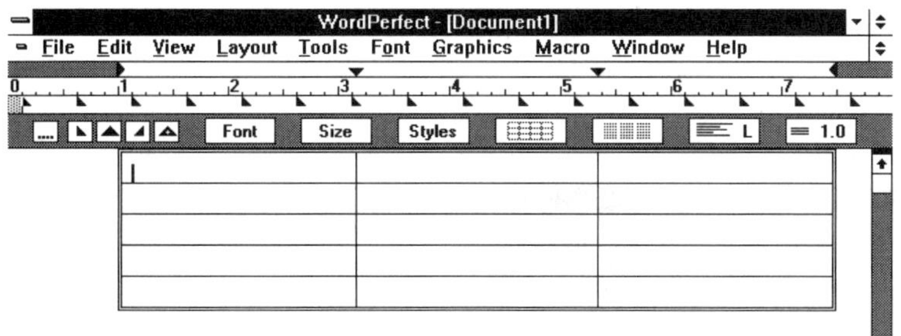

Figure 21x-3. The table is now on screen.

Whenever a table first appears, it will stretch from the left to the right margin. In Figure 21x-3 above, the margins are set at 1 inch on the left and 1 inch (7.5 inches on the ruler) at the right. You can change the actual width of the table using the *Tables* command in the **Layout** menu. For this exercise, however, you will be changing column widths using the ruler.

Hold the mouse button down on the marker just after 3 inches on the ruler, and drag it to a new position. The column width for this exercise is not strictly important, but make column one 1.125 inches wide. To do this, drag the appropriate marker to the first 1/8 graduation after the 2 inch mark on the ruler (Figure 21x-4).

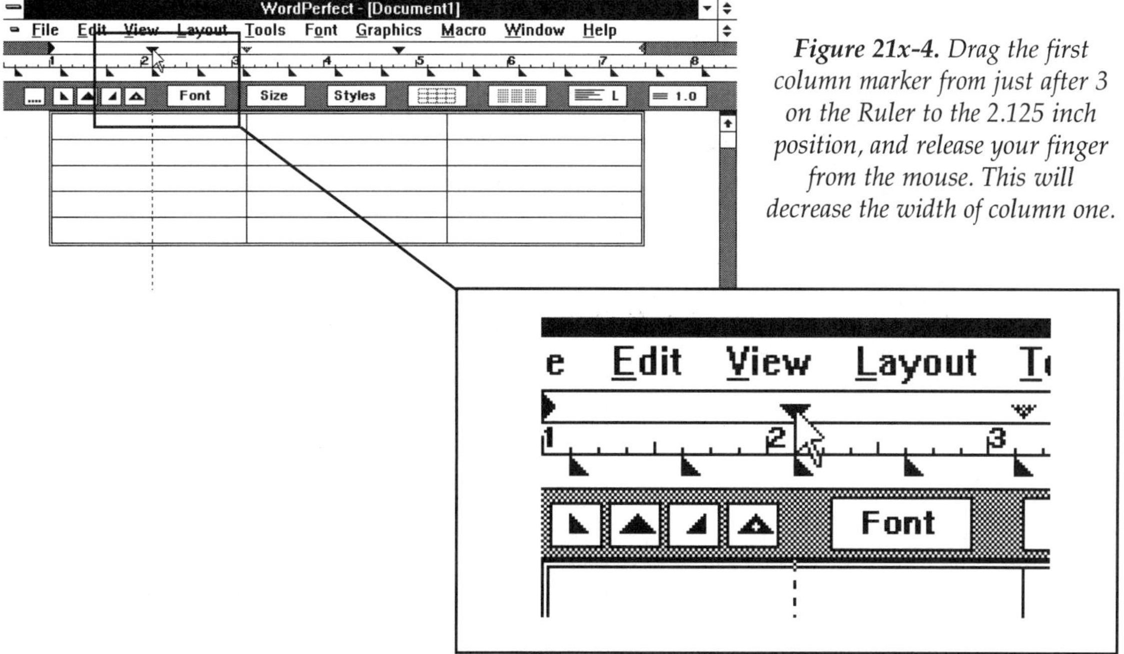

***Figure 21x-4.** Drag the first column marker from just after 3 on the Ruler to the 2.125 inch position, and release your finger from the mouse. This will decrease the width of column one.*

Make the next column 1.875 (1 7/8) inches wide. Drag the next marker to the 4 inch position on the ruler (Figure 21x-5).

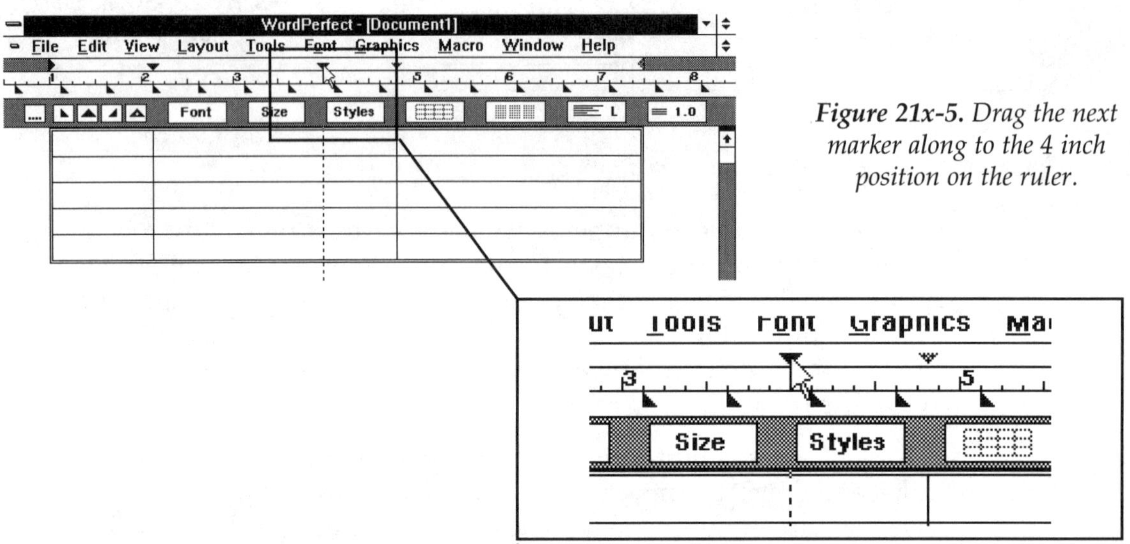

Figure 21x-5. *Drag the next marker along to the 4 inch position on the ruler.*

Drag the marker for the last column—the right margin—to the 5.75 inch position on the ruler as in Figure 21x-6; the third column is then 1.75 inches wide.

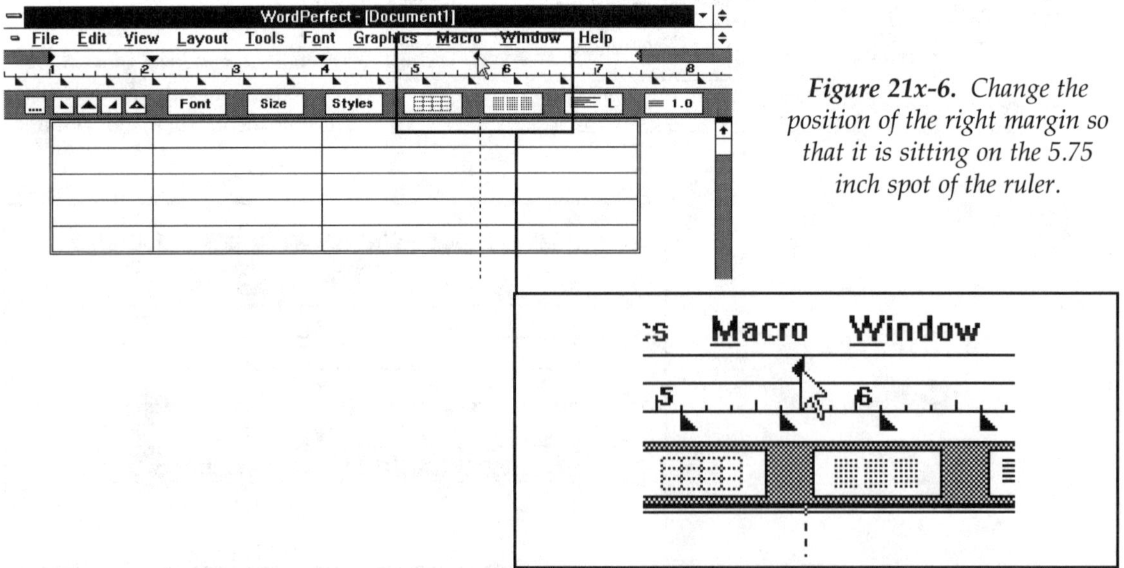

Figure 21x-6. *Change the position of the right margin so that it is sitting on the 5.75 inch spot of the ruler.*

Figure 21x-7. *Here is the table at its new size.*

The next task is to turn the top three cells into one cell. This is done with the *Join* command in the *Tables* fly-out menu in the **Layout** menu after you have selected all three cells. To select these cells, position the mouse in the top left cell and move it to the left of the cell, until the mouse becomes a left-facing arrow, as in Figure 21x-8.

Figure 21x-8. *When the mouse is moved to the left wall of the top left cell, a left facing arrow appears, allowing you to select the necessary cells.*

Now, hold the mouse down and drag it to the right across the top three cells, and release the mouse. They will all become selected as shown in Figure 21x-9.

Figure 21x-9. *Hold the mouse down, and drag it to the right over the top three cells, and they will become selected.*

Once you have selected the top three cells, choose the *Join* command from the *Tables* fly-out menu in the **Layout** menu (Figure 21x-10).

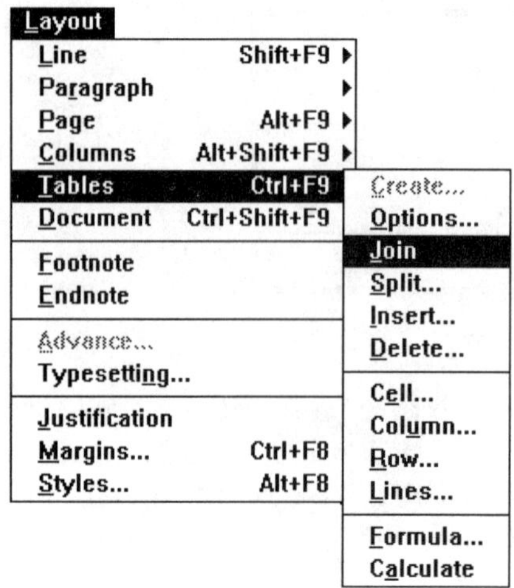

Figure 21x-10. *To combine the three selected cells as one, choose the Join command from the Tables fly-out menu in the* ***Layout*** *menu.*

Figure 21x-11 shows the change in the table after the *Join* command has been applied to the selected cells.

Figure 21x-11. *The top three cells are now one continuous cell.*

Now you can type the text into the cells. Click the cursor in the top cell and type "COOKIE SALE". Using the arrow keys on your keyboard, move the text cursor down and to the right one cell. In this cell type "Saturday". Move the cursor one cell to the right, this time using the Tab key, and type "Sunday". Now, move the cursor down one cell and to the left two cells and type the name "Bill". See Figure 21x-12 for the correct positioning of these words.

COOKIE SALE		
	Saturday	Sunday
Bil		

Figure 21x-12. *This figure shows a portion of the required text typed into the cells of the table. The arrow or Tab keys are used to move from cell to cell.*

Finish keying in the rest of the text in each cell and compare your table with Figure 21x-13 for accuracy.

COOKIE SALE		
	Saturday	Sunday
Bill	50 boxes	20 boxes
Peggy	10 boxes	35 boxes

***Figure 21x-13.** The text in your table should correspond with the text shown in this table.*

The cells in the bottom row of the table also need to be joined. The same procedure is followed for the joining of these three cells, as was used for the top three. Figures 21x-14 through 21x-17 summarize this procedure.

COOKIE SALE		
	Saturday	Sunday
Bill	50 boxes	20 boxes
Peggy	10 boxes	35 boxes

***Figure 21x-14**. The left facing arrow indicates that, by depressing the mouse, you can now select this cell.*

COOKIE SALE		
	Saturday	Sunday
Bill	50 boxes	20 boxes
Peggy	10 boxes	35 boxes

***Figure 21x-15**. Continue to hold down the mouse button and drag the mouse pointer across the bottom three cells. As the arrow moves over the cells, it selects each one in turn. Alternatively, with the arrow positioned as in Figure 21x-14, double-click the mouse. All cells in the row will then be selected.*

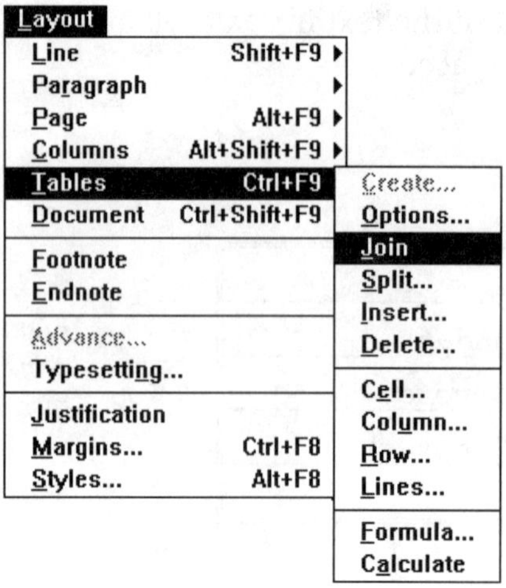

Layout		Tables fly-out
Line	Shift+F9 ▸	
Paragraph	▸	
Page	Alt+F9 ▸	
Columns	Alt+Shift+F9 ▸	
Tables	Ctrl+F9	Create...
Document	Ctrl+Shift+F9	Options...
Footnote		Join
Endnote		Split...
Advance...		Insert...
Typesetting...		Delete...
Justification		Cell...
Margins...	Ctrl+F8	Column...
Styles...	Alt+F8	Row...
		Lines...
		Formula...
		Calculate

***Figure 21x-16**. Once all three cells are selected, choose the Join command from the Tables fly-out menu in the **Layout** menu.*

COOKIE SALE		
	Saturday	Sunday
Bill	50 boxes	20 boxes
Peggy	10 boxes	35 boxes

***Figure 21x-17**. The bottom three cells have now been converted to one.*

The total number of boxes can now be calculated. Assign a formula to the bottom cell. First, place the cursor in the bottom cell and type in the word "Total"—be sure to include a blank space after this word as in Figure 21x-18.

COOKIE SALE		
	Saturday	Sunday
Bill	50 boxes	20 boxes
Peggy	10 boxes	35 boxes
Total		

***Figure 21x-18**. Before assigning a formula to the bottom cell, key in the word "Total" and then a space.*

Now that you have positioned the cursor in the cell in which you want the formula assigned, select the *Formula* command from the *Tables* fly-out menu in the **Layout** menu (Figure 21x-19).

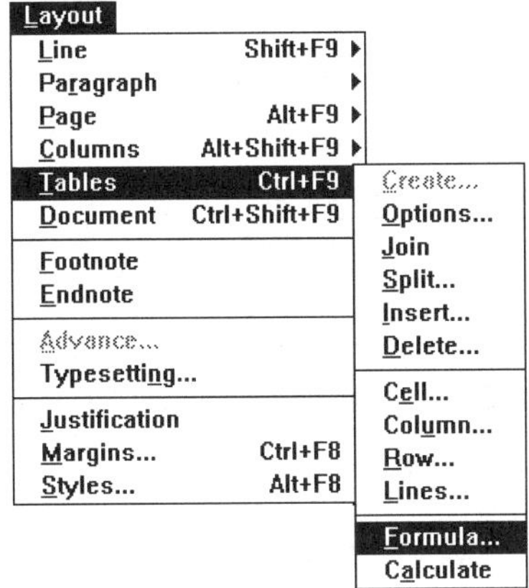

***Figure 21x-19.** Select the Formula command from the Tables fly-out menu, once the cursor is situated in the cell in which you want the formula assigned.*

The *Formula* command activates the *Tables Formula* dialog box of Figure 21x-20. For this exercise, the figures you keyed into the cells are to be added together to give you a result in the bottom cell. Because you selected the *Formula* command, with the text cursor in the bottom cell, the *To Cell* frame of the *Tables Formula* dialog box has the cell location A5 in it. This indicates the position of the cell.

For this example, the formula for the addition should include the positions of all cells that have figures in them. If the columns of a table are represented by letters and the rows are represented by numbers, the formula for the addition of the figures in this table will be b3+b4+c3+c4. These are the cells representing 50, 10, 20 and 35 boxes as shown in Figure 21x-13. If you wish to check the cell numbering, cancel the *Tables Formula* dialog box, go back to the table, and click your mouse into these different cells. The Status bar (bottom right of the screen) will indicate the cell numbers. Now key this *Formula* into the text box of the *Tables Formula* dialog box and click on the **OK** button.

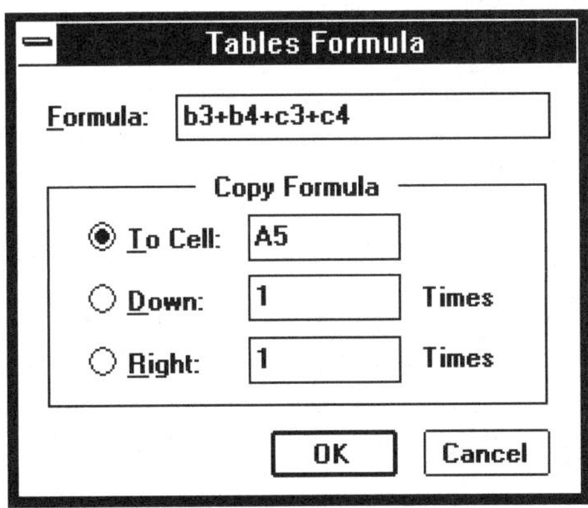

***Figure 21x-20**. After keying in the formula for the addition of the table figures, click on **OK**.*

After clicking on **OK** in the Figure 21x-20 *Tables Formula* dialog box, the result of the formula is shown in the bottom cell (Figure 21x-21).

COOKIE SALE		
	Saturday	Sunday
Bill	50 boxes	20 boxes
Peggy	10 boxes	35 boxes
Total 115.00		

***Figure 21x-21**. The result of the formula is now shown in the bottom cell.*

The figure in the bottom cell is 115.00. For this exercise, delete the decimal point and two zeros, and type the word "boxes" in its place. To do this, insert the cursor after the last zero and backspace over these zeros and the decimal point. Now key in a space and the word "boxes" (Figure 21x-22).

COOKIE SALE		
	Saturday	Sunday
Bill	50 boxes	20 boxes
Peggy	10 boxes	35 boxes
Total 115 boxes		

***Figure 21x-22**. After backspacing over the two zeros and the decimal point, key in the word "boxes".*

Now you are ready to format the text. To change the font of all the text, it must be selected first. To do this, move the mouse to the start of the first word in the top cell ("COOKIE"), as in Figure 21x-23.

COOKIE SALE		
	Saturday	Sunday
Bill	50 boxes	20 boxes
Peggy	10 boxes	35 boxes
Total 115 boxes		

***Figure 21x-23**. To select all the text, move the mouse to the beginning of the top cell.*

Hold down the mouse button, and drag it across the text in the top cell, as though you are selecting this text in a document. Then, move the mouse down and across, so that all cells become selected. Keep moving the mouse down past the bottom cell of the table, so the highlighting of the cells switches to the text (Figure 21x-24).

COOKIE SALE		
	Saturday	Sunday
Bill	50 boxes	20 boxes
Peggy	10 boxes	35 boxes
Total 115 boxes		

Figure 21x-24*. The difference between selecting all the cells in the table, and all the text, is to keep dragging the mouse down past the bottom cell, so the highlighting of the cells switches to the text.*

Once all the text is selected, choose a font from the *Font* button in the ruler. For this exercise, Palatino is being selected in Figure 21x-25. You may prefer to select a different font.

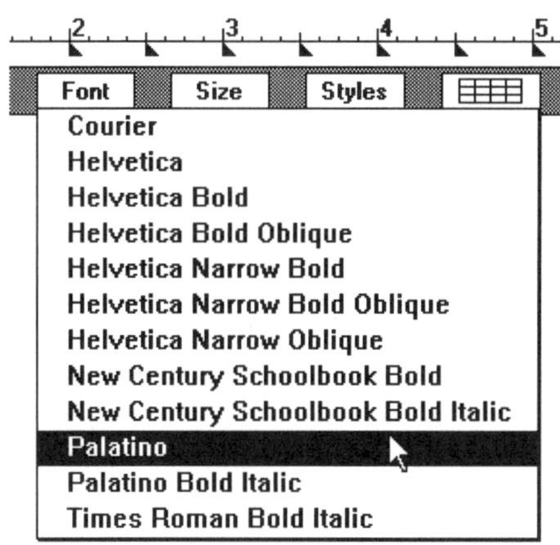

Figure 21x-25*. To apply a different font to all text in the table, select it from the* ***Font*** *menu in the ruler. Alternatively, you could use the Font dialog box from the* ***Font*** *menu.*

After selecting Palatino in Figure 21x-25, all text in the table changes to reflect the new font (Figure 21x-26).

COOKIE SALE		
	Saturday	Sunday
Bill	50 boxes	20 boxes
Peggy	10 boxes	35 boxes
Total 115 boxes		

Figure 21x-26*. All text in the table is now Palatino.*

Now, you can format the other cells individually. First, select the top cell by moving the mouse to the left side of the cell, so that an arrow appears. Then, click the mouse once to actually select the cell (Figure 21x-27).

OOKIE SALE		
	Saturday	Sunday
Bill	50 boxes	20 boxes
Peggy	10 boxes	35 boxes
Total 115 boxes		

Figure 21x-27*. Select the top cell by clicking the mouse once after the left-facing arrow appears.*

Once the cell is selected, choose the *Cell* command from the *Tables* fly-out menu in the **Layout** menu.

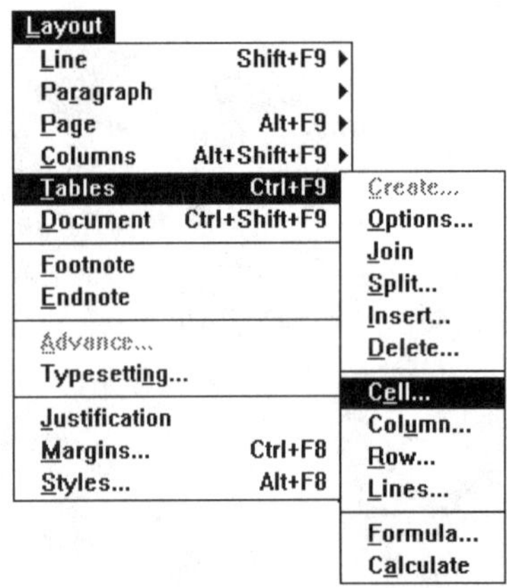

Figure 21x-28*. You are now going to further change the attributes of the text and change the appearance of the cell itself. Changes can be made to individual cells using the dialog box that is activated when selecting the Cell command.*

The *Cell* command activates the *Format Cell* dialog box of Figure 21x-29. The changes you can make here affect the text, its position, and certain other cell attributes. In the *Appearance* section of this dialog box, make sure that only the *Bold* and *Italic* options are selected. In the *Size* section, select the *Large* option.

The next option to select is in the *Cell Attributes* section of the dialog box. Click on the *Shading* option which turns *Shading* on. **Note:** The *Shading* percentage is altered in the *Table Options* dialog box. By default, a cell will have a shade of 10% black, as you will see if you select the *Shading* option in this dialog box. Keep the cell at 10% black for this exercise.

Change both the *Justification* and *Alignment* settings to *Center*. This is done by holding the mouse down on the button below these headings. This will activate a pop-up list where the mouse is used to select a new choice.

Make sure your dialog box is set up exactly as shown in Figure 21x-29, then click on the **OK** button.

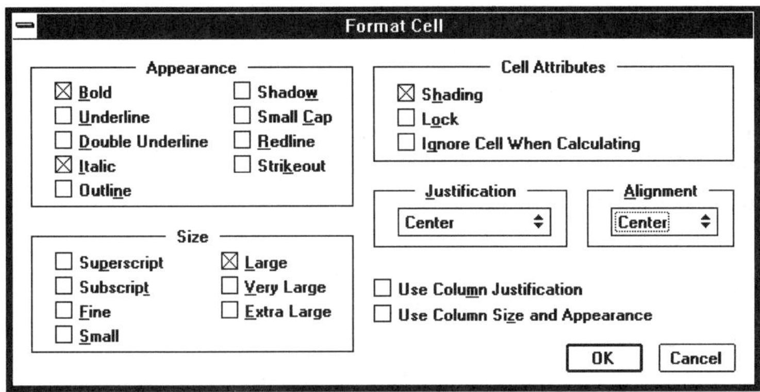

Figure 21x-29*. Changes made in this dialog box will affect the selected cell. Make sure your dialog box settings are the same as those shown here.*

After clicking on **OK** in the Figure 21x-29 dialog box, you will see the changes you set up in the *Format Cell* dialog box applied to the top cell in the table (Figure 21x-30). To apply the *Format Cell* settings to a cell, it need not necessarily be selected, as long as the cursor is inserted in the cell. The *Center Alignment* option can only be seen in the *Print Preview* window, and when the table is printed.

COOKIE SALE		
	Saturday	Sunday
Bill	50 boxes	20 boxes
Peggy	10 boxes	35 boxes
Total 115 boxes		

Figure 21x-30*. The top cell is now displaying the changes you applied to it in the Figure 21x-29 Format Cell dialog box.*

Now, go on to change the attributes of the cells that contain the text "Saturday", "Sunday", "Bill" and "Peggy", one at a time. Follow the same steps as you did to re-format the top cell; only this time in the *Format Cell* dialog box just select the *Bold* and *Italic* options under *Appearance*. Figure 21x-31 shows the results of these changes.

COOKIE SALE		
	Saturday	*Sunday*
Bill	50 boxes	20 boxes
Peggy	10 boxes	35 boxes
Total 115 boxes		

Figure 21x-31. *Change the format for the cells containing the words "Saturday", "Sunday", "Bill" and "Peggy" to look like the example shown here.*

Apply the *Bold* and *Italic* format options to the bottom cell and change its *Justification* setting to *Right*. After inserting the cursor in the bottom cell, set up the *Format Cell* dialog box as shown in Figure 21x-32 and click on **OK**. Figure 21x-33 shows the result of the changes made in the Figure 21x-32 dialog box.

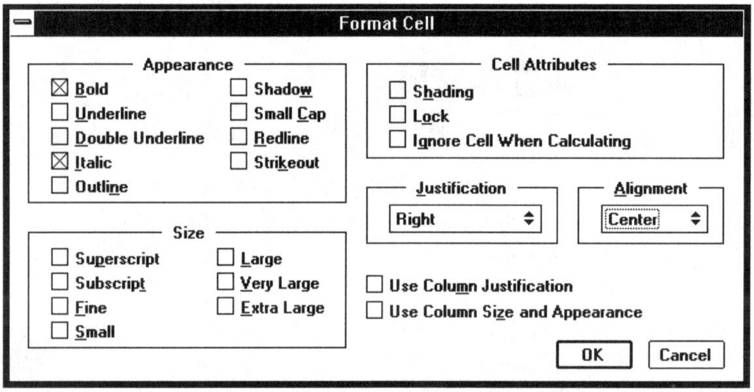

Format Cell

Appearance
- ☒ Bold
- ☐ Underline
- ☐ Double Underline
- ☒ Italic
- ☐ Outline
- ☐ Shadow
- ☐ Small Cap
- ☐ Redline
- ☐ Strikeout

Size
- ☐ Superscript
- ☐ Subscript
- ☐ Fine
- ☐ Small
- ☐ Large
- ☐ Very Large
- ☐ Extra Large

Cell Attributes
- ☐ Shading
- ☐ Lock
- ☐ Ignore Cell When Calculating

Justification: Right

Alignment: Center

- ☐ Use Column Justification
- ☐ Use Column Size and Appearance

OK | Cancel

Figure 21x-32. *Apply the Bold and Italic options to the bottom cell, as well as changing the Justification to Right.*

COOKIE SALE		
	Saturday	*Sunday*
Bill	50 boxes	20 boxes
Peggy	10 boxes	35 boxes
Total 115 boxes		

Figure 21x-33. *The text in the bottom cell is now bold, italic, and right justified.*

The last thing to do is give the table a thick outline. Select the whole table again by holding the mouse down in the top left cell, and dragging it down and across, until each cell becomes highlighted (Figure 21x-34).

COOKIE SALE		
	Saturday	*Sunday*
Bill	50 boxes	20 boxes
Peggy	10 boxes	35 boxes
		Total 115 boxes

Figure 21x-34. Select the whole table again so that you can then apply a different outline to it

Once the table is selected, choose the *Lines* command from the *Tables* fly-out menu in the **Layout** menu as in Figure 21x-35.

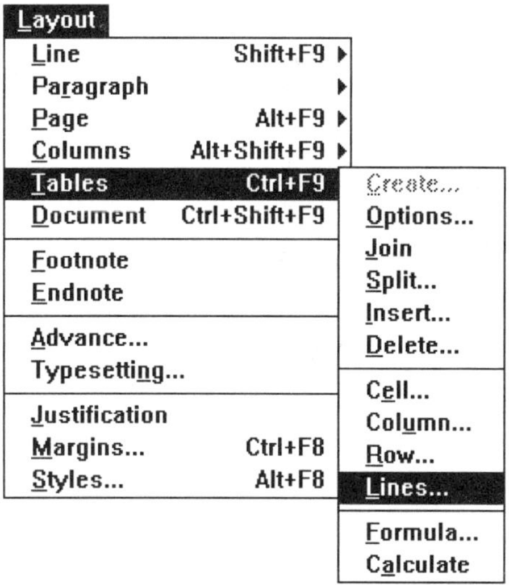

Layout		Tables
Line	Shift+F9	
Paragraph		
Page	Alt+F9	
Columns	Alt+Shift+F9	
Tables	Ctrl+F9	Create...
Document	Ctrl+Shift+F9	Options...
Footnote		Join
Endnote		Split...
Advance...		Insert...
Typesetting...		Delete...
Justification		Cell...
Margins...	Ctrl+F8	Column...
Styles...	Alt+F8	Row...
		Lines...
		Formula...
		Calculate

Figure 21x-35. The Lines command gives you access to the dialog box where it is possible to change the outline of a selected cell or cells.

Selecting the *Lines* command will activate the *Table Lines* dialog box of Figure 21x-36. To alter the outline for the whole table, hold the mouse down on the *Outside* button and, from the pop-up list box that appears, select the *Thick* option. Then, click on the **OK** button. The result of this change is shown in Figure 21x-37.

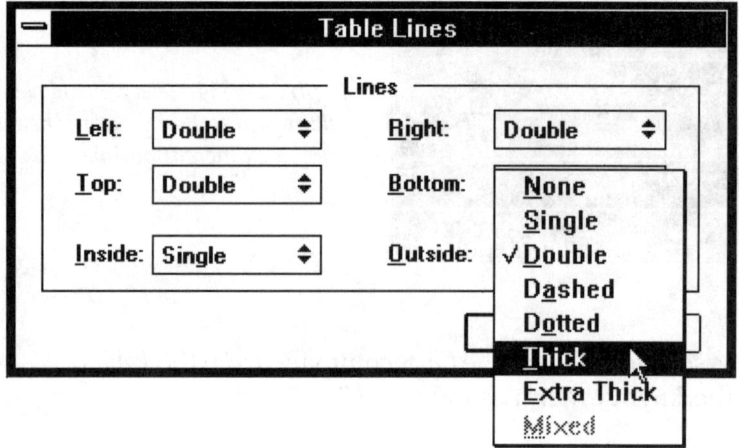

Figure 21x-36. In the Table Lines dialog box, change the Outside setting to Thick. Figure 21x-37 shows the result.

COOKIE SALE		
	Saturday	*Sunday*
Bill	50 boxes	20 boxes
Peggy	10 boxes	35 boxes
		Total 115 boxes

Figure 21x-37. The table is now bordered with a thick outline.

Advanced Features

This chapter examines many advanced and miscellaneous features within WordPerfect.

Widows & Orphans

When a single line of text is separated from the main body of a paragraph due to a page or column break, this line is known as a widow or an orphan. If the last line of a paragraph appears at the top of a new page or column, it is known as a widow. If the first line of a paragraph appears at the bottom of a page or column, this is known as an orphan.

Using the *Widow/Orphan* command from the *Page* fly-out menu in the **Layout** menu, you can prevent widows and orphans from appearing within a WordPerfect document. When the *Widow/Orphan* command is selected (this command is activated when a check mark appears next to the command name—Figure 22-1), WordPerfect will prevent the separation of single lines from the main body of a paragraph.

Layout

Layout menu	Shortcut
Line	Shift+F9 ▸
Paragraph	▸
Page	Alt+F9
Columns	Alt+Shift+F9
Tables	Ctrl+F9
Document	Ctrl+Shift+F9
Footnote	
Endnote	
Advance...	
Typesetting...	
Justification	
Margins...	Ctrl+F8
Styles...	Alt+F8

Page menu	Shortcut
Page Break	Ctrl+Enter
Center Page	
Headers...	
Footers...	
Numbering...	
Suppress...	
Paper Size...	
✓Widow/Orphan	
Block Protect	
Conditional End of Page...	

Figure 22-1. *The Page/Widow/ Orphan command from the* ***Layout*** *menu will prevent widows or orphans from appearing on a page.*

Conditional End of Page

The *Conditional End of Page* command from the **Page** fly-out menu in the **Layout** menu, forces WordPerfect to keep a selected number of lines together on one page.

A useful application for this command is to ensure that a heading, or subheading, is not separated from the paragraph immediately following, due to a page or column break.

To use this command, you insert the text cursor into the text on the line immediately *above* the lines you want to remain together. Then select the *Conditional End of Page* command from the *Page* fly-out menu in the **Layout** menu.

From the *Conditional End of Page* dialog box, key in the number of lines you wish to remain together, and press the **OK** button.

Block Protect

The *Block Protect* command in the *Page* fly-out menu is similar to the *Page/Conditional End of Page* command but is a little more specific. This command allows a specific block of text to always remain together on the same page.

Before using the *Page/Block Protect* command from the **Layout** menu, select a block of text on the page. The block of text selected must be smaller than one page in length, but it does not matter if the block of text is currently split by a page break.

Once the block is selected, select the *Block Protect* command in the *Page* fly-out menu in the **Layout** menu. The text currently selected will be moved so that it all appears on one page. Any page breaks currently in the selected text will disappear.

Sorting

WordPerfect provides a sorting facility for organizing data in WordPerfect documents. Select the *Sort* command from the **Tools** menu to access this feature. The *Sort* dialog box of Figure 22-2 will appear.

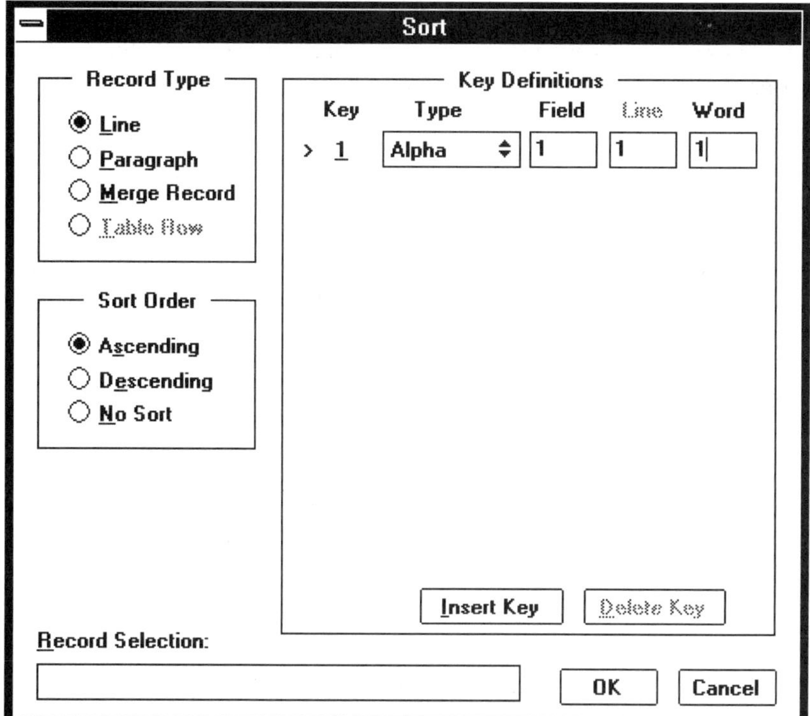

Figure 22-2. The Sort dialog box.

When preparing to sort a file, you must make several choices as to how this sort will occur.

First, select the text that you wish to sort. If no text is selected, the entire file will be sorted.

Second, select a *Record Type* to sort, from the top left-hand corner of the *Sort* dialog box (Figure 22-2). A *Line* is defined as text followed by a carriage return. A *Paragraph* is defined as text followed by two or more carriage returns. A *Merge Record* is text separated by *END RECORD* codes (used in a mail merge secondary file), and a *Table Row* is just that—rows in a table.

Next, select the *Sort Order*. The Sort Order options are: *Ascending*, *Descending*, or *No Sort*.

Finally, you can make some selections from the options under the *Key Definitions* section of the dialog box. The following paragraphs apply to these options:

The *Key* number cannot be edited, and simply numbers the sort keys from 1 to 16 (you can create several keys by which data can be sorted). By default, there will only be one key by which data is sorted.

The *Type* can be either *Alpha* or *Numeric*. The option you select here will depend on the data you wish to sort.

The three options following the *Type* are *Field*, *Line*, and *Word*. The order in which these options appears depends on the *Record Type* selected earlier in the dialog box. These options become *Cell*, *Line*, and *Word* when *Table Row* is selected in Figure 22-2.

If you are sorting *Lines* or *Paragraphs*, fields are strings of text separated by tabs or indents. When sorting *Merge Records*, fields are separated by the *END FIELD* code.

Lines are strings of text separated by a soft or hard return character.

Words are strings of text separated by a space, a slash (/) or a hard hyphen (-).

In the text box under the *Field*, *Line*, *Cell* or *Word* options, insert the number of the corresponding *Field*, *Line*, *Cell*, or *Word* by which you wish to sort. For example, say you wanted to sort the following file, using the last name of each full name:

```
FRED SMITH
JOHN COOK
LINDSAY WOODCOCK
DAVID JONES
CARRIE JONES
PETER DWYER
```

The *Record Type* to sort by here would be *Line*, as each name takes up one line. For the *Key Definitions*, insert the number "2" under *Word*. This setting ensures that the file is sorted based on the second *Word* in each *Line*. The result:

```
JOHN COOK
PETER DWYER
DAVID JONES
CARRIE JONES
FRED SMITH
LINDSAY WOODCOCK
```

Down towards the bottom of the dialog box, you can use the *Insert Key* or *Delete Key* dialog box. This allows you to add a key to the sort, so that the sort is based on two, or more, pieces of information.

If you take the previous names as an example, you will note the names were sorted by last name; there were two people with the name JONES in the file. Therefore, you may wish to sort primarily by the last name of each name but, after that, sort by the first name within each last name. To do this, you would need to set up two sort keys, by selecting the *Insert Key* button. The second key would sort based on the first *Word* in each *Line*.

JOHN COOK
PETER DWYER
CARRIE JONES
DAVID JONES
FRED SMITH
LINDSAY WOODCOCK

The *Record Selection* text box lets you use basic operators to select records in a file.

Labels

Creating labels within WordPerfect is managed slightly differently, depending on whether a Windows or a WordPerfect printer driver has been selected (see Chapter 9, **Printing**).

If a Windows printer driver is selected, you can define labels by selecting the *Paper Size* command from the *Page* fly-out menu in the **Layout** menu, and the *Add* button from the dialog box that appears.

If you are using a WordPerfect printer driver, select the *Paper Size* command from the *Page* fly-out menu in the **Layout** menu, the *Add* button from the dialog box that appears, and the *Labels* button from the resultant dialog box.

In both cases, the dialog box that finally appears looks very much the same (Figure 22-3).

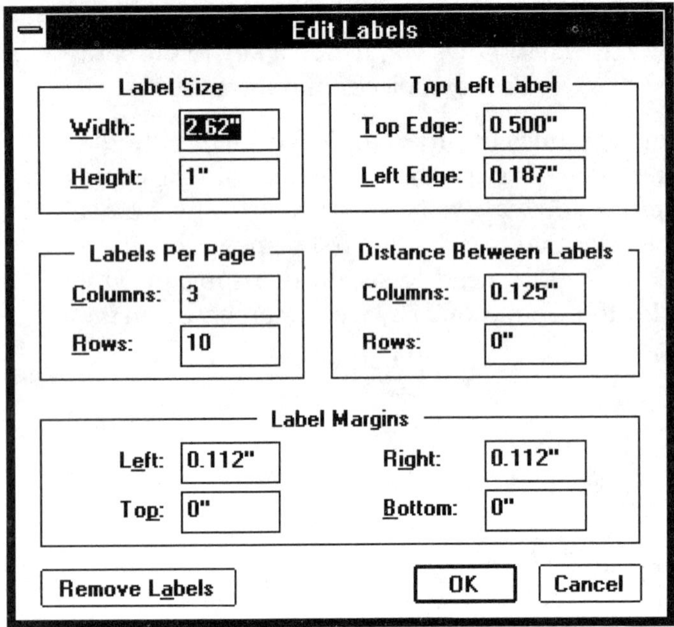

Figure 22-3. The Edit Labels dialog box.

Use this dialog box to provide the basic measurements for the labels. There may be quite a few numbers to fill in (if you do not want to accept the default labels form), but they are all quite straightforward.

Enter the size of the labels, the number of labels you wish to have across and down the page, the starting point of the labels, the distance between the labels, and the margins inside each label. WordPerfect handles the rest.

If you create a combination that will not fit on the current page size (for example, 10 labels across the page, each one ten inches wide), WordPerfect will warn you this is not possible.

Once you have defined the labels form, and selected it (from the *Page/Paper Size* dialog box), WordPerfect controls all label positioning and size. Your screen appears a little differently, letting you see how much information will fit into each label (Figure 22-4).

The only real way to get an idea of how the labels will look when printed is to select the *Print Preview* command from the **File** menu.

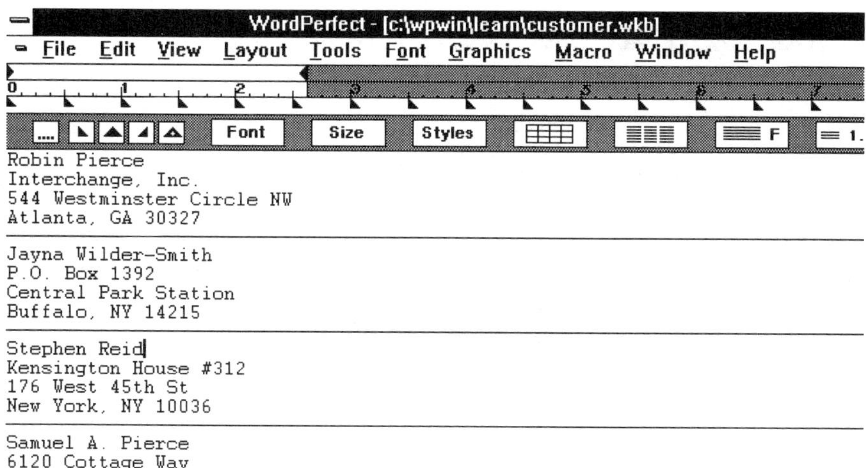

Figure 22-4. The lines on the screen indicate how much text will fit into each label as defined in the Figure 22-3 dialog box.

Word count

WordPerfect provides the *Word Count* command in the **Tools** menu, specifically to calculate the number of words in the currently active document. When you select this command, a dialog box informing you of the current number of words and file size in bytes, appears.

Special codes

Special codes are special formatting instructions you may insert into a document to ease or speed the formatting of that document.

To access these special codes, select the *Special Codes* command from the *Line* fly-out menu in the **Layout** menu, producing the dialog box of Figure 22-5.

Many special codes options are listed under the headings *Hard Tab Codes*, *Hyphenation Codes*, *Hard Tab Codes with Dot Leaders*, and *Other Codes*. Any particular code can be inserted into the text at the current text cursor position, by selecting that code and clicking on the *Insert* button.

Tab Codes should be inserted from this dialog box if you want to alter the tab settings for this line only. Tabs from this dialog box are forgotten as the line ends.

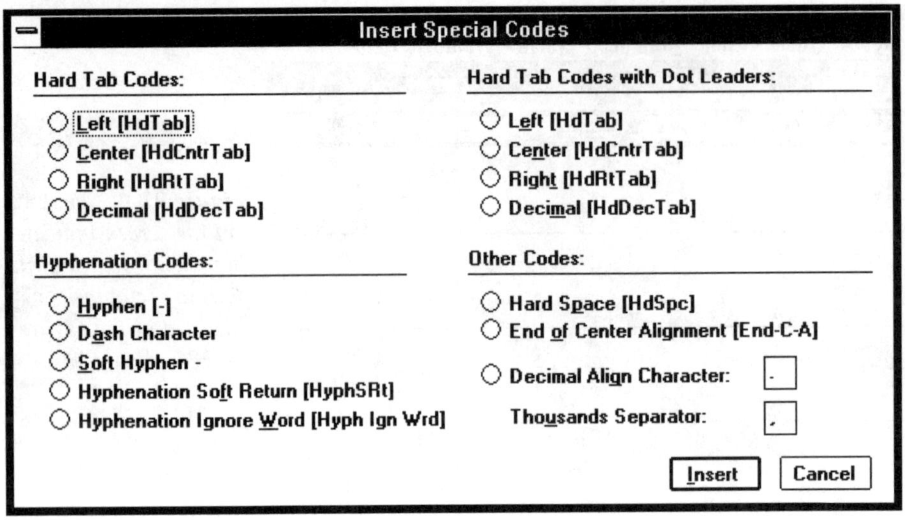

Insert Special Codes

Hard Tab Codes:
- Left [HdTab]
- Center [HdCntrTab]
- Right [HdRtTab]
- Decimal [HdDecTab]

Hard Tab Codes with Dot Leaders:
- Left [HdTab]
- Center [HdCntrTab]
- Right [HdRtTab]
- Decimal [HdDecTab]

Hyphenation Codes:
- Hyphen [-]
- Dash Character
- Soft Hyphen -
- Hyphenation Soft Return [HyphSRt]
- Hyphenation Ignore Word [Hyph Ign Wrd]

Other Codes:
- Hard Space [HdSpc]
- End of Center Alignment [End-C-A]
- Decimal Align Character: .

Thousands Separator: ,

Insert Cancel

Figure 22-5. The Special Codes dialog box.

If you select any *Hard Tab Codes* from this dialog box, the text cursor will proceed to the next tab stop. However, that tab stop will now have the properties designated by the tab code you selected. If you selected a *Right* tab code, the tab at the next tab stop becomes a hard right tab, rather than its original definition. Remember, this tab stop will return to normal on the next line.

Hard Tab Codes and *Hard Tab Codes with Dot Leaders* have the same properties, although, as you might have guessed, dot leaders will appear running up to the next tab stop if you select a tab code under the *Dot Leader* heading.

Hyphenation Codes are interesting. The *Hyphen* code is exactly the same as the hyphen on the keyboard—these codes are used to tell WordPerfect where to break a word should it need to be hyphenated.

A *Dash Character* is used to make a dash appear on the page. Two words on either side of a dash character are now treated as one word.

A *Soft Hyphen* will break a word and display a hyphen when it appears near the end of a line.

A *Hyphenation Soft Return* code can be inserted into words that may be separated by special characters (dashes or slashes for example) to indicate to WordPerfect where the word(s) can be broken if they occur near the end of a line. This code is similar to the *Soft Hyphen* code, but no hyphen will appear on screen with a *Hyphenation Soft Return* code—the word will simply be broken.

When the *Hyphenation Ignore Word* code is inserted as the first letter of any word, that word will never be hyphenated, and will wrap down to the next line.

Under the *Other Codes* heading, the *Hard Space* code, when inserted between two words, will force those words to remain together on the same line.

The *End of Center Alignment* code turns off center justification without requiring a return character.

The *Decimal Align Character* determines the character around which numbers are aligned at a decimal tab.

The *Thousands Separator* is the character used to separate large numbers (e.g. 1,000,000).

Comments

WordPerfect provides the extremely useful feature of allowing comments to be added to a document—comments that appear on screen, but do not print.

To insert a comment into a document, place the text cursor on the line where you would like the comment to appear, and select the *Create* command from the *Comment* fly-out menu in the **Tools** menu.

A dialog box will appear, into which you can enter comment text. Bold, italic, and underline facilities are available, as is a scroll bar for longer comments. After entering the text into the *Comment* dialog box, click on the *Enter* key to return to the editing screen.

The comment appears in the document in a distinctive box (Figure 22-6). The comment can be edited by inserting the text cursor just above the comment, and selecting the *Edit* command in the *Comment* fly-out menu in the **Tools** menu. A comment can be converted to text in the document by selecting the *Convert to Text* command in the *Comment* fly-out menu in the **Tools** menu.

Figure 22-6. This is a WordPerfect comment.

Footnotes

When creating a footnote in a document, WordPerfect automatically takes care of features such as numbering, positioning and spacing.

To insert a footnote into a document, you must first place the text cursor at the point in the text to which the footnote refers.

Select the *Create* command from the *Footnote* fly-out menu in the **Layout** menu. The *Footnote* screen then appears and displays the number of this footnote as shown in Figure 22-7.

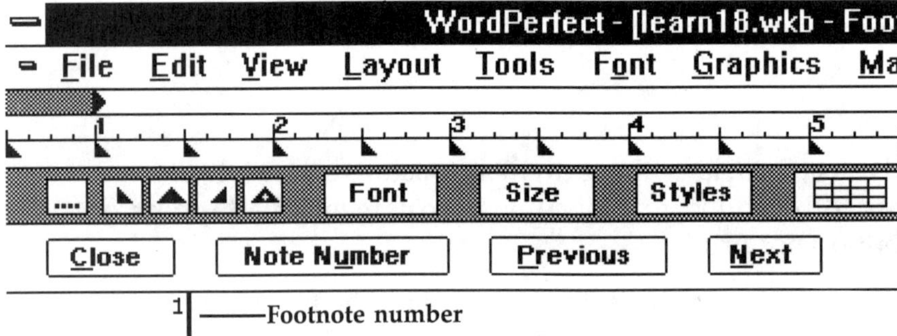

Figure 22-7. *The top left hand corner of the Footnote screen—displaying a small "1" (the footnote number), and the flashing text cursor, ready for you to insert the footnote text.*

Within the *Footnote* screen of Figure 22-7, insert the text that you wish to appear in the footnote. When the footnote text has been entered, select the *Close* button.

When the *Close* button is selected, the footnote number will be inserted into the document as seen here[1].

The footnote text will not appear on the editing screen, but can be seen using the Print Preview feature (see chapter 9).

Editing a footnote

Move to the page that contains the footnote you wish to edit and select the *Edit* command from the *Footnote* fly-out menu in the **Layout** menu. A dialog box appears, asking you the footnote number to edit. Key in the number and click on **OK**.

The selected footnote will then appear in the *Footnote* screen (Figure 22-7) ready for you to edit.

Footnote options

The *Options* command in the *Footnote* fly-out menu in the **Layout** menu, controls how the footnote appears on a printed page. Using this command (the dialog box is quite straightforward), you can control:

- The footnote numbering method (1,2,3,4; a,b,c,d etc.).
- The style of the footnote number as it appears in text (superscripted, subscripted, etc.).
- The style of the footnote number in the actual note on the bottom of the page.
- Whether numbering should be restarted for each new page.
- Line spacing and the space between multiple footnotes.
- How to handle long footnotes.
- Minimum footnote height.
- Where the footnotes should appear on the page.
- The line that separates the body text from the footnotes.

Endnotes

Endnotes are handled and created in almost exactly the same way as footnotes, but the *Endnote* command, rather than the *Footnote* command, from the **Layout** menu is used to create these notes.

The difference between footnotes and endnotes is that footnotes appear at the bottom of each page, while endnotes appear at the end of documents.

If you wish endnotes to appear before the end of a document, you can insert the text cursor at the desired position, and select the *Placement* command from the *Footnote* fly-out menu in the **Layout** menu. All endnotes created to this point will then appear.

Document Compare

The *Document Compare* command from the **Tools** menu, is provided to allow comparison between a currently open document, and a document on disk. This comparison will occur phrase by phrase (sentence by sentence), rather than character by character.

To use this command, open one of the documents you wish to compare. Then select the *Add Markings* command from the *Document Compare* fly-out menu in the **Tools** menu. An *Add Markings* dialog box will appear, asking you to select the document on disk to which you wish to compare the currently open document.

In a few moments, the currently open document will be marked with one of three types of markings:

- A phrase that appears in the document on disk, but not in the open document, appears with a strikeout through it: like~~ this~~.
- A phrase in a different position appears with the words "THE FOLLOWING TEXT WAS MOVED" before it, and "THE PRECEDING TEXT WAS MOVED" after it.
- A phrase that appears in the currently open document, but not in the document on disk, appears with Redline codes either side of it. On a color monitor, this text will appear in red.

Master document/subdocuments

When handling very large files, it is often easier to split the file into smaller parts. For example, in a book, each chapter may be contained in its own file.

You may, however, create a master document: a document that is made up of many subdocuments (like chapters in a book).

Assume you have a book made up of twenty chapters, each in its own WordPerfect file. You can create a master document, one that actually contains very little text but contains pointers to all the twenty chapter files. You can *expand* the master at any point to view all files, or *condense* the master to view only the text in the master file.

A master file is created like a normal file. When you reach the point in the master file where the first chapter file, for example, should fit in, select the *Master Document/Subdocument* command from the **Tools** menu. Select the first chapter file name from the dialog box that appears and that chapter file will become a subdocument; the file you are currently editing will become a master file.

At the location of the text cursor, a comment appears in the text, indicating the point at which a subdocument was inserted (Figure 22-8). The actual text of the subdocument does not appear.

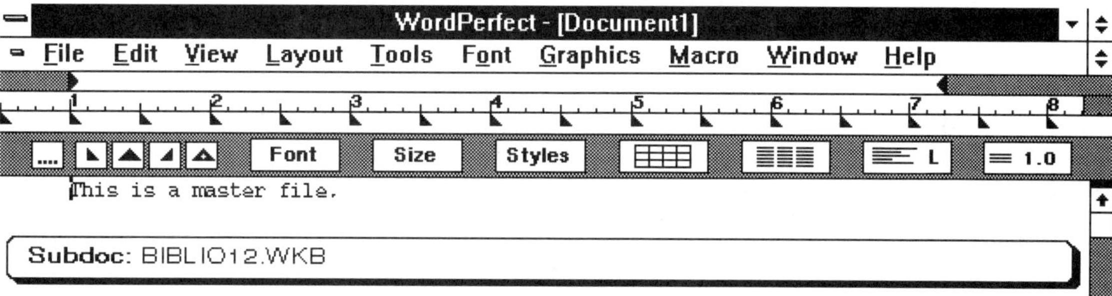

Figure 22-8. *This comment is inserted in the text after the Master Document/Subdocument command is selected, indicating that a subdocument has been inserted at this point.*

A range of subdocuments can be inserted into a master document in exactly the same method described above.

To view the master document, plus all the subdocuments, select the *Expand Master* command from the *Master Document* fly-out menu in the **Tools** menu. All subdocuments appear (between comments) and can be edited.

To remove the text of all subdocuments and just view the master, select the *Condense Master* command. You may be prompted to save the changes to some of the subdocuments before they disappear from screen and appear only as comments, as shown in Figure 22-8.

Any WordPerfect document that is a subdocument in a master document, can also be edited as a stand-alone file. Any changes made to any subdocument when it is edited as a normal file will be reflected in the corresponding master file, the next time it is opened or printed.

Advance

The *Advance* command, from the **Layout** menu, is designed to move the part of the document marked by the text cursor to specific positions on the editing screen. Using the *Advance* command is similar to scrolling without using the scroll bars.

To use this command, insert the text cursor into the area of the document that you wish to position. Then, select the *Advance* command from the **Layout** menu. The Figure 22-9 dialog box will appear.

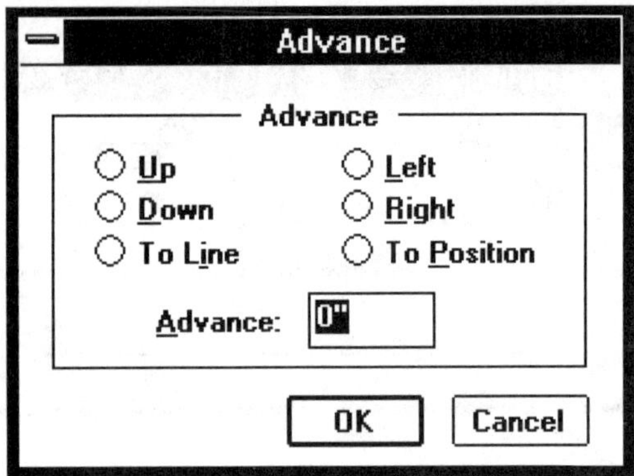

Figure 22-9. *The options within the Advance command dialog box allow you to move text almost anywhere on the page.*

As you can see, there are several directions in which text can be moved. *Up, Down, Left,* and *Right* all represent directions. The distance that the text will move is inserted in the *Advance* text box. If you attempt to move a distance in any direction that will force the text cursor outside of the editing window, WordPerfect will display an error message.

If you select the *To Line,* or *To Position* options, these are absolute measures. The *To Line* option will move the text from the top of the page the distance specified in the *Advance* text box. The *To Position* option will move text from the left of the page the exact position specified in the *Advance* text box.

Indexing

WordPerfect provides two methods of indexing documents: manually marking up words and phrases from a document to appear in an index, or a slightly more automated method, creating a *concordance file.*

Using the manual method, move through a document, select any word or phrase that you would like to include in an index, and select the *Index* command from the *Mark Text* fly-out menu in the **Tools** menu. From the dialog box that appears, you must decide whether this is a heading or a subheading (Figure 22-10). If it is a subheading you must decide under what heading will it appear.

```
Bananas                                Fruit
     Cultivation Methods   1                Apples   3
     Care of   3                            Bananas   1
     Skin  4,7                              Pears   7
```

Figure 22-10. *On the left, the word "Bananas" appears as a heading, with several subheadings under it. On the right, the word "Bananas" is a subheading, under the heading Fruit.*

If the word "Bananas" was located in a document, and you wanted it included in the index, you would need to know whether "Bananas" is a main topic (in which case it should be made a heading), or a minor topic (in which case it should be made a subheading). Figure 22-11 shows how the *Mark Index* dialog box is filled out for headings and for subheadings.

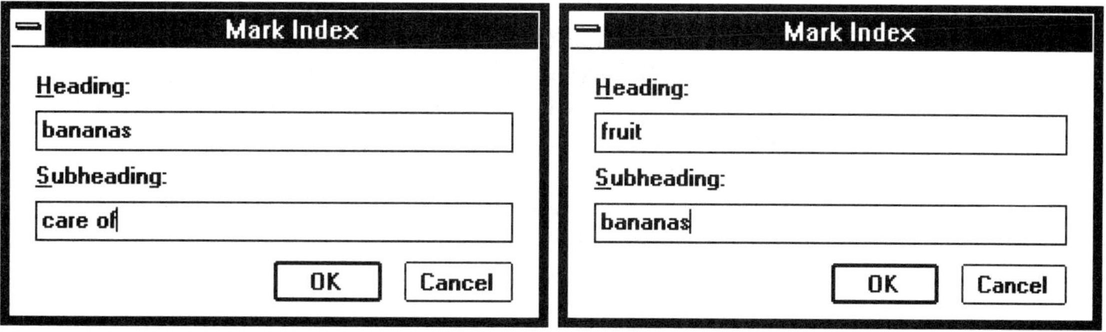

Figure 22-11. *On the left, "bananas" is a Heading. In the Subheading section, insert a word or words best describing what the selected area in the document is talking about in reference to bananas. On the right, a brief reference to "bananas" is being indexed and, hence, it is made a Subheading. The Heading under which this Subheading should fall depends on the rest of your document and on what index entries already exist.*

Any single word can be represented by both a Heading and a Subheading, if defined at different locations. Any topic that will appear on its own in an index should be created as a Heading, with no Subheading.

To complete the indexing procedure, move through the entire document, repeating the steps as outlined above for every word that should appear in the index.

If you wish to use the *concordance file* method, create a new file, listing all subjects to be cited in an index for a particular document. To organize this file into Headings and Subheadings, select each word in the *concordance file* and, using the *Index* command described above, mark all words as either a Heading or a Subheading. When it is completed, sort this *concordance file* alphabetically to speed index generation.

When the index is being generated, WordPerfect searches the selected document for every word listed in the *concordance file* and marks it automatically.

Positioning the index

Once all text has been marked up, or the *concordance file* completed, you must define the position in the document where the index is to appear. Insert the text cursor at the point where the index will appear (you may wish to create a new page for this step).

Select the *Index* command from the *Define* fly-out menu in the **Tools** menu. In the *Define Index* dialog box that appears, specify the name of the *concordance* file (explained above) in the *Optional Concordance File* text box. If a *concordance* file was not used, leave this text box empty. From the *Numbering Format* pop-up list box, select the style in which the index entries and their page numbers are to be displayed. A sample index entry in the dialog box will reflect the effects of these choices.

Generating the index

Once the index position has been defined, you must generate the index itself. Select the *Generate* command from the **Tools** menu.

The *Generate* command generates, and updates, a variety of document additions including indices, tables of contents, and endnotes.

These additions are all updated or created for the entire document using the *Generate* command.

Tables of contents

A table of contents is created for a document in a very similar method to an index.

To create a table of contents, move through a document and select each phrase, or paragraph, included in the table of contents.

After a phrase, or paragraph, is selected, choose the *Table of Contents* command from the *Mark Text* fly-out menu in the **Tools** menu. From the dialog box that appears, choose the level at which this selected text will appear in a table of contents. Each table of contents can contain up to five levels (Figure 22-12).

	Level
Chapter 1: Intro to Windows ....Page 1	1
What is Windows?...........................Page 1	2
The operating system ....Page 1	3
Microsoft Windows User Interface ....Page 3	3
Windows ....Page 4	4
Icons ....Page 4	4
Menus ....Page 4	4
The mouse ....Page 5	4

Figure 22-12. *This table of contents contains 4 different levels. The major entries (in this case, "Chapter 1: Introduction to Windows..." are level 1. As you move down the levels, the number moves up one each time. The lowest level in this table of contents (the words in italics) is level 4.*

After a level has been entered for the selected text, click on **OK** to insert a code into the text. Repeat this step for all text to be listed in the table of contents.

Positioning the table of contents

Once all the table of contents entries have been identified, determine the position in the document where the table of contents will appear. Insert the text cursor at this point (you may wish to create a new page for this step) and choose the *Table of Contents* command from the *Define* fly-out menu in the **Tools** menu. The *Define Table of Contents* dialog box will appear.

First, select how many levels this table of contents will have, and define how each level in the table of contents will be formatted. As with indexing, a visual guide is provided to make this selection easy.

Generating the table of contents

Once the table of contents position has been defined, generate the table of contents using the *Generate* command from the **Tools** menu.

The *Generate* command generates, and updates, a variety of document additions including indices, table of contents, and endnotes. These additions are all updated or created for the entire document using the *Generate* command.

Spreadsheets

Spreadsheet files from any of a range of compatible spreadsheet programs, including Lotus 1-2-3, Microsoft Excel, Quattro Pro, *et al*, can be imported into WordPerfect documents in one of two ways.

Importing a Spreadsheet

The first way to import a spreadsheet file is to select the *Import* command from the *Spreadsheet* fly-out menu in the **Tools** menu, and select the name of the spreadsheet file in the dialog box that appears. You may also, optionally, select a *Range*, or part of the spreadsheet to be imported. Finally, indicate whether this spreadsheet should come in as text (formatted with tabs) or as a table (automatically loaded into a WordPerfect table).

Linking a spreadsheet

A spreadsheet can be loaded while maintaining a live link with its original file so that it is easy to get an up-to-date version of the spreadsheet without having to reload it. To import a spreadsheet using the *Link* facility, select the spreadsheet using the *Create Link* command from the *Spreadsheet* fly-out menu in the **Tools** menu, rather than the *Import* command in the same menu. Both commands use the same dialog box.

If a spreadsheet is imported using the *Spreadsheet/Create Link* command, it is bound, top and bottom, by comments in the document indicating the name of the original spreadsheet file, and the directory from which it was originally loaded.

The spreadsheet can be updated to match the source file in one of two ways:—manually, or automatically.

With the manual approach, choose the *Update All Links* command from the *Spreadsheet* fly-out menu in the **Tools** menu to update every linked file in a document. Select the *Edit Link* command from the *Spreadsheet* fly-out menu in the **Tools** menu if you only wish to update a single linked file.

Alternatively, you can select the *Link Options* command in the *Spreadsheet* fly-out menu in the **Tools** menu. An option within the dialog box that appears is *Update on Retrieve*. If selected, this option will make sure all linked spreadsheets are updated every time this WordPerfect file is opened. Another option in this dialog box lets you hide the link comments from appearing in the text.

Outlines

The *Outline* feature of WordPerfect is a form of automatic or manual paragraph numbering, which allows you to create outlines up to eight levels deep and retain a good deal of flexibility and control over these outlines.

Creating outlines

To use outlines in their simplest form, select the *Outline On* command from the *Outline* fly-out menu in the **Tools** menu. An *Outline On* code is inserted into the text.

Each time the Enter key is now pressed, a number will appear at the start of each paragraph (initially numbering using roman numerals). If you press the Enter key, then the Tab key, the numbering system changes, reflecting the fact that the Tab key takes you to a new level in the outline. There may be up to eight different levels in an outline, as shown in Figure 22-13.

```
I.This is level 1.
II.This is also level 1
    A.This paragraph is on level 2
    B.This paragraph is also on level 2
        1.This paragraph is on level 3
            a.This is level 4...
                (1)...level 5...
                    (a)...level 6...
                        i)...level 7...
                            a)...and level 8.
```

Figure 22-13. This screen shot from WordPerfect reflects the eight different levels available in an outline.

When you have finished creating the outline, select the *Outline Off* command from the *Outline* fly-out menu in the **Tools** menu.

Any time a paragraph is deleted from an outline, all other paragraphs are re-numbered, if necessary, to compensate for the deletion. When a paragraph is added anywhere in an outline—all other paragraphs are re-numbered, where necessary.

Moving/copying & deleting families

A *family* consists of the line on which the cursor is positioned, plus any entries in lower levels. Figure 22-14 illustrates different levels of families in an outline.

```
I.This is level 1.
II.This is also level 1
    A.This paragraph is also on level 2          ——This is a family

III.This paragraph is on level 1
    A.This is level 2...
        1....level 3...                          ——This is a family
            a....level 4...
                (1)...level 5...
                    (a)...and level 6.
```

Figure 22-14. Some outline families.

Families, within an outline, can be selected and moved around the outline as one unit. To select a *family,* insert the text cursor into the paragraph that is the highest level in the outline you wish to select.

If you wish to move the family up in the outline, down in the outline, or even levels across in the outline, select the *Move Family* command from the *Outline* fly-out menu in the **Tools** menu. The entire family that the mouse cursor is inserted into becomes selected (highlighted). With a family highlighted, pressing any of the arrow keys on the keyboard will move that entire family in the direction of the arrow. Families can only be moved two levels to the left or the right, but can be moved up and down the outline as much as you wish. When you have finished moving the family, press the Enter key.

The *Copy Family* command from the *Outline* fly-out menu in the **Tools** menu works in the same fashion as the *Move Family* command from the same fly-out menu, but leaves the original family in its current position and moves only a copy.

To delete a family, select the *Delete Family* command from the *Outline* fly-out menu in the **Tools** menu. You will be asked to confirm the deletion via a *Yes/No* dialog box.

Paragraph numbering

WordPerfect offers a systematic outline feature, as well as a more manual paragraph numbering capability. Paragraph numbering can be used to create an outline or to number paragraphs individually.

To insert a paragraph number in a document, move the cursor to the paragraph that you wish to number and select the *Paragraph Number* command from the *Outline* fly-out menu in the **Tools** menu. If *Auto Code Placement,* from the *Preferences/Environment* command in the **File** menu is selected, the paragraph number will automatically appear at the start of the paragraph.

Selecting the above command, you will be asked to decide between *Auto,* or *Manual* numbering; in the latter case you must enter a number. Selecting *Auto* causes the paragraph number to act much as an outline—families may be created, levels changed, etc. Manual numbering does not allow levels to be altered (other than manually).

Paragraph numbers may be inserted while in outlines.

Defining paragraph numbers

If the *Define* command from the *Outline* fly-out menu in the **Tools** menu has not currently been invoked, then all numbering formats used to prefix all eight levels in an outline, or paragraph numbering style, have been determined by default settings. Using the above command allows the customization of all facets of outlines and paragraph numbering, through the Figure 22-15, *Define Paragraph Numbering*, dialog box.

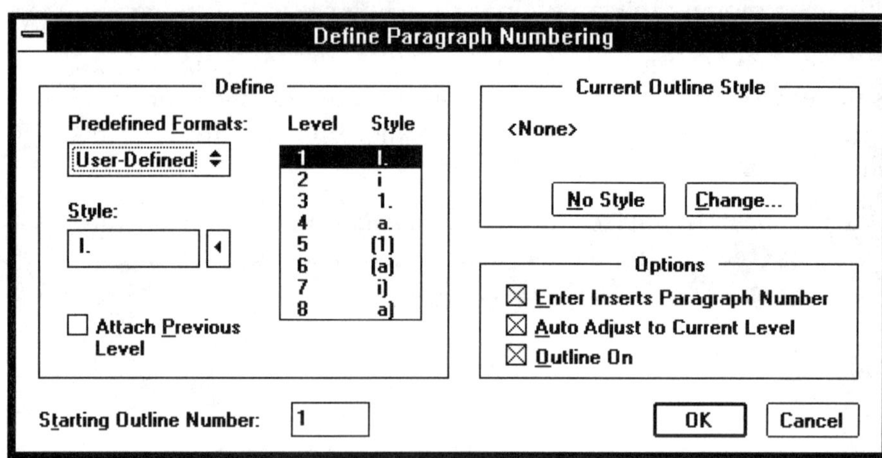

Figure 22-15. *The Outline/Define dialog box from the* ***Tools*** *menu.*

The dialog box of Figure 22-15 allows you to select a number of *Predefined Formats*, including a user-defined numbering *Style*. Other options within the dialog box allow you to start the outline number at any number you wish, or toggle a number of other options.

Outline styles

Using the *Current Outline Style* section of the Figure 22-15 dialog box, you can create, or retrieve, a style that may be applied to the current outline.

In Figure 22-15, the dialog box indicates that no Style is currently in use. To create a style, or to select a style, click on the *Change* button. The dialog box of Figure 22-16 will then appear.

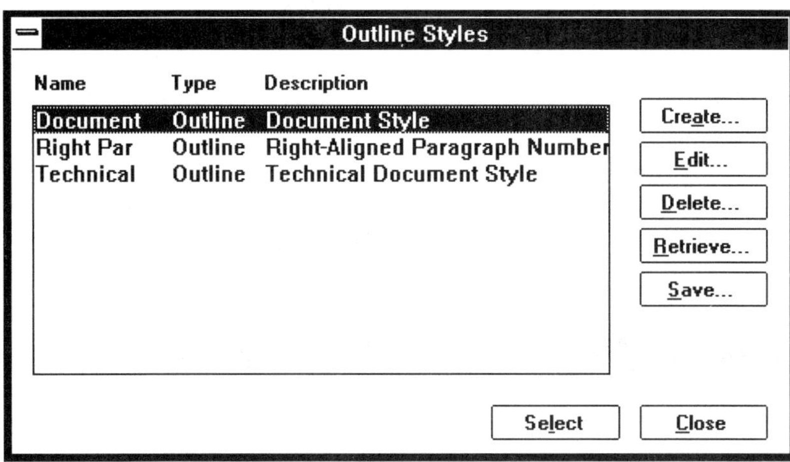

Figure 22-16. The Outline Styles dialog box is very similar to the dialog box that appears when creating traditional WordPerfect styles.

The *Outline Styles* dialog box of Figure 22-16 will be familiar if you have created WordPerfect styles before, as the idea is exactly the same (see Chapter 15, **Styles**). You may *Retrieve* existing style files from disk, select from any of the styles currently in the dialog box, edit any of the styles within this dialog box, or use the *Create* button to *Create* your own.

You will find, if you choose to edit or create a style, that formatting for all possible eight levels in an outline can be saved with the one style.

The Typesetting command

The *Typesetting* command, from the **Layout** menu, can be used to adjust and fine tune the appearance of text on the printed page. The *Typesetting* dialog box, invoked by the *Typesetting* command, is seen in Figure 22-17.

As most adjustments made using this command affect the printing of text, most changes are only visible when the *Print Preview* command is used or when the document is actually printed.

As with most other WordPerfect commands, this command will affect either selected text or, if nothing is selected, the text from the cursor position onwards.

Word Spacing

The *Word Spacing* options in the *Typesetting* dialog box adjust the spaces that appear between words on the printer. *Normal* and *WordPerfect Optimal* are similar settings. *Normal* word spacing is the word spacing designated by the font designer, and *WordPerfect Optimal* is the most appropriate spacing, as calculated by WordPerfect. Generally, there is very little difference between these two settings

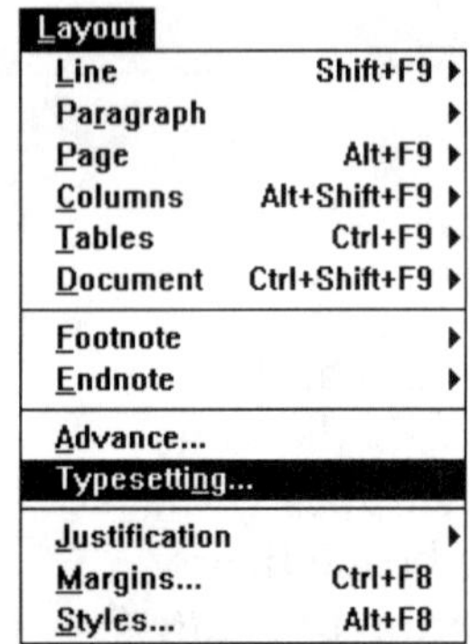

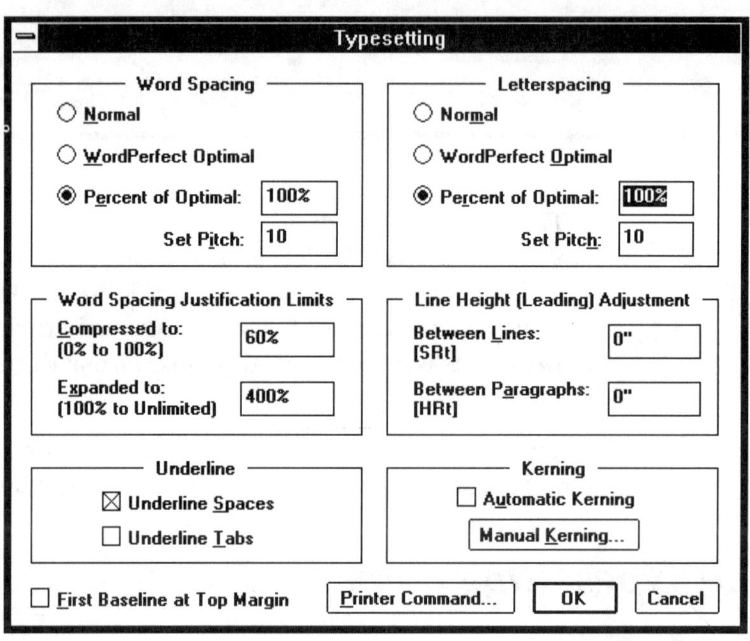

***Figure 22-17.** The Typesetting command, from the **Layout** menu, can be used to fine tune the appearance of text in a document.*

The *Percent of Optimal* option lets you insert a percentage value by which to increase, or decrease, the *Word Spacing*. Values here may range from 50% to 250%. Alternatively, if *Percent of Optimal* is selected, you may select a *Pitch*, by inserting a figure ranging from 20 (equivalent to 50% word spacing), to 4 (equivalent to 250% word spacing). Figure 22-18 shows examples.

This paragraph of text is here to demonstrate word spacing that has been reduced to 50%.

This paragraph of text is here to demonstrate word spacing that has been increased to 250%.

***Figure 22-18.** On the left, this paragraph has had Word Spacing reduced to fifty percent of optimal. On the right, the Word Spacing has been increased to 250%.*

Letterspacing

The *Letterspacing* options work much like the *Word Spacing* options—in fact the options in both sections are identical. Selecting *Normal* ensures that the amount of space that occurs between letters is as the font manufacturer intended. In *Letterspacing, Normal* and *WordPerfect Optimal* are identical.

The *Percent of Optimal* option lets you insert a percentage value by which to increase, or decrease, the *Letterspacing*. Values here may range from 50% to 250%. Alternatively, if *Percent of Optimal* is selected, you may select a *Pitch*, by inserting a figure ranging from 20 (equivalent to 50% letterspacing), to 4 (equivalent to 250% letterspacing). Figure 22-19 shows examples.

Thisparagraphoftextisheretodemonstrateletterspacingthathasbeenreducedto50%.

T h i s   p a r a g r a p h   o f   t e x t   i s   h e r e   t o   d e m o n s t r a t e   l e t t e r s p a c i n g   t h a t   h a s   b e e n   i n c r e a s e d   t o   2 5 0 % .

Figure 22-19. *On the left, this paragraph has had letterspacing reduced to fifty percent of optimal. On the right, the letterspacing has been increased to 250%.*

Word Spacing Justification Limits

The settings in this section of the dialog box affect only text that is fully justified, using both flush left and right margins. In order to justify text, WordPerfect must either increase, or decrease, the space between words to balance lines. The settings entered for *Compressed to*, and *Expanded to*, determine the minimum and maximum levels that WordPerfect may either decrease (*Compressed to*), or increase (*Expanded to*) word spacing. These values are also entered as percentages. The default values are shown in Figure 22-17.

Line Height (Leading) Adjustment

The options under this heading affect the amount of space added (or removed) from the current line spacing when a soft return (where WordPerfect automatically wraps a line) or a hard return (where the Enter key is pressed) code occurs. The figures entered for either of these options may have negative values.

For example, if the figure 0.25" were inserted into the *Between Paragraphs [Hrt]* text box, then a quarter of an inch of white space would be added below each paragraph.

Underline

The options involved in this section of the Typesetting dialog box affect only text that has been assigned the *Underlined* font attribute. If *Underline Spaces* is checked, then the spaces between words are also underlined. If *Underline Tabs* is checked, any spaces caused by tabs that occur in underlined text will also be underlined.

Kerning

Kerning may be described as the moving together of letters that may otherwise appear too widely spaced (Figure 22-20). This most often occurs when large font sizes are used, where the shapes of some letters exaggerate the space between them. Selecting *Automatic Kerning* will force WordPerfect to automatically adjust the spacing between specific letters (called 'kerning pairs').

Figure 22-20. *On the left, these two characters have been kerned. On the right are the same two characters as they appear without kerning.*

Clicking on the *Manual Kerning* button invokes the *Manual Kerning* dialog box (Figure 22-21).

Before selecting this command, insert the text cursor between the letters you wish to kern. Then, insert a negative figure (to decrease the spacing), or a positive figure (to increase the spacing). The small preview screen shows how the characters are affected by the settings.

It is possible that your printer may not support a kerning feature.

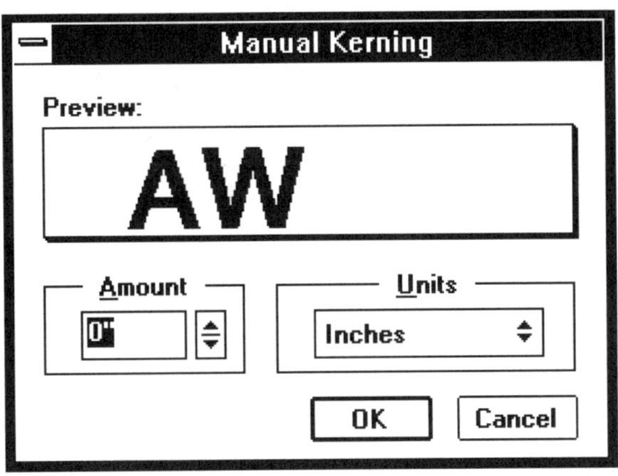

Figure 22-21. *This is the Manual Kerning dialog box. Before selecting the Manual Kerning command, insert the text cursor between the two characters to be kerned.*

First Baseline at Top Margin

The baseline of text is the imaginary line on which text rests. Normally, WordPerfect places the first baseline on the page below the current margin at the top of the page. Because the distance between baselines can vary, depending on the size of text and the font used, the actual position of the first baseline on a page will vary all the time.

To insure that text is positioned precisely on a page, the first baseline must be set at a fixed position on the page. Selecting *First Baseline at Top Margin* will ensure that the first baseline is exactly equal with the top margin of the page.

Printer Command

The *Printer Command* option (Figure 22-22) allows special printer commands, or printer files, to be sent to the printer every time a document is printed.

Figure 22-22. *The Printer Command dialog box.*

Index

D

G

H

I

J

K

L

M

Q

R

S

U

V

W